THE ROUTLEDGE COMPANION TO MEDIA AND CLASS

This companion brings together scholars working at the intersection of media and class, with a focus on how understandings of class are changing in contemporary global media contexts.

From the memes of and about working-class supporters of billionaire "populists", to well-publicized and critiqued philanthropic efforts to bring communication technologies into developing country contexts, to the behind-the-scenes work of migrant tech workers, class is undergoing change both in and through media. Diverse and thoughtfully curated contributions unpack how media industries, digital technologies, everyday media practices—and media studies itself—feed into and comment upon broader, interdisciplinary discussions. They cover a wide range of topics, such as economic inequality, workplace stratification, the sharing economy, democracy and journalism, globalization, and mobility/migration.

Outward-looking, intersectional, and highly contemporary, *The Routledge Companion to Media and Class* is a must-read for students and researchers interested in the intersections between media, class, sociology, technology, and a changing world.

Erika Polson is Associate Professor in the Department of Media, Film and Journalism Studies at the University of Denver, USA. Her research focuses on digital media and mobility in global contexts. She is author of *Privileged Mobilities: Professional Migration, Geo-social Media, and a New Global Middle Class* (2016).

Lynn Schofield Clark is Professor and Chair of the Department of Media, Film and Journalism Studies and Director of the Estlow International Center for Journalism and New Media at the University of Denver, USA. She is co-author most recently of the award-winning, *Young People and the Future of News: Social Media and the Rise of Connective Journalism* (2017). Clark serves as President of the Association of Internet Researchers.

Radhika Gajjala is Professor of American Culture Studies and Media and Communication at Bowling Green State University, USA. Her most recent book *Digital Diasporas: Labor, Affect in Gendered Indian Digital Publics* was published in 2019.

THE ROUTLEDGE COMPANION TO MEDIA AND CLASS

Edited by Erika Polson, Lynn Schofield Clark, and Radhika Gajjala

NEW YORK AND LONDON

First published 2020
by Routledge
52 Vanderbilt Avenue, New York, NY 10017

and by Routledge
2 Park Square, Milton Park, Abingdon, Oxon, OX14 4RN

Routledge is an imprint of the Taylor & Francis Group, an informa business

© 2020 Taylor & Francis

The right of Erika Polson, Lynn Schofield Clark, and Radhika Gajjala to be identified as the authors of the editorial material, and of the authors for their individual chapters, has been asserted in accordance with sections 77 and 78 of the Copyright, Designs and Patents Act 1988.

All rights reserved. No part of this book may be reprinted or reproduced or utilized in any form or by any electronic, mechanical, or other means, now known or hereafter invented, including photocopying and recording, or in any information storage or retrieval system, without permission in writing from the publishers.

Trademark notice: Product or corporate names may be trademarks or registered trademarks, and are used only for identification and explanation without intent to infringe.

Library of Congress Cataloging-in-Publication Data
A catalog record for this title has been requested

ISBN: 978-1-138-49361-2 (hbk)
ISBN: 978-1-351-02734-2 (ebk)

Typeset in Bembo
by Wearset Ltd, Boldon, Tyne and Wear

Printed and bound in Great Britain by
TJ International Ltd, Padstow, Cornwall

To the participants who came together for the NCA Media and Class Pre-Conference in Philadelphia on the challenging morning after the 2016 US Presidential Election

CONTENTS

List of Figures x
Notes on Contributors xi
Acknowledgments xvii

1 Introduction: Media and Class in the Twenty-first Century 1
  Erika Polson, Lynn Schofield Clark, and Radhika Gajjala

PART I
Class and Mass Media 15

2 Working-class Bodies in Advertising 17
  Matthew P. McAllister and Litzy Galarza

3 Class Hybridity and the *Habitus Clivé* on American Reality Television 27
  June Deery

4 Migrants Meet Reality Shows: The Class Representation of Non-Koreans in Reality Shows in Korea 38
  Hun-Yul Lee

5 Participation in Reality Television: Entertainment Mobilization in Dance Talent Shows 51
  Annette Hill and Koko Kondo

6 Love, Sex, Money: Gender and Economic Inequality in HIV Edutainment Programming in Kenya 63
  Renée A. Botta

PART II
Class in Interactive Digital and Mobile Media   75

7   Horse Racing, Social Class, and the Spaces of Gambling   77
     Holly Kruse

8   "Keep it Classy": Grindr, Facebook and Enclaves of Queer Privilege in India   90
     Rohit K. Dasgupta

9   YouTube-based Programming and Saudi Youth: Constructing a New Online Class and Monetizing Strategies   99
     Omar Daoudi

10   Mobile Technology and Class: Australian Family Households, Socioeconomic Status and Techno-literacy   110
     Will Balmford and Larissa Hjorth

11   Hanging Out at Home as a Lifestyle: YouTube Home Tour Vlogs in East Asia   122
     Crystal Abidin

12   Young People, Smartphones, and Invisible Illiteracies: Closing the Potentiality–Actuality Chasm in Mobile Media   132
     Sun Sun Lim and Renae Sze Ming Loh

13   Childhood, Media, and Class in South Asia   142
     Shakuntala Banaji

PART III
Labor in Digital/Media Contexts   155

14   The Roots of Journalistic Perception: A Bourdieusian Approach to Media and Class   157
     Sandra Vera-Zambrano and Matthew Powers

15   The Aspirational Class "Mobility" of Digital Nomads   168
     Erika Polson

16   Technologies of Recognition: The Classificatory Function of Social Media in Mobile Careers   180
     André Jansson

17   The Gig Economy and Class (De)composition   192
     Todd Wolfson

18   Digital Hierarchies of Laboring Subjects   203
     Kaitlyn Wauthier, Alyssa Fisher, and Radhika Gajjala

19 Between "World Class Work" and "Proletarianized Labor": Digital Labor
    Imaginaries in the Global South   213
    Cheryll Ruth Soriano and Jason Vincent Cabañes

PART IV
Media, Class, and Expressions of Citizenship   **227**

20 Class Distinctions in Urban Broadband Initiatives   229
    Germaine Halegoua

21 "Second-class" Access: Homelessness and the Digital Materialization of Class   242
    Justine Humphry

22 Marginality and Social Class in Moroccan Youth Media   253
    Mohamed El Marzouki

23 Reconsidering Mobility: The Competing Logics of Information and
    Communication Technologies Across Class Differences in the Context of
    Denver's Gentrification   266
    Lynn Schofield Clark

24 Class Interplay in Social Activism in Kenya   280
    Job Mwaura

Postscript   **293**

25 The Vivid Particularities of Class and Media   295
    David Morley

Index   302

FIGURES

5.1	Backstage at *Got to Dance*. Image by Tina Askanius	51
8.1	View of his "sacred thread" in Andy's profile distinguishes the man as belonging to the highest caste in India	94
8.2	Jash's post defends the club accused of discrimination	96
10.1	Mobile phones as recipe books. Image by authors	111
20.1	The living room at a Google Fiber sales center in Lee's Summit, Missouri. Image by author	230
24.1	A poster circulated on social media used for the #OccupyParliament protest	289

CONTRIBUTORS

Erika Polson is Associate Professor in the department of Media, Film and Journalism Studies at the University of Denver. Her research focuses on digital media and mobility in global contexts. She is author of *Privileged Mobilities: Professional Migration, Geo-social Media, and a New Global Middle Class* (Peter Lang, 2016).

Lynn Schofield Clark is Professor and Chair of the Department of Media, Film and Journalism Studies and Director of the Estlow International Center for Journalism and New Media at the University of Denver. She is author of *The Parent App: Understanding Families in a Digital Age* (Oxford University Press, 2012), *From Angels to Aliens: Teenagers, the Media, and the Supernatural* (Oxford University Press, 2003/2005), and coauthor of the award-winning, *Young People and the Future of News: Social Media and the Rise of Connective Journalism* (Cambridge University Press, 2017). Schofield Clark currently serves as President of the Association of Internet Researchers.

Radhika Gajjala is Professor of American Culture Studies and Media and Communication Bowling Green State University. Her most recent book is *Digital Diasporas: Labor, Affect in Gendered Indian Digital Publics* (Rowman and Littlefield International, 2019).

Crystal Abidin is a digital anthropologist and ethnographer of vernacular internet cultures. She researches young people's relationships with internet celebrity, self-curation, and vulnerability. Her books include *Internet Celebrity: Understanding Fame Online* (2018); *Microcelebrity Around the Globe: Approaches to Cultures to Cultures of Internet Fame* (2018, co-edited with Megan Lindsay Brown); and *Instagram: Visual Social Media Cultures* (2019, with Tama Leaver and Tim Highfield). She is listed on Forbes 30 Under 30 Asia (2018) and Pacific Standard 30 Top Thinkers Under 30 (2016). Crystal is Senior Research Fellow & DECRA Fellow in Internet Studies at Curtin University. She can be reached at wishcrys.com.

Will Balmford is a researcher within RMIT's Digital Ethnographic Research Centre and is part of the Design & Creative Practice Engaging Capabilities Platform. He also lectures within RMIT's Bachelor of Design (Games) program. His current research involves exploring the impacts of domestic videogame usage. With a keen interest in digital play, social exchange and the relationship between device and person, he examines the everyday use of new media through innovative ethnographic methods and an interdisciplinary approach to collaboration.

Contributors

Shakuntala Banaji is Associate Professor, Director of Graduate Studies and Programme Director for the Master's in Media, Communication and Development in the department of Media and Communications at the London School of Economics and Political Science. She lectures in development and communication, international media and world cinema, and is the winner of multiple teaching prizes including the fourth European Prize for Excellence in Teaching in the Humanities and Social Sciences (2015), awarded by Central European University. Her books include *Reading Bollywood* (Palgrave 2006/2011), *South Asian Media Cultures*, (Anthem Press, 2011); *The Civic Web* with David Buckingham (MIT Press, 2013), *Young People and Democratic Life* with Bart Cammaerts et al. (Palgrave, 2015) and *Children and Media in India* (Routledge, 2017).

Renée A. Botta is Associate Professor of Global Health Communication at the University of Denver, and has spent 16 years working in southern and eastern Africa and Haiti to improve health outcomes through health promotion and participatory communication. Her research focuses on communication in WASH projects and HIV/AIDS prevention and treatment, and includes health behavior change, health promotion campaigns, international and intercultural health communication, and family and peer communication about health and about health messages, and the role of CHWs in health education and outcomes. Focus areas include developing participatory communication models tailored to local socio-cultural contexts, as well as the motivational roles income generating activities and community driven social innovation play in sustaining behavior change and health outcomes.

Jason Vincent A. Cabañes is Associate Professor in Communication and Research Fellow at De La Salle University—Manila in the Philippines. He researches mediation of cross-cultural solidarities and intimacies, as well as conditions of digital labor in the Global South. He co-leads the university-funded research project "Between global aspirations and local realities: A viable future for digital labor in Philippine regional cities," and previously co-led the digital labor stream of the British Council-funded Newton Tech4Dev Network, from which he has published a public report and book chapters based on an ethnographic study of digital disinformation producers in the Philippines. His works have appeared in publications such as *New Media and Society*, *Media, Culture, and Society*, and the *International Journal of Cultural Studies*.

Omar Daoudi is a temporary media lecturer at West College Scotland, a freelance academic researcher and freelance Arabic interpreter at various law firms in Glasgow. Omar has recently obtained his PhD in Media and Cultural Policy at the Centre for Cultural Policy Research (CCPR) at the University of Glasgow. He has presented his academic works in several universities including University of Oslo, University of Westminster, University of Oxford and University of Glasgow. He is interested in media policy, cyber warfare research and global media studies. Omar worked as a freelancer filmmaker for two years, and he was an assistant producer for some Arab televisions prior to his academic path.

Rohit K. Dasgupta is a senior lecturer in global communication and development at Loughborough University. He is the author of *Digital Queer Cultures in India* (Routledge, 2017) and *Queer Studies* (Orient Blackswan, 2019). His co-edited volumes include *Queering Digital India* (EUP, 2018), *Styling South Asian Youth Cultures* (Bloomsbury, 2018) and *Friendship as Social Justice Activism* (Chicago, 2018). He is also an elected councilor in the London Borough of Newham.

June Deery is Media Professor and Department Head at Rensselaer Polytechnic Institute, Troy, NY. She writes about contemporary media and culture, particularly television and film, and has authored *Consuming Reality: the Commercialization of Factual Entertainment* (Palgrave, 2012) and *Reality TV* (Polity, 2015). She also edited the collection *Media and Class: TV, Film, and Digital*

Culture (with Andrea Press, Routledge, 2017). Currently, she is working on a book manuscript about political representation.

Mohamed El Marzouki is Assistant Professor of Communication at the Illinois Institute of Technology. His research interests sit at the intersection of youth citizenship, participatory media and politics, and creative cultural production in the Middle East and North Africa. His recent dissertation, "Young and creative: dissent, youth citizenship and participatory media on the Moroccan social web," investigates the role that social media platforms play in enabling youth in the Maghreb region to create spaces for a culture of political dissent. His work has appeared in *Information, Communication and Society, the International Communication Gazette,* and *Global Media and Communication.*

Alyssa Fisher is a doctoral candidate in Media and Communication at Bowling Green State University. Her current research focuses on the intersection of emerging and legacy media, mediated culture, and gender performance on YouTube.

Litzy Galarza is a PhD candidate in the Donald P. Bellisario College of Communications at Pennsylvania State University. Her research focuses on Latina/os in popular culture and interrogates the role of media discourses in shaping societal understandings of Latina/o citizenship in *Jane The Virgin* and the role of Latina/os as cultural translators in shaping first-generation American narratives in Disney/Pixar's *Coco*.

Germaine R. Halegoua is Associate Professor in the Department of Film & Media Studies at the University of Kansas. Her research focuses on digital media and place, urban informatics, and cultural geographies of digital media. Her work has been published in several anthologies, online venues, and journals including *New Media & Society, International Journal of Cultural Studies, Social Media + Society,* and *Journal of Urban Technology*. She is the co-editor of *Locating Emerging Media* and author of *The Digital City: Media and the Social Production of Place*.

Annette Hill is Professor of Media and Communication at Lund University, Sweden, and Visiting Professor at King's College London. Her research focuses on audiences and popular culture, with interests in media engagement, everyday life, genres, production studies and cultures of viewing. She is the author of eight books, and many articles and book chapters in journals and edited collections, which address varieties of engagement with reality television, news and documentary, television drama, entertainment formats, live events and sports entertainment, film violence and media ethics. Her latest books are *Reality TV* (Routledge 2015) and *Media Experiences* (Routledge 2018).

Larissa Hjorth is a Distinguished Professor, an artist and a digital ethnographer. Hjorth has two decades experience working in cross-cultural, interdisciplinary, collaborative creative practice and socially innovative digital media research to explore intergenerational literacies around play and sociality. Hjorth is currently the Design & Creative Practice ECP Platform director at RMIT University. The Platform focuses on interdisciplinary collaboration and creative solution to real-world problems, especially in relation to ageing well, careful and multisensorial methods. Hjorth is experienced in alternative ethnographic methods and also knowledge exchange.

Justine Humphry is Lecturer in Digital Cultures in the Department of Media and Communications at the University of Sydney. Her research is on the cultural and political implications of digital media in everyday life with a focus on mobile media cultures and marginalized publics, digital inequalities, and smart technology transformation. She has studied mobile communication and homelessness extensively and has conducted collaborative research on mobile anti-racism apps in

Australia, France and the United Kingdom. Her new project, Smart Publics, researches the social, design and governance implications of smart street furniture with a team from the University of Glasgow, building on her research on smart Wi-Fi kiosks in New York City.

André Jansson is Professor of Media and Communication Studies and Director of the Geomedia Research Group at Karlstad University, Sweden. His research is specialized on mediatization, communication geography and issues concerning social identity and power. His most recent books are Mediatization and Mobile Lives: A Critical Approach (Routledge, 2018) and Transmedia Work: Privilege and Precariousness in Digital Modernity (Routledge, 2019, with Karin Fast).

Koko Kondo is a senior lecturer at the University of Westminster, Westminster Business School, School of Management and Marketing after a post-doc at the School of Media, Arts and Design at the University of Westminster. Her area of research is audiences, including consumers and users, especially children and the media. Previously she worked at the media industry in Tokyo, Japan, managing the media productions, sales, and marketing.

Holly Kruse is Professor of Communications at Rogers State University. She is the author of Off-Track and Online: The Networked Spaces of Horse Racing (MIT Press: 2016) and *Site and Sound: Understanding Independent Music Scenes* (Peter Lang: 2003). Her research has been published in journals including *New Media & Society, Television & New Media, Popular Music, Popular Music and Society*, and *The Journal of Sport and Social Issues*.

Hun-Yul Lee is a professor at the School of Media and Communication, Korea University. He enjoys three major elements television offer: watching, studying, and teaching television. Dr Lee started his career as a producer in a cable network in Korea before moving to academia. His experience in television and his love for visual content has inspired him to continue his academic pursuits in the area. Additionally, Dr Lee's experience as a migrant has led his academic interest to the crossroad of migration, class, and media.

Sun Sun Lim is Professor of Communication and Technology and Head of Humanities, Arts and Social Sciences at the Singapore University of Technology and Design. She studies the social implications of technology domestication by young people and families, charting the ethnographies of their internet and mobile phone use. She also investigates technology domestication writ large, focusing on digital literacy, user perceptions, and public understanding of pervasive ambient technologies deployed in smart cities. She has conducted extensive fieldwork in Asia including in China, Indonesia, Singapore, South Korea and Vietnam, authoring over 70 articles, book chapters and books. She serves on the editorial boards of ten journals. Her latest book is *Transcendent Parenting—Raising Children in the Mobile Age* (Oxford University Press, forthcoming).

Matthew P. McAllister is Professor of Communications, Communication Arts & Sciences, and Women's Studies at Pennsylvania State University. His research focuses on the political economy of media and critiques of commercial culture. He is the co-editor of *The Routledge Companion to Advertising and Promotional Culture* (with Emily West, 2013) and *The Advertising and Consumer Culture Reader* (with Joseph Turow, Routledge, 2009).

Renae Sze Ming Loh graduated with a Master of Science in Sociology and Social Research from Utrecht University. Her Master's thesis examined students' educational performance in relation to their cultural capital and information and communications technology (ICT) usage. Her research interests include social influence, educational inequality, media literacy, and their policy implications. She has published work with the Tyndall Centre for Climate Change Research, and in journals such as *Telematics and Informatics* and *Body Image*.

David Morley is Professor of Communications, Goldsmiths College, University of London, and author of *Television, Audiences and Cultural Studies* (Routledge 1992); *Home Territories; Media, Mobility and Identity* (Routledge 2000); *Media, Modernity and Technology: The Geography of the New* (Routledge 2006) and most recently *Communications and Mobility: The Migrant, the Mobile Phone and the Container Box* (Wiley-Blackwell 2018). He is also the editor of *Stuart Hall: The Essential Essays* (Duke University Press 2019). His work has been translated into 18 languages.

Job Mwaura is Doctoral Fellow and Teaching Assistant in the Department of Media Studies at the University of the Witwatersrand (Wits), Johannesburg, South Africa. He holds a Master's Degree in Communication and Journalism. His PhD research is on Digital Activism in Kenya. His research interests include Social Media Studies, Online Activism, Data Justice and Media and Democracy. He teaches media studies at Wit, and he has previously worked as a researcher in Kenya for many years.

Matthew Powers is Associate Professor in the Department of Communication at the University of Washington in Seattle, and an Associate Director of the Department's Center for Communication and Civic Engagement. His writings have been published in *Journal of Communication*, *International Journal of Press/Politics*, and *New Media and Society*, among others. His first book, *NGOs as Newsmakers: The Changing Landscape of International News*, was published by Columbia University Press in 2018. With Sandra Vera-Zambrano, he is currently working on a book-length manuscript that examines how French and American journalists understand their professional purposes.

Cheryll Ruth Soriano is Associate Professor in the Department of Communication and Antonio Gocolay Professorial Chair in the Humanities, De La Salle University (DLSU), Manila. Her research focuses on digital cultures and marginality, exploring the dialectical tensions involved in digital media engagements by users from cultural, economic, and political margins and how these facilitate new modes of understanding culture/politics. She co-leads a digital ethnography project on digital labor in the Philippines under the Newton Tech4Dev Network, a networking collaboration funded by the British Council. She co-edited the book (with S.S. Lim), *Asian Perspectives on Digital Culture: Emerging Phenomena, Enduring Concepts*. Cheryll was awarded an Australia-APEC Women in Research Fellowship at the Center for Communication, Politics, and Culture at RMIT University.

Kaitlyn Wauthier is a doctoral candidate in the American Culture Studies program at Bowling Green State University where she has taught courses in Women's Studies, Ethnic Studies, and American Culture Studies. Her research interests include questions of access and mobility as they relate to critical disability studies, tourism, and immigration.

Todd Wolfson is Associate Professor in the Department of Journalism and Media Studies at Rutgers University. Trained as an anthropologist, Todd focuses his research on the convergence of technology, inequality and social change. He has published *Digital Rebellion: The Birth of the Cyber Left* (2014) and *The Great Refusal: Herbert Marcuse and Contemporary Social Movements* (2017) and is currently working on a book on organizing in the platform economy. Todd is co-director of the Media, Inequality & Chance Center (MIC), a partnership between University of Pennsylvania and Rutgers University. Alongside his research, Todd is co-founder and board president of the Media Mobilizing Project (MMP), and sits on the Executive Committee of 215 People's Alliance. Both organizations build the power of poor and working people across Philadelphia.

Contributors

Sandra Vera-Zambrano is Associate Professor in the Department of Communication at Universidad IberoAmericana in Mexico City. Her writings have been published in *New Media and Society*, *Journal of Communication*, and *International Journal of Press/Politics*, among others. Currently, she coordinates two research projects. The first analyses the increasing job insecurity of Mexican journalists (Proyecto de Investigación Científica Básica/DINV), revealing how precarious conditions are not evenly distributed in the social space. The second project, with Matthew Powers, examines how French and American journalists face recent economical constraints and technological transformations. They are now working on a manuscript that analyses how journalists from Toulouse and Seattle perceive their profession in relation to their social position and dispositions.

ACKNOWLEDGMENTS

As the dedication to this volume noted, this project began with a Pre-Conference on Media and Class, which met in Philadelphia, Pennsylvania the day before the 2016 annual meeting of the National Communication Association, and on what turned out to be the day the world awoke to the news of an unlikely new US President-elect. That day, many plenary presenters threw out or reframed their original notes, speaking spontaneously about how researchers needed to better understand the experiences, challenges, and fears of those being left behind in a global and digital economy, and critiquing how cultural and political media had neglected to cover or even understand the concerns and circumstances of so many. We are so thankful for the supportive, insightful, and motivating group of scholars who joined us on that day, and whose varied takes on media and class inspired the launch of this collection: Kishonna Gray, Meryl Alper, Jenny Korn, Matt Jordan, Jaelyn deMaría, Vikki Katz, Bryan Mercer (Executive Director of Philadelphia's outstanding Media Mobilizing Project), Demet Kassap, Doron Taussig, Michael L. Wayne, Louise Woodstock, Katie McCollough, Tasha R. Dunn, Deborah Creech, Jenna M. Grzeslo, June Deery, Melissa R. Meade, Lori Young, Andrew Calabrese, Aras Coskuntuncel, Doug Spielman, Lluis de Nadal, and Menglu Lyu; as well as the many others who filtered in to listen, ask questions, and provide camaraderie. While not everyone who attended was able to contribute to this volume, we remember that day and how what felt like a form of group therapy—in the moment—also became a call to renew a commitment to scholarship seeking to understand new class identities and mobilizations, to generate understandings rooted in history and articulated through the changing forms and connectivities of 'the' media, and to do so in diverse research contexts. We thank Erica Wetter, and her team at Routledge, for acknowledging the importance of this topic and lending us their patience and support. In addition, we recognize with gratitude the activists and organizers who launched many of the projects—online, in the streets, in workspaces, in creative communities, and more—that provided contexts for much of the research covered here.

Finally, as co-editors, we want to acknowledge each other and what we brought to our collaboration: Erika, for her ingenuity, her exciting research into mobile socialities, her dedication in organizing the NCA preconference, and for maintaining a steady focus that allowed us to bring this book to completion; Lynn, for her ability to see both the forest and the trees when it comes to media, class and cultural studies, and her commitment to seeking out emerging scholars to bring into the conversation; and, Radhika for her spot-on recommendations and constant encouragement to look deeply into the interconnections of gender, class, the national, and the digital.

1
MEDIA AND CLASS IN THE TWENTY-FIRST CENTURY

Erika Polson, Lynn Schofield Clark, and Radhika Gajjala

Class is ever present in contemporary public discourse. As growing inequality and the shrinking middle classes upend and reshape societies across many middle- and high-income countries, the rising middle classes in new powerhouse economies such as China and India (among other BRICS—Brazil, Russia, India, China, and South Africa—and MINT—Mexico, Indonesia, Nigeria, and Turkey—countries) create new necessities and demands in cultural and political spheres. Within these larger contexts, at the level of everyday life, disparate groups struggle to create and control narratives in shared mediated spaces, driven to obtain or protect opportunities and resources. From the memes of and about working-class supporters of billionaire 'populists', to well-publicized and critiqued philanthropic efforts to bring communication technologies into developing country contexts, to the behind-the-scenes work of migrant tech workers, class is undergoing change both in and through media.

There is no single agreed-upon definition of class, which makes the term both useful, and in need of explication. Generally speaking, class has been understood in relation to how certain groups of people share the same socioeconomic status and cultural tastes. But class is also a term that signals the need to pay attention to the systems of social stratification that hold these differences in place. Class and caste have long been understood in societies around the world in relation to social stratification—as cultural markers within a system in which the few have greater access than the many to status, power, and wealth. While English-language scholarship briefly turned away from class to focus more on rights movements around gender, ethnicity, and sexual orientation, attention to 'class' has returned, particularly as new forms of labor, migration/mobility, news and entertainment, and political communication are facilitated in and through ever-more interdependent communication and information technologies.

Class formations have always been intersectional, since class has been structured in relation to difference as it has played out in varied social, geographic, and material contexts, but new today is our heightened awareness of its intersectionality. As experiences of exploitation and oppression cut across race, gender, and geography, the specific experiences that feed into possible labor and social movements emerge out of local contexts and transnational/global production systems. Individuals encounter each other in work and leisure spaces and, although they might be expected to produce collective meanings, such encounters also continue to be fraught with tensions and contradictions based in the diverse and unique lived, experiential, socioeconomic, and cultural everydayness through which mediated and digital spaces emerge.

We argue that an examination of the everyday is an important place to start as scholars seek to better understand class in relation to how intersectional tensions around the mobility and digitization of media are mediated and negotiated in an era of globalization. A recent case in point is the various iterations and ways in which #MeToo emerged through Twitter publics. Very quickly, after a white Hollywood celebrity's #MeToo post sparked a viral outpouring of sharing, another wave of social media posts spread to bring attention to how a US-based Black activist, Tarana Burke, had been using "Me Too" to encourage women to support each other since 2007. Others chimed in with posts and media op-eds pointing out that #MeToo was more relevant (and risky) for working class women in factory, fast food, or janitorial jobs and encouraging supportive action and reform beyond hashtags. And while much of the global north was celebrating #MeToo as a moment of empowerment for women, MeToo movements in regions of the global south were also emerging through hashtag publics. In the case of China, they were being quickly squashed as they emerged through Chinese social media, but in the case of India, social media callout movements against sexual harassment revealed caste and class divides in how they were responded to—particularly when we make comparisons between the 2017 #LoSHA (list of sexual harassers in the Indian Academy) and 2018 #metoo-india movement.[1] In Indonesia, where one in three women has suffered physical and/or sexual violence, the corresponding #SayaJuga movement was mainly limited to middle-upper class women with social media savvy.[2] In addition, even while seeming to provide empowerment through callout and accountability movements by marginalized groups—whether women, transpeople, people of color, people from historically oppressed castes and races—the internet is still characterized by a proliferation of toxicity. We have encountered contradictions not only in relation to the hashtag publics around calling out sexual harassment, but also in relation to seemingly safe women-centered spaces, such as class, cis gender normativity, and race mediated discourses (for example, when discord emerged in the online "leisure oriented" but heavily entrepreneurial space of do-it-yourself *fibercrafting*, where those who spoke up about diversity and #BIPOC were accused of "bullying" and creating rifts within a peace-loving women-centered knitting space[3]).

As we survey this quickly evolving scene, we see new class formations and struggles reflected in media production, representation, and consumption/dissemination, and conceptions about class reconstituted with the new media industries, applications, and practices that have appeared. What roles are the media industries playing in relation to these changes? How are various changes in social class represented in media? How do media facilitate conversations across distance to challenge certain arrangements of economics and power while holding others in place? How might studies related to the media contribute to broader discussions of economic inequality, workplace stratification, the "sharing economy," and classed contexts of democracy, globalization, journalism, migration and belonging? To get at these questions, in this volume we frequently turn to specific examples, paying attention to the particularities of various milieux. And so, to set our context for this book, we might begin with a story about communication and transactional technologies in the city of Caracas.

The city of Caracas opened its first-ever crypto ATM in January 2019, with the digital currency trade publication CoinTelegraph predicting that cryptocurrency was set to enjoy impressive growth there.[4] As Venezuelan President Nicolas Maduro pledged the country's oil reserves to a digital currency known as the *petro*, and pegged the *petro* to the country's Bolivar currency in a last-ditch effort at economic recovery, the economic crisis in the country deepened. After shortages dating back to 2007, in the early months of 2019 Venezuelan hospitals went without running water, the country experienced a near-total electricity blackout, grocery store shelves stood empty, and the inflation rate for that country was projected to reach 10 million percent in 2019.[5]

Corruption, self-serving politicians, price-fixing schemes and a global commodity bust all played a role in Venezuela's problems, as did the steep decline in the price of crude oil, as oil accounts for 98 percent of Venezuela's exports.[6] Nevertheless, for a brief period some put their hope in the technological innovations of digital commerce. But while English language trade publications targeted to international investors were bullish on the rise of cryptocurrency in Venezuela, noting its alleged ability to lower financial transaction costs and give so-called average citizen-investors an alternative to banks and central bank policies, few in Venezuela were benefiting. A Reuters investigation then found that the *petro* was not available for trading on any major cryptocurrency exchange, further deepening the worries related to the attempt to shore up Venezuelan cash via digital currency.[7]

Catastrophic costs to the many and benefits for the few, particularly for those few who can withstand breathtaking financial risks: the recent story of Venezuela's deepening crisis and the failed bet on the promise of new technology near its core is in many ways an old story. And like many old stories of corruption and inequities, the genre of political satire served as an ideal venue as Maduro was alternatively paired with Homer Simpson, Eddie Murphy, and the absence of Wakanda in numerous memes and YouTube videos as people around the world collectively expressed their outrage and solidarity.

But what do cryptocurrencies and Venezuela have to do with 'media,' traditionally conceived, and how are ideas of class changing in an increasingly interconnected and volatile global economy? These questions, and the example at the heart of what is now an international humanitarian crisis, are illustrative of the concepts that this volume sets out to unpack. With globalization, the subjects of 'media' and 'class' are intertwined and evolving. As Aouragh and Chakravartty[8] have argued,

> Telecommunications networks and digital infrastructure regimes have become the lifeline of neoliberal globalization enforced by the World Trade Organization, multiple Free Trade Agreements, ensconced in the World Bank's Poverty Reduction Strategy papers (PRSPs) and advocated by multilateral governance regimes like the Internet Corporation for Assigned Names and Numbers.

Information and communication technologies are regulated and form the basis of contemporary infrastructures through the inherited inequalities of colonial infrastructures. The authors in this volume thus reconsider definitions of 'media' within the widened scope of technological change, exploring how various facets of information and communication technologies have come to serve as the foundation for the global economy and its emergent economic relations, both through technological capacity and through rapidly co-constructed narratives about its deployment, and how these technologies reproduce systems of privilege and oppression.[9]

We can no longer presume a sequence in which events and consequences occur, societal structures are solidified, and then media narratives explain or even parody them, if such a linear sequence could ever be presumed. With the rapid transactions and interactions made possible in and through the infrastructures of the digital realm, it is now the case that media, technologies, and class structures must be understood as co-constructed and as co-constituting. Caracas represents an extreme example, but many societies are experiencing widening gulfs between those who seek to leverage the speed of technologies and markets for their own benefit, and those who suffer sometimes direct consequences when hoped-for yields elsewhere in the world fail to materialize. And such changes and structural reorganizations can happen more rapidly than ever before, and amidst fewer societal guard rails. In the Venezuelan case, infrastructure moved from a site of shared expectation to a source of revenue that can be gambled away by the powerful.

Many in this volume argue that similar situations are emerging around the world as our traditional means of binding society together, such as through ideals and traditions of democracy and citizenship, are rapidly unraveling. Questions of media and class, then, require a broad understanding of a context in which rapid technological change is occurring in ways that are reconfiguring the expectations between differing members of societies with their variegated access to material and technological resources.

Historical Approaches Connecting Media and Class

Media have long been studied in association with modern class formations. In literary studies, the rise of the novel was considered a medium that promoted ideologies such as individual responsibility and delineated the roles and behaviors of middle-class subjects,[10] and historians linked the development of early media 'technologies' to concentration of power in particular classes, as well as the creation of shared practices and identities.[11] Taking an instrumentalist view of media and class, Cold War-era communication researchers sought to harness the so-called powers of mass media to foster 'modern' (in the image of the US American middle class) attitudes around work, health, and consumption through international development projects directed at disseminating television and radio in newly independent nations of the global south. Seen most notably in the work of Lerner,[12] Rogers,[13] and Schramm,[14] these efforts were later critiqued for actually furthering class divides and inequalities in those societies.

As mass media grew as sites for consumption in the 1950s and 1960s, the Frankfurt School critiqued mass entertainment culture as a form of social control that developed passive audiences,[15] while the rise of what has come to be known as the Birmingham School served as a counter to the top-down nature of such understandings of culture. These two differing perspectives spurred the advancement of divergent critical approaches: political economy and cultural studies. Political economists always held concepts of 'class' as central, in that they focused on how synergistic relations between media owners and regulators worked to maintain the dominance of existing economic and political power structures. Work in this area looked at how media products contained ideological messages that upheld the status quo, working, as Sut Jhally put it, to convince the majority to "support the present system of rewards and power rather than opposing it."[16]

Through cultural studies approaches, associated at the time with the work of Stuart Hall[17] and colleagues in Birmingham, scholars drew from Gramsci[18] to add a cultural dimension to what had been the primarily economic focus in Marxist critiques of power relations. Such work, inspired also by the semiotic analysis of Ferdinand Saussure[19] and Roland Barthes,[20] and the historical and critical reflections on the English working class put forward by Richard Hoggart[21] and Raymond Williams,[22] resulted in new arguments about the role of popular culture in the contexts of social movements, resistant to the messages of neoliberalism that were surfacing in the UK at the time. Whereas "popular culture" had been largely denigrated due to its association with the working classes, these scholars sought to explore how those in the working classes might find in popular culture the discursive tools for resistance to, as well as reproduction of, English class arrangements.[23]

Bringing this approach specifically into the realm of media studies, Morley's[24] research of how audiences from different educational and occupational backgrounds engaged the British *Nationwide* television show was able to demonstrate that while media messages may contain dominant ideologies, their messages were not necessarily read as intended. The idea that audiences bring class/socioeconomic status to bear when interacting with media helped transform narratives about 'false consciousness' to one about active audiences engaged in meaning making through media. Similar perspectives also attended to gender and race, as well as nation and ethnicity, to further elaborate on diverse audience interpretation strategies. For example, studies conceptualized in relation to 'reader-response theory' suggested that texts take on meaning through an interactive process of communities of viewers or readers interpreting them through common social and individual histories.[25] Integrating work by Pierre Bourdieu,[26] and drawing upon earlier reflections of Thorstein Veblen,[27] scholars were drawing more attention to the construction of a 'high brow/low brow' distinction[28] and the rise of 'middlebrow' culture, for example in the form of novel reading, noted above, and other acceptable mediated leisure pursuits of the middle classes.

Intersecting with Class and Media

For communication and media studies, approaches to class have long been fragmented. Across cultural studies, ruminations on digital labor, research on media and globalization, and work on media and migration, we have seen few attempts to pull together a conversation that crosses research paradigms to inform and interrogate class constructs. Even in efforts that consider the intersectionalities of race, class, and gender, few have foregrounded class and economic inequities in ways that explore historical contexts at the intersections of local, social and postcolonial hierarchies and media and technological systems. In conceiving of this book, we have intentionally avoided separating out 'race' and 'gender' into different topic areas, and have similarly avoided segregating essays focusing on the 'global south' versus the 'north,' or 'west' and 'east.' Rather, this collection acknowledges that a range of identities, religions, lifestyles, and geographies will intersect across all areas of media and class. It is the purpose of this collection to tease out how these intersections produce new understanding of power relations.

Various conjunctures reveal how class is produced through intersections of geography, race, gender, caste and labor. The conjunctural nature of class is noted even by Raymond Williams in a time that far predates the digital. In his famous 'Keywords' for instance, he notes how his personal encounter with Cambridge as a working class person allowed him to see how class was threaded through connections between art, industry and democracy. He writes of the term 'class' that:

> The words I linked it with, because of the problems its use raised in my mind, were class and art, and then industry and democracy. I could feel these five words as a kind of structure. The relations between them became more complex the more I considered them.[29]

While Williams is a key figure whose work allows us to see the situated, conjunctural nature of class—and the role of culture in the formation of economic structures—Stuart Hall[30] is key to highlighting issues of race and postcoloniality in the cultural studies field. For instance, he notes how race is "the modality in which class is 'lived,' the medium through which class relations are experienced, the form in which it is appropriated and 'fought through'."[31]

Critical race theory (CRT) has developed to recognize race as central to the making of the modern world and its distribution of power.[32] CRT locates the emergence of race, and of white supremacy, in relation to European imperialism, and hence also opens a critique for the relationship between theories of economic relations and the interests of those who have given articulation to those theories in a colonial context. White supremacy here does not refer to skin color, but to a historically constructed political system in which, as Mills has written, "one subset of humans, henceforth designated by (shifting) 'racial' (phenotypical/genealogical/cultural) criteria ... as 'white,'" has rendered a different subset "as 'nonwhite' and of a different and inferior moral status."[33] In order to advance understandings of class, then, we need to grapple with the ways that white supremacy has been an unnamed shaper of economic and political systems.

The focus on class in media studies was largely shaped by European social theory, as alluded to earlier in this essay. Yet several different factors have shaped the experience of class in nations and regions around the world.

In the Americas, relations of power and economic difference between groups of people have their roots in the sixteenth century, when a form of political, epistemic, economic, and subjective management emerged that Anibal Quijano[34] has termed the "colonial matrix of power." This was a system borne from a struggle over the conquest of the Americas by European monarchies. It legitimized a social classification of race, gender, and religion that in turn gave license to the confiscation of land and the destruction of cultures, and that set the terms for the relations of domination between the conquerors and the conquered. The logics of this colonial matrix of power thus justified hierarchical forms of knowledge, ranking the knowledge of the conquered as inferior and generating what Walter Mignolo[35] refers to as racial and patriarchal colonial wounds. Second, as persons were forcibly removed from their homes in Africa and brought into slavery in order to build the United States' agricultural economic system, the colonial matrix of power was extended to legitimize a racist system that justified the legalization of subjugation and relegated African Americans to a status devoid of rights to property, freedom of movement, and political agency.

For recent scholarship exploring African American intersections of media, race, and class, we suggest Catherine Knight Steele's[36] interrogation of how class and status are reserved for the more light-skinned characters in a television program meant to celebrate African American families and communities—finding that successful attributes are reserved for characters with Eurocentric phenotypic characteristics, and unsuccessful attributes given to characters with more Afrocentric features. Pointing to a long history of class-based colorism that brings higher status and better opportunities to lighter skinned African Americans, she suggests African American writers and producers be challenged regarding their roles in perpetuating these harmful mediated representations. And for an insightful exploration of the evolution of agency in creating *self*-representations, see Aisha Durham's[37] work tracing Beyoncé's formation over ten years—and three distinct periods—of performances differently embodying race, gender, and class. Durham argues that while perhaps beginning as a profitable object of the masculine-defined, white gaze, the star used her growing power within transnational culture industries to rewrite classed narratives about Black female bodies, and says that by the time of Beyoncé's 'Lemonade' album, her "music videos took up class in ways that critically reimagined Black belonging."[38]

As several chapters in this collection will demonstrate, class works very different in India and the Southeast Asian region, where there are intersecting areas of class and caste, impacting media regionally and globally. For example, the issue of caste in the Indian media space is further highlighted in global and transnational media as a contemporary issue partly because of the presence of what a Washington Post columnist referred to as the "Dalit Twitter." Thus, while Dalit activists have in fact connected transnationally—as in the case of Dalit Panthers and Black Panthers in the 1970s[39]—the need to see caste as a global, human rights issue is being revisited strongly through contemporary global/transnational mediation. There is insufficient understanding in the Western academic space (even within media research informed by postcolonial theory and transnational feminist work) about these conjunctures of caste and class.

There are vast gaps in media/class studies that can only unfold as more diverse intersections are researched from different socio cultural and geopolitical locations.

Global and Digital Disruptions to Media and Class

The terrain of media and class scholarship has changed dramatically with the introduction of digital and mobile media, and the global reach and impact of communication technologies.

Digital has disrupted everything from economic models to industry operations to everyday communications in work, consumption, personal relationships, healthcare and access to basic services, and the very way people move through space. And, indeed, "disruption" is the term used in the tech industry, for example how Airbnb *disrupted* hotels and Uber *disrupted* taxis. But these are not simply smart new technology companies; these innovations have also disrupted social class, with impacts on race and gender.

Even Facebook looks at us through the lens of class, particularly in relation to what we own and aspire to own. In the 98 data points that Facebook knows about us there are indicators as to whether or not we are thinking about buying a new car, what kind of home we own, did we recently use a travel app or participate in a timeshare and whether or not we carry a balance on our credit card.[40] Each of these categories contains assumptions about both economic capital and cultural capital. Similarly, when Facebook gathers information about people who are likely to need auto parts or services, and about people who have purchased auto parts or services recently, that, too, is information that locates us in relation to traditional economic and class markers. In response to new technology businesses that gather data on the most microscopic and private of practices and movements, we also see new forms of collective bargaining as workers rally to strike, registering their discontent. Whether Oracle workers in South Korea or podcasting upstart Gimlet media's employees in the United States, labor movements emanating from the digital economy are gaining steam and gaining ground. Stories and images of successful strikers circulate through digital and social media, inspiring others to collective action.[41]

Labor and movement are now more global and transnational—but also very contextual and local. And in the new digital economy, the Production/Text/Audience organization that once characterized media research is no longer clearly delineated. In this book, we wanted to rethink this structuring to consider new factors, such as the growing role of prosumption, neoliberal individual precarity, and the new form of labor across production, text, and audience participation. Sonia Livingstone notes the shift in media communication from "mass" (one to many) to "communication among peers (both 'one to one' and 'many to many')."[42] And indeed, in the turn to internet research, we see that while "mass" communication still happens, the proliferation of social media platforms gives rise to different forms of mass, many to many, as well as one to one communication. The shift to prosumption, for instance, serves to make invisible offline forms of labor—whether in production of gadgets, in home-based care-work or in coding work done to produce online platforms through which prosumption happens. Thus, not only has our relationship to text and the screen as media consumers and users shifted, there is also a shift in how traditional offline labor and class formations connect up with the larger socioeconomic and political infrastructures. For instance, even as we see the more visible callout movements or protests in global Twitter or Facebook spaces (such as the Arab Spring or Black Lives Matter), we also see that labor movements from offline factory sites are also being organized and mobilized through the everyday use of mobile phones and related gadgets.

As Jack Qiu, Melissa Gregg, and Kate Crawford[43] have noted, the contemporary trend of "the spatial separation between production and consumption in the global commodity chain" is a shift facilitated by moves to outsource work (where people working in different time-zones can contribute to the commodity chain of digital production). While a spatial separation in itself is not new per se—after all, historically the manufacturing processes have been spatially dispersed, particularly as a result of colonization—what is different now is the spacio-temporal continuum and the consumer–producer continuum that feeds into prosumerism. This shift, in some instances, is a result of the commodification of what might previously have been subsumed and made invisible as reproductive work or ancillary work. Qiu et al's useful "circuits of labor" model[44] shows how this works in the case of iPhone production and the Foxconn factory assembly lines.

As revealed in several of the chapters in this collection, arguments about the reproduction of class through digital mediation push on pre-existing definitions of class and indicate the need to rethink how status is accessed, created, represented, reproduced, and lost in relation to changing and proliferating digital media forms.

Contents of the Book

The Routledge Companion to Media and Class brings together scholars from many communication subfields working at the intersection of media and class, with a specific focus on how understandings of class are changing in contemporary media contexts. The volume foregrounds changing economic contexts, considering the role that various media industries and their products are playing in those societal changes. Contributors have been asked to make clear how they define and utilize the terms 'media' and 'class' in their work (e.g., what traditions of class are followed, and how is this contributing to the study of media?).

Since its earliest days, critical studies of communication have focused attention on the roles that mediated visual representations play in reinforcing taken-for-granted worldviews regarding class and social place. As the media industries continue to undergo change, so too does research into the role of mass media. In Part I of this book, which is focused on new conceptions of class in mass media, scholars foreground reality, fictional, and animated television, advertising, and music videos, developing new questions and new means of analyzing the role of visual media in relation to social change. This section's scholars adapt existing questions and methodologies to new situations emerging through contemporary mass media; their contributions add to studies of representation with a lens on contemporary popular culture, and improve understanding of material conditions underlying newer forms of entertainment.

In a study of English-language advertising by a variety of global brands, Matthew P. McAllister and Litzy Galarza argue that ads construct naturalized connections of working-class, male bodies in ways that range from loyal servitude, masculinity, physical abuse to disgust. In all these guises, representations of working-class men are mobilized to foster brand consumption, either by encouraging audiences to become associated with a 'masculine' product, or to avoid particularly negative/disgusting associations through their brand selections. Reflecting the growing presence of 'reality' shows produced for television markets around the world, a number of contributors consider how class works in this genre. June Deery surveys a range of reality TV shows that promise to bring viewers into the private and social worlds of a purported upper class, offering encounters with representations of people and lifestyles who viewers might never otherwise get to 'know.' Exploring relations between money and class as they play out in scenarios orchestrated for maximum drama, she demonstrates how these representations inform viewers about class performance. Considering reality television in Korea, Hun-Yul Lee analyzes representations of Non-Koreans in local television productions to demonstrate how low status becomes associated with particular migrant ethnicities, while Western expatriate professionals are attributed with cosmopolitan authority and status. Furthermore, he points out that although labor and/or marriage migrants make up the vast majority of the foreign population in the country, contemporary television shows now focus much more on the glamorous lives of professionals and travelers living in or visiting Korea, with the consequence that the working conditions and hardships faced by the majority of migrants go unnoticed.

Annette Hill and Koko Kondo take a different approach to representation in reality television, interrogating how the labor of performers and their supporters are mobilized as entertainment in a televised dance competition in the United Kingdom. Although the reality talent show is constructed as a resource for upward mobility and even stardom in the competitive world of professional dance, achieving this dream requires mobilization of considerable resources, including time, money, particular forms of training and skills, knowledge and experience with talent show formats, and an available support network of family and friends who can drive to performances and demonstrate enthusiasm for the contestant on television. This 'spectacle of labor' is woven into the show by producers.

In a chapter on how class and inequality are treated in representations of HIV and AIDS in Kenya, Renée A. Botta mobilizes findings on representation to make recommendations for improvements in how stories are told. Botta demonstrates how a popular edutainment program foregrounds the dominant class experience, ignoring the material and social realities of the majority of HIV-positive Kenyans. Through her interrogation of the program's representation of the intersection of class and economic inequality with gender in portraying HIV and AIDS in Kenya, Botta advocates for a more diverse and participatory approach to character and storyline development when trying to use entertainment to address real-life health concerns.

Part II considers class in interactive digital and mobile media, across varied international contexts but with a key concentration in Asia—a region characterized by high adoption of digital media into everyday life, quickly evolving new forms of class belonging, and understudied in overall English-language scholarship on media and class. Alongside excitement for interactive platforms to usher in a democratization of media has been a corresponding awareness of how these platforms may become contested by competing groups, exacerbate pre-existing tensions, and/or create new channels for domination and exclusion. As interactive websites and mobile devices proliferate to serve countless interests and needs, class becomes a significant differentiator among users who nonetheless are united within niche media communities. Essays in this part examine how old class divides structure practices in new ways within interactive digital media platforms. Building on the importance of private spaces to work in digital media studies, Holly Kruse looks at how horse race wagering practices are classed differently depending on the spaces in which they are enacted, and argues that classed divisions around gambling are maintained in and through various forms of interactive media. Rohit K. Dasgupta analyzes how, while mobile apps such as Grindr have opened up new private spaces for queer men in India, class and caste divides have continued to influence user experience and define community barriers. Omar Daoudi studies the emergence of Saudi YouTube celebrities, who have parlayed their stardom into financial and social gains. Daoudi cautions, however, that although the young stars have made names for themselves and gained a certain power over online discourse, in the greater context of a closed Saudi society their political impacts remain limited.

The development and growing ubiquity of mobile media add a new dimension to how media and class overlap. A key barrier and issue is how cost, affordability, cultural capital, and differentiated literacies shape appropriation, domestication, and use of digital media. The mobility of devices, content, and location-based access both shape and are shaped by class position. Will Balmford and Larissa Hjorth examine the roles that class, financial capacity and age play in how Australians navigate mobile technology in the home. By closely examining the influence class has on the household, they interrogate the multiple device literacies, daily habits and communicative scenarios of use across participant households from differing socioeconomic standings. Examining home-based media in East Asia, Crystal Abidin studies YouTube vlogs broadcast from and focused on the topic of 'home,' arguing that in these specific East Asian contexts, "domestic practices and leisurely pursuits convey *inconspicuous consumption* as an indicator of class." Indeed, against the backdrop of an overworked populace in expensive and fast-paced urban environments, Abidin finds the "slow living at home" focus of home vlogs to be a marker of class privilege.

Following this is Sun Sun Lim and Renae Sze Ming Loh's study of underprivileged youths in Singapore, which finds that although the youth are ostensibly connected to the internet, use is largely confined to social media accessed through mobile apps. They argue that these media literacies reproduce existing practices at the expense of developing new media literacies (and accompanying social and cultural capital). And, finally, critiquing the Western lens often given to discussions of class—particularly in relation to who is among the 'working class'—Shakuntala Banaji shares digital practices of working children and their parents in Southeast Asia. As Banaji points out, the affordances for which digital media are typically celebrated can seem trivial compared with what is required for basic dignity and daily survival.

In Part III of this volume, focused on labor in digital contexts, we have chapters that nuance and extend the idea of what 'class' means in the contemporary digital capitalist and neoliberal entrepreneurial moment as they map issues of labor from the production of gadgets such as smartphones to the production of affect in voluntourist platforms. These chapters also approach labor and the proletariat through different frameworks while also historicizing class and making connections with pre-digital labor formations. The part begins with Vera-Zambrano and Powers, who map a Bourdieusian concept of class to digital labor through an examination of journalism. They note how the difference in how 'excellence' on journalistic performance is viewed is a function of social status and access to social capital. Thus, their definition of class highlights "dynamic interactions between one's social origins and trajectories." Polson's chapter then takes up the issue of precarious labor, drawing on examples from "#digital nomad" lifestyles that are narrated through Instagram selfies and online forums. She notes how what she refers to as "lifestyle centric labor migration" represents a different kind of social mobility while simultaneously increasing forms of precarity.

Jansson's chapter then shifts the lens for examining mobile labor by moving our focus to the reproductive labor (citing Jarrat[45]) that is performed through the digital using the case of mobile women in the UN system.

In this section, we also see the historicizing of digital labor beyond just the digital. Wolfson examines class and historicizes labor in an examination of food delivery platforms, while elaborating on the "gig-economy" and "platform capitalism." In the chapter that follows, Wauthier et al. examine leisure migrants and philanthropy voluntourism; here, we can see resonances with both the digital nomads and the mobile women of the UN doing reproductive labor. Soriano and Cabañes historicize the study of digital labor and point to the global north/global south and neo-colonial hierarchies that emerge. Each of the chapters thus use specific context-relevant definitions of class. What we see in this set of chapters is an implicit and very clear laying out of ways in which neocolonial, transnational infrastructures shape contemporary forms of labor in relation to digital contexts functioning through gig economies, offshore labor and overlapping of leisure, work and philanthropy circuits that interweave certain populations within the global south and the global north who have particular kinds of access.

Part IV of this volume considers media and class in relation to expressions of citizenship. This part builds on the work presented in earlier chapters that explores class through the prisms of intersectionality, representation, labor practices, and traditional and digital media. By focusing on the practices that emerge as people and societal institutions navigate the new terrain of the digital realm, this part presents work situated in relation to questions of how various individuals, groups, and organizations in society participate in the collective actions of democratic engagement via, and in relation to, the representations proffered through, various media channels.

Germaine Halegoua addresses this question by examining the conflicts that emerge as those designing urban broadband initiatives, ostensibly to mitigate inequities of access, inadvertently participate in the reproduction of class distinction as planners fail to bring certain populations and their needs into consideration. Justine Humphry's chapter similarly looks at tensions in the urban context, focusing her analysis on the ways that those experiencing housing insecurities navigate the limitations of access that are largely held in place by designs that favor middle-class assumptions of digital platforms and their uses. Mohamed El Marzouki then introduces discussions of citizenship, analyzing the ways that young adults contest the discourses and institutions that sustain and reproduce inequities and social class distinctions as they utilize the social media platform of YouTube as a space for experimenting with the exercising of political voice as they build and lay claim to the respect of the people.

Lynn Schofield Clark's chapter extends this argument through an analysis of how young marginalized newcomers to US politics negotiated the political processes of governance and regional transportation planning by strategically deploying the youth voice in an effort to influence decision-making processes in their communities. Job Mwaura's chapter brings together contextual factors of media use with questions of civic and political action, offering an analysis of two youth-led instances of hashtag activism in Kenya.

Finally, in the Postscript, David Morley situates chapters from this collection into a broader spectrum of class theories, and argues that such intersectional, non-media-centric, and grounded approaches are a strength of the book and a necessity for critical inquiries of class structures in relation to media technologies and practices moving forward.

This collection includes approaches to class from many regions of the world (included are India, Kenya, Morocco, Saudi Arabia, Singapore, and a more general focus on Southeast Asia, South Korea, Europe, United States, Australia), and yet there are also gaps, for example, the lack of chapters focused on Latin American countries, Latinx and Indigenous communities, African-Americans, among others. Class/race/gender/nationality affect academic time and focus. For example, we understand that scholars who must write in English as a second or third language to participate in a project such as this may not find the resources to do so; and many scholars of color are working in institutions where not only must they produce impeccable work to avoid the micro and macro discriminations that structure the so-called 'meritocracy,' they also perform much more emotional labor to support students of color in predominantly white institutions, and are disproportionately called upon to serve on committees where the imbalance of white faculty becomes all too obvious. This "triple tax" can make it more difficult to say "yes" to producing original content for projects such as this one that take time and effort but do not count as much in scholastic economies.

It is our hope that this wide-ranging collection will inspire even wider ranging interrogations of class across diverse contexts in years to come. What is clear to us after spending much time and thought with the contributions to this collection is that: there is no one definition of class, and even less so when we think across cultures; there is no unifying theory of the relationships between media and class; and, finally, there is no doubt that media and class are co-constructed and continuously evolving.

Notes

1 See: Keertana K. Tella, "#MeToo: An International Conversation on Sexual Violence Impacting Feminist Discourse Across Borders," *Economic & Political Weekly* (October 25, 2018), accessed from www.epw.in/engage/article/metoo-international-conversation-sexual-violence-feminist-discourse-impact; Pallavi Rao, "Caste and the LoSHA Discourse," *Communication, Culture and Critique* 11, no. 3 (2018): 494–497.
2 Dyah Ayu Kartika, "#MeToo Has Skipped Indonesia: Here's Why," *The Conversation* (March 8, 2019), para 8, accessed from https://theconversation.com/metoo-has-skipped-indonesia-heres-why-112530.
3 Jaya Saxena, "The Knitting Community is Reckoning with Racism," *Vox* (February 25, 2019), accessed from www.vox.com/the-goods/2019/2/25/18234950/knitting-racism-instagram-stories.
4 Simon Chandler, "Ongoing Economic Crises in Venezuela and Beyond Show That the Idea of Bitcoin as a Store of Value is Increasingly Catching On," *CoinTelegraph* (February 20, 2019), accessed from https://cointelegraph.com/news/ongoing-economic-crises-in-venezuela-and-beyond-show-that-the-idea-of-bitcoin-as-a-store-of-value-is-increasingly-catching-on.
5 Megan Specia and Ana Vanessa Herrero, "Venezuela Crisis: Beyond the Political Drama, Normal People are Struggling to Survive," *Independent* (February 9, 2019), accessed from www.independent.co.uk/news/world/venezuela-crisis-food-inflation-refugees-life-people-maduro-a8762311.html.
6 Garth Friesen "The Path to Hyperinflation: What Happened to Venezuela?" *Forbes* (August 7, 2018), accessed from www.forbes.com/sites/garthfriesen/2018/08/07/the-path-to-hyperinflation-what-happened-to-venezuela/#5dae4c2715e4.
7 Brian Ellsworth, "Special Report: In Venezuela, New Cryptocurrency is Nowhere to be Found," *Reuters* (August 30, 2018), accessed from www.reuters.com/article/us-cryptocurrency-venezuela-specialrepor-idUSKCN1LF15U.
8 Miriyam Aouragh and Paula Chakravartty, "Infrastructures of Empire: Towards a Critical Geopolitics of Media and Information Studies," *Media, Culture & Society* 38, no. 4 (2016): 566.
9 Safiya Noble, *Algorithms of Oppression* (New York: NYU Press, 2018).
10 See: Ian Watt, *The Rise of the Novel: Studies in Defoe, Richardson, and Fielding* (Berkeley, CA: University of California Press, 2001); Myra Jehlen, "New World Epics: The Novel and the Middle-Class in America," *Salmagundi 36*, Winter (1977): 49–68; Patricia McKee, *Public & Private: Gender, Class, and the British Novel (1764–1878)* (Minneapolis: University of Minnesota Press, 1997).
11 For example, Harold Innis, *The Bias of Communication* (Toronto: University of Toronto Press, 1977); Benedict Anderson, *Imagined Communities: Reflections on the Origin and Spread of Nationalism* (London: Verso, 1983).
12 Daniel Lerner, with the assistance of Lucille W. Pevsner, *The Passing of Traditional Society: Modernizing the Middle East* (New York: The Free Press, 1958).
13 Everett M. Rogers, *Bibliography on the Diffusion of Innovations* (East Lansing: Department of Communication, Michigan State University, 1962).
14 Wilbur Schramm, *Mass Media and National Development: The Role of Information in the Developing Countries* (Stanford, CA: Stanford University Press, 1964).
15 For example, Theodor W. Adorno and Max Horkheimer, *Dialectic of Enlightenment* (New York: Continuum, 1972).
16 Sut Jhally, *The Spectacle of Accumulation: Essays in Culture, Media, & Politics* (New York: Peter Lang, 2006), 47.

17 For example, Stuart Hall, "Encoding/Decoding," in: *Culture, Media, Language: Working Papers in Cultural Studies, 1972–79*, eds. Stuart Hall, Dorothy Hobson, Andrew Lowe, and Paul Willis (London: Hutchinson, 1980), 128–138; Stuart Hall, "Gramsci's Relevance for the Study of Race and Ethnicity," in *Stuart Hall: Critical Dialogues in Cultural Studies*, eds. Stuart Hall, David Morley, and Kuan-Hsing Chen (London: Routledge, 1996), 411–440; Stuart Hall, "The Problem of Ideology: Marxism without Guarantees," in *Marx 100 Years On*, ed. Betty Matthews (London: Lawrence & Wisha, 1996), 57–85.
18 See: Antonio Gramsci, *Selections from the Prison Notebooks of Antonio Gramsci*, translated by Q. Hoare and G.N. Smith (New York: International Publishers, 1971); Antonio Gramsci, *Prison Notebooks: Volume I*, Translated by J.A. Buttigieg (New York: Columbia University Press, 1992); Antonio Gramsci, *Prison Notebooks: Volume 2*, Translated by J.A. Buttigieg (New York: Columbia University Press, 1996).
19 Ferdinand de Saussure, "Course in General Linguistics," in: *The Structuralists from Marx to Levi-Strauss*, eds. R. de George and F. de George (Garden City, New York: Anchor Books, 1972), p. 67.
20 Roland Barthes, *Elements of Semiology* (New York: Hill and Wang, 1964).
21 Richard Hoggart, *The Uses of Literacy* (Fair Lawn, NJ: Essential Books, 1957).
22 Raymond Williams, *Keywords: A Vocabulary of Culture and Society* (New York: Oxford University Press, 1976).
23 See: Dick Hebdige, *Subculture: The Meaning of Style* (London: Routledge, 1979); Paul Willis, *Learning to Labor: How Working Class Kids Get Working Class Jobs* (Aldershot, UK: Ashgate, 1978).
24 An earlier study published by Brunsdon and Morley involved textual analysis of the program (Charlotte Brunsdon and David Morley, *Everyday Television: Nationwide* (London: British Film Institute, 1978)) and Morley went on to write *The Nationwide Audience*, tying readings of the program to socio-cultural background: David Morley, *The 'Nationwide' Audience: Structure and Decoding* (London: British Film Institute, 1980).
25 For example, Ien Ang on soap opera viewing in the Netherlands; Janice Radway on romance reading in the US; Angela McRobbie on teen magazines in the UK; and Ondina Fachel Leal and Ruben George Oliven on telenovelas in Brazil: Ien Ang, *Watching Dallas: Soap Opera and the Melodramatic Imagination* (London: Routledge, 1985); Janice A. Radway, *Reading the Romance: Women, Patriarchy, and Popular Literature* (London: Verso, 1984); Angela McRobbie, *Jackie! An Ideology of Adolescent Femininity* (Birmingham, AL: The Centre for Contemporary Cultural Studies, 1978); Ondina Fachel Leal and Ruben George Oliven, "Class Interpretations of a Soap Opera Narrative: The Case of the Brazilian Novela 'Summer Sun'," *Theory, Culture & Society* 5 (1988): 81–99.
26 Pierre Bourdieu, *Distinction: A Social Critique of the Judgement of Taste* (Cambridge, MA: Harvard University Press, 1984).
27 Thorstein Veblen, *The Theory of the Leisure Class: An Economic Study of Institutions* (New York: The Macmillan Company, 1912).
28 Lawrence W. Levine, *Highbrow/Lowbrow: The Emergence of Cultural Hierarchy in America* (Cambridge, MA: Harvard University Press, 1988).
29 Williams, *Keywords*, 13.
30 Stuart Hall, "Race, Articulation and Societies Structured in Dominance" in *Sociological Theories: Race and Colonialism*, ed. UNESCO (Paris: UNESCO, 1980).
31 Ibid., 341.
32 Charles Mills, *The Racial Contract* (Ithaca: Cornell University Press, 1997).
33 Ibid., 11.
34 Anibal Quijano, "Coloniality of Power and Eurocentrism in Latin America," *International Sociology* 15, no. 2 (2000): 215–232.
35 Walter Mignolo, "Coloniality of Power and De-Colonial Thinking," *Cultural Studies* 21, no. 2–3 (2007): 155–167.
36 Catherine Knight Steele, "Pride and Prejudice: Pervasiveness of Colorism and the Animated Series Proud Family," *Howard Journal of Communications* 27, no. 1 (2016): 53–67.
37 Aisha Durham, "Class Formation: Beyoncé in Music Video Production," *Black Camera* 9, no. 1 (Fall 2017): 197–204.
38 Ibid., 201.
39 Diane Pien, "Dalit Panther Movement (1972–1977)" *Black Past* (August 17, 2018), accessed from www.blackpast.org/global-african-history/dalit-panther-movement-1972-1977/.
40 Stacy Liberatore, "Tired of Seeing Annoying Adverts on Facebook? Here's How to Fix It," *Daily Mail* (August 26, 2016), accessed from www.dailymail.co.uk/sciencetech/article-3753526/What-Facebook-REALLY-knows-Firm-reveals-98-pieces-data-uses-target-ads-them.html.
41 See: Sarah Attfield, "The Global Working Class Fought Back in 2018," People's World (December 17, 2018), accessed from www.peoplesworld.org/article/the-global-working-class-fought-back-in-2018/; Caroline O'Donovan, "The Staff of Gimlet Media is Unionizing," BuzzFeed News (March 13, 2019), accessed from www.buzzfeednews.com/article/carolineodonovan/gimlet-media-podcasts-spotify-union.

42 Sonia Livingstone, "The Challenge of Changing Audiences: Or, What is the Audience Researcher to Do in the Age of the Internet?" *European Journal of Communication* 19, no. 1 (2004): 75–86.
43 Jack Linchuan Qiu, Melissa Gregg, and Kate Crawford, "Circuits of Labour: A Labour Theory of the iPhone Era," *Triple C: Communication, Capitalism, & Critique* 12, no. 2 (2014): Para 22, accessed from https://doi.org/10.31269/triplec.v12i2.540.
44 Ibid.
45 Kylie Jarrett, "The Relevance of 'Women's Work': Social Reproduction and Immaterial Labor in Digital Media," *Television & New Media* 15, no. 1 (2014): 14–29.

PART I

Class and Mass Media

2
WORKING-CLASS BODIES IN ADVERTISING

Matthew P. McAllister and Litzy Galarza

In a US commercial for the home-delivery company Dollar Shave Club, which aired from 2016–2018, a thin white man in khakis and a Polo-style shirt stands in front of retail-store displays pondering between two faux razor alternatives. As he decides, two other white men, one at a time, walk by and quickly choose one of the two. "The Missile 12 Laser Chin Detection System" is selected by a snooty white man in a black turtle neck and blazer with steel-rod-straight posture and precise grooming. Although clearly a snob—he glances derisively at the undecided protagonist—his body type and face are not unlike that of the main character. When he exits another man shuffles more slowly in and chooses the second razor, the "Econo-Shave." His face, body and clothing are more distinct from either of the other two men. He is wearing sweat pants and an ill-fitting T-shirt that has a picture of a fried egg on it (with the slogan, "I Like 'Em Scrabbled"). He is balding, and the hair he does have is unkempt. He is also overweight—as his tight, food-themed T-shirt accentuates—and his shopping basket is filled with multiple bags of "Cheese Puffs" (in fact, he already is eating from one of the open bags). As he grabs several packets of razors, he smiles at the undecided one, revealing missing teeth. The dilemma for the conflicted consumer is resolved when the President of Dollar Shave Club—also trim, wearing a tailored if modest shirt with tie and slacks, and looking more like the first two men—bursts out of the retail displays and offers the consumer a third choice (the branded product).[1]

Although this ad is for a brand of razors, it is also about class (at least as commonly symbolized via white men). It explicitly contrasts strata of classes—upper, middle, and working class—in a way that is fairly rare in advertising. And while the ad clearly positions a preferred aesthetic/taste distinction[2] of a common-sense middle that rejects ridiculous extremes, the "Econo-Shave" consumer is the outlier of the group. The other three men all are thin, with nice hair and clothing. The "Econo-Shave" consumer's socioeconomic distinctiveness is shown by visual working-class markers prominent throughout media, including advertising. Some of this is communicated through clothing (sweat pants) and accessories (junk food). But class status is also communicated through the body itself, a symbolic physicality that is reflected in advertising's lessons about race, gender and sexuality.[3] These commercial lessons are fundamentally ideological, influencing—in the case of the Dollar Shave Club ad—our view of class in ways that have implications for the power inequities built into socioeconomic relations. Ads offer lessons, with and about class, about "who is in charge, how society is or ought to be, who is powerful, who is weak, who is dominant, who is subordinate."[4]

This chapter explores issues involved with the representation of working-class bodies in advertising. It will review some common incentives and tendencies of the portrayal of the working class in advertising, including intersectional portrayals involving connections of class to other social categories and inequities. Although commercial stories about the working class are not always as negatively stigmatizing as in the example above, they still circumscribe this group with particular reoccurring tropes that teach lessons about how we should think about the working class. In particular, these lessons include constructing naturalized connections of the working-class body to loyal servitude, masculinity, and physical abuse and disgust. These advertising-based portrayals are also always in service of consumption and capital and may be especially important in our changing economic times.

Class and Advertising

Paulson and O'Guinn observe that "social class is rarely the focus of advertising studies."[5] The lack of explicit scholarly attention is ironic given the key role of class dynamics in advertising. Because advertising funds our media to reach certain consumer groups who are defined by their socioeconomic status, and because advertising involves the portrayal of people's relationship to goods and services that involve economic transactions, class is inherently tied to advertising. In the case of the former, the economic incentives created by advertising often mean that our media system—looking to reach the ideal "audience commodity"[6]—underserves lower- and working-class audiences, opting instead to appeal to the middle and upper classes, given that advertising often prefers consumers in those strata.

The consumerist incentives built into advertising's political economy significantly affect the classed nature of all advertising-supported media.[7] As Butsch argues, this means that portrayals of the working class in mainstream, advertising-supported media, such as broadcast television, tend to be relatively rare, and, when occurring, may be ridiculing or non-sympathetic.[8] Stereotypes of white, working-class men, were solidified, if not constituted, by the enduring images of Ralph Kramden (*The Honeymooners*), Archie Bunker (*All in the Family*), Homer Simpson (*The Simpsons*), and Doug Heffernan (*The King of Queens*): loud, overweight, generally happy, not particularly ambitious or skilled. Other media, such as comics and film, offer similar stereotypes of the white working-class male.[9] This is in agreement with Diana Kendall's claim that television programs that do feature the working class "emphasize the workers' humble origins, lack of taste, proletarian lifestyle, and disgust with their work."[10] In news, Kendall adds, much of the framing of the working class historically focuses on corrupt or greedy unions that enable lazy and incompetent workers. When representations of working-class folk appear in television commercials, they flow with such entertainment and journalistic representations. The Maytag Repairman—overweight, uniformed, mostly physically inert, dissatisfied with his job, in this case because he is lonely, since Maytag never breaks down—could be the brother of Ralph Kramden.

A key connection of advertising to class is the lessons about, and representations of, class in the ads themselves. Messages about class were found from the early days of mass advertising and were even communicated by the sheer volume of goods on display in advertising. Both Gary Cross and Roland Marchand make this argument by noting that the abundance of branded products and their celebration in advertising promised class mobility as a benefit of consumer culture.[11] Marchand labels this lesson about class "The Parable of the Democracy of Goods"; it was punctuated by ads where the working class were shown to marvel over the access to the world of the rich: "his Tires are just like mine!"[12] Another promise of class mobility, as Marchand notes, was implied by white, female working-class bodies: during the depression of the 1930s, the body types of female servants in ads would mirror that of their employers, hinting that class mobility could also be possible with the right access to goods. Such "narratives of mobility" continued in many ads throughout the late twentieth century.[13]

However, class in advertising representations often does not call attention to itself. In advertising, the "normal" class position is coded as middle-class, and is so pervasive in advertising portrayals that it is simply assumed, and therefore nearly invisible.[14] Thus, the middle class may not be obviously "marked"—much like the "sensibly" dressed, and bodied, protagonist and benefactor in the Dollar Shave Club commercial described at the beginning of this chapter. Advertising characters who are coded as the working class are relatively rare, though, with barely above 10 percent of all characters in magazine ads in this category, according to studies by Paulson and O'Guinn.[15] Perhaps because of this, portrayals of the working class (and the rich as well) in advertising call attention to themselves with more showy or exaggerated iconography. Blue-collar workers may be literally wearing a blue work shirt, or be "plaid-collar workers" that signal the same status. In ads, white, working-class male bodies "are strong but not lean, their hair is short, sometimes graying. They have facial hair, wear plaid and overalls, and baseball caps."[16] They are often shown in their place of work,[17] unlike the typical middle-class advertising character.

The degree to which advertising does signal the working class may also vary by decade/era,[18] including tough economic times where privilege and hardship are especially noteworthy. Marchand notes that ads during the Depression especially foregrounded class, including class comparisons.[19] During the World Wars, more commercials may have celebrated men and women workers contributing to the war effort: "PARTS FOR TANK GUNS—made by Women" declared one print ad for Chrysler and accompanied by a photo of women on the assembly line.[20] In the Trump Era, the election of a rich man who brands his wealth in a variety of ways—and also ran on a platform that both celebrated the white working class while denigrating immigrants of color as threats to working-class jobs—combined with "post-recessionary" economic portrayals of the well-to-do, may also have triggered more explicit class comparisons and portrayals of class conflict in ads than is typical.[21] Two commercials during the 2017 Super Bowl reflected themes of immigration, in apparent response to President Trump's discriminatory policies, by portraying the traumatization of bodies trying to enter America: one ad for Anheuser–Busch and another for 84 Lumber.[22]

The common presumption of advertising characters as middle class, though, often means that the explicit placement of the poor, working class, and rich stand out more, and thus lessons about their nature are more affecting. Broad morals about class status in advertising are contradictory, being both "mutable and rigid."[23] On the one hand, advertising offers the enticement of upward mobility through the symbolic meanings of brands that can be acquired through purchasing rather than birthright; on the other, the stereotypes of classed people and hints about their innate behavior or solidified lifestyle choices imply it is an inherent aspect of their nature.

Intersectionality of Class with Race and Gender

Of course, representations of the working class in advertising are not just white and male. Crenshaw's concept of intersectionality shows that multiple aspects of an individual's identities including but not limited to class, gender, sexuality, race, and age are interconnected and should not be isolated in analyses seeking to more fully address their lived experiences.[24]

Intersections of race, gender and working-class signifiers characterize both past and current advertising. This was so even before the rise of national brand advertising. Although it involves not the "working class" but a class of human beings forced to work, one of the very first genres of newspaper advertising in the US was slave advertising. In what is often considered the first American newspaper, *The Boston News-Letter*, classified-style ads for slaves for sale could be found. Many other advertisements promised rewards for runaway slaves, and often would have detailed descriptions of their bodies: "6 Feed two Inches high short curl'd hair, his Knees nearer together than common" read one 1750 notice in a Boston paper.[25]

O'Barr's work details how, after the Civil War and with the beginning of mass consumer culture, US advertising depicted African Americans in service positions such as porters, luggage carriers, waiters, attendants, servants and shoe shiners. Many ads were embellished with specific language codes and imagery, such as dialects, bandanas, cotton-picking and watermelons, meant to invoke connections to the South. The presentation in ads of African American service workers as utterly devoted and loyal to the white middle-class fulfilled various hegemonic and promotional functions. They bowdlerized the abuses of slave relations, abuses that at the beginning of the branded era of consumer goods were very much in recent memory; they evoked images of a pre-industrial America to blunt the artificiality of mass-manufactured branded goods; they flattered non-rich consumers with the conceit that a servant would cater to them; and they established brand identities through visually distinct African American servant bodies.[26]

Aunt Jemima, for example, a brand for various breakfast foods, is one of the most enduring images associated with African American women in advertisements.[27] Like Uncle Ben's Rice, this commercial representation of a servant was euphemistically labeled with a family name, an "Aunt," belying the forced servitude that the character signifies. The character was the stereotypical "happy mammy"; she was overweight, very dark skinned, asexual (therefore, a non-threat to the white household), a master cook, with a wide smile, and used contrived racialized, colloquial speech. At the creation of the character in the 1910s, Aunt Jemima wore a bandana, a symbolic representation of slavery and cotton-picking that lasted in some form on the branded character until 1989. Her presence in advertising and on product packaging extended the reach of this character throughout the world. These images reinforced similar portrayals in film and television that could extend the depth of the stereotypes by adding dialogue that reinforced the loyalty and comedic delegitimization of the stereotype.[28] Although later versions of Aunt Jemima removed some of the most offensive characteristics (the bandana, the body type), Fuller argues for the endurance of some of the connotations of the African American woman servant in more later manifestations, such as in Pine-Sol advertisements of the late 1990s.[29] In the case of another character that was introduced much later, Mrs. Butterworth, the wide body type was literally the shape of the product packaging (in this case a bottle of maple syrup), although the voice in television commercials coded the character as white. With the backdrop of Aunt Jemima as a well-known predecessor, Mrs. Butterworth's dark, rotund body-shaped syrup bottle offers the strange example of a white advertising mascot in perpetual blackface.[30] In the post-WWII US, African Americans were included in the occasional group ensembles of service workers for companies' ads, signifying a harmonious multicultural America.[31]

Paradoxically, perhaps the most common representation of manual labor throughout the history of modern advertising comes from middle-class characterizations, in particular housewives. Advertising depicted women cleaning virtually every room and surface of a house, often unrealistically cheerful when using the branded product to assist their labor.[32] Here the brand is often presented as essentially doing much of the cleaning labor itself, downplaying the drudgery of such activity. In the case of the strangely orientalist Mr. Clean, the brand persona would clean a kitchen with a swipe of his magical Genie hand while a housewife smiled in delight. But in many cases, women were laboring in the ads. Such portrayals of housewife's work, of course, framed this labor as a natural part of femininity and gendered obligation rather than something for which economic compensation is expected.

White, working-class women were and are also portrayed at their place of employment. The wisdom of the common folk was celebrated by regularly occurring characters in television commercials from the 1950s to the 1980s. Paulson and O'Guinn argue that such characters were framed as altruistic and willing to share secret knowledge, having the consumers' interests at heart in helping them live better lives even if sometimes delivering "tough love" about the consumers' deficiencies. "Saucy" but good-hearted characters such as Madge, a manicurist who soaked her customers hands in Palmolive dishwashing liquid, and Rosie, the diner waitress who used Bounty paper towels, wore uniforms with their names embroidered or with a name tag. They would routinely, if benignly, insult their middle-class clientele for their bad hands ("My hands remind you of that sunset, Madge?" "Yep, red and sinking fast") or clumsiness that resulted in diner spills. Both dressed in their respective service uniforms, and talked with vaguely Brooklyn-ish accents. The moral of their common-sense wisdom was the superiority of their brand. Madge was also a global icon: Australia had a glocalized version of the character. Another character, Josephine the Plumber for Comet cleanser, wore white baggy overalls and an oversized cap; Josephine was notable for the rare representation of a woman working in a masculinist profession.[33] However, Hill argues that the makeup worn by Josephine on the job and her plumber's outfit that seemed more clownish than utilitarian undermined the character's professional legitimacy.[34]

Later working-class representations of Flo, the "Progressive [Insurance] Girl," Janice for Toyota, and Lily for AT&T are modern versions of the white-woman service worker. True to her roots in advertising characters from the 1960s like Madge, Flo offers a nostalgic vision of retail and loyal service. She wears a branded-white outfit with a nametag, and her hairstyle and red lipstick are a throwback to an earlier (and slightly kitschy) style. However, she combines these attributes with the "flexible labor" model of work that characterizes the digital age. Representations of Flo outside of the Progressive "Superstore," working odd hours and even wearing her white uniform at family dinners, diminish distinctions between modern workers' private and work lives. In this way, Flo becomes both a loyal Progressive spokescharacter and also a warning to salaried workers that they should always be on call in the "flexible economy."[35]

In the case of both African American and white women advertising spokescharacters, one element that is intersectionally reinforced is their loyalty to the middle class—enacted by their unwavering cheerfulness (in the case of traditional African American advertising icons) or their gentle wise-cracking (with white women in service industries)—that combines with their product wisdom and contentment in their station.

Symbolic Functions of White Working-class Males in Advertising

Like many semiotic tools available to advertisers, portrayals of the working class can be used to symbolize a variety of brand meanings. Two themes that appear in commercials will be explored below. The first examines masculinist connotations of a working-class body that are associated with brands, an exoticization that essentializes this body with strength and power. The second focuses on working-class bodies as a problem faced by consumers that brands can ameliorate; often such portrayals are associated with the highly undesirable, even disgust.

The Working-class Body as Naturalized Hegemonic Masculinity

bell hooks argues that white consumption of the racialized Othered body is pleasurable in part because of the dominant symbolic construction of such bodies as inherently tied to animalistic impulses, raw emotions, and nature.[36] "Eating the (racialized) other" in consumer culture, then, promises to add an exotic "spice" to the conventional (if dominant and privileged) world of whiteness. This ideological move helps to explain white appropriation of non-white cultural tropes and performances, such as the historical example of white actors in blackface, white teens' fascination with hip-hop, and in "going native" movies such as *Dances with Wolves* and *Avatar*.

One common intersectional representation of the working class in advertising is the use of male bodies to represent the brand and/or its targeted consumers as being traditionally masculine. Here we see a similar appropriation of "eating other bodies" by the dominant culture, but this one is rooted in white working-class images and assumptions. Linkages in advertising between male working-class bodies, masculinity, and the brand are accomplished through an assumed naturalness of both masculinity with physical strength, toughness and desirability that reinforces a hegemonic masculinity.[37] The connotations of working-class bodies as inherently strong, tough, and thus representing a particularly hard-working and authentic type of male is referenced by many products. These constructions of inherent masculinity in the working class—to use hooks' analytical framework—racialize the white working-class body, rooting them in a physicality that can be experienced through the brand (or so the ads promise).

Sometimes such classed masculinity is seen through brand icons and spokescharacters. Brawny paper towels, for example, emphasizes the durability of the brand not just through its name, but also its personification as a square-jawed, plaid-shirt wearing lumberjack-esque white male. One television commercial from 2001 showed a woman cleaning a messy kitchen. She reaches for the paper towel, saying "Hey Brawny, do your thing," and electricity flows from the paper towel to her arm, changing it to a giant muscle-man arm that yanks the woman from spill to spill, seemingly against her control.[38] This product, then, literally gives a middle-class woman a working-class masculine body (or at least part of one). A similar body switch occurred when the Brawny man was temporarily replaced, for a month in 2017, by a plaid-shirt wearing, if red-lipsticked, woman on packaging to "celebrate strong women" and with the hashtag #StrengthHasNoGender—although, as shown with use of the lumberjack outfit, it apparently does have a class.[39]

Another brand that, like Brawny, is targeted at consumers doing the shopping for domestic spaces, is Gorton's of Gloucester frozen seafood. On the package of these brands is a white, grey-bearded fisherman, at an old-fashioned ship's wheel (made of wood), wearing a yellow raincoat and with a steady gaze. In this case the icon represents the tradition, expertise, and hard-working dedication of the company; the fisherman is a nostalgic reference to an imagined, authentic, pre-industrial time that is connoted by the rugged sailor fishing off of the Massachusetts coast (although the brand is now owned by a Japanese conglomerate). A 2017 tongue-in-cheek TV commercial shows the Gorton's man sauntering into a bar, filled with sea-styled poseur/hipsters drinking craft beers, and ordering whiskey. "TRUST US TO BE THE REAL DEAL. NOT JUST LOOK THE PART," a graphic on the screen summarizes, highlighting authentic, masculine work connections and lifestyles.[40]

Brands that target men for traditionally masculinized products or those designed to appeal to a male market niche, of course, often use working-class male bodies to symbolize traditional hegemonic masculinity. In its switch from a female-targeted to a male-targeted brand in the 1950s, for example, Marlboro cigarettes visually associated its brand with a variety of traditionally male professions and occupations, including construction worker, sailor and of course the cowboy, which eventually became the brand's sole symbol of the "Marlboro Man." Surrounding this white, trim, male body with icons of the American west (cowboy hat, jeans jacket, chaps, horses), the character eventually became so iconic as the brand's symbol around the world that virtually no written text was needed in the ads, a technique that also reinforced the taciturn nature of this "man's man." Even in the TV commercials—before they were prohibited in the US in 1970—the Marlboro Man never spoke: commercial sound came from the ads' soundtrack, the theme from the western movie *The Magnificent Seven*, and from a male narrator. In TV and print ads, we saw the cowboy at work: roping cattle, corralling horses. Those wishing to emulate a traditional masculine lifestyle, then, knew these cigarettes exemplified it.[41]

Beyond the branded characters, commercials in the twenty-first century continue to use portrayals of working-class males as ways to emphasize masculinity. The Ford F-150 truck applies masculinized, classed bodies—coded as working class through clothing, speech patterns, or on-the-job settings—in its marketing to both hail and constitute its intended consumer niche.[42] One especially notable 2012 campaign was for the body spray "Axe Anarchy for Him and Her."[43] In these print ads, a working-class male encounters a middle- or upper-class sexualized woman, and both are presented as lustful for each other. The male's sexuality, though, is symbolized not just through square-jawed good looks, but also by his work implements that become an extension of his phallus. In one ad, a welder—facing a woman in a tight party dress gripping a bag of fireworks—holds a lighted blow torch that, given its pelvic placement, clearly symbolizes a double meaning of "working-class tool"; in another, an unshaven groundskeeper clutches a running edge trimmer, jutting from his crotch, as he faces a woman in a short, red dress, holding a tiny dog. In both cases, raw sexuality is communicated by a muscular working-class male body and his tools.

Male Working-class Bodies as Disgusting Consumer Problem

The ideological line between an otherness that is exotic and desirable, and an otherness that is strange, disgusting and offensive, is a commercially thin one. Class may be othered through affective representations that emphasize not just the intellectually disadvantageous, but also the emotionally disgusting. As Tyler writes, a way that social classes are differentiated "is through the repeated expressions of disgust for those deemed to be of a lower social class," including, in media, the use of "metaphors of sensation."[44]

So while the previously discussed theme focused on the working-class body as a positive brand attribute for consumers—representing a brand's toughness, linkage with a nostalgic past, or masculine authenticity/sexuality—other ads use the working class as representing problems for consumers to avoid. Sometimes these problems are the result of the body being acted upon in especially uncomfortable and humiliating ways; other ads imply the working-class body itself inherently has unpleasant characteristics that are not suitable for polite society. The consumer must avoid the visceral encounter with (or, worse, morphing into) the disgusting working class. In any case, the solution to the problem of working-class bodies is the consumption of the brand.

A 2017 State Farm television commercial told the story of an unjustly abused classed body, one that is solved through class mobility enacted by the right kind of privatized consumption.[45] In this commercial, a young white male rides the bus to his factory job every day. But things are not easy: we see a series of days where he has to wait in the rain and cold at the bus stop, where he runs after the bus only to miss it, where on the bus he endures uncomfortable heat, people rudely eating greasy sandwiches in front of him, and crowds invading his space and bumping his body. The humiliation his body endures because of the evils of public transportation—cold, heat, wet, crowds, smells—is reinforced by the lyrics of the commercial's soundtrack: "You'll break my bones, but you'll never break me." His "bones," then, are what ultimately suffer because of his class position. His discomfort is solved when he buys his own truck—a sign of class mobility through private property ownership—and can protect his purchase with State Farm insurance.

Commercials for Duluth Trading Company, which specializes in blue-collar work clothes, use simple animation of husky, mustached, and ball-cap wearing men to symbolize their clientele and the problems created by their bodies. "Crouchstrophobia," squatting in the wrong kind of jeans, can lead to such excessive sweating in a working-class male that it can flood a room; this is solved by roomier "Ballroom Jeans."[46] Another installment teaches us "HOW TO UN-PLUMBER A BUTT," or the dilemma of a butt-crack showing when a man sits and his shirt rides up. Essentializing this as literally a working-class condition ("Plumber's Butt"), this time the solution is a shirt, the "Duluth Longtail T" with "3 extra inches." The second commercial, especially, offers this physical problem not just as one of worker discomfort, but also as a public display that evokes disgust at the working-class body.[47] The butt that is found to be plumbered belongs to a wide man sitting on a stool at a diner counter sipping coffee. When the butt-crack is revealed, the facial expression of a second man—The Duluth Spokescharacter—shows irritation (or maybe light disgust), and he removes the offending shirt from the first man, rudely, with a shopvac.

Other advertisements use working-class bodies to symbolize problems faced by non-working-class people. We've already seen one example of this: The "Econo-Shave" customer whose fat, slovenly lifestyle can be avoided by instead buying Dollar Shave Club. Another, for Luftal anti-gas tablets that were advertised in Mexico in 2011, featured different people, working in smelly surroundings, who could pass gas with impunity (the slogan being "Not Everyone Can"). One featured an overweight garbage man farting near the back of his truck; another was a bloody-aproned fish monger surrounded by dead fish in a filthy kitchen. In both cases, the two men were leaning over with a strained look on their face.[48] These ads especially link the disgusting workplace (a garbage dump; a fish slaughterhouse) with smelly, dirty and overweight bodies of sanitation workers and food suppliers, respectively.

In a series of commercials for DirecTV from 2014–2015, actor Rob Lowe played two versions of himself: the suave DirecTV user, and a loser, cable TV-using version which was often marked by working-class iconography. "Peaked in High School Rob Lowe," for example, worked in a fast-food restaurant. A version that appeared in *Sports Illustrated* with supermodels representing the DirecTV vs. non-DirecTV versions offered "Lunch Lady Nina Agdal," with a hair-net, bad makeup, filthy work conditions, and smoking a cigarette. The ads didn't imply that one could change their class status because of a switch to DirecTV, but if one wanted to avoid being associated with such working-class versions—and their proletarian life choices, consumers needed to embrace the proper brand purchases.[49]

Conclusion: Trump, Increased Income Gaps, and the Importance of the Stories Ads Tell

This chapter has reviewed various tendencies and tropes involving the working-class body in advertising. Although the "default" class modality for ad representation is middle-class, the history of advertising has featured people specifically coded as working class. Intersectional portrayals often exploit particular manifestations of race, gender and the working-class, emphasizing ideological meanings that reinforce stereotypes especially of race and gender through their loyalty and product-wisdom as enacted by their centralization in service roles. Focusing on working-class males, advertising uses their bodies as naturalized access points for masculinity (that then become associated with the brand) or for symbols of disgust or humiliation that consumers may avoid through brand use.

As mentioned earlier, in the Trump era, issues of the working-class have been foregrounded in public discourse to a greater degree than many earlier modern times. Not coincidentally, wealth discrepancy is increasing, as the wealthiest 5 percent of Americans in 2013 controlled more than 60 percent of all assets, a significant increase from the 1980s.[50] In such a context, how we understand people in different economic situations is critical: do we see those in lesser economic circumstances, for example, as responsible for their own hardship, or as strata deserving of social safety nets? Or do we differentiate between different sub-categories within a socioeconomic class?

The stories that advertising tells may be influential in how we see class. What morals do we conclude about the working class from advertising? Do they have a secret wisdom that they altruistically share? Are they a tough bunch, and therefore self-sufficient? Do they cause others problems (that consumption may solve)? As this chapter argued, many of the messages of the working class seem to essentialize them: the ads imply males in this group are inherently masculine or have bodies that disgust, for example. Because of the volatile political and economic situation much of the world finds itself in, we should continue to monitor commercial stories for the messages they send about class, and how social changes and these messages may flow with, or against, other dominant ideologies that circulate about economic hardship and privilege.

Notes

1 This commercial is available at "Dollar Shave Club TV Commercial, 'The Smarter Choice,'" iSpot.tv, accessed April 1, 2019. www.ispot.tv/ad/AsqA/dollar-shave-club-the-smarter-choice.
2 Pierre Bourdieu, "The Aesthetic Sense as a Sense of Distinction," in *The Consumer Society Reader*, eds. Juliet Schor and Douglas B. Holt (New York, NYL New Press, 2000), 205–211.
3 See, for example, David Crockett, "Marketing Blackness: How Advertisers Use Race to Sell Products," *Journal of Consumer Culture* 8, no. 2 (2008): 245–268; Rosalind Gill, "Beyond the 'Sexualization of Culture' Thesis: An Intersectional Analysis of 'Sixpacks,' 'Midriffs,' and 'Hot Lesbians' in Advertising," *Sexualities* 12, no. 2 (2009): 137–160.
4 William M. O'Barr, *Culture and the Ad: Exploring Otherness in the World of Advertising* (Boulder, CO: Westview Press, 1994), 2.
5 Erika L. Paulson and Thomas C. O'Guinn, "Working-class Cast: Images of the Working Class in Advertising, 1950—2010." *The Annals of the American Academy of Political and Social Science* 644, no. 1 (2012): 53.

6 Dallas Smythe, "On the Audience Commodity and its Work," in *Media and Cultural Studies: Keyworks*, 2nd edition, eds. Meenakshi Gigi Durham and Douglas M. Kellner (Malden, MA, Wiley-Blackwell, 2012), 185–204.
7 Matthew P. McAllister and Anna Aupperle, "Class and Advertising," in *Explorations in Critical Studies of Advertising*, eds. James F. Hamilton, Robert Bodle, and Ezequiel Korin (New York: Routledge, 2017), 208–220.
8 Richard Butsch, "Ralph, Fred, Archie, Homer, and the King of Queens: Why Television Keeps Recreating the Male Working-class Buffoon," in *Gender, Race, and Class in Media: A Critical Reader*, eds. Gail Dines and Jean M. Humez (Los Angeles: Sage, 2011), 101–109.
9 Jayne Raisborough and Matt Adams, M. (2008). "Mockery and Morality in Popular Cultural Representations of the White, Working Class," *Sociological Research Online* 13, no. 6 (2008); Jeffrey Masko, "Neoliberal Transformations of 'White Masculinity' in Cinematic Media—1970–2015" (PhD dissertation, The Pennsylvania State University, 2017).
10 Diana Kendall, *Framing Class: Media Representations of Wealth and Poverty in America* (Lanham, MD: Rowman & Littlefield, 2005), 139.
11 Gary Cross, *An All-Consuming Century: Why Commercialism Won in Modern America* (New York: Columbia University Press, 2000); Roland Marchand, *Advertising the American Dream: Making Way for Modernity, 1920–1940* (Berkeley, CA: University of California Press, 1985).
12 Marchand, *Advertising the American Dream*, 294.
13 Paulson and O'Guinn, "Working-Class Cast," 63.
14 Gwendolyn Audrey Foster, *Class-Passing: Social Mobility in Film and Popular Culture* (Carbondale, IL: Southern Illinois University Press, 2005).
15 Paulson and O'Guinn, "Working-Class Cast"; Erika L. Paulson and Thomas C. O'Guinn, "Marketing Social Class and Ideology in Post-World-War-Two American Print Advertising," *Journal of Macromarketing* 38, no. 1 (2018): 7–28.
16 Patrick Callier, "Class as a Semiotic Resource in Consumer Advertising: Markedness, Heteroglossia, and Commodity Temporalities," *Discourse & Society* 25, no. 5 (2015): 587.
17 Paulson and O'Guinn, "Working-Class Cast".
18 Ibid; Paulson and O'Guinn, "Marketing Social Class".
19 Marchand, *Advertising the American Dream*.
20 Daniel Delis Hill, *Advertising to the American Woman: 1900–1999* (Columbus, OH: Ohio State University Press, 2002).
21 Matthew P. McAllister and Anna Aupperle, "Class Shaming in Post-Recession US Advertising," *Journal of Communication Inquiry* 41, no. 2 (2017): 140–156.
22 About the ideological dynamics of the 84 Lumber commercial, see Litzy Galarza and Lars Stoltzfus-Brown, "'Are You 84 Lumber Material?': Interpellation, Neoliberalism, and Immigrant Narratives in a Super Bowl Ad." Paper presented at the Annual Meeting of the Popular Culture Association/American Culture Association, Indianapolis, IN, April 2018.
23 Foster, *Class-Passing*: 8.
24 Kimberle Crenshaw, "Mapping the Margins: Intersectionality, Identity Politics, and Violence Against Women of Color," *Stanford Law Review* 43, no. 6 (1991): 1241–1299.
25 Quoted in Marilyn Kern-Foxworth. *Aunt Jemima, Uncle Ben, and Rastus: Blacks in Advertising, Yesterday, Today, and Tomorrow* (Westport, CT: Praeger, 1994), 10.
26 William M. O'Barr. *Culture and the Ad: Exploring Otherness in the World of Advertising* (Boulder, CO: Westview Press, 1994).
27 M.M. Manring, *Slave in a Box: The Strange Career of Aunt Jemima* (Charlottesville: University Press of Virginia, 1998).
28 Donald Bogle, *Toms, Coons, Mulattoes, Mammies, and Bucks: An Interpretive History of Blacks in American Films*, updated and expand 5th edn (New York: Bloomsbury Academic, 2016).
29 Lorraine Fuller, "Are We Seeing Things?: The Pinesol Lady and the Ghost of Aunt Jemima," *Journal of Black Studies* 32, no. 1 (2001): 120–131.
30 Thanks to Meredith Doran of Penn State for this observation. The class and race connotations of a 2018 television commercial featuring Mrs. Butterworth "dirty dancing" with Colonel Sanders of KFC—the latter evoking images of a pre-Civil War southern landowner—is particularly disturbing and ahistorical. This commercial is described and linked to at Jessica Wohl, "KFC's Colonel Goes 'Dirty Dancing' with Mrs. Butterworth to Promote Chicken and Waffles," *Advertising Age* (November 12, 2018), accessed on April 21, 2019 at https://adage.com/creativity/work/kfc-dance-hidden-language-stomach/957976.
31 Paulson and O'Guinn, "Working-Class Cast".
32 Jessamyn Neuhaus, *Housework and Housewives in American Advertising: Married to the Mop*, 1st Palgrave Macmillan pbk. edn (New York: Palgrave Macmillan, 2013).

33 Paulson and O'Guinn, "Working-Class Cast".
34 Hill, *Advertising to the American Woman*.
35 Matthew P. McAllister, Tanner R. Cooke, and Catherine Buckley, "Fetishizing Flo: Constructing Retail Space and Flexible Gendered Labor in Digital-Era Insurance Advertising," *Critical Studies in Media Communication* 32, no. 5 (2015): 347–362.
36 bell hooks, "Eating the Other: Desire and Resistance," in *Media and Cultural Studies: Keyworks*, 2nd edition, eds. Meenakshi Gigi Durham and Douglas M. Kellner (Malden, MA, Wiley-Blackwell, 2012), 308–318.
37 Raewyn Connell, *Masculinities* (Berkeley: University of California Press, 1995).
38 This commercial is available at "Brawny Paper Towel Commercial (2001)," YouTube video, 0:30, July 29, 2017, www.youtube.com/watch?v=ZjJ6sLW_27Q.
39 Madeline Farber, "The Brawny Paper Towel Man Has Been Replaced by a Woman," *Fortune*, March 6, 2017. http://fortune.com/2017/03/06/brawny-paper-towel-man-now-woman/.
40 This commercial is described at Heather Taylor, "The Return of the Gorton's Fisherman," *The Huffington Post* (February 15, 2017), accessed April 21, 2019 at www.huffpost.com/entry/the-return-of-the-gortons-fisherman_b_58a4bbede4b0fa149f9ac0ca.
41 For a discussion of Marlboro see Juliann Sivulka, *Soap, Sex, and Cigarettes: A Cultural History of American Advertising*, 2nd edn. (Boston, MA: Wadsworth, Cengage Learning, 2012).
42 Callier, "Class as a Semiotic Resource".
43 Duncan Macleod, "Axe Anarchy for Him and Her," *The Inspiration Room*, July 3, 2012. http://theinspirationroom.com/daily/2012/axe-anarchy-for-him-and-for-her/.
44 Imogen Tyler, "'Chav Mum Chav Scum': Class Disgust in Contemporary Britain," *Feminist Media Studies* 8, no. 1 (2008): 17–34.
45 This commercial is available at "State Farm TV Commercial: 'Backstory: Truck' Song by John Taylor," iSpotTV, accessed April 21, 2019 at www.ispot.tv/ad/wy2O/state-farm-backstory-truck-song-by-john-taylor.
46 This commercial is available at "Crouchstrophobia—The Onset of Squat Sweats," YouTube video, 0:44, August 30, 2016, www.youtube.com/watch?v=XGUguHKEs78.
47 This commercial is available at "Duluth Trading TV Commercial: How to Un-Plumber a Butt," YouTube video, 0:35, August 28, 2015, www.youtube.com/watch?v=yGn0WfKol3E.
48 Luftal campaign by FCB, *Ads of the World*. Accessed March 27, 2018. www.adsoftheworld.com/media/print/luftal_not_everyone_can_garbage_man.
49 McAllister and Aupperle, "Class Shaming in Post-Recession US Advertising".
50 Gil B. Manzon Jr., "How Rich Are the Rich?: If You Only Knew," *The Conversation*. Accessed March 1, 2018. https://theconversation.com/how-rich-are-the-rich-if-only-you-knew-89682?utm_campaign=Echobox&utm_medium=Social&utm_source=Twitter#link_time=1517858274.

3

CLASS HYBRIDITY AND THE *HABITUS CLIVÉ* ON AMERICAN REALITY TELEVISION

June Deery

The woman who calls herself "countess" and wrote a book on etiquette is one of the tackiest, ill-mannered, ungracious women I've ever seen.... There are no manners here. They seem to feel that money is the only prerequisite for being a lady. Far from it.... How much of a role model can any of them be? Poor breeding. Good grief![1]

Class Migration and Reality TV

In a society whose cultural geography indicates entrenched class segregation—expressed, for example, in separate neighborhoods, schools, and colleges—the media transmits representations of class identities that we might never encounter, and certainly never get to know, otherwise.[2] Despite narrowcasting and audience fragmentation, mutual cultural surveillance is still a key media function. But the question arises: does media entertainment recognize this burden of representation?[3] Do its producers marshal their resources to present a fair and representative sample of any given class? The answer is no, they do not. Nevertheless, the programming I will be examining does offer interesting glimpses into class performances *as performance* and prompts viewers to recognize, acknowledge, and publicly evaluate class identities. This is the largely inadvertent effect of some strains of reality television whose producers, for reasons we shall explore, are motivated to apply pressure right on the fault lines of class. Although this does not produce rounded and systematic studies such as would contribute to sociology, the popular thematizing of class identity does underline some of the problems of class identification and class transition. Viewer and participant reactions to on-screen behavior also suggest that Americans do notice, do monitor, and do care about class. The frustration of the viewer quoted in the epigraph above suggests that the inept performances of the newly rich, specifically the disconnect between money and class, is a particularly heated and therefore lucrative point of contention.

In contrast to the generally muted treatment of class demarcations in most American media, reality TV producers have for some time been exploiting class categorization—along with its uncertainties, anxieties, and ambiguities—for sub-tragic or comic effect.[4] Indeed, one could argue that observing classed behavior goes back to origins of reality TV in the 1970s,[5] which is not surprising since the extension of documentary into non-fictional entertainment incentivized producers to locate pre-existing social scripts. Class performance is one such script: by structuring and constraining social behavior, its rules and parameters offer producers predictable sources of tension and drama. In this essay, I focus on portraits of the newly rich and the accompanying class perceptions which energize prominent docusoaps—these being female-headed series about interpersonal relationships unfolding over multiple seasons in soap-like, interwoven narratives.[6] In particular, I will draw on Bravo TV, a channel whose marketing boasts it delivers the "affluencer" (i.e., affluent and influential), one who is "engaged, upscale and educated."[7] Several of Bravo's hit shows look closely and sometimes longitudinally at how class is subjectively enacted and understood, in some series for over a decade. Given that it is less visually marked than race or gender, class identification often proves difficult.

Even professional class categorization has always combined fact and judgement. While scholars can invoke quantitative factors such as income and wealth, judgement immediately comes into play in determining how these affect rank. Other criteria are even less objective or metricized. Many sociologists agree that occupation is a significant factor but its weighting becomes a matter of judgement with some historical and cultural variability: i.e., *which* occupations have *what* social prestige *when*. Then there are disagreements within and between cultures about temporal factors: the relative importance of upbringing and early socialization or how long before recently acquired wealth alters class rank. When individuals are in class transit many of these subjectivities and inconsistencies are particularly stark and it becomes clear the degree to which class attribution is a perception—not always universally shared but not arbitrary or individualistic either. This is where the morass of class confusion and class accusation among TV's nouveau riche proves interesting. Their postures and slippages allow us to see the fragility of some individual class identities and even of systematic attempts to adjudicate ranks.

Sociologists have recently begun to stress the need for personal narratives to better understand the subjective experience of class, as a supplement to traditional quantitative (and largely celebratory) analyses of large-scale data, such as the macro mobility studies conducted by John H. Goldthorpe and his colleagues at Nuffield College, Oxford.[8] Some have proposed a micro, qualitative-based research agenda which focuses on how class is lived and how individuals make sense of their class trajectories.[9] One perceived weakness in both academic and political discourse is an assumption that upward class mobility is a pure benefit, whereas individual narratives suggest more mixed blessings.[10] The filming of classed identities on reality TV—including newly acquired identities—gives millions of viewers some inner view of class experience not as scripted by writers but as lived by individuals, albeit in an exaggerated form for entertainment purposes and not with a great deal of introspection. Ordinarily, such portraits are written from the perspective of predominantly middle- or upper-middle-class media professionals,[11] whereas on reality TV this professional management is less complete and different classes are invited to represent themselves. Their combination of real-ness and *mediated distance* (as figures on a screen) means viewers feel licensed, even entitled, to publicly criticize or advise these individuals since they have signed on to expose themselves on a TV show (whereas advice for fictional social climbers such as Madame Bovary or Becky Sharp would fall on deaf ears). When the performances are regarded as flawed or risible, producers are able to evade charges of classism because while behavior may be managed to some extent it is not technically scripted.

The selling point of several popular series is offering access to an elite—or at least those who may appear to some viewers to be in this category. From its inception, the very successful *Real Housewives* franchise (2006–) was pitched as a glimpse into a higher social sphere (with hints at the imperfection that is another attraction). The original series is described thus:

> Welcome to one of the most exclusive neighborhoods in Southern California. Go behind the gates and meet the women who hold the keys. The Real Housewives of Orange County. Bravo introduces you to five women who are living lives of privilege and indulgence, replete with gorgeous homes, privileged offspring and fabulous bling. See how the other half really lives as The Real Housewives discover their Garden of Eden may not be so perfect....

Similarly, another Californian spin-off is marketed in this way:

> The series follows six of the most affluent women in the country as they enjoy the lavish lifestyle that only Beverly Hills can provide. Theirs is a world of luxurious wealth and pampered privilege, where being seen and who you know is everything. These women are in the center of it all and they have the mansions, the cars, and the diamonds to prove it. From heiresses to entrepreneurs to a family of child actresses—The Real Housewives of Beverly Hills deliver the star power and the drama.[12]

In addition, over many years the cast members' self-identifying taglines refer to the relative importance of money, class, and privilege. For example: "I was poor, I was rich, I was poor again and you know what? Having money is easier" (Lauri Waring Peterson, RH: OC); "I never feel guilty about being privileged" (LuAnn de Lesseps, RH: NYC); "I love the bling, I love the jewelry, I love it all" (Gretchen Rossi, RH: OC); "Money doesn't give you class, it just gives you money" (Brandi Glanville, RH: BH); "In Atlanta, money and class do give you power" and "People call me a gold digger, but they just want what I have" (Kim Zolciak-Biermann, RH: ATL); "I have a taste for luxury, and luxury has a taste for me" (Sonja Morgan RH: NYC); "If it doesn't make me money, I don't do it" (Lise Wu Hartwell, RH: ATL); "Beauty fades, class is forever" (Cynthia Bailey, RH: ATL); and so on.

A curiosity about how "the other half" (or 1 percent) lives is to some extent perennial but is also in tune with significant trends in American society today, which are the increase in the public naming and acknowledgement of class distinctions and a burgeoning awareness that the wealthy are pulling ahead, without a consensus about how fair or deserved this wealth distribution may be. American popular culture has periodically examined the ethics of naked capitalism through rapacious icons such as Gatsby or Gekko ("Greed … is good").[13] These contemporary docusoaps feature those with more ordinary ambitions but their leveraged lifestyles nevertheless raise questions about greed and narcissism, about class and culture and, what most concerns us here, about the relation between money and class. As a subset of the wealthy, the nouveau riche are generally good fodder for reality television because their being rich encourages voyeurism and their being new introduces vulnerability and dispute. When the topic is classed behavior, both viewer and participant engagement is often intense, in part because class categorization involves taboo and trauma, as when class labels are hurled about in the heat of battle. Even when the labeling is not explicit, the nouveaux riches' confusion and hypocrisy, as well as their enthusiastic display of new wealth, provoke a range of audience responses from a variety of class locations: some admire, others disdain, still others profess elements of both. It is the ambiguity of a nouveau riche status as a transitional category that encourages multiple viewer positions, and since class assessment requires judgement and opinion, viewers can become passionate, contentious, and, above all, engaged—to the delight and profit of producers and broadcasters and, to a lesser extent, of cast members.

A potentially far-reaching impact of these class portraits is that the self-consciousness of the behavior, and the disconnect between new and original class identities, allow many viewers to understand class *as a performance*. An often pronounced lag between the acquisition of financial and of cultural capital is often framed ironically to underline delusion, hypocrisy, and lack of self-awareness; especially when edited with "the Bravo wink" that implicitly suggests inconsistencies to savvy viewers.[14] In a kind of class misrecognition, the contrast between how well casts think they are performing and how they are assessed by editors and viewers opens up seams of dramatic irony. Adding to the comedy and condemnation is that, like much else on reality TV, these portraits are extrovert and exaggerated; for example, if the nouveau riche are to be characterized as avaricious, egotistic, and ostentatious then reality TV showcases pronounced examples of these traits. This is typical of reality TV's *extra*-ordinariness, its display of the recognizable but excessive. Judging by online commentary, not all viewers are critical however; not all notice the mockery and some accept the idea that they are gaining access to the lives of an elite. Those who identify these figures as "upper class" indicate that the real powerbrokers and wealth holders are misrecognized or under their radar: which in a system of universal suffrage is often to the elite's advantage. What is demonstrably true is that the lives of those in power—e.g., the networks of prep school–Ivies–finance/law/politics—are not being accessed or exposed here or, for that matter, elsewhere on TV. Set in a wider context, these ersatz versions of the upper class could be seen as a political distraction, concealing not only the existence of the real elite but also the effective suppression of the middle class who are *not* experiencing the upward mobility advertised on TV.

Thematizing Class

Class is brought to the public's attention in the first instance through market framing. Broadcasters are quick to promote the display of social status as a primary attraction or even raison d'être of these shows. Especially during a series launch, they routinely exaggerate the prestige of their nouveau riche cast, loosely employing words like "elite" and "socialite" to imply established upper-class status. Prior to this, casting plays a key role and in some instances class positioning is doubly marked when producers inject racial or cultural differences. For example, the *Ladies of London* (2014–2017) series points up contrasts between what some Americans think qualifies as upper class (predominately money) and the English version, which relies more on background and breeding. This series managed to cast some British upper-class characters (interested in media/appearance careers) and even a few aristocrats. It opens at a polo match where the restrained and sanguine British upper class is juxtaposed with loud and overly excited nouveau riche Americans. Class perceptions and the failure of Americans to understand or qualify as upper class thereafter remain strong themes. One British cast member (the upper-class Caroline Stanbury) spells out the difference:

> In America I think that if you become rich, you *are* society. Money and fame opens the door to society in the States. In England it's about the family name and breeding. Most of the old aristocratic families don't have money anymore.[15]

Given that the show's central dynamic is an almost Henry Jamesian narrative of boorish new money trying to assimilate into the British upper crust, producers foreground any societal rituals and conventions they can find: Ascot, afternoon tea, dinner at country manor, etc. Class and manners come up in regular discussions among participants regarding what is rude or inappropriate and here, as in other docusoaps, an offence such as being late to dinner or not RSVPing an invite can fester and drive the narrative for months.

The Real Housewives of Atlanta (2008–), *The Real Housewives of Potomac* (2016–) and *Married to Medicine* (2013–) center on African American women who claim to be in the upper echelon of the new South. Some of these are educated and professional but most are not, and, as with other casts, their claim to elite status is insecure: for example, even those who are touted as having earned professional degrees did so in institutions that are ranked from modest to low, or even unranked. Perhaps particularly tenuous is the claim to being a Southern Belle, which Phaedra Parks (*RH: ATL*) in particular has made a career out of, penning a book entitled *Secrets of the Southern Belle*.[16] Co-opting this historical designation elides the fact that the Southern Belle was valued for being the palest of the pale in a plantation culture where these women's African ancestors would have had a very different status. Even those who don't think of this as ironic will likely notice the gap between claim and practice: for Parks maintains that the demure Belle is quiet, restrained, always polite, self-controlled, non-confrontational, and pleasant. Yet, this model is subverted by her own behavior and that of other cast mates. One of these, NeNe Leakes, sweepingly co-opts the East Coast version of old white culture with the tagline: "I don't keep up with the Jones, I *am* the Jones," this being one of the best examples of pushing to the limits the idea of assigning one's own rank.

Upper-class whites enjoying the remnants of an elite Southern culture is the premise of *Southern Charm* (2014–), set in Charleston, South Carolina. Historically, this region was the closest America came to an aristocratic and feudal culture, but while there are occasional references to living in contemporary plantation houses, none of the cast acknowledges that some or most of their current wealth derives from a slavery economy. Most are quite conscious of wanting to behave in a "gentlemanly" or "ladylike" fashion but, while some do appear to be from old or oldish money, none are particularly illustrious members of the upper class (indeed, one is a felon). While some are self-conscious about their lineage and make great efforts to establish it with talk about ancestors, trust funds, and selective preschools, pride in their established lineages does not prevent bad behavior on camera and it turns out that some heritage and some rituals are fake or nouveau: for instance, the centrally featured and antebellum-sounding "Founders' Ball" was premiered in 2015 by a friend of some cast members.

Others who align themselves with old money are those who married it. This is the case in the East Coast *Real Housewives of New York City* (2008–) where some cast members secured husbands from old New York families such as the Morgans and Mortimers and others married into minor European aristocracy (Countess Luanne de Lesseps and Princess Carole Radziwill); reluctance to give up these illustrious names after divorce illustrates their social cachet. In such instances, viewers and participants have to consider whether an upper-class status can be transferred to a spouse and for how long. Or, more generally, whether it is acceptable to marry in order to boost one's status. Those who were *born* into the upper class rarely appear on TV presumably because, unless they are broke or desirous of celebrity, they simply have no incentive to appear. If a privilege of the elite is the ability to protect privacy and control personal information then they would be reluctant to sign a media contract (indeed, it seems Tinsley Mortimer's desire for publicity alienated her old-money husband and led to their divorce). Reality TV therefore faces class limits that fictional programming does not: a fate they share with sociologists who also find it difficult to access the elite.

Every one of these docusoaps reinforces the idea that the nouveau riche like to spend conspicuously: on caterers, florists, makeup squads, hairdressers, jewelry, formal gowns, cosmetic surgery, luxury cars, luxury vacations, private jets, spas, horse riding, gambling, etc. This consumerist address offers advantages to producers and cast through what we might call *affective commercial interactivity*, whereby producers build viewer engagement and loyalty in order to sell not just the broadcast series but also associated goods and services pitched by advertisers or cast members. Some of this promotion involves the massification of luxury, what I elsewhere refer to as the Godiva effect (referring to the mass distribution of a formerly exclusive chocolatier's brand).[17] In this case, ordinary viewers are offered a metonymic sampling of a greater whole: i.e., you may not be able to buy their houses or cars but you can buy the wine you saw them drink at the party you weren't invited to. And because these are real people in real situations, their use of products offers the advantage of what seems to be a personal testimony.

Financial competition among participants who are still in transit, who are still striving and jostling for position, is the main narrative in series such as *The Real Housewives*, *Married to Medicine*, and *Ladies of London*, where self-conscious social climbers openly discuss their strategies to advance in rank—at least in confessional interviews. Mutual status appraisal is ongoing and weaponized so that, in more explicit class terms than is usual in fictional drama, participants name-call and criticize each other, employing epithets such as "white trash," "ghetto," or "bougie." Using these distinctions as ways to injure and judge underlines the moral and emotional dimensions of class attribution. We see how quickly class difference becomes pathologized and class judgement becomes character judgement (as when we think of others as having "bad" taste rather than different or even lower taste). Ignoring more nuanced hierarchies, participants and viewers often judge others to be either "classy" or not classy, or to have or not have class, a simple binarism itself marked as déclassé.[18] In this usage, speakers will describe as "classy" an action they approve of as selfless or morally upright. Their class appraisal also includes assessment of each other's aesthetic taste, dress code, diction, mannerisms, and manners. Some participants undergo formal or informal etiquette lessons and others have written whole books on the subject. For example, former Countess LuAnn de Lesseps has made class and etiquette a major theme: after repeatedly instructing cast members, she produced the etiquette book *Class with the Countess*[19] and an auto-tuned song entitled "Money Can't Buy You Class." As many point out, it is ironic how often she fails to live up to her professed class rank.[20] The cast members who most often discuss the importance of manners and scold others for not complying are typically the older, dominant, and richest females, some of whom assume the role of the grande dame.[21] As part of their social monitoring they have more than once given a cast member the gift of an etiquette book as a putdown and condemnation of bad behavior.

The Drama of Dislocation: Class Hybridity and the *Habitus Clivé*

Docusoap portrayals of the rewards and vexations of the newly rich stand in contrast to a larger imperative mode in popular entertainment that counsels people on how to assimilate or to improve their situation. For example, numerous reality makeover or philanthropic formats intervene to help the subordinate to advance. Some formats offer unexpected help for the deserving poor who have been overlooked (*Undercover Boss*, 2010–), others school the lower classes in upper-class manners but actually encourage viewers to laugh at their lack of progress (*Ladette to Lady*, 2005–2010 or *Charm School*, 2007–2009). Many shows aid and applaud those who largely make their own way in the world, from competitive talent shows to business makeovers to financial partnerships (e.g., *Shark Tank*, 2009–). Indeed, as is often remarked, the world of reality TV is crowded with determined, neoliberal self-entrepreneurs.[22] But while they may model some forms of advancement, subjects in the nouveau rich dramas examined here are unaided, untrained, and largely left to their own devices. Some manage the difference between their original and current class identities through a deliberate and proud amalgam, but more commonly the shift in rank causes apprehension and doubt.

Hybridity

What I call hybrid class identities belong to those who acquire a new economic status but who deliberately, not inadvertently, maintain some social attributes of a different rank. This type is best illustrated by the popular *Duck Dynasty* (2012–2017) series whose originally lower-class Robertson family built a profitable business—before, and also because of, their media exposure. Their TV performance—and it *is* a performance—fully embraces and exploits the dual status of "redneck" and "rich": they are the wealthy who choose to maintain still the manners and rituals of a lower-class background. The germ of their on-screen license comes from a libertarian and self-conscious "redneck" culture, but their ability to live how they please is secured by their new wealth. A similar formula is found in Southern *Bayou Billionaires* (2012) where another rural family strikes it rich, this time due to natural gas being found on their land (à la *Beverley Hillbillies*); they, too, resist assimilation into a higher class.

When writing elsewhere about regionalism and class I have suggested that in the United States a Southern flavor softens class judgements through non-threatening exoticism.[23] On *Duck Dynasty*, the Robertsons' wry humor and self-mockery, as well as their "Southern charm," is sufficiently disarming that even the most sophisticated viewer can laugh *with* them as much as *at* them. This family is not trying to imitate the more privileged or pass as upper class and their upholding the values and rituals of a lower rank is framed as having a quirky integrity—although, as evidence of a lack of authenticity and playing to stereotypes, some viewers object that the Robertsons did not always sport their now iconic redneck beards. However, the degree to which their hybridity is genuine is not the point; the point is that a hybrid identity is what they are performing and capitalizing upon. Thanks to their TV income and a massive self-branding and merchandising effort the family was able to outplay the broadcaster who threatened to ban the patriarch for homophobic remarks: when all threatened to leave the show in solidarity, the executives backed down from losing so profitable an asset. The family went on to extend their influence into politics and specifically the Trump campaign. Speaking as right-wing populists, they appeared to echo Trump's wealthy-businessman-with-a-common-touch persona. The series' patriarch also starred in an apocalyptic, right-wing film by Trump's former chief strategist Steve Bannon. In fact, the Robertsons probably *were* effective spokespeople for Trump since pollsters discovered a strong correlation between Trump supporters and viewers of this series, stronger than those who voted for a previous Republican president.[24]

Habitus Clivé *and the Feminine Docusoap*

Other reality TV stars don't embrace but run from humble roots, yet these roots keep tripping them up. The regular faux pas and humiliations of the nouveau riche can be attributed to what Bourdieu[25] identified as a *habitus clivé*, a cleft or divided habitus where original class dispositions and current social position don't quite align. He used the term *hysteresis* (or lag) to describe the experience of those who, because their extant habitus has not yet adjusted to their new situation,[26] suffer the "double isolation" of not fitting in either within their original or new class group.[27] While mobility is an under-theorized area of Bourdieu's analysis—his focus being on a fairly stable and durable habitus formed during the primary socialization of childhood—he did at times acknowledge that one's habitus can and must adapt to new circumstances such as an upward class trajectory: indeed, his own life evinced such a transformation, although he was sparing in revelations about this personal experience.[28]

Subsequent accounts, such as that by sociologist Bernard Lahire,[29] have disputed the notion of a fixed or homogeneous habitus, especially when individuals are socialized in highly differentiated societies and draw on a plurality of dispositions in a variety of contexts. The specific effects of class mobility on individual subjects has, to a limited degree, been studied by other sociologists, some of whom suggest that any kind of social mobility (upward and downward) will have a "dissociative" effect on the individual[30] and produce an unease that may not be discernible from quantitative data sets.[31] Sennett and Cobb,[32] who famously explored the "hidden injuries" of class, found that the upwardly mobile can experience problems of isolation, vulnerability, and psychological distress that may disrupt the coherency of the self.

While there are some indications of trauma—erupting in breakdowns, addictions, divorces, family alienation, even suicide—generally speaking, Bravo's docusoap casts attempt to keep their deeper social insecurities under control and their pasts well-hidden. TV producers have a different agenda, however, and are more predisposed to exacerbate any misalignments in the habitus of their hapless casts. In addition, reality TV favors an extrovert and extreme modality that works against core ideas of higher-class behavior such as restraint and privacy: it is, in this regard, inherently vulgar. Producers therefore have to prop up the idea that they are offering access to an elite of some sort and offer viewers the pleasures of wealth voyeurism, but they are also motivated to cash in on the performance gaps and the social missteps that undermine their cast's material accomplishments.

If drama—and more specifically comedy—is found where there is maladjustment, dissonance, and disparity, then this basically describes the fate of the nouveau riche. It is hardly surprising, therefore, that producers should want to focus on their casts' class insecurity and their volatile combination of arrogance and insecurity. After selecting those who are ambitious but lack self-awareness, producers typically intensify pressure on their new identities in a variety of ways: with forced sociality and material display; with physical stressors such as alcohol and exhaustion; and by applying the financial pressure of selective contract renewals. While some expenses are covered, several participants have been under considerable pressure to spend beyond their means in order to merit inclusion on the show and in one case at least this may have led to suicide.[33] Even those who have adequate financial resources know they need to be outrageous to attract the camera and secure opportunities for onscreen branding of themselves and their products. But if their goal is to establish a genuinely elite status, then they are constantly being set up for failure. Many articulate their awareness that restraint in words and behavior is considered higher class, but the economics of reality TV are such that their salaries increase and their contracts are renewed if they are outlandish and vulgar. If (as they claim) being "classy" means thinking of others or putting others first then they fail ethically also, and if being upper class means resisting the temptation to share and to commercialize every aspect of their private lives then that battle is long lost.

Whatever their financial situation, these casts don't appear to have as yet an established or high cultural capital. Their most august ritual is not the opera but fashion week, and if they attend polo matches or tea parties they and their oversize hats are noticeably uncomfortable. When they attempt charity events such as the upper echelons use to consolidate their status, some of these have deteriorated into hair pulling and fist fights. And if they buy the physical structures or accoutrements of an older heritage, they don't preserve the original upper-class aesthetics, as in Dorinda Medley's garish makeover of a fine old home in the Berkshires; in a true rags-to-riches story, her father once worked there as a mason and when she later married a wealthy man his daughter acquired this aspirational object. These women are not Bourdieu's scholarly *transfuges* who rose through education and meritocratic, institutional selection.[34] More often their social elevation is due to a sexualized body: either its leveraging to marry wealth or to sell associated beauty products. Thus, another criterion these shows test is whether marrying money, especially new money, merits or guarantees class elevation. Typically, the husbands are not highly-educated or professional but are in careers such as sports, commerce, or real estate (an exception being *Married to Medicine*). Due to being on the TV show, a good number of the wives or ex-wives are now themselves entrepreneurs: given the possible stigma of marrying for money, many seem anxious to prove they have their own earning capacity. Typically, as entrepreneurs they focus on selling the attractive bodies and accessories they used to attract wealth in the first place, so it is a significant but not major change of direction.

The difficulties and fragility of class transition are particularly apparent when there is a sudden (and photogenic) social pratfall, most commonly when alcohol releases an original class identity and erases a more recent social veneer. For instance, the women will arrange some polite and aspirational event (formal dinner, social outing, pinkies-up tea party). Everyone starts out with good manners: fond greetings, mutual compliments, gratitude for the hostess's efforts. Language and postures are on guard. Then, after a few drinks, things begin to deteriorate. As perceptions of social slights and ill manners flare up, we witness the flinging of insults and class epithets (also the flinging of wine and tableware), before one or more participants wobble off to the limo in tears. The cleft is once again evident and the sudden code-switch comic because the participants trespass on taboos and puncture pretensions—a release of energy often associated with the comedy of manners, here in a markedly intoxicated version.[35]

One last means for securing social status worth mentioning is what can only be described as brand idolatry. In an effort to quickly and reliably translate financial into cultural capital, docusoap women are often seen buying or referring to their purchases of prestigious brands. In these circles, reverence is reserved not for Mozart or Rembrandt but for Louis Vuitton and Jimmy Choo; and a Birkin bag is not so much a purchase as an achievement. Global brands act as a prosthetic for what is missing: i.e., the individual's own elite taste palate and fluency in social signaling. Instead, these arrivistes appear convinced that acquiring these well-known retail talismans will accord automatic status—except for those who might judge this status unearned and crass.

Conclusion and Political Coda

Class incompetence draws attention to class performance. It also creates engagement and affect. Some viewers will miss the inept code switching but if Bravo, for example, claims that it attracts more sophisticated and affluent viewers, then there is a good chance that it is ultimately class slippage that is being sold. The extent to which cast members and viewers criticize individuals for not meeting class standards, and hurt or offend others in doing so, confirms that these standards do exist and that class recognition and affiliation do matter.[36] While some viewers might admire the aspirants' initiative and determination, when they overreach and seem to claim a higher rank than is merited this aggravates and even angers many, again supporting the idea that class calibrations still exist.

Yet confusion does remain, both on and off screen. Indeed, it may be that these TV productions mediate contemporary anxieties about the significance and identification of class, compounded now by a nouveau riche president who successfully exploited a weak understanding of class relations in order to persuade a disaffected underclass to support an oligarch. A stalling of the American Dream of class mobility is generally offered as one explanation for the success of Trumpist populism and the class inversion that secured him the election.[37] The real estate developer from Queens who now occupies the most prestigious address in the world, Trump specializes in selling the unsophisticated person's *idea of* wealth. His image as the successful business man was secured by his stint on reality TV where he sold his "high class" assets (even while many of his businesses had actually failed). Although born into some wealth, Donald Trump has always had affinities with the newly rich: flashy and ostentatious, a lover of fast food and easily digested television, he has long projected the narrative of being self-made. But he and his political persona may be most accurately described as a deliberate class hybrid since his performance capitalizes on a mixed identity of (supposedly) *regular* and (supposedly) *billionaire* by one who enjoys being considered authentically "ordinary" by the underclass whose interests he often does not, in fact, share.

Duplicity is too simple a concept to describe what is going on here. Nor does it encompass Trump's relentless media skepticism and destabilizing of fact, a maneuver that also possesses class dimensions. For it seems that pressures within postindustrial capitalism have emboldened this form of epistemological corruption, based on a loose ontological agnosticism that willfully discounts the distinction between "real" and "unreal." One pressure is the desperate desire among the old manufacturing and rural working classes to demolish the professional politics and professional journalism that have presided over a brutal economic divide. Trump has tapped into this frustration and, at the same time, his own iconic nouveau riche status appears to offer hope that the twentieth-century American Dream can still bridge this divide: individually if not collectively. If Trump does not adequately or consistently perform his elevated rank, if his hybrid identity means he is non-conforming and in class terms inconsistent and flawed, then among some groups his political performance is all the stronger. Inevitably, this raises the specter of whether reality TV not only gave Trump the name recognition and status to launch his campaign but also sowed the seeds of skepticism about what is real, a skepticism that threatens to destabilize nothing less than the democratic system.

Notes

1 Viewer Sarah Metzgar in a *YouTube* comment regarding RH: NYC. Available at: https://ru-clip.com/video/5XiW6zs7UC8/rhony-dorinda-to-sonja-shut-your-mouth-season-9-episode-4-bravo.html.
2 For an overview of scholarship on class and media see the Introduction to June Deery and Andrea Press, eds. *Media and Class: TV, Film, and Digital Culture* (New York: Routledge, 2017); for more essays specifically on reality programming see Helen Wood and Beverley Skeggs, eds. *Reality Television and Class* (New York: Palgrave Macmillan, 2011).
3 Ella Shohat and Robert Stam, *Unthinking Eurocentrism* (London: Routledge, 1994).
4 June Deery, "TV Screening: The Entertainment Value of Poverty and Wealth," in *Media and Class: TV, Film, and Digital Culture*, eds. June Deery and Andrea Press (New York: Routledge, 2017), 53–67.
5 Reality TV began with the overtly upper-middle-class *An American Family* (1973) and the working-class *The Family* (1974).
6 Other series featuring the nouveaux riches on Bravo Channel alone include: *Shahs of Sunset, Million Dollar Listing, Below Deck, Southern Charm, Flipping Out, Millionaire Matchmaker, Apres Ski, Princesses Long Island, Pregnant in Heels, Thicker than Water.*

7 "Affluencer" was coined by Bravo chief Zalaznick to describe Bravo's "young, chic, stylish, and upward-aspiring demographic." Susan Dominus, "The Affluencer," *New York Times Magazine*, November 2008, MM38–48.
8 For example, John H. Goldthorpe, John H., with Catriona Llewellyn and Clive Payne, *Social Mobility and Class Structure in Modern Britain* (Oxford: Clarendon Press, 1980); Robert Erikson and John H. Goldthorpe, *The Constant Flux. A Study of Class Mobility in Industrial Societies* (Oxford: Clarendon Press, 1992).
9 For more on arguments that support this type of research see Steph Lawler and Geoff Payne, eds., *Social Mobility for the 21st Century* (New York. Routledge, 2018). Also see Andrew Miles, Mike Savage and Felix Buhlmann, "Telling a Modest Story: Accounts of Men's Upward Mobility from the National Child Development Study," *The British Journal of Sociology* 62, no 4 (2011): 418–441; and Sam Friedman, "The Price of the Ticket: Rethinking the Experience of Social Mobility," *Sociology* 48, no 2 (2013): 352–368.
10 Steph Lawler and Geoff Payne, eds., *Social Mobility for the 21st Century* (New York: Routledge, 2018). And for a recent personal account of the difficulties of upward mobility see Lynsey Hanley, *Respectable: Crossing the Class Divide* (New York: Penguin, 2017). For how class origin can inform one's academic research see Beverley Skeggs, *Formations of Class and Gender: Becoming Respectable* (London: Sage, 1997).
11 For a recent and groundbreaking analysis of how middle-class and upper-class media producers affect class portrayals see David Hesmondhalgh, "The Media's Failure to Represent the Working Class," in *Media and Class*, eds. June Deery and Andrea Press (New York: Routledge, 2017), 21–37.
12 Both descriptions are found on the Google Play site: https://play.google.com/store/tv/show/The_Real_Housewives_of_Orange_County?id=MbnRbbBerOU&hl=en.
13 Gordon Gekko was the iconic 1980s stockbroker and defender of capitalism in Oliver Stone's *Wall Street* (1987).
14 Andy Cohen, the executive producer of multiple Bravo docusoaps, explains: "We wink at the audience when someone says I'm the healthiest person in the world, and then you see them ashing their cigarette." Andy Cohen, interview by Melissa Block, *All Things Considered*, National Public Radio, August 12, 2009.
15 Caroline Stanbury, "Caroline on the Fascinator Faux Pas," *Ladies of London* (blog), June 2, 2014, www.bravotv.com/ladies-of-london/season-1/blogs/caroline-stanbury/caroline-on-the-fascinator-faux-pas.
16 Phaedra Parks, *Secrets of the Southern Belle: How to Be Nice, Work Hard, Look Pretty, Have Fun, and Never Have an Off Moment* (New York: Gallery Books, 2013).
17 June Deery, *Consuming Reality: The Commercialization of Factual Entertainment* (New York: Palgrave Macmillan, 2012), 142.
18 June Deery, *Reality TV* (Cambridge: Polity Press, 2015).
19 LuAnn de Lesseps, *Class with the Countess* (New York: Gotham, 2009).
20 Michael J. Lee and Leigh Moscowitz, "The 'Rich Bitch': Class and Gender on *The Real Housewives of New York City*," *Feminist Media Studies* 13, no 1 (2013): 64–82.
21 Examples of the grandes dames of decorum are LuAnn de Lesseps, Lisa Vanderpump, Phaedra Parks, Heather Dubrow, and Patricia Altschul.
22 For example, Laurie Ouellette and James Hay, *Better Living Through Reality TV: Television and Post-Welfare Citizenship* (Blackwell: Oxford, 2008).
23 Deery, *Reality TV*.
24 Josh Katz, "'Duck Dynasty' vs. 'Modern Family': 50 Maps of the U.S. Cultural Divide." *New York Times*, December 27, 2016. Available at: www.nytimes.com/interactive/2016/12/26/upshot/duck-dynasty-vs-modern-family-television-maps.html.
25 Pierre Bourdieu, *The Logic of Practice*, translated by Richard Nice (Stanford, CA: Stanford University Press, 1990 [1980]); Pierre Bourdieu, *The State Nobility: Elite Schools in the Field of Power*, translated by Lauretta Clough (Stanford, CA: Stanford University Press, 1996 [1989]).
26 Bourdieu, *The Logic*, 62.
27 Bourdieu, *The State*, 107.
28 For a good overview of Bourdieu's personal transition versus his professional research see Sam Friedman, "The Price of the Ticket: Rethinking the Experience of Social Mobility," *Sociology* 48, no. 2 (2013): 352–368. For how this inconsistency can be leveraged to further critique Bourdieu's work see Tony Bennett, "Habitus Clivé: Aesthetics and Politics in the Work of Pierre Bourdieu," *New Literary History* 38 (2007): 201–228.
29 Bernard Lahire, *The Plural Actor* (Cambridge, UK: Polity Press, 2011).
30 For example, Earl Hopper, *Social Mobility: A Study of Social Control and Insatiability* (New York: Praeger, 1981).
31 See, for example, the early work of Pitrim Sorokin, *Social and Cultural Mobility* (London: Collier-Macmillan, 1941) and, more recently, Diane Reay, "The Cruelty of Social Mobility," in *Social Mobility for the 21st Century*, eds. Lawler Steph and Geoff Payne (New York: Routledge, 2018), 146–157.

32 Richard Sennett and Jonathan Cobb, *The Hidden Injuries of Class* (Cambridge: Cambridge University Press, 1977 [1972]).
33 It is thought that Russell Armstrong, a husband on *The Real Housewives of Beverly Hills*, committed suicide in 2011 due to financial pressures compounded by the show.
34 Bourdieu, *The State*.
35 There are some distinctions within *The Real Housewives* franchises, with the women of New York and Beverly Hills being more genuinely affluent and sophisticated than those of New Jersey or Atlanta.
36 Andrew Sayer, *The Moral Significance of Class* (Cambridge: Cambridge University Press, 2005).
37 For data on the economic decline of the American middle class see Pew Research Center, "The American Middle Class is Losing Ground," Washington, DC, December 9, 2015. Retrieved from www.pewsocialtrends.org. Some scholars disagree on the rates of mobility, depending on the main criterion selected; for example, whether income or occupation or lifestyle. For more on this see Will Atkinson, *Class* (Cambridge: Polity, 2015), 110–114.

4
MIGRANTS MEET REALITY SHOWS
The Class Representation of Non-Koreans in Reality Shows in Korea

Hun-Yul Lee

Globalization allows more people to move around and away from home, and the increased presence of non-natives brings about different opportunities and challenges to each society. Media play an important role in this change for people to recognize and understand each other. As this happens everywhere in the world, Korean society has experienced a rise in non-Koreans[1] in recent decades. This chapter discusses how Korean society deals with the influx in terms of class and media representation. The most significant groups of migrants in terms of history and size are migrant workers and marriage migrants. The others are professionals and travelers. While the first group, which comes to Korea to work and to support their families back home, is dominant in numbers and time spent in the country, they are not the most popular in media production and for viewers. Instead, those popular on television are professionals and travelers.

This chapter analyzes the implications of this phenomenon: why one group is underrepresented, while others are overrepresented, and what are the larger societal impacts of this representation. Viewers "learn some 'truths' about human interaction; thus, it is important to examine critically the representations of power and social interaction on these programs. How are they depicted, and how are they understood by audiences?"[2]

Migration to Korea began in the 1990s, as the country finished its phase of rapid economic development from the 1960s. It was a relatively new phenomenon in contemporary Korean society, as previous trends had seen emigration, not immigration. From the beginning of the twentieth century, people had been driven out of the country due to hard living conditions, such as poverty, colonization, the Korean War and a continuing confrontation in the form of an armistice and military dictatorship, to name the most significant factors. Existing migrants, most notably Japanese and Chinese, were driven out after the Korean War: the former because of colonial atrocities by Japanese colonizers and the latter due to governmental actions to treat them unfairly—politically, economically, and socially. In addition, the 'pure blood nationalism' propagated by the government during the economic development era under president Park Jeong-Hee's military government had been consistently used as the national identity to promote economic and, later, democratic development by the 1990s.[3]

With this nationalistic environment and emerging globalization as a backdrop, the first significant group of migrants in half a century to arrive were migrant workers primarily from Southeast Asian countries after the Seoul Olympic Games in 1988. The Games provided the first opportunities for Korean society to open its door to the world. That first wave of migrants was later followed by the second of 'marriage migrants,' as rapid industrialization brought a bridal shortage in rural areas in Seoul.[4] These two groups share many similarities such as where, how, and why they migrate. From the new millennium, migration to Korea has diversified to include highly skilled and highly educated migrants with a different array of backgrounds, but still workers and marriage migrants are the majorities. The rapid change from a military-ruled nationalist society, from the 1990s, to a globalized one with an increasing influx of migrants has caused a considerable cultural shock. It has not been an easy task to change public discourse from the nationalistic viewpoint to that of globalization in a decade.[5]

As it happened, Korean media initially played a very limited role, with scant attention being given to the 1990s' influx of early migrants. Korean media, especially terrestrial television broadcasters, have been at the center of shaping public discourse, as in any society. After more than 10 years of growing migration, the first major programs featuring migrants appeared in 2003 and 2005.[6] From being ignored by mainstream media and being strangers to the public, most migrant workers experienced unstable and unfair labor conditions upon arrival. They were given trainee status and later they started to be recognized officially as workers with labor permits. Their right to organize labor unions was not accepted until 2015. Labor problems caused large protests in the 1990s, as protestors sought to protect their rights as workers, and media coverage was so limited that migrants had to organize their own media outlets.[7] In comparison, marriage migrants received some media coverage, but these stories were criticized as patriarchal, orientalist, and Korean-centered.[8] Recently, Korean media have shown more interest in these stories, as non-Koreans entering Korea have become more diverse in their reasons and origins. Their presence has grown large enough that it has become normal to encounter non-Koreans in daily life and on television.

In this chapter, I survey the ways the migration-led demographic change has affected media representation of migrants in terms of class. Korea's recent experience with migration can provide an insight into other countries where change may happen in a short time period as the countries transition from being closed to open societies.

Between the Korean War and the 1990s, Koreans and the Korean media were exposed to a very limited number of non-Koreans. Thus, in a compressed timeframe, Korean society has faced the challenge of learning how to deal with unfamiliar faces in reality, and on television. This chapter chronicles the estranged relationship between media and class by examining the different ways migrants have been represented in Korea television reality shows.

Class Theory Applied to the Korean Context

Based on the Marxist approach, issues surrounding class have traditionally been understood in terms of economies of production and exchange. Marx divides classes based on ownership of the means of production. The bourgeoisies own the means of production; the proletariats don't. This division takes the form of collectivity. Marx states: "[T]here cannot be one capitalist for every worker, but rather there has to be a certain quantity of workers per capitalist, not like one or two journeymen per master."[9] This understanding of class as a collective based on possession of the means of production provides a clear picture, but it has been criticized for its simplicity in contrast with the complex approaches to class others have taken.

Others have taken more complicated approaches. For example, Weber and Bourdieu add social and cultural statuses as indicators of class distinctions.[10] Weber sees class not as a collectivity but as an element shared by people based on the possession of property.[11] To understand a group of people as a community, Weber develops the notion of the 'status group'—grouping people according to their specific lifestyles, which include "ideal and material goods and opportunities."[12] Status can link to class situation, but it does not necessarily do so. People from different classes can belong to the same status groups—and others can be excluded—based on shared style. For Weber, class is not the determinant of social group membership, just a part of it. In a similar way, Bourdieu finds that social classes are not only determined by economic factors, but also by one's social and cultural capital.[13] Taste proclaims his/her social class and distinguishes oneself from others. Weber and Bourdieu define class as a complex matter in combination with social, cultural, and economic factors.

Recently, Beck[14] takes a totally different position, asking about the validity of class. He regards class as increasingly obsolete when it comes to explaining social behaviors.[15] Identifying it as a "zombie category," he claims such a collective term as class cannot explain an individualized contemporary society. In his view, class was relevant when workers worked collectively in traditional industrial settings. However, individualized, consumer-oriented social forms have replaced the traditional collective form of class. Labor conditions have become more flexible in post-industrial environments, as individuals (are forced to) move easily and frequently from one job to another. As a result, it is hard to apply class as a collective term to contemporary social settings. This does not mean that Beck believes that class has totally disappeared. Rather, Beck argues that class in the form of social inequality has been de-structured and re-structured by the forces of individualization and globalization.[16] Beck considers human migration an important factor in the de-structuring of social class. Regarding the constitution of the working class, Beck states:

> In Germany, at any rate, it is the case that the cultural homogeneity of the so-called working class has been dissolved in a process of internal globalization and pluralization. This can be demonstrated by the explosive increase in the proportion of foreign or immigrant youth completing their school education at a Hauptschule, the lowest rung of the educational ladder. The constancy of social classes unreflectively assumes the constancy of the national membership of the members of these classes. Here too it is the case, that class culture and class position are being uncoupled; the multi-ethnic, multi-national working class is no longer a working class.[17]

A social class in the traditional sense is composed of a collection of people in the same nation-state. But as globalized post-industrial societies continually weaken national boundaries, they also weaken social classes. In this sense, for Beck, migrants serve as a contributing factor of class re-structuring.

In terms of analyzing reality shows in Korea, rather than following strict Marxist notions of class, it seems appropriate to take advantage of Weber's and Bourdieu's notions of social classes because reality shows display all possible facets of people's lives for entertainment. Among them, there must be signs of class identification. Beck's understanding of class dissolution in the context of globalization is also critical, since Korean reality shows hesitate and are confused when they portray non-Koreans. In that regard, the best way to treat them is to present them as others, not a part of social structure. Regardless of social status and working conditions, Korean reality shows portray non-Koreans as sacrificing father and mother, travelers, and exotic others. Although exposed clearly, signs of class, as shown below, are blurred and hidden within discourses of otherness.

Class and Migrations in Korea

This section examines how class has been de-structured in recent decades in relation to contemporary immigration in Korea. Rapid industrialization from the 1960s integrated Korea into the globalized capitalist system. The 1960s' Park military government utilized industrialization in tandem with the politics of nationalism to appease social discontent caused by rapid economic development and social and cultural restructurings. In the process, a huge population started to move from small villages to big industrial cities. While the percentage of non-wage workers (e.g., self-employed and unpaid domestic laborers) decreased from 69.5 percent in 1963 to 25.5 percent in 2015, employed wage workers increased from 2.3 million in 1963 to 19.2 million in 2015, an 8.2-fold increase.[18]

In this context, the Korean working class formed rapidly, concentrated in big *Chaebul* factories and industrial cities. It provided a foundation for persistent labor union movements from the 1970s to the 1990s. However, during the 1990s, especially after the 1997 economic crisis, the Korean economic system transitioned into a post-industrial, neo-liberal economic system under pressure from the USA and International Monetary Fund (IMF). One change in labor practices was more flexible labor conditions, where union protection was threatened, and firing workers became easier. Another outcome was globalized labor conditions, with the exportation of industrial factories to lower-wage adjacent Asian countries such as China and Vietnam, and the importation of cheaper workforces from these same countries. As a result, workers in Korea came to be working under precarious labor conditions as individuals. As of 2017, non-regular labor sectors employed a third of all workers in Korea, a mere 2.2 percent of whom had union membership.[19] As a result, the working class emerged during the economic development and, although being protected by labor unions, are slowly replaced by temporary and flexible workers. This has resulted in a fast-track social restructuring toward post-industrialization in workplaces from the 1990s.

Globalization began to be clear in Korea with the 1988 Seoul Olympic Games and the loosening of border controls that facilitated the entrance and exit of both Koreans and non-Koreans. The end of the Cold War meant fewer restrictions on people entering, especially from Communist countries such as China and Vietnam. These changes created waves of immigration to Korea for the first time in recent history, disturbing existing national social structures built around the ideology of 'pure-blood' nationalism.[20] In the beginning, migrants came individually without official working visas for better wages and stayed without governmental permission. In the 1990s, while the number of migrant workers doubled every year, undocumented workers were at one time more than three-quarters of all migrant workers.[21] On the one hand, more than two million immigrants currently reside in Korea, and the number has increased 9.26 percent annually over the last five years.[22] Among these immigrant residents, 75 percent are categorized as workers in factories and farms. On the other hand, the number of people undertaking short-term stays has doubled over the past decade, from 266,011 in 2007 to 518,902 in 2016. In sum, among the increasing number of migrants, the majority are workers, with the majority being short-term workers. Individualization and flexible labor also affect the migrant population.

Looking at class-related issues among migrants, the number of undocumented migrant workers from China and Southeast Asian countries doubled each year in the 1990s, prompting the Korean government to introduce a trainee program in 1991 that allowed migrant workers to stay for three years as trainees, not as workers. The program became controversial right away because it bestowed unsecure legal status for migrants with almost no protection, and led to labor exploitation by some Korean factory owners. Over the years, migrant workers have fought for fair legal and working conditions with continuous strikes and protests. One of the most noticeable ones occurred in 2003 when more than 2000 migrant workers organized country-wide sit-ins. In Seoul, about 150 workers staged a sit-in for 380 days. The protest eventually brought about a few changes. First, migrant workers organized their own labor union, which later received legal and industrial recognition. Second, the introduction of the Employment Permit System in 2005 made Korea the first Asian country to legally recognize the labor, pay, and benefit rights of migrant workers as equal to those of Korean workers.[23] Third, in 2015, the supreme court of Korea recognized equal labor rights for undocumented workers, even if they overstayed or worked without proper documents. Korean society finally took steps to embrace migrant workers in existing social structures.

Another critical group is marriage immigrants. International marriages between Korean men and women from other countries such as China, Vietnam, and the Philippines began in the 1990s when lower class and/or rural area male populations couldn't find brides among Koreans. It was believed that eligible Korean women moved to big industrial cities to work and eventually to find their partners there. Korean women generally didn't want to come back to their rural villages to get married and live. This became a social issue and international marriage provided a solution. As such, international marriages exceeded 10.9 percent of all the marriages in Korea in 2007 and have since settled around 7 percent.[24] This trend has serious social and cultural implications for Korean society. Marriage immigrants are to stay in Korea and raise the next generations. This relates directly to issues of national identity, citizenship, and tradition.[25] Furthermore, marriage migrants have become an important part of the Korean workforce. A government report found that, in 2015, about 60 percent of female migrants were employed, a lower but more rapidly growing employment rate than that of male migrants.[26] Marriage immigrants exist at the center of class, gender, family structure, and globalization issues.

The last area to briefly look at in terms of migration and the subject of this chapter is non-Koreans who stay temporarily for travel or business. According to government reports,[27] non-Koreans who visit Korea for short periods of time (less than 90 days) with/out visas account for more than 60 percent of all entrants into the country. The number of travelers visiting Korea has consistently increased since the mid-1990s, exceeding 10 million for the first time in 2012. In comparison, between 2012 and 2016, an average of 534,000 professionals, 49,000 non-professional residents, and 93,000 students entered Korea annually.[28] The number of non-professional workers who work in factories and on farms is five and ten times higher than the number of students and professional workers respectively. However, as shown below, they remain poorly underrepresented in Korean television shows.

A 2016 survey of immigration/entry to Korea shows an increasingly complicated trend. While most entrants are tourists, migrant workers and marriage migrants continue to exert substantial social and cultural impacts on Korean society. Most migrant workers are untrained laborers, who fill voids left by Koreans in the manufacturing and agricultural sectors. Professional workers and students form an insignificant part of the overall foreigner population. In terms of country of origin, about half of all immigrants to Korea are Chinese and Korean-Chinese (49.6 percent), followed by Vietnamese (7.3 percent), US citizens (6.8 percent), and Thais (4.9 percent).[29] This breakdown testifies to Korea's increasingly globalized population. This internal globalization[30] has introduced changes to conventional national social structures, such as class, family, and nationality. Efforts have been undertaken to embrace these migration-related changes through multicultural policies and labor movements.[31] Simultaneously, the identities of migrants as well as the perceptions of them by Koreans depend on the fair representation of migrants.[32] This is because media representation is always cultural, reflecting what a society has shared as common practices of understanding what is good or bad, and what is desirable or not.[33]

Reality Shows in Korea

In recent years, the popularity of reality shows has surged all over the world and Korea is no exception. Defining a reality show is not an easy task because the category has evolved to encompass nearly every part of the 'real' that television can deliver. Broadly, Ouellette and Murray locate reality TV in "the fusion of popular entertainment with self-conscious claim to the discourse of the real."[34] Originating from the documentary tradition, the real has evolved to encompass elements of social experiments for commercial television culture with a feeling of ordinariness.[35] In this regard, Hill summarizes the contemporary development of reality shows.

> There are a variety of styles and techniques associated with reality TV, such as non-professional actors, unscripted dialogue, surveillance footage, hand-held cameras, seeing events unfold as they are happening in front of the camera. However, the treatment of 'reality' in reality programming has changed as the genre has developed over the past decade. In the early stages of the genre, reality TV was associated with on-scene footage of law and order, or emergency services. More recently, reality TV is associated with anything and everything, from people to pets, from birth to death.[36]

Reality television can be summarized as the production of the real, taking advantage of available aesthetic styles to emphasize actions unfolding simultaneously in front of cameras and making mundane happenings entertaining and extraordinary in every possible way.

Sharing these characteristics with other cultures, reality shows in Korea have independently developed their own characteristics. Studies have identified the following traits as typical of Korean reality programs: celebrities as main participants, familism, emphases on fairness and equality, and production staff being revealed.[37] Each trait warrants brief explanation. First, Korean reality programs tend to feature currently popular talents as the main participants. Other countries differ in this regard, preferring recycled old celebrities and ordinary people for low production costs and reality.[38] The preference of popular talents is explained with the believed difficulty of training amateurs to look natural on camera and to act real.[39] Second, while global hit reality shows such as *Big Brother* and *Survivor* feature competition and conflict among participants, Korean reality shows emphasize camaraderie in the form of big pseudo-families and respect for age hierarchies.[40] Producers believe that Korean viewers don't enjoy conflict and competition in reality shows. As a result, Koreans reality shows feature a great deal of harmony, and following social rules diligently. Third, the presence of production staff and equipment are often exposed to reveal the constructed nature of the real in reality shows.[41] Directors and writers regularly describe the progress of the show in the form of pseudo-moderators. The peculiarities of Korean reality TV suggest that reality shows alter their forms to meet local preferences.

Non-Koreans on Korean Television

Non-Koreans were rarely shown on Korean television shows, although a lot of Hollywood television shows, from *The Man From U.N.C.L.E.* and *Six Million Dollar Man* to *X-Files*, had been imported and had become popular. This clear segregation on television between Americans in imported Hollywood shows and Koreans in Korean shows was maintained until the mid-2000s— even with a surge of labor and/or marriage immigration. The first desegregation happened in a Korean-style primetime reality show titled, *!Exclamation Mark* in 2003, and the second in a public service broadcaster's studio talk show titled, *Love in Asia* in 2005. The drama genre was the last to join with *Golden Bride* in 2007. Although the contemporary tide of immigration to Korea started around the time of the 1988 Seoul Olympic Games, it took almost 20 years for television to catch up with the emerging phenomenon of immigration. This section discusses how different categories of non-Koreans have been represented in the Korean media with examples from contemporary shows. Migrant workers and marriage migrants make up the first category, students and professionals the second, and short-term travelers the third.[42] Each group is represented distinctively in terms of production and presentation styles. Class elements are sometimes exposed so blatantly that they are taken for granted and look natural. In other instances, other social and cultural signs are foregrounded, working to hide issues such as class.

Migrants with (Un)clear Class Backdrop

The first category of Korean television shows features mostly marriage migrants and migrant workers (migrants, hereafter). Most of these migrants are from Southeast Asian and Central Asian countries.[43] The shows featuring them maintain the following basic narrative structure: first, they show that migrants (mostly male, father character) work hard under difficult circumstances and, second, they demonstrate that a family reunion at home or in Korea brings happiness to all. The narrative structure justifies the difficulties and the sacrifices migrants make in Korea, mostly for their families. The structure was introduced in 2003 in a primetime entertainment show, *!Exclamation Mark* on MBC, one of three major broadcasters in Korea. The show had a block titled *Asia! Asia!*, in which famous Korean entertainers went to the home countries of the week's featured migrant workers to find their families and bring them back to Korea for a temporary family reunion.

The family reunion format has been adapted by subsequent shows such as *Love in Asia* (KBS), and *Multicultural Mother- and Daughter-in-Law Stories* (*In-Law Stories*, hereafter, EBS). The fact that the former had 453 episodes over 10 years and the latter has more than 200 episodes and counting since 2013 illustrates that there is a certain appeal in the family reunion narrative among Korean viewers. The popularity prompted the launch of another show in 2015 that focused on migrant workers, but reversed the narrative structure. Titled *3000 Leagues in Search of Father* (*3000 Leagues*, hereafter),[44] the show normally starts by juxtaposing the life of a migrant worker, typically a male, working in an industrial setting in Korea with that of the worker's family in a rural village at home. The family later embarks on a trip to Korea to find the father on their own, experiences all kinds of troubles on the way, and finally meets him for a reunion.

These migrant shows have clear class implications. First and foremost, markers of economic status are distinct and pervasive. The migrants' background at home is always rural, while that in Korea is either industrial or rural. In Korea and at home, their low economic status is on clear display in every way from housing issues and educational difficulties to health problems. For example, trips to Korea in *3000 Leagues* are always difficult because the featured families always encounter problems of various kinds in Korea. The trip is always depressing and agonizing, and is the least adventurous of the travel shows. It is very different from what non-Korean travelers do in the third category. Marriage migrants in *In-law* also display hardship in their troubled relationships with their mothers-in-law. Migrants in this category shows are portrayed in need of help economically and culturally.[45]

These migrant shows present class in two ways. First, class is so obvious that it is a clear marker of migrant identity. However, this class marker overlaps significantly with ethnic representation, as most of these migrants are from Southeast Asian countries. As a result, class status among migrants is identified with ethnic/racial representation. Class and racial issues are confusingly represented together. Too much representation of certain racial/ethnic groups in very limited and repeated narrative lines makes those group identical with a certain class status. Class issues of migrants come to be owned and ghettoized by these repeated representations. Second, the issue of class becomes more complicated with the intrusion of family narrative. The shows regard family as a critical element with which to tell stories of migrants; family backgrounds are used to portray migrant difficulties. Mostly, these shows depict migrants as poor in Korea and in their home countries. They mainly come to Korea to support their families. Simultaneously, the shows portray family as a relief, if temporary, from the hardship. In *In-Law Stories*, marriage migrants return to their hometowns to find solutions for current conflicts between mothers- and daughters-in-law. In *3000 Leagues*, the joy of fathers meeting family at long last justifies the migrant workers' hard labor, sacrifices, and separation. Family is the alpha and the omega of the narrative, and nothing else. Class, obvious in every shot and crucial to the shows' plots, becomes just another backdrop in the show.

To summarize, class and migrants' ethnic/racial identities are displayed so obviously and consistently in these shows that class status becomes closely associated with ethnic/racial identity. Class issues become ethnic/racial issues, and vice versa. Furthermore, because the shows present family as both the source of, and solution for, migration, class becomes the backdrop, obscuring that class is the very reason for the separation.

Professionals

The second category of shows featuring non-Koreans is talk shows that invite non-Koreans as guests. Among the most significant of such shows was *Global Talk Show: The Beauties' Chatterbox* (*Beauties' Chatterbox* hereafter), where female guests with different nationalities talked about their experiences in Korea. The main difference between this show and those in the first category was the composition of the guests it featured. While the migrants featured in the first category were primarily low-income migrants from Southeast Asian countries, *Beauties' Chatterbox* guests were mostly female students, professionals, and models (professionals, hereafter) from all over the world. The second distinction of the show was its subject, which was about a non-Koreans' viewpoint on Korean society, the opposite of the previous category. *Beauties Chatterbox* aired for 5 years with 172 episodes. It generated frequent controversies due to guests' honest remarks on Korean society. Though cancelled, the show's popular format was later adapted for a new show, *Nonsummit*, a mock UN summit represented by 12 male participants from all over the world. *Nonsummit* replaces the female guests with males, who discuss slightly more serious cultural and political issues.

Since both *Beauties' Chatterbox* and *Nonsummit* belong to the talk show genre, the relationship between talk shows and reality shows warrants an explanation. Reality shows have had an affinity to talk shows; on a basic level, both depict ordinary people with interesting narratives[46] and both claim to provide access to 'real' stories unscripted. That is why, for example, Corner[47] observes that the style of new talk shows such as 'Jerry Springer Experience' influenced the practices of reality shows such as *Big Brother*. The environment in *Beauties' Chatterbox* resembled this new style of talk show because for entertainment purposes it focused primarily on real and entertaining elements in Korean culture. Its topics included, for example, "the shocking characteristics of Korean restaurants," "exotic jobs only available in Korea," "stereotypes among Korean men," and "moments when one wants to marry a Korean man." In addition, the show featured numerous guest activities and performances, such as cooking, dancing, and re-enactments in a competitive environment. These kinds of gameshow elements are also typical of reality shows, as the examples of *Survivor* or *Big Brother* illustrate. *Nonsummit* has been less active and sensational, but it has different elements of Korean reality shows, such as heavy editing and colorful subtitles and graphics. It eventually produced a spinoff reality show with the guests visiting their hometowns abroad.

Returning to the issue of class representation, shows such as *The Beauties' Chatterbox* and *Nonsummit* ignore any necessity of fair or equal representation. Obviously, they are produced for entertainment purposes. For instance, the guests of *Chatterbox Beauties* came from diverse countries, but the composition did not reflect the migrant population in Korea. Out of 117 guests who appeared on the show, 68 (58 percent) had European/American backgrounds, 43 (37 percent) had Asian backgrounds, and six (5 percent) African backgrounds.[48] In reality, in 2016, more than 70 percent of migrants were Asians while fewer than 10 percent were from Europe and America.[49] Eighty-two percent of the show's guests were students, who in reality make up only 6 percent of the immigrant population. The other guests were models, English language teachers, and white-collar employees. *Nonsummit* exhibits a similar degree of misrepresentation: 66.6 percent of regular guests are males from developed countries such as the USA, Germany, and France.[50] *Nonsummit* guests seem more fluent in Korean than *Beauties' Chatterbox* guests and most are professionals. There is clear misrepresentation of migrant population in the shows, but this did not affect their popularity. The fancy clothes and handsome faces of the professionals do not reflect the realities of the non-Korean population. They helped *Beauties' Chatterbox* record the highest rating in its timeslot, and *Nonsummit* aired for more than three years. The guests from both were invited to other television shows, landed book deals, and debuted as actors or actresses. They had clearly become the faces of new migrants in Korea, replacing those of migrants who had images of protesting and suffering.

This misrepresentation enables the professionals to act differently from the non-Koreans in the first category. While the migrants are portrayed as the ones who need to adapt and learn, the professionals are elevated to a social position where they can criticize Korean society. As equals, they are asked to make comparisons between their home cultures and Korea. One study[51] argued that the differences in representation originate from social status distinctions. The employment, educational, and ethnic backgrounds of professionals provide enough qualification for them to criticize Korean culture, whereas the social indicators of migrants block them from doing so.

This unequal representation in favor of the professional results in a few critical consequences: misrepresentation, manipulation, and discrimination. First, the overrepresentation of the professionals leads to underrepresentation of others—the majority of migrants. It conceals both the existence of underrepresented lower-class people and the issues they face. As they are dispersed to factories and farms in real life, shows about them are relegated to less popular status. Second, overrepresentation leads to a generalization that the lives of professionals are those of migrants in general. If they do have problems, migrants will be able to speak for themselves in Korean society. When there is no outcry, it is because there is no perceived problem. The issues faced by non-Koreans in general thus appear to be manageable. Finally, the positive and active images of the professionals surreptitiously, and maybe inadvertently, justify unfair discriminations against migrants to enhance racial stereotypes that privilege (Western) professionals. The visual cues from costumes and well-lit studio sets contrast clearly with the poor conditions in which migrants are shown to live. As a result, these shows naturalize the different treatment of migrants and professionals in society; they seem to justify discrimination.

Travelers

The last category of non-Koreans featured in Korean shows are foreign travelers. Such shows are a very recent phenomenon that began in 2017, when a minor cable network broadcast an observational reality show[52] titled *Welcome, First Time in Korea?* (*First Time* hereafter). Travelers had never previously served as main characters in Korean television shows. Travel shows in general have been popular since the 1990s when the restriction against international travel was lifted, but they have always been about foreign places and cultures from the viewpoints of traveling Koreans. *First Time* reversed this tradition, showing non-Korean travelers experiencing Korean culture while, in the studio, multinational guests observe and comment on the travelers' behavior on monitors. Korean viewers watch Korean culture through the eyes of foreign travelers and those of studio guests. There are three layers of reflexive observation on Korean culture: travelers, guests, and viewers. The sudden and unexpected popularity of the show despite the network's lower status and the program's low budget resulted in about half a dozen copycat reality shows featuring travelers to Korea.[53] For example, one show has Korean stars hosting travelers at their homes and showing them around. Another has Korean celebrities driving for travelers around Seoul as taxi drivers.

In its original format, a non-Korean, who lives in Korea, invites friends from home to stay for a few days in Korea.[54] Though invited, the travelers are on their own in terms of planning their schedules and traveling around. Sooner or later, their friends will join them to introduce them more fully to Korean culture. One trip produces a few episodes for programming. The travelers' countries of origin are as broad as possible, including France, Mexico, Germany, Russia, Finland, the United Kingdom, and India. Different from the professionals category, these travelers do not know much about Korea, so their reaction to Korean culture seems immediate and genuine. The popularity of the show seems to come from these 'real' reactions to Korean culture and the distinct cultural behaviors of the travelers.

While *First Time* seems to display no signs of class on the surface, this speaks to the complexities of social class in the era of globalization and migration. Class status seems to be eradicated; there is no clear class indicator because the travelers are out of their own social contexts. The show is not interested in sharing anything about their social backgrounds. Instead, it focuses on cultural differences, such as culinary cultures, shopping preferences, different choices in tourist destinations, etc. When class is based on a state system,[55] travelers are state-less and therefore class-less during their journey. Consequently, despite the popularity of such shows, travelers seem separated from any discussion of class and migrants.

The apparent absence of class signals in *First Time* exposes another side of the media representation of non-Koreans on television. First, traveler shows are interested in leisure and consumption, activities that implicitly reference class status.[56] For example, when groups of friends travel on their own, some groups rent cars and the others use public transportation. Some people are shown to have better language skills in English to enjoy fewer difficulties in communication. These scenes carry implicit signals about social class. One group brings out the class issue blatantly. In an Indian group episode (episode #13), the introduction starts with a luxurious house owned by one member of the group. In the scene, the owner states in an interview that with their urban culture and wealth, they want to change stereotypes of poverty associated with India. This is how representation of class is challenged and displayed in the era of globalization.

The traveler shows are different from other shows, especially compared with the first category of migrants. Although the travelers and the migrants both share that they have traveled from home to unfamiliar places, this common element highlights differences in terms of representation.[57] The travelers are portrayed enjoying strange places in affable manners, while migrants appear as troubled and in need of help. With their entertaining characters, travelers come across as more relatable, fun and cool. Their cultural skills and knowledge paint them like the second category professionals. They are funny and didactic in their cultural interpretations and representations.

In short, the travelers' apparent classlessness in the shows simply disguises class distinctions that emerge on closer examination. The significantly different representation of non-Koreans between the second and the third categories contrasts happy travelers with troubled migrants. Implicit class signs serve to further isolate migrants in television diegesis. At the same time, the shows fortify existing stereotypes about migrants by providing one more reference point for discrimination. In this way, these travel shows also hinge upon class, even if they seem indifferent to class.

Conclusion

Korean reality shows represent non-Koreans in varied ways, and these representations have class implications. Although class is ignored in the storylines, the ignorance works as a potential reference pointing to class in a broader scope. In the first category, shows about labor and/or marriage migrants, the class status of featured migrants is clear: migrant workers in a traditional Marxist sense and marriage migrants in social and cultural sense. However, their status becomes opaque when their class elements compete with others such as family and ethnicity.

In the second category, shows about professionals further obscure class signs. These programs represent students and professionals with beauty and fluency in Korean as the only interested and interesting non-Koreans. Their diverse backgrounds in nationality and culture highlight the globalized nature of contemporary Korean society and complicate class among non-Koreans. This obscurity seems to support the idea of class as a zombie category.[58] However, the fact that these shows put more emphasis on looks and speaking style, and overrepresent Westerners, only reveals that they are based on stereotypes. They hide the reality that most migrants in Korea have come for work in order to support their families back home. The classlessness reflects and reveals class.

Finally, the third category, shows about travelers, tries to make class status irrelevant, overshadowed by culture. The featured non-Koreans are travelers who come for leisure and consumption. However, their travel, compared with that of the migrants, provides clear class distinctions that further alienate migrants. Their temporary stay in Korea looks so enjoyable that the lives of labor and marriage migrants are made less desirable and less entertaining, leading them to be ignored.

Class representation in television is complicated, but it shows a clear direction. An array of elements refracts and reflects the representation of migrant's class status. Nationalism, familism, orientalism and cultural stereotypes, to name a few, affect how viewers watch these shows and understand class on television. Expected or not, shows featuring non-Korean deflect attention from the majority of migrants. The more favorable representation of other non-Koreans can work to justify existing unfair and underserved discriminations.

About a decade ago, migrants were at the center of social and cultural debates surrounding globalization in Korea. The debates addressed issues such as working conditions, ill-treatment, fraudulent marriage business, harassment, etc. Although controversial and confrontational from time to time, the issues of migrants were considered as critical challenges for Korea as it sought to be a member of the international community. Nowadays, however, finding stories about migrants (except occasional oddities regarding accidents and criminal activity) is not easy, at least on television. In their place, other kinds of non-Koreans appear. While good-looking, affable and educated professionals and travelers represent the happier faces of non-Koreans on popular television shows, migrant shows are relegated to the fringes of late-night educational programming, still flickering the images of hard-working mothers and fathers longing for their families.

Notes

1 Finding the right word to identify a certain group of people in the era of globalization is not an easy task, as their identities can be fluid. Although it sounds ethno-centric, I call all migrants as non-Koreans (temporarily-staying non-Korean citizens and travelers included).
2 David S. Escoffery, "Introduction: The Role of Representation in Reality Television," in *How Real Is Reality TV?: Essays on Representation and Truth*, ed. D.S. Escoffery (Jefferson, NC: McFarland, 2012), 1–3.
3 Nora Hui-Jung Kim, "Framing Multiple Others and International Norms: The Migrant Worker Advocacy Movement and Korean National Identity Reconstruction," *Nations and Nationalism* 15, no. 4 (2009): 678–695.
4 Andrew Eungi Kim, "Global Migration and South Korea: Foreign Workers, Foreign Brides and the Making of a Multicultural Society," *Ethnic & Racial Studies* 32, no. 1 (2009): 70–92.
5 Nora Hui-Jung Kim, "Korean Immigration Policy Changes and the Political Liberals' Dilemma," *International Migration Review* 42, no. 3 (2008): 576–596.
6 Kyung Sook Lee, "The 'Diaspora' Identity Represented in the Hybrid Reality Program: The Textual Analysis of 'Love in Asia' Aired on KBS 1 Channel," *Korean Journal of Broadcasting and Telecommunication Studies* 20 (2006): 239–276.
7 Hun-Yul Lee, "At the Crossroads of Migrant Workers, Class, and Media: A Case Study of a Migrant Workers' Television Project," *Media, Culture & Society* 34, no. 3 (2012): 312–327.
8 See Dong-Hoo Lee, "Korean TV's imagery of Asia," *Studies of Broadcasting Culture* 18 (2006): 9–35; and K. S. Lee, "The 'Diaspora'."
9 Karl Marx, *Grundrisse. Foundations of the Critique of Political Economy* (New York: Random House, 1973), 519.
10 June Deery and Andrea Press, eds., *Media and Class: TV, Film, and Digital Culture* (New York: Routledge, 2017).
11 Bert N. Adams and R.A. Sydie, *Sociological Theory* (New Delhi: Vistaar, 2002): 187.
12 Ibid.
13 Pierre Bourdieu, *Distinction: A Social Critique of the Judgement of Taste*. (Cambridge, MA: Harvard University Press, 1984).
14 Ulrich Beck, "From Industrial Society to the Risk Society: Questions of Survival, Social Structure and Ecological Enlightenment," *Theory, Culture & Society* 9, no. 1 (1992): 97–123; and Ulrich Beck, "Reframing Power in the Globalized World," Springer Briefs on Pioneers, in Ulrich Beck (ed.) *Ulrich Beck: Pioneer in Cosmopolitan Society and Risk Society* (New York: Springer International Publishing, 2014), 157–168.
15 Deery and Press, *Media*, 4.
16 Beck, *Ulrich Beck*, 102.
17 Ibid., 120.
18 Ha-Young Kim, *Onlnal Hankookeu Nodongkyekeup (Working Class in Contemporary Korea: Classic Marxist Approach* (Seoul: Chackgalpy, 2017), 122–127.
19 See Y.-S. Park, "Examining 'Statistical Differences' between Government and Labor Sector Reports." *Hankyoreh* (January 13, 2017). Retrieved from www.hani.co.kr/arti/economy/economy_general/778609.html. Park notes that 20 percent of regular workers have union membership.
20 N. H.-J. Kim, "Korean Immigration".
21 Han, Dong-Woo, "Migrant Workers in Korea Problems and Social Response," *Journal of Critical Social Welfare* (2002): 13–42.
22 See Statistics Korea, "2016 Report on Foreign Worker Employment Survey." Available online at http://kostat.go.kr/portal/korea/kor_nw/2/1/index.board?bmode=read&aSeq=356794 and Statistics Korea, "Status of Immigrants," 2018.

23 Amnesty International, "Migrant Workers Treated as 'Disposable Labour' in South Korea." October 2009. Available at www.amnesty.org/en/press-releases/2009/10/south-korea-migrant-workers-treated-e28098disposable-laboure28099-20091021/.
24 Danuri: Multicultural family support portal. "Status of Foreign Marriages and Divorces," (2017). Available at: https://liveinkorea.kr/portal/KOR/page/contents.do?menuSeq=295&pageSeq=290.
25 See A.E. Kim, "Global Migration"; and Timothy Lim, "Rethinking Belongingness in Korea: Transnational Migration, 'Migrant Marriages' and the Politics of Multiculturalism," *Pacific Affairs* 83, no. 1 (2010): 51–71.
26 Hae-Sook Chung, Yi-Seon Kim, Tackmeon Yi, Kyoung Hee Ma, Yunjeong Choi, Geonpyo Park, Cheyon Tong, Jung-Mee Hwang, and Euna Lee, *An Analysis on the National Survey of Multicultural Families 2015* (Seoul: Ministry of Gender Equality & Family, 2016).
27 Department of Justice, *2016 Annual Report: Status of Arrival and Departures of People & Migration Policies* (Gwacheon: Department of Justice, 2017). Available at: www.immigration.go.kr/indeximmeng.html.
28 Ibid., 40–41.
29 Ibid., 45.
30 Beck, *Ulrich Beck*, 102.
31 See: N. H.-J. Kim, "Korean Immigration"; H.-Y. Lee. "At the Crossroads"; and Lim, "Rethinking Belongingness".
32 Nora Hui-Jung Kim, "Multiculturalism and the Politics of Belonging: The Puzzle of Multiculturalism in South Korea." *Citizenship Studies* 16, no. 1 (2012): 103–117.
33 Stuart Hall, "The Work of Representation," in *Representation: Cultural Representations and Signifying Practices*, ed. Stuart Hall (London: Sage, 1997): 13–74.
34 Laurie Ouellette and Susan Murray, "Introduction," in *Reality TV: Remaking Television Culture*, eds. Susan Murray and Laurie Ouellette (New York: New York University Press, 2004): 3.
35 For example, see: Bill Nichols, *Representing Reality: Issues and Concepts in Documentary*, Vol. 681 (Bloomington, IN: Indiana University Press, 1991); Bradley D. Clissold, "Candid Camera and the Origins of Reality TV: Contextualising a Historical Precedent," in *Understanding Reality Television*, eds. Su Holmes and Deborah Jermyn (London: Routledge, 2004): 33–53; Laura Grindstaff, "Self-Serving Celebrity: The Production of Ordinariness and the Ordinariness of Production in Reality Television," in *Production Studies: Cultural Studies of Media Industries*, eds. Vicki Mayer, Miranda J. Banks, and John T. Caldwell, 72–86 (New York: Routledge, 2009): 72–86; and Chad Raphael, "The Political-Economic Origins of Reali-TV," in *Reality TV: Remaking Television Culture*, 2nd edn, eds. Susan Murray and Laurie Ouellette (New York: New York University Press, 2009), 123–140.
36 Annette Hill, *Reality TV: Audiences and Popular Factual Television* (London: Routledge, 2005), 41.
37 Joo-yeon Park, *Television Reality Programs* (Seoul: Korea Press Foundation, 2005); Sujeong Kim, "The Structure of Feelings and Cultural Politics in Korean TV Reality Shows," *Studies of Broadcasting Culture*, December (2011): 37; Hun-Yul Lee, "Securing Reality through Production Staff in a Korean Reality Program : Analyzing the Revelation Production Activities in Television," *Korean Journal of Broadcasting and Telecommunication Studies* 29, no. 6 (2015): 241–272.
38 Hugh Curnutt, "Durable Participants: A Generational Approach to Reality TV's 'Ordinary' Labor Pool." *Media, Culture & Society* 33, no. 7 (2011): 1061–1076.
39 Park, *Television Reality*.
40 S. Kim, "The Structure".
41 H.-Y. Lee, "Securing Reality".
42 I will use governmental categorizations, calling the first group migrants, the second professionals, and the third travelers to highlight the groups' different statuses and intentions for entering Korea (Department of Justice 2017). The first group come to Korea to stay; members of the second group have more professional backgrounds, work in white-collar environments, and are freer to move around the world; members of the last group, who obviously outnumber the other groups, come to Korea as travelers/tourists.
43 Interestingly, the Chinese migrants are almost non-existent in this category despite the fact the Chinese are the biggest majority. It is because most of them are Korean-Chinese who became Chinese nationals during the colonial era and the Korean War. There are still sensitive national, political, and diplomatic issues between two countries.
44 The title comes from a Japanese anime that tells the story of a young Italian boy trying to find his father after a long and hard journey.
45 K.S. Lee, "The 'Diaspora'."
46 Ouellette and Murray, "Introduction".
47 John Corner, "Performing the Real: Documentary Diversions," *Television & New Media* 3, no. 3 (2002): 255–269.

48 D.J. Kim, *Representation of Foreigner in a Variety Talk Show: A Comparative Analysis of JTBC 'Nonsummit' and KBS 'Beauties's Chattbox (Misuda)'* (Master's thesis). Sogang University, Seoul, South Korea (2015): 31.
49 Department of Justice, *2016 Annual*.
50 D.J. Kim, *Representation*, 33.
51 In-yung Kim, In-hee Lee, and Kwan-young Park, "Discourse Analysis on Multiculturalism in Korean Television Programs," *Oughtopia* 24 (2009): 69–95.
52 An observational reality show is another type of trendy reality show that has enjoyed significant popularity in the 2017–2018 season: observers, typically talents, watch footage and make comments in the style of a surveillance detail or a psychological experiment, according to Anna McCarthy, *"Stanley Milgram, Allen Funt, and Me": Postwar Social Science and the" First Wave" of Reality TV*, eds. S. Murray and L. Ouellette (New York: New York University Press, 2004).
53 A recent newspaper report indicates that some shows do not pay the travelers they feature; they merely cover travel expenses.
54 Some of them are from the second category shows to make this a good example of the star pool recycled in reality shows (see Curnutt, "Durable Participants") and recycled ones are only from the second category, professionals all the time, but never for the first category, migrants. The others are mostly professionals, fluent in Korean and living in Seoul. It provides another example for the second category, professionals.
55 Beck, "From Industrial".
56 See Thorstein Veblen, *The Theory of the Leisure Class* (New York: Penguin Books, 1994); and Bourdieu, *Distinction*.
57 The difference may also have an industry-related cause. The first show is produced by an educational terrestrial broadcaster and the second is produced by an entertainment-oriented cable network.
58 See: Will Atkinson, "Beck, Individualization and the Death of Class: A Critique," *The British Journal of Sociology* 58, no. 3 (2007): 349–366; and Ulrich Beck and Elisabeth Beck-Gernsheim, *Individualization: Institutionalized Individualism and its Social and Political Consequences* (London: Sage, 2002).

5
PARTICIPATION IN REALITY TELEVISION

Entertainment Mobilization in Dance Talent Shows

Annette Hill and Koko Kondo

Got to Dance is a reality talent format showcasing adult and child dancers. The combination of individual and ensemble dance acts creates physical and emotional performances, judged by a panel of professional dancers, live audiences, and people at home. This chapter draws on qualitative production and audience research from the fifth and final season of *Got to Dance* (Princess, Sky One 2010–2014, UK), with a focus on reality talent show participants and their supporters at auditions and live events (see Figure 5.1). Our case study highlights affective and material practices related to labor and mobility in reality television participation.

Figure 5.1 Backstage at Got to Dance. Image by Tina Askanius.

The analysis is based on two interconnecting arguments about the labor of participants and their supporters, and how this labor connects to mobility within the creative industries. The first part of our argument builds on the performance of selfhood in reality television, not only on an individual level with children and young adults as participants, but also at a collective level with production staff, family and friends, and local communities, providing practical and emotional support front and back stage. The visible performance of participants is a spectacle of labor,[1] one that suggests hidden labor that lies behind the televised dance performance. Thus, there is the visible performance of participants filmed for the show, and there is the invisible labor of family and friends, supporters and followers, who are mobilized to engender this dance performance for a televised reality event.

The second part of our argument is that this spectacle of labor reveals the material infrastructures and symbolic meaning making for what we call entertainment mobilization. This kind of mobilization includes the material conditions of being a reality TV participant, for example transportation for dancers, choreographers, teachers, dance mums and dads, and family supporters to and from venues. There are also the material objects, the props, makeup, hair, costumes, music, food and drink, all necessary to make these performances happen for a televised event. And there is the mobilization of fans and supporters through voting, social media, and as vocal crowds at the live events.

This entertainment mobilization is a key part of the television production of a talent show. Dance performances in this talent show are narrativized as a form of physical and emotional labor that will lead to personal and professional development, and opportunities for stardom. Kaufman[2] uses the term motility to refer to the unequal distribution of skills and resources for mobility, a category that can be expanded to include reality television participants. These participants come from a range of class, ethnicity, gender and regional backgrounds from the UK, and they have different skills and resources for competing in the dance industry, such as variations in dance technique, family help, community support, or financial assistance. The reality talent show is constructed as a resource to overcome obstacles and achieve success in a precarious labor market, to increase motility capital through this televised event. Overall, our research suggests that participation in a reality dance competition involves entertainment mobilization and that there are resources and barriers for mobility and success in the dance and reality TV industry.

Researching Reality Talent Shows

The empirical research of television producers and audiences involves the case study of *Got to Dance*, which was part of a larger project on media experiences, conducted in collaboration with the production company Endemol Shine and funded by the Wallenberg Foundation (2013–2016). This broader project examined how producers create experiences for audiences of drama and reality entertainment, and how audiences actually engage with these experiences.[3] A range of qualitative methods place listening and respect for producer and audience practices at the heart of the research, using cultural sociology to examine how culture is made and remade by producers and audiences.[4]

A pragmatic approach was adopted for the project, including participant-orientated and context dependent methodological routines for the research design and analysis. In particular, the pragmatic sensibilities of looking at cultural practices within situated contexts meant that attention was given to how parts and linkages connect with the whole.[5] Different types of original qualitative research and existing data were used in the fieldwork, including data collected by marketing teams, which are used to consider the performance metrics, alongside interviews with executive producers and creatives working on the series. The pragmatic approach of the fieldwork is connected with the analytic strategy of subtle realism adopted throughout the research;[6] subtle realism enabled the building of reflexive knowledge about how reality television is constructed within certain values and assumptions around reality participants. All interviews were transcribed and analyzed using qualitative data analysis, where descriptive and analytical coding was combined with critical reflection of interviews in the context of fieldnotes and participant observations. This multilayered analysis enabled an interpretation of the data across the sites of production, event, participants and audiences.[7]

For the production research, there were interviews and observations of the auditions, semi-finals and finals for *Got to Dance*, from May to August 2014. A team of four persons, including creative content consultant Julie Donovan, and academic researchers Annette Hill, Tina Askanius, and Koko Kondo conducted the research, sharing the work across the different sites of data collection; 10 production interviews took place with executive and creative producers; 30 interviews were conducted with performers at the auditions, and 10 interviews at the semi-finals and finals, including family and friends at the venues to support dancers. Observations took place front- and backstage for the auditions at The Roundhouse, London, and Earls Court, London during a two-week period, resulting in audio recordings, visual and aural data, and fieldnotes. All of the team took part in participant observations, taking notes, keeping diaries, and taking photographs and short videos as visual aids for the analysis of the data; the team discussed the participant observations at several moments of reflection during and after each production day was over. This continual reflection and analysis of the ongoing fieldwork allowed for flexibility in the data design, as each day the participant observations would be attuned to the production environment and the different kinds of participants at the venues. Such observations supported the theory building and analysis of entertainment mobilization within the production of a live reality event.

For the audience research, 50 individual and group interviews (one to five persons) were conducted with live crowds at the semi-finals and finals, in the queues, coffee shops, and on the street, outside and inside the venue. Each interview lasted between 5–20 minutes. Recruitment was focused on a range of participants and audiences, including professional dancers, individuals and dance troupes, dance teachers, family groups, people at the live show who received tickets as Sky subscribers, and people who were there to experience the filming of a reality talent show. Interviews were conducted individually and in groups in order to ensure both one-to-one and group interactions. The interviews were designed with a topic guide, including social contexts related, to routines surrounding attending the live show, or watching the series at home, and theoretically informed themes such as emotional and critical engagement with the series. Further follow up interviews were conducted with dance schools and at home audience, in order to explore issues raised by the fieldwork in August surrounding the final outcome of the series in the UK. Participant observations of the live shows where the venue was filled with crowds of 4000–6000 each day of filming followed the same pattern of flexible and pragmatic design, with notes, diaries, visual and aural recordings building a nuanced picture of reality television. The interviews and observations served as valuable sources of knowledge construction for reality talent show participants.

To reflect on the research, this is an ethnographic approach to the study of audiences, where agency is given to people and their interpretation and reflection on their experiences.[8] The aim is not to be critical of the people who took part in our study but to ask critical questions of the subject of the research and the context to their experiences. Our research addresses the production context of talent shows as a means to understand participation within the larger framework of socio-cultural values within the dance and television industry, and participants' everyday lives.[9] And our research addresses the reception context as an equally valuable data set to analyze entertainment mobilization and the resources and barriers for mobility and success in the dance and reality TV industry.

Performance in Reality Talent Shows

The notion of performance and the shaping of subjectivity is key for reality talent shows like *Got to Dance*. It has become something of a cliché that performers in talent shows brand themselves; their physical performances in auditions, semi-finals and finals are filmed in bite-sized form for commercial television and social media, including their own production of promotional videos. Producers in reality talent shows call this the 'Susan Boyle effect' (referring to Boyle's audition in *Britain's Got Talent*, ITV, Syco), a trope where a seemingly ordinary person starts a journey of discovery, rising from their local community to stardom through a reality television competition; in this case a participant's audition sparks a strong reaction from the judges and live crowds, ensuring social media attention. It is a 'moment's moment', showing performance and reaction as a highly mediated and sharable commodity.[10] These highly formatted performances signal just how integrated impression management is within the talent show production and participants' performances of selfhood. There are established tropes for the participants' journey through the competition, for example as amateur dancer, as a member of a community dance studio, or as street performer transformed into a semi-professional dancer. And these tropes become part of an emotional manipulation of public voting by talent show producers and participants. Douglas Wood (Head of Audience Research and Insight, Endemol Shine) noted that as talent shows developed during the 2000s, talent show performers "became fame hungry, carbon-copy talent show characters, just brazen about why they were there."[11]

In the case of *Got to Dance*, this talent show used the process of the performance of selfhood to shape a narrative of passion for dance within the series. The executive producer and casting director developed an anti-narrative to the 'fame hungry,' 'carbon-copy' talent show characters that dominated reality television; they wanted to cast young people who were already taking part in countrywide dance competitions, finding talented dancers in regional dance schools and local communities. The casting director explained:

> People who come on our show are used to hard work, training and discipline. They are not a showy type of person. We have to persuade the really talented people who want to be professional dancers and question "is it right that I go on a TV talent show?"

The production company Princess established trust in the dance community by offering flexibility to the winners—no contractual links with the company or the judges, and artistic freedom to participants—free style, free choice of music and costumes, for example. Such absence of contractual ties is rare in the labor conditions for reality participants.

The series established this narrative of passion for dance in its choice of judge, Ashley Banjo. He was the dance director for a street crew called Diversity, which had won *Britain's Got Talent* (the same year as Boyle). Every school child at the event knew the story of Banjo and his street dance crew Diversity. Banjo's story as a street dancer had become a legend for aspiring child dancers. One mum commented: "Diversity are normal people, not stuck up, just normal kids. They have done well for themselves and you don't begrudge them because they are talented young men." Another mum said, "Ashley is all for doing things in the community so he can inspire people to dance." Her focus on normal people, not stuck up, is significant as this is a means for Banjo to invite positive engagement with his personality and celebrity brand by the primarily working class audiences watching this show;[12] they relate to his perceived down to earth values, and the style of street dance he performs, which connects with aspiring child dancers watching the show at home. Thus, we can see how a strong narrative of talent as a resource for social mobility was established in the production by their hiring of Banjo, and this was further co-produced by prospective participants who knew to stage their own performance of selves to mirror the Banjo legend and marketing brand.

For example, in an interview with a dance teacher at the live event, they explained how the performance of selfhood in a talent show is connected to the narrative of self-transformation and social mobility. She noted:

> it's not all about winning ... these kids are based in London, they are street kids, they never go to school because they aren't interested in it, they hate their home, even there's

no family at home, so joining in a dance group and expressing themselves in this way, they can see opportunities. The programme is very good to encourage people to follow their dreams and follow what they believe in so it's good to have competitions like this.

Here, she follows the narrative journey of contestants in a talent show, a journey of self-discovery and social mobility. This personal value is connected to the benefits of making dance visible in the entertainment industry:

In this industry it is very, very hard to be seen. So many thousands of us are so talented and it is hard to get a job nowadays ... I mean Unity that we support tonight, they have had so many rehearsals to just get to the finals. Obviously their training is wicked and shows a certain standard of dancers who are very committed and work hard.

And such visibility has the added benefit of branding for dance schools in local communities. "I mean, tonight probably I'll get messages on Facebook or email from the public who wants to start dancing because they watched the show, so it is good for local businesses."

What we see in action is the performance of selfhood within a mediated space. The classic work by Erving Goffman[13] about how we perform ourselves in multiple ways, living life as part of a social drama, is reframed in relation to media environments. In John Corner's article titled "Performing the Real,"[14] he discusses the term 'selving' as "the central process whereby 'true selves' are seen to emerge (and develop) from underneath and, indeed, through, the 'performed selves' projected for us." This alternation between the true self and performed self invites "thick judgemental and speculative discourse around participants' motives, actions and likely future behaviour."[15] Corner's idea of selving connects with John McGrath's discussion of media space as "selves producing selves" in reality television.[16] In later work on class, the process of selving also includes the mediation of social classifications within reality television.[17]

The selves producing selves that McGrath sees as such a feature of mediated performance signals mixed narrative modes within talent shows. There is the narrative trope of the ordinary participant who has local community roots, uses dance as an expression of selfhood, and embodies dance as social mobility; and there is the narrative trope of the quick route to the promise of fame and wealth that reality television can offer. Both ways of performing selfhood invite thick judgmental description from audiences. The comment that dance is a means to follow your dreams is related to a value judgment regarding how a true self can be constructed through the physical performance of dance. And the awareness that such performances in a reality show offer commercial opportunities for dance highlights a value judgment about the economic incentives to making dance visible in entertainment television.

We saw these mixed narratives interwoven into how young children at the live events for *Got to Dance* articulated why the show mattered to them. In one example, we were on the street outside Earl's Court, waiting by the parking area, before beginning interviews in the queues to the venue. It so happened that a teacher from a London primary school was waiting with two of her pupils for a bus to arrive with the rest of her students. She explained how the school had organized a trip to see the live event because they loved *Got to Dance*: this was a pro social reality talent show, where positive values were embedded in the production. She noted how the positive gold star system and constructive comments by the judges were in sharp contrast to other talent shows. This was something her school had adopted, modelling their own amateur talent competitions on *Got to Dance*. We chatted with her and two young boys, and during the interview one of them spontaneously performed street dance for us. Six years old, he was practicing his break-dancing skills. We watched him perform, and then asked what he liked about the show. "What I like about *Got to Dance* is to tell us what to do, and ... so that we can be famous and make more money." His teacher tried to re-narrativize this, speaking about how dance is an expression of yourself, an authentic performance, whereas he was referring to an overt performance mode of reality television participation as a route to success and fame. These mixed narrative modes in the performance of selves in talent shows signal the tensions between dance as embodied meaning making for identity work and social mobility, and the commercialization of dance in the entertainment industries.

Entertainment Mobilization

This talent show connects the representation of creative performances with all the work of producers, dancers, choreographers, critics and supporters, that is to say the human work associated with the co-production of reality television. Roland Barthes,[18] writing about the performance of singing and dancing in music halls, describes this as a "subtle artifice," where the hard labor of an apprenticeship, long hours of training, and many examples of failure, is recreated in the moment of a stage performance. He describes this creative performance as "the aesthetic form of work"; creative labor is "memorialised and sublimated" in the spectacle of entertainment.[19] Although Barthes is talking about stage performance, there is a subtle artifice in the performance of affective labor and practical skills in television talent shows. People's hard work, dedication to their craft, and desire to improve is presented as a virtue; this is why audiences use phrases such as "dance takes dedication and hard work," or participants "follow their dreams" to signify the pro social values of the labor within a talent show such as this.

Alongside the work that is made visible in the televised performances, there is also an invisible labor. For every live performance, there was a support network of mums and aunts and best friends who sewed the sparkles on costumes, prepared hair, took a day off work, all to hold the hands and hold up the energy of those practicing for their big moment. This invisible workforce got up early and hired the bus to make sure the dance troupe arrived on time for rehearsals. The production company made sure to invite large groups of friends and family to auditions and the live shows, giving away free tickets, understanding that the support network for dancers is significant to the level of practice and training it takes to pull off a live dance performance.

We apply the idea of mobilization to this type of physical and affective labor. Mobilization means making something, or someone, mobile, or capable of mobility. It is a term usually associated with political mobilization, for example the mobilization of civic organizations to encourage participation in a social issue, or to vote in an election. There is a large body of work on the role of traditional and social media in enhancing political mobilization, including the use of internal networking via social media in grassroots movements, or video activism for particular critical events and social movements that aim to mobilize citizens into action regarding the environment, for example, or human and animal rights.[20] This kind of research examines the connections between participation and the media, with a focus on the mobilization of individuals and collective groups for participating in civic cultures, in the form of political dialogue, engagement, and active participation in online and street protests and elections. This meaning of political and social mobilization shifts when we consider an entertainment context. More relevant to this study is the mobilization of individuals and collective groups for sports participation and fandom, where the support of family and local communities, and the active engagement of fans, is part of understanding sport and its cultural significance. For example, football involves the mobilization of different people, from players, coaches, trainers, to supporters of the team in transportation and training, and the mobilization of fans to attend live matches, share comments via social media, and engage with sports media.[21]

Maren Hartmann[22] has recently explored what she calls banal mobilization within social and political contexts; for example, in her research on the homeless in Berlin she has looked at the practical and mundane ways mobile media are integrated into the everyday (im)mobility of homeless people. It is the practical side of mobilization that is of interest to our case study; the physical movements of participants and their supporters in their training, preparation, and live performance, for a reality talent show. To describe this mobilization as banal does not quite do justice to the degree of passionate physical and emotional labor of participants in a dance competition; this is a labor of love, and the passion work of participants is a resource for ensuring they are capable of competing and winning. But there is a more mundane side of the mobilization of participants which relates to the everyday routines necessary for training and performance, such as transportation, washing and ironing dance outfits, or the organization of food and drink during training and travelling to competitions. Certainly, this is an invisible labor that helps reality participants to mobilize for the live performance in the show. This is why we apply the idea of mobilization to entertainment because this invisible labor force enables the movement of dancers to participate in television entertainment.

The labor and the movements of participants intersects with another kind of mobilization, that of audiences and fans who through television and social media interact and vote for participants. The reality talent show integrates fan mobilization into their format, through the use of Facebook messages, and Facebook live spin-off digital shows, Twitter feeds screened live at the event, paratexts related to YouTube videos by past and present participants and fans, and the all-important online voting at the semi-finals and live finale. An experienced reality participant will know how to mobilize their fans to vote in order to keep them in the competition. This is where dancers who have appeared in other reality talent shows can carry over their knowledge from these past experiences to the ways they produce their performances, inviting fans to mobilize viewing parties and strategic voting. This kind of entertainment mobilization for fandom is a regular feature of reality talent shows. In such a way, we start to see the connection between the performance of selfhood for this dance talent show discussed earlier in the chapter with entertainment mobilization. The invisible labor of family and supporters helps to shape the creative labor of participants, and this in turn is "memorialized and sublimated" in the spectacle of entertainment in the live event.[23]

In one interview with a family (teenage sister, mother and father, August 27, 2014), they explained their support for one of the participants in Unity Academy. Unity is a dance school run by two former reality participants in *Got to Dance*. There were over 100 supporters for Unity at the semi-finals, wearing specially made T-shirts. "We are here to make a lot of noise." Their daughter started dancing at the age of four and, after she saw Unity perform in the series, she joined their academy. She regularly travelled three hours each way for training. The family were there to help with travel, competitions, training and live performances. Not only were they part of the 100 or so supporters, shouting, sharing on social media and voting, but at least 20 members of their extended family and friends were squeezed into their living room to watch it live on subscription channel Sky One and vote for Unity to win. There was recognition that to get this far in a dance competition was tough; her sister said "you have to really want it" to succeed as a dancer. Her parents added

> you have to have your parents behind you, for the travel and training. She has been down here every day, hours and hours and hours of training. You can forget your social life, there is no social life. It's all about dance.

There are several points of analysis in this example. We can see how performing in a reality talent show can act as branding for professional dancers and dance schools looking to reach out to a younger audience who might be inspired by the series to want to dance. There is a cyclical process to the selves producing selves, audiences transforming into reality talent show participants, and reality participants becomes actors in commercial culture.[24] This is a co-production of selving, both by audiences, participants and producers. The dancers in Unity understood the particular kind of performance of selfhood that this talent show produced as part of its brand. What we also see is the mobilization of family and supporters for reality talent performers. They traveled to the auditions, training studios, and live venue; they organized into groups of supporters at the live event, wearing branded T-shirts, providing vocal support to the performers on stage, back stage support in the form of hair and makeup, transportation to and from the venue and so forth. They mobilized people at home, coordinating live viewing and voting in a strategic move to combine access to this subscription channel and votes from the public. This form of entertainment mobilization highlights the considerable resources of family, time, money and personal sacrifice that come with being a participant in a talent show.

Kaufman[25] describes motility as the conditions under which mobility can take place. In an article on motility for qualitative research, Flamm and Kaufman explain "Motility can be defined as how an individual or group takes possession of the realm of possibilities for mobility and builds on it to develop personal projects."[26] They argue that motility involves access, skills and comprehension, and representation regarding mobility. If mobility is related to the freedom to move, then in this case there are the possibilities for mobility in the expression of dance as bodily movement, and the possibility of social mobility. The motility of participants in a dance talent show relate to access to the resources necessary to be a dancer, skills and training, and the representation of dance in the entertainment industries. For *Got to Dance* we see how individuals and groups work together in the co-production of the labor necessary to perform in a talent show. The personal passion project of a young dancer is made possible because of considerable resources mobilized to make this happen. In this example, the family have the economic ability, the time, access to transportation, and the emotional labor necessary to support this teenager in their dance career; and the reality talent show offers narrative modes and representations of dance as social mobility, an opportunity for creative and personal success, and fame within the entertainment industry.

Two examples of different participants in the show highlight the entanglement of performance of selfhood and entertainment mobilization. One dancer was a young freestyle performer from London, who made it through to the semi-finals. She was not sure how her style of dance would be interpreted by the judges or audiences: "I just lay myself out there and do my thing." Freestyle does not lend itself to the kind of commercial dance that talent shows tend to cast. When one of the judges in the auditions asked her why she came on this talent show, she explained: "why not, I am 19, my whole life would be nah, not yet not yet, I just thought why not?" Her performance of selfhood as an ordinary person hoping for their chance to shine was re-enforced by the judge Ashley Banjo who noted "you are really humble and sweet but you have real passion when you dance. I just absolutely loved what you did." Her narrative journey in the competition was represented through a video that highlighted her background as a street dancer in London, training hard in a local studio, and her 'humble and sweet' personality. On the day of her semi-final, she reflected in an interview on being in a talent show:

> Last night I was so nervous because I watched the TV episode and they showed the names, that was really surreal for me. I tried to have an early night but haven't slept much because I was just picturing things. It was ridiculous. Then when I woke up in the morning I felt OK, had breakfast and I felt calm and then just before rehearsals, I don't know why, I felt nerves were rushing in … literally I was in tears, even talking about it now upsets me. I can't watch myself on TV, I think my audition was rubbish.

We spoke with audiences who emotionally engaged with her performance: "She really, really moves me. You can tell that she has a backstory, that she was very, very nervous. You can tell from her performance. A lot of pain comes out in her performance" (20 to 30 year-old female viewer). Her performance was perceived as authentic to herself, her backstory, and her nerves were a sign of how genuine she appeared to live audiences.

Another act to make it to the semi-finals were a duo of an adult and child dancer. These participants had appeared in other talent shows and had performed as professional dancers. Duplic8 had a bone-breaking dance style, creating a spectacle of labor on stage, and memorable "did you see that moments" for social media. Their narrative journey through the competition was represented in a video that highlighted their collaboration, training and the physical style of dance. These participants mobilized online voting, carrying over fans from previous performances, gathering new fans, and ensuring vocal crowds at the live event. For the finale at Earls Court, crowds were cheering "Duplic8, Duplic8!" and stamping their feet. When one of the judges did not award a gold star for their performance, the crowd shouted back. They went on to win the series, mobilizing their fans at home to vote using a new online voting system just introduced by the production team for the first time. The social media performance metrics signal a successful strategy of entertainment mobilization: the top Facebook post (1300 posts, 7000 likes), top Snapchat post (2200 likes), and top post for Twitter (130,000 followers) were all congratulations to Duplic8. This act was not necessarily the best or most original dancers, but they were certainly the most aware of the strategic use of mediated performance, fans and online voting.

After the show was over, one producer muttered under their breath that Duplic8 were are more like winners of *Got Talent* than *Got to Dance*. This negative comment was echoed by other viewers interviewed at a dance school:

> Other acts were amazing, complex choreography ... I have to watch many, many, many times and that excites me, from a dancer's point of view ... and you can learn from them as opposed to be entertained by them ... Duplic8 had entertainment value, calling attention from everyone. The votes obviously took them in the position of winning.

For *Got to Dance*, the internal processes that led to the winners for Series 5 signified a wider problem that the series had lost touch with its core audience, the kind who positively engaged with dancers who performed what they perceived as an authentic self, rather than a more cynical talent show performer. The series was axed after its fifth season due to poor ratings. According to the BARB (Broadcaster Audience Research Board) figures, viewers disengaged with the series, dropping from 646,000 at the start of the auditions to 486,000 for the live finale, losing a percentage point in the share of audiences watching television at that time (from 3.4 to 2.2).[27]

If we return to the performance of selfhood with this talent show, then the comment by a six-year-old fan outside the venue encapsulates the creative and economic tensions within the series. His words, "What I like about *Got to Dance* is to tell us what to do, and ... so that we can be famous and make more money" signal the mixed narrative modes of passion for dance, social mobility and stardom in the entertainment industries. Duplic8 signified this mixed message, participants with talent, resources, and knowledge about how to perform and mobilize fans and win a reality show. Such success is also a mixed blessing: the winner of this final series went on to become a barber, "as seen" on *Got to Dance*, highlighting the precariousness of labor conditions in the entertainment industries.

Reflections on Participation in Reality Television

Through analyzing the intersections between production studies and participants and supporters for this reality talent show, we argue against research on reality television participants and amateur labor which sees this as exploitation and a form of enslaved labor relations. It is worth reflecting on this area of study in more detail before highlighting the significance of our findings on entertainment mobilization.

Within the area of reality television studies, the issue of participant labor and contracted work has been criticized, both in relation to the immaterial labor of participants,[28] the production labor of workers in a reality programme,[29] and the representation of class and labor in series.[30] Deery notes that "investigations are just beginning into the labour status of RTV participants and the extent to which they might be subject to same legal rights, protections, and compensation as other workers."[31] She refers to Hearn's[32] work on immaterial labor in an American reality series as one example of the exploitation of participants who "must obey explicit and tacit conventions," and who are expected to commodify their personal life experience for the benefit of entertainment.[33] Similarly, Andrew Ross[34] discusses the political economy of amateurs in reality talent shows, arguing that experts in the industry seek particular contestants at the final rounds who will be suitable for celebrity brands. Certainly, research suggests that talent show participants can find themselves locked into contracts in the production of the live event and in the period post transmission where further product placements, advertising deals, and live performances can bolster revenues for the production company. Although some manage their labor and contracts with television, entertainment and PR agencies to their advantage, others find themselves locked into a certain kind of career route, and without strong union representation, they have few opportunities to complain.

In her research on the legal ramifications of contestants and labor conditions in reality formats, Bowry[35] criticizes the "commercial dynamics" of *Australian MasterChef*, where the "authenticity of the human drama" activates "commodity relations," supporting corporate control over the "extended narrative of the enterprise" across the series, its paratexts, live events and social media. She argues that contestants provide access to not only texts and images but their whole person, seeing participants as "forced" into overtly competitive social relations, effectively locked into a "contract of servitude or voluntary enslavement."[36] This critical legal position sees contestants caught in the "logic of the reality TV game format" and that these conditions of confinement contribute to "feeding participant delusion about the nature and extent of the post-game opportunity on offer."[37] Bowry perceives not only this format but much reality television as supporting the production of global capitalism and consumption, and the commodification of affective labor.

The empirical research in this chapter on production, participant and audience practices for *Got to Dance* offers an alternative perspective to these criticisms of the labor of participants for talent shows. *Got to Dance* represents a local variation of the format with its own particular production and reception contexts. It is also a rather distinctive form of a talent show, with a history in talent competitions in British light entertainment for public service and commercial channels going back to the post-war period, a history that signals how young performers across dance, music, comedy and other entertainment areas use the route of television and radio talent competitions to further their careers in these industries. What is significant to this talent show is the focus on the practical skills of dance for individuals and regional dance communities which are not only about consumption and global corporations but also about pro social values associated with the meaning of dance as an expressive art form and an opportunity for cultural participation. What we find in interviews and observations of producers, participants and audiences for this series is more of an entrepreneurial labor relation for participants in the local production who understand the opportunities and barriers within a reality talent show. The dancers as participants, and their family and friends, are all too aware of the trade-off between their labor and the opportunity to be visible in a reality talent show. The participants in this show were also aware of the short-lived fame that arises from a reality talent competition, weighing up the value of visibility in a television event with the negative values associated with the commercialization of dance for an entertainment spectacle.

This suggests that a critical appraisal of talent shows can be challenged by an empirically led approach that recognizes the situated context to participation in talent shows.[38] By looking at the affective and material dimensions of reality television participation, we find alternative arguments for the agency of participants in the shaping of this reality talent show. The research suggests a form of entertainment mobilization. Participants who reach the semi-finals and finals are those with affective and material resources: they have familial, temporal, mobility and economic infrastructure and resources that enable them to be competitive in the dance industry. In addition, we find those participants with genre knowledge of talent shows, such as how to heighten their mediated performances, how to mobilize fans and users to vote and share social media, have the media resources to be competitive in the reality television industry.

Conclusion

The intersections of production and audience research for reality television highlight how the visible performance of participants in a talent show is only part of the story of the labor of producing these performances. In the production of a talent show such as *Got to Dance*, participants shape their performance of selfhood to highlight a narrative mode of down-to-earth values, hard work and dedication, and the possibility through dance to social mobility, performances that are enacted in videos, social media and within the live television event. We find a "spectacle of labour"[39] in talent show performances, indicating the physical and emotional labor of training that lies behind a screen performance. In addition, we also see the invisible labor of family and friends, and local communities, who are mobilized to support participants in the auditions process and live event; and the mobilization of fans through interactive voting, social media and vocal presence at live events. This is a form of entertainment mobilization, combining the movement of participants and their supporters in the realization of a passion project of dance and reality television. Thus, a spectacle of labor, which we see in the performances of participants on television, is contingent on the entertainment mobilization of participants and their supporters, fans and audiences.

There are uneven resources for participants, for example their access to dance schools and auditions, their dance skills and understanding of a reality talent show, and the representation of dance and their performance of selfhood in a talent show. Here, then, we see the opportunities and barriers regarding the material infrastructures to reality television participation, including transportation, time, finance, access to training studios and so forth, and the symbolic elements in the form of representation and artistic expression, the embodied meaning making of performance. The reality talent show offers itself as a resource for mobility, a space within which children and young adults from diverse backgrounds can realize their dream of being a professional dancer, and become a star, gaining recognition in the entertainment industries. In order to achieve such a dream, participants need considerable resources (time, money, skills, knowledge, and self-belief), the support network of their family and friends, and dance schools and local communities, and the knowledge and experience of how to perform in a talent show. Overall, the research highlights the visible and invisible labor of participation in a talent show, and the ways this spectacle of labor is both mobilized by television producers, and in turn mobilized by participants looking for recognition in the entertainment industries.

Notes

1. Roland Barthes, *The Eiffel Tower and Other Mythologies*, translated by Richard Howard (New York: Hill and Wang, 1979).
2. Vincent Kaufmann, *Re-thinking Mobility* (London: Ashgate, 2002).
3. Annette Hill, *Media Experiences: Engaging with Drama and Reality Entertainment* (London: Routledge, 2018).
4. See: Richard Sennett, *Respect* (London: Penguin, 2002); and Craig Calhoun and Richard Sennett, eds. *Practising Culture* (London: Routledge, 2007).
5. Clive Seale, Giampietro Gobo, Jaber F. Gubrium, and David Silverman, eds., *Qualitative Research Practice* (London: Sage, 2007), 6.
6. Martin Hammersley, *What's Wrong with Ethnography: Methodological Explorations* (London: Routledge, 1992).
7. See: Gillian Rose, *Visual Methodologies*, 4th edn (London: Sage, 2016).
8. Hammersley, *What's Wrong*.
9. John Corner and Jane Roscoe, "Outside and Inside Television: A Dialogue on 'Value'," *Journal of Media Practice* 17, nos 2–3 (2016): 162.
10. Annette Hill, *Reality TV: Key Ideas* (London: Routledge, 2015).
11. Ibid., 55.
12. See: Annette Hill, "Reality TV Engagement: Reality TV Producers and Audiences for Talent Format Got to Dance," *Media Industries* 4, no. 1 (May 2017): 1–17.
13. Erving Goffman, *The Presentation of Self in Everyday Life* (Harmondsworth: Penguin Books, 1959).

14 John Corner, "Documentary Values," in *Realism and 'Reality' in Film and Media*, ed. Anne Jerslev (Copenhagen: Museum Tusculanum Press, 2002), 263–264.
15 Ibid., 264.
16 John E. McGrath, *Loving Big Brother: Performance, Privacy and Surveillance Space* (London: Routledge, 2004), 17.
17 See: Beverly Skeggs and Helen Wood, *Reacting to Reality Television: Performance, Audience and Value* (London: Routledge, 2012).
18 Barthes, *The Eiffel*, 124.
19 Ibid., 124–25.
20 See: Peter Dahlgren, *Media and the Political Web* (Cambridge: Polity, 2013); W. Lance Bennett and Alexandra Segerberg, *The Logic of Connective Action: Digital Media and the Personalization of Contentious Politics* (New York: Cambridge University Press, 2013).
21 See: Ellis Cashmore and Kevin Dixon, eds., *Studying Football* (London: Routledge, 2016).
22 Maren Hartmann, "Banal Mobilisation," forthcoming journal article, 2019.
23 Barthes, *The Eiffel*, 124–125.
24 See: June Deery, *Reality TV* (Cambridge: Polity, 2015).
25 Kaufman, *Re-thinking Mobility*.
26 Michael Flamm and Vincent Kaufmann, "Operationalising the Concept of Motility: A Qualitative Study," *Mobilities* 1, no. 2 (2006): 167.
27 See Hill, "Reality TV."
28 Laura Grindstaff, "DI(t)Y, Reality-Style: The Cultural Work of Ordinary Celebrity," in *A Companion to Reality Television*, ed. Laurie Ouellette (London: Wiley Blackwell, 2014), 30–42.
29 Vicki Mayer, *Below the Line: Producers and Production Studies in the New Television Economy* (Durham, North Carolina: Duke University Press, 2011).
30 See: Anita Biressi and Heather Nunn, *Class and Contemporary British Culture* (Basingstoke, Hampshire: Palgrave Macmillan, 2016).
31 Deery, *Reality TV*, 78.
32 Alison Hearn, "Reality Television, *The Hills*, and the Limits of the Immaterial Labour Thesis," *tripleC* 8, no. 1 (2010): 60–76.
33 Deery, *Reality TV*, 79.
34 Andrew Ross, "Reality TV and the Political Economy of Amateurism," in *A Companion to Reality Television*, ed. Laurie Ouellette (London: Wiley Blackwell, 2014), 324–344.
35 Katherine Bowrey, "The Manufacture of 'Authentic' Buzz and the Legal Relations of *MasterChef*," in *Amateur Media: Social, Cultural and Legal Perspectives*, eds. Dan Hunter, Ramon Lobato, Megan Richardson and Julian Thomas (London: Routledge, 2012), 74.
36 Ibid., 81.
37 Ibid.
38 Helen Wood, Jilly Boyce Kay, and Mark Banks, "The Working Class, Ordinary Celebrity and Illegitimate Cultural Work," in *Media and Class: TV, Film, and Digital Culture*, eds. June Deery and Andrea Press (New York: Routledge, 2017).
39 Barthes, *The Eiffel*.

6

LOVE, SEX, MONEY

Gender and Economic Inequality in HIV Edutainment Programming in Kenya

Renée A. Botta

One of the mainstays for health intervention in the Global South has been entertainment education (edutainment) media programming designed to change attitudes about illness diagnosis, prevention and treatment, and to prompt healthy behaviors. In November 2009, MTV's Base channel launched *Shuga*—a sophisticated edutainment program filmed on the campus of an elite private university in Kenya, and designed to spread a message to young people about responsible sexual behavior and tolerance of those living with HIV. The intervention was co-sponsored by the MTV Staying Alive Foundation, the (US) President's Plan for AIDS Relief, Partnership for an HIV-Free Generation, and the government of Kenya; in the second season, some episodes were directed by Kenya's global superstar, Lupita Nyong'o. By industry standards, *Shuga* was a success: it won a Gold award at the 2010 World Media Festival in the Public Relations Health category, and it was so popular in its original two seasons in Kenya that the production and storyline then moved to Nigeria, where several more seasons have been produced. New spinoffs in South Africa, India and Côte d'Ivoire will begin soon.

Youth, who are most at risk of HIV/AIDS in Kenya, were the target audience for both Kenyan seasons, which were designed to promote single as opposed to multiple sex partners, condom use, and acceptance for people living with HIV.[1] Characters grapple with HIV stigma, poverty, multiple sexual partnerships, sugar daddies, and sexual assault. The program was extremely popular with youth: 60 percent of Kenyan 15–24 year-olds reported seeing and remembered the show,[2] and 52 percent of those who saw the show said they talked with a close friend about the characters or messages. Although fewer said they talked with romantic partners, the average intention to take an HIV test improved from 6.5 to 7.3 out of 10 after watching *Shuga*, and the intention to be friends with someone who was HIV-positive improved from 6.2 to 7.7 out of 10.[3]

HIV-prevention efforts targeting Kenyan youth and young adults frequently use media, including edutainment programming,[4] which involves "pro-social messages that are embedded into popular entertainment content."[5] Such programs often use aspirational characters and lifestyles, and yet because of this the dominant class's experience of HIV tends to be privileged while the lived experience for most Kenyans who are HIV positive is ignored. Indeed, according to Khalid and Ahmed, edutainment programs "are designed to promote and reinforce particular pro-social beliefs and values,"[6] with storylines written around "good" characters who are rewarded and "bad" characters who are punished as a way of encouraging viewers to imitate positive role models.

In this chapter, I will consider how class and inequality are treated in relation to HIV and AIDS in Kenya, focusing in particular on the ideologies used to socially construct HIV/AIDS in the popular edutainment program, *Shuga*. By interrogating the program's representation of the intersection of class and economic inequality with gender in portraying HIV and AIDS among youth in Kenya, this chapter demonstrates how critical media studies can contribute to the wider discussion of economic inequality in health.[7] Although there is much to commend in the *Shuga* program, this chapter will argue that a more diverse and participatory approach to character and storyline development would lead to more nuanced and effective use of this form of storytelling to address real life health concerns.

HIV/AIDS in Kenyan Socioeconomic Context

Inequality in Kenya is extreme, and, although the severity of poverty is greatest in rural areas, income inequality is more pronounced in urban centers. (Indeed, the poorest county is also the most economically equal county in Kenya.[8]) Although approximately 45 percent of people live below the poverty line, "the number of super-rich in Kenya is one of the fastest growing in the world … The rich are capturing the lion's share of the benefits, while millions of people at the bottom are being left behind."[9] Moreover, although Nairobi's Human Development Index (HDI)—a measure combining life expectancy, education, and standard of living—is comparable to higher HDI countries such as Seychelles and Mexico, parts of Kenya's Northern region compare to low HDI countries like Malawi and Afghanistan.

According to the World Health Organization (WHO), the lower an individual's socioeconomic position, the worse their health, and social rank is the strongest single predictor of health and well-being. As a health communication scholar, I draw from the Centers for Disease Control and Prevention's (CDC's) understanding that 'socioeconomic position' combines resource-based measures (income, wealth, education) with prestige-based measures (access to and consumption of goods, services, and knowledge, that are linked to their occupational prestige, income, and education level). In this measure, those on the lower end of the scale suffer the harshest consequences both physically in terms of their health status and psychologically in terms of the stigma attached to an illness.

In sub-Saharan Africa, HIV/AIDS tends to be higher for those with higher socioeconomic position, which is, in part, due to men with increased disposable income visiting prostitutes or entering into polygamous relationships without using condoms. However, emerging data suggest that this counterintuitive association with power and wealth is changing over time. Hargreaves, Davie and White theorized that current trends in new HIV infections may be following Julian Tudor-Hart's "inverse care law," which suggests that large-scale HIV prevention programs could paradoxically reinforce social inequalities in HIV infection through selective advantage to persons who are most able to respond to them—namely, the wealthier and more educated.[10] Indeed, as Tsai has argued, "the adverse health and psychosocial impacts of HIV stigma are likely concentrated among those with the fewest socioeconomic resources for managing and resisting it."[11]

In Kenya in 2017, 1.5 million people were living with HIV.[12] It is concentrated among the poor in urban areas but among wealthier adults in rural areas[13] and lower among higher educated women.[14] Disease progression is worse for those more entrenched in poverty in Kenya, with advancement "five times more likely to occur in study subjects with daily income available for expenditure of less than US$1 compared to those with more than US$5 available for daily expenditure."[15] Gender and age are also key factors: the epidemic exerts a disproportionate effect on young people under 24 and adolescent girls and young women aged 15–24 years have up to eight times the rates of HIV infection compared with their male peers.[16] Contrary to stereotypes, the main mode of transmission is through heterosexual sex, and university campuses as environments especially conducive to HIV transmission, because they bring young adults in their peak years of sexual activity into close physical proximity without any systematic supervision.[17] In response, the Kenyan government has recommended consistent safer-sex behavior, single sexual partnerships, and delayed sexual debut as messages to be promoted to Kenyan youth.

Shuga: A Kenyan Case Study

Shuga was filmed at US International University (USIU), an elite private university in Nairobi, and two of the first season's main characters, played by actors, were also students at USIU during filming,[18] yet the program has the look of an international program, including the glamour, expensive cars, fancy clothes and MTV video style that is recognizable among viewers and coded as "aspirational."[19] Thus, from its outset, the production of *Shuga* separated its story from the lived experience of the youth it was supposed to be targeting. Nairobi youth live vastly different lives based on their social and cultural backgrounds, economic means, and access to media and education. As Overbergh pointed out about the diversity of Kenyan society, it would be a mistake to "refer to 'the' Urbanites as belonging to 'one' homogenous group. They are a widely diverse pool of young people."[20] The reality of life for Kenyan youth is inextricably tied to socioeconomic position, including access to quality care for HIV prevention and treatment. Therefore, the ways in which an edutainment program such as *Shuga* depicts these youths becomes part of the identity of HIV and whether it speaks to them in ways that resonate with their experiences.

In Nairobi, those from a higher socioeconomic position are 50 percent more likely to have secondary education or higher than those from a lower socioeconomic position. And yet people in Nairobi also have 2.2 times more access to secondary education than an average Kenyan.[21] Thus, even putting characters in a university setting is a signifier of an elite social position. This constricted fantasy of class is connoted by expensive cars, elegant clothes, exclusive clubs, extravagant shopping, lavish homes, upscale places of employment, and their elite school. For the second season, many of the same things are shown but signifiers for the lower class are also introduced, including manual and daily labor, crowded living spaces, worn clothing, threat of violence, deference to the elites, and sporadic electricity.

As Menon argued, the production of such imaginary worlds risks glamorizing "the dull reality of sexual sickness" and viewers "may have been seduced not into visiting an HIV test center, but into trying to enter the framework imagined world of glamour depicted and endorsed by the show."[22] Viewers are meant to be entertained by the privileged lifestyles shown in media, yet they are also educated on how to mimic them,[23] which can also mean mimicking a careless lifestyle.

The Social Construction and Representation of HIV/AIDS in Shuga

The series opens in the first season with the message that gluttonous living filled with excessive sex, drinking, money, and partners is punished with the threat of HIV transmission. HIV is presented as a virus that is spread through heterosexual sex and on to innocent children by their HIV positive mothers. The virus seems to be inevitable due to the allure of a glamorous and exciting lifestyle, which is full of problematic temptation. For instance, a main character wakes up alone in a young woman's apartment hazy from a night of drunken partying and sex. His voiceover says, "It's the morning after the night before. You fight to get those eyes open…. Then the pieces keep coming back, slowly, slowly, like shards of glass. Then you're like, damn," he says as he sees an HIV/AIDS pamphlet taped to the bathroom mirror. The message is that those who are sexually promiscuous spread HIV.

Typical of edutainment programming, *Shuga* uses characters to model good and bad behavior to illustrate the conversation between what Kenyan youth might be doing versus what program producers want them to be doing. For example, a main character, Skola, banters about HIV with a famous Kenyan rapper, Madtraxx, on Skola's university radio show; they voice the reasons why Kenyans should but often do not engage in HIV prevention. Having a famous, local rapper unapologetically assert positive HIV prevention and testing messages establishes the idea that wearing a condom every time and knowing your status is aspirational; and, while knowing your status and getting tested remains a consistent message throughout both seasons, wearing a condom every time is more often spoken about than acted upon.

Another strong message in *Shuga* is that HIV is secret and stigmatized, even though it is treatable. For example, three young men discuss their HIV risk and decide together to get tested. However, when one's results are not good, he pretends all is well, and although this may be a more realistic reaction for Kenyan youth, it seems to suggest that your friends will support you to get tested but they might not support you if you are HIV positive. Another storyline from the first season reiterates this message when an HIV positive woman who is also a student at the university is portrayed as feeling separate, lonely and sad. She desperately wants love but avoids the chance because she fears she will be rejected if the young man she likes finds out she is HIV positive. Her father reinforces the silence of HIV when he tells her: "Virginia, you can live a normal healthy life as long as you continue to take your meds." But, he adds, no one is allowed to know. "I just don't want to hear gossip about the family," he says, buying her silence with a credit card to go shopping.

Another theme in *Shuga* suggests being unfaithful and having multiple sex partners is the cause of HIV. Although never directly stated, the head of an advertising agency seems to be HIV+ (his daughter is HIV+ and his wife died from AIDS). He pressures a much younger woman to not use a condom, who then doesn't use a condom with her boyfriend, implying that she might contract HIV and spread the illness to her boyfriend.

In some ways, the portrayal of HIV in season two is similar to the first season. Even the title "Love, sex and money" suggests how intertwined HIV is with lifestyle. Risky sexual behavior remains a temptation that leads to HIV. Moreover, questions of love and lust are bound up in loyalty and pressure to not use condoms, which increases the risk of spreading HIV. Condoms are mentioned frequently, mostly as something that is negotiable; some of the pressure is about power and gender, for example when an ad executive coerces his intern to go along with him not wearing one. Other examples are based on relational pressure coming from women who want their partners to prove they are faithful. Thus, condoms are not used every time, although this was preached by the Kenyan rapper. Indeed, men and women assert power in a relationship by pressuring their partners to not use a condom, and protected sex is shown to be a sign of infidelity.

Although the world of HIV remains tempting, glamorous, sexy, fun, wicked and heterosexual in the second season, the secretive and stigmatized nature of HIV is challenged. Pushing those boundaries is shown as going against cultural norms and against expectations. One character illustrates this need to fight norms when she writes an article revealing she is HIV positive. Her father is angry and pressures her to keep her status secret (the article has not yet been published). "Look, I'm a teacher. How do you expect parents to trust me with their children if they find out my own daughter behaves no better than a Kunanda Street prostitute?" When she decides to reveal her status after discussing it with a friend, her father demonstrates the way HIV is stigmatized in Kenya, asserting "get out. This family is not going to carry her shame."

Although more characters are openly HIV positive in the second season, HIV is also less inevitable. For example, HIV+ characters try to educate others about why they contracted HIV and to avoid the same mistakes. In the first season, the message seems to be "get tested because your behaviors are putting you at risk," whereas the second season seems to focus more on why they are engaging in risky behaviors, which I will discuss later.

An example of HIV being less inevitable is when after a main character gets drunk and has sex with a man without telling him she is HIV positive, a friend convinces her to tell him because he can take a post-exposure prophylaxis to help prevent him contracting the virus. HIV's preventability is tied to increased agency, but at the added expense of personal responsibility without recognizing structural barriers to the autonomy. With an exclamation point on self-efficacy, the second season ends with images of good and bad decisions from the season while a character says: "We have the power to make our own heaven. And, we have the power to make our own hell. The choice is yours." Although there is no mention of HIV in this message, those who have watched the program recognize the implied intent. Indeed, HIV is never explicitly mentioned in either of the last two episodes, which represents a preferred communication style for many Kenyans, particularly those from rural areas.[24]

Overall, the social construction of HIV and AIDS, in *Shuga*, is contradictory: the illness is constructed as both preventable and inevitable, threatening and treatable, worthy of conversation and a secret. Moreover, *Shuga* neglects to: (1) recognize men who have sex with men; (2) counter the notion that protected sex signals infidelity; (3) show a wider range of experiences relevant to Kenyan youth; and (4) discuss disparities in access to healthcare or access to quality healthcare.

Class and Economic Inequality in Shuga

Shuga attaches being rich and young to the identity of HIV/AIDS and privileges the dominant class experience of HIV and AIDS. Of course, upper class audiences and interests are more appealing to the networks who give airtime to edutainment programming, which then results in supporting the dominant class rather than educating marginalized communities. It is thus helpful to consider how these competing interests impact content.

In the first season, one of the main characters performs an upper-class lifestyle with the help of her "sugar daddy" (a much older man with whom she has sex in exchange for paying some of her bills and buying her nice clothes). Her roommate revels in drinking, dancing, and sex, and when questioned about the dangers of having unprotected sex, responds: "he is funny, he is smart, he comes from a good family." Another friend then says "money is not a condom, it won't save you from this disease." Thus, HIV does seem to be wrapped up in excess without protection from privilege.

Jaworski and Thurlow suggest that viewers rely on media stories "to inform and construct their identities, which has a profound effect on social relations."[25] Moreover, Hjarvard argues that media construct lifestyles that are offered up as "guidance for modern life."[26] The advice of *Shuga*, particularly in its first season, seems to say: look at this fun, glamorous, risky life, doesn't it look amazing? When Menon interviewed the executive producer of the first season of *Shuga*, Cathy Phiri, to ask about the disparity between the depiction of HIV among upper class elite youth in the first season and the reality for those most affected, she responded,

> We didn't necessarily consider the socio-economic as a key thing, we were intending the audience to be aspirational, and also to counter this belief that HIV/AIDS is only prevalent among those of lower socio-economic classes. On the visually creative side, it was also important for us to be able to reflect a different side of Africa than one which is normally seen.[27]

This response is important because she acknowledges the aspirational intent of the depiction of class. The notion of countering the belief that HIV/AIDS is only prevalent among those of lower socioeconomic class is important but invites the question of whether it was necessary to exclude all lower-class depictions in order to counter the misperception.

Class indeed functions aspirationally in the series, as female characters perform a class to which they do not really belong and use sex in an attempt to join the upper class, projecting symbolic capital. This is likely not the type of aspiration Phiri hoped to project, and research indicates that aspirational messages draw attention to the inequity. Kraus, Park, and Tan suggest we think of economic inequality as "the daily process of comparing one's own socioeconomic standing to that of others based on the dynamic observation of observable behaviors that signal social class."[28] This signaling reminds viewers of their own social standing and reinforces boundaries, while at the same time modelling behaviors that can be reproduced.

In surveys and interviews with Kenyan youth who fit *Shuga's* intended target audience,[29] Menon found more who recalled seeing the program were from the university where it was filmed than from a public, and more economically diverse, university, which makes sense given the relevance of the character's experiences to their lives and the fact that it was screened there twice. More important than who recalled seeing the first season of *Shuga*, though, were their reflections: "There was a general feeling that *Shuga* reflected the lifestyles of a certain socioeconomic demographic and excluded the realities of the majority of Kenyan youth, who live out of big cities and are usually from lower income brackets."[30] Many raised how unrealistic *Shuga* was given the rampant alcoholism and careless behavior. This reading is oppositional to the dominant (aspirational) reading Phiri suggests the producers were hoping Kenyan youth would take, suggesting the need for a more thorough reception analysis to understand the extent to which the target audience rejected the dominant reading in favor of negotiated and/or oppositional readings.

Whereas season one brushes the surface of class issues, the second season dives more deeply into social position and economic inequality. For example, speaking mostly English is a signifier of education and class in Kenya and although the first season has some Swahili and Kenyan slang, the characters mostly speak English. In the final two episodes of the second season, the focus is on two characters from a lower social position who speak much more Swahili and Sheng, which is a predominantly urban, lower class slang.[31] Take for example the story of Angelo, who lives in a poor neighborhood in a small one-room apartment. He used to be a "thug" but has changed his ways and works in a low-level job, cleaning floors and running errands, while making payments on a used computer. When his old connections cause him to lose his job, he is shown drinking alcohol with a prostitute, but a phone call distracts him, implying that he was vulnerable to HIV in that moment but made the "right" choice to walk away. Without a job, Angelo uses his last bit of money to purchase small items to sell on the street, which further signifies his lower class.

A lower class is further signified with a character in season two, who comes to the big city of Nairobi from a rural area after winning a singing contest. She has a small suitcase, no phone and no place to stay. Although she met Angelo only once, she knocks on his door for help, signifying that although she lacks economic capital she can rely on her social capital to survive. The characters at the university who are obviously upper class tell her that she's too rural and needs Nairobi swag, which asserts that her social capital will not be enough in Nairobi; she will have to find economic capital as well and so she eventually takes on a sugar daddy who buys her a beautiful wig made from real hair and upmarket clothes. Angelo tells her she looks like a sophisticated Nairobi woman. Now that she fits in with the university crowd, as signified by the diplomat's son's new interest, her choices have placed her within the dominant and elite class, but have also made her vulnerable to HIV. As it seems aspirations of class mobility make women vulnerable to HIV, a discussion about the intersection of gender and class is necessary in order to understand beliefs about inequality and HIV as depicted on *Shuga*.

The Intersectionality of Socioeconomic Position with Gender and HIV/AIDS on Shuga

In a study of Kenyan popular media, Ligaga[32] argues that narratives about women oscillate between the binaries of good and bad, rarely allowing for women to live in the gray areas between. Moreover, representations of women and men when it comes to sex also differ in the anxiety and public panic provoked by the suggestion of women's empowerment over their bodies, particularly within sexual contexts. A 2013 controversy over an advertisement in Kenya advocating condom use within polygamous relationships offers a clear example. The ad, sponsored by Kenya's ministry of public health, USAID and UKAID, had two versions, one which featured a woman who advises her female friend to practice safe sex after she confides that she is having an extra-marital affair, and a second that featured two men having a similar conversation. The ad featuring the women was banned in Kenya although the same ad featuring men was allowed to air after church members said that it was un-African to discuss bedroom matters openly, particularly for women. "The advert was encouraging women to cheat on their husbands, they claimed, and called for its ban," according to Ngina.[33]

Shuga's differences are less stark but women's positionality is still much more restricted than men's. Male desire for untethered sexual pleasure causes HIV, whereas for women, a need for love, attention, and money potentially causes HIV. In the final episode of season one, a character says to her boyfriend, "I'm just so fed up with struggling" to defend sleeping with an ad executive to get an internship. He responds, "you've got that upper-class taste and I will never be upper class enough for you." But it is more complicated than that. Another character writes an article titled "Vulnerable Girls and Missing Fathers" after reflecting on her own story as well as learning a teenage neighbor was raped by her uncle. This theme of girls being vulnerable because their fathers are missing from their lives runs through both seasons. One is distrustful of men due to her father's behavior and so she puts her career first, enters into the all too common scenario of inter-generation transactional sex and becomes vulnerable to contracting HIV. In a behind-the-scenes video from season one, the actress who plays this character, says she "is using her body to give her family a better life." Later, a male character voices something similar to his girlfriend who is about to engage in transactional sex: "I know what you're doing. I need to tell you that it's not worth it." He switches to Swahili, which seems to signal a switch to traditional values: "I understand you are trying to help your family. You know they won't touch that money if they knew how you earned it." Transactional sex is thus called out and problematized. The stark reality of transactional, inter-generation sex is also called out, in part, when the ad executive pressures his intern to have sex in the office, asserting "you got what you want, and now it's my turn."

Another gendered perspective shows up when a character becomes HIV positive and reflects on how her well-respected but distant father who focuses everything on his teaching and nothing on his daughter is part of what drove her to the life she has led. In reflecting on growing up wanting "the love he showed his students," she says: "I think love is a survival instinct, just like breathing, eating and sleeping. If you don't get that love at home, you're going to go into the world hungry." Reflecting on how she ended up being HIV positive, the images displayed are of her teenage neighbor, indicating that character is going down a similar path. Indeed, she says when she was young she discovered her "body had a mysterious effect on men" as the camera shows the 16-year-old dancing as she cleans the floor. After her much older uncle comes in and inappropriately touches her asking where she learned to dance like that, she tells her mom, who admonishes her to be grateful to the kindness of the men who allow her to live in that house. The uncle later rapes her, and after the neighbor tells the girl's mother, who still won't accept it, she finds the girl's estranged, rich father and tells him. In each of the seasons, a rich father abandons his daughter, however, the outcome changes in season two when the father does the right thing by rescuing his daughter from the abusive home, implying that this will "save" her.

Rape is just one way in which men claim an entitlement to sex in *Shuga*. Money is a device to control women's sexuality in ways that it does not control that of men—a reality in Kenya. A father gives his daughter a credit card to stop her from getting involved with men; an older man "buys" sex with a young woman with a job he gives her; and a rich man asks for sex in return for the friendship he offered by giving a young woman a phone and money. Men are portrayed as more entitled to sex in part because of their power and money.

Darlington[34] argues that HIV Campaigns often "do not address the gender inequalities and power relations that define the context in which both genders are being asked to engage in HIV preventative behaviors." Studies that examine the representation of women and HIV in African countries suggest women are often portrayed as passive receptors of HIV rather than active subjects with the agency and efficacy to effect change and improve their own lives.[35] Gibbs[36] argued that portrayals of the relationship between HIV and gender either pay no attention to the social context of women's lives, or portray women as passive and unable to act. This is not the case in *Shuga*. Women are frequently shown taking charge of their sexual health, which is counter to cultural and social norms. Moreover, men are often vectors for the spread of HIV in *Shuga*, which counters the stereotypical depictions of women as paths of HIV.[37]

Interestingly, mothers play a more direct role in HIV prevention in the second season. A rural mother hands her daughter a condom as she leaves for Nairobi and says "your beauty could be a blessing or a curse. You know men today" (a statement that also recognizes men's entitlement to sex). The female diplomat directly asks her son if he uses condoms (her directness compared with the rural mother perhaps suggesting a difference between mothers based on geography, class, and education). He responds affirmatively but she pushes to make sure it is every time. Her son explains that condom use is situational, adding, "If we've known each other for more than 3 months, we come to an agreement." His mother expresses further concern, but he brushes it off, responding, "Mom, I know what I am doing. Trust me." His decision-making is later called into question when he is pressured into not using a condom.

Discussion

Because Kenya's popular edutainment programs are made with the intent to affect individual viewers and societal norms, it is important to understand how they inform debate around key health issues. As Lewis and Lewis[38] point out, because of their "popularity with 'hard to reach' groups, people with low literacy and those who do not regularly access mainstream print media, EE [educational entertainment] approaches have an important role in addressing inequities in access to more traditional health promotion interventions." This analysis indicates that *Shuga* does a better job attempting to reach out to the broad diversity of Kenyan youth in its second season than its first. In its first season, *Shuga* does not allow for socioeconomic position, particularly of young women, to become part of the conversation around HIV/AIDS, in part because it does not problematize sugar daddies and the impending vulnerability to HIV for young Kenyan women. Moreover, it presents transactional sex and reliance on sugar daddies without critically pointing to the socio-economic disparities that create such a situation. Transactional sex through inter-generational relationships is a reality for Kenyan women that is less a choice than a necessity for many young women,[39] yet young women in these situations are portrayed with agency. This oversimplification of female empowerment condemns their behavior and assigns personal responsibility for contracting HIV without recognizing the structural conditions that create their "choices." This mirrors Asante's[40] findings on discourses used to rationalize skin toning in Ghana, where African women's empowerment was linked to neoliberal ideologies of individual choice and consumerism, seeming to pit gender equity against economic inequality.

In an ethnographic study of young women, HIV, love, and money in Kenya, Mojola[41] argues that "for young women, it was not the fear of getting HIV or AIDS that drove their sexual decision-making. Rather, entanglements of love and money underlay their choices of intimate relationships with the riskiest partners." She suggests a need to recognize the connections among economic need, gendered inequality in access to income, and HIV acquisition. *Shuga* addresses this but in problematic ways that echo Asante's and Daniel's[42] claim that this neoliberal form of female empowerment is meant to position African women to overcome patriarchy. They argue, "while African patriarchy continues to patrol women's bodies through specific policies, taboos, and cultural norms, the forms of resistance emerging against patriarchy and poverty also merit critical attention." In *Shuga*, having a sugar daddy is seen as a form of resistance to both patriarchy and poverty; however, women's resistance to poverty through the exchange of their bodies supports patriarchy as men are seen exerting control over women's bodies and even their health through the spread of HIV. Thus, neoliberal forms of female empowerment such as those shown in *Shuga* may encourage women to prop up patriarchy in the name of resisting poverty.

The dominant class's experience of HIV is privileged in the *Shuga* edutainment program and the lived experience for most Kenyans who are HIV positive is ignored. By focusing on the elite, the producers highlight income inequalities for the viewers who are not of this class, and this aspirational depiction becomes anxiety producing. Indeed, Rozer and Volker[43] found that income inequalities contribute to social anxiety which contributes to a decline in health. Thus, portrayals of class in edutainment matter not simply because they are an inaccurate reflection of the reality of HIV/AIDS but also because they may increase poor health. Desire for economic mobility creates increased risk of HIV for women. Popular programs become platforms for dialogue and need to start from the lived experience of the target audience to make that happen. Audiences need to recognize themselves rather than just recognize the disparity of their socioeconomic position from that of the characters.

In its second season, *Shuga* does ultimately point to how some inequities, particularly for women, are connected with the spread of HIV. These differences with the first season do not seem like an accident. Lupita Nyong'o (who starred in the first season and has since won an Oscar) was the supporting director on four of the six episodes in season two. Interestingly, the two episodes not involving Nyong'o are also most like the first season and thus centrally focused on the elite, glamorous lifestyle. One must wonder whether it was the decision-making power of Nyong'o that made the difference in portrayals of gender, class and culture, making the stories more relevant to Kenyan youth, especially young women.

Giving someone like Nyong'o central decision-making power in the production of edutainment programming speaks to scholars' call for more participatory health communication, which is grounded in listening to people and creating health communication for and by communities. Nyong'o's participation in the second season provides a glimpse of what giving voice to Kenyan youth can look like. Granted, she is only one person, and an elite, but Nyong'o voiced opinions about her character's story in a behind-the-scenes video before she became a star, and those opinions are reflected in changes seen in the second season. Allowing more Kenyan youth to gain access to the production process and make decisions would likely result in an even better reflection of the inequities in Kenya and the ways in which they impact their health. Lewis and Lewis argued,

> A participatory approach is community-driven in that it foregrounds the voices of community members and their own articulations of health problems facing their communities. It respects and emphasizes the agency (ability) of community members to frame solutions and communication strategies. Consequently, the role of experts is less about telling people what they need to 'do' or change, and instead involves listening, responding to and helping people give direction to their own change.[44]

When economic inequality matters to people impacted by a health issue, it should be a part of the messages created and presented in meaningful ways that resonate with their lived experience of the issue.

Edutainment programs need to consider audiences' positions in communicating about HIV. That fact that students who weren't from the elite university where *Shuga* was filmed completely dismissed the first season (as the stories reflected a position that was not theirs) demonstrates the importance of considering how socioeconomic position is part of identity, and part of what gets communicated about a health issue. How might edutainment audiences reinterpret what has been produced *for* them, rather than *by* them? Decoding what has been produced from the perspective of the intended audience is a necessary next step in understanding how class and gender impact the viewer's meaning-making process for health edutainment and the role it may play in their lives.

In this chapter, I have discussed how class is produced, represented and consumed in a popular HIV edutainment program in Kenya that is both groundbreaking and problematic. This analysis demonstrates how portrayals can normalize and problematize HIV behaviors and attitudes that are tied to gender and class. Moreover, I have argued for a more participatory approach in the production of edutainment programs for greater resonance, shared meaning, and impact among the

Kenyan youth for whom they are created. As Khan[45] points out, HIV/AIDS messages are "far from emancipatory" because they reinforce existing power relations structured by gender, sexuality, class and education, which could "hamper the very goal of HIV prevention." Ultimately, *Shuga* is groundbreaking and yet also suggests HIV portrayals still have much work to do in order to get it right.

Notes

1. Nancy Achieng' Booker, Ann Neville Miller, and Peter Ngure, "Heavy Sexual Content Versus Safer Sex Content: A Content Analysis of the Entertainment Education Drama Shuga," *Health Communication* 31, no. 12 (2016): 1437–446. doi:10.1080/10410236.2015.1077691.
2. Dina Borzekowski, "The Project Ignite Evaluation: Tribes in Trinidad & Tobago and Shuga in Kenya and Zambia," (2010). www.comminit.com/usaid/content/project-ignite-evaluation-tribes-trinidad-tobago-and-shuga-kenya-and-zambia.
3. No comparison was reported between attitudes of youths who did and did not watch *Shuga*, and no measures of behavior were taken in the evaluation (see Borzekowski, "The Project"), however, its producers deemed the program a great success.
4. Eliza Govender, "Working in the Greyzone: Exploring Education Entertainment in Africa," *African Communication Research* 6 (2013): 5–32.
5. Emily Moyer-Gusé, "Toward a Theory of Entertainment Persuasion: Explaining the Persuasive Effects of Entertainment Education Messages," *Communication Theory* 18, no. 3 (2008): 408.
6. Malik Zahra Khalid and Aaliya Ahmed, "Entertainment-Education Media Strategies for Social Change: Opportunities and Emerging Trends," *Review of Journalism and Mass Communication* 2, no. 1 (2014), 75.
7. Khan criticized the dearth of textual analyses of health media campaigns, suggesting the necessity to consider narratives of HIV and AIDS. See: Shamshad Khan, "Manufacturing Consent?: Media Messages in the Mobilization Against HIV/AIDS in India and Lessons for Health Communication," *Health Communication* 29, no. 3 (2014): 265.
8. Society of International Development, "Exploring Kenya's Inequality: Pulling Apart or Pooling Together?" (2013), accessed on August 15, 2018, http://inequalities.sidint.net/kenya.
9. See: Oxfam, "Kenya: Extreme Inequality in Numbers," accessed on August 15, 2018, www.oxfam.org/en/even-it/kenya-extreme-inequality-numbers.
10. James R. Hargreaves, Calum Davey, and Richard G. White, "Does the 'Inverse Equity Hypothesis' Explain How Both Poverty and Wealth Can Be Associated with HIV Prevalence in Sub-Saharan Africa?" *Journal of Epidemiology and Community Health* 67, no. 6 (2013): 526–529.
11. Alexander Tsai, "Socioeconomic Gradients in Internalized Stigma Among 4,314 Persons with HIV in Sub-Saharan Africa," *AIDS Behaviour* 19 (2015): 276.
12. See: Avert, "Aids and HIV in Kenya," accessed on August 15, 2018, www.avert.org/professionals/hiv-around-world/sub-saharan-africa/kenya.
13. Mohammad Hajizadeh, Drissa Sia, Sally Jody Heymann, and Arijit Nandi, "Socioeconomic Inequalities in HIV/AIDS Prevalence in Sub-Saharan African Countries: Evidence from the Demographic Health Surveys," *International Journal for Equity in Health* 13 (2014): 18.
14. James R. Hargreaves, Calum Davey, Elizabeth Fearon, Bernadette Hensen and Shari Krishnaratne, "Trends in Socioeconomic Inequalities in HIV Prevalence among Young People in Seven Countries in Eastern and Southern Africa," *PloS one* (2015).
15. Nyawira T. Gitahi–Kamau, James N. Kiarie, Kenneth K. Mutai, Beatrice Gatumia, P.M. Gatongi, and A. Lakati, "Socio-Economic Determinants of Disease Progression among HIV Infected Adults in Kenya," *BMC Public Health* 15 (2015): 733.
16. UNAIDS, *Kenya AIDS Indicator Survey* (Nairobi, Kenya: National AIDS Control Council, 2013); *AIDS Epidemic Update* (Geneva, Switzerland: Joint United Nations Programme on HIV/AIDS, 2013).
17. Abraham K. Mulwo, Keyan G. Tomaselli, and Lynn Dalrymple, "Condom Brands, Perceptions of Condom Efficacy and HIV Prevention among University Students in Kwa Zulu-Natal, South Africa," *African Journal of AIDS Research* 8 (2009): 311–320.
18. Kamini Menon, "The Role of the Imagined Worlds of Narrative in Social Change in Kenya: Exploring Narrative Consumption Tendencies amongst Youth in Urban Nairobi and their Interaction with Fictional Texts Geared at Altering Health Behavior," master's thesis in global communications at American University of Paris (2011).
19. Menon, "The Role".
20. Ann Overbergh, "Targeting Urbanites: Nairobi-Bred Audio-Visual Narratives in Sheng," *Journal of African Media Studies* 7, no. 1 (2015): 47.

21 Society of International Development. "Exploring Kenya's Inequality: Pulling apart or pooling together?" (2013) http://inequalities.sidint.net/kenya.
22 Menon, "The Role," 73–74.
23 Adam Jaworski and Crispin Thurlow, "Mediatizing the "Super-Rich," Normalizing Privilege," *Social Semiotics* 27, no. 3 (2017): 276–287. doi: 10.1080/10350330.2017.1301792.
24 Ann Neville Miller, "An Exploration into Kenyan Public Speaking Patterns with Implications for the American Introductory Public Speaking Course," *Communication* Education 51 (2002): 168–182; Julie Gathoni Muraya, Anne Neville Miller, and Leonard Mjomba, "Implications of High-/Low-Context Communication for Target Audience Member Interpretation of Messages in the *Nimechill* Abstinence Campaign in Nairobi, Kenya," *Health Communication* 26, no. 6 (2011): 516–524.
25 Jaworski and Thurlow "Mediatizing," 277.
26 Stig Hjarvard, *The Mediatization of Society* (London: Routledge, 2013), 149.
27 Menon, "The Role".
28 Michael W. Kraus, Jun Won Park, and Jacinth J.X. Tan, "Signs of Social Class: The Experience of Economic Inequality in Everyday Life," *Perspectives on Psychological Science* 12, no. 3 (2017): 423.
29 Menon, "The Role".
30 Ibid., 64.
31 See Overbergh, "Targeting Urbanities," for a discussion of Sheng.
32 Dina Ligaga, "Thinking around Genre: The Moral Narrative and Femininity in Kenyan Popular Media," *The Cambridge Journal of Postcolonial Literary Inquiry* 4, no. 2 (2017): 222–236.
33 Catherine Ngina, "Confessions of Women who Cheat on their Husbands," *The Star*, October 19, 2013, accessed August 15, 2019, www.the-star.co.ke/sasa/2013-10-18-confessions-of-women-who-cheat-on-their-husbands/.
34 Kay-Anne, Darlington, "Gender Representations, Cultural Norms and Message Features in Jamaican HIV/AIDS Advertisements: A Textual Analysis of Television Campaigns," Dissertation (2015): 33.
35 Darlington, "Gender Representations".
36 Andrew Gibbs, "Understandings of Gender and HIV in the South African Media," *AIDS Care* 22, no. 2 (2010): 1620–1628.
37 Andrew Gibbs and Geoff Jobson, "Narratives of Masculinity in the Daily Sun: Implications for HIV Risk and Prevention," *South African Journal of Psychology* 41, no. 2 (2011): 173–186.
38 Belinda Lewis and Jeff Lewis, *Health Communication: A Media & Cultural Studies Approach* (London: Palgrave, 2015), 172.
39 Kirsten Stobeanau, Lori Heise, Joyce Wamoyi, and Natalia Bobrova, "Revisiting the Understanding of 'Transactional Sex in Sub-Saharan Africa': A Review and Synthesis of the Literature," *Social Science and Medicine* 168 (November 2016): 186–197; Joyce Wamoyi, Kirsten Stobeanau, Natalia Bobrova, Tanya Abramsky, and Charlotte Watts, "Transactional Sex and Risk for HIV Infection in Sub-Saharan Africa: A Systematic Review and Meta-Analysis," *Journal of the International AIDS Society* 19, no. 1 (2016).
40 Godfried Asante, "Glocalized Whiteness: Sustaining and Reproducing Whiteness through "Skin Toning" in Post-Colonial Ghana," *Journal Of International and Intercultural Communication* 9, no. 2 (2016): 87–103.
41 Sanyu A. Mojola, *Love, Money, and HIV: Becoming a Modern African Woman in the Age of AIDS* (Berkeley: University of California Press, 2014), 110.
42 Godfried Asante and Rita Daniel, "(Re)defining Images of African Women: A Post-Feminist Critique of the Ghanaian YouTube Series, 'An African City'," Paper presented at the annual meeting of the International Communication Association (2018).
43 Jesper J. Rözer and Beate Volker, "Does Income Inequality Have Lasting Effects on Health and Trust?" *Social Science & Medicine* 149 (January 2016): 37–45.
44 Lewis and Lewis, *Health Communication*, 108.
45 Khan, "Manufacturing Consent".

PART II

Class in Interactive Digital and Mobile Media

7

HORSE RACING, SOCIAL CLASS, AND THE SPACES OF GAMBLING

Holly Kruse

Although analyses of media and social class are not as common in academia in the United States as they once were, they are still important. Notions of social class are implicit in popular discourses of media, which tend to celebrate early adopters of new commercial communication technologies and assume there are particular correct technologies to adopt and particular correct ways to use them. Historically, such determinations have been largely made along lines of class, age, gender, race, and dis/ability, with hegemonic modes of adoption and use positioned as the most worthy. Looking at the technologies of horse race wagering in both physical and virtual space provides us with examples of how practices and places are "classed," and of how class divisions are covered over and maintained in and through interactive media practices.

There are several ways to think about class. Raymond Williams[1] explains that in Marx's sense, class could be considered both an economic classification and a formation in which members are conscious of their economic condition and have developed various strategies for dealing with it. John Hartley, however, finds simple explanations of class problematic, arguing that class is "then made to explain matters external to economics, including values, politics, beliefs and culture."[2] Identity, Hartley notes, is composed of more factors than one's economic positioning relative to others in industrial society, including ethnicity, sexuality, and gender, and that differences within classes are as important as those between and among classes.[3] Still, Williams' discussion of class is useful in a historical analysis of class, media, and horse racing. According to Williams, contemporary notions of class originated during the Industrial Revolution, which is also the period during which the differentiation and mediation of space at racetracks emerged.

> Development of class in its modern social sense, with relatively fixed names for particular classes (lower class, middle class, upper class, working class and so on) belongs essentially of the period between 1770 and 1840, which is also the period of the Industrial Revolution and its decisive reorganization of society.[4]

As I will demonstrate in this chapter, a class-based understanding of which people—of the broadly understood lower class, middle class, or upper class—belong where in the spaces of horse racing has deep historical roots and persists to this day.

In the course of the twentieth century, for example, horse racing in the United States went from being a spectator sport popular across class lines to a sport whose defining spaces, like racetracks themselves and off-track betting facilities (OTBs), are avoided except on days when major stakes races are run. The everyday racetrack and/or OTB customer is likely older and less affluent than during racing's heyday. On ordinary days, racetracks and OTBs may be perceived as liminal, unwelcoming, and even dangerous spaces, populated by "degenerates" of the lower social classes. Racing's modern spaces, however, are highly mediated. They feature walls of screens that show races from racetracks across the country (and even around the world), carrels that include individual televisions, JumboTron screens in racetrack infields displaying odds and races, and self-service betting terminals.

These developments mean that while studies of technology users often focus on relatively young, affluent users of social media, streaming, and gaming platforms, less affluent and often older users of interactive media tend to be overlooked. My examination of horse racing and class illustrates how non-affluent (so, "lower" or "working" class) users have consistently adopted and effectively used new, complex media technologies and navigated these technologies' spaces. I argue that popular discourses bring these technologies into the mainstream when they appear to threaten the middle and upper classes. Online betting platforms provide an example. By the late 1990s in the USA, options for legal horse race betting in several states expanded to include online and interactive television betting, and therefore expanded into the private and semi-private spaces of the middle-class home. In the early twenty-first century the infiltration of gambling in the home via the internet led to a moral panic about online gambling and youth. As I will describe, the panic was at least partly well founded: access to gambling, much of it illegal, greatly increased, including and maybe especially among teenagers and young adults. This caused real harm.

The expansion of gambling continues. Twenty years after helping to bring betting into private spaces and onto private screens, several horse racing companies—such as Churchill Downs, Inc. and TVG—offer mobile betting apps for their customers. These companies would like to use new media platforms and renovated physical spaces to bring younger, more affluent customers to the sport, making clear the ways in which they consider certain technologies—such as the public screens and the betting windows of the racetrack or OTB—"classed" and "aged" in undesirable ways.

Horse Racing, Gambling, and Class

We can locate the prominent role of social class in horse racing's technologies and practices in the sport's modern origins. In Britain in the early nineteenth century, race meets were held in open areas where local people of all classes mingled. No attendance fee was charged, and a range of activities accompanied racing, from eating and drinking to cockfighting. As with many other local activities in Europe at the time, towns had carnival-like atmospheres during racing. Mike Huggins[5] argues that early meets allowed the kind of ludic play that was usually associated with carnivals. Yet, while horse racing has been associated with members of all socioeconomic classes, even in its earliest, fair-associated period, Wray Vamplew contends, "Any inter-class contact was solely for the duration of the event."[6] Further, Vamplew states,

> It is difficult to see how [racing] broke down class barriers when the upper ranks of society generally viewed the scene from the safe confines of private stands and carriages, or later the club enclosures, well segregated from the lower elements.[7]

Separation in physical space has been a defining feature of horse racing.

Racecourses in Great Britain became enclosed over the course of the nineteenth century, and this restricted carnivalesque activity and required paid admission. The enclosed racecourses affected the forms of social behavior that took place at the races, creating more physical segregation among classes of attendees, as Huggins notes,

> At the larger meetings grandstand accommodation increased through the century, allowing clearer social zoning. Beginning with a single grandstand in the 1820s, Doncaster later

added a jockeys and trainers' stand, Lord Wharncliffe's subscription stand, a second-class stand, Lord Astley's Lincolnshire stand and other private stands and boxes.[8]

Fellow racing historian Wray Vamplew agrees, claiming that not only were different sections of enclosed racecourses intended for different sorts of participants and meant to enforce order and maintain propriety, but that differential pricing was used to segregate groups from each other.[9]

Separation of racetrack spaces in order to segregate the sexes can be traced to the eighteenth century. In their book *Racecourse Architecture*, Paul Roberts and Isabelle Taylor observe that the earliest grandstand, built at York Racecourse in England in 1756, featured a separate area for upper-class women.[10] In the early nineteenth century, racetrack grandstands included dining rooms for middle-class women.[11] Whether partition of sexes and classes helped or hurt racetracks is a matter of dispute. Huggins contends that admission charges contributed heavily to declining attendance by women of all classes and by all members of the working class during the nineteenth century; Vamplew and David Schwartz disagree, with Schwartz writing that enclosed racetracks "actively courted both female and working-class spectators."[12] Huggins maintains that such efforts were unsuccessful.

In examining the role of social class in the origins of horse racing, it is tempting to overlook the urban middle class: yet its members were increasingly important in horse racing in Britain during the nineteenth century. By the century's end, members of the middle class were commonly found among racehorse owners and racing officials.[13] They also bet on racing, both on-track and off, although off-track betting was primarily identified with the working class.[14]

As in Great Britain, in the United States notions of class have significantly contributed to public understandings of horse racing, and to racing's histories and practices. In her ethnographic study of the lives of workers such as grooms and hot walkers who mainly occupy "the backstretch"—the stabling area of the track, usually located on the far side of the track and opposite the track's public areas—Carole Case states that racing's "stratification systems has elements of class and caste, some of which reflect racing's origins. If one is female, a member of a minority group, or a groom, one's chances of mobility [in the racing world] are generally limited."[15]

Members of ethnic minority groups in Case's study often mentioned that they were discriminated against. They were well aware that they were being paid less than others but were unwilling to file complaints, likely because of their immigration statuses.[16] Today workers from Latin American countries hold many if not most of the low status behind-the-scenes jobs, such as groom (the person usually responsible for cleaning stalls, grooming horses, feeding horses, and cleaning horses' tack) and hot walker (the person who walks horses by lead in the barn area after the horses have run in order to allow horses to cool down). These jobs were once mainly filled by African-Americans. Because many backstretch workers are undocumented, for many years the usually politically conservative horse racing industry lobbying association has repeatedly found itself in the position of supporting immigration reform, including amnesty for illegal workers already in the United States.[17]

Remarkably, there was a time in American horse racing when at least some members of minority groups were celebrated: during the nineteenth-century heyday of African-American jockeys. Early in that century, harness races that featured trotting horses pulling carts were the most popular kinds of races, but "running races" with riders on Thoroughbred horses soon became more popular than harness races.[18] People bet money and commodities, including slaves, on these informal competitions. Many of the jockeys were slaves who became regional celebrities and who sometimes won enough to buy their and their families' freedom. After the abolition of slavery in the United States, the winning jockeys of the first several runnings of the Kentucky Derby were black. At the peak of their visibility and popularity, however, black jockeys faced Jim Crow era discrimination, and they were largely pushed out of the United States to Europe if they wanted to pursue their riding careers.

Ideas of class, race, and the proper roles associated with particular social classes resonate in racing today. The sport's reliance on gambling as its primary source of revenue has made the sport seem "dirty" to many observers. But as I have already mentioned, racing was at one time a popular broadcast sport in the United States. Although major races broadcast by radio and television helped make the sport one of the most popular among all classes in the United States in the mid-twentieth century, by the end of the century horse racing in the United States had lost much of that popularity.

An exception to the decline in horse racing popularity is ongoing interest in the Kentucky Derby. The premier race for three-year-old Thoroughbred horses in the United States held on the first Saturday in May continues to air on a major broadcast network—NBC, as of this writing—and mainly attracts an audience of viewers who otherwise do not follow, or bet on, horse racing. Broadcast coverage has increasingly focused on celebrities at the Derby and at Derby parties, and on fashion worn by Derby-goers. The interest in fashion, especially women's extravagant hats, is a relatively recent phenomenon, emerging in the 1980s and 1990s. NBC has chosen to emphasize Derby fashion in parts of its racing coverage, arguing that features about fashion and celebrities attract to horse racing broadcasts female viewers (presumably white, middle-class viewers) who don't follow sports.[19] Media interest in and promotion of Kentucky Derby fashions has undoubtedly played a role in the growth of home-based Derby parties. With the televised running of the race the presumed centerpiece, Derby parties invite their primarily female participants to dress up, wear fancy hats, and drink mint juleps. It is not entirely clear though that such parties help draw these relatively affluent participants to the sport and physical spaces of horse racing, or whether they are merely epiphenomena of an annual event. Familiarity with the horses in field may be superficial for many, if not most, partygoers.[20]

The fascination with dressing up in a way that mimics the upper classes indicates how at its highest levels horse racing is still considered by many to be "The Sport of Kings." In the United States families such as the Phippses, Whitneys, and Janneys continue to have a presence in the sport, and some notable business moguls have high profiles as Thoroughbred breeders and owners: recent examples include Mike Repole, co-founder of Vitaminwater, and celebrity chef Bobby Flay. Although one is unlikely to find celebrity owners at the local off-track or inter-track wagering facility, the idea that horse racing includes participants of all social stations and helps eliminate class barriers is still prevalent. As a New York OTB patron states, "Wherever you have gambling, you're going to have rich guys and beggars next to each other ... and that's what makes these places unique."[21]

Implicit in this observation is the generally correct perception of many people inside and outside of the racing industry that, on the viewing and betting level, horse racing has become primarily a non-affluent older man's game. Industry concern about its aging customer base and its sport's lack of popular appeal has made it desperate to appeal to professional 20- and-30-somethings. And yet I must again note that racing's current customers are often adept technology users, whatever their age or class. By the end of the previous century, most horse race wagering took place offsite, at off-track facilities rather than at tracks where live racing was taking place, and where walls of screens simulcast races from across the country and around the world, while bets are transmitted to distant wagering hubs. That an older, non-affluent, apparently non-tech-savvy user base is able to successfully navigate a complicated new media environment is counterintuitive, but our intuitions are based on unexamined assumptions about age, class, and technology.

The propagation of simulcasting and off-track betting technologies, and now online betting, has meant that racetracks have struggled to attract customers of all classes to the track. Some tracks have aspired to become destinations for middle-class families, attempting to replace the received popular image of most tracks as seedy, urban places mainly frequented by members of the lower-class with an image of the racetrack as a modern facility with a range of amenities. Paul Roberts and Isabelle Taylor write that finally, facing competition for wagering dollars and onsite visitors, racetrack executives "woke up to the idea that they are in the entertainment industry."[22]

When Lone Star Park racetrack opened in the Dallas area in 1997, for example, its ownership and management team promoted the track to non-traditional attendees. Writing in the trade journal *Amusement Business*, Don Muret[23] listed as Lone Star Park's attractions its playground, giant slides, picnic pavilions and stage for live entertainment. At its opening, Lone Star Park promoted its 1200 member Kid's Club and its monthly meetings for games and barn tours. During its first race meet, Lone Star Park's attendance was, according to Muret, "60–40 male/female, compared with 80/20 at most tracks.... The average patron's income [was] $55,000. It [was] a family crowd."

Lone Star Park is just one example. Major renovations have taken place at premier tracks such as Churchill Downs in Louisville, Kentucky and Gulfstream Park in South Florida. Yet racing's efforts to attract an ostensibly more desirable customer base to the track have met with only marginal success. At the same time, online gambling—both legal and illegal—has become a massive source of revenue for its operators, and racing has begun tapping into this market with apps and other online platforms. Instead of bringing fans to the track, maybe the answer for the industry is to bring the track to fans. But there exists an obvious tension between the attempts of some tracks to make themselves attractive leisure destinations while communication technology makes it less necessary for people to travel to racetracks or off-track betting facilities to participate. As racetrack attendance is declining, in-home and mobile interactive wagering services are expanding, and thus expanding into the private and semi-private places of the broadband-connected middle class.

Gambling in the Home

Betting online on horse racing in the United States has helped usher in the era of open online gambling, using the internet, mobile apps, and, in some places, interactive television, to bring horse race betting to consumers. Online casino games, poker, sports betting, and lotteries are now sources of revenue, sometimes legally, but in the United States mostly illegally. In the USA, gambling is regulated at the state level rather than the national level. Many states run lotteries, and fewer allow casino gambling. Native American tribes are sovereign in regard to gaming, so many are heavily involved in the casino business.[24] Some states allow limited forms of non-tribal gaming beyond lotteries: Florida, for instance, allows some card and table games, such as poker and blackjack, but ban slot machines. Betting on horse racing, however, has been widely accepted by state governments, and it is legal in all but seven states.

In the USA, betting on horse racing is pari-mutuel, which means that the odds are set among the bettors themselves: the more money bet on a particular horse, the lower the odds, and thus the lower the payout for the wagerer should her bet be a winning one. While slot machines and roulette are considered games of chance, betting on horse racing is considered a game of skill because it requires the bettor to consider odds data as well as information about horses' past performances, bloodlines, trainer, jockey, competitors, and more in order to make an informed bet. Largely for this reason, in 1978 horse racing was granted an exemption from the Interstate Wire Act. The Wire Act become law in 1961 and was meant to target bookmaking over the phone by organized crime. Horse racing's exemption allows bettors at a racetrack or legal off-track wagering site in one state to bet on races in another state. In 2006 this exemption was extended to online pari-mutuel horse race betting.[25] No other form of online gambling has this explicit protection. Therefore, with few forms of legal online betting in the USA, many illegal forms are popular, including using illegal gambling sites, wagering through legal sites but from jurisdictions where certain kinds of internet betting are not legal, betting when under the age of 21, and failing to report winnings to the IRS. These "profane" uses invite disciplinary intrusions by the state into the "sacred" domestic sphere.

Many people view the very act of betting as morally debased and dangerous, even when it is legal, and therefore bringing it into the home challenges the dominant tropes of domesticity. At the same time, countless Americans engage in online shopping and other online financial transactions from the privacy of their homes in a relatively unproblematic way. So perhaps it is no surprise then that a familiar gambling card game, poker, was generally accepted when it gained online popularity in the early-to-mid-2000s. Betting on poker currently has much greater visibility online in the USA than horse race wagering, although both generate substantial revenue. Because relatively more has been written and said in the popular media about online poker than other forms of internet betting, when examining any form of online gambling it is useful to look at poker as representative of how the perceived boundary between public and private has been contested.

Extensive internet betting on poker began in 1998 with the appearance Planet Poker, which tried to replicate on the internet the in-person poker-playing experience.[26] Online poker's popularity quickly grew. Most online casinos offering poker were, and are, located offshore in the Caribbean and Central America to avoid being shut down by American authorities.[27] Initially, many casinos accepted credit card bets, but actions by the United States Department of Justice discouraged casinos from offering that option. In late 2006, President George W. Bush signed a bill that banned most kinds of financial transfers used to fund online bets. (Notably, this law exempted pari-mutuel horse race wagering.) The law had the effect of putting out of business most online poker casinos located in the United States that had hoped that continuing legal ambiguity would allow them to operate. In spite of the US law, internet poker continued to grow in popularity during the 2000s, and by the end of the decade it was bringing in an estimated $4 billion a year to its operators.[28]

The explosion in online poker's popularity began in 2003 when Chris Moneymaker won $2.5 million for his first place finish in the World Series of Poker. He prepared for the tournament by playing only online poker.[29] Moneymaker's win, televised on ESPN, is credited with drawing thousands of players worldwide to online poker and creating scores of poker websites in countries such as Malta, the Isle of Man, Antigua, and Costa Rica.[30] A few huge offshore sites, such as PokerStars and Full Tilt Poker, came to dominate the internet poker business.[31]

Lack of regulatory oversight means that offshore casinos are prone to cheating and fraud. In a *Washington Post* series on internet poker, reporter Gilbert Gaul notes of offshore sites:

> Millions of the bets originate in the United States, where online poker and gambling sites are banned, forcing players to reach out across the internet like modern-day bootleggers. Yet players have little way of knowing who is watching their bets or where their money is going. Often, owners hide behind multiple layers of limited partnerships, making it difficult to determine who controls the sites or to lodge complaints about cheating.[32]

Honest players can lose large amounts of money to cheaters with little recourse, although companies interested in maintaining customer loyalty have acted to compensate victims. Gaul cites a case in which AbsolutePoker's software was hacked, and the company refunded $1.6 million dollars to players who had lost money to the hackers.[33]

The most serious blow to the online poker industry in the United States came in early 2011 when the US indicted the founders of PokerStars, Full Tilt Poker and Absolute Poker. The sites' owners were charged with money laundering, fraud, and operating illegal internet casinos.[34] The accounts of all players were frozen, and, as of this writing, betting on online poker remains illegal in most states. However, offshore poker sites are easily accessible to anyone in the USA with an internet connection.

Unsurprisingly, the recent ease of gambling online from home has created anxiety. Victorian notions of the feminized middle-class home as a haven from the stresses of modern life are persistent, and they continue to shape discourse about domestic media use, even though a past in which the middle-class home was free of crass market relations is illusory. Further, no contemporary critic can realistically argue that an idealized feminine role in domestic space should be recovered or maintained, because it never existed in a pure form. For example, gambling commonly took place in the home in colonial America, and women participated.[35] In the centuries that followed, American women made bets, including on horse racing, in the streets, in their homes, and in masculine-defined spaces such as betting parlors: all seemingly in opposition to their expected roles as the civilizing, protective guardians of morality.

During the nineteenth century in the United States and Great Britain, the growth of industrialization in cities made moving from inner cities to suburbs attractive to members of the growing middle classes. Keeping the instrumental relations of industrialization out of the middle-class (and upper-class) home contributed to the notion of "separate spheres," in which the home was to be a feminized realm and a retreat from the masculine world of work and public life.[36] So, in large Victorian homes, rooms were often defined by the sex of their users: "the ladies' apartment," "the gentlemen's suite," and the "men's corridor," for instance.[37] Daphne Spain observes that the gendered segregation made explicit by room designations, along with features such as a separate entrance to the "masculine" library or office, excluded, middle- and upper-class women from the spaces where information related to the household's public status, such as legal and financial documents, was kept.[38]

Segregating rooms by sex fit the Victorian idea that an ordered home created ordered lives.[39] Indeed, the emergence of professional interior decorating in the late nineteenth century added even more strictness to Victorian conventions of household design. Rules regarding decoration of the middle-class home were key in maintaining a "proper home," which would presumably help defuse tensions between domestic space and public space, including in relation to new technologies. William Boddy states:

> It is important to keep in mind, however, that the late nineteenth century witnessed a sustained crisis in the cultural definitions of private and public space marked by a number of striking irreconcilable topographies conflating the domestic and the public, including Schivelbusch's public railway carriage appointed in the deeply upholstered style of the bourgeois living room, Benjamin's urban arcade presenting the street as furnished interior, and the domestic living room itself penetrated by the new industrial artifacts of the telephone, the stereopticon, and the magic lantern.[40]

If media technologies were to be accepted into the middle-class home, to eventually be integrated into family life, they would need to lose the "street" characteristics that so often carried working and lower class connotations. The technologies needed to be domesticated to be acceptable. Also, in truth the middle-class American home is not, and never has been, a pristine separate sphere of civilizing feminine influence. It is only in the past 150 to 200 years that the home has been transformed from a primary site of production to a site devoted to commercial consumption. In that time, we as a society have done much ideological work to maintain the symbolic boundary between domestic space and public space. In the case of media technologies, this has meant that we have "domesticated" them to accept them into our homes. Early twentieth-century phonographs could be placed in beautiful period cabinets, radios could be virtual hearths around which families purportedly gathered, high definition televisions are thin and flat and hung on walls like vivid pieces of art. Can the internet, with its myriad, perhaps unmanageable connections to licit and illicit activities, both public and private, be fully tamed to fit the idealized middle-class home?

Producers and sellers of industrially created in-home media technologies underscored the ability of new domestic entertainments to bring families together in increasingly fraught times. For example, early twentieth-century phonograph advertisements imagined families and friends gathering together around phonographs.[41] And by the early-to-mid-twentieth century, houses were designed to include communal areas—kitchens, living rooms, dining rooms—that opened onto each other and encouraged family togetherness, shunning the sex-specific spaces of Victorian homes.

Technologies, Class, and the Home

The feminized middle-class domestic sphere has never been isolated from the technologies and instrumental influences of the outside world. Transitional nineteenth- and early twentieth-century spaces included the aforementioned home-like upholstered railway car and the semi-public front parlor in the home, and transitional technologies brought lurid stories (such as the "yellow journalism" found in mass-produced newspapers) and morally suspect music (ragtime music played on a phonograph) into private spaces. Despite recent moral panics about online activities—gaming, pornography use, and gambling—might make it seem otherwise, the infiltration of mass-mediated vice into the home is not a new thing. And horse race wagering, including legal betting, has played a role in moving gambling into the home. Online gambling is now an enormous business, but because there are so many illegal online gambling sites, it is hard to know exactly how much money is being bet over the internet, although there have been several estimates. A *Washington Post* feature on online poker noted in 2008 that internet gambling revenue had "more than tripl[ed] over five years, to $18 billion annually, including about $4 billion from virtual poker."[42] Online wagers are forecast to total $950 billion in 2021.[43]

The popularity of televised poker tournaments and the ubiquity of online poker sites before the US government crackdown made a moral panic over online gambling seem inevitable. All of the ingredients were there: the perceived shadiness of the business of internet gambling; the availability of the internet and online gambling in the United States; the ease with which money can be spent through a web interface; the morally questionable status of even legal gambling; the proliferation of home entertainment and information media; the fragmentation, specialization, and privatization of domestic space; and the presumed vulnerability of teens. All of these factors contributed to widespread worries in popular media in the early 2000s over young people and online gambling.

Alice Marwick[44] describes societal concerns about young people and online predators and online pornography as "technopanics." A similar technopanic occurred over online gambling. The notion of technopanic comes from Stanley Cohen's definition and description of a moral panic, in which incidents of deviance—primarily youth deviance—become the focus of media coverage and public campaigns.[45] Cohen argues that media responses to these incidents tend to present them as a far greater social danger than the public previously believed them to be.[46] He also points out that the problematic behaviors are expressions of deeper structural problems that remain unaddressed.[47]

In a technopanic, the media express unease over the behavior of young people in relation to new technologies, behavior that is pathologized. In the case of panics over the internet, the purported ability of young people to understand computer technologies that baffle their elders contributes to the anxiety. Marwick argues:

> The trope of the teenager who possesses more technological knowledge than her adult counterpart and can program a VCR or set up a home computer is a powerful one. This image is furthered by movies from *Wargames* [sic] to *Hackers* to *Jurassic Park*, celebrations of young techno-entrepreneurs like Shawn Fanning and the wunderkinds of YouTube, and descriptions of the cultural competency demonstrated by teens as they blog, post digital pictures, talk to each other through instant messaging and interact through Facebook.[48]

The logic of the technopanic says that in order to stop young people's disturbing behavior, worrisome content must be restricted or banned.[49] There are usually valid concerns at the root of a technopanic, but these panics exaggerate the extent of the problem, or suggest solutions that are more far-reaching than what are justified by the reality of the problem.

In the case of online gambling, harms to victims are quite real, and I do not mean or want to diminish that. Importantly though, narratives of problematic online gambling are struggles, including in this case, over meanings of the private and the public, and of appropriate behaviors in the middle-class home. The protection of the middle-class family and domestic space is a central trope in dominant constructions of online gambling. The American Psychological Association's *Psychiatric News* published an article in 2002 that asserted a connection between internet use among young people and online gambling without evidence of a specific causal link. The article stated,

> Adolescents use the internet more than any other age group, and recent studies have found that about 3 percent of adolescents and 8 percent of college students have gambled on the internet, according to the National Council on Problem Gambling.[50]

The American Psychological Association (APA) had flagged the internet's accessibility to young people at home as a primary contributor to online gambling, concluding that lack of regulation meant that "there is no control on the hours of availability [or] age of participants," and that gambling sites targeted children, who were most likely using computers within the confines of their homes, with offers of discounts and free items on sports, adventure, and action figure websites.[51]

To be sure, with the explosion in online poker's popularity, news stories proliferated about the dangers of online gambling for teens, full of terrifying anecdotes about young men. A 2006 ABC News story describes how Greg Hogan, Jr., president of the sophomore class at Lehigh University and son of a minister, resorted to robbing a bank in Allentown, Pennsylvania in an attempt to get funds to pay off his online poker losses. Hogan told *Good Morning, America*:

> I started playing with about $50 ... I would deposit money from my checking account with an account at [an] online gambling site, mostly at PokerStars.com or Sportsbetting.com. I tripled my money the first few times so it seemed like easy money, but then I lost $300 and just felt this rage. Eventually, I spent it all.[52]

The assistant chief of police of Allentown let us know that it was online gambling that led Hogan, Jr. astray, that otherwise a good kid (i.e., white, middle-class) would never commit such a crime, when he said "The fact that he's a college student going, coming from an affluent family—he just does not fit your, your typical profile of, of someone robbing a bank."[53]

The college press added to the stream of student gambling addiction stories. A 2005 article in the California State University–Sacramento newspaper, for example, described cases of college students who stole to support their gambling habits, who dropped out of school because of gambling, who lost relationships, and who contemplated suicide. While the story featured the views of college students who gambled for fun and who claimed not to be addicted, it also cited a recovering compulsive gambler who was skeptical that those students' gambling practices would remain problem-free.[54] The gambler said that it "makes sense" that an estimated 15 to 20 percent of college students had bet online, "because many older people are not internet savvy. Students are smart, intelligent and have a better understanding of how to use the internet."[55] Interestingly, a subsequent survey funded by the National Institute of Mental Health found a correlation between non-student status and frequency of gambling but not between student status and frequency of gambling, contrary to popular press reports of a college gambling epidemic and in the tradition of media-driven moral panics.[56]

During the brief but significant technopanic over youth and online gambling, college students were not the only possible victims. High school and middle school students were also at risk. A 2006 Fox News report claimed that gambling was increasingly popular among pre-teens, and asserted that "The trend can be attributed to a growing acceptance of gambling in American culture, an increase in accessibility because of the internet and more betting shows on TV."[57] The story followed "Ross," who started betting online while he was in high school and who had a bookie by his senior year. "Ross" started selling marijuana to support his gambling habit, and he ended up $30,000 in debt before his parents learned of his problem and made him go to Gamblers Anonymous meetings. Parents were warned not to mistake dangerous activities that have infiltrated their suburban middle-class families for benign behaviors.

> "This looks very benign," said [neuropsychiatrist Lawson F.] Bernstein. "They're home playing cards with their friends, they're not drinking or doing drugs. It all looks very harmless. But the problem is for a certain number of kids, it's going to be the addictive equivalent of pot in that they're going to get in trouble with it."[58]

Teen gambling is far from innocent, said the researchers cited by the Fox News story. In fact, "adolescent-onset gambling is associated with more severe psychiatric problems, particularly substance use disorders, in adolescents and young adults."[59]

In all of these tales, the sacred domestic sphere is under threat. The webpage of the Columbia University Medical Center Gambling Disorders Clinic once warned that for teens, "online gambling is as close as their computer."[60] The problem posed by such narratives is one of mothers, and women in general, needing to re-establish their homes as spiritual centers. And yet how could the "civilizing' influence of women extolled as part of the "Cult of True Womanhood"[61] in an earlier era be asserted in the face of infiltration by undisciplined and profane online material?

When we travel online, we visit places that exist in a public arena and that may offer activities that were not previously easily accessible within the home or other private or semi-private places. Online gambling is just one phenomenon around which we can see active symbolic work done in and by popular discourse to maintain sense-making narratives in the face of a world in which public and private boundaries are shifting, and where the "sacred" space of the middle-class home is always already under threat from the "profane" and ostensibly lower-class influences that lurk outside.

Horse Racing, Media, and the Lives of Ordinary People

Today, horse racing and its followers are part of a broader cultural narrative that treats the sport as a relic of an earlier time. Interestingly though, the racing industry has been an innovator and/or early adopter of new media technology. For instance, racetracks used the nineteenth-century telegraph to transmit race results to remote locations, and they embraced the totalizator, an early twentieth-century racetrack computer, to calculate pari-mutuel odds and thus provide near-instant data processing. Horse racing was one of the most popular broadcast television sports in the United States in the 1950s, when television was a new medium. It pioneered the placement of screen media in public and semi-public places at OTBs in the 1970s and 1980s, and wagering through interactive television and the internet in the early 2000s. Yet despite its innovation in new media, the racing industry has often made poor decisions about media strategies. For example, it feared that providing racing programming to major television networks meant that people were watching horse racing at home rather than coming to the track to bet, which racing saw, and sees, as its fundamental source of revenue. In the 1960s it pulled much of its content from television, contributing to the decline in the sport's visibility and popularity.

Still, horse racing continues to exist in public and private places, in spaces where discourses of class, age, ethnicity, race, and gender intersect in tangible ways. The spaces of horse racing remind us to look at the work of the Annales School and Marxist historians, who studied the lives of ordinary people and their practices. Organized horse racing as entertainment and employment developed in clearly class-stratified societies. Horse racing's public settings—its everyday racetracks and its offsite betting facilities—continue to be primarily associated with the working and lower classes, and particularly with male senior citizens. Contemporary narratives often frame mere gambling in the spaces of horse racing as pathological, and the déclassé act of gambling a blight when it invades the middle-class home.

In studies of technologies, media, and society, we need to look at how older people, working class people, poor people, people of color, people who live in geographical marginalized spaces, and others generally considered late adopters use both new and old technologies. We need to consider the ways in which technologies are "classed" and "aged" in addition to how they are gendered and raced, and we need to examine how the discourses around technologies and their uses re-create rather than challenge our own scholarly assumptions and practices. The social and cultural histories and relations of horse racing and its technologies tell us that we, as media studies scholars, need to pay attention to how all sorts of people use media in all kinds of places, even if these users, their spaces, and their interests are not often made visible or seen as "sexy" in new media research.

Notes

1. Raymond Williams, *Keywords: A Vocabulary of Culture and Society* (New York: Oxford University Press, 1976), 58.
2. John Hartley, *Communication, Cultural and Media Studies*, 4th edn (London: Routledge, 2011), 44.
3. Ibid., 46.
4. Williams, *Keywords*, 51.
5. Mike Huggins, *Flat Racing and British Society, 1790–1914: Social and Economic History* (London: Frank Cass Publishers, 2000).
6. Wray Vamplew, *The Turf: A Social and Economic History of Horse Racing* (London: Penguin, 1976), 131.
7. Ibid., 130.
8. Huggins, *Flat Racing*, 121.
9. Vamplew, *The Turf*, 140.
10. Paul Roberts and Isabelle Taylor, *Racecourse Architecture* (New York: Acanthus Press, 2013), 26.
11. Ibid., 38–39.
12. David G. Schwartz, *Roll the Bones: The History of Gambling* (New York: Gotham Books, 2006), 180.
13. Huggins, *Flat Racing*, 12.
14. Ibid., 80, 101–106.
15. Carole Case, *Down the Backstretch: Racing and the American Dream* (Philadelphia: Temple University Press, 1991), 43.
16. Ibid., 44.
17. Ryan Conley, "Hickey: Good, Bad in Horse-Related Bills," *The Blood-Horse* (May 2, 2008), accessed April 19, 2018 from www.bloodhorse.com/horse-racing/articles/44979/hickey-good-bad-in-horse-related-bills.
18. David G. Schwartz, *Cutting the Wire: Gaming Prohibition and the Internet* (Reno: University of Nevada Press, 2005), 27.
19. I have seen and read of NBC executives make the argument that coverage of fashion, parties, and celebrities brings women to horse racing coverage, including at a racing industry symposium at which I was also speaking. Many women involved in the racing industry and/or who cover it dispute the claim and find the approach patronizing. NBC's lifestyle-and-feature-oriented coverage is routinely mocked by women and men who follow horse racing.
20. I have attended a few Kentucky Derby parties. At a 2018 Derby party held by a friend who competes in equestrian sports but is not involved in horse racing and who does not follow racing, none of the attendees had a deep knowledge of racing. Most were "horse people" who owned and rode horses, and they all watched the race. Most were women. Except for the hostess, few of the horse people dressed up. The two women at the party who wore the fanciest hats and dresses did not own horses or ride them, and they didn't come into the living room to watch the race with the rest of us. A few years earlier, the hostess of this party scheduled her wedding for the first Saturday in May—the day of the Kentucky Derby—and had a Derby-themed wedding. Many, if not most, of the female guests wore hats or fascinators (including me), and at the wedding reception guests watched the Derby on a large screen. Some members of the wedding party were concerned that many of the guests wouldn't know much about the race, so I was drafted to give a brief talk about the history of the Kentucky Derby. In addition to discussing the history of the race, including why and when the interest in fashion became a feature, I also talked about the main contenders.
21. Quoted in Corey Kilgannon, "If OTB Goes, so Would a Relic of a Grittier City," *New York Times* (February 22, 2008), accessed April 18, 2018, www.nytimes.com/2008/02/22/nyregion/22otb.html.

22 Roberts and Taylor, *Racecourse Architecture*, 137.
23 Don Muret, "Texas' Lone Star Park horse racing facility charges to front …" *Amusement Business* 109, no. 52 (1997): 12–12.
24 In Tulsa, Oklahoma I live within a 15-minute drive of three large casinos: the Hard Rock Hotel and Casino, operated by the Cherokee Nation; the River Spirit Casino Resort, operated by the Muscogee (Creek) Nation; and the Osage Casino, operated by the Osage Nation.
25 Holly Kruse, *Off-track and Online: The Networked Spaces of Horse Racing* (Cambridge, MA: The MIT Press, 2016), 122–123.
26 Chris Matthews and Amanda Zamora, "Timeline: Internet Poker and the Law," *Washington Post* (December 1, 2008), accessed April 19, 2018. www.washingtonpost.com/wp-srv/investigations/poker/time.html?sid=ST2008112902159&s_pos=list.
27 Gilbert M. Gaul, "Confusion Surrounds Legal Status of Online Bets and Firms That Handle Them," *Washington Post* (December 1, 2008), accessed April 19, 2018, www.washingtonpost.com/wp-dyn/content/article/2008/11/30/AR2008113002006.html.
28 Gilbert M. Gaul, "Cheating Scandals Raise New Questions about Honesty, Security of Internet Gambling," *Washington Post* (November 30, 2008), accessed April 19, 2018, www.washingtonpost.com/wp-dyn/content/article/2008/11/29/AR2008112901679.html.
29 Matthews and Zamora, "Timeline: Internet Poker".
30 Gaul, "Cheating Scandals".
31 Virginia Heffernan, "Flop," *New York Times* (March 6, 2009), accessed March 9, 2009, www.nytimes.com/2009/03/08/magazine/08wwln-medium-t.html?_r=2.
32 Gaul, "Cheating Scandals".
33 Ibid.
34 Patricia Hurtado and Beth Jinks, "Online Poker Customer Accounts Frozen as U.S. Indicts Operators," *Bloomberg* (April 19, 2011), accessed April 19, 2018, www.bloomberg.com/news/2011-04-18/online-poker-player-accounts-frozen-amid-fbi-gambling-probe.html.
35 Schwartz, *Roll the Bones*, 142.
36 Lynn Spigel, *Make Room for TV: Television and the Family Ideal in Postwar America* (Chicago: The University of Chicago Press, 1992); Ruth S. Cowan, *More Work for Mother* (New York: Basic Books, 1983).
37 Daphne Spain, *Gendered Spaces* (Chapel Hill: University of North Carolina Press, 1992), 113–117.
38 Ibid., 124.
39 Ibid., 123.
40 William Boddy, *New Media and the Popular Imagination* (New York: Oxford University Press, 2004), 14.
41 Holly Kruse, "Early Audio Technology and Domestic Space," *Stanford Humanities Review* 3, no. 2 (1993): 1–14.
42 Gaul, "Cheating Scandals".
43 Juniper Research, "Global Online Gambling Wagers to Approach $1 Trillion by 2021," *Juniper Research*, accessed April 18, 2018, www.juniperresearch.com/press/press-releases/global-online-gambling-wagers-to-approach-$1-trill.
44 Alice E. Marwick, "To Catch a Predator? The MySpace Moral Panic," *First Monday* 13, no. 6 (2008), accessed http://firstmonday.org/htbin/cgiwrap/bin/ojs/index.php/fm/article/view/2152/1966.
45 Stanley Cohen, *Folk Devils and Moral Panics* (New York: St. Martin's, 1972).
46 Ibid., 65–66.
47 Ibid., 204.
48 Marwick, "To Catch," para 40.
49 Ibid.
50 Christine Lehmann, "Internet Gambling Alarms Addiction Experts, Government," *Psychiatric News* (August 2, 2002), accessed April 19, 2018, https://psychnews.psychiatryonline.org/doi/full/10.1176/pn.37.15.0004.
51 Ibid.
52 "Student Says He Was Driven to Crime by Gambling Addiction," *ABC News* (July 25, 2006), accessed April 20, 2018, http://abcnews.go.com/GMA/LegalCenter/story?id=2232427&page=1.
53 Ibid.
54 Vincent Gesuele, "College Students Struggle with Gambling Addiction," *The State Hornet* (October 5, 2005), accessed July 19, 2014, www.statehornet.com/college-students-struggle-with-gambling-addictions/article_f6975b47-096a-5911-b343-74fd7469534f.html.
55 Ibid.
56 John W. Welte, Grace Barnes, Marie-Cecile O. Tidwell, and Joseph Hoffman, "The Prevalence of Problem Gambling Among U.S. Adolescents and Young Adults: Results from a National Survey," *Journal of Gambling Studies* 24, no. 2 (2008): 131.

57 Catherine Donaldson-Evans, "Junior Jackpot: Teen Gambling on the Rise," *Fox News* (May 17, 2006), accessed April 19, 2018, www.foxnews.com/story/2006/05/17/junior-jackpot-teen-gambling-on-rise.html.
58 Ibid.
59 Ibid.
60 Columbia University Medical Center Gambling Disorders Clinic, "Teen Gambling" (December 19, 2006), Accessed July 8, 2014. www.cumc.columbia.edu/dept/gambling/teen.html.
61 Spigel, *Make Room*.

8

"KEEP IT CLASSY"

Grindr, Facebook and Enclaves of Queer Privilege in India

Rohit K. Dasgupta

This chapter[1] is based on five years of ethnography (between 2011 and 2016) conducted with queer men mostly in West Bengal and New Delhi.[2] The popularity of mobile applications such as Grindr/Planet Romeo and queer groups being set up on Facebook have opened up new spaces for interaction, socializing and romantic intimacy for queer men in India. However, I argue that these spaces, far from removing barriers of class, race, and gender, create new barriers, thus catering to a 'classed' community of users. Economic and social inequalities remain embedded within the communication, creating enclaves of privilege which puts several queer men "out of place."[3] Class location and identification are significant in India and, as Henderson puts it, is the prism through which often painful, sometimes shameful, experiences and feelings are pressed into recognition.[4]

Mary Chayko argues that it is common for time spent online to have an intimate and emotionally rich dynamic.[5] Intimacies and forging of intimate connections are common in digital settings. Even the most fleeting of relationships online can be quite intimate. Digital texts can be saturated with intimacy. As Adi Kuntsman notes, there is an increasing need to think about feelings, technologies and politics together and through each other.[6]

This chapter will critique the invisibility of class and look at the role social media plays in perpetuating class-based bias within queer digital spaces in India. I use three ethnographic vignettes from my research to explore how class and caste based discrimination operates and exists within queer media spaces in India. The three vignettes come from different time periods of my ethnography but share common themes around class- and caste-based exclusion from digital queer spaces.

Keep the Riff-Raffs Away

Between 2011 and 2013 I was traveling frequently between New Delhi, West Bengal and London to carry out fieldwork on queer men's digital culture in India. Grindr, a geosocial networking mobile application geared mostly towards gay men, had been launched in the United Kingdom a few years earlier. Using geolocation it allowed users to locate other gay men nearby for friendship as well as "hook ups." Initially launched only on iTunes it catered to a small group of people who could afford iPhones. Over time it rolled to other smartphones, thus creating a larger pool of users. Various authors[7] have written about how social media has been helping the LGBTQ community find love and acceptance against the backdrop of section 377, an archaic law that criminalized homosexuality until as recently as 2018. Whilst this utopic view is definitely true within some quarters of the queer male community it also continues to create new spaces of exclusion and difference.

I met Haider[8] during my field work in 2013 in New Delhi. Haider was 26, an English teacher, liked to party and was in the process of moving to Europe with his new partner. Haider lived in Hauz Khas Village, a popular trendy destination for middle-class professionals. He was fluent in English and we had met quite by chance on Grindr during one of my Delhi visits. Haider's profile was pretty interesting. It said:

> Classy Men this way. Into Gym, Films and nice lads along the way. With Place. For the few.

I made the first conversation with a polite hello and small chitchat. In the beginning, Haider did not seem to be too interested in talking to me, especially when he heard I was a researcher. However, when he found out I was from London and we discovered a few friends in common, Haider became more interested. We started talking about friends, gay culture in the UK and the party scene. Very soon, Haider was interested in meeting up for a cup of coffee. We met the next day in a café in Hauz Khas Village which Haider described as "full of wannabes but sexy waiters."

Haider was waiting for me when I arrived. In his Levis jeans, Benneton T-shirt and Ray Ban sunglasses, there was no doubt he was conscious of fashion trends but also most probably had a good income/economic background. Haider was pleasant. We started talking a little more about him and then my research. I was quite interested as he was one of the few Indians who was using Grindr in that locality. Most of the other people were either white expatriates or lived almost a city away. This is of course a far cry from today when almost all the Indian cities have sizeable number of Grindr users brought about with the increase in smartphone uptake and cheaper data tariffs.[9]

When I asked Haider about him using Grindr over PlanetRomeo which was a much more popular gay social networking site he smiled at me and said that he definitely found Grindr much more preferable as it acted as a filter which "keeps the riff-raffs away." I was quite intrigued by this and he explained that given the cost of buying a smartphone it catered to only a certain "class" of consumers, who Haider described as classy.

As his own profile text explained he was only looking for classy men. His declaration of having a place is also important. Given the lack of social spaces for queer men and most adults still continuing to live with their families, having a place gestures towards a level of economic privilege as well as privacy from the surveillance of parents and relatives. Thus, having a 'place' works as a social capital within the gay dating world of New Delhi and most other cities of India. Social capital, Bourdieu and Wacquant argue is "the sum of the resources, actual or virtual, that accrue to an individual or a group by virtue of possessing a durable network of more or less institutionalized relationships of mutual acquaintance and recognition."[10]

Social capital in the gay dating world of New Delhi, as Haider explained, comes in many forms—speaking English, dressing up in high-street labels, possessing smartphones and, of course, having an independent place. Haider belonged to a group of professional gay men who have moved to New Delhi over the last few years in search of better jobs and opportunities. Given the anonymity afforded to large cities, it was easier for Haider to be open about his sexuality and also create privileged enclaves of gay belonging. Critiquing the nature of queer subjectivity and queerness, Chatterjee notes that the politics of queerness determines what falls within the field of queer politics and outside it, and differentiates between who comes to be seen as a queer subject at the cost of erasing others. Chatterjee is quite right in pointing out the limits of queer subjectivity.[11] With the growth of debates around sexual citizenship, which uses a rights-based assimilationist agenda that represents all queer men as oppressed minorities seeking access to marriage, family and the military (as in the case of the USA), what we see is a rise of neoliberal politics of normalization which privileges the 'good gays' from the 'bad gays.'

In the context of India, as academics such as Paul Boyce, Ila Nagar have argued, there exists an erasure of trans bodies and voices. With most kothis and jananas[12] coming from economically backward and unprivileged backgrounds, there exists little to no acknowledgement and recognition of the power differentials that exist between certain queer groups over others.

In fact, as Haider went on to explain, he did not like kothis at all. Not only were they undesirable given their gender attributes but also most of them were "low class scum who cannot speak English and are only trying to cheat the rich." Haider described himself as a "closet activist." I found this quite interesting and pressed him further to explain what he meant. Haider said that he was not a "jhande baaz [flag carrying] activist" but he believed gay men and women should be allowed to live "normal respectable lives." As he explained:

> I live on my own and earn a pretty decent salary. Do you know, quite a bit more than some of the other migrants who have moved here from Pune. I contribute a lot in taxes and am not a burden on the State like some of these hijras. The day this country understands the power of the pink rupee they will give us equal rights.

Haider is self-aware of his privilege and is also aware that many gay men like him have that economic privilege. He is actually differentiating his own queerness from that of others who he feels are not deserving of the same rights as him because they "don't contribute" as much as he does. Class and sexuality are intimately connected. It would be useful to cite Sherry Ortner's "class project" in this case.[13] Despite the recognition of class as historical it is also connected to cultural representation, which is recognizable in everyday cultural practices calibrated to economic and institutional hierarchy. Lisa Henderson argues that queer class distinction is visible through four gestures:

> (1) good queers (protagonists, familiars) are moved from the class margins to the class middle, where practices of bodily control are maximized; (2) bad queerness and powerlessness are represented as class marginality and are signified by performative excess and failures of physical control; (3) wealth becomes the expression of fabulousness, in a limited version of the good life legitimately achieved; and (4) class is displaced onto family and familialism as the locus of normalcy and civic viability.[14]

Haider's narrative is indicative of the nature of assimilationist politics within queer subjectivity which renders some more worthy of rights than others. Class marginality is expressed by those who do not have the technological affordance to be a part of the fast changing digitally connected India where social media and mobile applications have become central to socialization and being part of a "queer community" which is meditated through technological and social differences.

Sexual Threads of Caste

One area of queer studies that has received little critical attention in recent years is the role of caste and its connection to sexuality and class. Patil notes that the sexuality of dalit women is regulated by the constraints on their social mobility devised by hegemonic, non-dalit men and women.[15] Given the vitriolic caste oppression faced by Dalits even today in contemporary India it is no surprise that queer Dalits continue facing erasure from the larger queer movement in India. Whilst 2015 saw the Chennai Pride Walk stating the queer movement's solidarity with the anti-caste movement; intersectional class/caste-based struggles remain marginal when it comes to media representations. Rachel Dwyer argues that even within Bollywood, the largest film industry in the world, there is no major dalit star.[16] Caste purity is effectively related to class given the ways in which capital has moved exclusively within the higher castes, with major jobs still held by those belonging to people in higher castes.

The year 2015 saw the entrenchment of caste discrimination within queer liberal politics when a now famous matrimonial advertisement was placed in a popular daily by the mother of queer activist Harrish Iyer. The advert read:

> Seeking, 25–40, well placed, animal-loving, vegetarian groom for my SON (36. 5 11) who works with an NGO. Caste no bar (Though Iyer Preferred)

There is much to be gleaned by this small advertisement. Iyer claimed that three major newspapers refused to carry the advertisement because it was "illegal" (on the basis of pertaining to a same-sex relationship). While several newspapers and media outlets both in India and the West have celebrated this advertisement as a significant and provocative exemplar in queer rights actions (one signified through hetero-normative marriage), on closer inspection the advertisement reveals some of the complex ways in which queerness and social identity are reflected in contemporary India. The advert openly seeks a "well placed" (read upper class) and "Iyer preferred" (read upper caste) groom, for sanctioned matrimony at a time when the State criminalized consensual non-heteronormative sex under the guise of Section 377. Caste preference far from subverts tradition. The Iyer caste are Brahmins at the very top of the caste hierarchy. The imagined queer (homonormative) utopia then in this case might be read as building on the endurance of class and caste discrimination. Queer activists had heated debates on social media regarding this advertisement and came from both sides of the debate. While some were supportive of the gesture, others were quick to admonish it.[17]

I would like to take a nuanced view on this. The politics of coming out is not easy in a socially conservative society as India. Whilst caste, class and religious dimensions do make a difference, overall, under the aegis of section 377, discrimination and harassment have been rife for most queer people. However, it is also true as we discussed earlier, some queers are more discriminated than others, be it because of their class, caste or even religion. In the case of Iyer, what we see is how the trappings of heterosexual privilege through economic power (class) and caste are also practiced within queer communities.

Desirable subjects within queer social media are also constructed through some of these trappings. Andy (pseudonym) is 26 years old. I came across his Grindr profile in 2016. In his profile text he describes the kind of guys that he desires and wants to socialize and "hook up" with. There are various cues in his profile that signal his class trappings. From the fact he mentions himself to be sophisticated with an interest in art and culture to wanting to meet "decent and civil" men. Shaka McGlotten calls this construction of profiles as "image labour." He argues:

> Men work hard to produce and manage their Grindr avatars … the profile creation process is laden with affective demands and effects…. The labor that goes into one's profile or being online isn't simply about creating a profile and then waiting to see what happens, or getting online, chatting with someone, and meeting. Rather, it enters one into a marketplace of desire, of sexual value and existing hierarchies.[18]

Andy's profile invites our gaze on to his headless but gym-toned torso, inviting interaction and interpretation. One of the other things clearly visible in Andy's profile is his "sacred thread." The thread that is presented to Brahmin men at their *upanayan*, which is an elaborate process signaling the child's entry to formal education, also distinguishes the man as belonging to the highest caste in India (see Figure 8.1).

I realized Andy was quite close by and started chatting to him. Like all other 'good' ethnographers, I made it very clear on my profile that I was only looking to chat and not any 'fun'—fun of course being the code word for having sex. Of course, that did not stop me from having a smiling wink at the bottom of my profile text to signal a bit of ambiguity, if only to get more people to

Figure 8.1 View of his "sacred thread" in Andy's profile distinguishes the man as belonging to the highest caste in India.

come and chat to me. Andy's profile intrigued me, not just the fact that he was only 15 minutes away but specifically I was interested in knowing more about the decision-making that he had invested in making his profile the way he had. Overall, the prospect of going out for coffee with a complete stranger after only a day in Kolkata and finding about the queer scene was high on my list. Andy invited me to meet him at Roxy, a swanky five-star club in the middle of the city, almost an hour away from my home. I had been there a few times when I lived in Kolkata but wasn't sure if it was a conducive environment to chat to someone, but Andy was insistent and even offered to have his driver pick me up on the way. I finally relented. Andy was waiting for me in the car and at once went into a long introduction about himself and how he was finally happy to have met me. He said the fact that I lived in London was what clicked the deal. The joys of social capital that living in London brought me aside, I was by now getting slightly irritated with him. His constant reference to his work and his love for wine was more than what I had signed myself up for. The club itself was pleasant. Andy knew the bouncer and got us entry. As he walked in a group of his friends came to greet us and showed us to an area that they had comfortably settled in. As his friends went to get the drinks, Andy stretched out his legs and started asking me about myself, what I did, a little bit about the project and of course the obligatory question of which school I went to (to determine my social class). Over the course of time I actually started to enjoy my time with his friends who all seemed very chatty and very unhappy about the 2014 Supreme Court judgment recriminalizing homosexuality.

I told Andy that I was intrigued by his profile especially the fact that he had his thread on his profile picture. I asked him if this was deliberate. Andy did not disappoint. He mentioned that he was very proud of his *poite* (the Bengali word for scared thread)—"Why should we not be proud of our heritage"—but also it was seen as being quite erotic to some who enjoyed having sex with the thread on. Whilst telling me this he started showing me some of the messages he had received on Grindr. Over the course of that month I met Andy a couple of more times. Given our backgrounds—we both went to private Christian missionary schools and had a few acquaintances in common—I became a regular person who he started including in his social life. My own class privilege and caste identity played a role in this acceptance. For Andy I was recognized as "one of them." In fact, Henderson[19] has noted that "class recognition is not an immediate distributive remedy but filtering class subjectivity and subjection out of the domain of recognition, including queer recognition, makes the harm and privilege of class hierarchy inarticulate."

Our discussion on caste remained quite elusive. It was not something that he mentioned much during our meetings over the month. Whilst he was proud of his heritage he did not seem to understand or recognize his caste privilege. He mentioned his hard-working family a couple of times. I asked him, given his sacred thread was fetishized by some on Grindr, did it bother him that this adulation for his caste could be problematic? His response now was a bit more interesting.

> I am not sure what you are on about, If someone likes me for my caste or class background that is not my problem. At the end of the day we do stick to people like us don't we?

In many ways Andy was right. We do stick to our own and, in fact, however much solidarity we might profess with those from minoritarian identities, dismantling supremacism requires more than just critiquing those practices. As an ethnographer I chose to remain muted in my criticism of Andy's caste privilege, if only to gain entry into his world for my research. This was my own complicity with that hierarchy.

Speak Proper English

In this case study I move away from Grindr to a popular mainstream social networking platform—Facebook. I will briefly discuss a particular closed group (whose name I am lightly disguising) called Pink Kolkata Party. Pink Kolkata Party was started by a Kolkata based fashion designer and a social activist. Its description reads:

> A need to find a regular place to socialize during weekends for the LGBT community in Kolkata has led to the formation of this group....
> Regular updates about Events will be put up here....
> Please spread the word and invite people in to make this network grow continuously.... Lets reach out to the rest of our diverse communities and friends and allies....

In July 2011, there was a big controversy on the page when a regular pink party which was organized by the administrators in a five-star venue was called out for discriminatory practice. Several members complained that they had been screened by the club bouncers and, given what clothes they were wearing, they were denied entry into the venue. Whilst some members argued that the club authority might not have known about the queer party and was being homophobic, on closer inspection it showed that it was only a handful of members, especially those who were trans identified or came from a lower socioeconomic background who were denied entry. The administrator put up a post asking for people to tell them about their experience and it would be taken up with the club authorities. The post received multiple responses. What was interesting however is to see how several people came in to defend the club's position.

One particular posting was made by Jash (see Figure 8.2).

There are various ways in which Jash's statement can be read. Jash does not recognize or see himself as one of the members who were being deprived entry. As such, his swift gesture, to resist any kind of discussion on the issue, registers the difficulties that subaltern queer voices face from

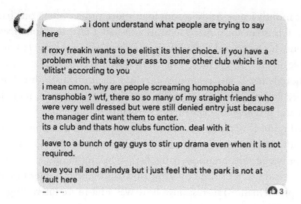

Figure 8.2 Jash's post defends the club accused of discrimination.

within and outside the community. Jash's own queer elite position (which was evidenced by his Facebook profile)—the acceptable face of queer India and the club's own position in terms of class—signal the different forms of marginality working within this space. It was surprising that only two people who were denied entry actively discussed this on the thread. Most of the others were silent or did not participate in this dialogue. Drawing on the work of Spivak, as discussed, I would argue that the issue is not only the lack of an opportunity to speak and be heard, but also the discursive mechanisms such as Jash's comment, which through equating the club's policy as acceptable renders any oppositional statements (such as class-based bias) useless. The subaltern's voice, as Spivak has argued previously, is only mediated and represented but never fully replicated.[20]

Following the incident, I spoke to Subir who was one of the people denied entry to the club. Subir was humiliated when he was told he could not go in. He remembers the way in which he was looked at by the bouncer. He recalls:

> I felt like a complete piece of trash. My existence meant so little to them and I was very embarrassed that I was one of the people screened and denied entry.

Subir however did not present his story on the Facebook thread where people were being encouraged to share their stories of discrimination. As Subir explained to me, the group dynamics were very elitist. It is where "people speak proper English—do you think I really belong here?" Jin Haritaworn describes how, despite the visibility of queerness, liberal Europe has also seen a renewed increase in racism where migrants are seen as the new hateful bogeyman. In this case, queer migrants are seen as disposable to society. In current neoliberal times, certain bodies are marked as unwanted and not needed. Haritaworn further argues that certain queer bodies are rendered worthy of protection whilst others are marked for erasure.[21] Subir's experience of being in this group resonates with these concerns. Coming from a lower middle class family with little to no disposable income he was aware that his T-shirt, picked up from the roadside, could not compete with the designer labels needed to enter the club.

Subir laments how, belonging to the queer community, he has faced multiple levels of discrimination. Did having access to social media change any of that? He was quick to angrily respond:

> Facebook and PlanetRomeo are from the ingrezi [English] babus [boys]. Amra laker dhare ghuri [We cruise by the lakesides].

Despite the proliferation of early literature[22] around the utopic possibilities of social media in creating a classless/genderless society, what has happened is how these very identities become central to the ways in which social media spaces are experienced by different groups of people. For people like Subir, social media makes apparent even more the class differences that exist between him and other gay/queer men like Jash. Jash's inability to see class elitism puts off people like Subir from engaging in a space like Pink Kolkata Party.

Moving Forward

My attempt in this chapter was to critique class- and caste-based discrimination practices that exist within queer digital spaces in India. I have also argued that universalizing queer subjectivity is to erase narratives of queer people who come from different class backgrounds and whose experience remains vastly different from urban English speaking users. This universalizing and English enclave building is most apparent on gay social media spaces. As Judge explains, this also promotes the unrealistic promise of solidarity that queer identity politics cannot deliver.[23]

All three ethnographic vignettes in this chapter affirm that class and caste (in the case of India) remain extremely important in navigating queer spaces and the politics of who gets included and excluded in this space. Whilst it is true that digital queer spaces have indeed changed the landscape of queer intimacy and socializing with far reaching impact on sexual health outreach and activism, the effort remains incomplete. The public visibility of the queer community in India has grown exponentially in the last decade, with queer prides in almost all the major metropolises (Bangalore, New Delhi, Mumbai and Calcutta) and smaller cities such as Bhubaneswar and Madurai. This, however, should not be seen as some form of tacit endorsement/acceptance. We must also remember that queer struggles in India are far from being intersectional. Issues such as class and caste are especially compelling within the 'Indian context'. As Arvind Narrain and Gautam Bhan remarked in their landmark anthology *Because I Have a Voice*:

> Perhaps the most relentless construct which assaults queer people is the conceptualisation of their lives as the preoccupations of a small, Western educated, and elite minority, whose understanding of sexuality is thus aped from the West.[24]

The various examples of queer digital cultures that my research explored are the responses from the community. Whether they are queering mainstream spaces (through active presence and participation) like Facebook, establishing user profiles on PlanetRomeo, accessing Grindr from their family room, or using these spaces to mobilize people for protests—they are taking part in the process of visibility and representational politics. But before the celebrations can begin in earnest, the fight for intersectional rights remains far from over. It is perhaps fitting given the latest Supreme Court decision in 2018, which has now read down Section 377, that the fight for equal rights goes beyond marriage, children and the right to own property. It is only when all discriminatory practices are eradicated that queer politics can emerge from neoliberalism again.

Notes

1 A version of this chapter was presented as a keynote at the Queer Youth and Media Cultures Symposium at Bournemouth University, UK. I am grateful to Dr Chris Pullen who organized it, and to other presenters for their useful feedback on that version. This chapter has further benefited from the feedback of reviewers and editors for this volume.
2 Rohit K. Dasgupta, *Digital Queer Cultures in India: Politics, Intimacies and Belonging* (London: Routledge, 2017).
3 Adi Kuntsman and Esperanza Miyake, "Introduction" in *Out of Place: Interrogating Silences in Queerness/Raciality*, eds. A. Kuntsman and E. Miyake (New York: Raw Nerve Books, 2008), 7.
4 Lisa Henderson, *Love and Money: Queers, Class and Cultural Production* (New York: New York University Press, 2013).
5 Mary Chayko, *Superconnected: The Internet, Digital Media and Techno Social Life* (New Delhi: Sage, 2017).

6 Adi Kuntsman, "Introduction: Affective Fabrics of Digital Culture," in *Digital Cultures and the Politics of Emotions*, eds. A. Karatzogianni and A. Kuntsman (Basingstoke: Palgrave Macmillan), 1–19.
7 For example see, Rohit K. Dasgupta, *Digital Queer Cultures in India: Politics, Intimacies and Belonging* (London: Routledge, 2017); Rohit K. Dasgupta and Debanuj Dasgupta, ed., *Queering Digital India* (Edinburgh: Edinburgh University Press, 2018); Rohit K. Dasgupta and Kaustav Bakshi, *Queer Studies: Texts, Contexts, Praxis* (Hyderabad: Orient Blackswan, 2019); Parmesh Shahani (New Delhi: Sage, 2008); Rahul Mitra and Radhika Gajjala, "Queer Blogging in Indian Digital Diasporas: A Dialogic Encounter" *Journal of Communication Enquiry* 32, no. 4 (2008): 400–423.
8 All names used are pseudonyms to protect the anonymity of my respondents. Ethical clearance for the research was provided in 2011.
9 Rohit K. Dasgupta and Pawan Dhall, *Social Media, Sexuality and Sexual Health Advocacy in Kolkata, India* (New Delhi: Bloomsbury, 2017).
10 See Pierre Bourdieu and J.D. Loic Wacquant, *An Invitation to Reflexive Sociology* (Chicago: University of Chicago Press, 1992).
11 Shraddha Chatterjee, *Queer Politics in India; Towards Sexual Subaltern Subjects* (London: Routledge, 2018), 2.
12 Kothis and Jananas are usually biological men who display effeminacy. They are usually underprivileged and enact passive sexual roles. Researchers such as Paul Boyce have however rightly pointed out there is no cultural coherence of the category. Whilst kothi as a term is used more frequently in West Bengal, Jananas are more widely used in places such as Lucknow. See Ila Nagar, "Digitally Untouched, Janana Invisibility and the Digital Divide," in *Queering Digital India*, eds., R.K. Dasgupta and D. Dasgupta (Edinburgh: Edinburgh University Press), 97; Paul Boyce, "Moral Ambivalence and Irregular Practices: Contextualising Male to Male Sexualities in Calcutta/India", *Feminist Review* 83 (2007): 79–98.
13 Sherry B. Ortner, *New Jersey Dreaming: Capital, Culture, and the Class of '58* (Durham, NC: Duke University Press, 2003).
14 Henderson, *Love and Money*, 34.
15 Smita Patil, "Reading, Caste, Gender and Sexuality in Dalit Writings", *Intersections* 34. Available at: http://intersections.anu.edu.au/issue34/patil.htm.
16 Rachel Dwyer, *Bollywood's India: Hindi Cinema as a Guide to Contemporary India* (London: Reaktion Books, 2013).
17 Rohit K. Dasgupta and Paul Boyce, "Utopia or Elsewhere: Queer Modernities in Small Town West Bengal," in Urban Utopias, eds. M. Varghese and T. Kuldova (London: Palgrave Macmillan, 2017), 220.
18 Shaka McGlotten, *Virtual Intimacies: Media, Affect and Queer Sociality* (Albany: SUNY Press, 2013), 127.
19 Henderson, *Love and Money*, 100.
20 Gayatri Chakravarti Spivak, "Can the Subaltern Speak," in *Marxism and the Interpretation of Culture*, eds., C. Nelson and L. Grossberg (Urbana, IL: Illinois University Press, 1988), 271–313.
21 Jin Haritaworn, *Queer Lovers and Hateful Others* (London: Pluto, 2015).
22 Howard Rheingold. *The Virtual Community: Homesteading on the Electronic Frontier* (Reading, MA: Addison-Wesley Publishing Company, 1993).
23 Melanie Judge, *Blackwashing Homophobia: Violence and the Politics of Sexuality, Gender and Race* (London: Routledge, 2018).
24 Gautam Bhan and Arvind Narrain, "Introduction," in *Because I have a Voice*, eds., G. Bhan and A. Narrain (New Delhi: Yoda Press, 2005), 15.

9

YOUTUBE-BASED PROGRAMMING AND SAUDI YOUTH

Constructing a New Online Class and Monetizing Strategies

Omar Daoudi

The massive changes in media technology have become extremely prominent to the extent that they have been integrated into the daily practices of individuals, communities and even society as a whole. The affordability and reach of media technology have facilitated this influential change, and have also introduced a new culture and norms that may shape the social hierarchy and power relationships within certain settings or communities.[1] For instance, Turner conceptualizes the public visibility attained by ordinary people through digital platforms as the "demotic turn,"[2] which can be attributed to several factors, including the interactivity of web 2.0 and the pervasiveness of celebrity culture. The public visibility of ordinary citizens, Turner argues, creates a new research domain that examines the new relationship between media and culture. As a result, this may lead to the formation of a new social class that has not previously existed, creating economic, cultural and social capital for certain new class members.

Drawing particularly on the original findings of a funded PhD project by the Centre for Cultural Policy Research (CCPR) at the University of Glasgow, which explores the economic, political and cultural context of YouTube-based programming in Saudi Arabia between 2010 and 2016, this chapter briefly and critically examines how Saudi youth have monetized their labor through the creation of YouTube-based programming. It seeks to foreground the economic context of YouTube-based programming in Saudi Arabia to understand its role in the social change for Saudi content creators.

By adopting grounded theory methodology,[3] the analysis presented in this chapter is drawn from ten semi-structured online interviews with influential young Saudi content creators at a range of leading YouTube-based programs and channels including *Uturn Entertainment, Myrkott Production, SceenTV, TakkieSeries* and the film *Monopoly*. The interviews were conducted in Arabic, transcribed in Arabic text and then translated into English. The chapter explores the formation of Saudi YouTube celebrities and how they capitalize on their roles to reap financial rewards by taking into account the economics and political sensitivity of the Saudi context.

For the sake of clarity, the discussion begins by defining the research problem in order to help the reader to understand the application of terms throughout the analysis, before highlighting the significance of this contribution to media studies. Second, it briefly contextualizes the social, cultural and economics contexts of Saudi Arabia in order to provide a clear background for the research problem. After that, it explores the formation and development of YouTube-based programming by conceptualizing it into three main business phases—*Abstract*, *Concrete* and *Innovative*—in which the Saudi YouTube laborers have interacted and reacted differently to capitalize on their fame and popularity. Finally, the chapter concludes by pulling together the main findings and illustrating how these social, cultural and economic intersections produce new understandings of social dynamics and power relationships within the Saudi digital sphere.

YouTube-based Programming and Class

Media critics such as Van Dijk,[4] Sandoval,[5] Meikle,[6] Fuchs,[7] and Burgess and Green[8] have voiced concerns over particular issues in relation to corporate social media platforms, including the commodification of data and culture, privacy, economic surveillance and digital labor. Others, such as Lang[9] and Strangelove,[10] however, positively perceive online platforms including YouTube, in that they break the traditional monopoly of information systems, creating new communities, constructing identities, and facilitating cultural participation.

Keeping this complexity in mind, the focus of the chapter is on what Kim conceptualizes as professionally generated content (PGC) on YouTube.[11] The analysis focuses on the bottom-up professionally generated content created exclusively for YouTube, as a publishing platform, between 2010 and 2016 by Saudi content creators, who were 'ordinary' people before launching careers through YouTube productions that garnered millions of views, subscribers and followers online.[12] YouTube-based programming in Saudi Arabia is defined as "the process of constructing and organizing new critical interpretations of Saudi public discourse, reflecting the thoughts of ordinary Saudi youth in the form of localized [professional] video products."[13] The Saudi creators treat YouTube as a broadcasting platform, similar to television, with production roles including directors, actors, presenters and editors to overcome the traditional media restrictions in Saudi Arabia and to give voice to their aspirations. YouTube-based programming tends to be different from that of traditional media outlets in terms of the tone of coverage, format, language, and aesthetics.

Importantly, there are three dimensions with which this chapter is not concerned. First, it avoids investigating top-down professionally generated content that is produced, for instance, by Saudi media outlets that treat YouTube as a secondary publishing window. Second, it eschews investigating bottom-up user generated content (UGC) such as, for example, personal video blogs or family diaries. Finally, it does not focus on the income generated through the partnership agreements between the platforms and creators, but rather on the strategies developed externally by Saudi creators to capitalize on their fame and to generate income for themselves.

As for class, by drawing on Bourdieu's scholarship in which he theorizes the forms of capital,[14] highlighting specifically the significance of the cultural capital concept for contemporary society, the work of Savage et al.[15] adopts Bourdieu's approach and argues that social classes are formed out of three distinctive circles of capital. The first is economic capital, which refers to wealth and income. The second is cultural capital, which is concerned with tastes, activities and interests. Finally, social capital indicates one's social network, friendships and associations. This conceptualization is extremely significant because, when applied to content creators in Saudi Arabia, there is a correlation between their socioeconomic backgrounds and their publicity and visibility online. For instance, some of the content creators who have taken the lead in managing and producing content from 2010 onwards tend to be males in their mid-to-late 20s who speak English as a second language and a number of them have been educated in Western institutions. It is worth suggesting here that this particular social group has grown with the internal educational expansion in Saudi Arabia, with several public and private universities being available to the young population where almost 7.3 million out of 20 million Saudis are between 15–34 years old.[16]

More importantly, the liberal policy of late King Abdullah (2005–2015) who established the scholarship abroad program, which included women,[17] has exposed young people to various cultural, social and commercial settings and so it might have a role in initiating and probably imitating YouTube-based programming as well as taking advantage of the digital growth in Saudi Arabia.

Erik Wright argues that class formation can be understood as "the formation of collective actors organized around class interest within class structure".[18] By also applying Turner's concept of the demotic turn,[19] this chapter argues that the organized production activities of Saudi youth have led to the creation of a new online class of YouTube celebrity. It forms its own distinctive identity, behavior, social space and attempts later to pursue its commercial returns by capitalizing on its members' influence and popularity online. Bourdieu states that class construction can be characterized by agents who occupy similar positions in a social place and are subject to similar social conditions, which can result in the development of similar practices and the construction of practical groups.[20]

Based on this discussion and considering the restrictive public sphere in Saudi Arabia,[21] the organized production activities of the Saudi youth have formed a new online-celebrity class that is responsive to its cultural and political specificity, and which is commercially and culturally oriented, exchanging its online influence and prestige for online and offline rewards, for instance advancing their economic and social capital.

Contribution to the Study of Media

The significance of this contribution stems from its ability to produce a critical account of the economic context of YouTube-based programming in Saudi Arabia specifically, which, it would appear, no one has investigated before. Very few studies have attempted to examine the economics and the participatory aspect of YouTube itself, investigating the business model of the platform or the partnership agreements between YouTube and content creators.[22] Nevertheless, this study contributes to our understanding of how the platform is utilized and monetized by Saudi content creators without their directly engaging with YouTube. It investigates the youth perspective to understand how the platform can be employed in different settings.

The analysis also contributes to the development of international media theories and particularly to the Arab media field as it examines the global platform of YouTube in the local setting of Saudi Arabia.

Contextualizing Saudi Arabia

The total population of Saudi Arabia is 31.7 million including 11.6 million non-Saudi residents; and the Saudi female population is 9.8 million. Saudi Arabia is relatively young and almost 7.3 million Saudis are between 15 and 34 years old. The country is the largest exporter of petroleum, where the sector accounts for almost 87 percent of the budget revenue, and so Saudi Arabia became, in 2014, the 19th largest economy in the world.[23] However, the fall in international oil prices has had a negative impact on the economic activities. In response, a national project called 'Saudi Vision 2030' was proposed to build a sustainable economic system for the state in order to move gradually from an oil-based economy to a non-petroleum based economy through diversifying economic activities.[24] Nevertheless, its implementation invited controversy amongst the public because of, for example, the increasing privatization of the service sector and the hostile tone towards non-Saudis, where tough financial measures were placed upon non-Saudis, forcing a large number of foreign workers to leave the country.

The paradox of Saudi Arabia consists of various complex socioeconomic factors including traditional tribal culture, the oil, the challenge of modernization, the liberal economic approach, and the authoritarian model of governance. The political and cultural systems are labelled as closed, totalitarian, and intolerant of voices critical towards the Government and its policies.[25] The

Government is also sensitive towards researching and distributing information that may undermine its legitimacy in the eyes of the public; for example, the poverty in the country is in contrast to the private wealth of the members of the Royal Family. John Peterson maintains that the Saudi Royal Family has complete control of the public sphere, including the political and economic arenas.[26] Senior members of the Royal Family control the distribution of oil income, which enables them to abuse their public role and to enjoy greater privileges than ordinary citizens.

The political and religious sensitivity of the state has shaped the public spheres and has led to cultural struggles between liberals and conservatives over the public narrative and everyday life practices. The voice of the conservatives has been dominant, especially between the 1930s and the 2000s. However, the liberal voice has been empowered by certain political wings in the Royal Family, especially during the reign of the late King Abdullah (2005–2015) and the current King Salman (2015–present) when the country underwent major liberal developments, which displeased the traditional conservative class.

In terms of the media, the overall number of state-run media outlets is nine television stations and six public radio channels, all serving the interests of the Government, which made it unattractive for audiences.[27] Saudi Arabia, nevertheless, gave a fresh look to the national media network in 2010, including its own national children's television Ajyal, which translates as *generations*.[28] The focuses of the television channels vary from religion to news to sport to economics. The employees are employed by the state, which suggests the nature, culture and aims and outcomes of these media outlets. In addition, the political motivation of the Royal Family to influence the private Pan-Arab channels through proxy investors is evident.[29] The goal is to advance the state narrative and exclude critical voices by acquiring private Saudi and Pan-Arab channels. As a result, the state controls the public Saudi channels and the most prominent private Saudi and Pan-Arab channels to order to, then, control the hearts and the minds of the Saudi and Arabic public.

The Government's monopoly over the Saudi public sphere has resulted in the construction of a social class that adheres publicly to the traditions and norms of Saudi political-religious institutions, privileging those who are in line with the state policy, economically and socially, but also marginalizing and delegitimizing another segment that is critical to the official public policy. The voices of women and young citizens are absent from public discussion. However, the ubiquity of social media platforms, along with the political unrest that swept the Arab countries from 2010 onwards, has stimulated online and offline youth movements and provided them with new opportunities to construct new social positions for themselves.[30]

The Creation of Saudi YouTube-based Programming Celebrity

Empirical data show that there is a strong relationship between the tight offline restrictions on the public and the creation of YouTube celebrity in Saudi Arabia. However, this on its own was not enough to construct such a class without certain conditions that could nurture and advance the phenomenon, including the digital surge in the country and, more importantly, the local and regional political climate that reshuffled social and power relationships in the region. These factors resulted in empowering the youth and expanding the freedom margin, especially between 2011 and 2013, before the counter-revolutions sponsored by deeply Arab states restored their power and ensured the maintenance of the traditional status quo from 2013 onwards.

The tone of Saudi YouTube-based programming echoed its political context, offering highly critical political content between 2011 and 2013 before softening its tone and focusing on cultural and social matters as a result of the counter-revolutions. In both cases, the content creators offered the audience an alternative narrative that caught their attention and interest. Consequently, the creators gained authority and popularity in the Saudi digital public sphere, enabling them to construct a celebrity-like class with millions of followers and fans online, and also enjoying regional and international media attention. The background of this celebrity-like class consists mainly of young

Saudis who tend to be males in their mid to late twenties, educated, and employed in various sectors including the media. In addition, some of the participants were non-Saudi young people who were born and had lived in the country all their life, but had not been granted a Saudi nationality by the Saudi Government. It is extremely difficult to distinguish between Saudis and non-Saudis, who were born and have lived in Saudi Arabia, because they share the same culture, traditions, customs and even the same accent. However, non-Saudis are subject to a sponsorship system and they usually need to renew their residence permit annually, which makes them vulnerable to state control.

The tight restrictions on freedom of expression and freedom of assembly, along with the state- and privately-controlled media outlets in Saudi Arabia have left the vast majority of the young population unrepresented and unheard, with no access to public platforms available to them. This was a significant factor that pushed some content creators to explore new avenues to voice their concerns and aspirations. This is a very interesting phenomenon to observe because the analysis reveals that Saudi YouTube celebrity was not constructed initially out of commercial interests, but rather out of the social and cultural demands of ordinary young people in 2010. It took them some time to amass their digital prestige and fan-base before triggering new business-oriented thinking to monetize and capitalize on their digital labor.

A number of participants, interviewed in 2016, confirm that participating in public discussions and voicing their critiques were the main motivations for them to form the phenomenon of YouTube-based programming. For instance:

> [We] were doing the programme out of fashion and out of interest, and [we] were not driven by any financial motivations.
>
> One of the main incentives was that we [were] doing something that mattered to us. [Our] team used to work in [a private traditional] media [channel], and we were able to see certain opportunities [between 2009 and 2010]. However, due to the complexity and the politics of [our channel], we were unable to do anything.... [YouTube] programming offered us an opportunity to create things that we believed in.

This quote from one of the interviewees implies that having an interest and passion for certain public matters does not facilitate public participation for ordinary people in Saudi Arabia unless they are equipped with mechanisms to convey their thoughts within the public domain. The traditional media organization in which the respondent worked adhered to the general policy of Saudi media, which seemingly blocks any attempt to provide the youth with a relatively free public platform. The behavior of the media organization acted as a trigger to push young people away to form their own paths, utilizing YouTube as a public platform to engage with society.

The novelty of the practice along with the bravery of content creators who reported critical, previously unreported, stories all drew attention to YouTube as a publishing platform. In addition, this invited new producers to construct and collectively organize their own celebrity class by producing diverse and professional content that fulfilled the audience's needs. Consequently, original and diverse content was introduced to the emerging phenomenon, including animation-based series, drama series, satirical mockumentary films, talk-shows and factual programs, all of which deal with the social, cultural and political specificity of Saudi Arabia on YouTube.

YouTube-based programming flourished and developed drastically as its original and representative professionally generated content became popular amongst the audiences who moved to YouTube and other online platforms in searching for content that resonated with their expectations. This made Saudi Arabia the world's top per capita user of YouTube, according to Google,[31] which provided the content creators (for instance, the presenters and directors) with a social and cultural boost, making them online stars with influence.

Monetization of YouTube-based Programming

As discussed previously, Saudi YouTube celebrity was born out of the urge to participate in the public discourse; although some critics may argue that there was also a hope of celebrity when this phenomenon emerged, according to the interviewees' own accounts there was no financial motivation initially because they were unaware of that potential outcome at the time. However, the digital advancement and quality growth of YouTube-based programming reached the point later where it became economically viable for content creators to capitalize on their online stardom. Digital growth may play a role in introducing new players to the media industry and their cultural products can usually create employment opportunities and make a cultural impact on the targeted audience.[32]

The process of monetization has undergone various stages, each of which has different characteristics and features in terms of the strategies employed to secure financial rewards. The three business stages are conceptualized as follows: first, the *Abstract* stage (2010–2011); second, the *Concrete* stage (2012–2013); and finally, the *Innovative* stage (2014–2016). Saudi content creators have utilized a two-sided market practice[33] throughout the various stages to monetize their labors. They were keen to keep the audience interested in order to maintain a balance between their popular visibility and economic viability.

The Abstract Stage

This marks the first attempt of the content creators to monetize their visibility and publicity on YouTube as they had recently become aware of their economic viability. This phase reflects the period between 2010 and 2011, when the number of influential YouTube-based programs that attracted the vast majority of the audience ranged between three or four programs.

First, the rise of online stars is a significant aspect of the abstract stage, as the class of YouTube celebrity became recognizable amongst the online audience. One of the interviewees demonstrates that "the idea of stars in Saudi Arabia was exclusive to singers and to actors, but the idea of making stars of the presenters was very new because of that breakthrough in 2010." This, in fact, explains the new cultural and social norms introduced to the Saudi public sphere through the cultural products of content creators. This illustrates the emergence of a new class capable of defining its relationships with the audience and, more importantly, it gained a considerable amount of influence online because of the representative nature of the content.

The second main feature of this phase is that the monetization is based on experimenting with the revenue-making process because of the lack of experience and the novelty of the phenomenon. The content creators adopted a trial and error approach, experimenting with different strategies to develop the business side of their cultural products. One of the presenters describes the uncertainty the content creators faced during the monetization process: "[The business model] was not fully clear [for us at the beginning] and [we] were unaware of it in a professional way."

Although this may invite questions in relation to the role of state, civil society or the private sector in supporting digital business enterprises for Saudi youth, it highlights that self-reliance and copying similar practices in other countries can be considered to be an efficient strategy in developing financial mechanisms. Nevertheless, it indicates a particular form of capital struggle[34] for the youth over the cultural infrastructure that is controlled by the Saudi Government, in the search for symbolic power for the young content creators.

As a result, the content creators responded to the business model's challenges and developed a basic framework that enabled them to commodify their viewership. One of the interviewees explained this as follows:

> It is a very simple model that is based on viewership. We create content that is extremely relevant to audiences, which can generate a lot of views, and then [we] embed the

advertisements within the content only because we do not have control over the platform. Basically, we sell based on 1,000 views.

This establishes a basic framework to generate income out of the popular content by utilizing a traditional advertising-based model that targets the audience segment. There is, however, one essential dimension to observe in the above quote, which is the direct relationship between Saudi YouTube celebrities and brands—excluding YouTube as a platform from the monetizing process. This means that this business model could be not in line with the general policy of YouTube as they remove the platform from this process.

The third feature of this stage is the absence of engagement between YouTube as a platform and Saudi content creators and the Middle East region in general. This analysis echoes the tone of Saudi YouTube celebrities who argue that they initially created their own stardom and income, utilizing the platform without any partnerships or agreements being made with YouTube. For instance, a number of interviewees assert that "[YouTube] did not pay enough attention to the region [at the time] and it was underdeveloped" and that "[YouTube did not] monetize the Middle East for the first two years."

This neglected an attitude by the platform. YouTube has extended opportunities for content creators, enabling them to externally build their social and economic capital online, enhancing the monetization and the growth of the YouTube market in Saudi Arabia.

The Concrete Stage

The time framework for this stage is between 2012 and 2013, when the growth of YouTube-based programming became a global trend, with several Arabic and Western media outlets attempting to report on and understand the phenomenon.[35] This attention, along with the experience accumulated during the *Abstract* Stage, improved the conditions for the monetization of Saudi YouTube celebrities, pushing them to adopt various mechanisms to capitalize on their popularity.

The first feature of this stage is the transition from utilizing basic business models to employing a market-oriented strategy to maximize the financial value of their products. As discussed previously, the creators treated YouTube as a broadcasting channel, borrowing non-Saudi TV formats for Saudi YouTube-based programming. What emerges here is that they also employed television's methods in the revenue-generating process. For instance, sponsorship, product placement and branding content strategies all emerged at this stage, which represents a mature business attitude on the part of YouTube celebrities. The interviewees provide insights:

> The model of sponsorship is completely new, not only for us, but even for companies in Saudi Arabia … [For example,] the overall revenue we received in [our three] seasons from sponsorships was about [100–110 k GBP] and I assure you this is now attainable for just one season for a successful programme.

Another said,

> [YouTube celebrities] provide [brands] with product placement and branding content. Also, [they] provide ad samples in the introduction. These are the three forms we deal with.… We [developed significant] relationships with many [firms in the telecommunication sector].

These quotes reveal that the wide audience reach and the professionally generated content nature of the programs were considered high enough that big brands felt comfortable associating their products with YouTube-based programs, strengthening the relationships between the parties, developing the cash flow and the professionalism of YouTube celebrities in Saudi Arabia.

The second feature of the *Concrete* stage is the institutionalization of YouTube-based programming after going through a period of trial and error. The newly constructed market and class managed to overcome the logistical obstacles that had previously affected them; for instance, generating sufficient income and building a systematic approach to their production outputs. One of the factors that enhanced this institutionalization was the intervention of the investors whose capital supported the infrastructure of the productions; for example, establishing production houses dedicated to YouTube. This resulted in widening the scale of employment opportunities to include, for instance, marketing managers and administrative roles. Their presence also affected the structure of production because of the ability of investors to acquire or sponsor influential YouTube-based programming or stars. There is a strong empirical basis for suggesting that the intervention of the investors could play a role in shaping the editorial policy of YouTube stars and therefore utilizing economic influence to control the creators and limit their criticism of the state.

The final feature concerns the role of YouTube as a platform as a result of global trends and the boom of YouTube in Saudi Arabia. The massive surge in YouTube production and consumption drew the platform to the attention of the region, motivating corporations to start building relationships with Saudi content creators. In so doing, YouTube began regulating the MENA (Middle East and North African) region and intervening to monetize the market, imposing its policies and regulations upon the creators. The regulations seemingly limit the financial freedom of YouTube stars, creating new conditions for their businesses. For instance,

> [YouTube] forces us to use [our external ads] less ... YouTube accepts [advertisements] as long as the [they] are indirect. If you use explicit advertisements such as "this show is sponsored by" or have a break in the middle for ads, then YouTube will take the video down.

This challenged the financial prosperity created by the stars as the new regulations affected their external monetization and led to certain changes that will be explored in the third phase.

The Innovative Stage

This stage covers the period between 2014 and 2016. Saudi YouTube celebrities came to interact and behave differently following the intervention of the platform in the business of YouTube-based programming. The regulation of YouTube constrains some Saudi celebrities and limits their financial scope, which inspired some of them to think more broadly in terms of capitalizing on their fame. Various features are associated with this stage.

First, this stage marks the shift of some celebrities from being YouTube-based to becoming media-based enterprise celebrities who utilize other platforms to produce cultural products and generate income, getting away from YouTube's policy. Some of them consequently moved to private Saudi television, for example, to present TV programs or to act in televised drama series, enjoying wider publicity and so advancing their social and economic capital.

Others moved to develop their own media enterprises, capitalizing on their experience, relationships with the creative industry and stardom which marks the construction of media entrepreneurship[36] by YouTube celebrities in Saudi Arabia. Examples of the newly constructed businesses include media and marketing companies, premium content production houses and media business developers, all of which have been set up by YouTube celebrities. For instance, one of the interviewees who established a media production firm states that:

> I [established my own company to] focus on [producing] premium content ... to invest in storytelling; to produce content that we can export globally. [YouTube-based programming] produce[s] freemium content that is available freely online.

Second, other celebrities who decided to stay in the business of YouTube filled the gap and started to offer their prestigious YouTube channels as distribution windows for other new emerging YouTube-based programs. This was an attempt to diversify content and to introduce new actors to the YouTube market as it started to fall in popularity. For example:

> Our plan is to make [our YouTube channel] a platform for various content. Many of our programmes come to us via creators who present their ideas for a specific price ... and so we allow them to produce their own programmes and use our platform officially.

This may reflect the hidden struggle of YouTube-based programming to stay popular and relevant to the audience in light of recent changes, exploring new avenues to maximize the value of their content following the move of some influential celebrities to other media platforms.

All in all, the market in this phase (2014–2016) became mature and well established for both YouTube celebrities and the audience. The content became diverse as newcomers joined the YouTube market. However, the market started losing popularity as prominent stars moved to other media platforms as a result of YouTube's constraints upon the content creators.

Conclusion

This chapter has briefly and critically explored the conditions that helped form the Saudi YouTube celebrity class before examining how the Saudi youth monetized their labor, commodifying their popularity and stardom into financial rewards. The chapter conceptualized the monetization process as three stages, where each stage has a different time framework with various strategies employed by YouTube celebrities in order to capitalize on their online fame.

The *Abstract* stage (2010–2011) is based on simplicity and trial and error approaches to establish a business framework to monetize their cultural products. The *Concrete* stage (2012–2013) shows advanced progress in utilizing advertising strategies and dealing with brands to maximize financial returns. The regulating intervention of YouTube in this stage followed its previous absence and affected the cash flow for the stars, motivating some of them to consider alternative options. The *Innovative* business stage (2014–2016) witnessed the shift for many from being YouTube-based celebrities to media-based enterprise celebrities.

The change in media technology produced a new culture and constructed a new online class in Saudi Arabia, which is well known for its closed cultural and social systems. The platform of YouTube transformed ordinary people into YouTube stars because it helped them to manufacture new interpretations of Saudi public discourse, a phenomenon that created a fan base for Saudi YouTube celebrities. Although the focus of this chapter was on the economic context of the celebrities, it could be argued that their online influence empowered these stars and repositioned their place in society. This created a new social order online which, to a certain degree, affected the power relationships within the young population of Saudi Arabia. By being transformed from ordinary marginalized people to online celebrities, the young people have become the pioneers who have constructed a new social class, creating a new symbolic position of power in the Saudi digital space with a considerable amount of influence over their online followers and over the digital public sphere, influence that was also extended to offline commercial gains. More importantly, it currently opens up new complicated avenues and relationships between creative labor, creative work and the state, by creating new sub-areas in the undeveloped cultural industries because of the state monopoly.

However, one should not exaggerate the impact of such changes, especially in a restrictive environment such as Saudi Arabia. YouTube and other platforms invite considerable financial freedom, but their impact on politics and culture remains very limited.

Notes

1 danah boyd and Nicole Ellison, "Social Network Site: Definition, History and Scholarship," *Journal of Commuter-Mediated Communication* 13, no. 1 (2008): 210.
2 Graeme Turner, *Ordinary People and the Media: The Demotic Turn* (London: Sage, 2010), 1–2.
3 See: Kathy Charmaz, *Constructing Grounded Theory* (USA: Sage, 2014), 320; Juliet Corbin and Anselm Strauss, *Basics of Qualitative Research: Technique and Procedures for Developing Grounded Theory* (USA: Sage, 2015), 25.
4 Jose Van Dijck, *The Culture of Connectivity: A Critical History of Social Media* (Oxford: Oxford University Press, 2013), 12.
5 Marisol Sandoval, *From Corporate to Social Media: Critical Perspectives on Corporate Social Responsibility in Media and Communication Industries* (UK: Routledge, 2014), 125.
6 Graham Meikle, *Social Media: Communication, Sharing and Visibility* (New York: Routledge, 2016), 141.
7 Christina Fuchs, *Social Media: A Critical Introduction* (London: Sage, 2017), 161.
8 Jean Burgess and Joshua Green, *YouTube Online Video and Participatory Culture* (Cambridge: Polity Press, 2018), 45.
9 Patricia Lange, "Publicly Private and Privately Public: Social Networking on YouTube," *Journal of Computer Mediated Communication* 13, no. 1 (2007): 362–363.
10 Michael Strangelove, *Watching YouTube Extraordinary Videos by Ordinary People* (Toronto: University of Toronto Press, 2011), 103.
11 Jin Kim, "The Institutionalization of YouTube: From User-generated Content to Professionally Generated Content," *Media, Culture & Society* 34, no. 1 (2012): 61.
12 Gilbert Ramsay and Sumayah Fatani, "The New Saudi Nationalism of the New Saudi Media," In *Political Islam and Global Media the Boundaries of Religious Identity* (New York: Routledge, 2016) 188–191.
13 Omar Daoudi, "YouTube-Based Programming and the Saudi Youth: Exploring the Economic, Political and Cultural Context of YouTube in Saudi Arabia," (PhD thesis: University of Glasgow, 2018), 18.
14 Pierre Bourdieu, "The Forms of Capital," in *Handbook of Theory and Research for the Sociology of Education* (USA: Greenwood Press, 1986), 241.
15 Michael Savage, *Social Class in the 21st Century* (UK: Penguin, 2015), 4–53.
16 General Authority for Statistics, "Population and Demography," April 2017. www.stats.gov.sa/en/930.
17 Caryle Murphy, *A Kingdom's Future: Saudi Arabia Through the Eyes of its Twentysomethings* (Washington, DC: Wilson Centre, 2013).
18 Erik Wright, *Class Counts: Comparative Studies in Class Analysis* (UK: Cambridge University Press, 1997), 3.
19 Turner, *Ordinary People*, 1–2.
20 Pierre Bourdieu, "What Makes a Social Class? On The Theoretical and Practical Existence of Groups," *Berkeley Journal of Sociology* 32, (1987): 5.
21 See: Amnesty International, "*The State of the World's Human Rights,*" February 2017. www.amnesty.org/en/documents/pol10/4800/2017/en/.
22 For example: Van Dijck, *The Culture*, 12; Pelle Snickars and Patrick Vonderau, *YouTube Reader* (Stockholm: Logotipas, 2009), 10.
23 McKinsey Global Institute, "*Saudi Arabia Beyond Oil: The Investment and Productivity Transformation,*" December 2015.
24 Saudi Vision 2030, "*Thriving Economy Rewarding Opportunities,*" August 2018. http://vision2030.gov.sa/en/node/8.
25 Asad AbuKhalil, *The Battle for Saudi Arabia: Royalty, Fundamentalism and Global Power* (New York: Seven Stories Press, 2004), 173.
26 John Peterson, *Saudi Arabia and the Illusion of Security* (USA: Oxford University Press, 2002), 49.
27 Marc Lynch, *Voices of New Arab Public: Iraq, Al-Jazeera and Middle East Politics Today* (New York: Columbia University Press, 2006), 31.
28 Naomi Sakr and Jeanette Steemers, *Children's TV and Digital Media in the Arab World: Childhood, Screen Culture and Education* (London: I.B. Tauris, 2017), 9.
29 See: Douglas Boyd, *Broadcasting in the Arab World: A Survey of Radio and Television in the Middle East* (Philadelphia: Temple University Press, 1982), 127; Madawi Al-Rasheed, *Kingdom Without Borders: Saudi Arabia's Political, Religious and Media Frontiers* (London: Hurst & Company, 2008), 2–6; and Marwan Kraidy, "Television Reform in Saudi Arabia: The Challenges of Transnationalization and Digitization," in *National Broadcasting and State Policy in Arab Countries* (UK: Palgrave Macmillan, 2013), 28–29.
30 Mohamed Zayani, *Networked Publics and Digital Contention: The Politics of Everyday Life in Tunisia* (Oxford: Oxford University Press, 2015), 3–11.
31 Nahlah Ayed, "Nahlah Ayed: Why Saudi Arabia is the World's Top YouTube Nation," *CBC*, April 1, 2013. www.cbc.ca/news/world/nahlah-ayed-why-saudi-arabia-is-the-world-s-top-youtube-nation-1.1359187.

32 Gillian Doyle, *Understanding Media Economics* (London: SAGE, 2002), 143.
33 Joelle Farchy, "Economic of Sharing Platforms: What is Wrong with Cultural Industries," in *The YouTube Readers* (Lithuania: National Library of Sweden, 2009), 363.
34 Nick Couldry, "Media Meta-capital: Extending the Range of Bourdieu's Field Theory," *Theory and Society* 32, no. 5–6 (2003): 23.
35 For example, Ayed, "Why Saudi Arabia"; Bianca Britton, "Why Women are Taking to YouTube in Saudi Arabia," *CNN* April 5, 2017; Simeon Kerr, "YouTube Taps Fast-growing Saudi Arabia Interest," *Financial Times*, March 17, 2014. www.ft.com/content/2407aa1a-adc3-11e3-9ddc-00144feab7de.https://edition.cnn.com/2017/04/04/middleeast/saudi-arabia-youtube/; and Carla Marshall, "Top 5 Most Influential Female Saudi Arabia Creators On YouTube," *Tubular Insight*, November 28, 2016. http://tubularinsights.com/saudi-arabia-female-creators-youtube/.
36 See: Ann Hoag, "Measuring Media Entrepreneurship," *The International Journal on Media Management* 10 (2008): 75; David Hesmondhalgh and Sarah Baker, Creative Labour: Media Work in Three Cultural Industries (USA and Canada: Routledge, 2011), 141; and Leona Achtenhagen, "Media Entrepreneurship—Taking Stock and Moving Forward," *International Journal on Media Management* 19, no. 1 (2017): 2.

10
MOBILE TECHNOLOGY AND CLASS
Australian Family Households, Socioeconomic Status and Techno-literacy

Will Balmford and Larissa Hjorth

A high school student chats to ten of her best friends through *WhatsApp* in the backseat of the car, recapping the events of the school week. Next to her, her brother plays *Minecraft*[1] on his Nintendo Switch, digging an immense pit into the bowels of a digital Earth. In the front passenger seat, their father goes to check his emails on his tablet, only to be distracted by a notification that he has lost the lead in *Words with Friends*.[2] Behind the wheel, their mother is following driving directions from her smartphone announced through the car stereo to take the next left to best avoid peak hour traffic. Across town, a youth laments that his ageing phone isn't able to play the latest *FIFA Ultimate Team*,[3] leaving him out of touch in the schoolyard. His mother turns her phone's cellular data off at home, concerned about her data use and trying to save money for the iPad her son will need for school next year.

These opening vignettes illustrate the complex ways in which social interactions, co-presence, financial cost, gameplay and techno-literacy play out in everyday life. An interesting example of this is seen in Figure 10.1.

From smartphones to tablets, laptops, e-readers and even portable gaming consoles, the mobile devices we use to negotiate media have become crucial to how we move through our daily routines.[4] Figure 10.1 shows a scenario of use highlighting how mobile devices can be adapted into new household roles. Similarly, when and where we interact with these devices has become a complex balancing act that involves socioeconomic factors, cultural capital and techno-literacy. Such factors will be explored in this chapter as informed by ethnographic data from the *Games of Being Mobile* study.

Games of Being Mobile (*GoBM*) was a three-year longitudinal study into mobile games around Australia. It employed ethnographic methodology involving interviews, home tours, participant observation and play sessions in an effort to understand mobile games as part of broader cultural and media practices in the home. Over three-years the study ethnographically engaged with ten households in six Australian capital cities—60 households in total. The anecdotes of this chapter come from several key participants in the study, from a variety of socioeconomic backgrounds in Melbourne, Sydney and Brisbane.

Figure 10.1 Mobile phones as recipe books. Image by authors.

Framing Class

Class is one of the most contested and complex notions—complicated by the rise of individualism[5] and lifestyle media DIY vernaculars.[6] Within this chapter, class is discussed in terms of the relationship between socioeconomic inequality and technology—similar to Sonia Livingstone and Magdalena Bober's identification of the links between technology use (and access) and socioeconomic differences in UK homes.[7] Class is constituted by many factors and has been one of the most contested concepts in disciplines such as cultural studies through Bourdieu's notion of "cultural capital."[8] Bourdieuan cultural capital holds that culture, measured as a form of capital, is critical to how class relationships are established and consolidated.[9] Bourdieu's notion of capital has also been defined as "knowledge," operationalized by several scholars as "knowledge of high culture and educational attainment."[10] These definitions begin to unpack how literacy in particular topics can be a powerful indicator of cultural status. Entangled in these indicators of class relationships are other structural factors; such as the economic distinctions highlighting class divisions.[11–13]

The collected volume, *Culture, Class, Distinction*, offers insight into the myriad ways class is engaged and disputed within cultural studies.[14] Tony Bennett and his co-authors argue that there is "no doubt regarding the significance of age, gender and ethnicity in organizing complex patterns of socio-cultural division."[15] In addition, the authors break down Bourdieu's notion of cultural capital into sub divisions of "cultural assets"—cultural resources reorganized and mobilized across different kinds of social relations.[16] Such "cultural assets" are a useful frame of analysis for technology such as mobile devices.

Beverley Skeggs analyses cultural assets in relation to moral value in her work exploring reality television consumption in the UK.[17] In particular, she highlights how the significant popularity of "working class self transformation" reality television shows indicates a societal discourse where "certain people and cultures are positioned, evaluated and interpreted as inadequate, deficient and requiring improvement."[18] Such an approach privileges middle class values of "polite and proper" and the use of cultural assets (such as clothing attire) to highlight these values[19] as "universal and normative" across much of UK society.[20]

In our ethnographic examples, similar phenomena emerge, with middle-class forms of mobile media usage and access to mobile media being upheld and instilled as the norm through practices such as Bring Your Own Device (BYOD) school programs and expensive personal mobile data packages.

Looking closer at mobile usage and class within the Australian context, much of the recent work in this area considers the role of lifestyle and modes of informal citizenship in and through media practices that serve to constitute particular types of moral values and constructions of class.[21] Tania Lewis arrives at a similar endpoint to Bennett et al.'s "cultural assets" through an analysis of internet usage to retrieve health information in Melbourne, Australia.[22] Lewis's work engages Ulrich Beck's writings on "risk society" to critically assess "a decline in the relevance of traditional social categories".[23] Beck's "risk society" theory contends that a societal shift from managing the unequal distribution of wealth to managing risk has turned the modernization process upon itself in what he calls "reflexive modernization."[24] He argues that reflexive modernization is a process that cuts through class and social divisions to become a more generalized experience linked to individualized forms of cultural and social identity.[25,26] Lewis discusses how Beck's approach unnecessarily dismisses class.[27] Instead Lewis argues that reflexive modernization increases individual pressures, leading to a greater dependence upon "the possession of certain forms of socially-valued cultural capital and social hierarchy."[28] These "certain forms of socially-valued cultural capital" have distinct similarities to Bennett et al.'s "cultural assets."[29,30] These terms are conceptualized throughout this chapter as mobile devices and technology. In our ethnographic anecdotes, the cultural standing of these assets is heavily linked to the financial costs associated with mobile device ownership and subsequent engagement with mobile media.

Another example of these moral values is seen in Clifton Evers, Kath Albury, Paul Byron and Kate Crawford's work into sexual health communication in Australia through social media.[31] Their research used focus groups to explore how social media (with particular attention to mobile media) was accessed in relation to sexual health education in Australia.[32] The authors caution against "impinging on young people's rights to 'intimate citizenship'."[33] Their work highlights how class divisions can impact personal construction of informal citizenship, a potential link between mobile media usage and class. *Disposed to Learn: Schooling, Ethnicity and the Scholarly Habitus* by Megan Watkins and Greg Noble also highlights such links.[34] Watkins and Noble explore the relationship between class, ethnicity and education, exploring how schools serve as sites that reproduce cultural capital, instilling "class based knowledge and power."[35] The authors extend Bourdieu's cultural capital to include educational capital; a critical factor in how learning dispositions are instilled and social practices are reproduced.[36]

In a similar vein, our chapter explores how mobile media literacy and learned practices can inform class structures. In particular, our ethnographic examples present situations where financial burden creates unequal access to mobile media, generating a class-based "digital divide."[37] Digital divide terminology refers to access to digital media technology.[38] Where the term originally referred to whether or not individuals had internet access, it has now become a more nuanced term that explores the levels of internet and digital media access available to individuals.[39] Research suggests that as levels of access have become the focal point of analysis the digital divide has become increasingly linked to socioeconomic capabilities and, in turn, the generation of cultural capital.[40,41]

In this chapter, we engage with the digital divide through these lenses, linking the financial costs of mobile media ownership and literacy to cultural capital and the promotion of particular class norms. We explore such phenomena through ethnographic examples focused on three key themes;

the multiple device literacies required in the modern Australian home; daily mobile routines and data usage costs in relation to class standing and digital divides; and the influence of BYOD programs upon such digital divides. The chapter will use these three themes to explore how mobile media access and usage can be a potential expression of class difference in Australian homes.

Household Demographics and Multiple Device Literacy

Within the home, mobile phones are rarely used in isolation. Instead, they are part of complex configurations that include other devices and members of the household. Human, non-human and more-than-human actors such as household pets all play a role in the life of mobile media. Frequently, mobile phones are used co-presently—both with other devices and with others physically or virtually present. A useful example of this is in the all-female shared house of Viola, a Melbourne based *GoBM* participant.

At Viola's[42] home, a combination of older media technologies and new digital social media helps facilitate interactions between the housemates. Viola and several of her housemates are still studying; budgeting is often tight. However, all members of the household place a priority on device ownership. Despite being students living on limited income, all of Viola's housemates have smartphones and laptops. In addition, a further two (out of five) of them also own iPads. There are times when they are sitting on the couch, watching television through a Chromecast Netflix stream from a computer. At the same time, all of them are also looking at their devices, playing a game and comparing scores, swiping through social media or answering emails and swapping work shifts. All of these actions require device literacy, and the simultaneous enactment of them is a tangled interaction of social cues and technology. Within Viola's youth-orientated shared house, multiple device literacy is a ubiquitous phenomenon.

In contrast to Viola's household is the domestic media usage of Paul and Zelma. The two are retirees living in Melbourne's outer suburbs. For Paul and Zelma, device literacy and ownership are not of primary importance. Although they have significantly more disposable income than Viola and her housemates, Paul and Zelma do not prioritize device ownership. While Zelma owns an iPhone 6, it is only for "emergencies." Paul does not own a mobile phone, as he believes it is "unnecessary and stops people from actually talking." Paul intentionally excluded himself from mobile phone ownership in an attempt to limit the entry of unwanted social interaction into his domestic space.

The social aspects of device literacy have been an important focus of many media scholars. One critical early example of this focus is the work of communications scholar Ronald Rice. Rice's examination of device literacy focused on the social aspects of new media, stressing its impact on choice, innovation and the push and pull of social forces.[43-45] Rice's work acknowledges the dual significance of technological affordances and existing social practices. It is here that a critical feature of mobile and new media technologies can be seen—new media technologies can entangle these topics, meshing the spheres of social choice together, creating links and blurring public and private spaces, work and leisure.[46-50]

Examples of this blurring can be seen in the Australian context, where a common area of research in new media studies concerns the ways in which new media technologies such as mobile devices in Australian homes can reshape behaviors, spaces and locations. The work of Elaine Lally argues that the physical placement and use of new media devices within the home impacts how the space is navigated and perceived by those using it.[51] Practical examples of this reshaping model can be seen in the evolution of dedicated media spaces such as computer desks, console hubs, and wireless router requirements, and, more recently, mobile phone ownership and data plans. Recent scholarship such as the work of Donnell Holloway, Lelia Green, and Carlie Love builds on this body of research to explore how domestic mobile device use can reflect or alter the household.[52] Their work describes scenarios of parental mediation of childhood device use and explores how such technologies are managed in family life.

Work exploring household management of device use is also heavily influenced by "domestication theory"—an approach that focuses on how technology is shaped by domestic environments. A key text in domestication theory is *Consuming Technologies: Media and Information in Domestic Spaces*.[53] Central to this book is an emphasis on the nuanced relationships that take place in—and help to define—domestic life in the modern world.[54] Similarly, Leslie Haddon's work into domestic use of mobile technology engages domestication approaches to explore differences in mobile phone use across generations, and the financial entanglement involved in such differences.[55] In a similar way, this chapter examines how differing socioeconomic household structures can influence the relationships between mobile technology and users.

These relationships with mobile technologies come at a financial cost, which impacts the organization and cadence of everyday family life around mobile device engagement. How a mobile media user interprets and manages these costs depends on their literacy across devices and platforms, and the extent to which these become integral to their communicative practice, relationship maintenance and social identity.[56] Despite the access and use of such technology being relatively expensive, ownership and data use is more often prioritized by media literate groups (such as Viola and her housemates) as large portions of their social relationships are enacted through mobile devices and technology. Furthermore, for Viola and her housemates, mobile devices inform their social standing by enabling them to display class membership through possession of a "cultural asset"[57,58] and an ability to engage in "intimate citizenship" through personal communication.[59]

Within Viola's shared house, multiple device literacy is an important tool in maintaining the social cohesion of the home. Being literate in several mobile media and digital technologies enables Viola and her housemates to enact the variety of domestic social scenarios outlined above. In contrast, Paul and Zelma do not use mobile media as part of their domestic social configurations. Instead, they orientate their home away from device use, intentionally restricting usage across a variety of devices in order to maintain their current domestic configuration and its social rhythms. Their reasons for doing so also revolve around cultural capital, with Paul in particular interpreting mobile phone ownership as a negative cultural asset that would limit his communication with others in his social circles. These two examples portray very different notions of mobile media literacy within two distinctly socioeconomically disparate homes. Interestingly in these two examples, the digital divide's relationship to cultural standing is expressed both ways, with ubiquitous access generating positive cultural capital in Viola's household and limited access a positive in Zelma and Paul's.

While socioeconomic brackets and percentage of income spent on mobile media usage differs between the households of Viola, and of Zelma and Paul, the differing levels of techno-literacy of mobile devices are particularly important in households with younger children.[60,61] During the *GoBM* research, some participants with young children explained they felt the financial costs of mobile media more significantly due to the educational requirements of many Australian schools. These examples will be explored in a later section of this chapter that discusses the BYOD programs present in many Australian schools. Intergenerational differences in device literacy often result in internet parenting anxiety around children's use of digital technology. Within academic literature there is a significant history of research into parent anxiety concerning the relationships their children have to digital technologies and new media.[62,63]

One of the key projects in this area is the report "UK Children Go Online: Listening to Young People's Experiences" undertaken by Sonia Livingstone and Magdalena Bober.[64] Their work specifically explores "internet literacy" among UK children, and provides several important insights into childhood internet usage and literacy. These included several categories of "dangers" related to use including content, exclusion, engagement in "risky behavior" and the "digital divide" potentially widening to leave children who cannot adequately engage with the internet unable to pursue online opportunities.[65] They conceptualize the modern digital divide along lines of opportunity; those "for whom the internet is an increasingly rich, engaging and stimulating resource and those for whom it remains a narrow, unengaging, if occasionally useful, resource."[66]

Livingstone, along with media scholar Julian Sefton-Green, has also published significant scholarly work examining the use of digital technology in and around the classroom.[67] Their work details adolescent social spheres in relation to digital technologies, and the "public hyperbole about digital media."[68] The authors push against this hyperbole, arguing that adolescent use of digital technology is reframing, rather than simply replacing, face-to-face interactions.[69]

Within the Australian context, Green has undertaken significant work exploring the risks and benefits of online interaction for children.[70,71] Her work explores the relationship between potential risk and harm, and highlights the responsibility of policy makers to address these online risks.[72]

Similar to anxieties around videogames, there have been media concerns about the impact television might have upon children.[73] These anxieties began to emerge when television was the new media the previous generation was uninitiated into.[74] Such fears were also seen in the early days of arcade videogames and home computers.[75,76] Research indicates that parental anxieties around new technologies stem from a lack of knowledge and know-how—a distinct difference in techno-literacy between generational groups.[77] As Gustavo Cardoso, Rita Espanha and Tiago Lapa point out in their work concerning family mediation of new media, it is very difficult to create systems and rules around use of technology a parent doesn't understand.[78]

Several ethnographic examples from the *GoBM* project presented a link between device purchase and techno-literacy with regard to purchasing criteria for school devices. The rise of mobile devices capable of playing videogames, such as smartphones, tablets and laptops has created tensions between the devices a child requires literacy in to negotiate everyday social life and the economic feasibility of such purchases for parents. This tension will be explored in the next section of this chapter through ethnographic examples involving the Australian BYOD program.

Cultural Capital, BYOD and Financial Costs

The BYOD program in place at many Australian schools has created a potential "digital divide" for Australian school children from lower socioeconomic backgrounds, with several state governments now developing school guidelines with a specific focus on "equitable access."[79] BYOD programs involve parents being required to purchase a device for their child's schooling, such as an iPad. This device is then linked to the school and is often restricted in usage (such as network access or game playing) despite being taken home by children overnight, on weekends and during school breaks. Although the BYOD is attempting to limit unequal access in Australian homes, ethnographic data from the *GoBM* project provided examples where device usage remained a cultural asset linked to financial purchasing power.

Felix and Grace Smith are the parents of primary school child Oli. The three live in Melbourne, where Oli attends primary school. In Felix and Grace's case, the BYOD was a significant financial cost. Alongside this financial cost, Oli's use of the iPad at home is problematic to monitor as neither Grace nor Felix are particularly literate in the device. To save money, they each use old Android OS phones—hand-me-downs from Grace's parents. The two parents expressed difficulty in monitoring Oli's use habits due to their lack of knowledge around how content is stored on an iPad. However, Oli's school required all children to have the same form of tablet to facilitate easier learning in the classroom. In situations such as this, "necessary device" purchases exacerbate issues of inter-generational multi-device literacy in domestic family homes with limited financial capabilities.

Felix and Grace were also worried about the exposure to mobile videogames the BYOD program might have on the health of their son Oli. They were concerned that Oli's social life at school would not revolve around "running around the playground and backyard" but rather be "lived and limited through the iPad." Oli's parents worried that mobile media usage would constrict Oli's social interactions—limiting him from developing the social skills they understood as necessary. The two parents did not believe a mobile device was necessary to their child's primary education. Instead they were required to purchase the device to adhere to social norms, with Grace lamenting that the purchase of a mobile device was now required to give Oli a "proper education." This terminology recalls Skegg's recognition of middle class cultural assets and values being interpreted as the universal norm in Australia.[80] For Felix and Grace, adherence to this social norm (expressed here through mobile device ownership) came at a significant financial cost and created further issues around domestic management of Oli's mobile media usage.

The Richards family of Brisbane also drew attention to parental management of child device usage in relation to the BYOD program. However, in comparison with the Smith family's single iPad and hand-me-down Android phones, the Richards family has a greater variety of devices in the home. Amanda, 8, plays *Minecraft*[81] on the family iPad. In contrast to the Smith family, the iPad is a shared device between Amanda and her sister Penelope. Heather and Chris, Amanda's parents, also have an iPad, and are competent in using and monitoring Amanda use of it. Amanda's school does not have a single device BYOD program, instead allowing parents to select from several devices. Therefore, Heather and Chris decided to purchase a device they were experienced with as they are more comfortable enabling their children to use devices and software they are literate in and can adequately monitor. For the Richard's family, the flexibility of their school's BYOD enabled easier navigation around a potential digital divide, lessening the tension between class norms and financial burden.

Throughout the research of the *GoBM* project, issues of intergenerational literacy frequently related to the extensive variety of devices used in everyday life. As this section has shown, some *GoBM* participant parents raised concerns in relation to their ability to monitor the usage habits of their children when their children are using devices the parents are not competent in. These issues were further exacerbated in situations where to school BYOD programs mandated purchases of particular device types—itself a requirement aimed to limit the device literacy required by teachers to monitor student usage. These scenarios created tension in two ways; first, they highlighted the financial burden felt by some families to adhere to normative conceptions of class standing (i.e., a child needs a "proper" education, with such terminology now associated with mobile device ownership) and second, they created parental issues around domestic management of childhood device usage of technology they were unfamiliar with.

The next section of this chapter explores how Australian households from various socioeconomic backgrounds interpret and manage their mobile data "caps" and costs. It will engage with ethnographic evidence of household routines, exploring examples how mobile phone usage and associated data costs are linked to cultural capital and socioeconomic circumstances.

Data Usage, Management, and Scenarios of Use

This section explores how mobile technology is accessed and the influence of socioeconomic factors upon such access. These ethnographic observations help to highlight mobile technologies' changing roles within household structures, and subsequent reconfiguration of routines around socioeconomic capabilities. In particular, this section explores reconfigurations of domestic routines in relation to Australian mobile data usage through an analysis of how data "allowances" afford higher socioeconomic households greater agency in their mobile technology usage. In Australia, mobile phone (and many tablet device) plans come with a data allowance in the form of Gigabytes per month (GB/month). When these limits are exceeded, device owners are automatically charged extra for more data.

However, the current state of Australian internet access appears to make issues of data allowances a more pressing concern than in other countries. In particular, the lack of full speed unlimited mobile data packages in Australia means that mobile data continues to be a highly controlled and limited commodity, with Australians paying $313 million a year in excess data charges.[82] Common excess data costs are around $10 a GB, which can quickly double the cost of monthly mobile phone bills.

Livingstone and Sefton-Green explore similar experiences in their research into social media usage among disparate socioeconomic groups in their work *The Class: Living and Learning in the Digital Age*.[83] The authors discuss how online interactions among student groups were frequently stratified into homogeneous groupings of "socio-economic position, ethnicity, and gender."[84] These notions of limiting social interactions link back to the danger of "exclusion" identified by Livingstone and Bober.[85] Fear of exclusion was similarly a frequent topic of discussion among *GoBM* participants—both parents and children. Parents expressed fears of "messy" socioeconomic discussion, paralleling the findings of *The Class*.[86] However, child and adolescent participant fears of exclusion revolved around being socially outcast as a result of being unable to adequately use mobile phone technology to consolidate social relationships. These examples link closely to Bennett et al.'s recognition of media as a potential cultural asset required to belong to certain class divisions.[87] Several *GoBM* participant homes also engaged management strategies around their children's mobile device usage to limit financial burden, with parents strictly controlling the data consumption of their children (as well as their own) in order to avoid excess data charges.

Lynn Schofield Clark has explored the impact of socioeconomic class upon parental management strategies of children (and household) mobile media usage.[88] Her book *The Parent App: Understanding Families in the Digital Age* used interviews with mothers and fathers to explore how parental management of device usage and internet consumption approaches might differ according to family income.[89] Clark identifies several differing criteria for "internet parenting"; while parents in upper-income families encouraged child engagement with media in order to increase self-development and independent education, lower income families prioritized the use of digital and mobile media in "family focused" ways, stressing compliance and respect towards parents.[90]

Within the *GoBM* research, "internet parenting" methods concerning mobile technology usage appeared to vary between participant households. Families from lower socioeconomic backgrounds had more engaged parental monitoring than affluent households. Sonia Livingstone, Giovanna Mascheroni, Michael Dreier, Stephane Chaudron, and Kaat Lagae found similar phenomena in their research into parental management of child device usage, positing that one reason for this increased monitoring may be due to the significant financial cost of many digital devices.[91] These cases also parallel Clark's findings in *The Parent App*, that lower income families seek management strategies that promote family engagement, often linked to lower levels of device usage.[92] Within the Australian households of the *GoBM* project, discussions of mobile technology usage in households with less financial income often centered on balancing financial factors such as the cost of data plans against social requirements.

For example, the Bailey family struggled with technology costs in relation to data usage on the family's limited data "allowances." As mentioned earlier, Australian internet and mobile plans are often "data restricted," meaning users have a limited amount of data consumption per month before they begin incurring additional costs. Restricted in both cellular and home internet usage, the Bailey family established differing days of access to data intensive services such as Netflix for their children and limited the playing of internet-dependent mobile games to within the household to avoid incurring excess data costs by "burning through all their data on the school bus." The Bailey family also said they felt the technological requirements demanded by schools disadvantaged less affluent families such as themselves. The Bailey family's position reflects a common discourse on the usage of digital media being employed to ensure children "stay ahead" of the learning curve.[93] Furthermore, their usage parallels the balancing act between allowing children their social interactions and the associated financial costs detailed by Livingstone et al.[94]

For families such as the Baileys, fear of excess data costs often limited their daily mobile usage outside of the home. Mother Sarah Bailey explained how she did not use her music streaming service *Spotify* outside of the home, in order to avoid going over her 2GB of mobile data a month. Instead, Sarah reserved her mobile data for "potential emergencies" such as needing to use Google Maps to navigate to an unfamiliar location.

In contrast to the Bailey family, more affluent households were much less concerned about their mobile data consumption. Xavier and his family, based in Sydney, each have 30GB of data a month on their mobile phone plans, 15 times the amount of Sarah Bailey. Xavier explained that, despite being aware of the data limit, he was never worried about it, as he "never even got close to using that much." These disparate data allowances create vastly different scenarios of mobile technology use. One of Xavier's preferred commuting activities was to watch *Netflix* on his mobile, a highly data intensive activity, offering a stark contrast to Sarah Bailey's limiting of her *Spotify* usage to the home Wi-Fi. The data packages of mobile phone plans were one of the clearest demarcating lines of financial difference that emerged during the *GoBM* research, affording those with the financial capacity to have larger data allowances (or not worry about excess data costs) significantly greater mobile technology agency.

These costs were of importance to many *GoBM* families as, within many of our participant households, mobile phone devices were the primary means of telephonic communication—several households had eliminated their landline connection altogether. Other households still had a landline connection, but informed us that it was rarely used, continuing to exist only as part of their home internet plan. Instead, families used mobile devices for a variety of domestic communications; as their home contact numbers, to send text messages, to access social media or other communicative apps.

Nick, a 20-year-old participant from Melbourne, exclusively used the messaging app *WhatsApp* to communicate with his brother while he was overseas. Nick's usage highlights an intriguing scenario of use. Despite many Australian mobile phone plans now coming with significant or "unlimited" national calls per month, Nick and his brother preferred the messaging format for their communications. Nick's data allowances largely restricted his usage of the messaging application to within his home. The use of messaging services as a communication tool was common among *GoBM* participant households, especially when communicating with individuals over a long distance, such as internationally. In international communication, *WhatsApp* was the most frequently used communication method—due largely to it bypassing international carrier charges by going through data.

The above anecdote offers an interesting example where data was perceived as "cheaper" than cellular. How financial costs are related to international mobile device communication is an area that could be well served by further research. While Nick's example does offer a counterpoint to the Australian perception of mobile data as "expensive," Nick and his brother's international communication was still facilitated through mobile media. To this extent most of the participant households in the *GoBM* research, from both affluent and low-income homes, primarily relied on their mobile devices as their method of external communication from within the home.

This section has provided examples from the *GoBM* research where domestic mobile phone usage is heavily mediated through financial costs such as data consumption, with this consumption is also balanced against what is interpreted as "normal" usage within Australian society. Data packages and their significant costs had a noted impact upon how several *GoBM* participant households used mobile phones, paralleling Livingstone and Bober's digital divide of opportunities.[95] Restrictive data allowances and expensive excess charges caused participant families with less disposable income to be far more conscious of mobile phone data consumption, frequently restricting such usage to within the home.

Conclusion

This chapter has explored how financial income, class and techno-literacy intersect with regard to Australian domestic mobile phone usage. It has explored three areas of enquiry; the significant variety of device literacies present within the home, BYOD programs and associated financial costs, and data allowances and subsequent management strategies. A key finding of this chapter concerns the data usage practices of Australian homes. Mobile data usage, particularly in family homes, provided one of the starkest examples of socioeconomic difference among *GoBM* participant households.

Participant households with less financial income also expressed greater anxiety around parental management strategies of children. BYOD programs exacerbated this issue not only by placing financial stress on several participant homes but also reinforcing class boundaries around digital access. Current government policy inefficiently engages with this issue, only offering "guidelines" for BYOD purchasing and affordability, and no guidelines for data usage. Such lack of a clear Australia-wide policy leads to socioeconomic based inequality of mobile device usage that perpetuates differences in techno-literacy between Australian family households of various income levels.

In the ethnographic fieldwork of *GoBM*, the role of both the socioeconomic standing of a household and the generational groups present within it are key factors influencing behavior. The *GoBM* research provides examples where younger groups are more techno-literate in a greater variety of devices, and employ this techno-literacy in more scenarios. Compared with other countries, Australia's expensive data costs indicate the relevancy of state policies in creating greater class mobility in relation to technology engagement and accompanying levels of techno-literacy.

Further research into this area could explore these brackets in greater detail, such as more detailed ethnographic work into migrant families' communication habits with international family members and the associated links to financial costs to international communication facilitated through mobile media. A comparative analysis of how data and cellular charges are interpreted in different communicative scenarios would be a useful starting point for such future research.

Through its examination of the influence class has upon the domestic home, and the growing relevance of techno-literacy, this chapter has examined the changing landscape of domestic mobile phone usage within Australia. Through an interrogation of multiple device literacies, data costs and usage and communicative scenarios of use, this chapter has explored the interactions and contestations between socioeconomic class and intergenerational techno-literacy. Such interactions are central to the types and forms of mobile technology use within the Australian household. The findings of the *GoBM* project explored in this paper offer useful ethnographic examples that point to a need to more equitably promote techno-literacy of mobile technology across Australian socioeconomic class lines.

Notes

1. Mojang. *Minecraft* (Mojang, 2011), videogame.
2. Zynga. *Words with Friends* (Zynga, 2009), mobile videogame.
3. EA Sports. *FIFA Ultimate Team* (EA Sports, 2018), mobile videogame.
4. Larissa Hjorth and Ingrid Richardson, *Gaming in Social, Locative and Mobile Media* (New York: Palgrave Macmillan, 2014).
5. Ulrich Beck, *Risk Society. Towards a New Modernity* (London: Sage, 1992).
6. Beverley Skeggs, "The Moral Economy of Person Production: The Class Relations of Self-Performance on 'Reality' Television," *The Sociological Review* 57 (2009): 626–644.
7. Sonia Livingstone and Magdalena Bober, "UK Children Go Online: Listening to Young People's Experiences," *London School of Economics and Political Science* (2003), http://eprints.lse.ac.uk/4035/1/UK_children_go_online.pdf.
8. Tony Bennett, Alan Warde, Elizabeth Silva, Mike Savage, Modesto Gayo-Cal, and David Wright, *Culture, Class, Distinction* (New York: Routledge, 2009).
9. Pierre Bourdieu, *Distinction: A Social Critique of the Judgement of Taste* (London: Routledge, 1984).
10. Michèle Lamont and Annette Lareau, "Cultural Capital—Allusions, Gaps and Glissandos in Recent Theoretical Developments." *Sociological Theory* 6 (1988): 153–168.
11. Bourdieu, *Distinction*.
12. Bennett et al., *Culture, Class, Distinction*.
13. Lamont and Lareau, Cultural Capital.
14. Bennett et al., *Culture, Class, Distinction*.
15. Ibid., 3.

16 Ibid., 3.
17 Skeggs, The Moral Economy of Person Production.
18 Ibid., 626.
19 Ibid., 628.
20 Ibid., 639.
21 Tania Lewis, "DIY Selves? Reflexivity and Habitus in Young People's Use of the Internet for Health Information". *European Journal of Cultural Studies* 9 (2006): 461–479.
22 Ibid.
23 Ibid., 463.
24 Beck, *Risk Society*.
25 Lewis, DIY Selves.
26 Beck, *Risk Society*.
27 Lewis, DIY Selves.
28 Ibid., 477.
29 Ibid.
30 Beck, *Risk Society*.
31 Clifton Evers, Kath Albury, Paul Byron, and Kate Crawford, "Young People, Social Media, Social Network Sites and Sexual Health Communication in Australia: 'This is Funny, You Should Watch It,'" *International Journal of Communication* 1 (2013): 263–280.
32 Ibid.
33 Ibid., 271.
34 Megan Watkins and Greg Noble, *Disposed to Learn: Schooling, Ethnicity and the Scholarly Habitus* (London: Bloomsbury Academic, 2013).
35 Ibid., 6.
36 Ibid.
37 Livingstone and Bober, UK Children Go Online.
38 Benjamin Compaine, ed., *The Digital Divide: Facing a Crisis or Creating a Myth?* (Cambridge: MIT Press, 2001).
39 Martin Hilbert, "Technological Information Inequality as an Incessantly Moving Target: The Redistribution of Information and Communication Capacities between 1986 and 2010," *Journal of the Association for Information Science and Technology* 65 (2014): 821–835.
40 Christine Clark and Paul Gorski "Multicultural Education and the Digital Divide: Focus on Socioeconomic Class Background," *Multicultural Perspectives* 4 (2002): 25–36.
41 Mark Warschauer, *Technology and Social Inclusion: Rethinking the Digital Divide* (Cambridge: MIT press, 2004).
42 All participants have been given pseudonyms to ensure anonymity.
43 Ronald Rice, "Task Analyzability, Use of New Media, and Effectiveness: A Multi-site Exploration of Media Richness." *Organization Science* 3 (1992): 25.
44 Andrew Shapiro, *The Control Revolution: How the Internet is Putting Individuals in Charge and Changing the World We Know* (New York: Public Affairs, 1999).
45 Frank Webster, *Culture and Politics in the Information Age: A New Politics?* (New York: Routledge, 2001).
46 Ann Moyal, "The Gendered Use of the Telephone: An Australian Case Study," *Media, Culture & Society* 14 (1992): 51–72.
47 Bram Lievens, Wendy Van den Broeck, and Jos Pierson, "The Mobile (R)evolution in Everyday Life: A Border Crossing between Public and Private Space?" in *Mobile Media*, ed. Gerard Goggin and Larissa Hjorth (Brisbane: Watson Ferguson & Company, 2007): 23–33.
48 Michael Bittman, Judith E. Brown, and Judy Wajcman, "The Cell Phone, Constant Connection and Time Scarcity in Australia," *Social Indicators Research* 93 (2009): 229–233.
49 Manuel Castells, Mireia Fernandez-Ardevol, Jack L. Qiu, and Araba Sey, *Mobile Communication and Society: A Global Perspective* (Cambridge, MA: MIT Press, 2009).
50 Melissa Gregg, "Do your Homework: New Media, Old Problems," *Feminist Media Studies* 11 (2011): 73–81.
51 Lally, Elaine, *At Home with Computers* (Oxford: Berg Publishers, 2002).
52 Donell Holloway, Lelia Green, and Carlie Love, "It's All About the APPS': Parental Mediation of Pre-Schoolers' Digital Lives," *Media International Australia* 1 (2014): 148–156.
53 Eric Hirsch and Roger Silverstone, *Consuming Technologies: Media and Information in Domestic Spaces* (London, UK: Routledge, 2003).
54 Ibid.
55 Leslie Haddon, "Domestication and Mobile Telephony" (Machines that Become Us Conference, Rutgers University, NJ, April 18, 2001).
56 Gerard Goggin and Larissa Hjorth, *Mobile Media 2007* (Brisbane: Watson Ferguson & Company, 2007).
57 Bennett et al., *Culture, Class, Distinction*.

58 Skeggs, The Moral Economy of Person Production.
59 Evers et al., Young People, Social Media.
60 Sonia Livingstone, *Young People and New Media: Childhood and the Changing Media Environment* (London: London School of Economics and Political Science, 2002).
61 Sonia Livingstone, "The Changing Nature and Uses of Media Literacy" (Media@lse Electronic Working Paper, No. 4, 2003), http://eprints.lse.ac.uk/id/eprint/13476.
62 Chas Critcher, "Making Waves: Historical Aspects of Public Debates about Children and Mass Media," in *The International Handbook of Children, Media and Culture*, eds. Sonia Livingstone and Kirsten Drotner (London: Sage, 2008): 91–104.
63 Eugène Loos, Leslie Haddon, and Enid Mante-Meijer, *Generational Use of New Media* (Farnham, UK: Ashgate, 2012).
64 Livingstone and Bober, *UK Children Go Online*.
65 Ibid.
66 Ibid.
67 Sonia Livingstone and Julian Sefton-Green, *The Class: Living and Learning in the Digital Age* (New York: NYU Press, 2016).
68 Ibid., 104.
69 Ibid.
70 Lelia Green, "Internet Savvy? Children and Online Risk," *Proceedings of Communications Policy and Research Forum* (Network Insight Institute, Sydney, NSW, 2010).
71 Donell Holloway, Lelia Green, and Sonia Livingstone "Zero to Eight: Young Children and their Internet Use," *EU Kids Online* 1 (London: LSE, 2013), http://eprints.lse.ac.uk/52630/.
72 Green, "Internet Savvy?"
73 Lynn Spigel, *Make Room for TV: Television and the Family Ideal in Postwar America* (Chicago: University of Chicago Press, 2013).
74 Ibid.
75 Haddon, *Domestication and Mobile Telephony*.
76 Sherry Turkle, *The Second Self: Computers and the Human Spirit* (Cambridge, MA: MIT Press, 2005).
77 Leslie Haddon "Parental Mediation of Internet Use: Evaluating Family Relationships," in *Generational Use of New Media*, ed. Eugène Loos, Leslie Haddon, and Enid Mante-Meijer (Farnham, UK: Ashgate, 2012): 1–28.
78 Gustavo Cardosp, Rita Espanha, and Tiago Lapa "Family Dynamics and Mediation: Children, Autonomy and Control" in *Generational Use of New Media*, ed. Eugène Loos, Leslie Haddon, and Enid Mante-Meijer (Farnham, UK: Ashgate, 2012): 48–70.
79 Victorian Government "School Policy Advisory Guide," accessed August 10 2017. www.education.vic.gov.au/school/principals/spag/management/Pages/personaldev.aspx#top.
80 Skeggs, *The Moral Economy of Person Production*.
81 Mojang, *Minecraft*.
82 Yolanda Redrup, "Deloitte Suggests Unlimited Mobile Plans as Aussies Pay $313m a Year in Excess Data Charges," *Australian Financial Review*, November 14, 2017, accessed June 12, 2018. www.afr.com/technology/deloitte-suggests-unlimited-mobile-plans-as-aussies-pay-313m-a-year-in-excess-data-charges-20171114-gzlmav.
83 Livingstone and Sefton-Green, *The Class*.
84 Ibid.
85 Livingstone and Bober, *UK Children Go Online*.
86 Livingstone and Sefton-Green, *The Class*, 108.
87 Bennett et al., *Culture, Class, Distinction*.
88 Lynn Schofield Clark, *The Parent App: Understanding Families in the Digital Age* (Oxford: Oxford University Press, 2013).
89 Ibid.
90 Ibid.
91 Sonia Livingstone Giovanna Mascheroni, Michael Dreier, Stephane Chaudron, and Kaat Lagae, "How Parents of Young Children Manage Digital Devices at Home: The Role of Income, Education AND Parental Style," *EU Kids Online* 1 (London: LSE, 2013), http://eprints.lse.ac.uk/63378.
92 Clark, *The Parent App*.
93 Sonia Livingstone, "What are Pre-schoolers Doing with Tablets and is it Good for Them?" *Parenting for a Digital Future* (blog), February 29, 2016, accessed June 10, 2018. http://blogs.lse.ac.uk/parenting4digital-future/2016/02/29/what-are-pre-schoolers-doing-with-tablets-and-is-it-good-for-them.
94 Livingstone et al., *How Parents of Young Children Manage Digital Devices at Home*.
95 Livingstone and Bober, *UK Children Go Online*.

11
HANGING OUT AT HOME AS A LIFESTYLE

YouTube Home Tour Vlogs in East Asia

Crystal Abidin

The locus of the home is one of the earliest and most common settings and backdrops for YouTube vlogs. In the decade since YouTube creators and Influencers have flourished in the industry, new strategies, mechanisms, and vocabularies of self-presentation have emerged across various social media, resulting in the emblem of the home emerging as a topic, genre, and setting in YouTube vlogs. Several studies have studied the proliferation of various genres of vlogs on YouTube—generally surveying how the medium is used for diary-keeping, sharing one's identity, or constructing one's self[1]—but very few focus on the spatiality of the home as a locale and topic of content production.

Three studies on YouTube vlogs, in particular, have focused on the home as a topic, genre, and setting for discussion. Juliano Spyer's thesis looked at YouTube vloggers in the beauty genre and the creation of a social order, and in one chapter focused on the spatiotemporality of their video content. Specifically, they point out that room tours are a popular *topic* among beauty gurus on YouTube and provide "an introduction to the person's room including explanations about the meaning of certain objects of decoration and about how different kinds of products … are organized and stored."[2] Building on Spyer's work, Gala Rebane has focused on the *genre* of home tour vlogs in their paper that defines room tours as "short, amateurish or semi-professional videos [in which] predominantly female teenagers put their bedrooms on show, painstakingly commenting on furniture and decoration"[3] and "flaunting material possessions" as an extension of their "narcissistic tendencies on social media."[4] Drawing up a literature review-based conceptual history of visiting the parlor, Rebane argues that YouTube home tours are a similar interstitial space between privacy and public socialization within the locus of the home, where symbolic capital can be put on display for viewers as "virtual guests"[5] to take in. Rebane further contrasts the room tour genre with DIY videos, in that while the latter is "concerned with interior decoration" and "practical guidance", the former "only boasts [of] the results of that process."[6]

Perhaps most relevant is Rainer Hillrichs' broader study on the history of the earliest vlogs on YouTube and how they managed the bedroom as a *setting* for their content. Hillrichs observes that prior to YouTube's culture of rapid professionalization, bedrooms were not merely unthoughtful, convenient backdrops for producing content, but were already "motivated by particular video projects" and were "willingly, consciously, and performatively"[7] captured on film. Focusing on the teenagers whose videos comprised the earliest YouTube archives, Hillrichs argues that the arrangement of bedrooms in the absence of the camera are already manipulated for "a private local audience"[8] such as one's friends and parents, thus challenging the idea that such home vlogs are mere extensions of "home movies and home videos" that had more accurately captured life 'as is' pre-social media.[9]

Following from these three key works, this chapter presents a subset of work from an exploratory study to survey other formats, demographics, and genres of home tour vlogs and vlogs that privilege the home as a locus, specific to the East Asian context, in relation to performances of class in domestic spaces. This diversion is a reflexive decision considering that Hillrichs' study has focused on American YouTubers by nature of the history of YouTube, that Rebane's survey of videos that were "chosen randomly" is (still) dominated by the figure of a "girl in her mid-teens, mostly white and middle- to upper-middle class,"[10] and that Spyer's study focused on British YouTube microcelebrities.

East Asian Context and Methodology

Topically, research on Asian cultures on YouTube can be grouped into three categories. The first group of studies predominantly focus on the East Asian diaspora, usually from the US, who are parsed as 'Asian American' in relation to discourses of cultural hybridity.[11–14] Although sometimes claiming to focus on the 'Asian community', these studies are still largely Anglo-centric in their sampling, for instance, by focusing on YouTube channels where content creators primarily generate English language content. This reflects the larger Anglo- and Euro-centricity of studies on YouTube videos, where studies have claimed to draw from a "random sample" via search terms on YouTube only to exclude those that are not in the English language,[15] for instance. The second group of studies focus on how YouTube is used as a medium to document and disseminate knowledge about various practices in East Asia, such as the promotion and remixing of legacy media productions,[16–18] documenting and discussing cultural heritage,[19] consuming news,[20] and producing and discovering identity.[21] At times considering nation-specific issues such as media censorship or state authoritarianism, these studies have also explored the potential for YouTube to be a site of participating in politics, political campaigning and to hold politically subversive content.[22–26] The third group of studies has focused specifically on socio-cultural practices on YouTube content that is based on East Asian cultural phenomena, such as the experience of expatriates in these countries,[27] East Asian specific memes[28] and internet celebrities.[29]

This chapter is oriented to the third group of studies and focuses on YouTube videos produced by East Asian content creators in East Asian languages. Specifically, this chapter looks at YouTube vlogs that focus on the home as a topic and locale of content production, and how these creators' domestic practices and leisurely pursuits convey inconspicuous consumption as an indicator of class within their East Asian contexts. Responding to social theorist Raewyn Connell's call to decolonize social thought by interrogating our practices of knowledge production and methodological application in research,[30,31] the data in the chapter are purposively sampled to discuss two specific genres of home vlogs or domestic space vlogs that are popular among Chinese, Japanese, South Korean, and Taiwanese YouTube creators but have not otherwise been covered in the literature of YouTube home vlogs thus far. The YouTube creators in this study are drawn from a larger set of East Asian YouTube channels that are being observed by the author in an ongoing pilot study on East Asian Influencers as producers and gatekeepers of knowledge, and have been studied via immersive digital ethnography from June 2018 to April 2019.

The survey of YouTube home vlogs in the larger study can be classified into three broad categories: *Recreational* home vlogs displaying YouTube creators flaunting their houses or holiday homes; *Procedural* home vlogs documenting YouTube creators cleaning, organizing, or upgrading their space; and *Milestone* home vlogs detailing YouTube creators progressing in their domestic living space, such as moving into a college dormitory or a new house. This chapter concentrates on the recreational genres of 'slow living at home' and 'home cafés.'

Each channel is screened weekly for new video updates and announcements, the content of the videos and comments section, and the rhythm and shape of the discourse in the comments section, all of which are observed and recorded with thick description in ethnographic fieldnotes. Each of the videos in this chapter was precisely selected from the YouTube creators' channels to demonstrate the core features of the genres. They contain spoken and written Chinese, Japanese, and Korean and are usually complemented by English subtitles provided by the creator, or, in a few instances, crowd-sourced and volunteered by other viewers; some of the video titles are auto-translated by YouTube while others are bilingually titled by the creators. Although it is difficult to generalize the demographic of these YouTube creators given that the variety of videos and channels is diverse across the cultural and language groups, the sample in this chapter and in the larger study do not reflect Rebane's[32] claim that home tour vlog creators are usually teenagers and differ from Spyer's[33] focus on microcelebrities, as they primarily comprise adults in their 20s–30s and include an assortment of internet celebrities[34] and non-celebrity, non-monetized YouTube creators.

Slow Living at Home

'Slow living at home' generally features YouTube creators who share sentiments about preferring to stay in and spend recreational time at home rather than venturing outside. These videos tend to focus on reducing one's conspicuous consumption, being more mindful about waste, and resisting societal pressures such as overworking. Many of these channels include YouTube creators who reveal that they have resigned from high paying, fast-paced corporate jobs to pursue better wellbeing, or that they are recovering from mental health conditions such as burn out, stress, and exhaustion, which are urban conditions that proliferate in fast-paced, commercial-driven cities such as Shanghai, Tokyo, Seoul, and Taipei, to name a few. Unlike traditional displays of class and wealth that are performed through "conspicuous consumption"[35] these YouTube creators boast the valuable asset of time and the ability to juggle both their work lives and a degree of "conspicuous leisure"[36] within the confines of their homes. Their capacity to opt out of the rat race in their countries by pursuing alternative mostly home-based freelance work and their dedication to the conscientious keeping up of their domestic spaces signify a "pecuniary ability to afford a life of idleness"[37] at least to a certain extent.

One such channel is 슛뚜 sueddu. Based in South Korea, the videos feature a young woman whose face is generally obscured and whose movements are filmed from the neck down. Even then, the focus of the videos is less on her body and more on her household environment. Like many videos in this genre, dialogue and speech in these videos are minimized and diegetic sounds of various actions on screen are emphasized. Occasionally, some of these videos feature a soft and gentle narrative complementing certain scenes in post-production, layered over the diegetic sound. They almost always feature brief captions describing the YouTube creator's actions or thoughts in small, slim, simple white script placed in the middle of the screen. At times, some scenes are complemented with light background music.

Narrativizing Visual Rhythms of Everyday Routines

In an early video, 슛뚜 sueddu explains at the beginning of one of her standard house tours that she has recently moved house: "I move to a new house. It's a new house but feels familiar. It's because I used to live here till a year ago."[38] She explains in another video that her "Home is a precious place with many meanings to me. Where I can be MY SELF."[39] With the house as her primary locus of inhabitation and where she develops her personhood the most, 슛뚜 sueddu explains how she went to great lengths to return to this previous apartment. Her videos generally follow the rhythm of her daily life, starting from when she wakes up, makes her bed, and makes herself some breakfast. The rest of the video usually spotlights routine activities such as doing the laundry and cleaning, or other home-based lounging practices such as reading or enjoying a coffee.

The scenes pan across different areas of her house in each video, and zoom in on different corners or artifacts to complement the slow living practice captured on film. 숯뚜 sueddu's videos of the daily mundane usually emphasize diegetic sounds completed with superimposed white Korean script on screen as descriptors: the pouring water into a flask from making a cup of coffee ("This moka pot that I bought in Spain is really useful"), the crinkling of plastic from unwrapping packages that arrive by post ("The items I ordered last night arrived this afternoon"), or the pitter-patter footsteps of her dog around the living room ("Bebe [name of her dog] eats a snack while I work").[40] Set against the culture of "conspicuous consumption"[41] that is prevalent throughout East Asia, the wares 숯뚜 sueddu displays around her home may not always connote "pecuniary beauty"[42] per se—a status elevation and distinction accorded to goods desired by people by virtue of its prohibitive financial cost—as they are often mere household products. However, the short captions she shares often subtly point to their distinction as 'exotic' or 'exclusive' wares by referencing the holiday destinations from which she acquired her goods, and indirectly highlight her relative wealth as such.

Aestheticizing the Principles of Housekeeping

In other videos, 숯뚜 sueddu is focused on specific house-bound recreation activities such as painting,[43] and explains how these activities allow her to appreciate the locus of her home—in one scene where her camera fixates on a sunray on her carpet, her caption reads "I like today's sunlight."[44] Other videos turn to very specific steps of routine household chores such as loading up a washing machine with clothes, starting it up, listening to water gush through the pipes, and watching the machine spin rounds.[45] Like other channels in her genre, 숯뚜 sueddu also espouses some principles of housekeeping, which in her instance include minimalism and recycling[46] through demonstrations of her practices in these home tour vlogs. In a handful of videos where she has to go for a grocery run or go to work, the scenes cut from her morning routine to short snippets of her commute on public transport, where the camera continues to focus on the scenery to reflect her daily rhythms, until it culminates in her return home. Here, she regularly refers to her home as a refuge, as encapsulated in one video where she is seen preparing an elaborate meal in the kitchen upon coming home at nightfall; the captions accompanying her cooking and winding down at home read "It is late ... but I bake meat for me who suffered all day."[47] In these examples, YouTube creators such as 숯뚜 sueddu demonstrate their "habitus"[48]—a conditioned set of dispositions, preferences, practices, and habits that are ingrained and embodied in persons as a sum of their upbringing, social exposure, and personal experiences—through the decisions they make about mundane routines such as housekeeping and preparing a home-cooked meal. Building on Veblen's notion of "pecuniary beauty",[49] she displays a "pecuniary taste"[50] in that her lifestyle patterns refute the mainstream 'big city' culture of outsourcing household chores to casual cleaners and substituting the labor of home-cooked meals for convenient take-out. Instead, 숯뚜 sueddu is able to afford spare time during regular working hours to focus on her chores, and some leisurely time after her freelance work to invest in an extent of culinary extravagance.

Slow Home Living as Recuperation

Slow living at home is not just a lifestyle choice but also a recuperation device. The home has long been designated as a space where people calibrate their "moral standards, happiness, and success in the outside world."[51] Studies in the medical and health fields have promoted home-based care for people with serious mental illness,[52] found that the elderly who stay at home are able to receive better social support and increase morale alongside good material and emotional needs,[53] and that the elderly who have deteriorating mobility can still lead meaningful lives at home when they experience: independence from the privacy and control over their environment, familiarity with their surroundings, the presence of a stable social network, home maintenance as productive exercise, a conducive space to provide hospitality, and the home as a locus of meaning-making during crucial milestones.[54] Although she is a young person, some of these principles similarly apply to 숫뚜 sueddu: the desire to have control over one's environment is exactly why she painstakingly moved back to her former apartment; her stable social network is not focused on other human actors, but more on routine places of familiarity such as the grocery store or the regular coffee shop she frequents in her videos; home maintenance is portrayed as a mindful and even enjoyable activity rather than a chore; and although more rare, hospitality is practiced through the deliberate sprucing up of the home and preparing of a meal for visitors, and the house becomes a locus for meaningful seasonal celebrations through a change in décor such as table settings. Further, juxtaposed against the networks of South Korean home improvement vlogs that often focus on inevitable clutter from a lack of time to clean, space constraints in a crowded city like Seoul, and the struggle to personalize one's domestic space given the prevalence of transient renting practices over the more secure home ownership, 숫뚜 sueddu's class is further accentuated through the meta message in her vlogs: she has the financial capacity and temporal ability to cultivate her home into a leisurely space wherein she is able to pursue pecuniary hobbies such as calligraphy and painting, and slow living at home can be a way of life.

Subtle Integration of Monetization

In early 2019, 숫뚜 sueddu's channel began to make sponsored videos for collaborations with clients, although still keeping in theme with her ethos of slow living: in the first of these videos, she records her house cleaning routine and focuses on clearing her closet, using this opportunity to showcase a new machine for sterilizing fabrics. Her integration of the sponsored message feels seamless and unforced, as her videos maintain their usual aesthetic and only lightly reference the product. For instance, in one scene the camera pans on her dog sniffing the foot of the machine, with a caption that reads "Samsung Air Dresser I just brought home last weekend. Bebe is sniffing at the new stuff." She then shows herself hanging up a few heavy clothes in the machine, and explains in the captions that "It removes dust and chemicals that are left on the lining of the clothes", and continues the video with other household chores. There is minimal overt promotion or mentioning of the brand or product, apart from the video information that reads: "Hello everyone! I've got so many request about making Home cleaning video. And finally, here it is! ★ This video was made with support from Samsung Electronics, and contains AD." Comments on this first sponsored video are still focused on how peaceful and calming her videos her, and how viewers feel relaxed and soothed once again.[55] This marked the beginning of some conspicuous consumption practices in her videos as these products come with a hefty price-tag, and provide non-essential middle-class housekeeping. Other channels of 'slow living at home' include South Korean cardsu 까르슈[56] who tends to focus on plant care and culinary skills, and South Korean 해그린달 haegreendal[57] who focuses on cooking for her children and decorating her home.

Home Cafés

Home cafés are a subgenre of 'slow living at home', wherein the logic is to be able to simulate café-style ambience and foods in the comfort of one's own home. Through detailed home tour vlogs focused on the kitchen where food is prepared and the dining and living areas where meals are consumed, such YouTube creators as Cafe709 showcase their homewares through immaculate kitchen and dishware, flaunt their home décor through beautiful backdrops and props on the dining table, and feature long montages of themselves slowly enjoying a proper home-cooked meal in their homes. Although it has been offered that women tend to be "more attached to memorabilia and men to items of instrumental value, such as furniture and appliances,"[58] home café

YouTube creators tend to blur these demarcations by concentrating care towards and highlighting the sentimental value of functional objects such as coffee machines or wooden tea spoons. In various videos, they explain how a specific item of dishware is meaningful for its visual aesthetic or the associated memories of previous pleasant experiences. In other words, despite the temptation to maximize convenience and ease, eating alone at home can still be designed to be mindful and enjoyable. These behaviors constitute a form of "aspirational class" where the elite class in society are defined less by their "economic position" than their "acquisition of knowledge and culture."[59] Such YouTube creators "reveal their social position through much more subtle behaviors and goods that are not necessarily expensive but imply a rich cultural and social capital relegated to aspirational class membership."[60]

Eating Alone but Eating Well

Various news reports posit that the rise of people eating alone in East Asian countries is due to the growth of single-person households, a falling birthrate, an aging society, time constraints due to a hectic pace of life, and the lack of company due to anomie in city life.[61–63] While such phenomena has resulted in digital trends like the collaborative eating practice of *mukbang* in South Korea, where users livestream themselves eating while socializing with followers via a screen,[64] home café YouTube creators turn away from the notion of convenient takeaway foods and instead channel their energies into preparing "proper meals" comprising "fresh" and "natural" ingredients that are "cooked rather than cold or heated up."[65] Such elaborate cooking, plating, and eating is experienced as a privilege and luxury in the climate of fast paced East Asian cities—considering their "conspicuous leisure" as the "ability to use time for something with no productive purpose"[66] (given that quicker and cheaper alternatives abound)—as evidenced in the comments section where viewers consistently query what these YouTube creators do for work to be able to afford this time, how much effort each home café experience takes, and the financial sink of such a lifestyle choice. Like the 'slow living at home' genre, these videos usually obscure one's face and focus on diegetic sound.

Slow Cooking and Slow Eating

One such channel is the South Korean Cafe709. A typical video such as "Sunday late lunch"[67] catalogues the process of the YouTube creator slicing, dicing, and mixing ingredients with the camera focused on the kitchen top, before moving to focus on pots boiling and pans frying as the camera fixates on the stove top. Once the food is ready, it is carefully plated onto dishware, artfully garnished, and conscientiously set on a table alongside various matching utensils. As if to accentuate "conspicuous leisure,"[68,69] around three minutes of footage (which is rather long in the context of YouTube vlogs that average 11–15 minutes), which is often comprised of longer scenes that have been truncated and spliced to speed things along, is then dedicated to the camera fixated on the Cafe709 creator and a family member dining, with the frame capturing their bodies from neck down, and focused on their hands and dishes. There is some light small talk in the background, but emphasis is on the diegetic sound of crunching on vegetables, slurping on soup, and chewing on meats. Each video usually ends when their plates are emptied, and they clear and clean the dining table to end the scene.

Care around Dishware

Some videos may cast a spotlight on special dishware, such as teacups and tea plates,[70] or elaborate Japanese wooden dishware including matching trays, bowls, chopsticks, and chopstick holders.[71] They may focus on variations of their daily meals such as "Sunday lunch," which appears heartier than the usual fare,[72] or "Simple breakfast," which seems to require less preparation time for lazy days.[73] Still other videos focus on special occasions with more extravagant meals such as "New Year's Morning,"[74] or culturally specific dishes that necessitate very distinctive kitchenware such as "Sukiyaki"[75] which requires a continuously boiling ceramic pot on a portable stove on the dining table. Other channels in this genre include South Korean 아이비 키친 Ivy Kitchen,[76] or Chinese-Australian 子时当归[77,78] that focuses especially on the grocery shopping experience prior to meal preparation.

Hanging Out at Home as a Lifestyle

While prior Anglo- and Euro-centric studies on YouTube home vlogs have deliberated how they are being integrated into commercialized Influencer content,[79] how they may convey continuums of privacy and publicness,[80] and whether the nature of such footage is simulated or manipulated to convey semblances of privacy,[81] this chapter is an exploratory study into the other genres of home vlogs that abound among East Asian creators on YouTube, and how their domestic practices and spaces can be read as displays and affirmations of social class. Unlike other studies on microcelebrity[82] and ordinary users[83] on YouTube home vlogs, these videos discard the primacy of person-based fame by obscuring the facial identity of the creator, choosing instead to focus on the feelings of spatiality and temporality within the locus of the home through camera pans over spaces, objects, routines, and practices, and in the process, reveal the "conspicuous leisure"[84,85] and "pecuniary taste" and lifestyles[86,87] of a leisurely aspirational class. Specifically, the chapter draws from a purposive sampling of video styles that are popular among YouTube creators in China, Japan, South Korea, and Taiwan to outline the core elements of 'slow living at home' and 'home café' home vlogs as emblems of class displays against the backdrop of fast-paced living, overwork culture, and lifestyle decisions tending towards convenience and affordability in big cities in East Asia. Reflecting on the social conditions and cultural routines of the East Asian region, the chapter also shows how such YouTube home tour vlogs foreground households in situ, domesticity as a privilege, and hanging out at home as a lifestyle.

Notes

1 Maggie Griffith and Zizi Papacharissi, "Looking for You: An Analysis of Video Blogs." *First Monday* 15, no 1–4 (2010).
2 Juliano Spyer, "The Fame of Vloggers: Value Production and Spatiotemporal Expansion among YouTube Beauty Gurus." Chapter in dissertation, "Making Up Art, Videos and Fame – The Creation of Social Order in the Informal Realm of YouTube Beauty Gurus, Department of Anthropology, University College London, 2013. www.academia.edu/2526400/THE_FAME_OF_VLOGGERS_Value_Production_and_Spatiotemporal_Expansion_Among_YouTube_Beauty_Gurus.
3 Gala Rebane, "A 'Parlour of One's Own'? The YouTube Room Tour Genre," *Continuum* 33, no. 1 (2019): 51–64, p. 52.
4 Ibid, 51.
5 Ibid, 52.
6 Ibid, 52.
7 Rainer Hillrichs, "From the Bedroom to LA: Revisiting the Settings of Early Video Blogs on YouTube." *NECSUS: European Journal of Media Studies* 2: 107–131, p. 107.
8 Ibid, 111–112.
9 Ibid, 107.
10 Rebane, "A 'Parlour of One's Own'?," 54.
11 Stuart Cunningham and David Craig. *Social Media Entertainment: The New Intersection of Hollywood and Silicon Valley* (New York: New York University Press, 2019), 191–202.
12 Lei Guo and Lorin Lee. "The Critique of YouTube-Based Vernacular Discourse: A Case Study of YouTube's Asian Community," *Critical Studies in Media Communication* 30, no. 5 (2013): 391–406.
13 Lei Guo and Summer Harlow, "User-Generated Racism: An Analysis of Stereotypes of African Americans, Latinos, and Asians in YouTube Videos," *Howard Journal of Communication* 25, no. 3 (2014): 281–302.

14 Roger Saul, "KevJumba and the Adolescence of YouTube." *A Journal of the American Educational Studies Association* 46, no. 5 (2010): 457–477.
15 Heather Molyneaux, Susan O'Donnell, Kerri Gibson, Janice Singer, "Exploring the Gender Divide on YouTube: An Analysis of the Creation and Reception of Vlogs," *American Communication Journal* 10, no. 2 (2008): 1–14.
16 Marc L. Moskowitz, "Seeing Sound: Perhaps Love, YouTube, and Hong Kong's Cultural Convergence," *Visual Anthropology* 27 no. 1–2 (2014): 149–165.
17 Cameron David Warner, "Hope and Sorrow: Uncivil Religion, Tibetan Music Videos, and YouTube," *Journal of Anthropology* 78, no. 4 (2013): 543–568.
18 Hui Yu and Sary Schroeder, "Distribution and Popularity Patterns of Chinese Music on YouTube: A Case Study of Local Music's Representation on a Global Internet Platform," *Journal of New Music Research* 47, no. 1 (2018): 68–77.
19 Peter R. Petrucci and Katsuyuki Miyahira, "'Can You Call it Okinawan Japanese?': World Language Delineations of an Endangered Language on YouTube," *Journal of World Languages* 3, no. 3 (2016): 204–223.
20 Francis L.F. Lee, "News from YouTube: Professional Incorporation in Hong Kong Newspaper Coverage of Online Videos," *Asian Journal of Communication* 22, no. 1 (2012): 1–18.
21 Chih-Ping Chen, "Forming Digital Self and Parasocial Relationships on YouTube," *Journal of Consumer Culture* 16, no. 1 (2014): 232–254.
22 Nur Amali Ibrahim, "Everyday Authoritarianism: A Political Anthropology of Singapore," *Critical Asian Studies* 50, no. 2 (2018): 219–231.
23 David Chison Oh, "'Racist Propaganda': Discursive Negotiations on YouTube of Perceived Anti-White Racism in South Korea," *Atlantic Journal of Communication* 26, no. 5 (2018): 306–317.
24 Carol Soon and Siti Nadzirah Samsudin, "General Election 2015 in Singapore: What Social Media Did and Did Not Do," *The Commonwealth Journal of International Affairs* 105, no. 2 (2016): 171–184.
25 Kenneth Paul Tan, "Choosing What to Remember in Neoliberal Singapore: The Singapore Story, State Censorship and State-Sponsored Nostalgia," *Asian Studies Review* 40, no. 2 (2016): 231–249.
26 Weiyu Zhang, "Social Media and Elections in Singapore: Comparing 2011 and 2015," *Chinese Journal of Communication* 9, no. 4 (2016): 367–384.
27 Yueh-ching Chang and Yu-jung Chang, "Identity Negotiation in the Third Space: An Analysis of YouTube Channels Hosted by Expatriates in Taiwan," *Language and Intercultural Communication* 19, no. 1 (2019): 77–92.
28 Weiai Wayne Xu, Ji Young Park, Ji Young Kim, and Han Woo Park, "Networked Cultural Diffusion and Creation on YouTube: An Analysis of YouTube Memes," *Journal of Broadcasting & Electronic Media* 60, no. 1 (2016): 104–122.
29 Donna Chu, "Collective Behavior in YouTube: A Case Study of 'Bus Uncle' Online Videos," *Asian Journal of Communication* 19, no. 3 (2008): 337–353.
30 Raewyn Connell, *Southern Theory: Social Science and the Global Dynamics of Knowledge* (London: Wiley, 2007).
31 Raewyn Connell, "Using Southern Theory: Decolonizing Social Thought in Theory, Research and Application," *Planning Theory* 31, no. 2 (2014): 210–223.
32 Rebane, "A 'Parlour of One's Own'?"
33 Spyer, "The Fame of Vloggers."
34 Crystal Abidin, *Internet Celebrity: Understanding Fame Online* (Bingley, UK: Emerald Publishing, 2018).
35 Thorstein Veblen. *The Theory of the Leisure Class: An Economic Study of Institutions* (Laxmi Nagar, Dehli: Aakar Books, 1899).
36 Veblen, *The Theory of the Leisure Class*.
37 Veblen, *The Theory of the Leisure Class*, 33.
38 슛뚜 sueddu. 2018a. "My New House Tour." YouTube.com, August 18. www.youtube.com/watch?v=1By_P265oHs.
39 슛뚜 sueddu. 2018b. "Room Tour;)" YouTube.com, May 12. www.youtube.com/watch?v=1FQA1qRaEq8.
40 슛뚜 sueddu. 2018c. "Staying all Day at Home." YouTube.com, March 25. www.youtube.com/watch?v=RXr8X6vF1rk.
41 Veblen, *The Theory of the Leisure Class*.
42 Veblen, *The Theory of the Leisure Class*.
43 슛뚜 sueddu. 2018d. "Staying all Day at Home/Painting." YouTube.com, March 31. www.youtube.com/watch?v=FHVBjxukEwU.
44 슛뚜 sueddu. 2018d.
45 슛뚜 sueddu. 2018e. "Invite a Friend to My Home." YouTube.com, April 4. www.youtube.com/watch?v=82li-WaN56M.

46 숫뚜 sueddu. 2018f. "Become a Minimalist. Minimalism." YouTube.com, July 15. www.youtube.com/watch?v=6tcdDZh6K_c.
47 숫뚜 sueddu. 2018g. "일하는 숫뚜 일상 브이로그 (Work day vlog/ENG)." YouTube.com, March 16. www.youtube.com/watch?v=Ebwv8gGnu5U.
48 Pierre Bourdieu. 1984. *Distinction: A Social Critique of the Judgement of Taste* (Cambridge, MA: Harvard University Press, 1984).
49 Veblen, *The Theory of the Leisure Class*.
50 Crystal Abidin. 2014. "#In$tagLam: Instagram as a Repository of Taste, a Brimming Marketplace, a War of Eyeballs." in *Mobile Media Making in the Age of Smartphones*, eds. Marsha Berry and Max Schleser (New York: Palgrave Pivot, 2014), 122.
51 Marilyn Ferris Motz, "Introduction," in *Making the American Home: Middle-Class Women & Domestic Material Culture 1840–1940*, eds. Marilyn Ferris Motz and Pat Browne (Ohio: Bowling Green State University Popular Press, 1988), 1.
52 I.M. Marks, J. Connolly, M. Muijen, B. Audini, G. McNamee, and R.E. Lawrence, "Home-Based Versus Hospital-Based Care for People with Serious Mental Illness," *The British Journal of Psychiatry* 165, no. 2 (1994): 179–194.
53 Yang Gyeong Yoo, "Perceived Social Support and Morale of the Elderly Staying at Home," *Journal of Korean Academy of Nursing* 34, no. 2 (2004): 297–306.
54 Barry S. Fogel, "Psychological Aspects of Staying at Home," *Generations* 16, no. 2 (1992): 15.
55 숫뚜 sueddu. 2019. "House Cleaning Day. My Closet." YouTube.com, April 27. www.youtube.com/watch?v=YYMD9RN5Mjg.
56 cardsu 까르슈. 2018. "#3.일상 브이로그 Weekday in Korea 식물과 살림, 영문 캘리그라피가 있는 일상." YouTube.com, September 18. www.youtube.com/watch?v=9EL4-EOUL24.
57 해그린달 haegreendal. 2019. "(SUB) Mom's Daily Life Vlog, How to Spend my Own Time Beautifully. Time for Me." YouTube.com, April 13. www.youtube.com/watch?v=QF26vsH_qSg.
58 Fogel, "Psychological Aspects of Staying at Home."
59 Elizabeth Currid-Halkett. *The Sum of Small Things: A Theory of the Aspirational Class* (Princeton and Oxford: Princeton University Press, 2017), 6.
60 Currid-Halkett, *The Sum of Small Things*, 22.
61 Japan Times, "More Japanese Eating Alone Amid Aging Society: Report," *Japan Times*, May 29, 2018. www.japantimes.co.jp/news/2018/05/29/national/japanese-eating-alone-amid-aging-society-report/#.XN5PLxMzY_U.
62 Claire Lee. 2016. "Why More Koreans Are Eating Alone." *Asia One*, May 30. www.asiaone.com/asia/why-more-koreans-are-eating-alone.
63 *Straits Times*, "Table for One Please! More Chinese Done Alone When Eating Out." *Straits Times*, December 24, 2018. www.straitstimes.com/asia/east-asia/table-for-one-please-more-chinese-dine-alone-when-eating-out.
64 Hanwool Choe, "Eating Together Multimodally: Collaborative Eating in *Mukbang*, a Korean Livestream of Eating," *Language in Society* 48, no. 2 (2019): 171–208.
65 Gill Valentine, "Eating In: Home, Consumption and Identity," *The Sociological Review* 47, no. 3 (1999): 491–524, p. 492.
66 Currid-Halkett, *The Sum of Small Things*.
67 Cafe709. 2019a. "Cafe709 일요일 늦은 점심. 계란을 풀어 넣은 폭신폭신 칠리 새우. 간단 레시피" YouTube.com, March 13. www.youtube.com/watch?v=SBLzRhBwbXk.
68 Veblen, *The Theory of the Leisure Class*.
69 Currid-Halkett, *The Sum of Small Things*.
70 Cafe709. 2019b. "Cafe709 Vol. 31 티타임, 영상속 음악과 사라진 영상" YouTube.com, February 27. www.youtube.com/watch?v=HtGRd568GEs.
71 Cafe709. 2019c. "Cafe709 남편이 구운 일본 찹쌀떡(餅)과 인스턴트 일본 단팥죽(おしるこ), 일본 일상" YouTube.com, January 9. www.youtube.com/watch?v=OCSDtIlcZkQ.
72 Cafe709. 2019d. "Cafe709 일요일 점심 준비. 계란요리(카니타마:かに玉). 감자 미소시루. 냄비밥. 함께 먹는 식탁. 일본가정요리" YouTube.com, April 3. www.youtube.com/watch?v=V2KhXhcbDqI.
73 Cafe709. 2019e. "Cafe709 간단하게 준비해서 먹는 아침식사. 양배추 소세지찜. 양배추요리. 남편과의 소소한 대화" YouTube.com, March 20. www.youtube.com/watch?v=oLshjewxecQ.
74 Cafe709. 2019f. "Cafe709 2019 년 새해 아침, 오세치요리(おせち料理), 남편이 내린 커피와 카마쿠라 치즈케익, 원플레이트 아침" YouTube.com, January 2. www.youtube.com/watch?v=JfEYsWS9Zlk.
75 Cafe709. 2018. "Cafe709 일요일의 스키야키, Sukiyaki, すき焼き, 일본 가정 요리" YouTube.com, December 12. www.youtube.com/watch?v=LrMgHdX4TV0.

76 아이비 키친 Ivy Kitchen. 2018. "미역국라면과 참치마요 오니기리 | Ivy Kitchen" YouTube.com, December 28. www.youtube.com/watch?v=tfQ0Cm7VbfU.
77 子时当归. 2018a. "当归 Vlog.01 | 跟我一起买菜做饭吃早餐 | A Morning In The Life: Make & Eat Breakfast With Me" YouTube.com, July 17. www.youtube.com/watch?v=2c5dWDTQTjA.
78 子时当归. 2018b. "当归 Vlog.10 | 两日生活：做饭，买菜，穿搭 | Two Ordinary Days In My Life: "Fat" Sandwich Tutorial | 沼三明治怎么做" YouTube.com, August 20. www.youtube.com/watch?v=e5-w7EiV798.
79 Spyer, "The Fame of Vloggers."
80 Rebane, "A 'Parlour of One's Own'?"
81 Hillrichs, "From the Bedroom to LA."
82 Spyer, "The Fame of Vloggers."
83 Rebane, "A 'Parlour of One's Own'?"
84 Currid-Halkett, *The Sum of Small Things*.
85 Veblen, *The Theory of the Leisure Class*.
86 Veblen, *The Theory of the Leisure Class*.
87 Abidin, #In$tagLam.

12

YOUNG PEOPLE, SMARTPHONES, AND INVISIBLE ILLITERACIES

Closing the Potentiality–Actuality Chasm in Mobile Media

Sun Sun Lim and Renae Sze Ming Loh

There has been considerable euphoria surrounding smartphones and their ability to make mobile internet access a reality for previously disconnected communities, offering them exciting possibilities in terms of communication, education, health and consumer services. However, is this optimism warranted or is there a chasm between the inherent potentiality in how these devices can be fully exploited and the actual ways in which they are utilized by individual adopters? In the current chapter, we report our findings on underprivileged youths in Singapore, a country with affordable and widespread internet access. We find evidence of young people who are ostensibly connected to the internet, but whose online repertoire is relatively limited compared with that of their peers. Eschewing laptops and computers in favor of smartphones, these young people's internet use is largely confined to social media and communication apps such as WhatsApp, Snapchat and Instagram, and entertainment apps such as YouTube, Dubsmash and Musical.ly, with minimal exploration of the World Wide Web's rich offerings. While statistical measures would classify these youths as internet users, their limited navigation and usage of the online space does not fully optimize the medium's affordances for learning, participating, creating and "produsing." To rectify these trends and symptoms of "invisible illiteracies," media literacy education in mobile-only or mobile-heavy media environments needs to be urgently refined to better prepare young people for the full complement of online opportunities. We explain our study's approach and findings against the broader context of class distinctions in Singapore.

The Changing Face of Digital Literacy

The notion of digital literacy is not new. Indeed, arguments for computer literacy date back to at least the 1980s. Computer literacy entails the proficiency to operate a computer and perform various everyday tasks using email, internet browsers, word processing software and others.[1] It constitutes a part of digital literacy, a much broader concept that involves the ability not only to handle computing devices and consume computer-based entertainment and interactions, but also to critically consume the content presented on various digital platforms.[2] This critical awareness of distinguishing authoritative from non-authoritative and relevant from irrelevant sources[3] calls not only for users to possess multi-modal literacy, the ability to make sense of all forms of media including graphs, images and videos, but also for information literacy, the ability to analyze and assess the information.[4] Underlying this critical awareness is discernment about information—sourcing, creating and evaluating information—which contributes to an individual's options for participating in the political, social and economic spheres of modern societies as a citizen.[5]

Indeed, a new dynamic order is forming, as is a new mode of how society functions. Where we were previously constrained to a desktop computer with an internet connection, today the permanent and ubiquitous connection to data networks has granted portable digital devices and mobile applications a high degree of accessibility and convenience. Additionally, with Wi-Fi infrastructures installed in many public spaces and buildings, and the growing saturation of smartphones and tablets, we are never "disconnected." We seem to live in an age where our actions are frequently mediated by digital tools, and the objects we encounter are frequently shaped by digital intervention.[6] For example, we now use digital devices to manage work obligations, schedule our meetings, search for directions, keep up with friends, consume content, and purchase physical goods, among many other activities. We also use global digital platforms such as LinkedIn to apply for jobs, Coursera to attend courses, Wordpress to chronicle our lives, Dropbox to store our files, and Facebook, Instagram and Twitter to build our digital profiles and personal networks. At the global level, the world is more connected than ever. The amount of cross-border bandwidth has increased by 45 times since 2005.[7] Flows of users, information, communication, video, transactions and other digital traffic look set to increase as digital device use and ownership proliferates. These streams of information and ideas enable the movement of goods, services, capital, and people. Some 900 million people have international connections on social media, and 360 million take part in cross-border e-commerce.[8] Much like our daily lives, almost every type of international action now consists of a digital component. However, to assume that this growth in digitalization is homogeneous across the globe would be to neglect some critical issues pertaining to inequalities in internet access and usage.

Whither Literacy and Class

Indeed, as the subsequent discussion will seek to demonstrate, social inequality and class divides are both reflected in and exacerbated by uneven patterns in young people's internet usage. The field of research surrounding digital literacy can be said to be dominated by two threads. One sheds light on how internet usage could play a key role in addressing socioeconomic issues. From this salutary perspective, the internet helps us to connect with people and resources from all over the world, and interact across different socioeconomic backgrounds.[9] Social media, in particular, makes it easy for lay users to publish diverse content—in the form of texts, pictures, videos or audio—to a (potentially) sizeable audience,[10] regardless of one's own socioeconomic background. Furthermore, the content disseminated via the internet is often blind to one's cultural, economic and educational background. The internet and digital devices are thus regarded as facilitators and promoters of communication, bridging all backgrounds. On the other hand, the second thread views internet access through the lens of social barriers.[11] Some scholars have raised critical concerns about how internet usage and the new emphasis on digital literacy, particularly in education, may well be deeply imbricated with economic inequalities and power relations. These inequalities occur at two levels—access and skills.

The first level concerns the extent and nature of access. In order to gain access to the wealth of online information, fundamentally, one must first have access to ICTs (Information and Communications Technologies). Considerable academic work has been undertaken on this aspect, and this division between ICT haves and have-nots has been widely referred to as the digital divide.[12] Lack of access has been found to correlate with disadvantages in financial, educational or cultural resources that extensive research has revealed to exist between nations,[13] and within developed nations and regions,[14] as well as along the lines of age,[15] ethnicity[16] and income differences.[17] Most studies however, have focused mainly on adult populations. Yet, the degree to which young people's lives are increasingly mediated by ICTs at home, at school and in the community, certainly warrants greater academic attention. While scholarly fervor has been trained on the consequences of internet use, particular attention should also be paid to the reasons why some avidly utilize the internet while others do not, and the discrepancies in ways they use the internet.[18] The relative paucity of youth-centered research is perhaps attributed to the common perception of this generation as "digital natives"—the generation who were born into the internet era, where their technological inclinations and skills are (often mistakenly) assumed.[19]

And while many "digital natives" revel in the presumption that they are online experts, research has shown this to be misplaced.[20] The legitimacy of assuming that a whole generation would possess common digital traits in terms of access and use of technologies has been challenged at the theoretical[21] and empirical levels.[22] For example, Livingstone, Bober and Helsper[23] found that differences in engaging in online communication, information-seeking and peer-to-peer connection occur along the lines of gender, class and age. Lim[24] found that in Singapore, at-risk youths, as compared with their more academically achieved peers, did not fare significantly worse in their access to ICT. While both groups of youths had access to the same range of apps, the differences lay in how they used their devices and which apps were considered their mainstay. Their uses of technology primarily centered on socializing and entertainment, and manifested less information-seeking behavior. These studies indicate that simply belonging to the generation of "digital natives" does not automatically vest individuals with digital literacy or access to digital tools. A further assertion that this generation can be characterized by active online engagement also fails to capture how many young people's uses of digital technologies are actually far less extensive in scope, and actually more passive, pedestrian, and mundane than is widely believed.[25] Such claims also gloss over the huge variation between what youths are able to do with technology and what they know about technology.[26] What persists here is a secondary digital divide[27] which occurs on the skills level, separating those with the competencies to benefit from computer use, from those without.

Delving deeper into technology-related practices of youths can further illuminate the discussion. There are two kinds of online activities that have been identified as having the potential to enhance one's economic, social and cultural capital.[28] The first kind is capital-enhancing use, which involves marshalling online resources to improve educational outcomes, seek employment, advance careers, and enhance physical and mental health. The other kind of internet use mainly involves using the internet for entertainment, such as gaming, shopping and gambling online. Such use is generally believed to have little potential for increasing economic, social and cultural capital.[29] Bourdieu's research on social inequalities suggests that individuals tend to develop practices and dispositions that reflect their social positions and thereby reproduce existing advantages and disadvantages.[30] In the case of the internet, disadvantaged youth not only have less access to devices but also may be less likely to use the internet to enhance their education, and more likely to use the internet for entertainment. Previous research has provided some evidence for disadvantaged youths' greater propensity to use the internet for entertainment and converges on several explanations.[31] Principally, it is argued that lower engagement in capital-enhancing use of the internet reflects socioeconomic inequalities. These inequalities are further perpetuated because digital literacy levels affect their performance in school, thereby being systematically encoded into disparities in educational credentials. Going beyond these general trends, it is worthwhile exploring the nexus of digital literacy and socioeconomic differences in the specific context of a highly digitalized country such as Singapore.

Technology Adoption in Singapore

Singapore has amongst the highest internet and mobile phone penetration rates in the world. As of 2017, the overall wireless broadband penetration rate stands at 206.7 percent and residential broadband penetration rate at 94.5 percent. With 8.46 million mobile phone subscriptions for its approximately 5.61 million residents, Singapore's mobile phone penetration rate stands at 150.8 percent[32] and household computer ownership was 86 percent in 2014.[33] These statistics give a good indication of a preference for, or perhaps the greater accessibility of, mobile phones for the general population.

In recognizing ICTs' impact on the economy and workplace of the twenty-first century and its potential to enhance learning, the Singapore government committed S$2 billion to provide, in its initial phase (1997–2002), one computer per five students, and subsequently, one for every two students. To further integrate ICTs into learning and teaching, the Ministry of Education stipulated that up to 30 percent of instruction time should be enriched through the use of ICTs. All teacher trainees have compulsory and elective modules to equip them with ICT skills.[34] These efforts are geared towards development of what the Ministry of Education terms "21st Century Competencies," which encompasses communication, collaboration and information skills—these emphasize the development of skills required to function and indeed to thrive in a society and workplace permeated by ICT and internet-enabled services.

Given Singapore's technology adoption climate, and the evidence uncovered by extant research on how young people's digital literacy is imbricated with issues of class, the current study seeks to address the following two research questions.

1   What was distinctive about the technology use of disadvantaged youths?
2   How does the nature of their technology access influence their digital skills?

Research Method

For this study, a qualitative research method was chosen over a quantitative one in order to allow for more in-depth understanding of internet and device use of youths from disadvantaged families. More specifically, we conducted semi-structured in-home interviews. The approach of in-home interviews has been used in other studies regarding media usage among less-advantaged populations and yielded appreciable results.[35] A semi-structured approach affords the interviewer the flexibility needed to follow any relevant trajectories that arise during the interview, while still maintaining a focus on the core issue at hand. This proves beneficial in two ways—interviews become opportunities for gleaning new ideas, and it encourages two-way communication, making the interviewee more comfortable and thus more willing to share.

The interviews were conducted in the homes of these youths between November 2015 and April 2016 by the two authors, either individually or together, in the presence of a social worker. The social worker was always someone who had visited the family before and therefore known to them, and this greatly contributed to how comfortable the family was with having interviewer(s) in their home. This previous experience with the social worker further helped the interviewees, especially the younger ones, feel more at ease and less under scrutiny. Disadvantaged youths were chosen as our primary focus because relatively little academic attention has been paid to this demographic group in comparison with that for mainstream youths. The interviews opened with an introduction to the research, and an assurance that there were no right or wrong answers. In order to learn about their technology use, the respondents were first requested to note down their media use via a media map to represent how they were connected to the most important people in their lives through their devices and apps. As this is not a common concept, the interviewer would first construct her own media map by drawing it out on a piece of paper. The interviewee's mind map served as a springboard for further discussion and ensured that the interviewer did not overlook any aspect of their media use. A complementary list of questions regarding their media usage and practices was also prepared beforehand. A total of 18 youths, aged 12–17, were interviewed. Although a larger number was targeted, the challenges of soliciting participation and parental support from this group, which had very unpredictable schedules and relatively limited communication channels, made it difficult to attain the target. Each interview lasted between 45 to 90 minutes and was audio-recorded and later transcribed.

Findings and Discussion

This section will first provide an overview of the respondents' internet access, device ownership and environment, followed by their technology use, and digital skills. Where appropriate, illustrative interview excerpts will be furnished, with respondents indicated by their first initial, and the interviewer by the letter 'I'.

In terms of internet access, all of our respondents owned smartphones and had internet access mostly at home, at school, tapping into Wi-Fi hotspots such as those in fast food outlets, or with prepaid phone packages. Many of them preferred smartphones to laptops and desktops, manifesting a mobile-first user behavior. Their phones were mostly rewards for doing well in school or gifts vested upon crossing significant milestones such as birthdays. Most used prepaid packages funded by their parents, while the older interviewees tended to pay for their own phone bills using their savings or income from part-time jobs. There were also respondents who would pay for their own phone bills if and when they could afford it, especially if they had exceeded certain limits such as mobile data allowances. Paying for their own phone bills seemed to be a badge of honor for most of the respondents, perhaps as a potent indicator of their independence and maturity.

S: For me, I pay by myself. Because I am working part-time.
I: And then if you don't have enough savings?
S: That won't happen.
I: Because you plan your money well?
S: Yeah, I think so. I think because of the faith that I get from my mom, my dad also give me allowance every month. And then I always save the money, use it wisely, depends on what I need to buy.

(Interviewee S [17 years old], upper secondary school student, working part-time)

Most of the younger interviewees reported that their parents regulated their smartphone usage through rules such as "no phones when working on homework," and the confiscation of the phone was often used as a form of punishment.

With regard to other devices, not all respondents had access to either desktops or laptops at home. Of the few who did, it was access to laptops rather than desktops. The laptops often either belonged to another family member, such as a parent or older sibling, or was a shared family laptop. Shared laptops tended to be placed in common areas such as the living room so that usage could be monitored by authority figures such as parents or older siblings. A handful of respondents who did not have access to desktops or laptops at home stated that they could borrow a tablet belonging to their older sibling. However, their older sibling was often already working, so they would have to wait for them to return from work before asking for permission to use the tablet. Even then, use of the tablet was not always guaranteed. On the other hand, there were also those who lived in device-rich households.

I: Do you have any other devices at home besides everybody's phones? Any laptops, tablets?
S: Yes. Tablet, laptop. For my siblings, my father has a laptop. My mother has a phone. My younger siblings like my second brother, he have phone. My third one have a tablet. Even my younger sister, she's only 7, she has a tablet. So everyone has their own.

(Interviewee S [17 years old], upper secondary school student, working part-time)

Consistent with other studies of less-privileged youths, our respondents' online repertoire was largely confined to social media and communication apps such as Facebook, WhatsApp, Snapchat and Instagram, and entertainment apps such as YouTube, Dubsmash, Ask.fm and Musical.ly. Briefly, Dubsmash is a video messaging mobile app where users can choose from a range of audio clips from movies, TV shows, songs and the like and film themselves while dubbing over the audio clip. Ask.fm is a social networking site, with an accompanying mobile app, where users can ask each other questions that, in essence, prompt disclosure of some degree. For example, some may post questions such as "what do you want to do in the future?" and "what is your favorite food?" Musical.ly is a video 'prosuming' social media site, which also has an associated mobile application. Users can create videos that last from 15 seconds to a minute, which they can also edit with inbuilt video editing tools such as filters, speed adjustments (for example, time-lapse, slow-motion) and tack on an accompanying soundtrack. Our respondents used these services primarily, if not solely through the mobile apps, instead of the website. Overall, Facebook, WhatsApp, YouTube, Snapchat and Instagram were by far the most common and widely used mobile applications among our respondents. However, Facebook was sharply decreasing in popularity as numerous respondents indicated that they did not check or use Facebook as much given that their peers were also slowly withdrawing from Facebook, especially among the younger respondents.

Many of our interviewees reported that they often turned to social media, and in some cases, mobile games, when they were bored. Previous studies have suggested that disadvantaged children may play games to escape from the drudgery of school work, poor peer interaction and other life stresses.[36] However, this may be well true for youths from any socioeconomic background.

Beyond entertainment, our respondents' online activities mainly revolved around communicating with peers and family members. Not surprisingly, their communication with peers was principally social in nature, including activities such as keeping up with friends after school and engaging in gossip. With their family, it was mostly to keep the family updated on their whereabouts.

We noted that our respondents' mobile-centered and indeed, app-centric usage had implications for the development of their digital skills. While most if not all of our respondents were adept with social media, video splicing apps and other entertainment apps and platforms, not many were as skilled with the computer. Some would use the laptops at home or computers in their school libraries to complete school assignments, mostly if the assignment required use of the school's e-learning platform, or if it was a group project involving collaborative platforms such as Google Docs. If they required any assistance, either with the homework or the computer itself, their first instinct was to turn to their peers, parents, older siblings and perhaps relatives rather than searching for help online. This was often done face-to-face with parents, but more frequently via communication apps with friends.

I: Let's say you need help with your homework, do you normally google for information or do you ask your parents or friends?
A: Sometimes I did ask my parents, but they … she [my mother] doesn't really know. Then I say never mind, I try by myself.

(Interviewee A [13 years old], lower secondary school student)

A rare few do turn to Google should they require information, such as to obtain definitions and formulae. This was mostly if their other mobile applications, such as dictionary apps, did not work or if their parents or older siblings could not answer their questions. This was despite their having Wi-Fi access at home. Their use of Google was more to retrieve certain pieces of information such as formulae they had forgotten, rather than for more extensive research. Most used Google in order to access other entertainment platforms such as YouTube, Tumblr and online streaming services in order to watch content ranging from anime to Korean dramas.

Instead of using Google, other search engines or crowdsourcing platforms such as Wikipedia, our respondents revealed a preference for app-based communication tools such as WhatsApp to solicit information from people in their personal networks. Some of the respondents brought up how many of their classes had group chats hosted on apps such as WhatsApp, where students and sometimes teachers were included. These served as avenues not only for students to seek updates from the teacher or perhaps a student representative of the class, but also provided them with the opportunity to ask questions regarding homework. There was thus a reliance on seeking solutions from friends rather than independent information-seeking that leveraged the internet's repository of knowledge.

P: I will ask my friends for answers, then we share.
I: So, how do you normally ask for answers?
P: WhatsApp.
I: WhatsApp. And, let's say your homework, for example, you come to a very difficult question that you don't know how to do. Who do you ask?
P: My friends.
I: You'll ask your friends. If all your friends don't know?
P: If like ... If it is very urgent, I will text the teacher. If not, I will just wait until the next morning. If there's class, I will ask the teacher.
I: Then do you go on the internet and Google for answers, like how to do the questions.
P: No. No.
I: Okay. Do you ask your parents for help?
P: No.

(Interviewee P [16 years old], upper secondary school student)

In terms of access to news, our interviews also revealed that Facebook was the primary source of news and information, although the older interviewees tended to also watch the news on television. Their fact-checking practices were based on what their peers share, comment and say in real life or via communication apps or social media platforms. A handful of the interviewees discussed the news with their friends, older siblings or a parent. The older youths in particular showcased an awareness of what constitutes an authoritative and reliable source and what does not.

S: If I'm not sure it's real, I'll ask my sister if she has learnt this. And if she has heard it, then okay. Then maybe talk about it.
I: Do you use Google for more information or search for news?
P: Uh, no. I don't google. I just like ... because I follow the news, like ChannelNewsAsia, and also the Malay Berita [news] on Facebook. So they will just update what is happening in the world, so I will just read it and open and they will give all the information.

(Interviewee S [17 years old], upper secondary school student, working part-time)

Due to our respondents' mobile-first user profiles, the digital skills they possessed, while not limited, centered on smartphones and their app centric ecosystem. Communication apps such as WhatsApp, Snapchat and Instagram, and entertainment apps such as YouTube, Dubsmash and Musical.ly were thus their mainstay. Of the respondents interviewed, a handful were satisfied with using just these apps, and shared them with their peers. They were adept at producing short clips, and were quick to pick up these skills. Unfortunately, these are not necessarily the skills that are well-appreciated in educational or vocational settings. In Singapore, as with other developed countries, digital skills that are more valued in the school or workplace tend to relate broadly to research skills such as the gathering, compilation and critical evaluation of information as well as effective communication and online collaboration.

Even as our respondents possessed rich digital skills of a particular entertainment-centric nature, they manifested illiteracies in more academically- and professionally-valorized digital skills. Yet these youths' digital illiteracies are "invisible" because their active use of the smartphone and internet access qualifies them as internet users by broad statistical measures of online activity. Conventional data on internet access and use belies the relatively superficial and narrow nature of these youths' digital repertoire. Indeed, the common fallacy of equating internet access to digital literacy means that these underprivileged youths' digital illiteracies are not effectively identified and, regrettably, not consequently addressed.

Our interviews thus indicate that, for our respondents, these digital devices seem to be just another conduit to entertainment and an avenue for keeping in contact with family and friends. Given the limited range of their online activity, we observe that they did not actively harness the internet and its rich stock of information to enhance their learning or employment opportunities. This echoes Bourdieu's[37] observation that individuals tend to develop practices and dispositions that satisfy their social positions and thus reproduce existing advantages and disadvantages.

In view of our respondents' family profiles, there was also the absence of "warm experts"[38] to share their expertise with them. Our findings revealed that the parents and older siblings in these households did not themselves possess extensive technological skills. Some of our interviewees noted that they would not instinctively turn to their parents for help regarding their smartphone because their parents would not know enough to offer any substantial aid. This echoes the findings of Hollingworth and colleagues[39] that children in disadvantaged families may lack supervision and guidance in enriching the use of the internet because their parents have limited technological skills themselves. For some of our respondents, their parents had long working hours, or worked two jobs, and were thus are not available when help was needed.

The nature of mobile-only internet usage should also be taken into consideration. Desktops and laptops allow for the use of multiple applications at a time. For example, internet browsers on laptops permit users to open multiple tabs concurrently, thus allowing for better cross-referencing. Conversely, internet browsers on the small screens of smartphones permit only one application to be open at any one time, and only one tab at a time. In both cases, users are accessing the internet, however with a stark difference in efficiency and quality of engagement. Our respondents' mobile-first usage behavior was therefore shaping their technological repertoires in particular (limiting) ways.

Conclusion

As technological advancement charges ever rapidly forward, and technology becomes more pervasive in our everyday lives, it would be specious to claim that internet access would necessarily lead to an enhancement of technological skills. Consistent with extant literature,[40] our research has revealed that there can be great variability in the digital skills of the purported digital natives. A number of factors, rooted in one's socioeconomic background, come into play when assessing media literacy skills, even in a hyperconnected urban city-state such as Singapore. Whereas access inequalities were not salient, the digital divide in Singapore relates more to the quality of internet use and engagement. Most jarringly, the digital practices of disadvantaged youths tend to be mobile-centered and highly app-centric, and mostly extending and reproducing their existing practices of communication and entertainment rather than for capital-enhancing purposes, as postulated by Bordieu.[41] Corresponding to their disadvantaged circumstances, the absence of "warm experts" for guidance and supervision further exacerbates and reinforces the existing situation. These inequalities in turn affect their performance in an educational system and professional environment that appreciates a different set of digital skills, one revolving around information-based competencies that prize the effective and critical marshalling of diverse bodies of knowledge. Set against a backdrop of extant research indicating how one's socioeconomic background has a profound impact on educational attainment and career trajectories, we could perhaps see how the seemingly innocuous disparities in device usage which stem from socioeconomic inequalities can in turn manifest as disparities in educational achievement.

More broadly, our findings suggest that the nature of the digital divide has changed along with technological advancement, diffusion and usage. Consequently, our research efforts should also evolve accordingly so as to better capture and represent current digital divides, with a view towards effectively addressing these invisible illiteracies. To begin with, a revision of current statistical measures would enable us to more accurately reflect the extent and quality of internet use. Greater granularity in data on internet use should be sought so as to offer clearer distinctions in the usage patterns of mobile-only versus mobile-first users who complement smartphone use with devices such as laptops and desktops. Furthermore, given the increasingly mobile-centric media environments youths inhabit, media literacy education and perhaps technology-enhanced education approach in general, is in need of an urgent review and revamp. It has to take into account how today's youths access, utilize and understand the internet, in order to better equip them for exploiting the plenitude of online opportunities. In so doing, they can more effectively maneuver in an increasingly complicated digital landscape, regardless of their socioeconomic background.

Notes

1 Estelle Taylor, Roelien Goede, and Tjaart Steyn, "Reshaping Computer Literacy Teaching in Higher Education: Identification of Critical Success Factors," *Interactive Technology and Smart Education* 8, no. 1 (2011): 28–38.
2 Christoph Klimmt, "Key Dimensions of Contemporary Video Game Literacy: Towards a Normative Model of the Competent Digital Gamer," *Eludamos. Journal for Computer Game Culture* 3, no. 1 (2009): 23–31; John Potter, "New Literacies, New Practices and Learner Research: Across the Semi-permeable Membrane between Home," *Lifelong Learning in Europe (LLinE)* 3 (2011): 174–181.
3 Sonia Livingstone, Magdalena Bober, and Ellen J. Helsper, "Active Participation or just more Information? Young People's Take-up of Opportunities to Act and Interact on the Internet," *Information, Community & Society* 8, no. 3 (2005): 287–314.
4 Markus Appel, "Are Heavy Users of Computer Games and Social Media more Computer Literate?" *Computers & Education* 59, no. 4 (2012): 1339–1349.
5 Zizi Papacharissi, "The Virtual Sphere: The Internet as a Public Sphere," *New Media & Society* 4, no. 1 (2002): 9–27.
6 Allan Martin, "Digital Literacy and the 'Digital Society'," *Digital Literacies: Concepts, Policies and Practices* 30 (2008): 151–176.
7 James Manyika, Susan Lund, Jacques Bughin, Jonathan Woetzel, Kalin Stamenov, and Dhruv Dhingra, "Digital Globalization: The New Era of Global Flows," *McKinsey Digital*, February 2016, www.mckinsey.com/business-functions/digital-mckinsey/our-insights/digital-globalization-the-new-era-of-global-flows.
8 Ibid.
9 Peter Kearns and John Grant, *The Enabling Pillars: Learning, Technology, Community, Partnership: a Report on Australian Policies for Information and Communication Technologies in Education and Training* (Australia: Global Learning Services, 2002).
10 Grant Blank and Bianca C. Reisdorf, "The Participatory Web: A User Perspective on Web 2.0," *Information, Communication & Society* 15, no. 4 (2012): 537–554; Eszter Hargittai and Gina Walejko, "The Participation Divide: Content Creation and Sharing in the Digital Age," *Information, Community and Society* 11, no. 2 (2008): 239–256.
11 Janis Wolak, Kimberly J. Mitchell, and David Finkelhor, "Escaping or Connecting? Characteristics of Youth who Form Close Online Relationships," *Journal of Adolescence* 26, no. 1 (2003): 105–119; Michele L. Ybarra and Kimberly J. Mitchell, "Youth Engaging in Online Harassment: Associations with Caregiver–Child Relationships, Internet Use, and Personal Characteristics," *Journal of Adolescence* 27, no. 3 (2004): 319–336.
12 Neil Selwyn, "Apart from Technology: Understanding People's Non-use of Information and Communication Technologies in Everyday Life," *Technology in Society* 25, no. 1 (2003): 99–116; Neil Selwyn, "Reconsidering Political and Popular Understandings of the Digital Divide," *New Media & Society* 6, no. 3 (2004): 341–362; Neil Selwyn, "The Information Aged: A Qualitative Study of Older Adults' Use of Information and Communications Technology," *Journal of Aging Studies* 18, no. 4 (2004): 369–384; Mark Warschauer, "Dissecting the "Digital Divide": A Case Study in Egypt," *The Information Society* 19, no. 4 (2003): 297–304.
13 Pippa Norris, *Digital Divide: Civic Engagement, Information Poverty, and the Internet Worldwide* (New York: Cambridge University Press, 2001).
14 Wenhong Chen and Barry Wellman, "Charting and Bridging Digital Divides: Comparing Socio-economic, Gender, Life Stage, and Rural–Urban Internet Access and Use in Eight Countries," *AMD Global Consumer Advisory Board (GSAB)* (2003).
15 William E. Loges and Joo-Young Jung, "Exploring the Digital Divide: Internet Connectedness and Age," *Communication Research* 28, no. 4 (2001): 536–562.
16 Donna L. Hoffman, Thomas P. Novak, and Ann E. Schlosser, "The Evolution of the Digital Divide: Examining the Relationship of Race to Internet access and Usage over Time," in *The digital Divide: Facing a Crisis or Creating a Myth?* ed. Benjamin M. Compaine (Cambridge, MA: MIT Press, 2001): 47–97.

17 Ronald E. Rice and Caroline Haythornthwaite, "Perspectives on Internet use: Access, Involvement and Interaction," in *The Handbook of New Media: Social Shaping and Social Consequences of ICTs*, 2nd edition, eds. Leah A. Lievrouw and Sonia Livingstone (London: Sage, 2006), 92–113.
18 Agnetha Broos and Keith Roe, "The Digital Divide in the PlayStation Generation: Self-efficacy, Locus of Control and ICT Adoption among Adolescents," *Poetics* 34, no. 4–5 (2006): 306–317.
19 danah boyd, *It's Complicated: The Social Lives of Networked Teens* (New Haven: Yale University Press, 2014); Marc Prensky, "Digital Natives, Digital Immigrants Part 1," *On the Horizon* 9, no. 5 (2001): 1–6.
20 Keri Facer and Ruth Furlong, "Beyond the Myth of the 'Cyberkid': Young People at the Margins of the Information Revolution." *Journal of Youth Studies* 4, no. 4 (2001): 451–469; Ellen Johanna Helsper and Rebecca Eynon, "Digital Natives: Where is the Evidence?" *British Educational Research Journal* 36, no. 3 (2010): 503–520; Livingstone et al., "Active Participation,".
21 Sue Bennett, Karl Maton, and Lisa Kervin, "The 'Digital Natives' Debate: A Critical Review of the Evidence," *British Journal of Educational Technology* 39, no. 5 (2008): 775–786; Neil Selwyn, "The Digital Native–myth and Reality," *Aslib Proceedings* 61, no. 4 (2009), 364–379.
22 Mark Bullen, Tannis Morgan, and Adnan Qayyum, "Digital Learners in Higher Education: Looking beyond Stereotypes," in *Proceedings of EdMedia+ Innovate Learning* (Lisbon: Association for the Advancement of Computing in Education, 2011), 678–687.
23 Livingstone et al., "Active Participation,".
24 Sun Sun Lim, "Young People and Communication Technologies: Emerging Challenges in Generational Analysis," in *Communication Across the Lifespan*, ed. Jon F. Nussbaum (New York: Peter Lang, 2016), 5–19.
25 Sonia Livingstone, *Children and the Internet* (Cambridge, MA: Polity, 2009); Selwyn, "The Digital Native–myth,".
26 Eszter Hargittai, "Digital Na(t)ives? Variation in Internet Skills and Uses among Members of the 'Net Generation'," *Sociological Inquiry* 80, no. 1 (2010): 92–113.
27 E. Dianne Looker and Victor Thiessen, "Beyond the Digital Divide in Canadian Schools: From Access to Competency in the Use of Information Technology," *Social Science Computer Review* 21, no. 4 (2003): 475–490.
28 Jan A.G. van Dijk and Alexander J.A.M. van Deursen, *Digital Skills: Unlocking the Information Society* (New York: Palgrave Macmillan, 2014).
29 Ibid.
30 Pierre Bourdieu and Jean Claude Passeron, *Reproduction in Education, Society and Culture* (Thousand Oaks, CA: Sage, 1990).
31 Seth Gershenson, Seth, "Do Summer Time-use Gaps Vary by Socioeconomic Status?," *American Educational Research Journal* 50, no. 6 (2013): 1219–1248; Doug Hyun Han, Young Sik Lee, Churl Na, Jee Young Ahn, Un Sun Chung, Melissa A. Daniels, Charlotte A. Haws, and Perry F. Renshaw, "The Effect of Methylphenidate on Internet Video Game Play in Children with Attention-deficit/Hyperactivity Disorder," *Comprehensive Psychiatry* 50, no. 3 (2009): 251–256; Sumi Hollingworth, Ayo Mansaray, Kim Allen, and Anthea Rose, "Parents' Perspectives on Technology and Children's Learning in the Home: Social Class and the Role of the Habitus," *Journal of Computer Assisted Learning* 27, no. 4 (2011): 347–360; Linda Jackson, Alexander Von Eye, Frank Biocca, Gretchen Barbatsis, Yong Zhao, and Hiram Fitzgerald, "How Low-income Children Use the Internet at Home," *Journal of Interactive Learning Research* 16, no. 3 (2005): 259–271.
32 "Infocomm Usage-Households and Individuals," Infocomm Media Development Authority (IMDA), accessed May 1, 2018, www.imda.gov.sg/industry-development/facts-and-figures/infocomm-usage-households-and-individuals.
33 "Data.gov.sg," Government of Singapore, accessed May 19, 2018, https://data.gov.sg/.
34 Saravanan Gopinathan, "Globalisation, the Singapore Developmental State and Education Policy: A Thesis Revisited," *Globalisation, Societies and Education* 5, no. 1 (2007): 53–70.
35 Sun Sun Lim, Shobha Vadrevu, Yoke Hian Chan, and Iccha Basnyat, "Facework on Facebook: The Online Publicness of Juvenile Delinquents and Youths-at-risk," *Journal of Broadcasting & Electronic Media* 56, no. 3 (2012): 346–361.
36 Han et al., "The Effect of Methylphenidate on Internet Video Game Play,"; Jackson et al., "How Low-income Children Use the Internet,".
37 Bourdieu and Passeron, *Reproduction in Education*.
38 Maria Bakardjieva, *Internet Society: The Internet in Everyday Life* (London: Sage, 2005).
39 Hollingworth et al., "Parents' perspectives on technology,".
40 Bullen et al., "Digital Learners in Higher Education"; Livingstone et al., "Active Participation".
41 Bourdieu and Passeron, *Reproduction in Education*.

13
CHILDHOOD, MEDIA, AND CLASS IN SOUTH ASIA

Shakuntala Banaji

There is little consensus on the size of the South Asian middle-classes, about whose media practices the most has been written.[1] Business-oriented accounts report much higher figures than anthropological scholarship does; and far more attention is devoted to India than to its neighbors. What is rarely discussed is the idea that whether the South-Asian middle-classes number two or three hundred million people, they are still a minority of the now approximately 1.7-billion-strong South Asian population, who nevertheless access a vast majority of South Asian communication resources. In fact, the media and communications tools available to urban upper-middle class and middle-middle class South Asian children have kept pace with those available to their peers in the global north. These include tablets, computers, smartphones and apps, the internet of things, as well as sound systems, games consoles, television, books and comics. Analysis of World Bank and Asian Development Bank data on household income, technology ownership and media use suggest that, despite receiving a disproportionate amount of coverage in regard to their media consumption and technological abilities, children in these groups make up around 20 percent of the child population in India and between 15 and 20 percent of the child population in Bangladesh, Nepal, Pakistan, and Sri Lanka.

According to Asian Development Bank Key Indicators Asia[2] in 2015, in India alone:

> 59.2 per cent … live on less than 2 dollars per day with 23.6% living on less than 1.25 dollars a day…. Based on a total population of 1.21 billion in 2011 (Census data), this indicates that approximately 716 million Indians are very poor, i.e., are living on less than 2 dollars a day and, of these 286 million are living on less than 1.25 dollars a day.[3]

Adding together such evaluations across South Asia, it is clear that more than 500 million children in South Asian countries live in poverty,[4] facing a lack of food and clean water, limited access or no access to leisure media and communications technologies. In India alone, there are more than 3000 child deaths per day and levels of hunger across rural areas mean that children who do not get midday meals at school will often have to work or forage for their families if they want to eat.[5] Literature searches on such communities of children yield information on material health, child mortality, a range of infections and medical conditions and child labor, but rarely anything on their leisure pursuits. Over two decades ago, Anura Goonesekara suggested that when it comes to low income families in Asia,

[t]he lack of information on children and media is indicative of the lack of interest among research community and the ruling classes about this issue. It is also indicative of the absence of an accepted policy regarding communication for children. This situation becomes all the more glaring when one considers the fact that in many poorer countries in Asia, a large proportion of children who should be in school are not in school. The proportion is particularly high in the case of Asian girls.[6]

My own research over the past decade[7] suggests that the media environment of these hundreds of millions of low-income and very poor children, especially in towns and villages, comprises some radio, music cassettes, occasional comic books, sporadic access to television and video, rare sightings of a computer in a village school or NGO center, rare access to the internet or to cinema, rare access to mobile phones through a parent or relative. While much has been written in recent years about digital childhoods, this vast group appears to hold little intellectual excitement for media and communications scholars, except in the intersecting fields of education, health communication, and ICT for Development (ICT4D).[8] And yet this is a fascinatingly diverse cohort, who do not fit easily into received categories of "early adopters," "digital natives," "hanging out," and "geeking around" with media tools. Redressing imbalances in the literature, this chapter builds on a targeted literature review[9] of research on children, youth, schooling, media and class in Bangladesh, India, Nepal, Pakistan, and Sri Lanka over the past two decades to answer the question: how does social class inflect South Asian children's encounters with and experiences of media? Vignettes from qualitative ethnographic and interview-based fieldwork with 7–17 year olds in India illustrate how class differences across the subcontinent overlap with other axes of inequality such as caste and gender in children's lives.[10] These intersecting differences position children with regard to the media they encounter and with regard to representations possible via or entrenched within those media.

Class and Caste

One of the key ways in which the South Asian middle classes differ from those in contemporary Western Europe are the many shades of middle-class—clinging on, lower, middle-middle and upper-middle class, salaried or small business owning, urban, small-town and rural, old or new money, largely vernacular or anglophile, and with differing religious and caste affiliations. Literature on the interconnection between cultural consumption or production and social class from other parts of the world yields insights about the connections between social class, culture, and education as well as wages and types of labor—be these manual or knowledge-based.[11] Using combinations of these, in Western Europe, quite distinct classes—working, lower, and upper middle—can be arrived at, with most children in each of these conforming to normative sets of values that distinguish their class. While the framework offered is a starting point, the class-based identities of children in South Asia cannot be categorized so smoothly via aspects of family life, such as wages or parental education and occupation. In order to understand how children in South Asia experience media and class, one has to consider also how class is inflected by practices of labor, caste, and religion as well as geography and gender, and how encounters with media filtered through these other factors entail different positionings within capitalist labor relations and social reproduction.[12]

Sub-groups that intersect traditional classes—lower-middle, middle-middle and upper-middle; blue-collar, urban dispossessed; rural smallholders, rural landless—are frequently characterized by stringent sets of caste-linked customs and markers of caste distinction, oppression and intimidation.[13] These oppressive, discriminatory customs—and the structural prejudices and individual biases that attend them—apply to types of work and remuneration, land, use of space, material objects that can be touched, owned and consumed, as well as sexuality and marriage. Dalit children are still—despite decades of legislation aiming to reduce caste discrimination—being inducted into manual scavenging, or treated as dirty and uncouth. Many Adivasi children suffer the same exclusion and mistreatment, and displacement from land, that their parents endure. Attempts to break out of ethnic and caste divides to initiate class mobility or social justice—whether collective or individual—are met with traumatic violence, which is both disciplinary and punitive.[14] Caste-related oppression, caste identities and conflicts affect South Asian children in material and psychic ways as they grow up and participate in social reproduction through their own forms of affective and material labor. School and media are two fora in which these forms of learning about self and society might potentially be challenged or entrenched.

Education and Schooling

Although schooling is hugely prized in the lower-middle and middle-middle classes, especially for boys, the education systems of these five countries cannot comfortably accommodate all the children who need school places; government-run rural schools are under-resourced and often don't even run to books or boards and chalk for poorer children, while urban schools—both private and government-run—vary dramatically in pedagogy and in what access to media and technologies they can offer, depending on how much they charge in fees, and on what the goals of their curricula are. Therefore, while some boarding schools and private schools in urban metropolises now have internet connected computer labs into which older children can go for research, libraries with computers, and iPads that children can borrow, many schools don't even have a regular supply of electricity. In between are schools that ostensibly have computers for teachers' use, but where these machines rarely get turned on, and where there is neither a dial-up nor a broadband connection, let alone wireless access. As in many high and middle income countries, even where the middle class children can afford smartphones and bring them to school, their use is prohibited.

Further, while some teachers work incredibly hard to transmit knowledge to all the children under their care, and are much loved, as indicated by these recent stories,[15] caste-class or religion-class hierarchies are often reinforced by teachers through their daily interactions with children from working class, lower caste, Dalit, Adivasi or minority sects and religious backgrounds. (Discriminated groups include Muslims and Christians in India, Hindus, Buddhists, Ahmedis in Pakistan, Hindus in Bangladesh, Tamils and Muslims in Sri Lanka and so on.) The spectrum of behaviors ranges from direct insults to children from minority religions and sects, violence towards these children, jokes or insults about their names, leaving working-class and/or Dalit children out of activities, leaving them to sit on the dusty ground or making them clean the plates of their classmates, to the more subtle prejudice of neglect and silencing of indigenous knowledge through activities that value differentially the dialects, literacy, and cultural capital of children from upper castes, majority religions and affluent families. For instance, a child who can sing a folk song about a crop harvest or about preserving the forest in a local vernacular, or who can raise a baby or fix a tractor engine, and one who reads aloud from and explains a written narrative about accepted national history in Sinhala, Bengali, Urdu, Hindi or English, might be rewarded differently and would certainly be treated differently in assessment regimes.

Chalk and talk is still the most common mode of instruction, and memorization and rote learning as methods are reinforced by the expensive and time-consuming private tuitions and after-school classes that many lower- and middle-class secondary-age schoolchildren must perforce attend.[16] Matthan et al. also argue that schools frequently contribute to structural inequalities by reinforcing caste and religious divides[17]; they describe how in India Muslim girls in Hindu-run schools are othered in ways that have deep implications for their citizenship. In parts of Pakistan, girls risk their lives on a daily basis going to school, as the now famous case of Malala Yousafzai made explicit; and Pakistan is also the venue of one of the most terrible school massacres of the past decade: in the Army school in the city of Peshawar, where gunmen killed 132 children.

Textbooks are a form of media that are seen and studied by an enormous number of South Asian children—including working class and lower caste children. As such, the representations in them, the language in which they are written and the discourses therein, constitute a significant site for identity formation or contestation as well as, of course, for alienation and boredom. For instance, previous generations of children experienced the complex changes in the telling of the history of Bangladesh in its textbooks before and after the war of liberation from Pakistan, that saw its name change from East Pakistan to Bangladesh and the move from Urdu to Bengali. These textbooks as read out by teachers, along with popular films that were watched by whole families, were a key site of the transmission of Bangla nationalist stories to children with low literacy.

In Sri Lanka and Nepal, decades of civil war and insurgency have devastated education systems that were already groaning, leaving children from communities targeted by the state traumatized, with significant gaps in their schooling and often, also, large gaps in their families. Further, disasters such as the 2004 Tsunami—which hit Southern coasts in India and the whole of Sri Lanka in devastating ways—as well as the Nepal earthquake of 2015, have disrupted still more the schooling and media access of children in affected areas, leaving many extremely traumatized.[18] These are also familiar circumstances for many children from Kashmir, from parts of North-West Pakistan and North-Eastern India. It should also be noted that where other factors are equal, teenage girls in all of these situations face the most significant difficulties in accessing educational institutions. Even where religious schools such as Madrasas have been set up and are the norm in Pakistan, Bangladesh and parts of India, they often cater primarily for boys, and teach a limited range of subjects. Equally worrying are the thousands of Hindutva schools set up around India to engage children in a Hindu nationalist discourse that encourages suspicion of and violence towards Muslims, Christians, and atheists. Partly because these schools require little financial input from parents, they can afford to cater to working class and Adivasi (tribal) populations in places poorly served by the government.

More recent changes to the curricula in each South Asian nation are politicized in different ways, with the Sinhala Buddhists in Sri Lanka and Hindu Right in India vying with the Pakistani religious right in their efforts to replace secular histories with mythology in textbooks;[19] and to downplay the role of women in all spheres.[20] These sorts of changes, exclusions and myths are experienced by the children in government schools or private religious trust schools more extensively than they are by children whose parents send them to secular private schools that follow international curricula such as the IGCSE. Informal schooling and NGO projects, which are deliberately initiated with the aim of bringing children into contact with new technologies or with media education are few and far between, generally short-lived, and usually centered on a single medium—and staff employed in these also sometimes hold prejudices towards the groups they are working with.[21] So, South Asian schools certainly cannot be considered a leveler in terms of allowing working class South Asian children to access new media, or to develop enthusiasm for or critical accounts of culture accessed through whichever medium.

Social Class and Everyday Media Use

Relative poverty, gender, and geography intersect to determine access to media, and the role of media within everyday routines of economic production and social reproduction. Even without the stressors of war and insurgency, the need to contribute to family income or to provide free labor for care-giving structures South Asian working class children's everyday life. In *Children and Media in India*, I focused on the ways in which media made an appearance in children's accounts of their daily routines. Accounts by Shiv who is 9 years old and from an upper working class family in an urban slum, and Kadam and Durga, both rural children aged 12 but in different parts of the country, exemplify the presence or absence of media in everyday routines:

SHIV: I woke up at 7.00 am today, bathed, had breakfast and watched TV for a while. I went for my Hindi tuitions at 9.00 am for an hour, then came home and got ready for school and went to school at 11.00. *I don't like school.* I came back home at 3.30 pm. Watched TV for a bit and had lunch. I took a nap from 4–5 pm. Had snacks. Went for English tuition classes at 18.00. I *hate English*. I don't get it at all. At 7.15 pm I went straight off to my aunt's place because she has an *old computer*. I *played a few car racing games* on that. Then I came home at 9.30 pm. Had dinner, then went into the road to play with my friends. We jumped stairs today. The one who could jump from the highest step would be the winner. I couldn't. I came home at 11.00. *Played snake on my father's phone. It's not a smartphone.* And finally went to sleep.

KADAM: My mother woke me up at 5 am. We prepared tea, then I walked to (school as the school is several kilometers away). We sang songs on the way to school. I sat in the school. *I didn't learn anything* because teacher gave writing and was smoking and chatting outside. I came back by one with my friends from the village, we *listened to a match on the radio while walking*; then I went to collect wood and leaves and help my mother. Then I went to play with my friends: we built a big pile out of stones, and played a battle, to see who could destroy it with throwing stones, then I came home and finished my homework; and I filled water. I had some snacks and *saw some television* with my brothers. Then I helped my mother with making dinner, we ate dinner, then I fell asleep around 11.

DURGA: I got up before the light and made tea for the family. We walked to the fields, I don't know how long it takes, but it is far. Then we were there all day working. We—the children came back when the sun was setting—again walking, and I went to fill water—that is a long walk. Then I helped my sisters to prepare dinner which is rice, we chatted while we were cooking. My parents returned later and we ate together. There is no electricity in our place. We were very tired, so we went to sleep.

Although the two boys who attend school either say that they 'don't like school' or 'don't learn anything' it is clear that they are learning—about what education is and what is valued, about their position in a social system, about legitimate adult behaviors. Outside school, simple tasks such as collecting wood and leaves, going to school and filling water can involve rural children in walking for up to five kilometers, leaving little daylight time for other activities. Eschewing both pastoral romanticism, which contrasts such "freedom" and "outdoors activities" with the new media lethargy of all-night online game playing, and a straightforward categorization of this labor as parental exploitation, it is important to see both how its routine nature prevents questioning, and how the performance of these tasks allow the children to situate and value themselves as part of families and communities. Without being fetishized as gateways to independence, all available old and new media are described matter-of-factly alongside other types of leisure.

Seasonal laborers such as Durga's family often live in encampments between towns and rural areas, where there are no water or electricity connections; and that in turn means that they do not access any media for the months they are travelling and sowing or harvesting. However, some of these migrant labor families also return to their native villages for part of the year, where the children will attend school in a desultory manner—going for a few hours a day or a few days a week over the winter months—and might well have access to television. The picture when it comes to mobile phone ownership is similarly complex.

A family from the rural poor—whether categorized as a below the poverty line (BPL) or not—may own an outdated mobile phone, which is used by the men in the family for receiving texts about work and the occasional phone call, but often will not have a smartphone or any money to spend on data, despite the pressures of new digital identification systems in India and Pakistan. In such households, which outnumber the ones that can afford to buy children iPads or give them smartphones, girls are also far less likely to be given access to a phone owned by a parent, and older boys the most likely to be given an outdated mobile. In these households, an average day for a rural girl of 12 might consist of six to eight hours of seasonal labor with her parents in the fields, household labor such as cooking, cleaning and childcare, looking after livestock, a couple of television serials in electrified settlements or listening to the radio with elders in the family.

In peri-urban communities and when it is not harvest season, children might attend an informal school or a government school for a few hours a day, and intersperse household tasks such as washing clothes, looking after younger children and cooking with television viewing and games on discarded mobile handsets. Younger boys between seven and 11 will often be sent out to mind animals or stalls, collect things, repair things, or assist men from the family.[22] Older boys are often expected to earn as well as to attend school if that is an option. Nevertheless, unemployment is so high that often after graduating from school these older boys and young men will either end up hanging around doing nothing or going back to seasonal labor and manual labour.[23]

Cricket, sketching and coloring, singing, skipping, marbles, carrom, card games, and television form the major leisure activities of many urban and rural upper working class and lower middle class children. Arora[24] describes some of the ways in which rural school children incorporate their television viewing into imaginative activities at school and in informal educational programs. The routines of children from the more impoverished and insecure working classes, however, vary massively depending on the presence or absence of adults, and the types of institutional circumstances they encounter,[25] with enforced work routines and child labor often leaving them too exhausted for leisure activities.

Middle class urban children's routines now usually incorporate old and new media into multiple aspects of their leisure. Take, for instance, this account by 12-year-old Shilpa:

SHILPA: I woke up at 6 today as I had to study for my tuitions test. I went for a bath and then I *checked my WhatsApp*. I had a bath *listening to my favorite songs on radio*.... The test was long and boring. After the test I took a walk with my tuition buddies and then I went to my friend's house and *edited a few pictures of mine* because I wanted to get a *new Facebook DP* (Display Picture, outdated name for a profile picture). I came home by 10 am and spent around an hour chatting with school friends *on our WhatsApp group* and at 11 mom made Maggi [noodles] for me. Then I watched *music videos on television*. Around 12:30 pm *I checked my Instagram account* and I started following my friends who have recently joined Instagram. They were uploading nice pictures. Even I *commented*. Then I had my lunch and studied again. By 5 pm I went down to walk the dog and play with my friends then travelled by metro with my mom to my cousin's place. There we *watched television* for some time and then went out for dinner. We *clicked many images*. Some of them were uploaded on Facebook by my cousin. At night we watched television for some time and then we played card games. It was very fun. Before sleeping I took dog for a walk, then spent more than *an hour chatting on WhatsApp* and then I checked *my Facebook account* before sleeping and was surprised to know that all the pictures that I had uploaded were appreciated by a lot of people![26]

Although many older middle class teenagers read blogs on subjects that interest them, look for information on health and sexuality online, play digital games, circulate memes, post in multiple Facebook, Instagram and Snapchat accounts, use WhatsApp continuously, follow celebrities, and watch comedy, news or music on You Tube, this activity includes a range of misogynist and sectarian content accessed and circulated by teenagers but often produced by powerful adults.

In line with Shilpa's personal account, Sharma and Sharma's research on urban high school and college students in Nepal discusses a savvy, connected and highly culturally literate group, who have domesticated digital technologies in intelligent ways to fit their own circumstances[27]—for instance, the constant load shedding power outages which might impede Skype or phone charging are expected and surplus charged batteries or individual generators are ordered into middle class homes. In Nepal, as in the other four South Asian countries, film music and popular songs in English, Hindi, Bengali, Urdu and other vernaculars, as well as rock and roll and heavy metal, are central features of children's, teenagers' and young people's leisure in larger villages, towns and cities. Where connectivity and smartphones are easily available, these are being accessed and customized via mobile phone playlists, digital radio, and apps. However, for children of all classes across South Asia, the most common ways of accessing popular music remain radio, cassettes, CDs and music shows on television, as well as ambient songs sung or played through loud speakers at festivals and celebrations.

Except in rare instances where an NGO—or Negroponte's One Laptop per Child project—has decided to donate cheap laptops to a set of schoolchildren or to a small community for participation in some program, the games console, iPad, or personal computer with broadband access is primarily an urban- and middle-class phenomenon. During my research in India, I encountered many rural children had never handled a mobile phone, and many who had not seen a laptop, used an iPad or a desktop computer.[28] Numerous reports and studies[29] suggest that in almost all middle and working class urban communities, television remains the most used form of media, with digital games and the internet lagging far behind mainly because of the cost of upkeep to hardware and software, and only secondarily because of issues of connectivity. In cases where educational digital games are provided through a project or NGO, working class children show a significant degree of enthusiasm.[30] Therefore, although radio reaches a number of children in remote regions of India and Pakistan, and is still very popular in Nepal and Sri Lanka, as the medium in South Asia that reaches the largest number of middle and working class, urban and rural children and contains the greatest proportion of content made for children, television remains central. It is therefore worth dwelling, as the coming section does, on children's relationships to television: their viewing rituals, popular genres, storylines and representations.

Media Content and Child Audiences

To varying extents, all five South Asian countries have witnessed massive changes in their media systems over the past 30 years with moves—generally in the 1990s—from highly controlled, limited, state-owned channels—Nepal Television, BTV, PTV, Doordarshan, Sri Lanka Roopvahini Corporation—that aired one or two hours of children's programs, to a significantly privatized electronic media in which market forces have brought in a dozen or more channels in English, Bengali, Hindi, Urdu, Sinhala, Tamil and other regional languages that are directed primarily at children but also contain vast amounts of advertising and advertorials. While India has had the most written about children and television,[31] dubbed, indigenized or subtitled sit-coms and cartoons form a significant portion of children's television programming across all five countries. Amongst the channels airing cartoons and children's shows, some of the most popular are Animax, Cartoon Network, Discovery Kids, Disney, Disney XD, Hungama, Nick, Pogo and Sonic; A Plus Kids TV airs children's content in Sri Lanka. Pogo claims to target ages between four- and 15-year-olds,[32] Discovery Kids says it is aimed at 4–12 year-olds,[33] Animax, a Japanese subsidiary of Sony, targets 'teens' and adults aged from 15- to 40-year-olds and started broadcasting across South Asia in 2004; Disney creates special weekend content targeting children and adults in the age group of four to 34.

Several of these channels have had their content taken off air in Bangladesh and Pakistan over the years and particularly around 2010–2011, ostensibly because of controversies around their content (Westernization, media imperialism) but most evidently because of the way in which the Hindi dubbed versions from India were aired without changes in Bangladesh and Pakistan. Many of them are also unaffordable for families who cannot purchase satellite packages or diviboxes. Most working-class children, therefore, would tend to watch less tailored children's content and more content aimed at everyone on local vernacular channels.

Where they are accessible, cartoons are so popular with South Asian children and teenagers that a conservative Pakistani lawmaker tried to enforce a ban on the dubbed Japanese cartoon *Doraemon* (about the everyday life of a mischievous little boy and his robot) on the grounds that it is 'corrupting' Pakistan's children. This action provoked a number of satirical pieces on *Doraemon*'s demerits. Older children (13–17) with access to televisions watch cartoons and a range of other content such as soaps and serials from the US, Canada, the UK, and in vernacular, films made for adults, game-shows, comedy programs, music videos, sport and news. In a rare study of Sri Lankan television's children's content, Atugala explains the popularity of melodramatic serials as well as the ways in which children question some representational frameworks:

> The participatory observation of children of age 11 to 13 years old has shown that they strongly identified with the plots and characters of programmes that were perceived as a dramatic rehearsal of moral and social problems with which they would have to grapple in real life. However, observation among the 15-to-17-year-olds further revealed serious concerns about misrepresentations of "reality", under-representation of ethnic minority groups, and a desire that youth television should be explicit about issues such as horrors of conflict, sexual behaviour, drug addiction etc.[34]

However, Atugala points out,

> one of the major problems with regard to media professionals is that children themselves are not taken seriously enough, since their target is the adult market. Conventionally, children are regarded as a subgroup of society to be protected if not cosseted.[35]

So, the problematic situation exists in which children, many of whom have been and are being exposed to violent events and trauma in their daily lives both within and outside the family, and to varied forms of structural inequality in communities and if they happen to go to school, are targeted by marketers and media producers who imagine a homogeneous, mischievous, carefree, middle-class (usually urban) boy child as the South Asian norm. While the cartoons made outside South Asia—in Canada or Japan—at least imagine a somewhat egalitarian family, and where children have some rights, representations of children and childhood in most South Asian soap operas are extremely narrow and limited with children primarily being vehicles for adult melodrama or for the unfolding of an aspect of the plot.

Further analysis of the types of communities and central characters most frequently represented in South Asian-made programs suggests that these tend to be male, tend to be from ethnic majority communities and tend to be from upper castes and middle-class backgrounds.[36] The girls and women in these programs are often introduced and framed as the sisters, mothers or wives—or occasionally the friends, cousins and girlfriends—of male protagonists, and tend to fall into stereotypes of "good mother," "evil step mother," "sister who gets into trouble and has to be rescued." A recent spate of soaps with female protagonists, also tend to depict middle-class central characters, and if there is class conflict—as in the Hindi Sarabhai versus Sarabhai—it is conflict between the middle-middle classes and the upper classes.

With rare exceptions—such as the high quality, cutting-edge Pakistani serials such as *Zindagi Gulzar Hai* and *Humsafar*, which air on the Hindi-Urdu Zee channel Zindagi TV—the daytime soaps, sitcoms and serials on NTV, BTV, PTV, Doordarshan, Roopvahini, Star and Zee channels that are most popular with children and families represent a highly stratified community with an almost-feudal view of the working classes, who appear to exist either to serve or thwart the schemes of the rich and occasionally to give the audience a laugh or a cry at their foolishness, but have little autonomous existence. The majority of family homes are depicted as palatial spaces consisting of endless color-coordinated suites to accommodate joint families, kitted out with expensive objects and fittings, milling with extended kin, great grandmothers, aunts in law, elderly uncles dressed in absurdly opulent clothing and finery who all have a say in how children and young people should behave and live their lives.

Particularly amongst working-class and lower-middle-class children, most of these exclusionary, regressive and highly stereotyped representations of gender and family relationships are not counterbalanced by a diversity of other mainstream or alternative media content. In Bengali, Urdu and

Hindi—as well as other vernaculars—films and soaps which are watched by large numbers of teenagers, "good" girls and women are predominantly represented as pious, amenable, long-suffering and beautiful—although they will occasionally fight their elders on behalf of a man they love or a child they need to protect and will sacrifice themselves for the country they are loyal to. Hindi, Tamil, Malayalam, and Telegu films in India, and Pakistani films from the Punjab region, all frequently interlink successful masculinity with caste identities and dominance over characters from despised religions or castes. As Sevea writes of Punjabi films, "approaching gender in relational terms entails the study of how codes of masculinities are established by demonstrating their superiority not only over women but also over 'other men,' especially those from subordinated social groups."[37]

Crucially, cross-caste and cross-class romances, and poverty are depicted in many televised dramas, and in Hindi, Bengali, Tamil, and Urdu films as dreadful states that a families might "suffer from" or "fall into" because a loss of Gods' grace, laziness, the wiles of another family or of an evil nemesis. As in the cases of audiences of Hindi films, the responses of children and teenagers watching these programs vary between credulity, unquestioning enjoyment and irony or mistrust;[38] but whatever their attitude, they are certainly learning things from the shows. South Asian serials and soaps on daytime television contain almost no representations of working class children or teenagers going about their everyday lives, and rarely show them working or falling in love. Unsurprisingly, then, when working-class teenagers in South Asia fall in love with someone "taboo" in the eyes of their family or community, they have little recourse except to try to handle matters themselves. This can be seen in the tragic story of teenage sweethearts from different religions who apparently committed suicide when kept apart by their families in Agra[39] and the tragic report of the lesbian working-class lovers who committed suicide by drowning themselves and their toddler because they could not envision an acceptable future together in the world of the living.[40]

There are, of course, instances of television programs that show teenagers and children in real settings dealing with complex contemporary issues involving gender discrimination, sexuality, religious differences, class and caste stigma and disabilities. In India, *Balika Vadhu* (*The Child Bride*), which deals with the story of a woman who was a child bride and *Naa Aanaa Is Desh Laado* (*Don't Come to This Country, Darling*) have been named by more working-class child participants in interviews alongside expected "family" serials such as *Kahani* (Story) and *Ek Nayi Pehchaan* (*A New Identity*). The Tamil drama *Kana Kaanum Kaalangal* airing on Vijay TV was set in a high school, and depicted the friendships of a supposedly mixed social class group of school children, before becoming increasingly melodramatic and being discontinued. Although *Deweni Inima* (*Second Innings*), about the lives and loves a group of high school cricket champions, is arguably now the most popular televised soap, some years ago *A9* was an attempt by a primetime teledrama to reflect the experiences of war and peace of a cross-section of Sri Lankan society. In Bangladesh a child-centered news program *Amra Korbo Joy* airs regularly on the private satellite channel ATN Bangla.[41] But, here too, the child reporters tend to be highly literate from affluent urban schools.

Overall, then, middle- and upper-class children from majority religions and higher castes who speak national languages, and those who identify with urban and Western fashion and speak English, are most likely to see themselves represented on television and to be able to find representations of young people and children like them online. Although they do introduce significant moral dilemmas and new cultural modes that can be very attractive to children and young people, the genres such as mythological serials and animations or manga don't represent or deal with contemporary South Asian working-class issues or problems. While showing a greater range of ideas and values about non-South Asian cultures, mental health and sexuality, middle-middle class and upper-middle class urban teenagers who have the greatest degree of exposure and access to non-South Asian content via the internet are not significantly more likely to question class, sectarian, and caste prejudice, to have progressive opinions about people from other religions and countries, or to share feminist values than their less media connected, working-class and rural peers.[42] I interviewed a range of middle-class Indian teenagers who go online regularly but few of whom show a penchant to question political misinformation, fake health news, or sexist memes on WhatsApp; and many of whom, moreover, hold particularly strong prejudices towards Dalits and Scheduled Castes and Tribes, working class people, Muslims, and "bad girls" compared with their peers in villages who have never been online, but who use life experience to navigate the social world.

Conclusion

This chapter has given only an overview of the dynamic and exciting discussions around children, class and media in South Asia. It is limited, on the one hand by space, and on the other by the dearth of studies on this topic undertaken in all five countries: where social class and caste are discussed or media is the issue, childhood is rarely the focus. There is a burgeoning literature on small-scale child-centered interventions in the development and education fields, and these would in themselves warrant a significant study. However, it is possible to use the conclusions of this chapter as a starting point and guide for framing additional research.

The intersection of social class, caste, gender, and geography structures not only *how much media* South Asian children have access to and *how many formats and genres* they encounter, but also *what meanings* different technologies and representations hold in their imaginaries and daily routines. While there are a small number of better-off families in villages whose children have access to digital gadgets, if not in their own homes then at least via neighbors or relatives, the overall tendency is for diminishing access to media based on family income, caste or ethnic status, and more rural and more interior locations. For instance, in the Chittagong hill tracts, in the interior of Chattisgarh, Jharkhand, and Orissa, in Balochistan, entire villages exist with very limited access to communication technologies amongst adults, and none amongst children. In such circumstances, the appellation "digital natives" appears deeply problematic, erasing as it does the geographically unstable, classed and gendered nature of children's interactions with all media.

The aptly named neoliberal field of "cyberlibertarian developmentalism,"[43] shows concern for the progress of the poor and deprived in South Asia as described in some of the studies quoted in this chapter, but does so in ways that center technologies, private companies and governments, while silencing or side-lining campaigns for a more far-reaching economic and social justice. Scholarship that celebrates the digital through e-education, digital citizenship and other means, simply adds to the representational abyss that currently encompasses working class South Asian children's diverse lives and identities. Meanwhile, mainstream media representations across most genres privilege older boys and young men, with only a third of central characters being female or played with female voices. Men's sporting events are covered with far more regularity than women's sports; and much news and sporting coverage is bound up with nationalist discourses which pit South Asians against each other. Indigenized South Asian children's and family-oriented programs usually include children with visible caste names, wealthy quasi-feudal families who follow implicitly conservative patriarchal practices in regard to gender, caste, religion and class interactions. As Mankekar and Rajagopal have shown in their work on cultural gendered and nationalist imaginaries circulating through television in India,[44] the fewer alternative representations people have available to them, the greater the salience of available media in inflecting the formation of social identities and reproducing social structures. My research agrees with this to an extent, but also questions the idea that an abundance of media access counter-balances the religious, national or gendered propagandist role of much South Asian community socialization.

In stark contrast to middle-class urban male teenagers, significant numbers of South Asian working class children and lower middle class girls have little or no access at all to smartphones, the internet and online digital games but participate in very "adult" forms of labor and social reproduction on a daily basis using a plethora of non-communications technological tools. The idea of a personalized playlist or of paying for and downloading songs from the internet might seem like science fiction, but, more importantly, it is trivial or irrelevant compared with the need for dignity, sustenance and safety, and the ability to look after a baby, mend a stove, plough a field, and service a motorbike. Although older teenagers might go to "internet cafes" in adjacent towns, that kind of travel is not common even amongst adults in farming communities. And, despite the fact that the internet is repeatedly touted as the medium where all children and youth congregate, when it comes to South Asia, this is true only for a highly connected minority in the under-17 age group. This does not mean that this minority is not a vast number in absolute terms or that these technologies are not spreading fast. They are, and in some cases perforce, as governments adopt digital identification systems that will punish remote marginal communities who fail to use digital technology to authenticate their identities. It does mean, however, that scholarship on digital movements, online civic initiatives, information dissemination systems, and educational and representational content in South Asia needs to be far more alert to the ways in which social class—overlaid by gender, geography, religion, and caste—structures and inflects children's connections with and through media and communications technologies.

Notes

1 Notably, the following: Christine Brosius, *India's Middle Class: New Forms of Urban Leisure, Consumption and Prosperity* (London and New York: Routledge, 2010); Amita Baviskar and Raka Ray, *Elite and Everyman: The Cultural Politics of the Indian Middle Classes* (London: Routledge, 2016); Ritty Lukose, *Liberalization's Children: Gender, Youth, and Consumer Citizenship in Globalizing India* (Durham: Duke University Press, 2005); Teresa Platz-Robinson, *Cafe Culture in Pune. Being Young and Middle Class in Urban India* (New Delhi: Oxford University Press, 2014) and Brian Shoesmith, Jude William Genilo, and Md Asiuzzaman (eds), *Bangladesh's Changing Mediascape: From State Control to Market Forces* (Intellect Books, 2013).
2 Asian Development Bank Key Indicators (2015), 207.
3 Cited in Shakuntala Banaji, *Children and Media in India: Narratives of Class, Agency and Social Change* (London: Routledge, 2017), 47.
4 Asian Development Bank, "Key Indicators for Asia and the Pacific, 2017," accessed July 8, 2018 www.adb.org/publications/key-indicators-asia-and-pacific-2017.
5 See: Shakuntala Banaji, "Behind the High-Tech Fetish: Children, Work and Media Use Across Classes in India," *International Communication Gazette* 77, no. 6 (2015), 519–532; Ali Khan, *Representing Children: Power, Policy and the Discourse on Child Labour in the Football Manufacturing Industry of Pakistan* (Oxford: Oxford University Press, 2007); Lieten G. Kristoffel. *Working Boys and Girls at Risk: Child Labour in Urban Bangladesh* (Dhaka: Dhaka University Press Limited, 2011).
6 Anura Goonasekera, "Children's Voice in the Media: A Study of Children's Television Programmes in Asia," *Media Asia* 25, no. 3 (1998), 123.
7 See: Shakuntala Banaji, "Adverts Make Me Want to Break the Television": Indian children and their audiovisual media environment in three contrasting locations. In *South Asian Media Cultures: Representations, Contexts and Audiences* (London, UK: Anthem Press, 2010), 51–72; also Shakuntala Banaji, "A Tale of Three Worlds: Young People, Media and Class in India," in ed. Christine Hensler, *Generation X Goes Global: Mapping a Youth Culture in Motion* (New York: Routledge 2012), 33–50; and Banaji, *Children and Media in India.*
8 L. Bartlett, W. Akala, R. Semyalo, and T. Stafford, "ICT in education study." (Earth Institute at Columbia and Connect to Learn with Ericsson, 2013).
9 Databases such as JSTOR and SCOPUS were used in addition to Sage and Taylor & Francis journal collections. It should be noted that where studies in medical and psychiatric journals referenced the media, these studies were discarded in the main as their hypotheses were far too constrained, and findings often limited to a single item to do with the influence of advertising on smoking, body-image or the like.
10 See: Banaji, "Behind the High-Tech Fetish," and Banaji, *Children and Media in India*; Jenny Huberman, *Ambivalent Encounters: Childhood, Tourism, and Social Change in Banaras, India* (New Jersey: Rutgers University Press, 2012); Hia Sen, *"Time-Out" in the Land of Apu: Childhoods, Bildungsmoratorium and the Middle Classes in Urban West Bengal* (Freiburg: Springer, 2014).
11 See discussion in Pierre Bourdieu, *Distinctions. A Social Critique of the Judgment of Taste*, translated by Richard Nice (Harvard: Harvard University Press, 1984); Also: E.P. Thompson, *The Making of the English*

Working Class (Harmondsworth: Penguin, 1980; third edition with new preface) and Erik Olin Wright, *Understanding Class* (London: Verso, 2015).

12 Susan Ferguson, "Children, Childhood and Capitalism: A Social Reproduction Perspective," in ed. Tithi Bhattacharaya, *Social Reproduction Theory: Remapping Class, Recentering Oppression* (London: Pluto Press, 2017), 112–130.

13 Ahsan Abdullah, "Digital Divide and Caste in Rural Pakistan," *The Information Society*, 31, no. 4 (2015), 346–356; Christophe Jaffrelot, *Religion, Caste and Class in India* (Chennai: Primus Books, 2010).

14 Hugo Gorringe, "'Banal Violence'? The Everyday Underpinnings of Collective Violence," *Identities: Global Studies in Culture and Power* 13, no. 2 (2006): 237–260; Anand Teltumbde, *The Persistence of Caste: The Khairlanji Murders and India's Hidden Apartheid* (London: Zed Books, 2010).

15 "Tamil Nadu: Students Protest Transfer of 'beloved' English Teacher, School Forced to Defer it by 10 days," *Financial Express*, accessed July 8, 2018 www.financialexpress.com/india-news/tamil-nadu-students-protest-transfer-of-beloved-english-teacher-school-forced-to-defer-it-by-10-days/1215788/.

16 Khan, *Representing Children*; Sen, *Timeout in the Land of Apu*; Mahrouf Shohel and Tom Power, "Introducing Mobile Technology for Enhancing Teaching and Learning in Bangladesh: Teacher Perspectives," *Open Learning: The Journal of Open and Distance Learning* 25, no. 3 (2010), 201–215; Arathi Sriprakash, "New Learner Subjects? Reforming the Rural Child for a Modern India," *Discourse: Studies in the Cultural Politics of Education* 34, no. 3 (2013), 325–337.

17 Tanya Matthan, Chandana Anusha and Meenakshi Thapan, "In Quest of Identity: Student Culture in a Religious Minority Institution," in ed. M. Thapan, *Ethnographies of Schooling in Contemporary India* (Los Angeles & Washington: Sage, 2014), 225–271.

18 Claudia Catani, Abigail H. Gewirtz, Elizabeth Wieling, Elizabeth Schauer, Thomas Elbert and Frank Neuner, "Tsunami, War, and Cumulative Risk in the Lives of Sri Lankan Schoolchildren," *Child Development* 81, no. 4 (2010): 1176–1191.

19 Mushirul Hasan "The BJP's Intellectual Agenda: Textbooks and Imagined History," *South Asia: Journal of South Asian Studies* 25, no. 3 (2002), 187–209.

20 Manabi Majumdar and Jos Muuij, *Education and Inequality in India: A Classroom View* (London: Routledge, 2011); Vivimarie Vanderpoorten Medawattagedera, "Representing Women 'Our way': An English Language Teaching Television Programme in Sri Lanka," *Society and Culture in South Asia* 4, no. 1 (2017), 94–122.

21 See: Matthew Kam, Anuj Kumar, Shirley Jain, Akhil Mathur, and John Canny, "Improving Literacy in Rural India: Cellphone Games in an After-School Program," Paper presented at Third IEEE/ACM Conference on Information and Communication Technology and Development (Doha, Qatar, 2009); Also: Sugata Mitra, Dangwal, Ritu Chatterjee, Shiffon Swati Jha, Bisht Ravinder S., and Preeti Kapur "Acquisition of Computer Literacy on Shared Public Computers: Children and the 'Hole in the Wall,'" *Australasian Journal of Educational Technology* 21, no. 3 (2005), 407–426.

22 Banaji, "High-Tech Fetish"; Jane Dyson *Working Childhoods: Youth, Agency and the Environment in India* (Cambridge: Cambridge University Press, 2014).

23 Craig Jeffrey, *Time Pass: Youth, Class and the Politics of Waiting in India* (Stanford, CA: Stanford University Press 2010).

24 Payal Arora, "Instant Messaging Shiva, Flying Taxis, Bil Klinton and More: Children's Narratives from Rural India". *International Journal of Cultural Studies* 11, no. 1 (2008), 69–86.

25 See: Sarada Balagopalan, *Inhabiting 'Childhood': Children, Labour and Schooling in Postcolonial India* (Basingstoke: Palgrave Macmillan, 2014); Also: Khan, *Representing Children*.

26 Banaji, *Children and Media in India*, 130–131.

27 Ghanashyam Sharma and B.K. Sharma, "Leapfrogging in the Global Periphery," in eds. T. Williams and A. Zenger, *New Media Literacies and Participatory Popular Culture across Borders* (London and New York: Routledge, 2012), 151–166.

28 Banaji, *A Tale of Three Worlds*; Banaji, "High-Tech Fetish"; Banaji, *Children and Media in India*.

29 A.M Rozario, V. Masilamani, and S. Arulchelvan, "The Case of the Missing Girls: Distribution of Gender Roles in Indian Children's Television Programming," *Journal of Children and Media* 12, no. 2 (2018), 125–142; Ariyaratne Atugala, "Sri Lanka: Success of Children's TV Programmes in the Ratings," *Media Asia* 35, no. 1 (2008), 40–46.

30 Kam et al., "Improving Literacy."

31 Ruchi K. Jaggi, "An Overview of Japanese Content on Children's Television in India," *Media Asia* 41, no. 3 (2014), 240–254; Usha Nayar and A. Bhide, "Contextualizing Media Competencies amongst Young People in Indian Culture: Interface with Globalization," in eds., Kirsten Drotner and Sonia Livingstone, *International Handbook of Children, Media and Culture* (London: Sage, 2008), 328–335; Manisha Pathak-Shelat and Cathy DeShano, "Digital Youth Cultures in Small Town and Rural Gujarat, India," *New Media and Society* 16, no. 6 (2013), 983–1001.

32 Bipin Chandran and Jai Arjun Singh, "More Channels for Indian Eyeballs," *Rediff.com* (December 13, 2003), accessed July 8, 2018. www.rediff.com/money/2003/dec/13channels.htm.
33 "Discovery Networks Asia-Pacific Makes Its Foray into Kids," *Discovery* (14 March 2002), accessed July 8, 2018. http://corporate.discovery.com/discovery-newsroom/discovery-networks-asia-pacific-makes-its-foray-into-kids/.
34 Atugala, "Sri Lanka," 45.
35 Ibid., 47.
36 Banaji, *Children and Media in India*; Rozario et al., "The Case," 125–130.
37 Iqbal Sevea, ""Kharaak Kita Oi!": Masculinity, Caste, and Gender in Punjabi Films," *BioScope* 5, no. 2 (2015): 129–140.
38 Arora "Instant Messaging"; Banaji *Adverts*; Sen *Time out*.
39 Naveed Iqbal, "How a Hindu-Muslim Love Story that Started in Agra School Ended in Flames," *The Indian Express* (May 24, 2016), accessed July 8, 2018. https://indianexpress.com/article/india/india-news-india/how-a-hindu-muslim-love-story-that-started-in-agra-school-ended-in-flames-2807944/.
40 Annie Banerji, "Lesbian Couple's Suicide Note Reveals Stigma They Face in India" (June 12, 2018), accessed July 8, 2018. www.reuters.com/article/us-india-women-lesbian/lesbian-couples-suicide-notes-reveal-stigma-they-face-in-india-idUSKBN1J82CH.
41 www.youtube.com/watch?v=7DGy9vHbo_g.
42 Banaji, *Children and Media in India*.
43 It was named thus by T.T. Srikumar in a 2006 paper entitled "ICTs for the Rural Poor: Civil Society and Cyber-Libertarian Developmentalism in India," in ed. G. Parayil, *Political Economy and Information Capitalism in India: Digital Divide Development and Equity* (London: Palgrave Macmillan, 2006), 61–87.
44 See: Purnima Mankekar, *Screening Culture, Viewing Politics: Television, Womanhood and Nation in Modern India* (New Delhi: Oxford University Press, 2000) and Arvind Rajagopal, *Politics after Television: Hindu Nationalism and the Reshaping of the Public in India* (Cambridge: Cambridge University Press, 2001).

PART III

Labor in Digital/Media Contexts

14
THE ROOTS OF JOURNALISTIC PERCEPTION

A Bourdieusian Approach to Media and Class

Sandra Vera-Zambrano and Matthew Powers

Consider four journalists. When asked to describe recent work they are proud of, two (one French male, one American female) discuss detailed investigative reports that took months to develop and which explore the impact of government policy on social issues such as homelessness and urban development. The other two journalists (one French male, one American female) talk about human interest stories that, in their view, manage to simultaneously interest audiences while also accurately portraying their subject matters. The biographical characteristics of the respondents immediately suggest that these differences cannot wholly be explained via nationality or gender. How, then, can these differences in work about which these journalists are proud be explained?

In this chapter, we argue that differences in what journalists perceive as professional excellence derive in part from their social origins and professional trajectories. Drawing on the sociological work of Pierre Bourdieu, we analyze these differences in "class" terms, with class understood as the outcome of dynamic interactions between one's social origins and trajectories, the position one holds in social space, and one's perceptions of this position. In particular, we argue that place of birth, parents' occupations, and educational attainment correlates with job titles, beats, and the organization for which a journalist works, as well as one's understanding of journalists' purposes and visions of quality. We illustrate this framework by analyzing how social "roots" (i.e., individual origins and trajectories) shape the different views of journalistic excellence described briefly above. In doing so, we suggest that news values—long of interest in the sociology of news[1]—are neither neutral nor entirely the result of individual choices; instead, such values reflect the unequal opportunities available to journalists for realizing differing ideals of professional excellence.

We differentiate this understanding of class from two traditions more commonly found in studies of media and class: Marxist-influenced approaches to political economy and Gramscian-inspired forms of cultural studies. Where Marxists generally emphasize the relationship between labor and class, a Bourdieusian perspective broadens the analysis to social space more generally, including the symbolic aspects of relations of production, in order to make visible the links between social origins and professional trajectories. And while cultural studies usefully demonstrates the importance of issues such as gender and race in shaping the ways individuals produce and consume media, Bourdieu's framework embeds these identities in a relational perspective that specifies the contexts in which particular identity traits (e.g., gender, race, class) do or do not become salient.

While we draw on profiles of journalists from our own work on journalists in France and the United States, we suggest that the approach articulated here could be utilized by scholars examining other aspects of media and class. This might include other sorts of media producers (e.g., musicians, filmmakers), as well as media consumers. Our aim is not to prove some mechanical argument about class and journalists (i.e., to demonstrate definitively that class shapes roles and perceptions more than other determinants); rather, we seek to show how the Bourdieusian approach might aid empirical analyses of media and class. To achieve those ends, we proceed below by (1) describing a Bourdieusian approach to media and class; (2) distinguishing this approach from Marxist and cultural studies traditions in media and communication scholarship; and (3) illustrating the Bourdieusian approach through an analysis of the ways that class shapes individual journalists' understandings of professional norms and ideals.

A Bourdieusian Approach to Media and Class

Bourdieu is well-known for, among other things, his many studies in the sociology of culture. Rather than look at media *per se* in these studies, his work explored the way culture is produced across a range of discrete social fields, like literature[2] and journalism,[3] as well as the social organization of different cultural practices such as museum attendance[4] and amateur photography.[5] Across each of these studies, he sought to link aesthetic tastes (i.e., judgments held about the beauty of any object or practice) with an individual's social position (i.e., their origins and trajectory). By doing so, he explored the social roots of seemingly abstract values. This effort can be seen most clearly in *Distinction*, his massive study of cultural tastes and lifestyles in France during the 1960s and 1970s.[6]

Three basic principles underpin Bourdieu's[7] approach to class. First, he conceives of class as a *relational* concept. It is not the "real" group—i.e., the specific number of individuals in a given segment of the population—or skill or activity with which Bourdieu concerns himself. Instead, what matters is the way individuals define themselves vis-à-vis individuals located higher or lower than them in "social space" (understood as the juxtaposed relationships that comprise a field of activity). Familiarity with a newspaper like *Le Monde*, to take an example from *Distinction*, constitutes a sign of upper-class status in 1960s France because individuals with greater resources use it to distinguish themselves from less cultured groups. Therefore, one important empirical task for the researcher is to understand how the judgments that any individual or group adopts are related to the judgments taken by others in social space.

Second, Bourdieu[8] views class as *dynamic*. Despite his tendency to emphasize the degree to which classes reproduce themselves,[9] Bourdieu's conceptual approach remains open to the way individuals might challenge their social origins and move in different directions. His early work, for instance, sought to account for what Jurgen Ruesch[10] called "the climbers" (individuals trying to ascend socially) or "the strainers" (individuals trying in vain to ascend); or even what Harold Wilensky and Hugh Edwards[11] termed "the skidders" (individuals in decline). Furthermore, Bourdieu was open to biographical "ruptures"[12] that lead individuals to find themselves in social conditions where they cannot fully master their own behaviors. Here, too, for Bourdieu the empirical question is always how people respond to conditions in which they find themselves, and how their prior experiences shape their capacities to respond.

Finally, Bourdieu views class as containing as much a *symbolic* dimension as an economic one. It is not merely one's wage, salary, or overall economic assets that defines one's class position in an economically-derived hierarchy. Various other assets such as educational attainment, technical knowledge, and social networks, which are symbolic in nature, must also be considered. This symbolic hierarchy can be seen in journalism, for example, in terms of the legitimacy accorded to some forms of reporting (e.g., investigative reporting, long-form storytelling) vis-à-vis less legitimate forms (e.g., clickbait news). Partly because such hierarchies are made to appear natural (i.e., it appears obvious that investigative reporting *is* "better" than clickbait news), Bourdieu sees these struggles over classification as a crucial space of class struggle (as the individuals who produce clickbait are likely to hold fewer economic and symbolic assets than those capable of producing investigative reporting, and to accept the judgments of those with more assets as the appropriate definition of journalistic excellence).

Through this relational, dynamic, and symbolic approach, Bourdieu offers an account of class that defines class itself as the outcome of (dynamic) interactions between one's social origins and trajectories, the (relational) position one holds in social space, and one's (symbolic) perceptions of these positions. Empirically, this leads him to gather data that can assess these interactions (e.g., including empirical indicators found on surveys, such as place of birth, parents' occupations, educational attainment, and professional title, as well as data derived from interviews identifying aesthetic preferences and judgments). His general hypothesis about class in contemporary capitalist democracies is that such interactions tend to be structured homologously.[13] By this, he means that individuals' social origins often correlate with the social position they hold as well as their perceptions of social space. This homology simultaneously reproduces and legitimates social inequalities, by transforming differences in social origins into differences of aesthetic judgment.

Scholars of French journalism use Bourdieu's framework to shed light on various aspects of class. Lafarge and Marchetti,[14] for example, show that journalists from upper-middle class backgrounds tend to work for national news media, while those from lower-middle class origins are more likely to work for regional outlets. Grossetête[15] shows that journalists tend to report the same event differently depending on the social position of the individuals involved. News coverage of equivalent types of automobile accidents, for example, tends to emphasize irresponsibility when working class individuals are implicated. Professionals (e.g., lawyers, doctors), by contrast, are viewed as having a reason for their behavior (e.g., in a rush to get to a meeting).

While Anglophone researchers also examine class-based aspects of journalistic perception, they tend not to study this issue through a Bourdieusian lens. By using such a lens, we seek to move beyond familiar Anglophone use of concepts, such as field and capital, and instead explore how Bourdieu's relational, dynamic and symbolic approach to class can inform analyses of journalistic ideals.

Bourdieu vis-à-vis other Approaches to Media and Class

Bourdieu's approach to media and class is of course simply one among many. For the purposes of clarity, we briefly review what distinguishes this approach from others commonly used to make sense of media and class. As Bourdieu himself noted,[16] one could easily minimize the differences between his approach and these Marxist-influenced traditions. We distinguish them here not to establish Bourdieu's approach as better or more preferable, but to clarify how and in what ways his approach might inform scholarship on this topic.

The political economic tradition, rooted in the work of Marx, offers one point of contrast. This tradition has long explored media and class in relation to the capitalist mode of production. From this standpoint, the major questions concern how those in media businesses (i.e., the capitalists) accumulate capital while exploiting workers. These workers are sometimes conceived as the individuals employed within a given firm, whether they be journalists,[17] knowledge workers[18] or factory laborers producing digital devices.[19] Other times they are conceived as the individuals whose attention is packaged and sold as a commodity to advertisers.[20] Across both, attention is given to the way capitalists use legal regimes (e.g., intellectual property) and political alliances to further their accumulation of capital via exploitation of working classes.[21] Throughout these inquiries, emphasis is placed on exploitation as it occurs in relations of economic production.

Bourdieu's approach to class differs in two key ways from this Marxist perspective. For starters, he views class not only in terms of relations of production. Rather, for Bourdieu, class pertains to the structure of people's assets, which as noted above include both economic and symbolic dimensions. Thus, he pays little attention to whether or not certain activities count as labor (e.g., whether social media users can be viewed as workers), and instead focuses on how individuals draw on their various assets to exert power in a given situation (e.g., how a subset of social media users draw on their educational and cultural skills to create jobs for themselves online). Furthermore, Bourdieu, again drawing on his symbolic and dynamic principles, sees class itself as a categorization struggle, where the legitimate definition of the phenomena is a struggle among individuals with differential resources at their disposal to influence the debate.

A second tradition of media and class analysis is found in cultural studies. Often (though not always) inspired by Gramscian theories of hegemony, this tradition documents the ways lower classes interact with and sometimes resist dominant ideologies of the ruling class. Exemplars in this tradition include Hoggart's pioneering work[22] on the relation between attitudes in popular papers and magazines and the working-class readers to whom they are addressed; Morley's examination of the ways the same television program can be interpreted differently by audiences from different class backgrounds;[23] and Skeggs' analysis of the ways women challenge, modify and sometimes reformulate their understanding of both class and gender.[24]

Bourdieu is in substantial affinity with this approach, and in fact helped introduce the early work of Hoggart and others to French audiences.[25] However, his emphasis on a relational understanding of class is one point of difference between the two. Whereas many cultural studies analyses focus primarily on popular or working classes, Bourdieu insists on linking their perceptions to those found across the social space. In Hoggart's reading of class, for instance, the bourgeoisie are largely absent. Additionally, the two approaches likely differ in their reading of resistance. Inspired by Gramsci, cultural studies approaches tend to place more weight on the capacity of lower classes to resist dominant ideologies and find spaces for autonomy. By contrast, Bourdieu, drawing on his theory of symbolic domination,[26] often portrays the judgments of lower classes as influenced by those above them (e.g., in his theory of "cultural goodwill" that lead middle class individuals to admire legitimate culture despite being only somewhat familiar with it).

Thinking with Bourdieu: French and American Journalists' Perceptions of Excellence

In our work, we seek to think with—rather than mechanically apply—Bourdieu's approach to class. Our specific project examines transformations in local journalism in France and the United States.[27] We selected two cities—Toulouse and Seattle—that share a number of affinities. They are of similar size and have comparable levels in the citizenry of education and technology use. They are both home to a number of technology and aeronautics firms (Toulouse is home to Airbus, Seattle to Boeing). Their news media also face parallel pressures. In the past decade, the two have—like those in many cities throughout Western Europe and North America—undergone major transformations. Media have lost considerable proportions of their advertising revenues, and have witnessed large declines in audience share. In both cities, too, internet access is high and growing over time. While job losses have been greater in Seattle, precarious employment is a feature of journalism in both cities, and journalists generally accept that the future of journalism is online.[28]

One dimension of the project examines journalists' perceptions of "good journalism." Given prior research showing that these perceptions vary over time and across space, we conducted interviews with journalists aimed at eliciting these perceptions. In these interviews, journalists were asked to talk about work of which they were especially proud, and to explain why they were proud of it. Additionally, and in keeping with the Bourdieusian premises described above, journalists were asked about other journalists they admired, as well as forms of journalism they disliked. In order to link these perceptions to individual positions and trajectories, we asked each journalist a range of questions about their backgrounds and professional trajectories, including their place of birth, their parents' occupations, the education they received, and their paths into (and, in some cases, out of) journalism.

Below, we provide narratives of four journalists—mentioned at the chapter's outset—that link each's view of professional excellence to their social origins and professional trajectories. Our presentation of these narratives mirrors those found in Bourdieu's work. Each narrative begins with a quotation from the interviewee, which captures a core aesthetic judgment in the person's own words. The narratives then describe the individual's social origins and trajectory, ensuring that readers see the dynamism and particularity of a given individual's professional trajectory. They culminate with descriptions of journalistic excellence, with individuals discussing work they are proud, as well as journalism they admire or dislike.

The two journalists that describe being proud of long-form reporting on social issues are featured first. They have several biographical features in common. Both come from professional families and attended prestigious universities. Both experienced tensions early in their journalism careers that arose from a disconnect between what they were then doing and what they wanted to do, which led both to make major moves (away from New York and Paris, respectively). Both ultimately found themselves in Seattle and Toulouse—cities outside of their nation's media capitals—doing work they were proud of, even as ongoing cutbacks in the media industry create instability for each. For each, we can see a homology between their social origins, professional trajectories, and vision of quality journalism.

The two journalists that take pride in human interest stories they reported accurately also share several biographical features. Both come from working class families and attained higher levels of education than anyone else in their families. Their professional trajectories from working to middle class simultaneously reflect their relative ascent from their social origins, as well as their greater precarity vis-à-vis other journalists. Both articulate a tension between the journalism they are proud of and the journalism they would ultimately like to do, with the latter often corresponding to the more legitimate forms of journalism that emphasize long-form investigations. Such tensions, we suggest, indicate a form of "cultural goodwill," whereby they admire symbolically more legitimate forms of journalistic work that they do not have the working conditions to do. As with the other two journalists, we can see a homology between their social origins, professional trajectories, and visions of quality journalism.

"I Do Long-form, Deeply Reported Stories About Social Issues"

Esther[29] was born in a city in the American Midwest. Her father was a university history professor who studied civil rights. As a doctoral student, he wrote a dissertation about the history of "muckraking" journalism in the United States. Esther attended college at an elite liberal arts school on the East Coast, and did internships at elite, progressive news magazines that emphasize deep reporting and stylistic writing. One summer, she worked for the *New Yorker*. Another summer, she did fact-checking at *The Nation*.

After graduating, Esther started as a reporter for a community newspaper in Brooklyn, and then quickly got a job at a community newspaper "across the river" in the state of New Jersey. This was a "very intense boot camp in journalism" where she wrote three news articles a day. Listening to her describe this early work, one gets the sense that this was important training but not entirely enjoyable given the focus on "hard core daily turnaround" that drove the coverage.

From there, Esther moved to Africa and freelanced from Zimbabwe and South Africa for two years during the time in which the African National Congress (ANC) was banned and Nelson Mandela was freed from prison. She wrote for several newspapers. While there, she sought to do a different form of journalism: "I had really tried to move myself from doing that kind of really hardcore daily turnaround kind of journalism to doing more thoughtful features." After a few years of living and working in South Africa, she returned to the United States and moved to Seattle because her brother—a university professor in the life sciences—lived there.

She found work at an alternative weekly newspaper. During this time, Esther says that she moved "towards this longer magazine style journalistic" reporting. She worked there "for a really long time" (20 years) doing "long-form, deeply reported stories about social issues." She does not mention it in the interview, but that newspaper changed owners in 2013 and proceeded to lay-off many of the staff. In 2015, for example, nearly a third of employees were laid off. During that same year, what she describes as "this wonderful job" opened up at the *Seattle Times*, "which was very similar in a lot of ways" to what she was already doing (social issues focused, enterprise reporting). "It was just perfect for me and that is where I am now."

When asked to discuss work she is proud of, she talked about a mother on the verge of homelessness who struggled to find housing:

> I really liked it because I love to do those kinds of stories that are able to tell a larger story through one person's life. So, it's a way of making it very real for people and also you are bringing a narrative in getting people involved emotionally but you are also talking about a much larger issue. So, in that case I talked about a whole array of issues including recent shifts in homeless policy and the way the nonprofits were handling homeless people, and problems with the system, and the way the federal government was dealing with this subsidy program and all sorts of larger issues that could be told through one person's life. So, I was very glad to be able to do that in a story for the *Times*, which is something that they—that was part of why they hired me to bring this kind of stories.

When asked about other news she reads, she responded: "I canvas a lot." She mentioned her old newspaper, as well as social media feeds "to see some of the breaking [news] stuff that might be going on." She doesn't watch television news nor read a local alternative publication. Instead, "I … read national news, which is often just as important not only because it will have some local stuff…." But, she explained, because it is "important to know all the national trends going on because that interacts very much with what's happening here—whether a local version of it is happening here or know something to look into or whatever." To emphasize the point, she concluded the thought with the following remark: "I always read the *New York Times* and the *New Yorker* and stuff like that."

"I Am the Only One who Knows all the Details About That Story"

Pierre was born in downtown Toulouse and grew up in an upper-middle-class neighborhood. His father was a prestigious lawyer in the region, his mother a housewife. His early education took place in a private Catholic school. His family expected him to become a lawyer; however, Pierre disliked the university and got what he described as bad grades. His only passion at that time was his participation at a well-regarded private local radio station. After a push from his father to obtain a degree, he enrolled at a recognized private journalism school. After graduation, he moved to Paris and worked for a prestigious private radio station where he found a "very comfortable position." He earned some prestige in Paris because he offered a left-political perspective on a right-oriented station. He is proud of himself because he "made [his] way living in Paris, having money, recognition … and [his] father would listen to [him] on the radio".

After seven years in Paris, his boss proposed that he become a "multimedia journalist" (MMJ) in southern France. He accepted because he would have a lot of money with "his upper Parisian income and very low costs of living down there." Two years after, he realizes he hates breaking news and burns out. "I was kind of frustrated … and tired. You never fully sleep, actually. One night out of two someone calls you at any time and tells you to go to the event, even on weekends." He explained that this job focused only on productivity. "The only thing you need is productivity. The accent is on the quantity, never the quality. You are nothing but an executant." Summing up that segment of his life, he said: "I am one of those who did a burnout in [that media company]. That's why I left … I was not the only one. Among MMJ, we are many to have "cracked" under the pressure".

Worried about his health, his parents proposed that he return to Toulouse with his wife and small daughter. They did, and Pierre decided to launch a magazine based on investigative "slow" journalism with some journalist friends. Doing so allowed him to produce journalism he could be proud of again:

> This is it. This relation to time is marvelous. When you move from breaking news to a monthly magazine ... you have the time to have perspective, to really be sure of weighting every word and to *say something* about our society. Now we're printing subjects we decided 1 or 2 years ago ... this gives me the chance to show my writing talents. [...] To me, true journalism is the one you show with your *belle plume*. I am very proud of showing that I can write interesting and deep things. I am not only the guy from the breaking news who is perceived to be a scavenger.

When asked about the story he is most proud of, he talked about a local government proposal from the 1960s and 1970s to culvert the city's main canal. He said that what interested him was the intellectual work required to make sense of government actions. "What's interesting there is that you can tell how much mentalities have changed in 40 years and how difficult it is to understand the machinery of public policies." He takes pride in the time he dedicated to the project: "I spent a lot of time writing it [...]. The inquiry took several months. I found many witnesses from that time. I made a lot of interviews to specialists. I spent a lot of time in the archives." Finally, he emphasizes his grasp of the subject matter and his attention to detail: "I am the only one who knows all the details about that story. And I put a lot of attention to details."

Asked to describe journalists he admires and follows, Pierre focused entirely on those based in Paris: the online news site *Mediapart* and magazine *Revue XXI*, which were started by the famed investigative journalists Edwy Plenel and Patrick de Saint-Exupéry, respectively. "They are passionate and audacious," he says. "They have embodied their ideals and I really appreciate that." He also admires the result: "Because *Mediapart* is the symbol of the press freedom. They give life to the left press (*la presse de gauche*). I don't know if it's correct to say left, I mean alternative ... free. It's a real free press." Explaining further, he says: "They are a little bit left oriented but they criticize everyone, one side or the other. They are free. It is freedom that amazes me. Mostly in a place like Toulouse where journalists are not really free."

"I Think I Told the Story Well"

Emily was born in a small town—population just under 2000—in the American west. Her mother was a county clerk who filed birth certificates, marriage notices and death announcements; she attended a regional public university but did not graduate from it. Her father, now retired, was a welder.

Emily attended the major state university. When she arrived there, she was unsure what she should study. During freshman orientation, her mother heard the dean of the journalism school tell the parents that if their kids were rebels, they should send them to him and he would make a "hell of a reporter" out of them. "My mom was like, 'You should check out the journalism school.'" Initially, Emily had thought about studying Communication. Ultimately, she decided on journalism because a Communication degree required a class on interpersonal communication whereas journalism required only drama. "I was like, oh drama sounds like an easier A, so let's do that. And once I got there, the professors got me interested in what I was doing and I got sucked in." She focused on broadcast journalism because a print-journalism professor told her she was "talentless" and unfit for print journalism.

After graduation, Emily got a job at a production company doing entertainment and sports-related programming. In her view, it was an OK first job but she wanted to travel and get out of the state. She left and took a job in Denver as a flight attendant, then got a job at Alaska Airlines. "Great benefits, union jobs, but I just wasn't passionate about it. I wasn't intellectually challenged. I was bored." When asked to expand on what that meant, she replied: "I just missed writing and talking to people, having a job that I like going to every day. It sounds crazy when you look at the paychecks and the benefits. But I love what I do."

Emily then got a job at a newspaper in rural Washington, and did community reporting for two years. She was writing 7–10 stories per week, and a reporter's job came up at a suburban daily outside Seattle that focused on Boeing. She decided to apply for it. "And they did not like me for that job. But they liked me." She therefore got a job focused on rural communities around the suburb. At the time of the interview, she was working on this beat. In the two years since, she moved on: first, to a newspaper in another state, but also in a metropolitan setting, where she worked for six months; later, she returned to Washington state and reported for a chain of weekly newspapers on the coast. This lasted just under a year and a half. Now she is based again in Seattle as a freelancer.

When asked to describe a story she is proud of, she talked about a "little Iraqi boy" who was blinded at the age of two when he got shot in the face. A local family in the Seattle area adopted him, and Emily was tasked with doing a profile about him.

> It was the first story that I have gotten and spent a good amount of time on. I went there [to the boy's home] several times over the course of reporting, and it took months and months to build [a] relationship with the boy. And I really got to slow down and go in more depth with something. So I really enjoy working on that and this story came out really nice. I think I told the story well. And I have seen other reporters cover him and call him disfigured and stuff like that. And I just thought that that was completely, I mean he is a kid. You do not say that. Even though his face is severely disfigured, I did not think it was really necessary to point that out seven times in the same story.

Questioned about media she likes, initially Emily responded by naming a colleague at her newspaper, who is "a terrific writer." But she also followed up quickly by mentioning Matt Taibbi, a well-known contributing editor at a national magazine whose writes about politics. ("I really do not know how to spell his last name properly. He writes a lot of good stuff"). When asked what she likes about his reporting, she responds: "I really like his long form reporting. I would love to write some of the political features he does, like [in] *Rolling Stone*." Later in the interview, she said that her beat is challenging. "I really wish that I had a larger subject area to write about." She explained that an editor thought every story should take four hours to produce. "I was like, well, I like more time." She also stated she would like to make public records requests without asking for permission.

We ask her if there is anything she would like her news organization to do. She replied pithily: "Pay people better." We ask if there is anything we ought to know. She said: "No. I mostly just want to tell you how much people work on their own time ... I was really surprised when I came from a union job to journalism." She described her surprise upon learning that "everybody thinks that it's totally fine to just work 12 hours and put down 8 on your time card, when you are making 27,000 dollars a year in the first place. That was really shocking to me." She paused, but continued by noting the difficulty of even having a job in journalism. "We are lucky to have one anyway. We are getting paid at least enough to make it a part-time job." When asked if she ever put down the full hours worked on her time card, she replied: "I was told you just have to write yourself into a better job."

"I Will Never Tell Sordid Details"

Victor was born and raised in a social housing area in Bordeaux. His father used to be a worker and his mother still is a nursery assistant. Growing up, he was a good student. In high school, a teacher encouraged him to attend university. While he did not score well enough on his entrance exams to go to the country's most prestigious universities in Paris or Bordeaux, a public program (*Egalité des chances*) for students with good grades and limited resources led him to be accepted at Sciences Po Toulouse. It was the only "Grande Ecole" to which he gained entry.

Victor liked the idea of a broad-based education in the Humanities and Social Sciences rather than a narrow technical specialization. He also knew that students coming from Grandes Ecoles tend to get better jobs than those that do not. He entered into journalism immediately after graduation, which is somewhat unusual in France as the specialization for a journalism degree starts after undergraduate studies are completed. He explained his reason for entering the workforce immediately, and reflected on how it impacted his career:

> When I finished Sciences Po, I got some information about continuing in a prestigious journalism school ... but ... I really didn't want to keep on studying. I was tired, and besides ... I'm in [a relationship] with someone who has worked since the age of 16. It became harder and harder to still be the eternal student whereas my wife kept working. So, I wanted to do something else and get to work and not keep studying. [...] Perhaps if I had studied more, I would do another type of journalism ... I would love having the time to do more interviewing, to have the time to cross different points of view ... which I cannot do at the radio. There, we literally work day-to-day. When we have something to write, it should be ready in the next hour.

Initially, Victor found work as a freelancer for an online news startup and a magazine. Both are now out of business. He then secured a one-year contract at the local radio station, and he did not contain his excitement about this during our interview. "I have a contract that lasts for one year! This is my second one-year contract, and it will last until May." The contract removes some of the uncertainty associated with freelancing. Victor described himself as "grateful" for having it. He said this despite having a salary that is scarcely more than minimum wage and comes with difficult conditions (he works from 4 am until noon). Thinking of his wife and parents, who work standing all day long, he says that at least he has an "office, a computer, and I sit."

When asked about something he had done and was very proud of, he couldn't think of anything in particular. He tries to do his best every day on every note. After thinking, he said he's proud of never speaking about crime in a sordid or sensationalist way. He hates doing news that is oriented to gossip or sensationalism.

> So, for example, for me ... crime stories ... I'm not interested. If they ask me to add crime stories, I will adapt myself. Sure. Because sometimes you have nothing else, and you have two minutes to be filled ... so ... voilà. Sometimes in the local dailies crime stories are extremely well detailed, and that's something I do not like. So, if I have to say that someone was found dead, I will only say that one person was found dead [...] I will never tell sordid details! I believe that sordid details are awful for the radio ... I find them inappropriate. Even some words in radio, violent terms as blood, members, someone dismembered.... To use those terms in the radio, or explicit sexual terms ... I think it might offend the listener.... So, sometimes there's something like the self-censorship [in terms of sensationalism]. But it's me who does not want to talk about that. I will try to say something different ... something people will feel concerned about beyond the gossip.

When asked about the media he likes, he stated the difference between what he likes and what he uses at work. "If we talk about dailies, I read *Le Monde*, *Rue 89* and of course *Le monde diplomatique*. I even pay for the subscription.... It really does not correspond to the editorial policy of the radio I work for." For his job, he explained he uses Agence France Presse and *Le Parisien*. When asked why, he answers:

> It is very simple. I work for a music-oriented radio station. A station where news is not that important. We are not opening with international news ... we will open with the gas price ... those kind of things ... things that journalists call "concerning". This means that it concerns, it interests the average listener who is listening to the music and that listens to a 2-minute flash. This means, the essential stuff ... we will not open with the news in *Le Monde* or in *France Culture* ... Indeed, we limit ourselves to something "white" ... meaning ... banal. On my side, I do listen to the radio to get the news. I listen to France Inter and FIP.... They do not really correspond to the editorial policy of the organization I work for ... by the way, these preferences have produced some little problems in my job but I've learned how to adapt myself.

Conclusion

The above interviews suggest that journalists' social origins and trajectories can shed light on their professional ideals. Doing so, we suggest, enables a view of the social roots of journalists' perceptions. Victor's trajectory, for example, is one of ascent from working class origins (he is the first person in the family to get an office job), and his university experience cultivated an appreciation for dominant journalistic ideals (as evidenced by his news consumption habits). Yet these origins also limit his ascent and shape his understanding of professional excellence. While further education would increase his chances of professional advancement, Victor didn't want to be the "eternal student" because it would be unfair to his partner. And because his current job sometimes requires him to cover crime news, he focused on accurately portraying the events while avoiding "sordid" details.

Esther's rather different social origins and trajectory also shape her professional ideals. Born into a family of liberal professionals, her university experience exposed her to internship experiences that emphasized deep reporting and stylistic writing. These ideals reflect an upper-middle class emphasis on justice and civil rights, as does her decision to leave the "hard core daily turnaround" of community newspapers for the "more thoughtful" reporting possible in South Africa. This vision of journalistic excellence largely ignores the unequal opportunities available for journalists to achieve it. Esther talked, for example, about the "wonderful job" she found doing exactly the type of reporting she values in Seattle at a time of massive layoffs for other journalists.

By empirically examining the links between social origins, trajectories and perceptions, the Bourdieusian approach suggests that journalists' norms are neither neutral nor abstract. Instead, they reflect the unequal opportunities afforded to journalists to realize specific values. Beyond the case of journalists' perceptions, Bourdieu also offers a framework for thinking of class as relational, dynamic, and symbolic. This does not suggest other variables like national origins or gender do not matter; it also does not imply that any homology occurs mechanically.

Scholars of media and class, especially in the Anglophone world, have increasingly integrated Bourdieu into their theoretical toolkits. His concepts of field, habitus and capital, for example, are increasingly utilized to explain who produces and consumes various forms of media. Somewhat surprisingly, Bourdieu's attempt to rethink class, and move beyond what he considered some of Marxism's limitations, remain relatively underutilized in media and communication. The current chapter offers a small step to addressing this gap by explaining the Bourdieusian approach to media and class, contrasting it with Marxist understandings, and briefly illustrating it with some of our own empirical research.

Notes

1 Michael Schudson, "The Sociology of News Production," *Media, Culture and Society* 11, no. 3 (1989): 236–282.
2 Pierre Bourdieu, *The Rules of Art: Genesis and Structure of the Literary Field* (Stanford: Stanford University Press, 1996). Please note that, where possible, we provide citations to the English-language version of Bourdieu's writings.
3 Pierre Bourdieu, *On Television* (New York: New Press, 1998).
4 Pierre Bourdieu and Alain Darbel, *The Love of Art: European Museums and their Public* (Cambridge: Polity, 1997).
5 Pierre Bourdieu, Luc Boltanski, Robert Castel, Jean Claude Chamboredon, and Dominique Schnapper. *Photography: A Middle-brow Art* (Stanford, CA: Stanford University Press, 2005).
6 Pierre Bourdieu, *Distinction: A Social Critique of the Judgement of Taste* (Cambridge: Harvard University Press, 1984).
7 Pierre Bourdieu, "The Social Space and the Genesis of Social Groups," *Theory and Society* 14, no. 6 (1985): 723–744.
8 Pierre Bourdieu, "Condition de Classe et Position de Classe." *European Journal of Sociology* 7, no. 2 (1966): 201–223.
9 Bourdieu, *Distinction*.
10 Jurgen Ruesch, *Chronic Disease and Psychological Invalidism* (New York: Paul Hoeber: 1946).
11 Harold Wilensky and Hugh Edwards. "The Skidders: Ideological Adjustments of Downwardly Mobile Workers," *American Sociological Review* 24 (1959): 215–231.
12 Jean Claude Passeron, *Le Raisonnement sociologique. L'espace non-poppérien du raisonnement naturel* (Paris: Nathan, 1991) and Pierre Bourdieu, *Sketch for a Self-analysis* (Chicago: University of Chicago Press, 2008).
13 Bourdieu, "The Social Space and the Genesis of Social Groups".
14 Gérauld Lafarge and Dominique Marchetti, "Les hiérarchies de l'information. Les légitimités professionnelles des étudiants en journalisme," *Sociétés Contemporaines* 106, no. 2 (2017): 21–44.
15 Mathieu Grossetête, *Accidents de la route et inégalités sociales. Les morts, les médias et l'Etat* (Vulaines sur Seine: Editions du Croquant, 2011).
16 Bourdieu, "The Social Space and the Genesis of Social Groups."
17 Hanno Hardt, *Newsworkers: Towards a History of the Rank and File* (Minneapolis: University of Minnesota Press, 1995).
18 Vincent Mosco and Catherine McKercher, *The Laboring of Communication: Will Knowledge Workers of the World Unite?* (Lanham: Rowman and Littlefield, 2008).
19 Christian Fuchs, *Social Media: A Critical Introduction* (London: Sage, 2014).
20 Dallas Smythe, *Dependency Road: Communications, Capitalism, Consciousness, and Canada* (Norwood: Ablex: 1981) and Nick Dyer-Witherford, "Digital Labor, Species Being, and the Global Worker," *Ephemera* 10, no. 3/4 (2010): 484–503.
21 Robert McChesney, *Corporate Media and the Threat to Democracy* (New York: Seven Stories: 1997).
22 Richard Hoggart, *The Uses of Literacy: Aspects of Working Class Life* (London: Penguin, 1957).
23 David Morley, *The Nationwide Audience: Structure and Decoding* (London: British Film Institute, 1980).
24 Beverley Skeggs, *Formations of Class and Gender: Becoming Respectable* (London: Sage, 1997).
25 Philippe Coulangeon and Julien Duval, eds., *The Routledge Companion to Bourdieu's Distinction* (London: Routledge, 2015).
26 Bourdieu, *Distinction*.
27 Matthew Powers and Sandra Vera-Zambrano, "Explaining the Formation of Online News Startups in France and the United States: A Field Analysis," *Journal of Communication* 66, no. 5 (2016): 857–877.
28 See the overview in Matthew Powers, Sandra Vera-Zambrano, and Olivier Baisnée, "The News Crisis Compared: The Impact of the Journalism Crisis in Toulouse, France and Seattle, Washington," in *The Uncertain Future of Local Journalism*, ed. Rasmus Kleis Nielsen (London: IB Tauris: 2016), 31–50.
29 In order to protect identities, all names have been changed, and cities outside of Toulouse and Seattle have been described in general terms (e.g., a Midwestern city).

15
THE ASPIRATIONAL CLASS "MOBILITY" OF DIGITAL NOMADS

Erika Polson

The Instagram feed (2.6 million posts and counting) looks indistinguishable from a number of those with hashtags related to vacation or adventure travel: Yoga headstands on the sand; a view of a woman's back as she stares at a distant volcano; a man riding an electric scooter along a row of palm trees. Pyramids, ruins, and brightly painted row houses; bicycles, parasails, and boats; waterfalls, sunsets, and rice paddies. The few photos that include images of laptops or other work-related technologies feature them as accessories, used on beaches or from lounge chairs alongside a swimming pool. As such, one could be forgiven for not realizing that the feed's organizing hashtag—#digitalnomad—refers to a burgeoning trend in online labor.

In the late 1990s, developments in wireless internet and portable devices enabled professionals in a variety of occupations to begin working at home or in coffee shops; celebrating their liberation from the office, journalists referred to these mobile workers as "digital nomads."[1] Recently, however, the nature of professional nomadism has changed, and a growing new generation of remote workers seeks to be liberated not just from the office but from the home. By combining online labor and personal motility, today's digital nomads work to build itinerant lifestyles involving temporary work-life stints in cultural and nature hotspots around the world. As sociologist Annika Müller explains, this might mean working in Berlin one month and Chiang Mai, Thailand, the next, because the nomads "can essentially work anywhere, as long as they have their laptop with them and access to a good internet connection."[2] Coming mainly from North America, Europe, and Australia/New Zealand, but increasingly from Southeast Asia as well, they are motivated by the opportunity to embrace the mobilities enabled by techno-society and to become free from the stasis associated with being settled in one place. If this sounds like a philosophy more than a trend, in many ways it is. And the philosophy has inspired a (literal) movement, which calls on people to "free" themselves to roam the world and to realize they don't have "to be trapped to get paid."[3] That this discourse proliferates and gains laudatory media coverage at the same time that the number of forcibly displaced people in the world has reached an all-time high[4] illuminates an irony of our era and the deep privilege embodied by these welcomed leisure migrants.

A growing transnational infrastructure is increasingly converging to provide nomads with spaces and services for work, lodging, transportation, and community. Online forums abound for sourcing digital employment gigs, accessing resources abroad, and sharing information and concerns with fellow nomads. In recent years, a host of co-working and co-living businesses (sometimes combined) have opened in locales such as Budapest (Hungary), Berlin (Germany), Medellín

(Colómbia), Ubud (Indonesia), Chiang Mai (Thailand), and many more places around the world—sites considered attractive for the low cost of living, availability and affordability of high-speed internet, beautiful nature or hip urban environments, and the presence of a like-minded "nomad community." Many of these companies were founded by people who are themselves nomads, and a key sector of the digital nomad economy appears to be driven by those who have created businesses serving other nomads directly. One of the largest target markets in this field seems to be aspirational nomads, and a great many seminars, websites, blogs, and books are devoted to helping people figure out how to achieve the "location independence" that is their ultimate goal.

Although there have always been segments of the labor market whose work requires travel, seasonal migration, or expatriation, the phenomenon of digital nomadism represents a novel mode of lifestyle-centric labor migration enabled by developments in technology, infrastructure, and employment models, but also, importantly, represents a new stage in the elevation of global mobility as a middle-class asset. Bourdieu identified the attribution of value (in the form of *status*) to particular cultural competencies, or "distinctions," as one of the ways that people within the middle-class and upper-middle classes both distinguish themselves from lower classes and achieve social mobility in competition with others within their class.[5] As Lawler points out, this concept sees class not as "a set of static and empty positions waiting to be filled by indicators such as employment and housing" but rather as a contested and dynamic process through which classificatory boundaries are continually remade.[6] In Bourdieu's view, assets are constituted not only by economic capital but also through the status-bearing competencies, knowledge, and symbolic practices referred to as 'cultural capital.'[7] Within the aspirational middle classes, travel has long been pursued as a status asset,[8] the nature of which has changed over time to reflect an evolution in what counts as cultural capital, with new distinctions continuously sought as the status becomes the status quo. For example, as tourism grew into one of the world's largest industries, travel trendsetters revolted against the theme parks, all-inclusive resorts, cruises and bus tours of the masses, seeking more 'authentic,' adventurous, and unique travel experiences.[9] This ante has been considerably upped by the digital nomads, who advocate for a lifestyle of permanent travel sustained by working remotely. The growing popularity of digital nomadism (or nomadic aspirations) points to the status that increasingly accrues to those who are able to most take advantage of the 'promise' of the techno and global age by becoming frequent and comfortable world travelers.

This chapter explores discourses of digital nomadism through news articles, blogs, social media, and online forums in conjunction with a variety of online and offline businesses developing to provide a networked infrastructure in support of people who want to be free-floating yet connected, and considers them in the context of the new, globalizing middle classes. Analysis of discursive practices around this mobile lifestyle shows how a swath of professionals from a range of national backgrounds is developing aspirations that diverge from those of traditional middle and upper-middle classes, in that they privilege membership over ownership and visiting over belonging. Digital and mobile media prove to be at the center of this process in many ways, in terms of inspiring the pursuit of the lifestyle and selection of locations; organizing travel and stays; seeking and conducting remote work; communicating with distant loved ones; finding new social connections on-the-go; and performing the nomad lifestyle on social media.

Drawing from theories of the middle classes, as well as literature on professional migration, travel/tourism, and the gig economy, the chapter traces how the identity of the digital nomad is being constructed and sold as an advanced mode of living through liberation from societal constraints, and considers what this discursive trend indicates about changing values and perhaps a growing restlessness of a younger and more globally-focused fraction of the middle classes. Finally, I consider what the notion of "location independence" underlying the digital nomad movement might imply about how this segment of the middle class is increasingly valorizing detachment from the commitments that once defined social mobility in terms of community investment, yet without developing new obligations to the places where they land.

Professional Mobilities: From Expatriates to Digital Nomads

When I began to study the use of geo-social media by mobile professionals ten years ago (with ethnographic research of expatriates in Paris, which in later years expanded to Singapore and Bangalore and became the book, *Privileged Mobilities*[10]), I was focused on how a new generation was increasingly moving abroad alone (rather than with a family) and explored how this single, more diverse, and more gender-equal cohort of expatriates used a variety of online platforms to access offline social events in cities around the world. Noting that these expatriates avoided the tradition of segregating themselves into communities of co-nationals—attending events for "international people" instead—I argued that the online and offline communities created through geo-social media platforms significantly supported the construction of a new form of global middle-class identity, with competencies such as international experiences, language capabilities, and a certain "global mindset" being performed, negotiated, and reproduced as cultural capital.[11]

As Anne-Meike Fechter found in her ethnography of expatriate communities in Indonesia, this younger generation of expats considers themselves to have "an international outlook with regard to their professional and social lives, which is unencumbered by national boundaries."[12] She added that while traditional expats accepted a period abroad as a step toward advancement back home, the new expats explicitly aim to work abroad—not only to gain international work experience, "but because a 'global' lifestyle is seen as attractive and exciting."[13] For contemporary expatriates, that global lifestyle can mean moving to a new country every few years, either through the circulation policies/plans of their corporate or NGO employers, or by leveraging international experience to change jobs along with an attractive country relocation. Acknowledging the extent to which this generation of expats values mobility, Nowicka referred to their "geographic promiscuity"[14] and Favell found that movement was valorized as "a permanent state of mind."[15]

Professional migration has recently entered a new phase with the emergence of digital nomads pushing for even more frequent and wide-ranging mobility, and with less direction from employers regarding where they go and how long they stay. For expats, an employer normally has a branch office or regional headquarters in the location to which the professional has been posted for a period of time, which can span multiple years. The nomads, however, are either freelancers or entrepreneurs, or work for companies to whom their geographic location is not important as long as they are responsive to electronic communications and meet deadlines and quality of deliverables. As part of their nomadic philosophy but also because they often enter a country on tourist visas, they tend toward shorter stays in any one site. Thus, although the digital nomads use various types of employment to fund their mobile lives (often in addition to savings and/or family money, as de Vaujany and Aroles have discovered[16]), this employment does not specifically connect them to the places where they are (temporarily) based. This is clear, for example, in an ad for a job-search engine aimed at digital nomads, called Remote OK, that invites members to use its services in order to "Work anywhere; Live everywhere." Because of the continuous nature of the nomads' movements, in many ways they have more in common with travelers than expatriates, although work remains an important part of their lives on-the-go.

The mobile lifestyle of the digital nomads is one where, as Reichenberger points out, "the boundaries between work, leisure and travel appear blurred."[17] In fact, as nomadism grows more popular as an ideal, it is increasingly featured by mainstream media and in the internal blogs of global organizations where its promise is frequently summed up with the slogan: "Get paid to travel the world." Despite connections between frequent travelers and digital nomads, Cohen, Duncan, and Thulemark argue that "lifestyle mobilities" (which include the nomads) differ from the temporary mobility of travelers through the "higher significance placed on physical mobility itself as a defining aspect of one's identity."[18] Part of that identity is built on affirming intentions to keep moving on, rather than to 'return' to an originating home; in this context, professional labor is key to providing stability and purpose to what might otherwise be seen as an unmoored lifestyle.[19]

Cohen et al. also point out that the growth of these voluntary ongoing mobile lifestyles is connected to the increasing collapse of "a binary divide between work and leisure."[20] The idea that such collapse is a positive occurrence has been key to developing ideological justifications for freelance work and the so-called "gig economy," supported by slogans such as "Do what you love" or "Work to live, don't live to work."

Recently, Sutherland and Jarrahi conducted an extensive content analysis of the three largest online groups for digital nomads, and interviewed remote workers.[21] While their study found that members of the communities performed a broad variety of jobs across diverse industries, they observed a very cohesive digital nomad identity built around the commonalities of "digital work, an extreme form of mobility and travel, and independence from organizations."[22] The nomads were highly motivated "to combine travel adventurism and an escape from the office atmosphere," and travel destinations were chosen for being places the nomad wanted to visit, rather than for specific work or professional reasons.[23] At the same time, they noted that professional challenges such as networking, maintaining productivity in an effective workspace, developing new skills, locating Wi-Fi, and self-promotion and marketing took up considerable time—even more so considering the nomads must begin anew in each location and do so without the support functions that are provided by internal corporate services in traditional work contexts. In addition to finding/creating suitable workspaces in each new location, Sutherland and Jarrahi noted that the nomads must also find places to live and socialize. In meeting these needs, the personal and professional frequently overlap—for example, by attending social meet-ups or accessing nomad-centered temporary lodgings which also provide networking opportunities. Digital media are fundamental to accessing and managing these mobilities and moorings.

Digital Media and Global Mobility

The popularity of the work/travel lifestyle has expanded alongside technologies that allow people to feel more 'at home' and connected while traveling. Many tourism businesses have drawn on the capacity of location technologies to connect mobile users to local people and services, moving the concept of travel away from a sojourn in a separate world and toward models that emphasize immersion into everyday life while abroad. This is notable in the growing short-term home rental market (Airbnb's 2016 advertising slogan was "Don't go there, live there"), as well as an array of new apps for connecting travelers to local social events and other experiences that attempt to provide a semblance of life as a 'local.'[24] Access to 'everyday life' while on the move is additionally aided by electronic communication technologies used to keep in touch with relationships and media, compressing the gap between home and away[25] and producing a sense of immediacy as people feel that their social networks are actively traveling with them.[26] Such services are taken up by the digital nomads on a more permanent basis to support mobile lives and, indeed, Germann Molz finds that media communications may help constant travelers to develop a sense of "global abode," where they are able to be at home in mobility and thus, "at home in the world."[27]

Digital communication technologies are also implicated in significant changes to how travel yields status—the power of which has increased with the ability to circulate images of one's foreign experiences among online audiences. Today travel content is among the most viewed on social media,[28] which points to how, for many, aspirations have shifted from the accrual of material goods to the pursuit of unique, adventurous, or meaningful *experiences*. Economists refer to this as the "experience economy,"[29] where spending shifts from buying things to *doing* things; and, of course, "telling the world about it online afterwards."[30] Trend forecaster James Wallman argues that experiences have greater potential than material goods for boosting status on social media platforms, partially because their actual price tags are more fungible and in part because "posting pictures of what you just bought is gauche, [but] posting pictures of something you're doing is fine."[31] In this context, social media seem to have changed the very way travelers take photographs, in many cases making it more about communicating an experience to others than about creating a memory of the moment for oneself.[32] This tendency finds its ultimate expression in the use of selfies to insert oneself into exotic backdrops, an act that shifts the focus away from "fetishizing the extraordinary at the tourist destination" and instead seeks to "capture the extraordinary within themselves."[33] The cachet of travel is further transmitted online through the ability to broadcast locations, whether through check-ins, place-based hashtags, or the geo-tagging that can be enabled to accompany posts to most social media platforms, which in this case allows digital nomads to spatially represent their mobility to others.[34]

However, the fact that this sharing (and feedback from friends) can occur instantaneously has meant that people more "selectively present their travel stories" as part of strategic self-presentation,[35] which can lead to a profound disconnect between the 'story' and the reality of lived experiences with mobility. Although a life of constant travel may sound like the experience economy's version of "having it all," many recent blog posts from people who have given up on, or are questioning the sustainability of, the digital nomad lifestyle demonstrate the downside to an uprooted life on the move and the difficulties of building a mobile sense of home. For example, nomadic blogger Mark Manson recently wrote,

> To many back home, we are living the dream. We have access to an unspeakable freedom of choice and boundless personal opportunity.... Last year I visited 17 countries ... I saw the Taj Mahal, the Great Wall of China and Machu Picchu in a span of three months.... But I did this all alone.... [T]he price of overwhelming freedom is often my isolation.[36]

And in a high-profile defection, NomadList founder Pieter Levels moved back to a full-time life and lease in Amsterdam in 2016. As he explained in an interview:

> "I was standing in my apartment in Medellin, Colombia looking out the window, and I realized I don't know anyone here," he recalled. "I was thinking this is not what I should be doing. Like, this looks really great if I take a photo, but I don't feel any connection."[37]

As Michael Thomas, the fellow nomad who interviewed Levels above, explained, "Life as a digital nomad is much more complicated than those beautiful Instagram tableaus might imply."[38]

These quotes from the ex- or questioning-nomads demonstrate two issues key to critically evaluating digital nomad culture. First, the fact that it is a highly aesthetic lifestyle—the value of which is deeply interconnected with the traction it gains on social media ("looks really great if I take a photo")—is significant for understanding how cultural capital is created through performances of global mobility. Second, the idea that the reality of loneliness and disconnection is very different than what the beautiful photos might imply suggests the need to further examine the discourses that celebrate and perhaps inspire/compel this form of mobility. The following two sections analyze a variety of these discourses, first considering them in light of the new business models emerging to recruit and service nomads and, second, considering how they are representative of evolving tensions between the status attached to traditional and emerging middle-class lifestyles.

Selling the Nomadic Life

Digital nomads have been featured in newspapers and magazines around the world, and a review of coverage shows that mainstream media have tended to emphasize a celebratory view. The topic is often covered as a lifestyle feature about an innovative community of people who have figured out how to exist on continuous vacation—an idea that is presented as obviously superior to the middle-class professional's normal life. For example, a 2015 article in *The Sunday Telegraph* (London), asked, "Fed up with spending the 9 to 5 in a stuffy office with only a long commute to look forward to?" and went on to advise:

> Well, pack your Mac and head to Bali to join the 'digital nomads'. Why put up with pollution, urban squalor, rain and high rent when you could open your laptop in Thailand, Australia or Germany—and move on to another hot-desking set-up and Airbnb rental when you get bored of the view?[39]

Similarly, an article from the *Sunday Times* (London) pointed out that, "Nowadays, you can be on a beach with your laptop, Skype someone back in Ireland, close your laptop and go back to drinking your mojito."[40]

The common-sense tone of these essays—which implies that all one needs to do is simply *decide* to choose the nomad life and a sort of universally-defined happiness will fall into place—obscures not only the emotional challenges of continuous mobility, but also the economic ones (not to mention the political, economic, and cultural concerns arising in the locations that increasingly cater to nomads—and their money—over local residents). The fact that many nomads begin their journeys with significant financial support, whether savings from successful previous careers or from family backing or trust funds, is "significantly downplayed if not outright excluded" from reporting.[41] In fact, as a review of the media coverage makes clear, many of the people either writing (as freelancers or opinion writers) or being interviewed in the press about nomadism are those who have a financial stake in the remote work industry itself.

An eager new business sector has coalesced around inspiring people to become nomadic workers, and to serve their needs once they've embarked. A growing book genre encourages disaffected professionals to follow in the footsteps of the authors, themselves nomads. With names such as *Diary of a Digital Nomad: How to Run Away with Your Responsibilities* and *What is Your Moonshot?*,[42] the books are mainly self-published and tend to be one part of cross-promotional endeavors that can include a travel advice blog, YouTube channel, workshops, and/or event series. A long list of events, hosted in locations around the world, promises to prepare (paying) attendees with the information and skills they need to become (or continue as) digital nomads. For example, Coworkation[43]—hosted in Indonesia, Thailand, and Spain in 2018—is advertised as a series of "coworking retreats that are designed to inspired and motivate location-independent professionals" as well as provide valuable networking opportunities just by being there; and DNX, a weekend of talks, workshops and networking held twice a year in Berlin is "aimed at nomads and people thinking about becoming one."[44] These types of conferences abound, and tend to be hosted in the glamorous locations that might prove enticing to the future nomad, such as Bali, Vietnam, India, and Mexico, or a "Nomad Cruise" across the Mediterranean[45] and "Nomad Train ride" on the Trans-Siberian Railway.[46] Additionally, a host of immersion programs helps prepare people to enter nomad life. For example, Remote Year is one of many packages that brings together groups of people who spend one year working in cities around the world; for a fee of around $27,000, a cohort of participants gains access to workspaces, lodging, community, and travel to various locations while they learn whether remote working might be for them.[47] And an assortment of coding camps, such as Hacker Paradise, offers courses in programming in far-flung locations so that participants might develop a taste for nomadism and the skills to support the lifestyle.

The above is just a glimpse of the many ways that entrepreneurs or influencers are supporting their own nomadism by selling the idea to others in what might be considered a mobile lifestyle 'pyramid scheme.' The pyramid operation can be glimpsed through the experience of Kate Smith, described by the English-language Middle Eastern newspaper, *Arab News*, as "a former project manager at an advertising agency in Canada [who] left her dreary nine-to-five cubicle job to pursue the nomadic lifestyle and has not looked back since."[48] Ms. Smith participated in the Remote Year program, mentioned above, and during that experience started WiFly Nomads, a three-month intensive program (hosted in Bali) that trains people to become digital nomads.[49]

Although it's impossible to know how many people are actually traveling and working remotely, social media memberships give a glimpse of those who are, have been, or are thinking of becoming nomads. The digital nomad community on Reddit had 498,000 subscribers as of summer 2019, and more than 60,000 people are members of the active NomadList chat/forum. On Instagram, over three million posts contain hashtags with the digital nomad phrase (such as #digitalnomad, #digitalnomads, #digitalnomadlife, etc.), and the Digital Nomads Around the World group on Facebook has over 111,000 members. New businesses work to provide the nomads with a cohesive global network experience, combining drop-in workspace, lodging, and community, with business models that in many ways grow out of (and inform) already developing trends in co-working, professional development, and short-term travel accommodation. As an enthusiastic article in Singapore's *The Business Times* pointed out,

> There are apps to help you: find co-working spaces on the fly; rank the quality of WiFi speed and friendliness in cafes ... swap houses; list remote jobs; and give you the comparative cost of living in different countries. There are even digital nomad dating apps and ones which help you find a roommate ... and now, there's even "flexible housing" which offer hard-to-turn-down designer locations.[50]

In one example of the synergies developing to create a unified digital nomad services sector, the co-working company WeWork has launched flexible (no lease/temporary) housing, called WeLive, and in 2017 bought the online social organizing tool, meetup.com, as a strategy to shore up the 'community' offering in its all-encompassing labor/leisure/life business model. Another example is the company, Roam, which has launched "a network of global co-living spaces that provide everything you need to feel at home and be productive the moment you arrive,"[51] with rent *starting* at $500 per week. A *New York Times* article argues that services such as Roam's are helping to make this once-alternative lifestyle much more conventional:

> [T]he early digital nomads were pioneers, planning solo trips around the world, seeking out spare rooms and spotty connections in the name of escaping drudgery back home. Roam aims to make dislocation easy and glamorous, transforming digital nomadism into a mainstream, off-the-rack proposition.... The idea is that you never have to leave the system.[52]

The *Times* article illuminates some tensions around the budding digital nomad society. First, the fact that more people are becoming nomads, and that translocally networked services are making it easier to manage, could mean the loss of some of the prestige that stems from doing something meant to be unique and adventurous. Similarly, the idea of "never leaving the system" belies the promise of personal freedom on which the lifestyle is based. On the other hand, even if the nomadic life is becoming more mainstream, it is still presented as something glamorous—superior to the supposed "drudgery" of being "back home." Such has been a significant selling point aimed at, and perpetuated by, a growing group of young professionals with the ability to work online and the desire to accumulate experiences in locations around the world. In digital nomadism, the experience and gig economies converge, and this convergence has implications for how we might understand connections between mobile media and class.

Class Mobility and the Mobile Class

As Liechty points out, one of the challenges to conceptualizing the middle class is that it is an "extraordinarily complex culture with myriad forms of competing cultural capital," as well as "intricate systems of dissimulation (whereby it hides its class privilege in everyday practice)."[53]

Discourses around becoming a digital nomad demonstrate how cross-border mobility has become a form of cultural capital that—as with so many other status bearing symbols—obscures its privilege through the language of individual effort and merit. This can be seen in the tone of blogs and articles that portray nomadism simultaneously as an obvious choice, accessible to anyone who decides to go for it, yet also the distinctive accomplishment of unique individuals. As the section above has shown, accounts that depict nomadism as preferable to a sedentary alternative take for granted that nomads have achieved a better lifestyle than those masses who have acquiesced to "the drudgery back home." A profile from the 'Lifestyle' section of *The Business Times Singapore* serves as an illustrative, and typical, example of how such coverage portrays the path of the individual nomad:

> Mr. Rogers has been a digital nomad for about two years, after reading a blog about remote working and was inspired to quit his job at a software agency [*sic*]. Though he had left without a concrete plan, he later managed to find work as a software engineer through an online freelancer database.... Now, Mr. Rogers works remotely for a start-up in the US, and lives in a different country every month or so.... He says: "I lead a much better life now; I didn't realize how little I was taking care of myself—both mentally and physically—back in my office job."[54]

The feature story does not question the privilege underlying Mr. Rogers' choices, for example, how he was able to finance his initial effort before finding employment, or how he could assume his passport would allow him access to a different country every month or so. Additionally, at the same time the article assures us that Mr. Rogers leads a "much better life now," it also explains that he had to take a risk in order to achieve it ("he left without a concrete plan").

Such stories of risk/courage are typical in tales of nomadism, suggesting that while many would obviously prefer digital nomadism, only select people have the courage to do it. As an article in the *Free Press Journal* (India), claims, "Working and travelling at the same time is on everyone's wish list but very few *dare* to opt for it."[55] This fundamental aspect of constructing the digital nomad's distinction suggests that personal characteristics—rather than financial or political concerns—are the tickets to entry. Remote work voyages and fluid border crossings are portrayed as accessible to anyone who takes a few simple steps and has the right level of motivation and courage, rather than as privileged mobilities reserved for the most economically and culturally advantaged citizens from countries with the most powerful passports. For example, in a feature story written for the 'Smarter Living' section of *The Hartford Courant* (USA), a professional nomad explains that, "digital nomadism is possible for almost everyone but getting started takes a proper plan ... and a bit of determination."[56] This is a constant theme: acting as a balance to the Instagram photographs of laptops on the beach is the consistent message that, "although we have attained the best life, we have earned it through hard work and personal struggle." The idea infuses almost every profile I read about digital nomads; for example, in a newspaper interview where the author describes an Indian woman who gave up her job with the global consulting firm, Accenture, to become a nomad, and explains: "comfort makes her uneasy and that is why she started hopping from one place to another."[57] However, noting the gap between celebrations of nomadic life and the lamentations noted earlier from many who have been living in mobility for some time, it's important to question the ideological work done by these pro-mobile discourses.

The malaise that has become associated with the idea of professionals' daily reality in the digital economy seems to have found its solution in the pursuit of (or aspirations to) the life of the nomad.

Rather than asking for meaningful work, a proposed solution suggests accepting the banality of digital labor in exchange for a more exciting work environment: the dreaded cubicle traded for the palm-lined beach, the long commute home for the temporary live-work bungalow. In this context, it's worth considering how the status around the lifestyle compares with older indicators of middle-class mobility. One key difference is in the way that cultural and economic capital intertwine around the issue of home-ownership. In many national contexts, the ability of citizens to own homes has been a main component of class mobility (although in the US, this 'American dream' prioritized white homeownership). The way people sacrificed financially to buy a home (over non-necessities such as luxury cars)—as well as how they decorated and maintained their homes—has been found to be a contested area representative of class status.[58]

Although digital nomads make up a just a fraction of the millennial generation, the rarely-questioned status attached to their lifestyles in mainstream and social media indicates that a recognizable 'global dream' is emerging based on travel and continuous movement, lack of place-based commitments, convergence of labor and leisure, and eschewing homeownership in favor of drop-in housing. Although this lifestyle is often discussed in ideological terms (leaving the daily grind, becoming a citizen of the world), the infrastructure developing to support it coalesces around a business model rather than a new politics. The nomads are not connected enough to their temporary locales to invest social capital in those societies (nor are they necessarily welcome to), and their frequent mobility means they must be able to pay their way in to the communities of 'likeminded' people that will ensure their social and professional comfort. The lifestyle does not so much resist ownership (by, for example, creating a non-profit cooperative housing network) as support a set of businesses where people will pay extra to come and go as they please. The nomads are part of a generation who's move away from ownership is often explained by a belief in 'sharing' and being 'asset light'; however, new research finds that changes in their consumption are in fact due to the economy having priced them out of those traditional trappings of middle-class life.[59] The story of the digital nomads demonstrates how, for a middle-class generation with dwindling financial assets, the accrual of cultural capital is increasingly called to stand in for that of economic capital—in this case, through an ideological project and labor market built around the status attached to becoming 'location independent.'

Conclusion

This chapter has focused on mediated discourses around the growing digital nomad movement. While critically examining how nomads construct their mobility as a form of cultural capital, I've also critiqued how the ideologies that celebrate digital nomadism ultimately serve a new set of entrepreneurs (who target and exploit desires for uniqueness and distinction in the process of developing profitable experience markets) while also aiding the cost-cutting efforts of employers. The gig economy that emerged with the growth of digital work, which for the first time allowed labor to be separated from place on a mass scale,[60] has led to employment innovations impacting and creating new economic hierarchies (e.g., tech outsourcing to developing economies; growth in freelance and on-demand work). The digital nomads have a unique spot in this hierarchy, particularly considering they often earn North American or European salaries that go farther in the lower cost-of-living countries where they roam. In this broader context, it's worth taking a final look at the meaning of 'location independence.'

In "Notes Toward a Politics of Location," Adrienne Rich argues that race, class, gender, and nationality are points of location for which we must each take responsibility; acknowledging her own location, she says, means recognizing "the places [my body] has taken me, the places it has not let me go."[61] The mantra of location independence omits such awareness. To bring it back in would mean acknowledging: location independence means making a wage from one location and spending it in another (less expensive) location, where one does not pay local taxes; and location independence means a lack of political and cultural investment in creating and sustaining local communities, which thus means the efficiencies of local life are mainly accessed through consumption. It follows then that location independence means the creation of local markets serving the needs of those who are location independent, often at the expense of investments to serve those who are located. Location independence also means a presumption of "location welcome"—to enjoy the status of having access to every place, to having one's capacity inherently recognized and accepted. It means taking for granted the privilege to imagine stepping into and experiencing other worlds—worlds that others have labored to produce and maintain. The production of location independence occurs in a political economic context where some can move freely and others cannot, where some movements can be posted on social media while those of others must be obscured. This gap, which grows as mobility yields status and social media shape how the currency of mobility is represented, shared, and reproduced, represents a social field where class differences and perhaps class struggle will increasingly be seen.

Notes

1 For example, see Michael S. Rosenwald, "Digital Nomads Choose Their Tribes," *Washington Post* (July 26, 2009), A01.
2 Annika Müller, "The Digital Nomad: Buzzword or Research Category?" *Transnational Social Review* 6, no. 3 (2016): 344.
3 See Marianne Cantwell interview in Monty Majeed, "Work from Anywhere: What it Takes to be a Digital Nomad," *Yourstory.in* (September 13, 2016).
4 United Nations High Commissioner for Refugees. *Global Trends: Forced Displacement in 2016.* Geneva: UNHCR, 2017. www.unhcr.org/globaltrends2016/.
5 Pierre Bourdieu, *Distinction: A Social Critique of the Judgement of Taste* (Cambridge, MA: Harvard University Press, 1984).
6 Stephanie Lawler, "Disgusted Subjects: The Making of Middle-Class Identities," *The Sociological Review* 53, no. 3 (August 1, 2005): 430.
7 Bourdieu, *Distinction*.
8 See Chris Rojek. *Ways of Escape: Modern Transformations in Leisure and Travel* (Lanham, MD: Rowman & Littlefield, 1993).
9 For example, see: Ian Munt, "The 'Other' Postmodern Tourism: Culture, Travel and the New Middle Classes," *Theory, Culture & Society* 11 (1994): 101–123; Deepti Ruth Azariah, *Tourism, Travel, and Blogging: A Discursive Analysis of Online Travel Narratives* (New York: Routledge, 2017); Eric G.E. Zuelow, *A History of Modern Tourism* (London: Palgrave, 2016).
10 Erika Polson, *Privileged Mobilities: Professional Migration, Geo-Social Media, and a New Global Middle Class* (New York: Peter Lang, 2016).
11 Erika Polson, "Belonging to the Network Society: Social Media and the Production of a New Global Middle Class," *Communication, Culture & Critique* 4, no. 2 (2011): 144–163.
12 Anne Mieke Fechter, *Transnational Lives: Expatriates in Indonesia* (Hampshire, UK: Ashgate, 2007), 134.
13 Ibid., 128.
14 Magdalena Nowicka, *Transnational Professionals and Their Cosmopolitan Universes* (Frankfurt, Germany: Campus, 2006), 20.
15 Adrian Favell, *Eurostars and Eurocities: Free Movement and Mobility in an Integrating Europe* (Oxford, UK: Blackwell, 2008), 104.
16 François-Xavier de Vaujany and Jeremy Aroles, "Is the Future of Work Necessarily Glamorous? Digital Nomads and 'Van Life'," *The Conversation* (January 14, 2018): para 6. https://theconversation.com/is-the-future-of-work-necessarily-glamorous-digital-nomads-and-van-life-89670.
17 Ina Reichenberger, "Digital Nomads—A Quest for Holistic Freedom in Work and Leisure," *Annals of Leisure Research* 21, no. 3 (2018): 364.
18 Scott A. Cohen, Tara Duncan, and Maria Thulemark, "Lifestyle Mobilities: The Crossroads of Travel, Leisure and Migration," *Mobilities* 10, no. 1 (2015): 158.
19 For example, see: Cohen et al., *Lifestyle Mobilities*; Müller, *The Digital Nomad*; Reichenberger, "Digital Nomads," 364–380.
20 Scott A. Cohen, Tara Duncan, and Maria Thulemark, "Introducing Lifestyle Mobilities," in *Lifestyle Mobilities: Intersections of Travel, Leisure and Migration*, eds. Tara Duncan, Scott A. Cohen, and Maria Thulemark (London, UK: Routledge, 2013), 155.

21 Will Sutherland and Mohammad Hossein Jarrahi, "The Gig Economy and Information Infrastructure: The Case of the Digital Nomad Community," *Proceedings of the ACM Human–Computer Interaction* 1, no. 1 (January 2017), 97.1–97.24. https://doi.org/10.1145/3134732.
22 Ibid., 97.7.
23 Ibid., 97.6.
24 See Erika Polson, "Doing Local: Place-Based Travel Apps and the Globally Networked Self," in *A Networked Self and Platforms, Stories, Connections*, ed. Zizi Papacharissi (London, UK: Routledge, 2018), 160–174.
25 André Jansson, "A Sense of Tourism: New Media and the Dialectic of Encapsulation/Decapsulation," *Tourist Studies* 7, no. 1 (2007): 5–24.
26 Jennie Germann Molz, *Travel Connections: Tourism, Technology and Togetherness in a Mobile World* (London, UK: Routledge, 2012).
27 Jennie Germann Molz, "Global Abode: Home and Mobility in Narratives of Round-the-World Travel," *Space and Culture* 11, no. 4 (2008): 325–342.
28 Monica Watson, "*Instagram Analysis Reports: August 2015*," *Get Chute*, Chute Corporation. 15 Octobre 2015. Accessed at http://blog.getchute.com/insights-outlook/instagram-analysis-reports-august-2015/.
29 See B. Joseph Pine II and James H. Gilmore, "Welcome to the Experience Economy," *Harvard Business Review* (July–August 1998): 97–105. https://hbr.org/1998/07/welcome-to-the-experience-economy.
30 Simon Usborne, "Just Do it: The Experience Economy and How We Turned Our Backs on 'Stuff'," *Guardian* (May 13, 2017): para 1.
31 Ibid., para 12.
32 Jacob Silverman, "'Pics or it Didn't Happen': The Mantra of the Instagram Era," *Guardian* (February 26, 2015), www.theguardian.com/news/2015/feb/26/pics-or-it-didnt-happen-mantra-instagram-era-facebook-twitter.
33 Anja Dinhopl and Ulrike Gretzel, "Selfie-Taking as Touristic Looking," *Annals of Tourism Research* 57, no. C (2016): 126.
34 See Raz Schwartz and Germaine R. Halegoua, "The Spatial Self: Location-Based Identity Performance on Social Media," *New Media & Society* 17, no. 10 (2015): 1643–1660.
35 Jeongmi Kim and Iis P. Tussyadiah, "Social Networking and Social Support in Tourism Experience: The Moderating Role of Online Self-Presentation Strategies," *Journal of Travel & Tourism Marketing* 30 (2013): 87.
36 Mark Manson, "The Dark Side of the Digital Nomad," *Mark Manson* (blog), para 25–26. https://markmanson.net/digital-nomad.
37 Michael Thomas, "Don't Believe Instagram: Ditching the Office to Work in Paradise as a 'Digital Nomad' has a Hidden Dark Side," *Quartz* (September 8, 2016), para 8. https://qz.com/775751/digital-nomad-problems-nomadlist-and-remoteok-founder-pieter-levels-explains-why-he-has-quit-the-nomadic-lifestyle/.
38 Ibid., para 15.
39 Anna Hart, "Now This is What We Call Hot-Desking," *Sunday Telegraph* (London), May 17, 2015.
40 Gabrielle Monaghan, "Remote Trip is just the Job," *Sunday Times* (London), August 5, 2012.
41 For example, Vaujany and Aroles, *Is the Future*; Paris Marx, "Digital Nomads are Not the Future," *Medium* (July 19, 2018). https://medium.com/@parismarx/digital-nomads-are-not-the-future-be360c7911b4.
42 Amy Molloy, *Diary of a Digital Nomad: How to Run Away with Your Responsibilities* (Self-published, 2015). John Sanei, *What is Your Moonshot? Future Proof Yourself and Your Business in the Age of Exponential Disruption* (Kenilworth, South Africa: Mercury, 2017).
43 https://coworkation.com/.
44 Sheryl Garratt, "The World is their Office," *Telegraph Magazine* (London), July 25, 2015.
45 www.nomadcruise.com.
46 www.nomadtrain.co/.
47 https://remoteyear.com.
48 Shaistha Khan, "The Life of a Digital Nomad: Is It for You?" *Arab News* (Saudi Arabia), November 12, 2017. www.arabnews.com/node/1192241/offbeat.
49 www.wiflynomads.com/.
50 Cheah Ui-Hoon and Rachel Loi, "Nomad's Land," *Business Times Singapore*, April 29, 2017, para 22.
51 "Homepage." Roam, accessed July 18, 2018. www.roam.co/.
52 Kyle Chayka, "When You're a Digital Nomad, the World is your Office," *New York Times* (February 8, 2018). www.nytimes.com/2018/02/08/magazine/when-youre-a-digital-nomad-the-world-is-your-office.html.
53 Mark Liechty, *Suitably Modern: Making Middle-class Culture in a New Consumer Society* (Princeton, NJ: Princeton University Press, 2002), 20.
54 Ui-Hoon and Loi, *Nomad's Land*, para. 33–36.

55 Roshani Shinde, "The Digital Nomad: The New Way to Work," *Free Press Journal* (India), April 2, 2017, para. 2, emphasis added.
56 Arianna O'Dell, "Dreaming of being a Digital Nomad?" *Hartford Courant* (USA), December 31, 2017.
57 Shinde, *The Digital Nomad*, para. 4.
58 These issues are explored in a variety of essays, based on research in varied country and cultural contexts, in: Daniel Miller (ed.), *Home Possessions: Material Culture Behind Closed Doors* (Oxford: Berg, 2001). On the role of home decorating choices and housekeeping, see: Ruth Madigan and Moira Munro, " 'House Beautiful': Style and Consumption in the Home," *Sociology* 30, no. 1 (February 1996): 41–57; and Ian Woodward, "Divergent Narratives in the Imagining of the Home amongst Middle-class Consumers," *Journal of Sociology* 39, no. 4 (2003): 391–412. In addition to décor, the following also considers the symbolic quality of neighborhoods: Kirsten Gram-Hanssen and Claus Bech-Danielsen, "House, Home and Identity from a Consumption Perspective," *Housing, Theory and Society* 21, no. 1 (2004): 17–26.
59 See Christopher Kurz, Geng Li, and Daniel J. Vine, "Are Millennials Different?" *Finance and Economics Discussion Series* (Washington: Board of Governors of the Federal Reserve System, 2018).
60 See Mark Graham, Isis Hjorth, and Vili Lehdonvirta, "Digital Labour and Development: Impacts of Global Digital Labour Platforms and the Gig Economy on Worker Livelihoods," *Transfer: European Review of Labour and Research* 23, no. 2 (May 1, 2017): 135–162.
61 Adrienne Rich, "Notes Toward a Politics of Location," in *Blood, Bread, and Poetry: Selected Prose 1979–1985* (New York: Norton, 1986): 215–216.

16
TECHNOLOGIES OF RECOGNITION
The Classificatory Function of Social Media in Mobile Careers

André Jansson

Corporate leaders are often told to teach their employees to use social media in ways that are good for their organizations and their own careers. This is a matter of strategic control. In times when social media are everywhere and the logic of spreadability[1] may cause viral effects (some of which are both unpredictable and undesirable) brand building and reputation management are bound to be critical undertakings. There are today numerous handbooks, reports and research articles proclaiming how responsible leaders should act in order to reduce the risk of employees messing up the image of their organization, or even the whole industry.[2] Social media visibility should be turned into an asset, realizing the inherent potential of employees to become "credible and authentic representatives of their organization."[3] Such strategies testify to how the so-called connectivity imperative[4] is often imposed through organizational management, turning social networking and self-branding into key elements of work as such.[5]

Yet, it would be too simplistic to explain the expansion of social media in contemporary work environments by just looking at structural imperatives and top-down processes. Social media flourish also in environments where neither employers nor professional guidelines explicitly ask for it. They are also appropriated in different ways in different sectors, more or less organically without formal prescriptions or strategies from organizations. Universities are a case in point, where researchers and teachers often work out their own individual ways of managing social media in ways that should gain their career development. We should thus assume that people feel that there is something in it for them too, beyond the fact that they might feel more secure if they follow established rules and standards.

This chapter aims to show *why* and *how* the appropriation of social media in contexts of professional work becomes a critical element of class formation, and to unpack the multiple forces at play in such processes. The point of departure is Bourdieu's[6] understanding of class formation as a matter of everyday praxis, where the value of different classificatory properties is defined in relation to the agents who appropriate them and their classified positions in particular social fields and/or social space at large. The point here is thus that there is no intrinsic value attached to a certain property (which may refer to an object, a commodity/brand or a particular type of practice, e.g., using Facebook), but that value and meaning are continuously negotiated through everyday activities. As such, the social history of media is also a history of classification; certain film genres, certain newspapers and certain communication technologies have been classified as more prestigious than others and thus also embraced by those people who want to associate themselves with more "refined" values. Conversely, popular media forms (e.g., commercial radio and television), those used by "the masses", have been classified as "vulgar" and associated with lower social standing.

The classificatory value of social media (in general, as well as individual platforms) thus depends on who uses them, for what purpose and under what socio-cultural conditions. However, these classificatory processes are far from clear-cut. They cannot be explained only in terms of organizational imperatives or which individual capacities are encouraged within different professions or work sectors (e.g., the value of visibility or availability), especially not when it comes to such complex phenomena as "social media" that incorporate and mediate a variety of different practices and transcend boundaries of private/public, work/leisure, home/away, and so forth. Rather, we should aim for an inside view that could reveal how people negotiate these matters in the concrete settings of daily life. We should take into account what it means to be a woman or a man, what kinds of values people live by, where they live, and where they are going.

For this reason, this chapter advances *recognition theory* as an entry-point for reaching more complex understandings of the bottom-up processes through which social media are normalized in work settings and enter into processes of class formation. It is argued that social media use expands largely as a consequence of *recognition work* that concerns more than professional aspirations, but life in general. As held by recognition theorists,[7] the complexity and unpredictability of modern society accentuate the desires among individuals to seek out recognition from people and institutions around them. While social media offer an unprecedented range of alternatives for fulfilling such desires, however, they also nurture the imperative of connectivity. People's engagement with social media is thus both a potential solution to the problem of "recognition deficit" and a source of commercial exploitation, premised on the very reproduction of recognition deficit. At the same time, certain fields and organizations maintain a rather restrictive view of (certain kinds) of social media use. Altogether, this means that the modulation of social media use is today a *critical* and *ambiguous* part of career development. While social media are increasingly taken as indispensable *technologies of recognition*, it is often difficult for individuals to know what are the most appropriate—classified and classifying—ways of using them, especially since the logics of social media spur the collapsing of different contexts of recognition.[8]

This chapter presents an analysis of a certain fraction of the well-educated middle class; professional women employed within the United Nations (UN) system. This class fraction is marked by high levels of international mobility both in their jobs (regular business trips) and *between* jobs, meaning that if they want to succeed in their professional careers they must be willing to take up positions in different offices and different countries. While UN careers are associated with privilege and prestige (including relocation services, tax reductions, etc.), they also entail elements of precariousness. Positions are most often based on limited-term contracts (normally 2–3 years) and mobility pressures can be tough on family life, especially for women, since they are still (more often than men) expected to take the main responsibility for the household.

The analysis provides an inside view of the lives of Scandinavian women living in Geneva and working for UN organizations. The author conducted two waves of fieldwork in 2014, interviewing 13 individuals among which ten were women. The case of mobile women in the UN system provides a pertinent illustration of how the normalization of social media platforms takes place in-between the imperative of *strategic recognition work* (demands on professional visibility) and the need for handling private relations of recognition (especially domestic care work) under strained life conditions. This is a difficult balance. In order to "play the game" and consolidate their positions within the field, UN women are expected to pursue both kinds of recognition work without overdoing either of them. Social media thus provide tools for flexible career development while at the same time imposing the risk that agents who use them "too much" or in the "wrong way" are seen as less serious-minded, less reliable, etc., and thus declassified.[9]

Recognition Theory and the Coming of Strategic Recognition Work

Work and social recognition are closely connected. People find work particularly rewarding if there are others paying attention to what they have achieved or to the fact that they are willing to take care of things in a responsible and/or creative way. This is also why work is crucial to emancipation. According to recognition theorists, the development of autonomous human beings occurs through self-esteem and respect, which in turn requires that people are part of meaningful social relations where recognition is mutually given and received.[10] Honneth[11] asserts that recognition should be positively affirmative, based on a concrete activity directed towards another individual or group, and explicitly intended for recognition rather than any other end. Such "pure" acts of recognition are to be found especially in *love* relations and in social settings where individuals and groups develop a "cooperative frame of mind"[12] and gain *esteem* from one another through mutual encouragement and support. Work is obviously a social realm where positive recognition can make people grow, not just nurturing a sense of security and dignity but also widening the social horizon in ways that enable people to set up new visions in their lives.[13] At the same time, however, work is also a contested sphere of discrimination and competition where individuals and groups are held back because of their backgrounds, values or lifestyles. Even behind the façades of seemingly well-functioning and harmonious work environments, the threat of misrecognition and subordination is lurking. To be misrecognized means that individuals are judged negatively based on their group identity and "denied the status of a full partner in social interaction, as a consequence of institutionalized patterns of cultural value that constitute one as comparatively unworthy of respect or esteem."[14]

Recognition theory can thus help us scrutinize work and career-making as sites of social reproduction, struggle *and* change. As Smith[15] argues, recognition theory differs from instrumentalist views of self-preservation as well as more determinist versions of critical theory where social conflicts are linked to class domination and the control over the means of production. Recognition theory "offers the prospects of a phenomenologically more nuanced critique of the sphere of work [...] as well as a more complex conception of what emancipation might mean in relation to work."[16] Smith's view resonates with Bourdieu's reflexive sociology in its aim to challenge the division between theories of structural determination and phenomenological approaches to the dynamics of everyday life.[17] While the dispositions of individuals and groups are always socially produced, materialized through the invisible guidance of *habitus*, which most often preserves the stability of social structures, recognition is a social resource that may also engender modulations of *habitus*. According to Bourdieu, there is always a space of creative agency, a "margin of freedom,"[18] in people's lives, which is particularly obvious when people find themselves in unexpected situations or achieve new kinds of recognition from people around them. It may happen, for instance, when they move within or across social fields, or, if there appear new job offers or opportunities for education.[19]

The close relation between work and recognition does not only concern the prospects of gaining recognition *through* work, however. It also concerns the fact that some forms of work per se are oriented towards the creation of social value through the *recognition of others*. This especially includes taking care of fellow human beings; a social sphere traditionally associated with "women's work" and unpaid domestic duties.[20] As argued by feminist thinkers,[21] these forms of affective work and the fundamental values created in terms of social communion and solidarity have been marginalized in dominant theories of work and labor in modern societies. Recognition theorists have acknowledged the same problem, stressing the generally weak social esteem given to the informal economy of care-work compared with paid work.[22]

Beverly Skeggs,[23] who has brought together feminist perspectives and conceptions of class-based orders of recognition, found in her study of British working-class women that one of the main routes to respectability was to be recognized as a caring person, somebody who in a natural, even altruistic, manner recognized the needs of others and performed well to satisfy those needs. The women in Skeggs' study developed such skills not just professionally through their orientation towards jobs in healthcare and domestic care. They also took on unpaid caring duties, making *a gift* of caring for others, in order to "prolong the recognition of themselves as caring."[24] Recognizing others thus attained an intrinsic value based on mutual relations. However, Skeggs also found that while these women wanted to recognize themselves with neither traditional femininity, nor the subordination of the working-class from which they came, their caring performances had a tendency to hold them back in these positions since this was how their performances were institutionally legitimized.[25] While they could work with, and thus invest in, the recognition of others, they could not control how others classified them.

Voluntary, unpaid care-work can be seen as the archetype of *recognition work*. However, it would be a mistake to reproduce the simplified view of such recognition work occurring only within the domestic, informal economies of work (mainly carried out by women). Just as the division between paid work and freely given work has often been too rigidly drawn, we should acknowledge that recognition work also takes place, and has always taken place, in professional settings, also beyond the caring sectors. If the sphere of paid work, labor, is a place where people can grow and achieve a sense of autonomy, this also means that there must be mutual relations of recognition in place. As Sennett[26] argues, recognition in the workplace, whether directed toward fellow workers or customers or clients, is often spontaneously given as a way of making other people grow, which in turn contributes to the building of trust and durable relations of cooperation. These practices may transcend the boundaries of formally salaried work-hours, as when colleagues meet in their free time to discuss work-related problems or just socialize, or when an employee volunteers to help a customer who has run into trouble during the weekend.

Recognition is a complex matter to analyze, however. A particularly salient problem is to identify whether a certain social act is to be regarded as recognition in the "true" sense of the word, or if there are other causes and motives involved. First, if the *giving* of recognition spurs processes of social and personal growth then it is not a far-fetched assumption that individuals, groups and organizations would also develop and implement this type of behavior strategically as a tool for other types of value creation. Second, the positive consequences of *receiving* recognition might also be subjected to strategic calculation and instrumentalizing work, such as "self-branding." For this reason, we should distinguish recognition work in the original sense, understood as freely given recognition through care or cooperation, from *strategic recognition work*, referring to the instrumentalized forms of giving or seeking out recognition for the maximization of extrinsic values.

Strategic recognition work is a typical example of the social pathologies that critical recognition theorists have discussed and associated with the flexible economies of late capitalism. While capitalist societies have always struggled with social pathologies in terms of ideological misrecognition, for instance when workers are not recognized for what they accomplish but for who they are, the coming of post-Fordism has led to a new pattern, marked by the kind of "reversal" of recognition that we find in strategic recognition work. People are not merely given the opportunity to express their identities and set up goals for their lives; they are *expected* to do so, especially through the strategic molding of their lifestyles and careers, both professionally and throughout life. Honneth[27] calls this overarching imperative *organized self-realization*. Whereas the post-Fordist economy rests upon a mythology of new types of independent jobs where life and work melt together within the project of the self, especially within the creative sector,[28] there is also a vast under-vegetation of the "gig-economy," including anything from Uber drivers to "Gigsters" and "Insta-workers", for whom reputation management and self-promotion, that is, mediated visibility, is literally the only route to job security there is.[29] Individualization shifts from emancipation into a new form of oppression.[30]

We may now assess how social media play into and alter the relations between recognition and work. The structural expectation on individuals to manage recognition work cannot be uncoupled from the more deeply felt need to maintain a sense of ontological security and direction in times of uncertainty, which together provide the basis for the continuous engagement with social media. Taken as *technologies of recognition*, then, social media do not have to be imposed, but are appropriated by workers as a convenient way to ensure that they have a future in their professions, or in the labor market at large. At the same time, social media are associated with the indirect commoditization of unpaid recognition work during "free time". Mundane activities such as commenting or "liking" on Facebook underpin and reproduce social relations and conditions that are in turn constitutive of the capitalist.[31] Accordingly, they attain a position reminiscent of "women's work" in bygone eras.[32] Whereas participating in these social exchanges may entail the intrinsic value of recognizing and being recognized by others, the abstract accumulation of such exchanges constitutes the raw material for datafication and algorithmic user profiling.[33] Recognition work thus fuels the capitalist attention economy in the sense that it indirectly produces advanced models for predicting media users' preferences and feelings about other people and properties. As these models get implemented, in turn, they tie media users closer to the logics of platforms and turn recognition work into something mandatory, even measurable, rather than a spontaneous gift.[34] Ultimately, they contribute to the reproduction of the classificatory structures through which people navigate in social space.

In sum, recognition theory can help us see how social media contribute to the destabilization and instrumentalization of relations of recognition up to the point where the giving and receiving of recognition, in professional as well as private spheres of life, are all subsumed under the ideology of organized self-realization and the normative framework of strategic recognition work. This should not be mistaken for a linear or unequivocal development, however. Rather, it is full of negotiations and ambiguities related to classificatory orders and the concrete circumstances of everyday lifeworlds.

Career Making in the United Nations System

Working for the United Nations per se carries symbolic capital. Its value transcends the value of particular professions (e.g., being a public health expert, a lawyer, or an information officer) and identifies its possessor as somebody with cosmopolitan ambitions and the whole world as his or her working field. The longstanding status of the UN as a global development and peace-making project makes it an institution that legitimizes certain skills and values. As found in previous research,[35] these assets are typically of an embodied, immaterial nature, including language skills, university degrees and international work experiences and networks, and thus are acquainted with cultural capital.[36] The fact that the UN incorporates approximately 44,000 employees working for a range of UN agencies and organizations, which are in turn closely associated with numerous collaborating NGOs and political and diplomatic entities around the world, makes it relevant even to conceive of the UN as the center of a relatively autonomous social field of international development, politics and diplomacy where career opportunities and orders of recognition gravitate around the accumulation of *cosmopolitan* capital.[37] This type of capital comprises all those resources that enable people to move and communicate across cultural boundaries and establish new social relations and a sense of home under mobile conditions, whether in temporary dwelling places or during business trips. Having a UN career not only manifests that somebody possesses cosmopolitan capital; UN jobs also turn these embodied resources into recognizable symbolic capital.

Cosmopolitan capital is not easily achieved, however. The kinds of skills and orientations that it incorporates are more accessible to some people than to others, depending on *habitus* (which may lead to certain types of education and mobile life experiences) and the ability to continuously invest in one's career. As to the latter, the UN system is marked by longstanding patriarchal structures. There are formal hierarchies defining salary levels, expected career paths and demands on mobility. Many organizations, such as the UNHCR, maintain strict rotation policies, which means that employees must change job and location after a few years and make sure to spend time both in receiving regions (in "the field") and in UN headquarters. Other UN organizations have less strict, but still demanding, mobility policies that encourage employees to change positions on a regular basis. Such conditions are obviously not easy to combine with family life and have traditionally made it difficult for women to reach higher positions in the UN system. Current statistics speak the same language; the higher you get in the hierarchies, the fewer women there are.[38] This is particularly true for those UN organizations that involve demanding work in crisis regions where UN workers are not even allowed to bring their families (if they have any).

The interviews conducted among Scandinavian UN expats in Geneva provide evidence of these structures, while at the same time illuminating how women navigate and try to subvert the patriarchal system as a matter of recognition work. They have all gone through higher education and obtained degrees with a focus on subjects such as international relations, political science, global health and communication for development. In the typical case, they have planned for an international career since they were very young and are driven by activist visions of being part of building a more equal world. Gender rights are part of the picture, and thus their own career paths also become the object of reflexivity and negotiation. While aware of the privileges attached to UN jobs—not just in terms of symbolic capital but also in a material and economic sense, and especially in comparison to the people they are destined to help—there is a lingering experience of being disadvantaged as a woman. The women interviewed have "played the game" in order to reach their current positions in Geneva. They have gathered experiences from UN postings around the world and sometimes from associated NGOs or political entities. They have thus created their CVs according to the UN *doxa* and adapted their lives in ways that work towards this end.[39]

However, combining family life with work-related mobility is a tricky feat. Owing to the inherently international nature of UN work it is difficult to sidestep the professional demands on being mobile and "ready to go." Entering the family stage imposes a challenge that sometimes ends up with women giving up their UN career to find a more stable job. A survey conducted by Impactpool[40] among current and previous UN staff members found that more women than men were singles and that divorce rates were significantly higher among women than among men. Furthermore, while 84 percent of men over 40 had children, the corresponding rate among women was 46 percent. The Geneva study contains numerous examples that confirm this picture and illustrate how it is experienced by women in the UN system:

> Sure, this system is constructed around old ideas, around old family constellations, and it's basically a way of making sure there is a man working and, you know, one hardly gets any parental leave. It's very short.
>
> *(Camilla, program communicator)*

> You should not go home at 5 pm, and it's not nice to confess that you have a family. You should put the organization first. If you look at the people on the top they are men that can be accepted by the patriarchal system. The patriarchal system accepts that men reach the top without caring for the family. If we look at the women who sit on the top they have either one child or no children at all.
>
> *(Linn, technical officer)*

Camilla and Linn are both mothers of young children. Their careers are reliant on relatively non-traditional, flexible family conditions. They live with men who have agreed to take the main responsibility for the household. Linn's husband is a cultural worker who can spend much time at home. Camilla's partner combines sporadic consultancy with taking distance-learning courses. Sometimes there are also other family members and relatives involved in taking care of children. Other women have had to solve the challenges related to parenting in other ways. Leena lives in

Geneva with her two-year-old son but travels about 10 to 12 times per year. The father lives in Scandinavia. In the interview, she emphasizes that travelling is the key to success for her; it is part of the job and the best way to get to know the right people. Thus, it cannot be negotiated to any extent. When Leena has to be away for a couple of days she calls a girl that works extra with baby-sitting and with whom she feels confident. But sometimes she must find extraordinary solutions.

> One time I had to go to Torino for a week. And then I took the kid with me. I have a friend in Madrid who took vacation to go to Torino and do baby-sitting. So I have very good friends. That's how we solved it.
>
> *(Leena, program officer)*

Managing mobile careers thus involves a lot of recognition work, both paid and unpaid, locally anchored as well as spatially negotiated. The UN system produces not just mobilities but also entire support networks built on mutual trust and emotional involvement in the lives of others. The existence of such networks—which basically reflect what women's unpaid domestic work has traditionally been about—allows for a certain degree of *elasticity* in relation to mobility pressures.[41] They ensure that travelling is less an emotional hassle and take away some of the stress stemming from flexible work. These are also the conditions that shape the classificatory function of social media in the UN sector.

Social Media and the Ambiguities of Recognition Work

The women in the study describe media mainly in positive, emancipatory terms and appropriate them in ways that enhance the elasticity of their lives. They describe how different devices and platforms are given particular meanings in relation to different types of relations and different communicative situations. Media thus comprise a complex polymedia environment.[42] For instance, Skype is singled out as an important channel for maintaining a sense of proximity with children, whereas WhatsApp occupies a more logistical and socially lubricating function in distributed family life.[43] WhatsApp is described as a particularly quick platform that is "always on" and enables immediate responses to practical issues and mundane forms of recognition or phatic communication (e.g., just sending an emoticon).[44] Similarly, Instagram is presented as a way to stay in touch with geographically dispersed friends, allowing for visual snapshots of everyday life. Compared with Facebook, the women use Instagram in a more private and intimate manner; they have not as many "followers" on Instagram as they have "friends" on Facebook.

> I use Instagram simply to show pictures from my everyday life. It makes me feel closer to my friends. Or if I have visited someone or if someone is visiting me and there is a mutual friend, then it sparks off a kind of exchange and comments that create a sense of co-presence. It really means a lot.
>
> *(Linn, technical officer)*

Practices of sharing and commenting on social media are thus constitutive of recognition work that strengthens *and* loosens up the social bonds that economic circulation and individual careers depend upon.[45] This capacity of social media to generate elasticity is a fundamental reason for their growing indispensability *across* social spheres, which in turn leads to the fusion of productive and reproductive spaces, professional and domestic life. This tendency is likely to be particularly strong among *mobile women*; not in any essentialist sense, but through the combined significance of mobility as a driver of mediatization[46] and the general pressure on women to entertain relations of mutual care and family support in spite of their professional aspirations. Freely given recognition work, the need to care for others and entertain networks of mutual support, is thus an important avenue through which social media and the so-called connectivity imperative[47] spread and eventually affect professional life.

Social media are also important for making oneself visible to others within the UN system. Strategic recognition work is a way of maintaining a sense of autonomy within the field[48] and, more concretely, paving the way for new job opportunities. These endeavors are intricate matters to the women in the study. They emphasize the potential of social media when it comes to establishing a professional reputation. As Leena puts it, "it's not enough to do one's job in a good way, one must also make sure that people are aware of that good work". While this attitude is reflected in the long-established convention to copy emails to a great number of people[49]—which is also a way of securing that strategic persons do not feel sidelined—social media have brought along more sophisticated opportunities for self-branding. However, as Linn explains, these opportunities must be reflexively managed since visibility may not be all positive.

LINN: I have blocked some colleagues [from Facebook] that I prefer not to take part of things I feel are more private. And then I post things, activist things about workers' rights, HBT [homosexual, bisexual and transsexual] rights in working life and about gender and HIV, but I probably don't develop that much further. But then there are people in organizations that I perhaps want to see these things and think "well, she seems to be active in this subject area" and then it might lead to a work-related discussion at some point later on. But there is also prestige in all this, like if you go on a business trip you may see people making status updates, a classic way of seeking attention.

INTERVIEWER: How do you feel about that?

LINN: I feel ambivalent. I don't want it to look like I want to prove something, even though it's nice to display what one is doing. So I've become more restrictive.

At some point there is thus a price to pay for strategic recognition work, either because the wrong people might get exposed to certain types of material, or because of the general erosion of authenticity that follows from the staged exposition of the self. This is certainly a more sensitive matter in the UN system than in most other businesses because of the ethically and politically oriented nature of this sector. Camilla stresses that it is important that everything she does on social media is true to the values of the UN and to her own ideals, and that she wants to justify her accountability in relation to those she works for, that is, local partner organizations and ultimately people suffering from poverty, war or global epidemics.

> There are many different layers in this. Many try to use social media to build some kind of movement and all that. But I think there is often much slackness to it. A lot of PR junk in it. A lot of people try to do things like "collectivism" even though it's not much of collectivism to it, which I think is problematic. […] I believe that the type of idea that is truly built upon some kind of democracy, built around theories of social organization, built around some kind of counter-system, it demands some kind of authenticity. There has to be a point of departure that works for that kind of ambition. It concerns all platforms, both Twitter and Facebook. Instagram is also important. It feels more personal since it's almost only good friends I have on Instagram, and people I work with who are also close friends, with photos of my kids and so forth.
>
> *(Camilla, program communicator)*

Staging the self through social media thus evokes two main forms of ambiguity, which both point to the risk of social declassification. On the one hand, there is the risk of undermining the intrinsic value of UN work, and thus also jeopardizing the prospects of accumulating cosmopolitan capital. This is typically what happens when the staging of mediation is exaggerated up to the point where underlying values are obscured and turned into simulation.[50] On the other hand, there is the risk of exposing too much authenticity, for instance through circulating images of a private nature via professional networks, which may lead to harmful situations of context collapse.[51]

As to the latter problem, the normalization of social media implies that both individuals and organizations are forced to find ways to manage mediated visibility in mutually beneficial ways. While the *doxa* of UN organizations, in comparison to most other organizations, prescribes restrictive norms when it comes to communication that crisscrosses private and professional realms, there is also growing awareness of the benefits of social media and collaborative platforms (Skype and Basecamp are mentioned in the interviews) for building communities and running collaborative projects that involve multiple stakeholders. Gradually, and largely because of informal transitions within teams and projects (as opposed to central monitoring), social liquidity becomes the normal state and something that should be strategically managed rather than prohibited. Still, these strategies work out differently in different organizations, and individuals have to find their own routines.

> There is some kind of policy around social media and all that. They have loosened it up a bit now, but if you have a Twitter account you must write "this message is sent by, etc...." Then you can be active there, but I'm not. Because it's too much of a hassle, since there can always be someone saying "you shouldn't have said that".
>
> *(Linn, technical officer)*

> I stay in touch with many youth organizations through Facebook. And there is the chat too. I'm logged in as myself. We just talked about that the other day, my boss and I, and he thinks it's a bit problematic that I mix private and professional things on Facebook and wonders why I'm doing that. But to me Facebook is a place for me to be personal. What I'm doing is such a big part of who I am personally. [...] It's important for me that these youth organizations can see that the same values are part of my personal life.
>
> *(Camilla, program communicator)*

While Linn points to the risk of social media practices, and especially certain elements of strategic recognition work, colliding with the image of the UN, and potentially damaging her career, Camilla depicts how social media can be used to underline the correspondence between her own life and UN values. These contrasting stances represent the current instability of the communicational *doxa* in the UN system,[52] the fact that there are yet no clear policies or taken-for-granted conventions that monitor individual agents in their day-to-day communication. This instability is largely due to the rapid alteration of the media landscape, whereby the logics of social media (e.g., the so-called popularity principle)[53] have come to saturate recognition work. While social media platforms are normalized, reinforced by mobile life conditions and the imperative to make oneself visible (as described above), their wider consequences for individuals and the UN at large are difficult to overlook. The working conditions of Linn, Camilla and their colleagues are in a state of flux, as are the classificatory status of social media. UN employees are in the midst of an open-ended process of mediatization whose future directions they are part of shaping through everyday praxis.

As women whose positions are relatively more precarious due to ingrained expectations on domestic care work, they also have to engage more deeply than male colleagues in these negotiations. As shown in this analysis, social media offer a communicative space that bridges the divide between private and professional recognition work and thus empower the forms of mobile careers that the UN prescribes. At the same time, however, it is not clear to what extent these changes in terms of intensified social media engagement and the increasing liquidity of social regions amount to more substantial alterations when it comes to gender relations and the countering of ideological forms of recognition. While social media contribute to more elastic entanglements, these entanglements are still largely constitutive of the patriarchal structures of the UN. Elastic entanglements, as we have seen, also demand high degrees of reflexive monitoring in order to avoid "exaggerated" expressions of strategic recognition work and thus situations of social declassification.

Conclusion

This chapter introduced recognition theory as a tool for reaching deeper understandings of how social media get normalized in social life as a classified and classifying property. The chapter also applied this approach to a study of professional women working for UN organizations under expatriate life conditions. It was shown that social media were largely appropriated without any formal prescriptions; on the one hand, as a means for enhancing the elasticity of private relations of recognition (i.e., to maintain social bonds with family and friends), and, on the other hand, to manage strategic recognition work. Social media can thus be described as *technologies of recognition*, entailing a capacity not just to mediate the social intentions of the users but also to classify the nature of their careers. On the whole, the women in the study maintained that social media were good for their careers, potentially contributing to women's emancipation and possibilities to keep up a UN career on equal terms with men. At the same time, however, social media contributed to keeping up rather than disrupting dominant orders of recognition and the logic of the field, especially the internalized desire to accumulate cosmopolitan capital. Accordingly, the growing reliance on social media evoked high demands on the women to be continuously self-reflexive in order to use different platforms in ways that neither opposed the (largely unspoken) *doxa* of the field, nor damaged their own reputation or family life.

A further conclusion of this chapter is that more complex understandings of the relationship between media practices and class formation deserve analyses that take into account not just the specificities of different media and platforms, but also the situated and intersectional nature of those power relations that media enter into. It is only through detailed analyses of the conditions and experiences of *appropriation*—that is, the social processes through which something *becomes a meaningful property* of somebody—that we can explicate the *classificatory* function of media. In the case of social media, as shown here, recognition theory provides a viable entry point for such situated and intersectional approaches, enabling us to highlight both the possibilities and the growing vulnerability involved in contemporary career-making.

Notes

1. Henry Jenkins, Sam Ford, and Joshua Green, *Spreadable Media: Creating Value and Meaning in a Networked Culture* (New York: NYU Press, 2013).
2. For example, Nancy Flynn, *The Social Media Handbook: Rules, Policies, and Best Practices to Successfully Manage Your Organization's Social Media Presence, Posts, and Potential* (San Francisco, CA: John Wiley & Sons, 2012); Anne Linke and Ansgar Zerfass, "Future Trends in Social Media Use for Strategic Organisation Communication: Results of a Delphi Study," *Public Communication Review* 2, no. 2 (2012): 17–29; Anne Linke and Ansgar Zerfass, "Social Media Governance: Regulatory Frameworks for Successful Online Communications," *Journal of Communication Management* 17, no. 3 (2013): 270–286; Sonja Dreher, "Social Media and the World of Work: A Strategic Approach to Employees' Participation in Social Media," *Corporate Communications: An International Journal* 19, no. 4 (2014): 344–356.
3. Dreher, "Social Media," 345.
4. Melissa Gregg, *Work's Intimacy* (Cambridge: Polity Press, 2011).
5. Alice E. Marwick, *Status Update: Celebrity, Publicity, and Branding in the Social Media Age* (New Haven: Yale University Press, 2013).
6. Pierre Bourdieu, *Distinction: A Social Critique of the Judgement of Taste* (Boston, MA: Harvard University Press, 1984 [1979]).
7. For example, Axel Honneth, *The I in the We: Studies in the Theory of Recognition* (London: Polity Press, 2012).

8. Cf. Alice E. Marwick and danah boyd, "I Tweet Honestly, I Tweet Passionately: Twitter Users, Context Collapse, and the Imagined Audience," *New Media & Society* 13, no. 1 (2011): 114–133.
9. This study is part of the research project "Kinetic Elites: The Mediatization of Social Belonging and Close Relations Among Mobile Class Fractions," funded by the Swedish Research Council (2012–2016). Portions of this chapter also appear in: Karin Fast and André Jansson, *Transmedia Work: Privilege and Precariousness in Digital Modernity* (London Routledge, 2019).
10. Axel Honneth, *The Struggle for Recognition: The Moral Grammar of Social Conflicts* (Cambridge, MA: MIT Press, 1996).
11. Honneth, *The I in the We*.
12. See also: Richard Sennett, *Together: The Rituals, Pleasures and Politics of Cooperation* (New Haven, CT: Yale University Press, 2012).
13. Honneth, *The I in the We*, 83.
14. Nancy Fraser, "Rethinking Recognition," *New Left Review* 3 (2000): 113–114.
15. Nicholas H. Smith, "Work as a Sphere of Norms, Paradoxes, and Ideologies of Recognition," in *Recognition Theory as Social Research: Investigating the Dynamics of Social Conflict*, eds. Shane O'Neill and Nicholas H. Smith (Basingstoke: Palgrave Macmillan, 2012), 87–108.
16. Ibid., 90.
17. Pierre Bourdieu and Loïc J.D. Wacquant, *An Invitation to Reflexive Sociology* (Chicago: University of Chicago Press, 1992).
18. Pierre Bourdieu, *Pascalian Meditations* (London: Polity Press, 2000 [1997]), 234.
19. See also: Lois McNay, *Against Recognition* (Cambridge: Polity Press, 2008), 180–185.
20. For example, Arlie R. Hochschild, *The Managed Heart: Commercialization of Human Feeling* (Berkeley: University of California Press, 1983).
21. For example, Leopoldina Fortunati, *The Arcane of Reproduction: Housework, Prostitution, Labor and Capital* (New York: Autonomedia, 1995); Kathi Weeks, "Life Within and Against Work: Affective Labor, Feminist Critique, and Post-Fordist Politics," *Ephemera: Theory and Politics in Organization* 7, no. 1 (2007): 233–249.
22. Beate Rössler, "Work, Recognition, Emancipation," in *Recognition and Power*, eds. Bert van den Brink and David Owen (Cambridge: Cambridge University Press, 2007), 135–164; Smith, "Work as a Sphere," 94.
23. Beverly Skeggs, *Formations of Class & Gender: Becoming Respectable* (London: Sage, 1997).
24. Ibid., 63.
25. Ibid., 162–165.
26. Richard Sennett, *Together: The Rituals, Pleasures and Politics of Cooperation* (New Haven, CT: Yale University Press, 2012).
27. Axel Honneth, "Organized Self-Realization: Some Paradoxes of Individualization," *European Journal of Social Theory* 7, no. 4 (2004): 463–478.
28. For example, Alice E. Marwick, *Status Update: Celebrity, Publicity, and Branding in the Social Media Age* (New Haven, CT: Yale University Press, 2013); Brooke E. Duffy and Emily Hund, "'Having it All' on Social Media: Entrepreneurial Femininity and Self-Branding among Fashion Bloggers," *Social Media+Society* 1, no. 2 (2015), 2056305115604337.
29. Cf. Ngai Keung Chan and Lee Humphreys, "Mediatization of Social Space and the Case of Uber Drivers," *Media and Communication* 6, no. 2 (2018): 29–38.
30. Smith, "Work as a Sphere".
31. Mark Andrejevic, "Social Network Exploitation," in *A Networked Self: Identity, Community, and Culture on Social Network Sites*, ed. Zizi Papacharissi (New York: Routledge, 2011), 82–101; Karin Fast, Henrik Örnebring, and Michael Karlsson, "Metaphors of Free Labor: A Typology of Unpaid Work in the Media Sector," *Media, Culture & Society* 38, no. 7 (2016): 963–978.
32. For example, Kylie Jarrett, "The Relevance of 'Women's Work': Social Reproduction and Immaterial Labor in Digital Media," *Television & New Media* 15, no. 1 (2014): 14–29.
33. For example, José Van Dijck, *The Culture of Connectivity: A Critical History of Social Media* (Oxford: Oxford University Press, 2013); Ted Striphas, "Algorithmic Culture," *European Journal of Cultural Studies* 18, no. 4–5 (2015): 395–412.
34. Van Dijck, *The Culture*; José Van Dijck and Thomas Poell, "Understanding Social Media Logic," *Media and Communication* 1, no. 1 (2013): 2–14.
35. André Jansson, "How to Become an 'Elite Cosmopolitan': The Mediatized Trajectories of UN Expatriates," *European Journal of Cultural Studies* 19, no. 5 (2016): 465–480.
36. Pierre Bourdieu, "The Field of Cultural Production, or: The Economic World Reversed," *Poetics* 12 (1983): 311–56.
37. Paul Kennedy, "The Middle-Class Cosmopolitan Journey: The Life Trajectories and Transnational Affiliations of Skilled EU Migrants in Manchester," in *Cosmopolitanism in Practice*, eds. Magdalena Nowicka and

Maria Rovisco (Farnham, UK: Ashgate, 2009), 19–36; André Jansson, "Cosmopolitan Capsules: Mediated Networking and Social Control in Expatriate Spaces," in *Online Territories: Globalization, Mediated Practice and Social Space*, eds. Miyase Christensen, André Jansson, and Christian Christensen (New York: Peter Lang, 2011): 239–255; Jansson, "How to Become"; Felix Bühlmann, Thomas David, and André Mach, "Cosmopolitan Capital and the Internationalization of the Field of Business Elites: Evidence from the Swiss Case," *Cultural Sociology* 7, no. 2 (2013): 211–29; Hiroki Igarashi and Hiro Saito, "Cosmopolitanism as Cultural Capital: Exploring the Intersection of Globalization, Education and Stratification," *Cultural Sociology* 8, no. 3 (2014): 222–239.

38 United Nations, *Improvement in the Status of Women in the United Nations System: Report of the Secretary-General* (United Nations General Assembly, A/72/220, 2017).
39 Cf. Henrik Rydén, *Are Women Paying a Higher Price for a UN Career?* (Stockholm: Impactpool White Papers, 2017).
40 Rydén, *Are Women*.
41 Karin Fast and Johan Lindell, "The Elastic Mobility of Business Elites—Negotiating the 'Home' and 'Away' Continuum," *European Journal of Cultural Studies* 19, no. 5 (2016): 435–449.
42 Mirca Madianou and Daniel Miller, *Migration and New Media: Transnational Families and Polymedia* (London: Routledge, 2012).
43 Toke H. Christensen, "'Connected Presence' in Distributed Family Life," *New Media and Society* 11, no. 3 (2009): 433–451.
44 Vincent Miller, "New Media, Networking and Phatic Culture," *Convergence* 14, no. 4 (2008): 387–400; Vincent Miller, "Phatic Culture and the Status Quo: Reconsidering the Purpose of Social Media Activism," *Convergence*, 23, no. 3 (2017): 251–269.
45 Cf. Jarrett, "The Relevance".
46 André Jansson, *Mediatization and Mobile Lives: A Critical Approach* (London: Routledge, 2018).
47 Gregg, *Work's Intimacy*.
48 Cf. Bourdieu and Wacquant, *An Invitation*.
49 Gregg, *Work's Intimacy*.
50 Jean Baudrillard, *Simulations* (New York: Semiotext(e), 1983).
51 Marwick and boyd, "I Tweet".
52 André Jansson, "Using Bourdieu in Critical Mediatization Research: Communicational Doxa and Osmotic Pressures in the Field of UN Organizations". *MedieKultur*, 58 (2015): 13–29; Jansson, "How to Become".
53 Van Dijck and Poell, "Understanding Social Media".

17
THE GIG ECONOMY AND CLASS (DE)COMPOSITION

Todd Wolfson

In August of 2016, hundreds of take-out delivery couriers in London assembled outside the headquarters of Deliveroo, a three-year-old Australian, platform-based food courier company. The couriers had all received a text or email earlier in the day from Deliveroo management. In the message, employees were unceremoniously told that their hourly wage would be abolished and they would instead be paid on a per-delivery basis. At the time, Deliveroo drivers were making £7.00 per hour and £1.00 per delivery, which had many workers making less than the London living wage. However, after a series of trials, the company declared that they were moving to a new system where they would pay couriers on a £3.75 per delivery basis with no guaranteed hourly wage.

It was clear to the couriers that by moving from an hourly wage to a per delivery wage, the company was attempting to shift all of the risk of this growing start-up on to the backs of the couriers. In addition, the company's move to pay workers by the task was compounded by the fact that Deliveroo had secured over £250 million as part of a recent round of venture capital fundraising.[1] Recognizing that their work conditions were exploitative, some couriers had already begun talking to leadership at the Independent Workers Union of Great Britain (IWGB) about launching an organizing campaign for Deliveroo couriers. The sudden announcement of the new wage structure however, enraged couriers and accelerated the organizing process, quickly setting off strike action across London.

Deliveroo couriers, like most workers in the gig economy, perform their jobs alone, picking up pizza or curry from a local restaurant and dropping the food off for customers at home or work. However, unlike Uber "partners" or TaskRabbit "taskers" who truly work in isolation, Deliveroo couriers congregate at "local hubs" to await their food pickup. These points of physical assembly naturally led couriers to develop relationships while forging lines of communication.[2] Specifically, couriers began using the text-messaging app WhatsApp (owned by Facebook). Detailing how this happened, Ali, a courier and organizer explained that couriers used WhatsApp to chat "about stuff, where people are, funny videos, lots of spam … as well as bad restaurants and problems on the routes." Once established however, as Ali described, the line of discussion amongst couriers organically became a critical channel for workplace organizing.

Once the change in salary structure was declared, Deliveroo employees quickly harnessed these pre-existing lines of communication to call for a wildcat strike. A few short hours after the original text from management, hundreds of workers converged on the company's UK headquarters demanding that their hourly wage be reinstated. In one video that went viral, Deliveroo's Managing

Director in the UK, Dan Warne, came out of headquarters to appease the growing throng of couriers. In an attempt to calm the crowd, Warne contended that the new pay scale was merely "a trial," to which he was quickly met with jeers. He also told couriers: "We're happy to speak with each and every one of you. We have a team upstairs to do that.... We want the chance to listen to everyone individually...."[3] At this point the crowd of couriers erupted with boos. It was clear that while Deliveroo management wanted to enter into dialogue with individual workers, the couriers were focused on acting and bargaining collectively. Unsuccessful in his bid to de-escalate the situation, Warne left the couriers as chants broke out outside of Deliveroo Headquarters.

After a six-day strike, Deliveroo couriers won some concessions from the company and eventually returned to work. In particular, couriers that were threatened with "deactivation" if they did not sign up for the new program, were not fired, and all couriers were given a choice to either take part in the new "experimental" wage program or alternatively they could return to the previous hourly wage, albeit, in a different zone of work in London. While the couriers were not entirely satisfied, they decided to get back on their bicycles and mopeds and return to delivering food.

Since this initial strike, Deliveroo has successfully moved most couriers onto a per delivery pay scale. At the same time however, workers throughout the food courier industry have consistently fought back regarding work conditions. Since 2016, we have seen a wave of strikes and work actions among Deliveroo couriers (and couriers for similar food delivery platforms) in Hong Kong, and throughout both continental Europe and the UK that were inspired by this first action in London.[4] In fact from 2016 to 2017, according to Callum Cant[5] we have seen at least 42 work actions against food delivery platform companies, such as Deliveroo, in Europe alone. As couriers continue to take on gig companies regarding terms of employment, they have become one of the front lines in the struggle over the future of work in this digital, platform-driven economy.

I begin with this moment in London as it opens a window onto the changing nature of class, work, and worker organization in the gig economy. In the case of Deliveroo, workers were able to organize and win some concessions. The norm for this growing class of workers however—who find themselves conscripted into a precarious army paid by the task, and receiving work orders through online platforms based on algorithms that are controlled by companies that do not claim them as employees—is that they do not organize and therefore they have little control over their labor. For the most part, the growing rank of precarious gig workers are isolated and at times alienated from one another as they compete with one another for jobs. And all too often they do not have the tools, connections or communication infrastructure to organize and, thus, have little recourse as companies set the terms and conditions of work in the sector.

With this reality in mind, in this chapter I look at the process of class composition, and importantly decomposition of workers in the gig economy. I argue that in the gig economy it is increasingly difficult to organize because of the lack of social relations, lines of communication and ultimately worker organization. Moreover, I argue that the technological developments that have facilitated the gig economy are not natural developments but rather, emerged as part of a process to diminish the power and collectivity of the working class. To make this argument, first, I look at Marx's analysis of the French peasantry and the conditions, or lack thereof, for organizing amongst this group of workers in the nineteenth century. Building on this, I argue that the rise of the gig economy is not merely the result of benign technological innovation, but is compelled by the ideological, political and importantly economic domains. Following this, I detail the Autonomist Marxist concept of class composition. Specifically, I look at how the transformation to the gig economy or what some have called "platform capitalism"[6] is part of a historical process, where the goal of the capitalist class is to weaken the composition of the working class, through the introduction of technological tools and labor processes that undermine working class power. This process of worker decomposition, which has been taking place across the last 40 years, has accelerated with the rise of the gig economy, leaving gig workers in a uniquely precarious position while hinting at the nature of work and resistance in years to come. Finally, given the political conjuncture, I conclude by looking at some problems and possibilities for worker organization in the gig economy.

Class and the Curious Case of the Peasantry

In order to understand the lived experience of gig workers today, it is important to take a brief historical detour to the mid-nineteenth century to develop a comparative vantage. In *Eighteenth Brumaire of Louis Bonaparte*, Karl Marx offered a detailed analysis of Louis Bonaparte's coup d'état in 1851, and in so doing he presented a more nuanced account of class formation than can be found in the majority of his work. In a widely cited passage, Marx set out to outline the difference in circumstance between the peasantry and proletariat in France. While the below passage has famously been harnessed by Gayarti Spivak[7] to dissect the concept of "representation," there is much left to probe, as Marx lays out some of the differences between peasants and industrial workers, outlining the inherent advantages the proletariat possessed in forging class power. Specifically, Marx focuses on the lack of social relationships amongst peasants owing to the isolating and redundant features of work in feudalism, which, he argued, separates peasants from one another, "much like a potato in a sack creates a sack full of potatoes." Along these lines Marx writes:

> The small-holding peasants form a vast mass, the members of which live in similar conditions, but without entering into manifold relations with one another. Their mode of production isolates them from one another instead of bringing them into mutual intercourse. The isolation is increased by France's bad means of communication and by the poverty of the peasants. Their field of production, the small holding, admits of no division of labor … no wealth of social relationships.[8]

In the above, Marx details how the process of work in a feudal economy does not create an interlinked community of farmers. Instead, each peasant works alone and therefore, aims to meet his or her needs in a singular fashion. The segregated process of work has material consequences, as peasants do not naturally forge collective relationships with one another through the process of production, and consequently they do not form a tight-knit community. A few passages later, building on this argument, Marx sets forth an often-overlooked axiom of class theory:

> In so far as there is merely a local interconnection among these small peasants, and the identity of their interests begets no community, no national union and no political organization, they do not form a class. They are consequently incapable of enforcing their class interest in their own name, whether through a parliament or through a convention. They cannot represent themselves, they must be represented.[9]

The significance of this statement is that in Marx's analysis it is the lack of social relations, lines of internal communications infrastructure and ultimately political organization of the French peasantry that hinder the peasants' ability to become a class. In essence, the inability to forge relationships and lines of communication ultimately made it impossible for the peasantry to build collective organization that can be the basis of class power. Ultimately for Marx, the barriers to building class organization lead to a group of people that, although oppressed by their lived conditions, cannot effectively forge collective consciousness and change their conditions.

Hardt and Negri[10] seize on this line of argument to develop their theory on the role of communication in resistance. Hardt and Negri explain:

> Communication in this sense, is the key to the political significance of the traditional division between city and country and the political prejudice for urban political actors … not

so much idiocy but incommunicability defined rural life. The circuits of communication that gave the urban working class a great political advantage over the rural peasantry were also due to conditions of work. The industrial labor force, working in teams around a common machine, is defined by cooperation and communication, which allows it to become active and emerge as a political subject.[11]

Hardt and Negri argue, in their interpretation of Marx, that it is the lack of an internal communications infrastructure and circuits of social cooperation of the French peasantry that hinder their ability to be a class and represent their interests to the larger French community. This led Hardt and Negri to argue that lines of internal communication are necessary for establishing political subjectivity and identity. Thus, it is not some ideological backwardness forged through rural life, but instead lack of social cooperation and lines of communication that differentiate the peasantry from the proletariat.

I highlight Marx's initial analysis and Hardt and Negri's interpretation as it offers a compass for delineating some of the core conditions that must be in place for a sector or group of workers to form into a class. What becomes clear, at least for Marx, is that social relationships and lines of communication are critical to building political organization, and it is political organization that plays a decisive role in representing workers and thus enabling workers to solidify into a class for itself. These are the critical characteristics that differentiate the proletariat from the peasantry in nineteenth century France.

Returning to the current conjuncture, as we begin to analyze the conditions of work in the fast-growing gig economy, whether in a rural or urban setting, one thing that emerges more often than not is the isolation of the work and the lack of an interconnected division of labor. This lack of circuits of social cooperation, where people work together in teams and forge relations, is not present for most gig workers. Much like the peasantry, each gig worker is primarily in charge of his or her own labor and subsistence, and therefore the work is not formed relationally. Correspondingly, organic circuits of social cooperation are harder to build. This reality leads to thin social relations and correspondingly, fragile lines of communication and ultimately anemic political organization. Thus, in many ways this precarious sector of the working class is more akin to the peasantry than to the proletariat, a point we will return to later in the chapter. Next though, it is critical to discuss the rise of the gig economy, as the conditions that precarious workers find themselves in today are neither an accident nor the outcome of some "neutral" technological advances.

History and the Rise of the Gig Economy

The common narrative about the rise of the gig economy is that technological advances led to new systems of production and consequently new labor relations. In this line of argument, the terms and conditions between companies and workers are organically set in motion, we are told, by the increase in the power of computing, advances in Artificial Intelligence and the emergence of big data and the Internet of Things. These technological breakthroughs have allowed for the efficiencies of a "just-in-time" workforce, where customers receive goods and services at breakneck speed and workers are afforded the flexibility to operate as mini-entrepreneurs, working on their own time with the freedom to choose when and how to work. The underlying implication is that platform capitalism and the resulting labor processes that have emerged in recent years are not the result of human or social intervention, instead messianic machines and big data sets are prodding us forward towards a new societal age.

While this narrative about the rise of the gig economy is quite intoxicating, with observers breathlessly extolling the possibility of market "disruptions" and new flexible ways of making a living, if we step back, it is clear that this description conjures up the specter of a new "invisible hand"—this time the invisible hand of technology, that silently guides social progress. This is not the first time that technological shifts have been accompanied by tropes of organic transformation. In his social history of automation, historian David Noble[12] discussed the development of technological innovation on the factory floor in New England. In reference to increasing automation in the factory Noble argued, "technology has come to be viewed as an autonomous process, having a life of its own which proceeds automatically, and almost naturally, along a singular path...." Challenging this perspective Noble continued:

> Rather than showing how social potential was shaped by technical constraints, ... I examine how technical possibilities have been delimited by social constraints.... For when technological development is seen as politics, as it should be, the very notion of progress becomes ambiguous: What kind of progress? Progress for whom? Progress for what? And the awareness of the ambiguity, this indeterminacy, reduces the powerful hold that technology has had on our consciousness and imagination, and it reduces also the hold upon our lives enjoyed by those whose social power has long been concealed and dignified by seemingly technological agendas.[13]

Bringing this argument to life, Noble detailed how corporations and the military shaped the development of automation in the factory, highlighting the social and political aspects of technological innovation. Specifically, Noble outlines how the process of automation was guided by the desire of managers to take control away from workers and this led to specific decisions about technological design. Thus, technological breakthroughs were made with the specific intent to weaken the power of workers on the factory floor. In a corresponding theoretical analysis first printed in 1961, Raniero Panzieri,[14] argued: "The technology incorporated in the capitalist system at once destroys the old system of division of labor and consolidates it systematically, 'in a more hideous form' as a means of exploiting labor-power."

Building on Noble and Panzieri, it is critical to underscore that the gig economy did not emerge as a consequence of the benign evolution of human technology. As scholars have argued,[15] the transformation in the logic of contemporary capitalism began well before the "information revolution." In the 1970s, as many scholars have detailed,[16] capitalism faced a crisis of growing worker strife as well as over-production/under-consumption. This crisis led to a drastic reduction in the incomes and assets of the elite classes and, in collaboration with the neoliberal state, led to a broad reorganization in the logic of capitalism and specifically the regime of accumulation.

David Harvey[17] famously characterized this as a transformation from a Fordist regime of accumulation to a flexible regime of accumulation. In defining flexible accumulation and building on the scholarship of the *Regulation School*, Harvey wrote:

> Flexible accumulation ... is marked by a direct confrontation with the rigidities of Fordism. It rests on flexibility with respect to labor processes, labor markets, products and patterns of consumption. It is characterized by the emergence of entirely new sectors of production, new ways of providing financial services, new markets and, above all, greatly intensified rates of commercial, technological and organizational innovation.[18]

Specifically speaking to the changing nature of work in late capitalism, Harvey continued, "The labor market has, for example, undergone a radical restructuring ... employers have taken advantage of weakened union power and the pools of surplus (unemployed or underemployed) laborers to push for much more *flexible work regimes and labor contracts*."[19]

As Harvey and others detail, over the last 40 years, this economic transformation has advanced as the state has moved towards policies of deregulation, privatization and globalization, allowing capital more flexibility, and this has happened while unions and the labor movement have become increasingly weak. The consequence of this new regime of accumulation is that workers have gradually seen their work become casualized, flexible, and temporary, while companies look to stay lean by employing fewer workers, in an effort to lower operating costs. This new temporary work arrangement has led to temporary work contracts that have been lionized as the "freedom to work when you want," but in all practicality, it has resulted in longer hours and more precarious work conditions for most.

In her book on digital labor, Ursula Huws[20] builds on this analysis detailing three critical moments that have taken place within this broader economic sweep of the last 40 years—from the oil shock of 1973 and the fall the Berlin Wall in 1989 to the economic crisis of 2008. Each of these moments, she argues, has led to social and economic transformations that have altered labor processes, and further weakened the working class. This series of economic transformations set the stage for the gig economy, as the type of work—low-wage, temporary, casualized and precarious—quickly emerged as a preferred means of employment.

While Huws keenly asserts that the 2008 economic crisis is a moment where draconian austerity measures changed the employment landscape, Srnicek adds another element to her argument, detailing one of the specific catalysts for the emergence of the gig economy, "asset-price Keynesianism." By this, Srnicek argues that in the wake of the economic crisis of 2008, the fixed low-interest rate enforced by states led to low returns for capital from more traditional financial assets. As such, capital and in particular venture capital was desperate for a high-return investment. This led to investments in new assets and, as Srnicek details, this led to heavy investment in companies such as Uber, Airbnb, and other online mediated work platforms. These companies were particularly attractive as they do not employ many people (or so they claim) and dramatic growth was possible in sectors such as housing and transportation as these businesses were harnessing already existing infrastructure (personal homes and automobiles). These realities led to heavy investment, and thus the meteoric rise of companies that epitomize the gig economy, from Airbnb to Uber.

This broad analysis, from Harvey and Huws to Srnicek, helps clarify that the intent to create flexible and precarious work arrangements is something that first emerged as a political and economic strategy for capital accumulation, it was not an outcome that was compelled by technological advances. In this sense, in the same way that Noble illustrated that certain automation technologies were chosen, not because of efficiencies, but rather because they undercut the role of skilled workers, the last 40 years illustrate that there were a set of economic and political conditions that were the primary engines for the rise of platform capitalism and the gig economy.

The massive economic transformation has led to both a shrinking labor movement and isolated workers that, more often than not, do not have the relationships, lines of communication or political organization to control their conditions of labor.

Understanding the Gig Economy

While there are many definitions of the gig economy, for the purpose of this chapter we are defining the gig economy by short-term or temporary work contracts defined by specific tasks. Most workers in the gig economy are classified, fairly or not, as independent contractors so they are not eligible for most of the protections afforded employees. Moreover, the gig economy and the majority of new gig companies are reliant on harnessing online or mobile platforms to connect consumers with contractors. The intermediary role of platforms is a critical component of this new gig economy.

Given this broad definition of the gig economy, it is critical to make a few points about the historical rootedness as well as novelty of the current conjuncture. First, it is important to note that paying workers by the task, or gig, is not a new development. In fact, in *Capital Volume 1*, which was published in 1867, Karl Marx devotes a chapter to "Piece-Work," where he argues that piece-work is more naturally aligned with the capitalist mode of production than daily wages, because, on average, workers make less when paid by the task. As such, one of the early struggles of the industrial proletariat in the nineteenth century was to challenge piece-work and win hourly wages, as Marx touched upon.[21] In fact, the struggle to win daily wages took place throughout the nineteenth and twentieth centuries. And while hourly wages became the norm due to shop floor organizing and the growing power of the working class, there have always been industries where workers (usually with less protections) were paid by the task—from pickers paid by the pound, adjuncts paid by the course, or sex workers paid by the "john."

While it is critical to note the history of piece-work, by the same token it is important to tease out some novelties in the emergent digitally-driven gig economy. The first novelty is that workers in the gig economy tend to receive their tasks through one or multiple online platforms. Accordingly, many of these workers are given their tasks, not directly by a human manager, but instead tasks are distributed by an algorithm (written by humans) that has no physical interaction with the workers undertaking the task. Another novelty is that these gig workers are not receiving their work orders in the informal economy or by a farm outsourced by McDonalds, but instead these tasks are delegated by some of the giants of the contemporary economy, from Amazon to Uber. This leads to a final point, that while gig work is in no way a dominant form of work in the United States or globally,[22] it is a growing form of labor and one we can argue is creating the logic for how work might look in the future.[23] We have already begun to see platform-based gig work creeping in to new sectors, such as the sciences,[24] and more recently we have seen retail companies beginning to utilize gig platforms for short-term workers.[25] Most recently, Uber announced the launch of Uber Works in Chicago, where they are planning to harness the platform to match prospective workers with businesses that need short-term labor.

Recognizing the historical, economic and political factors in the emergence of the gig economy, in the next section I will detail the concept of the cycle of struggle to show how technology and transformation of labor processes have been utilized to undermine the power of the working class. In *A Brief History of Neoliberalism*, David Harvey[26] makes this argument, detailing how neoliberalism is not successful as a regime of accumulation but it is successful as a class project which both facilitates the largest redistribution of wealth from the poor to rich in history, while also dismantling working class institutional power in the form of workers' rights and labor unions. The strategy of capital to weaken the working class is one that autonomist Marxists have identified as a constant battle throughout history, as I now turn to discuss.

Cycle of Struggle

To explore this issue of the changing nature of worker organization in the gig economy, it is critical to discuss the *operaismo (workerist)* or autonomist Marxist concept of the cycle of struggle and specifically the composition, decomposition and recomposition of the working class. Building on Marx and Engels' conception that class struggle is the engine of history, the cycle of struggle is built on the insight that the working class and the capitalist class are in a constant "now hidden, now open, fight." This struggle can be understood by analyzing the strength and composition of the working class and the strength and composition of capital. The cycle of struggle is an effective concept in that it adds an element of dynamism to our understanding of processes of class formation. In particular, the concept of class composition allows us to see that the process of class struggle is a historical fight over the nature and strength of the working class. Autonomists analyze both the technical composition of the working class as well as the political composition of the working class. The technical composition describes how the capitalist regime of accumulation forges a workforce from the process of production to the division of labor as well as forms of social reproduction such as the broader community and family structure.[27] Correspondingly, the political composition is the way that workers organize themselves to build power, which includes worker organization and political parties.[28]

The class composition of the working class is most potent when members recognize their collective self-interest, they have established strong bonds of communication and cooperation and they have built robust political organizations that are able to fight both for reforms and at times a revolutionary program. Correspondingly, the forces of capital aim to decompose the working class. By decompose, autonomists argue that the capitalist class aims to diminish the cohesiveness of the working class by breaking the bonds of collective consciousness, solidarity, channels of communication and social cooperation and political organization. As many autonomists argue,[29] this is often done by introducing new labor relations and conditions of work and oft times this is compelled through technological transformations.

Among other things, these new relations and conditions of work are meant to isolate and alienate members of the working class. In *Cyber Proletariat*, Nick Dyer-Witheford[30] examines the cycle of struggle across the twentieth century through the lens of the composition of the working class. Building on autonomist scholarship, Dyer-Witheford identifies two figures, or ideal-types, of the working class over the last 150 years: the professional worker (late nineteenth, early twentieth century) and the mass worker (mid twentieth century). Each of these figures is dominant in a specific historical moment and epitomized by certain traits.

The professional worker is characterized by highly skilled workers that have the ability to control the emerging industrial factory because of the expertise they exhibit over the production process. This capacity for control of the early factory floor makes the professional worker the main protagonist for workplace struggles in this period. Recognizing the power of the professional worker to control the production process, capitalists worked to decompose, or deskill the workforce, through the introduction of Taylorist and later Fordist practices, which broke the work process into small tasks and erased the influence skilled workers enjoyed over production.

While the introduction of new strategies of management and technological practices were aimed at weakening the professional worker, with the introduction of the Fordist production line and the complex division of labor that emerged in these economies of scale, the dynamics within industrial capitalism began to shift. Over time, the working class re-composed as the mass worker. The mass worker, which was characterized by density, social cooperation, lines of communication and mass organizing quickly developed political organization and the ability to halt the production process through broad control of the factory floor. In this case, instead of a specific skill that brought power, it was mass organizing and shared conditions of work that brought power.

In this cyclical process, we see that as the working-class gains power, and challenges the mechanisms of production, capitalism transforms, often through control of technology and other adaptive processes, to break the power of the working class. Mario Tronti has likened this to a spiraling "double helix" where, as Dyer-Witheford explains, "working-class composition and capitalist restructuring chase each other over an ever widening and more complex expanse of social territory."[31]

In the case of the industrial capitalism, the mass worker grew in power and organizational capacity leading to increased strife across the late 1960s and 1970s. The response of capital, as discussed above, was marked by massive transformations in the regime of accumulation from a stable fixed regime of accumulation to a flexible regime of accumulation. In this new regime, which was enabled by the state and catalyzed by technological breakthroughs, we see a global division of labor and a correspondent deindustrialization of the USA and Europe; smaller more flexible sites of production; the privatization of public goods; and deregulation and flexible work relationships that allow the employer more latitude over workers. Through this process of transforming the regime of accumulation, or the dominant logic wherein capital makes profit, one of the key outcomes has been transforming the labor process. In this case, through the introduction of technology and the aim of creating a just-in-time workforce as well as lean corporations that do not employ a lot of workers, it has led to growing precarity, where work is increasingly isolated and atomized.

As Huws[32] remarks, the emergence of the gig economy is not a separate moment in this history, but instead part of a broader wave in the cycle of struggle between capital and labor. As we look at the growing gig economy, it is clear that workers are more isolated and atomized than ever before. Workers get their work through an app on their phone, and the work is parceled out through an algorithm that has been programmed by a computer programmer in another city. There is little recourse when workers have a problem with the decision of an algorithm, as the managerial class has largely been eliminated. Moreover, there is virtually no worker-to-worker interaction, and thus no point of assembly to build connections, which consequently lessens the basis of organizing.

The shift towards piece-work has had a destabilizing effect on workers. On a material level, workers are making less money and working longer hours. Moreover, they have become increasingly isolated and the ability to organize and build power has become a difficult task. That said, in the last year we have seen new strategies for building solidarity within and across sectors of work and we have also witnessed new forms of worker organization, as I discuss in the concluding section.

Organizing in the Gig Economy

The argument thus far is that the rise of the gig economy and correspondent transformations in the nature of work are not solely economic transformations, but also that these changes are meant to weaken the power of the working class or decompose the working class. In this sense this is a moment in the cycle of struggle between the two classes and one where the capitalist class is seizing on the weakness of labor and the possibilities embedded in new technologies to impose new work conditions. These work conditions have forged a new type of worker, the gig worker that is increasingly isolated and alienated.

This reality is crystallized if we return to Deliveroo and food couriers in London. While the workers had some success, and are still fighting, the company's tactics have also transmuted. Since the 2016 strike, Deliveroo has abandoned the concept of local hubs, the same local hubs that played a critical role in establishing some of the relationships that led to worker organizing. It could be argued that getting rid of the hubs was a response to a court case that the Deliveroo couriers and IWGB brought to win worker status in London. It is also possible that Deliveroo has abandoned the local hubs because management recognized the role the local hubs play in facilitating bonds of trust, lines of communication and ultimately worker organization.

While we are witnessing shifting strategies among gig companies like Deliveroo, we are also beginning to see new types of worker organization developing in response to the conditions within the gig economy. One example is the aforementioned Independent Workers Union of Great Britain (IWGB). IWGB represents food couriers in the UK, but it has also organized across multiple sectors of precarious and gig economy workers such as Uber drivers and Deliveroo couriers as well as outsourced custodial staff, medical couriers, video game programmers and foster care parents. This sundry mix of workers were all represented in a massive rally and series of demonstrations in October 2018, aptly named "The Rise of the Precarious Worker." The Rise of the Precarious Worker action took over six hours as the procession traveled to over five work sites across London to hear about the struggle of Uber drivers, food couriers, medical couriers, foster care parents and outsourced custodial staff at the University of London. The seemingly diverse organizing strategy of IWGB, and the precarious worker action, together illustrate the goal of the union to call or hail this new emergent and coalescing worker into a classed form. In this sense, IWGB is an example of a new form of worker organization that is working to re-forge class composition among gig workers and a broader section of the precarious workforce.

Alongside the IWGB and in a more sector specific sense, food couriers across Europe launched the Transnational Courier Federation (TCF) in the fall of 2018. The inaugural meeting was held in Brussels and included 34 organizations from 12 countries across Europe. The goal of TCF is to build a network of projects across the globe focused on organizing food couriers. As one courier argued, companies such as Deliveroo are transnational so resistance must be transnational as well. In a video that was taken during the inaugural meeting in Brussels, one London-based food courier, Ali Chugthai, captured the goal of TCF and courier organizing to build solidarity and the collective power of the food courier. He explained:

> Our struggles are part of the same struggle, it's is all part of the continuum of neoliberalism atomizing people and making us feel alone. And the solution to that is, that community, and that global community on a European level and a global scale. Like this is it, these are the factories of our time. This is the same struggle the dockers went through, just in … new clothes. That perspective you get from meeting people from different countries in very, very, very similar situations, um, yeah it gives you that perspective and that perspective lets you build the solidarity, that is how we win … we win by coming together.[33]

In this succinct and thoughtful analysis, Ali offers the vision of organizing among food couriers in the gig economy. He details the goal to break isolation through lines of communication and solidarity, which is the basis for building collective power and winning. It is through these projects, from the IWGB to TCF that we begin to see how workers are responding to the current conjuncture. Building on this, as we think through the life and conditions of work for Uber drivers, food couriers or domestic workers that receive work via online platforms, it will be critical to tease out how gig workers can re-compose as a new organized sector of the working class.

Notes

1 Facility Waters and Jaime Woodcock, "Far From Seemless: A Worker's Inquiry at Deliveroo." *Viewpoint Magazine*, September 20, 2017. www.viewpointmag.com/2017/09/20/far-seamless-workers-inquiry-deliveroo/.
2 Ibid.
3 Retrieved from www.facebook.com/uvwunion/videos/1127800247288213/.
4 Callum Cant, "The Wave of Worker Resistance in European Food Platforms 2016–2017," *Notes from Below*, January 29, 2018. https://notesfrombelow.org/article/european-food-platform-strike-wave.
5 Ibid.
6 Nick Srnicek, *Platform Capitalism* (London: Polity Press, 2017).
7 Gayarti Spivak, "Can the Subaltern Speak," in *Marxism and the Interpretation of Culture*, eds. Cary Nelson and Lawrence Grossberg (Urbana, IL: University of Illinois Press, 1988), 217–316.
8 Karl Marx, Friedrich Engels and Robert C. Tucker, *The Marx and Engels Reader* (New York: Norton, 1972), 608.
9 Ibid., 608.
10 Michael Hardt and Antonio Negri, *The Multitude* (New York: Penguin Press, 2004).
11 Ibid., 123.
12 David Noble, *Forces of Production: A Social history of Industrial Automation* (New York: Knopf, 1984).
13 Ibid, xiv–xv.
14 Raniero Panzieri, "The Capitalist use of Machinery: Marx versus the Objectivists." Libcom.org, August 10, 2017. Accessed at https://libcom.org/library/capalist-use-machinery-raniero-panzieri.
15 Ursula Huws, *Labor in the Global Digital Economy* (New York: Monthly Review Press, 2014); Srnicek, *Platform Capitalism*.
16 Gary Teeple, *Globalization and the Decline of Social Reform: Into the Twenty-First Century* (Amherst, NY: Humanity Books, 2000); William I. Robinson, *A Theory of Global Capitalism: Production, Class and the State in a Transnational World* (Baltimore, MA: Johns Hopkins University Press, 2004); David Harvey, *A Brief History of Neoliberalism* (New York: Oxford University Press, 2005).
17 David Harvey, *The Condition of Postmodernity* (Malden, MA: Blackwell Publishing, 1990).
18 Ibid., 147.
19 Ibid., 150 (emphasis added).
20 Huws, *Labor*.
21 Marx et al., *The Marx*, 692–700.

22 Lawrence F. Katz and Alan B. Krueger, *The Rise and Nature of Alternative Work Arrangements in the United States 1995–2015*, The National Bureau of Economic Research, September, 2016. www.nber.org/papers/w22667.pdf.
23 Hanna Johnston and Chris Land-Kazlauskas, *Organizing on Demand: Representation, Voice and Collective Bargaining in the Gig Economy*, International Labour Office, March 29, 2018. www.ilo.org/travail/whatwedo/publications/WCMS_624286/lang-en/index.htm; Huws, *Labor*.
24 Roberta Kwok, "Flexible Working: Science in the Gig Economy," *Nature*, 550 (October 19, 2017), 419–421. Accessed www.nature.com/nature/journal/v550/n7676/full/nj7676-419a.html.
25 Abha Bhattari, "Now Hiring for a One-day Job: The Gig Economy Hits Retail," *Washington Post*, May 4, 2018. www.washingtonpost.com/business/economy/now-hiring-for-a-one-day-job-the-gig-economy-hits-retail/2018/05/04/2bebdd3c-4257-11e8-ad8f-27a8c409298b_story.html?utm_term=.cb3b620fe743.
26 Harvey, *A Brief History*.
27 Kolinko. Class Composition, *Nadir*, April, 2001. Accessed from www.nadir.org/nadir/initiativ/kolinko/engl/e_klazu.htm.
28 Ibid.
29 Mario Tronti, "The Strategy of Refusal," in *Working Class Autonomy and the Crisis*, ed. the Red Notes Collective, 7–21 (London: Red Notes, 1979); Antonio Negri, *Revolution Retrieved: Selected Writings on Marx, Keynes, Capitalist Crisis and New Social Subjects* (London: Red Notes, 1988).
30 Nick Dyer-Witheford, *Cyber Proletariat: Global Labour in the Digital Vortex* (Toronto: Pluto Press, 2015).
31 Nick Dyer-Witheford, *Cyber-Marx. Cycles and Circuits of Struggle in High-Technology Capitalism* (Urbana, IL: University of Illinois Press, 1999), 72.
32 Huws, *Labor*.
33 Retrieved from: www.facebook.com/labournet.tv/videos/european-riders-form-the-transnational-federation-of-couriers/516413332161000/.

18
DIGITAL HIERARCHIES OF LABORING SUBJECTS

Kaitlyn Wauthier, Alyssa Fisher, and Radhika Gajjala

In this chapter, we note how the three concepts of "digital domesticity," "digital housewife," and "digital subalternity" work together at the site of online philanthropy (philanthropy 2.0) to produce a gendered class (layered and intertwined) hierarchy between digital consumer and laborer.[1] In doing so we use examples from two startups: one is the online microfinance site Kiva (kiva.org) and the other is the site Workaway (workaway.info), both of which connect global volunteers to places where they can contribute their labor in social, ecological, or other care-related projects. By exploring the concepts of digital domesticity and digital housewife, this chapter illustrates how online philanthropy motivates forms of reproductive labor. Because of this, we argue that the sites Kiva and Workaway, as examples of online philanthropy, depend on this reproductive labor to produce digital subalternity, the decontextualized, individualized incorporation of subaltern populations into a global financial infrastructure based on immaterial labor.

In 2005, Matt and Jessica Flannery co-founded Kiva as "an online lending platform that allows individuals in the developed world to loan to small business people in the developing world."[2] Matt Flannery describes Kiva as a partnership program between investors and entrepreneurial-minded people, despite having the ostensible attributes of benevolent paternalism-driven philanthropy. Evidencing Flannery's claim that the platform supported a mutually beneficial financial relationship to lenders and borrowers, the Flannerys tested out their financing model during their beta launch. Friends of the Flannerys loaned money through the site to seven entrepreneurs in rural Africa. Several months later, all of the loans were repaid in full.[3] From there the platform continued to grow while keeping the Flannerys' original business model.

Kiva remains embedded within a philanthropy 2.0 context, where images of poor individuals from the Global South proliferate the screens of potential lenders from the Global North (this is a process of digital subalternity). These images are the primary strategy Kiva uses to hail potential lenders as philanthropists-in-waiting. Paired with third-person narratives crafted by Kiva fellows (field workers) about the borrower, profiles emphasize carefully selected details about the individual's skills, business plans, and life experiences, and serve to mobilize affect and build connections between lenders and borrowers. We call this representative strategy "staging." By staging, we refer to the site's representations of subaltern, unbanked persons as "entrepreneurial borrowers." In some ways, the borrower appears to have agency and ownership of their representation as entrepreneurs or business persons. However, these representations are static reproductions of who Kiva field workers and lenders imagine subaltern borrowers to be. Thus, we refer to them as stagings to problematize the ostensible "true" narratives that profiles produce about each individual borrower.

Similarly, Workaway offers its site visitors opportunities to support local infrastructure initiatives in Global South communities. Those who wish to volunteer with Workaway, or "Workawayers," exchange a few hours of work on projects in those communities for free "food and accommodation" during the duration of their stay in that place.[4] The site clearly states the benefits for individuals who are interested in becoming Workawayers:

> You can use Workaway to enable you to travel around a country for very low cost, you can use it to practice a language you have spent many years learning ... or use it to learn new skills and meet new people![5]

Workaway attempts to make site visitors into Workawayers by highlighting the benefits of volunteering for the volunteers themselves, not for the communities with which Workaway partners. Volunteers get to travel at a reduced cost, they get to learn new skills, and importantly, they are told that they will make a difference.

In approaching Kiva and Workaway as sites to explore the concepts of digital domesticity, digital housewife, and digital subalternity, we employ a visual analysis of images typical of each of the platforms. We look at the framing of the image itself, its color, perspective, etc., and the image's context, both on the platform (as juxtaposed against both textual narratives and lender/voluntourist conversations) and in its larger social location. In the next section, this chapter turns to a discussion of the concepts at play in online philanthropy (like Kiva and Workaway).

Class and Labor in Online Philanthropy

This chapter uses a socio-cultural and labor-based view of class, where the organization of and contribution to class is largely involuntary and embodied through traditions, experience, and unconscious modes of performance.[6] For example, class can be understood through daily tasks. Reay's illustration of class through the act of mothering identifies mothers who enact education within the home as middle class, while those who enact more practical tasks such as lunch making are conceptualized as working class.[7] These same concepts of class can be illustrated through the women who seek business support through online philanthropy. Those who engage in what could be construed as craft that is limited to their local geography may be positioned lower in a class hierarchy, while the conception that a woman who engages in the same craft-based activities, but as a business owner with sights set further away geographically, has the potential to be in a higher class. This is conceptualized through a Global North perspective where labor in the home and for more casual profit is considered a hobby while registering the same work as a legal business and setting up an online shop is classified as business owner.[8]

This view of class extends to our understanding of online identities, subalternity, and how labor is positioned within a hierarchy in online spaces. In "Epistemologies of Doing: E-merging Selves Online," Radhika Gajjala, Natalia Rybas, and Melissa Altman discuss the impossibility of separate online and offline identities.[9] Their creation of a practice of cyber ethnography through a study of the space and identity performances reveals technological infrastructures, coded subtext, and context that create normed practices within an online society. The study of cyber identities allows for a nuanced understanding and reduction of identity essentialism online, and tries "to unravel the relational nature of online/offline, virtual/real, place/space, subject/object, local/global, urban/rural, east/west and so on through praxis at and beyond the interface, focusing on how tacit knowledge is first produced through everyday practice in techno-mediated environments."[10] As such we see the difference between how a Global North blogger's labor, for example, is understood differently compared with the types of labor performed by artisans or entrepreneurs from the Global South.

Gina Chen's article, "Don't Call Me That: A Techno-Feminist Critique of the Term *Mommy Blogger*," which explores "mommy blogging," demonstrates how digital labor not only moves along class lines, but also gendered expectations. Mommy blogging, according to Chen, creates a new sphere of "digital domesticity," where women's labor in the home is gendered feminine, and therefore subordinate to masculine forms of labor.[11] Chen's study focused on women in the mommy blogging sphere, as readers or writers, debating the term "mommy blogger" using phrases such as "cutsey," "childish," "accurate," and "innocuous."[12] Mommy blogging, according to Chen, reinforces the social act of mothering, wherein one's instincts are not to be relied upon, but instead knowledge about becoming and being a mother is found within society. Chen suggests that mommy blogger can be a term and gaze performance that is both empowering and limiting. As some find power in the collective community of mommy bloggers, others find pressure to perform perfect mothering practices.

Chen argues that the term directs focus to the nurturing act of parenting, and represents digital domesticity, wherein a hegemonic frame of motherhood is focused on daily actions rather than the "radically empowering act" that writing about the experience of family and parenting could be.[13] The act of writing about one's experience can be co-opted by those who feel free to critique the author's parenting skills. When located within a Global North context, then, mommy blogging is gendered feminine and illustrates how certain types of labor are undervalued or dismissed as hobbies.

Jarrett broadens this view of digital domesticity and applies a domestic metaphor to emotion work performed online. Previous work from Jarrett, such as her 2014 article in *Television and New Media*, discusses emotional labor from a gendered perspective, and its increasing effects on our lives, relationships, and perceptions of productivity, and her book *The Digital Housewife* extends this work.[14] Jarrett establishes quickly that the housewife imagery is meant to be a metaphor to encourage the reader to make comparisons between housewives' work as physical and emotional, tied together under added pressure from society, and the constant social pressure to use and contribute to social media. Jarrett focuses on immaterial labor in terms of a blurring of boundaries between work and home life. Here, we can easily connect the metaphor from housewife to user generated content to our identities as we perform them online, at work, at home, or in other environments. However, Jarrett shows that digital labor in the Global North has capitalized on forms of labor historically performed by housewives.

Jarrett argues that the rise of immaterial capitalism has produced an effect she calls "presence bleed": intellectual labor often extends past the workday because of mobile communications technologies that blur boundaries between work and intimate personal life.[15] Much in the way that housewives' jobs were both personal and required a sense of professional pride, Jarrett states that contemporary jobs require the worker to have a blurred line between the professional and personal, whether it means actually bringing tasks home, maintaining availability to answer questions on-demand via text, or even participating in work culture on social media sites. The emotional labor that makes up the online commercial spheres is not purely female—it is gendered through what feminist critiques of Marx have called "reproductive labor," based upon the action of the labor and the contextualization of it as traditionally female performed. Therefore, persons of any identifying gender who perform immaterial labor, like blogging, perform undervalued, yet identifiably Global North-located, reproductive labor. Silvia Federici indicates how a global gendered class hierarchy persists despite the proliferation of undervalued emotional/domestic reproductive labor in the Global North:

> Neither the reorganization of reproductive work on a market basis, nor the "globalization of care," much less the technologization of reproductive work have in any way "liberated women" and eliminated the exploitation inherent to reproductive work in its present form. If we take a global perspective we see that not only do women still do most of the housework ... the amount of domestic work paid and unpaid they perform may have actually increased, even when they had an extradomestic job.[16]

So, while women in the Global North can hire out material reproductive labor, women globally have to perform both material and immaterial forms of reproductive labor. Often these tasks are unvalued and unacknowledged as labor, whether they are physical housework, work brought home to be completed, or emotion work done in the workplace or social platforms online. This connects us to the final concept illustrated by online philanthropy: digital subalternity, a condition of this gendered class hierarchy that depends on reproductive labor.

In regard to the final concept, Gajjala writes about cyberculture, subalternity, and particularly online philanthropy/philanthropy 2.0 within the production of digital subalternity.[17] The concept of the subaltern is connected to historic caste, class, and colonized populations. It is tied to a traditional lower class population as a generalized group, and often discussed as such a group in reference to efforts to rise above or against high castes.[18] Digital subalternity transitions this caste system into populations who are often outside of technological developments, either because the devices and infrastructure have not reached their physical location or an economic inability to acquire the means to participate. In the example of our case studies, the interaction of consumer labor, marginalized populations, and their marketability as an object to consumers creates digital subalternity as an ostensibly mutually satisfying relationship between the producer and consumer. Furthermore, digital subalternity is an enactment of the so-called subaltern presence in global digital space and forms a portal for the emergence of a particular decontextualized (staged with selective context and background narration and images), individualized, global labor force. In the sites we examine below, we specifically expand on how online philanthropy produces digital subalternity through the platforms' visual reproductions of subaltern populations.

Kiva and Workaway use tactics of staging digital subalternity to motivate consumer labor that in turn creates a layered, gendered class hierarchy between consumers and the digital subaltern laborer, firmly rooting the sites within online philanthropy/philanthropy 2.0. Through blending the best of the private and philanthropic sectors by investing in social enterprises that seek returns through market approaches,[19] sites such as Kiva provide an online shopping experience to find a cause to help, and promise a return of money while providing the feel-good endorphins of charity. According to Brainard and LaFleur,

> the public has become an active participant in financing development and a growing contributor to development activities on the ground. Individual donations from the United States to the developing world have surged to approximately $26 billion a year, and innovative models promise to further facilitate this exchange.[20]

By bringing Silicon Valley business models to charity, typical citizens feel they are buying for good. This decontextualized marketing strategy then mobilizes affective circuits among consumers, which compels emotional, reproductive labor that continues to produce an understanding of the digital subaltern.

In short, startups such as Kiva and Workaway work in concert with nonprofit organizations that serve to privatize the provision of "aid" to the poor and delink the public sector from having to be responsible for these sorts of financial relationships.[21] The responsibility for the empowerment of the poor is now on the individual who is told they can and should participate in digital giving (i.e., reproductive labor) because now it has been made easy. Giving has not only been made easy, it is now marketed as fun for the individual and a way to form affective links and networked sociality through communities engaged in digital giving and voluntourism. Regardless, the work of folks in the Global North who lend money and actively engage on these sites is a form of reproductive labor in the vein of digital domesticity/the digital housewife and it also serves to decontextualize subaltern populations from the global financial infrastructure to create digital subalternity.

Reproductive Labor on Kiva and Workaway

In this and the following section, we turn to an analysis of Kiva and Workaway as sites to understand how the concepts of "digital domesticity," "digital housewife," and "digital subalternity" interweave through online philanthropy. On these platforms, expressions of feeling and of connection serve to elicit an emotional attachment to the communities that lenders/volunteers are supporting. Kiva's profiles use visual and textual "stagings," for example, to authenticate the reality of the borrower's story—these feelings spread across lender groups and in lender profile posts, as well as in blog posts in a way that constantly recirculates and reaffirms the affective linkages between lender and borrower. The lenders perform the immaterial labor that Jarrett writes about, where the personal and professional overlap and reproduce gendered class hierarchies. They participate in the circulation of knowledge about the digital subaltern and extend their subject positions as Global North citizens into this digital space wherein their personal beliefs are reified, but also become mechanized components of neoliberal capitalism.

As Jarrett describes in "'Let's Express Our Friendship by Sending Each Other Funny Links instead of Actually Talking': Gifts, Commodities, and Social Reproduction in Facebook," the way lenders communicate on Kiva emulates the types of interactions available on social media platforms.[22] Through these exchanges, lenders enter into affective interactions among themselves around the borrower profiles. At the same time, the borrower profiles must be produced as having the potential to transform into "happy objects" after being presented first as simultaneously deserving of investment and charity.[23] This means that the subaltern borrower is presented as an entrepreneur attempting to lift themselves out of poverty by their bootstraps. Both parties perform labor in this constructed exchange even as the labor performed by lenders is hierarchically positioned in relation to borrower labor.

For example, Workaway's mission asks subjects located in the Global North to invest their time and emotional labor in building relationships with racialized and classed communities in the Global South. Testimonials by volunteers communicate the positionality Workaway seeks from its user-participants. One example from Workawayer Gemma reads:

> The work is easy and shifts are well organized ... as a workawayer you need to take a bit of initiative to help the place run smoothly, but there's always other volunteers to help out and Mari or Elias are always on hand to help you out. The volunteer team became like a family ... sharing meals or adventures![24]

In this review, the Workawayer talks about how they needed to step in as a leader in a Puerto Viejo de Talamanca, Costa Rica hostel where they volunteered. While they mention the hospitality of the Global South hosts, they are more interested in the relationships they made with other volunteers and that they are there to help, not learn from the business owners.

This positions the Workawayer as a white savior who has to teach the business owners how to properly operate. Furthermore, in making more substantial relationships with other Workawayers, this volunteer has maintained race and class dynamics and a hierarchy between the volunteers and hosts. The volunteers forge relationships with each other (like the mommy bloggers Chen writes about) while ignoring the other labor that goes into the process of running the hostel (like maintaining relationships with government entities, marketing the hostel, etc.). And in the writing and reviewing of their trip, the Workawayer performs reproductive labor for the Workaway platform, attracting more volunteers to the site who pay Workaway to get access to these voluntourism opportunities. While it is well intentioned (this reviewer gave the hostel owners a five star, "excellent" review), this review does more to ensure Workaway's intermediary presence as a philanthropy-focused tech startup than support the growth of independent businesses in the Global South.

Thus, we see in the discussed examples that the site produces a vision of philanthropists within a certain middle class location that plays on expectations of middle-class mobility, leisure, and web-based global connectivity. By crafting this image of what qualifies a person as a voluntourist (their Global North location, etc.) and how they enact that subject-position through reproductive labor, we see how Workaway functions similarly to Kiva within the model of philanthropy 2.0. We expand on this interaction in the next section, discussing ways that on the one hand, the site extracts reproductive labor from the voluntourist/philanthropist through an interplay of leisure and feel-goodness associated with the writing of reviews and chatting in a blog/forum space. On the other hand, as with Kiva, Workaway produces an iteration of digital subalternity and internet tourism that invokes a desire to contribute labor. As Lisa Nakamura contends, internet-based leisure "not only reinforces the idea that cyberspace is not only a place where travel and mobility are featured attractions, but also figures it as a form of travel which is inherently recreational, exotic, and exciting, like surfing."[25] So the key really is not the giving of money alone (neither in Kiva nor here), but in the "giving" of reproductive labor—framed as leisure—for free to prop up the tech startups. As noted earlier this also gives rise to a hierarchy in the digital and affective labor performed that privileges the Global North participants as consumers of the digital subaltern.

In this way, Workaway is implicated in a cycle of peril and poverty whereby businesses like the hostel featured in Gemma's review rely on Workaway's supply of volunteers. Likewise, Kiva's borrowers are also brought into a system whereby they rely on the system of finance created and maintained by the Global North. Megan Moodie writes in regards to this: "it does not work sufficiently to actually mitigate peril (that is, to take people out of cycles of anticipating and living through crises of food and shelter), and microfinance can itself exacerbate the condition of peril."[26] As such, these sites frame the lenders'/volunteers' position as one of risk (hierarchically gendered as masculine), whereby they may lose money or time invested, but the platforms create conditions of peril for the borrowers/hosts, where the risk is gendered as feminine because most of the funding is used "in the realm of the domestic and through the feminized work of getting by."[27] In the case studies that follow, this dichotomy is evident in Nasiba's profile on Kiva and in Workaway's repurposing of the image of the Madonna of Humility.

Case Studies

Kiva

In addition to the lender networks that create knowledge about its borrowers, Kiva pairs visual stagings with textual narratives in order to persuade the site's visitors to enter into lending relationships with borrowers. The stagings reproduce representations of borrowers as feminized and their work as extensions of their domestic responsibilities. For example, Nasiba's profile, which was active in May 2018, emphasizes her family dynamics immediately. She is married with three children and her husband's "income is small," because he "is an ordinary worker."[28] Right away, potential lenders understand that because her husband is unable to provide financially for their family, Nasiba has stepped in and now manages both her family's domestic and financial well-being. Readers then learn that she is now sick and needs medical treatment that she cannot afford; therefore she requires a loan of $2050 to pay for care.[29] She can no longer work because of her illness, either. By juxtaposing her hard work outside of the home with her illness, Nasiba's profile suggests that somehow the two are connected. Whether or not there is a connection between the two, Nasiba's illness returns her to a sphere of domesticity that she transgressed by working outside of the home. The profile suggests, too, that Nasiba's priority in recovery will be to spend time with her family: "She hopes she will pass through the surgery very well and will be able to participate in all the happiness of her family."[30] Potential lenders are helping Nasiba return as a caring mother to her children and a wife to her husband; the profile does not re-emphasize her career aspirations as a motivation to fund her loan.

In the image that accompanies the textual narrative, Nasiba's pose and facial expression support her position as an individual who needs care. She stands alone in a stark white hallway that is sparsely furnished. The photograph frames Nasiba as its focus. She is in the center of the image and there is nothing else in the photograph to draw the spectator's attention. Her facial expression is neutral, but importantly she directs her gaze straight at the camera and returns the spectators' gaze. The image seems rather clinical and almost like the photographer took it as an afterthought. Perceptive viewers can make out the barely visible words on the right side of the image's frame, "IMON International," one of Kiva's field partners—organizations that serve as intermediaries between Kiva and individual borrowers. Coupled with Nasiba's winter coat and hat and her position in front of a door, the image looks hurried and impersonal. Unlike other stagings on Kiva's website, this image does not show Nasiba's work or her achievements as part of her staging. Nasiba's enfleshed embodiment is the only tool spectators/lenders have when assessing her profile and making decisions whether or not they want to lend her money.

This is where Kiva extracts reproductive labor from the lenders themselves as an iteration of digital domesticity. Kiva's profiles draw lenders into an identification process with borrowers. While Nasiba might appear tired and while she has no visible support system with her in the IMON International office, there is no indication in the photograph that she is ill. The image diverts attention away from the specific reason Nasiba needs care—spectators see that Nasiba can be a strong and steady individual laborer in the economy. If she gets funding for the surgery as she requests, she will return to the microfinance economy as a returning borrower. This prompts lenders to envision Nasiba as an important component of the system in which they themselves participate.

In bold letters, the profile writes, "It helps families pay for potentially life-saving medical expenses."[31] Nasiba's story is extrapolated to represent the need of a collective community for medical care. Lenders are called into action to provide this care and save Nasiba and others in her geosocial location. As mentioned above, this informs the construction of peril as part of Kiva's commodification of its borrowers. Despite having a job, Nasiba needs money to "get by" in the moment; her loan is not for the development of long-term economic and entrepreneurial goals.

Workaway

On workaway.info, images compel site visitors to understand systems of labor and care in ways that similarly perpetuate relational dynamics between members of the Global North and South. For example, when a site user navigates to the "Our Mission!" page on workaway.info, they are confronted with an image of a Workaway volunteer sitting with a young boy on her lap. The page's design leads viewers to look at this image as an illustration of the textual description of the organization's mission. However, the image's meaning-making capacity moves independently beyond the text on the page. According to the text, Workaway's mission is: "Building a sharing community of global travelers who genuinely want to see the world whilst contributing to the places they visit."[32] To us, this mission statement elicits images of young, urban, socially mobile individuals from the Global North—"global travelers"—who see themselves as conscientious consumer/producers and who understand themselves as uniquely able to positively influence individuals and communities in the Global South. In the phrasing of this text, the act of "contributing" flows one-way from those travelers with the means to move in and out of spaces with ease and without restriction to those "places they visit."

Upon first viewing, the image of the woman sitting with child shows a positive cultural interaction between a white (possibly Western) woman and a black child from the Global South. The woman, who we understand to be a Workaway volunteer, physically supports the child as he leans back into her torso and she raises his legs off the ground with her hands. She carries his weight through this physical act. By embracing the child in this way, the volunteer also provides emotional support to him through the transfer of touch. She sits on the dirt to lift him and ease his burden, even if only for the duration of the photo shoot.

However, the image also moves our understanding of Workaway's mission beyond the textual description. Sitting in front of what looks like a domestic structure, the female volunteer simultaneously guards the doorway from and invites the photo's viewers into the seemingly private space, a place for reproductive labor and family mediation. She becomes the keeper of the space and the person who turns the reproductive activities of the home space into a productive marketing tool for Workaway.[33] Importantly, she sits at the front line of interaction between Workaway's operations and the communities they access. And, she usurps the roles of other adults in the young boy's community.

Evidencing the volunteer's positionality is a sign that leans against the home's door frame. The sign reads, "When we share our food, we are sharing our culture," and its presence stands in contrast to the rest of the photo's figures. The sign is bright white and clean; the text is clear and carefully cast on the sign. A blue, cursive font emphasizes the words *food* and *culture*, linking the domestic practice of making food to cultural exchange. In a way, the sign almost looks like it was Photoshopped into the photo after it was taken. It belies the impression of candidness the rest of the image suggests. The sign reveals the photo's artifice—the work that went into the figures' poses and situatedness in front of the door.

The boy and woman are visual stagings that operate similarly to the ones that appear on Kiva's site. Their poses, directed by an invisibilized photographer, work to suggest the types of interactions prospective voluntourists will experience during their own travels. First, the image indicates that the adult volunteers spend most of their time with children, acting as ostensible surrogate guardians for the children they meet. The boy's relaxed pose and beaming smile in this image indicate his willingness to share his affection with the volunteer. Her smile suggests that she, too, is fulfilled by the interaction, playing on feminized ideals of caregiving. She easily accepts the role of caregiver as the boy becomes a natural extension of herself.

The figures' staging is a visual homage, whether intentional or not, to the figure of the Madonna and Child, particularly in the lineage of the Madonna of Humility. In their poses, the woman assumes the position of the virgin selected by God to care for his children on Earth. This photo assures spectators that she is a virgin by contrasting her light skin with the boy's darker pigmentation; she is not his biological mother, but she has welcomed him without question into her life. The image further evokes the Madonna of Humility with the woman's seated position on the dusty, dry ground, which according to Gretchen Hirschauer, the Associate Curator of Italian and Spanish Paintings with the National Gallery of Art, "emphasiz[es] her humanity, almost as if she were a peasant woman and not an elegant Queen of Heaven."[34] The Madonna of Humility also highlights the intimacy between mother and child through physical touch and emotional connection.[35] Finally, in Workaway's rendition of the Madonna of Humility, the pair are seated in front of a fabric patterned with yellow flowers and wide green leaves. In the small frame of the photograph, the flowers take on the appearance of bright yellow suns, forming celestial halos behind the woman and child. The sun-flowers then juxtapose the figures' groundedness on Earth, and remind spectators of the woman's divinity, despite her humble appearance.

Where Workaway's Madonna of Humility departs from its historical antecedents is in the way the two figures address the gaze of the spectators. Both the Workaway volunteer and the boy look directly at the camera. In the historical versions of the Madonna of Humility, the figures typically address each other, the mother gazing down, consumed by the child's needs. The figures' staging in the Workaway version of course reflects typical contemporary photography styles: when we take photos of friends and family, they pose and smile toward the camera. However, the figures' staging also directs the spectators' gaze towards the volunteer and the young boy. Spectators are not meant to linger on the image of the dirt floor or the building's rough exterior; instead, spectators are meant to look directly at the interaction of the woman and child, ignoring the markers of Otherness that persist despite the volunteer's presence in the community.

Focusing the spectators' attentions on this interaction supports the entanglement of leisure and labor that Workaway facilitates through its platform. The image emphasizes the joy these two figures experience through their interaction: the volunteer gains satisfaction from the knowledge that she is helping/supporting the boy, and the boy is joyous because he is the ostensible beneficiary of this service. Their expressions and, more importantly, the iconographic lineage of their staging by Workaway demonstrate how the site, like Kiva, operationalizes gendered mechanisms of reproductive labor to mobilize participation in its venture.

Conclusion

Social and economic divides along class and access lines are both recontoured and reinstated through the digital. Can we say these access lines are purely along economic and/or along lines of access to higher education? Are the boundaries along lines of metropolitan versus rural? Are they along boundary lines formed around vernacular languages or English? In this chapter, we note how a *digital* subalternity is produced visually while keeping invisible the systemic and infrastructural socio-political dominance of inflexible global financial structures.

The question is not of access or inclusion in "the digital" but of mechanisms of subjugation within a neoliberal techno-governmentality that works to produce "generic institutions and generic subjects while systematically dismantling the will to critique."[36] On the one hand there is a discourse of equalizing difference, through a discourse of entrepreneurial and individualized aspiration towards mostly gendered subaltern autonomy in local social space through economic access. On the other, there is a highlighting of difference between the Global North and Global South, the urban and rural, and the socio-cultural haves and the have-nots because the economic can now be accessed through connectivity per the discourse offered up. The visual and discursive flattening of digital labor relies on the invisible labor of those producing the interface through offline and technical work (volunteers who blog, the NGO workers who find the potential borrowers and plug them into the interface, the technical computer coding and hardware maintenance staff, and so many others) and on highlighting the consumer labor of the digital housewives as philanthropy. The founders of these tech startups on the other hand are celebrated as both philanthropists and as business rock stars. However, as the founders create online portals to philanthropic giving, they extend the material infrastructure of inequality to new arenas. While they are lauded for giving avenues of financial borrowing or voluntourist labor to Global South business owners, for example, philanthropy 2.0 platforms do not reroute global inequality. The sites ensure the founders' wealth and celebrity, continue to demand the reproductive consumer labor of a middle-class Global North population, and perpetuate the production of digital subalternity for such consumption. In this way, online philanthropy's hierarchy of labor persists.

Notes

1 Gina Masullo Chen, "Don't Call Me That: A Techno-Feminist Critique of the Term *Mommy Blogger*," *Mass Communication and Society* 16, no. 4 (2013): 510–532, https://doi.org/10.1080/15205436.2012.737888; Kylie Jarrett, *Feminism, Labour and Digital Media: The Digital Housewife* (New York: Routledge, 2016); Radhika Gajjala, *Online Philanthropy in the Global North and South: Connecting, Microfinancing, and Gaming for Change* (Lanham, MD: Lexington Books, 2017).

2 Matt Flannery, "Kiva and the Birth of Person-to-Person Microfinance," *Innovations* 2, no. 1–2 (2007): 31.

3 Alice Garrard, "5 Questions for Jessica Flannery, Co-founder/Chief Marketing Officer, Kiva," *Philanthropy News Digest*, May 8, 2008. http://philanthropynewsdigest.org/5-questions-for-jessica-flannery-kiva.

4 "Our Philosophy is Simple," *Workaway.info*, accessed December 27, 2018. www.workaway.info/.

5 "Information for Workawayers," *Workaway.info*, accessed December 27, 2018. www.workaway.info/information-for-travellers.html.
6 E.P. Thompson, "Preface from *The Making of the English Working Class*," in *Cultural Theory and Popular Culture*, ed. John Story, 3rd edn (London, UK: Pearson/Prentice Hall, 2006), 41–45; Lawrence Grossberg, ed., "On Postmodernism and Articulation: An Interview with Stuart Hall," *Journal of Communication Inquiry* 10, no. 2 (1986): 45–60, https://doi.org/10.1177/019685998601000204.
7 Diane Reay, "Doing the Dirty Work of Social Class? Mothers' Work in Support of Their Children's Schooling," supplement, *The Sociological Review* 53, no. S2 (2005): 104–116, doi: 10.1111/j.1467-954X.2005.00575.x.
8 Kylie Jarrett, "The Relevance of Women's Work: Social Reproduction and Immaterial Labor in Digital Media," *Television and New Media* 15, no. 1 (2014): 14–29, https://doi.org/10.1177/1527476413487607; Kylie Jarrett, "Through the Reproductive Lens: Labour and Struggle at the Intersection of Culture and Economy," in *Digital Objects, Digital Subjects: Interdisciplinary Perspectives on Capitalism, Labour and Politics in the Age of Big Data*, ed. David Chandler and Christian Fuchs (London, UK: University of Westminster Press, 2019), 103–116, https://doi.org/10.16997/book29.
9 Radhika Gajjala, Natalia Rybas, and Melissa Altman, "Epistemologies of Doing: E-merging Selves Online," *Feminist Media Studies* 7, no. 2 (2007): 209–213, doi: 10.1080/14680770701286714.
10 Ibid., 212.
11 Chen, "Don't Call Me That".
12 Ibid.
13 Ibid., 511.
14 Jarrett, "The Relevance of Women's Work."; Jarrett, *Feminism, Labour and Digital Media*.
15 Jarrett, *Feminism, Labour and Digital Media*, 31.
16 Silvia Federici, "The Reproduction of Labour-power in the Global Economy, Marxist Theory and the Unfinished Feminist Revolution" (seminar reading, UC Santa Cruz, Santa Cruz, CA, January 27, 2009). https://caringlabor.wordpress.com/2010/10/25/silvia-federici-the-reproduction-of-labour-power-in-the-global-economy-marxist-theory-and-the-unfinished-feminist-revolution/.
17 Radhika Gajjala, ed., *Cyberculture and the Subaltern: Weavings of the Virtual and Real* (Lanham, MD: Lexington Books, 2012); Gajjala, *Online Philanthropy in the Global North and South*.
18 Ludden, D. ed., *Reading Subaltern Studies: Critical History, Contested Meaning and the Globalization of South Asia* (London: Anthem Press, 2002).
19 Lael Brainard and Vinca LaFleur, "Making Poverty History? How Activists, Philanthropists, and the Public are Changing Global Development," in *Global Development 2.0: Can Philanthropists, the Public, and the Poor Make Poverty History?* ed. Lael Brainard and Derek Chollet (Washington, DC: Brookings Institution Press), 9–41.
20 Ibid., 12.
21 Gajjala, *Online Philanthropy in the Global North and South*.
22 Kylie Jarrett, " 'Let's EXPRESs our Friendship by Sending Each Other Funny Links Instead of Actually Talking': Gifts, Commodities, and Social Reproduction in Facebook," in *Networked Affect*, eds. Ken Hillis, Susanna Paasonen, and Michael Petit (Cambridge, MA: MIT Press, 2015), 203.
23 Sara Ahmed, *The Promise of Happiness* (Durham, NC: Duke University Press, 2010).
24 Gemma, December 27, 2018, comment on "Help Needed in a Hostel in Puerto Viejo de Talamanca, Costa Rica," *Workaway.info*, accessed December 27, 2018. www.workaway.info/712942856812-en.html.
25 For discussion of internet tourism, see: Lisa Nakamura, "Race In/For Cyberspace: Identity Tourism and Racial Passing on the Internet," *Works and Days* 13 (1995): para 9. http://faculty.humanities.uci.edu/poster/syllabi/readings/nakamura.html.
26 Megan Moodie, "Microfinance and the Gender of Risk: The Case of Kiva.org," *Signs* 38, no. 2 (2013): 288. www.jstor.org/stable/10.1086/667448.
27 Ibid., 289.
28 "Nasiba," *Kiva*, accessed April 11, 2018. www.kiva.org/lend/1486904.
29 Ibid.
30 Ibid.
31 Ibid.
32 "Our Mission!" *Workaway.info*, accessed December 27, 2018. www.workaway.info/mission.html.
33 Moodie, "Microfinance and the Gender of Risk," 280.
34 Gretchen Hirschauer, "In Depth: Madonna and Child," National Gallery of Art. www.nga.gov/research/in-depth/madonna-child.html.
35 Ibid.
36 Chandra Talpade Mohanty, "Transnational Feminist Crossings: On Neoliberalism and Radical Critique," *Signs* 38, no. 4 (2013): 972, doi: 10.13060/12130028.2015.127.2.216.

19
BETWEEN "WORLD CLASS WORK" AND "PROLETARIANIZED LABOR"
Digital Labor Imaginaries in the Global South

Cheryll Ruth Soriano and Jason Vincent Cabañes

This chapter's focus[1] lies in the nexus between the ethical challenges of labor exploitation as well as the conditions surrounding complex imaginaries of agency in the digital economy. The increasing global connectivity and the relative affordability of technology have heralded the rise of online platform labor or digitally-mediated service work. Platform workers (also referred to as online freelancers in this chapter) engage in digitally-mediated work through online labor platforms and microwork intermediaries such as *Freelancer.com, Onlinejobs.ph, Sama-Source* and *Upwork* (formed from a merger of *Odesk* and *Elance* in 2015). Although these workers are largely concentrated within the Global South, the demand for platform work comes from the Global North.[2]

Marketed as a geographically-flexible and competitive source of income, digital labor is touted as a highly viable and attractive option, especially in countries where employment conditions are fraught with financial stagnation and socioeconomic tensions. The "globalization" of business services propelled by the development of information and communication technology (ICT) allowed for the relocation of voice-based call centers and other back-office processes from the Global north to the Global south. Ranked as having the worst unemployment rates in Asia but with a large English-proficient population, the Philippines has become one of the prime sites of Business Process Outsourcing (BPO) work.[3] Data on the labor supply in the gig economy show that the country, together with India, Bangladesh, and Pakistan are the major sources of labor supply. The Philippine government champions digital labor as a way to overcome the various employment woes faced by countless Filipino professionals across age groups and educational background. The government sees platform labor as a complement to other forms of BPO work, an alternative to overseas labor migration, a catalyst for urban and rural development, and an attractive option for young graduates. In the same vein, some of the Filipino online platform "gurus" whom we interviewed for this research say that many Filipino professionals are also migrating to online platform labor in exchange for autonomy, spatial flexibility, and the possibility for higher earnings. Indeed the focus of this chapter is on our interviews with these very individuals who are engaged in the gig economy and who obtain work through digital labor platforms. Many of them have moved to platform labor and online freelancing from the "drudgery" of call center work. It is also important to note, however, that those who were once deemed as undesirables under traditional labor standards—such as those with physical disability, chronic illnesses, or low educational attainment—are now able to compete for jobs based on skills and project portfolio in these digital labor platforms.

In contrast to local aspirational narratives, the "Western"-based literature on digital labor in the Global South has been critical of the realities of such work.[4] In many ways, these studies echo the scholarship on digital labor in the Global North, which describe the pernicious conditions that digital workers face, from exploitation to isolation to the colonization of personal space.[5] Although these studies do the important work of training their lens on the problematic realities of digital labor in the Global South, they at times insufficiently address how workers might negotiate with, resist, and even challenge their unfavorable work conditions.[6]

This chapter attempts to avoid both overly optimistic and pessimistic accounts of the "on-demand" global economy and of "platform labor" in the Global South. To do this, it goes beyond simplistic explanations of un- or under-employment. We consider how the socio-cultural and economic complexities of the worker environment might drive the attractiveness of this form of labor and how histories of colonialism might make local employment and upward mobility less of a viable option for workers from the Global South. The chapter draws from an ethnographic inquiry on online freelancing in the Philippines, examining the experiences of Filipinos who engage in online freelancing and the entwined imaginaries of class and coloniality that draw them to this work. Rooted in the meanings that workers themselves ascribe to their working engagements, the affective elements of digital labor may perhaps be understood through various perspectives other than rigid concepts long associated with exploitation. Digital migration is possibly one of the limited ways workers from the Global South can participate in a globalization that is still Global-north centric. In the context of Filipino workers, these ways include imaginaries that underscore how it is that, as a result of their cultural embeddedness, workers might have alternative and more positive perceptions of their work.

Digital Labor in the Global North and South

There is already an established set of research about digital labor in the Global North. Much of this research stems from a critique of Richard Florida's notion of the rise of the "creative class," which was about this new group of socioeconomic subjects who had jobs based on creativity and individual talent and who could usher cities into a new era of economic development and prosperity.[7] This notion became quickly popular with policy makers and city planners who started to imagine the development of "creative cities." But, just as quickly, scholars have roundly challenged its celebratory vision. They say that this notion neglects social inequalities and class divisions as well as the many forms of exploitation that are experienced in the world of creative labor.[8]

Recent works on creative labor have talked about "flexible exploitation," which pertains to the double-edged nature of creative work that affords people new ways of working but also brings with it new kinds of precariousness.[9] For example, the temporal and spatial flexibility that has come to be one of the most powerful selling point of contemporary labor has also resulted in "presence bleed," where the always on phenomenon in the context of creative and digital work is brutally colonizing the personal space of contemporary workers.[10] There is also "self-exploitation" that describes how workers in creative fields are willing and prepared to take the risks of precarious creative work in hopes of obtaining fulfillment and even fame.[11] This notion goes hand in hand with the prevalent culture of "free labor" among creative industries, which then subjects workers to carry out unpaid labor in hopes of reaping the benefits of these "gifts" somewhere along the career line.[12] There is also emerging scholarship that is particularly focused on "microwork" or "platform labor," which is accused of effacing the long history of racialized and gendered exploitation of low-income workers.[13]

Parallel to the above-mentioned studies, there is a relatively small but growing collection of works on digital labor in the Global South. Taking a largely critical position, most of these works express concern about how people engaged in digital labor in the less-developed regions of the world have even more precarious experiences.[14] Because demand is geographically concentrated in the Global North, workers from the global South and other parts of the world find themselves competing for hyper-specialized, undervalued, and low-paying jobs. Idealistic notions of the value of affect and self-fulfillment, subjectivity, autonomy, and solidarity were found to have been directly challenged by accounts of anxiety from financial and career instability, physical exhaustion, increasing levels of stress, and social isolation.

Whereas online labor platforms have empowered workers to perform skill arbitrage or the process of selling their labor to whoever is willing to buy it for the best price, the asymmetry of the labor market as engendered by the fierce competition results in an environment conducive for the exploitation of "labor arbitrage," or the process of sourcing for the cheapest labor available.[15] As the majority of digital workers hail from the Global South, where the currency and standard of living is relatively low, cases of underbidding and a generally unstandardized pricing process characterize the online labor platforms, much to the advantage of clients.[16] Consequently, researchers have noted how these conditions severely diminish the bargaining power of digital workers. In particular, workers note feelings of isolation as a result of working long and irregular hours at intense speeds along with concerns about their job security and, sometimes, low income, all of which are issues that researchers attribute to the ubiquitous discrepancy of wages in platform labor.[17] Because of the dispersed geographic nature of digital work, clients are able to exploit workers from low-income countries in that they can buy labor at significantly lower rates in the guise of being considered above average in the context of the worker's geographic position. Furthermore, the dispersed geography of digital work engenders irresponsible market practices by clients who end up taking advantage of the lack of mandated wage regulations on digital work.

These conditions have led some quarters to call such working environments as "digital sweatshops."[18] Many of the concerns about platform labor involves the low pay and the absence of bargaining and organizing capability of workers in the platform that leave them prone to abusive work conditions. Yet, confronted by overwhelming accounts of exploitation in the various sociotechnical ecosystems of digital labor, one would ask, what draws thousands of workers from the Global South to such forms of labor? Are these to be characterized simplistically as "forced" labor due to perilous unemployment conditions in economically marginalized countries? What explains the striking contrast in the narratives drawn from these scholarly works with local articulations on digital labor?

Class, Coloniality, and Digital Labor Imaginaries in the Philippines

This chapter argues that in the case of the Philippines, the entwined imaginaries of class and coloniality are crucial to understanding why many workers are attracted to digital labor and to online platform work. Here we define class beyond the narrow concept of the economic, but through the broader lens of the social.[19] This entails including two complementary ideas about contemporary social class. One is the Weberian idea of class as "a social category pertaining to individuals or groups sharing comparable behaviours, characteristics, and way of life."[20] The other is the Bourdieusian idea of class as "reproduc[ing] social divisions [through] individual practices, subjectivities, and perceptions."[21] Meanwhile, we take coloniality to mean "long-standing patterns of power that emerged as a result of colonialism, but that define culture, labor, intersubjective relations, and knowledge production well beyond the strict limits of colonial administrations."[22] We also acknowledge its contrapuntal postcolonial consciousness, that pertains to how subjects possess a history and a way of being that resists or subverts being entirely defined by coloniality and capital.[23]

Given this polysemic nature of class and coloniality, we define these imaginaries through a poststructuralist lens, that is, as sets of socially shared representational assemblages and practices that function as contingent anchor points in terms of emerging relationships of individuals to their conditions of existence.[24] As an embodied practice of transcending both physical and sociocultural distance[25] and empowered by mediated images and discourses, colonial imaginaries about economic, social, or cultural mobility have changed the way people collectively envision their world and the possibilities within it. In the case of the Philippines (and potentially in other Global South contexts), these entwined imaginaries can simultaneously cast the middle class status of digital workers as marginal and aspirational.[26]

To be sure, some quarters in the Philippines rightly claim that while digital labor in the country offers many Filipinos the possibility of making it to the middle class, they are only marginally so.[27] In sheer economic terms, the salaries of digital workers place them within the country's middle classes whose monthly income ranges from PhP15,780.00 (approximately US$308.00) at the lower end to PhP157,350.00 (approximately US$3071.00) at the higher end.[28] But at the same time, digital workers are often thought of as being akin to the "marginal middle class," who are "wage- and salary-earning clerical workers."[29] They are compared less favorably to the so-called "new middle class," who are "professional and technical workers on the one hand, and wage- and salary-earning administrators, executives, and managers on the other hand."[30] And this less than favorable comparison also holds with the "old middle class," who are "nonprofessional, nontechnical self-employed workers other than those in the informal sector and the primary industries, as well as employers outside the primary industries except for those holding administrative, executive, and managerial positions."[31]

What makes the precariousness and "marginal middle class-ness" of digital labor in the Philippines distinct is the jobs mismatch that predominate this kind of work, which is often characterized as "low prestige" in the Global North.[32] This labor is primarily comprised of offshored low-skilled occupations being taken up by the country's highly educated and young workforce.[33] The country's business process outsourcing (BPO) industry in particular is dominated by work in call centers, transcription, and content moderation, which are taken up by college graduates, including those from the top universities. They are "based on a narrow job description and offer only limited opportunities for acquisition of knowledge and skills replicable in other professions" and, crucially, often have poor "longer-term employment prospects."[34]

As a counterpoint, however, it is also important to consider the perspectives of the digital workers themselves. By this we mean taking into account their "worker agency," which pertains not only to their act of making choices and or acts of resistance, but also to the process of their subject (re)formation.[35] And the latter is replete with conflicting logics and contradictory impulses, where workers may collude with, inasmuch as challenge, existing structures. For many Filipino workers who do digital labor, for instance, the downbeat class imaginary of "marginal middle class-ness" runs alongside a more positive colonial imaginary of being a "global worker." They see themselves as holding not just any white-collar job, but one that is linked to the global flow of industries and, as such, to a global and flexible lifestyle.

BPO work, for instance, is described as happening in "hip workplaces, situated in upscale business districts, utilizing latest technology, and servicing top global corporations ... [they] offer the chance to build a career with a growing company catering to international clients."[36] Many of its workers are proud of their proficiency in English, which is a "high prestige" language in the country, owing in part a history of American colonization and in part to English being the lingua franca of contemporary globalization.[37] These workers also appreciate how their jobs afford them access to some of the perceived markers of a global middle-class lifestyle, such as wearing fashionable clothes to parties and hanging out for coffee in Starbucks.[38]

In the ensuing discussion, we go beyond the often-studied BPO workers and present the digital labor imaginaries that predominate particularly with online freelance workers in the Philippines. We show how the imaginaries of this specific subgroup of digital workers articulate an assemblage of classed and colonial perspectives of agency and false aspirations created by the digital economy. To view these online freelance workers as mere victims implies positioning them within an interpretive framework of either oppression or resistance to normative structures and discursive constructions. In exploring the motivations, meanings, and values that digital workers ascribe to their jobs, we discuss how norms and discourses are inhabited in order to understand what makes individuals both identify and resist certain subject positions. Imaginary relations are managed by individuals who are culturally and historically located and hence embedded within specific relations of power.[39] A critical analysis of imaginaries may thus also offer a deconstruction device of ideological, political and cultural stereotypes.

The Digital Labor Imaginaries of Filipino Online Freelance Workers

Drawing from in-depth interviews and analysis of multiple texts circulating in online freelance forums, Facebook groups, and freelancer events, we looked at how freelance workers and platform managers enacted and articulated classed and colonial digital labor imaginaries. We have identified three such interconnected imaginaries and label them as follows: that of 'distinction,' 'transcendence,' and 'flexibility'. In fleshing out these digital labor imaginaries, we also discuss the role of virtual spaces, online communities, and the influencers who help push these imaginaries within the digital platform. In exploring digital labor in the context of its socio-political and cultural embeddedness, we aim to show how workers constituted a sense of self and agency while being embedded in aspirations that were fraught at best and false at worst.

Imaginary of 'Distinction'

One key classed and colonial imaginary of online freelance workers we interviewed was that of 'distinction.' This pertained to their belief in the exceptionality of Filipinos when it came to skilled global service work. They situated themselves within the long history of their compatriots fulfilling labor shortages throughout the world, as nurses and domestic workers, as seafarers and agricultural workers, and as cooks and cleaners.[40] They saw themselves in particular as a special class of workers who possessed distinct traits that matched the requirements of digital labor as "world class service workers." Crucially, they often articulated this idea in comparison with individuals from 'competitor countries'—such as India and their Southeast Asian neighbors—drawing on cultural stereotypes that put down other nationalities for being less professionally skilled than them.[41]

In an article, "Why Pinoys and BPOs are a Good Fit," this 'goodness-of-fit' is attributed to unique Filipino values:

> It's the values in our culture that make Filipinos suitable for the job. We are known to be hospitable, accommodating, and empathetic, and these are vital traits to have for a job that requires a lot of interaction.... Filipinos are willing to adjust their lifestyles, which is asked of many BPO employees.[42]

A majority of the workers we interviewed did talk about having a distinct suite of skills attractive to the digital economy, which included English proficiency, digital literacy, willingness to serve, and an entrepreneurial spirit. Some of them narrated that this was what actually led them to digital work. Online freelance work allowed them to break free from the difficult or abusive work conditions they faced in their previous jobs as call center workers, overseas labor migrants, and even advertising and TV production staff. And they were happy that in their new work, they had achieved a comparative level of success by "earning the same or higher amount of salary" (Gino, male, 42) or "building a diverse portfolio of skills useful to the global economy" (Cris, female, 43). The continuity from BPO or media-related work and online freelance work also added to this imaginary of distinction. As freelance worker turned coach Gino (male, 42) shared,

> It is about the experience of talking to foreign people and of course the customer service culture you know, serves us well. So although it is not a direct continuation, those with BPO experience have a good chance of thriving in this career because of entrepreneurial skills that prepare us for online freelancing, and that's an advantage.

This imaginary of 'distinction' was, in key ways, also driven by how the Philippine government has used labor brokerage as one of its neoliberal strategies to bring in much-needed foreign currency inflows.[43] This government has actively branded the nation as one that systematically trains and exports service workers for the global market. And this is predominantly constructed as a "natural global order of things" that Filipinos should accede to and benefit from. This mirrors what Irani retells as the illusion created by the eighteenth-century Mechanical Turk with that of the "joyful optimism" and "celebrations of creativity" being sustained by the precise invisibility of microworkers who are tasked to take on the unwanted jobs in high-technology workplaces.[44] By marketing the nature of microwork platforms as "human-as-a-service," these microworkers are rendered as mere "standing reserve," faceless and as dispensable as the other.[45]

In the last decades, the Philippine government has continually touted the mantra of Filipinos being "world class service workers" and "modern heroes," helping drive labor export despite the precariousness associated with such work. As former Philippine President Gloria Arroyo said in a 2003 speech,

> I am not only the head of state responsible for a nation of 80 million people, I am also the CEO of a global Philippine enterprise of 8 million Filipinos who live and work abroad and generate billions of dollars a year in revenue for our country.[46]

Digital labor has been envisioned to address unemployment and rural development in the country, but also as an alternative to foreign labor migration. The labels of "modern heroes" and "world class workers" that have been previously attributed to overseas Filipino workers were in fact being gradually conferred on online freelance workers too. They were thought to be the OFW 2.0; no longer the 'Overseas Filipino Worker' but the 'Online Freelance Worker'. This was because through digital labor, one still earns dollars and performs as a 'global worker,' only this time without having to be away from home.

The ambiguous construction of the 'good service worker' was heightened by the expectations that foreign clients had about Filipinos. According to Mr. NJ (male), founder of an online labor platform primarily catering to Filipinos,

> We only work in the Philippines because it's a different experience working with Filipinos than with anybody else in the world. Filipinos are honest, they are loyal, they are hardworking, they speak really good English ... Filipinos will do all kinds of stuff to make their employer happy. Also, generally, across the board Filipinos are not entrepreneurial either and that's a big deal for a lot of entrepreneurs to be able to hire someone who is not, they don't have to fear who is going to steal their business. So the Philippines provides a unique situation, a unique setup of cultural difference that makes it different than anywhere else in the world.

But Cynthia (female, 39), a freelance worker who had achieved an influential position in the freelance community, disagreed that Filipino workers should necessarily subscribe to these expectations and ideals. She said:

> We Filipinos, we are hardworking, we complain about different things but usually not to the foreign client. Also we are willing to do everything, even overtime to please a client. I think this makes us preferred workers but also makes some of us prone to abuse.

Clearly then, articulating the characteristics of 'distinction' enables the fashioning and nation-branding of Filipino online freelancers as highly valuable and competitive 'world class workers.' At the same time, however, it constructs Filipino subjects not only as a global commodity and a colonized subject, but also as pliable servants unlikely to steal clients' ideas.

Imaginary of Transcendence

A second classed and colonial imaginary that the online Filipino freelance workers had was of 'transcendence.' Many of them subscribed to the idea that having to overcome difficulties was not only demonstrative of their positive qualities as a digital worker, but was also crucial to their overall self-development. Contemporaneous with modern capitalist thought, the freelance workers saw the experience of triumphing over tough work conditions not only as a means to career success, but also "as self-realization, as human self-fulfillment and development."[47] Unfortunately, this belief easily became co-opted into the earlier discussed idea of 'self-exploitation' in creative industries,[48] which is about this internalized belief that to be competitive and attain success, one should be able to tolerate pay that is often non-commensurate with one's skills and effort, and work conditions that are often unfair. This belief in transcendence also aligned easily with the related idea of 'free labor,' where workers agree to do unpaid labor in hopes of reaping the benefits of these 'gifts' somewhere along the career line.[49]

The imaginary of 'transcendence' of the freelance workers also seemed to be tied to the Filipino colonial experience of being stereotyped as indolent.[50] They wanted to show that, above other workers from other countries, they could turn in high quality work even in the most trying of circumstances. What further reinforces this thinking is the culture of audit and accountability in digital platforms, crystallized in the ratings systems that enable employers to give feedback on the freelancer's "service."[51] Indeed, the on-demand model of platform labor "conjures an all-too-familiar colonial imaginary of pliable servants" who may be "disassembled, reassembled, exploited as a reserve labor force and thoroughly surveilled and mined for value."[52]

The freelance workers often expressed the imaginary of 'transcendence' by building a resilience-based reputation and, subsequently, visualizing the success that results from this. As Cris (female, 43) narrated, "I used to get the lowest rate just to get the job when I was starting." She further shared that many of her peers have done the same with the belief that the rate will later increase when one has proven oneself. However, increasing one's rates is not always realized. As Karen (female, 26) puts it,

> In terms of pay … people don't know you so you have to lower your fees but if you're established already as a good worker and have the skills you can raise your fees. But it becomes a dilemma whether to raise their fees or not because in freelancing there are lean and peak seasons, if it's lean season some people just want to get clients even when the rates are not ideal.

In the end, working hard and earning a reputation did not really give all workers full control, as they still had to deal with the structural limits of labor arbitrage or constraints of labor oversupply. Certain workers who managed to take advantage of reputational capital are able to secure the trust of loyal clients, move from labor platforms to being directly hired, or turn into coaches and trainers. It is these people who appear to feel more fulfilled and gain a sense of stability.

This practice of building a reputation around resilience had strong classed and colonial inflections. It reinforced a dynamic that made the workers feel that their drive for self-improvement and social mobility were in line with what was deemed desirable by global capital.[53] Reputation here shaped the workers' idea of resilience and is crucial in their imaginary of transcendence. In an economy characterized by the diffusion of project-based employment and visible, quantified, and accumulated client ratings, the rise of online freelancing highlights the importance of reputation-building and resilience. Often, the workers legitimized both the need for hard work and resilience by visually instantiating the promise of success. This further reinforced the idea of an alignment between the workers' self-improvement and social mobility on one hand and the desirable qualities of workers needed by global capital on the other hand.

Indeed, visualizations of success were actively crafted, shared and circulated by the online freelance workers and also by influencers. Take for instance "*Katas ng freelancing*" (Fruits of Freelancing), a thread in one of the Facebook online freelancing community groups that was meant for posting "what one is able to buy or achieve" with digital work. The header of this thread stated,

> Here we can share to other freelancers all that we have worked hard for. The fruits of our hard work from being a freelancer. Here we can share what we have managed to acquire: car, house, business, etc. This is not to boast about our material possessions but we want to look back at the hard work and what we managed to accomplish. That in freelancing, THESE ARE ALL POSSIBLE.

Under this thread, digital workers shared photos of the 'fruits' of their freelancing career that ranged from the material (from house to car to a new laptop) as well as the immaterial (such as having their children graduate from good private schools) and actively commented on each other's posts to show support. The fact that such ideas needed to be articulated and visualized implied that there was a need to assuage the doubt that some potential freelancers had about the legitimacy and reliability of online work. This was particularly salient because our interviews showed that some freelancers remained ambivalent about whether online freelancing was gainful or sustainable. As online freelancer Red (male, 24) admitted, it is hard to predict sustainability because one always fears that "foreign clients will come and go" and "freelancing work is becoming seasonal and more and more competitive."

Here one can see the crucial role that coaches and influencers in the online freelancing community took not only in creating aspirations of middle classness, but also in articulating the norms of global capital as constitutive of good work. Online freelancing coaches and community leaders, a growing league of influencers in the local digital labor economy, also expanded the fruits of hard labor to the 'immaterial.' They created the notion that anyone can be like them, successful, entrepreneurial, well-networked, and "contributing to bigger social good," but achieved all these through sacrifice and hard work. In reality, some of these influencers achieved their status by harnessing other forms of capital, such as educational attainment, strong social or familial networks, or some financial wealth. Unfortunately, such skills and assets that allowed one to flexibly navigate across digital labor spaces and achieve a negotiating position with clients were not as easy to come by for the others.

Clearly, the freelance workers have an imagination that upon crossing a certain threshold one can perhaps achieve the reality of the "global knowledge worker class," one characterized by the recruitment materials of digital labor platforms. At the same time, Filipino workers see this performance of extra labor, patience, and suffering beyond the economic and the material and instead as a reflection of virtue and values of care, self-worth and meaning that connects work with inner notions of being (i.e., "producing a better version of oneself" as one worker has put it). Unfortunately, it is also true that sometimes, they end up competing and sacrificing for jobs that are relatively insecure and unprotected.

Imaginary of Flexibility

Finally, online Filipino freelance workers also articulated the classed and colonial imaginary of flexibility. For many of the workers we interviewed, their job brought into focus how they were connected to the infrastructures of global connectivity that drove the digital labor platforms in which they worked. It also highlighted how they were able to find ways of avoiding the infrastructural immobility—heavy traffic, bad roads, inefficient public transport—that characterized contemporary middle class life in the congested urban landscapes of the Philippines.[54]

Online freelancing has made the freelance workers rethink their standards of 'good work'[55] since they have experienced digital work as a site for negotiating flexibility and the attractive fluidity of 'work-leisure-care spaces' that might challenge 'traditional' models and cosmologies of professionalization of work. As online freelance worker Mark (male, 27), content writer and specialist in search engine optimization narrated,

> You get to work at the comfort of your own home. Traffic is invisible to you, you don't really care about traffic as much and you get to enjoy perks of working in your house clothes. You don't have to dress up for anyone. In that sense, you'd get to save money from buying clothes because you don't have to impress your boss anymore … and you also get to save money from travel fees—no need to pay for jeep or UV express [modes of public transportation in the Philippines]. And no more sudden corporate hangouts. No more Friday nights, you can just schedule it whenever you are comfortable. No longer peer pressured in spending money in unnecessary [ways].

Our respondents shared the amount of time wasted from commuting to and from work with their previous corporate jobs: "It used to be about 3 hours from my house to work, if I'm lucky, 2.5 hours one way, so that's about 5 hours wasted" (Anne, 41, female, Virtual Assistant and former online transcriber and book question writer). She believes that savings in terms of travel time has afforded her the space to flexibly take on more jobs which in turn helped broaden her skillset.

Many of the workers we interviewed appeared to attach more value to these flexible work arrangements that online freelance work afforded them, than the absence of health benefits and job security.

Other workers, Virtual Assistant Red (male, 24) and Clara (female, 28), expressed satisfaction with the flexibility afforded by freelance work conditions that allowed them to explore the country and other parts of the world. Clara said it allowed her family to "travel with our child in a lot of places while earning sufficiently."

The imaginary of flexibility also encompassed imaginaries of limitless social mobility and diversity in the nature of work. For example, online freelance writer Karen (female, 26) shared,

> In my previous job, they can throw as much deliverables to you as they can because you signed a fixed contract for a fixed amount of time, and they can even exceed that beyond office hours. In freelancing you can expand your earning as much as you work.

Freelancing work presents multiple possibilities to a worker. In a Freelancer Forum we attended, the speaker/coach advised the workers to explore new work possibilities by "faking one's skills," anyway, one can "learn new tasks on the job."

Interestingly, for some workers, the trope of flexibility attributed to online freelancing stretched to the capacity to flexibly circumvent traditional labor expectations and norms. Karen (female, 26) said that in more traditional jobs,

> You were fighting (with other candidates) over a full-time job or it's you versus people from the bigger universities, then the employer would be very biased to the graduates of those schools.

In online freelance work, however, she continues, overseas clients did not have the same considerations.

> They may also look if you're a college graduate or if you study in a university, but it boils down to your skills and your track record. They look if you can do their job, if you have good work ethic, if they can get along with you on a personal level.

The interesting aspect with "imaginaries of flexibility" was that it could be negotiated depending on the specific values to which a worker ascribed importance. And this could be about diversifying the nature of work, expanding one's earning capacity, designing one's office space as a leisure space, having more travel opportunities, or spending more time with family.

Despite imaginaries of flexibility, however, many workers also shared the need to work within inflexible and predetermined schedules due to work monitoring systems (for example, *Hubstaff*), and the need to constantly be on the email and provide immediate responses to clients. Whereas 'flexibility' and mobility have come to be two of the most powerful selling points of digital labor, the professional habitus that workers have created around these "always-on networks of communication" has forged new standards and a basis of professionalism that continues to be legitimized by the valorization of various institutions, including that of the media and technological brands.[56] This in turn leads to an unspoken yet compulsory need for today's workers to assume the habit of a constantly performing presence, whereby the office is no longer a place but "an idea to be enacted."[57] The negative affective component of "presence bleed" is also underscored in this form of contemporary work; one that generates anxiety and compels workers to develop an extra sensitive attunement to stay on top of one's work alongside the ability to anticipate what needs to be done.[58] More specifically, a transcriptionist, Em (female, 31) shares the tension between flexibility and constraint in the nature of her online freelance work:

> Yes, I work fulltime at home. I have something like a bundy clock like that [laughs]. Can you imagine? Hubstaff. It's an app that was given by my boss.... Since I'm putting in 40 hours and it's a must that I complete the 40 hours per week. It's not like you will get paid even if you don't work, no that's not the same for me. But you see you are tied in a way but also *flexible* in a way because you can start like 10 am or 1 pm as long as you complete the total 8 hours [per day].
>
> *(Emphasis ours)*

Together with the above, some of the workers articulated the need to work at cafes or co-working spaces. This clearly contradicted arguments about traffic avoidance or saving money, especially as co-working spaces and cafes were also often located in central business districts of Manila. Interestingly, this was necessary for some workers as physically 'working at home' was still not fully recognized as a legitimate job for family members. Their laments included relatives thinking that "I am lazy" and asking them to "find a serious job" (Cris, female, 43), to their neighbors interrogating them about "how we were able to buy a car, yet we are always just here at home" (JR, male, 27). This concern about the non-recognition of online work as legitimate work appeared to be important for a number of Filipino online freelance workers as it also constantly emerged as an issue raised during online freelancer events.

The above examples show the value of the imaginary of flexibility as one of the major drivers compelling Filipino middle class workers to embrace online freelance work. Through their classed interpretations of flexibility attached to the nature of digital freelance work, we see that digital labor, although understood to be facilitating a precarious form of labor, is actually fulfilling for some in relation to previous work conditions that tied them to past experiences of constraint and control. At the core of this trope of flexibility are the neoliberal ideologies of "individual entrepreneurial initiative" or "individual self-realization"[59] that compel the workers to break free from the controls of traditional corporate institutions and inefficiencies of local institutions to seize multiple unlimited opportunities. However, flexibility remains an imaginary, for as we see from the examples above, digital labor presents its own forms of control and constraint. As Peck[60] has argued, it is important to avoid the dangers of a narrative that "glorifies and naturalizes the contracted-out, 'free-agent' economy without regard for the exploitative tendencies of a highly flexible working environment that arise from this economic system."

Conclusion

This chapter sought to provide a grounded account of the realities of the 'on-demand' global economy and of 'platform labor' in the Global South. In paying particular attention to the experiences of online Filipino freelance workers in one context, we showed how locally situated contexts of class and coloniality foreground the imaginaries of digital labor. At the same time, we see the global scale of the digital labor experience and we find that some of these experiences echo findings on digital labor in other parts of the Global South[61] and the Global North.[62] We argued that in order to go beyond oppositional binaries or overly optimistic or pessimistic accounts of these experiences, we need to consider the socio-cultural and economic complexities of the worker environment that might drive the attractiveness of platform labor. As a framework for understanding this, we conceptualized the entwined imaginaries of class and coloniality. Drawing from in-depth interviews and analysis of multiple texts circulating in online freelance forums, Facebook groups, and 'freelancer' events, we identified three such imaginaries: that of 'distinction,' 'transcendence,' and 'flexibility.'

The key insight from our data is how Filipino online freelance workers experience digital labor in contradictory ways. We argue that it is important to understand more deeply the classed and colonial imaginaries that frame whether and how these workers embrace platform labor as an appealing work option. While this work hides a horde of conflicts that starkly resemble both old and new manifestations of exploitation and self-exploitation, its connections to the abovementioned notions of distinction, transcendence, and flexibility nevertheless possesses deeply affective dimensions that provide workers with a sense of fulfillment.

Seeing online platform labor merely as digital sweatshops tells us only a part of the real picture of how digital transactions unfold, are lived, experienced, and imagined, particularly in less economically advanced regions. Together with a continued interest in the global dynamics of inequalities that structure this labor, we also need to capture the local articulations of these global work realities and, crucially, the globally inflected but locally rooted meanings that workers ascribe to them. Making sense of all these is a crucial precondition to exploring possibilities for interventions that can improve the conditions of digital workers, both in the Philippines specifically and in the global South more broadly.

One other emerging insight from our data has to do with the role of the digital environment as well as the rise of 'influencers' in shaping the enactment and circulation of these imaginaries. We contend that this deserves a more focused study in the future. Digital labor in the Philippines has produced its own micro-celebrities that work—indirectly and directly—in pushing for these imaginaries in blogs, Facebook groups, and physical gatherings. These influencers who have become successful as some of the early takers in the field attempt to cascade imaginaries of success and mobility to their subscribers that also create rosy aspirations for the workers who now have to compete with thousands of new aspirants. Norms and values held by these influencers who are spatially, and gender located, suggest what is appropriate or good digital work. In turn, workers embrace and perform the imaginaries by sharing their own experiences, memes, and playing coach for other freelancers who cannot afford professional coaching. These imaginaries are also reinforced by government in its pronouncements, forums, and efforts to promote digital labor as a viable employment opportunity. Unfortunately, this allows government to elide its responsibility of addressing the many underlying labor and infrastructure issues that make digital labor, with all its imperfections, become palatable.

Notes

1 The chapter is an output of the Newton Tech4Dev Network, funded by the British Council. We thank the online freelancers interviewed for this study as well as the members of the network for the comments and suggestions during the preliminary presentation of findings.

2 Mark Graham, "Digital Labor and Development," *Oxford Internet Institute* (October 22, 2014). Accessed 1 January 2018. www.oii.ox.ac.uk/blog/digital-labor-and-development/; Alex Wood, Mark Graham, Vili Lehdonvirta, Helena Barnard, and Isis Hjorth, "Virtual Production Networks: Fixing Commodification and Disembeddedness," *The Internet, Policy, and Politics Conferences* (2016): 1–33.

3 Anna Charmaine Abara and Yoon Heo. "Resilience and Recovery: The Philippine IT-BPO Industry During the Global Crisis," *International Area Studies Review* 16, no. 2 (2013): 160–183, doi:10.1177/2233865913493282; Emmanuel David, "Purple Collar Labor: Transgender Workers and Queer Value at Global Call Centers in the Philippines," *Gender & Society* 29 no. 2 (2015): 169–194; Alinaya Fabros, *Outsourceable Selves: An Ethnography of Call Center Work in a Global Economy of Signs and Selves* (Quezon City: Ateneo de Manila University Press, 2016).

4 See for example, Antonio Casilli, "Is There a Global Digital Labor Culture? Marginalization of Work. Global Inequalities, and Coloniality," *Second Symposium of the Project for Advanced Research in Global Communication*, (2016): 1–42. Accessed January 15, 2018. https://hal-mines-paristech.archives-ouvertes.fr/halshs-01387649v1; Alex Wood et al., *Virtual Production Networks*; Mark Graham, Isis Hjorth, and Vili Lehdonvirta, "Digital Labor and Development: Impacts of Global Digital Labor Platforms and the Gig Economy on Worker Livelihoods," *Transfer: European Review of Labor and Research* (2017): 1–28; Mark Graham, Vili Lehdonvirta, Alex Wood, Helena Barnard, Isis Hjorth, and D.P. Simon, *The Risks and Rewards of Online Gig Work at the Global Margins* (Oxford: Oxford Internet Institute, 2017), accessed February 2, 2018. www.oii.ox.ac.uk/publications/gigwork.pdf; and Sarah Roberts, "Commercial Content Moderation: Digital Laborer's Dirty Work," in *The Intersectional Internet: Race, Sex, Class and Culture Online*, eds. Safiya Umoja Noble and Brendesha Tynes (New York: Peter Lang, 2016).

5 For example, see the works of Melissa Gregg, *Work's Intimacy* (Cambridge, UK: Polity, 2011); Melissa Gregg, "Presence Bleed: Performing Professionalism Online," in *Theorizing Cultural Work: Labor, Continuity and Change in the Cultural and Creative Industries*, eds. Mark Banks and Rosalind Gill (New York: Routledge, 2013), 122–134. See also Niels Van Doorn, "Platform Labor: On the Gendered and Racialized Exploitation of Low-Income Service Work in the 'On-Demand' Economy," *Information, Communication & Society*, 20 no. 6 (2017): 898–914; Lily Irani, "The Cultural Work of Microwork," *New Media & Society* 17, no. 5 (2013): 720–739. doi:10.1177/1461444813511926.

6 David Hesmondhalgh and Sarah Baker, "'A Very Complicated Version of Freedom': Conditions and Experiences of Creative Labor in Three Cultural Industries," *Poetics* 38, no. 1 (2010): 4–20. doi:10.1016/j.poetic.2009.10.001; Helen Kennedy, *Net Work Ethics and Values in Web Design* (New York: Palgrave Macmillan, 2012).

7 Richard Florida, *The Rise of the Creative Class: And How It's Transforming Work, Leisure, Community and Everyday Life* (New York: Basic Books, 2006).

8 See for example, Rosalind Gill and Andy Pratt, "In the Social Factory?: Immaterial Labor, Precariousness and Cultural Work." *Theory, Culture & Society* 25 nos 7–8 (2008): 1–30; Hesmondhalgh and Baker, "*A Very Complicated Version of Freedom*"; Christian Fuchs and Sebastian Sevignani. "What is Digital Labor? What is Digital Work? What's their Difference? And Why Do These Questions Matter for Understanding Social Media?" *TripleC: Communication, Capitalism & Critique. Open Access Journal for a Global Sustainable Information Society* 11, no. 2 (2013): 237–293. doi:10.31269/triplec.v11i2.461.

9 Alessandro Gandini, *The Reputation Economy: Understanding Knowledge Work in the Digital Society* (London: Palgrave Macmillan, 2016).

10 Gregg, *Presence Bleed: Performing Professionalism Online*.

11 Hesmondhalgh and Baker, "A Very Complicated Version of Freedom"; Arvidsson, *The Ethical Economy*.

12 Adam Arvidsson, Giannino Malossi and Serpica Naro. "Passionate Work? Labor Conditions in the Milan Fashion Industry," *Journal for Cultural Research* 14, no. 3 (2010): 295–309.

13 For example, Irani's study on US-based Amazon Mechanical Turk (AMT) argues that by marketing the nature of microwork platforms as "human-as-a-service," these microworkers are rendered as mere "standing reserve," faceless and dispensable. Irani, *The Cultural Work of Microwork*, 2.

14 Casilli, *Is There a Global Digital Labor Culture?*; Alex Wood, Mark Graham, Vili Lehdonvirta, et al., *Virtual Production Networks: Fixing Commodification and Disembeddedness*; Mark Graham, Isis Hjorth, and Vili Lehdonvirta, "Digital Labor and Development"; Mark Graham, Vili Lehdonvirta, Alex Wood, et al., *The Risks and Rewards of Online Gig Work at the Global Margins*; Sarah Roberts, *Commercial Content Moderation: Digital Laborer's Dirty Work*.

15 Niels Beerepoot and Bart Lambregts. "Competition in Online Job Marketplaces: Towards a Global Labor Market for Outsourcing Services?" *Global Networks* 15, no. 2 (2014): 236–255. doi:10.1111/glob.12051.

16 Wood et al., *Virtual Production Networks*.

17 Ibid.; Graham, et al., "Digital Labor and Development"; Graham, et al., *The Risks and Rewards of Online Gig Work*.

18 See for example, Ellen Cushing. "Amazon Mechanical Turk: The Digital Sweatshop," *Utne Reader* (February, 2013). Accessed on 15 December 2017. www.utne.com/science-and-technology/amazon-mechanical-turk-zm0z13jfzlin; Fiona Graham. "Crowdsourcing Work: Labor on Demand or Digital Sweatshop?" *BBC News* (October 21, 2010). Accessed 15 December 2017. www.bbc.com/news/business-11600902; Emiko Jozuka. "As More Work Moves Online, the Threat of 'Digital Sweatshops' Looms," *Motherboard* (March 22, 2016). https://motherboard.vice.com/en_us/article/qkjk35/as-more-work-moves-online-the-threat-of-digital-sweatshops-looms.
19 Asuncion Fresnoza-Flot and Kyoko Shinozaki. "Transnational Perspectives on Intersecting Experiences: Gender, Social Class and Generation among Southeast Asian Migrants and Their Families," *Journal of Ethnic and Migration Studies* 43, no. 6 (2017): 867–884. doi:10.1080/1369183x.2016.1274001.
20 Ibid., 871.
21 Ibid.
22 Casilli, *Is There a Global Digital Labor Culture*, 31.
23 Ibid., 139; see also J.K. Gibson-Graham, *The End of Capitalism (as We Knew It): A Feminist Critique of Political Economy* (Minneapolis, MN: University of Minnesota Press, 2006).
24 Rossi Braidotti. *Metamorphoses: Towards a Materialist Theory of Becoming* (Cambridge: Polity Press in Association with Blackwell, 2002); Rutvica Andrijasevic. *Migration, Agency and Citizenship in Sex Trafficking* (Basingstoke: Palgrave Macmillan, 2010).
25 Noel B. Salazar, "The Power of Imagination in Transnational Mobilities," *Identities: Global Studies in Culture and Power* 18, no. 1 (2012): 576–598. doi:10.1080/1070289X.2011.672859.
26 Niels Beerepoot and Emeline Vogelzang. "Service Outsourcing to Smaller Cities in the Philippines: The Formation of a Local Emerging Middle Class," in *The Local Impact of Globalization in South and Southeast Asia: Offshore Business Process Outsourcing in Services Industries*, eds. Bart Lambregts, Niels Beerepoot and R.C. Kloosterman (London, New York: Routledge, 2014), 29–45.
27 For example, see Emmanuel David, *Purple Collar Labor: Transgender Workers and Queer Value at Global Call Centers in the Philippines*.
28 Caroline S. Hau. *Elites and Ilustrados in Philippine Culture* (Quezon City, Philippines: Ateneo De Manila University Press, 2017).
29 Ibid.
30 Masataka Kimura. "The Emergence of the Middle Classes and Political Change in the Philippines," *The Developing Economies* 41, no. 2 (2003): 265. doi:10.1111/j.1746-1049.2003.tb00941.x.
31 Ibid.
32 Kingsley Bolton. "Thank You for Calling: Asian Englishes and 'Native-like' Performance in Asian Call Centres," in *The Routledge Handbook of World Englishes*, ed. Andy Kirkpatrick (London: Routledge, 2010): 550–564.
33 See Nedelyn Magtibay-Ramos, Gemma Esther Estrada, and Jesus Felipe, "An Analysis of the Philippine Business Process Outsourcing Industry," *Asian Development Bank* (2007). Accessed on February 1, 2018 from www.adb.org/sites/default/files/publication/28359/wp093.pdf; see also Ceferino Rodolfo, "Sustaining Philippine Advantage in Business Process Outsourcing," *Philippine Institute for Development Studies*, 28 (2005). Accessed on February 1, 2018. https://serp-p.pids.gov.ph/serp-p/download.php?d=4101&s=1; Roberts, *Commercial Content Moderation*.
34 Niels Beerepoot and Mitch Hendriks. "Employability of Offshore Service Sector Workers in the Philippines: Opportunities for Upward Labor Mobility or Dead-end Jobs?" *Work, Employment and Society* 27, no. 5 (2013): 824. doi:10.1177/0950017012469065.
35 Andrijavesic, *Migration, Agency and Citizenship in Sex Trafficking*, 15–17.
36 Fabros, *Outsourceable Selves*, 13.
37 Kingsley Bolton, "Thank You for Calling: Asian Englishes and 'Native-like' Performance in Asian Call Centres," in *The Routledge Handbook of World Englishes*, ed. Andy Kirkpatrick (London: Routledge, 2010), 550–564.
38 Carlos Luis Santos. "The New Trends in Urban Lifestyle in Manila," *Research Institute for High-Life* (2013). Accessed February 2, 2018. www.hilife.or.jp/asia2012/Manila4eng.pdf.
39 Andrijasevic, *Migration, Agency and Citizenship*.
40 Nicole Constable, *Maid to Order in Hong Kong: Stories of Filipina Workers* (Ithaca, NY: Cornell University Press, 1997); Rhacel Salazar Parrenas. *Servants of Globalization: Women, Migration, and Domestic Work* (Stanford, CA: Stanford University Press, 2001).
41 Jason Vincent Cabañes. "Pinoy Postings: On the Online Cultural Identity Performances of Young Filipino Professionals in Singapore," in *Changing Media, Changing Societies: Media and the Millennium Development Goals*, ed. by Indrajit Banerjee and S.R. Muppidi (Singapore: Asian Media Information and Communication Centre, 2009), 158–190.
42 Therese Reyes, "Why Pinoys and BPOs are a Good Fit," *Rappler* (April 6, 2016). Accessed February 2, 2018. www.rappler.com/brandrap/finance-and-industries/124981-filipinos-bpo-good-fit.

43 Robyn Magalit Rodriguez, *Migrants for Export: How the Philippine State Brokers Labor to the World* (Minneapolis, MN: University of Minnesota Press, 2011).
44 See Irani, *The Cultural Work of Microwork*, 18.
45 Ibid., 12–13.
46 Former President Gloria Macapagal Arroyo's speech cited in Rodriguez, *Migrants for Export*, ix.
47 See George Kovacs. "Phenomenology of Work and Self-transcendence," *The Journal of Value Inquiry* 20, no. 3 (1986), 199. doi:10.1007/bf00148299.
48 David Hesmondhalgh and Sarah Baker, "A Very Complicated Version of Freedom".
49 Arvidsson, *The Ethical Economy*.
50 See Jose Rizal, *On the Indolence of Filipinos* (Madrid: La Solidaridad, 1890); see also Emmanuel de Dios, "Indolence, Incentives, and Institutions," *The Philippine Review of Economics* 20, no. 2 (2011): 41–78.
51 For a discussion on rating systems in online labor platforms, see Graham et al., "Digital Labor and Development," 150.
52 Van Doorn, *Platform Labor*, 907–908.
53 For more on the idea of reputation and capital see Gandini, *The Reputation Economy*.
54 On the global and cosmopolite Manila middle class life in the late 1990s and early 2000s, see Neferti Xina Tadiar, *Fantasy-Production: Sexual Economies and Other Philippine Consequences for the New World Order* (Hong Kong: Hong Kong University Press, 2004).
55 Anne Kalleberg, "Nonstandard Employment Relations: Part-time, Temporary and Contract Work," *Annual Review Sociology* 26, no. 1 (2000): 341–365. doi:10.1146/annurev.soc.26.1.341.
56 Gregg, *Work's Intimacy*, 4.
57 Gregg, *Presence Bleed*, 10.
58 Ibid.
59 Gandini, *The Reputation Economy*; Van Doorn, *Platform Labor*, 900.
60 Jamie Peck. "Struggling with the Creative Class," *International Journal of Urban and Regional Research* 29, no. 24 (2005): 756.
61 Jack Qiu, *Working Class Network Society: Communication Technology and The Information Have-Less in Urban China* (Cambridge, MA: The MIT Press, 2009); Mark Graham, et al., "Digital Labor and Development".
62 Adam Fish and Ramesh Srinivasan. "Digital Labor is the New Killer App," *New Media and Society* 14, no. 1 (2011), 137–152; Gandini, *The Reputation Economy*; Irani, *The Cultural Work of Microwork*.

PART IV

Media, Class, and Expressions of Citizenship

20
CLASS DISTINCTIONS IN URBAN BROADBAND INITIATIVES

Germaine Halegoua

The public announcement posted on the "Google Fiber for Communities" (more commonly known as Google Fiber) events site invited Kansas City residents to "Enjoy a drink or two on us, plus appetizers and live music by the Zach & Michelle band, as we toast to gigabit speeds. Come early for a chance to pick up your very own yard sign." This was an invitation to recurring "happy hour" events open to the public since Kansas City neighborhoods began signing up for Google Fiber service in 2012. Residents could show up at the bar, event space, or golf club and enjoy free beer or wine as they perused Google Fiber products and were encouraged by perky millennials to sign up for one gigabit internet speeds. Although the event was free, someone at the door asked for an email and home address in order to verify whether or not your neighborhood qualified for Google Fiber service. The spaces were brimming with logos and branded paraphernalia such as Google Fiber water bottles, sunglasses, and yard signs as well as displays that offered speed tests of Google's service and compared the gigabit network with "basic Internet" connections. Expansive sign up stations and customer representatives in matching blue T-shirts that read "That's What Speed Do" fluttered between MacBook Air laptops and iPads in order to sign up interested customers. Google Fiber maintained its presence at other community events as well, hosting booths at block parties, marathons, holiday celebrations and special events hosted at the Fiber Space and Google Fiber retail outlets. These promotional events were intended to demo Google Fiber speeds and consumer products and give away free Google Fiber swag and snacks in order to encourage people to sign up for the service.

There were similarities in the branding of these events. Large blue signs with white custom sans-serif font announced the products displayed on sleek, high-definition, flat screen monitors. The primary colored Google Fiber rabbit made an appearance on brochures or the yard signs handed out at the door. And where space allowed, there was a replica of a living room that served as the focal point of the demo and display (see Figure 20.1).

The living room replica was not exclusive to happy hour events, but is a setting found in Google Fiber spaces and demonstrations across the country. The Kansas City living room resembles the one in Salt Lake City, Charlotte, or Nashville. The staged living room serves as a space for potential Google Fiber users to sit down, get comfortable, and test out gigabit technologies and services in a setting reminiscent of the places in which the services would be installed and used. The living room is an area set up to mimic a trendy, middle class or upper-middle class living space equipped with gigabit connection and "Fiber TV": Google's high-definition television, DVR, and streaming service. These spaces are outfitted in Scandinavian modern furniture (possibly from Ikea) oriented

Figure 20.1 The living room at a Google Fiber sales center in Lee's Summit, Missouri. Image by author.

toward a flat-screen TV atop a sleek console. The spacious, mock living room offers Fiber TV viewers one to two matching full-size couches or multiple classically modern womb or egg-shaped chairs, coffee or side tables, and at least one carefully arranged plant or centerpiece on each surface. There is no clutter in the room and no wear on the couches, throw pillows, or chairs. The aesthetic choices in interior design replicate the discriminating minimalism and modern yet functional decor on the pages of a CB2 catalog with splashes of Google's signature primary colors.

The room used in these displays and demos is significant because it is ubiquitous, but also because it has symbolic power. The visual and material cultures on display in our domestic spaces express and are shaped by our identities and preferences as well as access to and accumulation of capital. Sociologists have analyzed the choice of housing and design of domicile interiors as materializations of political economies as well as symbolic exercises in taste, desire, and distinction.[1] Living room furnishings and other home décor have been read and analyzed as signals of social status and social mobility in addition to indicators of income or wealth.[2] Aesthetic commodities manifest distinctions of class in the realm of leisure and the living room is a central location through which to understand class distinctions.[3] The living room is encoded with objects, decorations, and furnishings that imbue meaning and identity for the household and act as an interface between public and private worlds.[4]

Google's mock living rooms evoked taste cultures that reinforced ideas of the imagined Google Fiber user as middle to upper middle class. The organization of these living rooms with designated seating areas and entertainment systems were spaces where the consumer had time to dwell. The absence of a dining area or furnishing and appliances for other domestic activities implied that there were other rooms where eating and laundry and sleeping take place. These staged rooms were not spaces of the imminent future, but the dens of the already connected enjoying even faster connection on digital devices in the comfort of their homes. The modern minimalist, design-centered, barely lived-in room on display alongside Google Fiber products and services was just one of the many ways that Google Fiber for Communities symbolically hailed particular types of consumers and discursively constructed and codified hierarchical classes of urban broadband users.

Urban broadband initiatives, including Google Fiber, promise to improve services, connect communities, and enhance economic development and entrepreneurship in designated metropolitan areas. More often than not, these broadband plans aim to enable social mobility and ameliorate digital divides by offering more affordable, comprehensive, and high-speed internet connection for diverse populations—including those who have never had internet access at home. Based on ethnographic analysis of Kansas City's Google Fiber for Communities initiatives, this chapter investigates class-based encodings of internet access that are common among urban broadband projects within the United States. Although urban broadband initiatives that address digital divides attempt to lessen economic barriers to internet connection in terms of cost and affordability of access, representations of internet use and the spaces in which members of the public might use the internet emphasize class distinctions that value certain social and economic classes and taste cultures over others.

Drawing on cultural studies understandings of media and class I trace the making of a broadband upper class alongside the erasure of the experiences of a broadband underclass. In the Kansas City region, there is an overlap between the urban underclass and the "broadband underclass." I categorize the broadband underclass as a socioeconomic class of people who are non-adopters of the internet or who lack a consistent home broadband connection. The urban broadband underclass may not use the internet at all, but more likely, these populations access the internet on mobile devices or at locations other than their home. Therefore, their experience of using the internet is routine, but also subpar, circumscribed, and peripatetic.

Through an analysis of marketing materials and demos, meetings and interviews with broadband users and non-users, and the public and private spaces in which urban broadband projects are implemented, I highlight specific and repeated instances of class-based constructions of connectivity, mobility, and home and identify patterns of broadband adoption that are encouraged by these representations.[5]

Class and Classification

Social classes are structured by an unequal distribution or variations in access to economic, social, and cultural capital. These groups are composed of people who share similar positions and experiences within systems of economic and cultural production. Many scholars have understood and analyzed class by focusing on the power and processes of classification and the structures and the outcomes of these processes. Most notably, one of the outcomes of classification is inscribed divisions. As Raymond Williams notes, since the Industrial Revolution (if not before) "class" has been used as a term to delineate and distinguish groups of people based on access to resources, power, and authority in economic as well as social terms.[6]

Processes of classification encode private or personal practices and preferences with socioeconomic position.[7] Taste preferences and aesthetic dispositions, culture and cultural practices, knowledge and expertise are all "classified" and become indicators or signals of class status. Furthermore, these taste preferences and cultural practices that are shared among members of a social class are exhibited publicly in the form of aesthetic sensibilities or a "lifestyle." As other scholars have proposed, when a person talks about or marks their class, they are symbolically expressing their experiences of power and prestige both past and present.[8] Or, as Bourdieu explains in *Distinction* (1987), "Taste classifies, and it classifies the classifier."[9] For example, Bourdieu proposes that the working class "taste for necessity" or appreciation of "function over form" is exhibited in the objects, fashion, and art consumed by members of this class, which simultaneously signal or mark people as conforming members of a particular class (and the economic or cultural capital ascribed therein). Through everyday practices of consumption—eating, dressing, choice of housing or décor, practices of leisure or entertainment—a person is distinguished and distinguishable from members of other social classes.

Bourdieu's focus on class fosters awareness of the cultural processes that systematically marginalize, oppress, and codify social life. For example, symbolic power or symbolic violence work to delineate and codify boundaries between different classes and naturalize or internalize inequalities through social practices. According to E.P. Thompson, class "happens" through human relations over time and is a contested and relational concept defined in association and opposition to other social groups.[10] Class and processes of classifications are structured through conflict and hierarchies of dominance which are evident in the labels commonly applied to social classes: upper class, middle class, lower class with "ruling" or "dominant" classes at one end of the spectrum and "working" classes on the opposing end. Similar to the hierarchical status inscribed in the labels assigned to different social classes, "lifestyles" or taste cultures are also hierarchically ranked. While the definition of "legitimate culture" is perpetually contested, the hierarchical status of certain lifestyles is codified based on their proximity or distance from the legitimated culture of the moment.[11]

Privileged classes or upper classes possess accumulations of capital and knowledge that legitimate their social position within society, but also yield social power to discern and validate who and what counts as culturally legitimate. Populations considered working class, working poor, or poor, and those who Wilson describes as the "truly disadvantaged" are sometimes referred to as "the underclass".[12] The "underclass" or "urban underclass" have been classified by structures and experiences of inequality, social exclusion, economic insecurity and disadvantage due to discrimination, unemployment or underemployment, changing labor markets, environmental and economic or social welfare conditions. More generally, the underclass is defined as a class of people who are systematically excluded or have unequal access to institutional and cultural resources, and where populations' "constraints and opportunities" are shaped by these structures and experiences.[13]

In addition to commonly documented structures, policies, and social relations that shape the urban upper and underclasses, I argue that we should also recognize the discourses, materialities and implementation of urban broadband networks as structures that codify class relations. As digital divide and digital inclusion research has shown, many populations experience privilege or extreme marginalization from access to broadband infrastructures as well as the economic, social, and technological systems that support these services. The remainder of this chapter is an effort toward investigating the systems of opportunities and constraints that influence and/or curb access and adoption of broadband systems among social classes and may determine which types of broadband networks these classes adopt. In addition, this chapter illustrates the ways in which urban broadband networks are inflected with class encodings or markers of class and simultaneously interpellate and exclude certain populations from participating in broadband connectivity efforts.

Class and Urban Broadband Networks

Socioeconomic class influences access to the internet and the types of internet access available to certain populations. Studies have shown that low-income, marginalized, or socially excluded populations are more likely to be disconnected or disconnect from internet services.[14] The ability to afford or willingness to pay for broadband access has continually been cited as a major obstacle to broadband adoption and the persistence of digital divides. Along with education, race, age, and geographic location, cost is seen as a reason for both non-adoption as well as un-adoption of internet and/or broadband access. Non-adopters or internet "nevers" are typically defined as people who have never had at-home broadband or internet connection. These populations are generally characterized as low-income communities who might rely on public computer labs or public

Wi-Fi (libraries, computer centers, school or work, commercial spaces, etc.) or have mobile-only connections to the internet.[15] According to recent studies, mobile dependent or mobile-only internet users tend to be minorities and lower-income groups with lower education levels than other types of internet users.[16]

Although the number of households with broadband connection has exponentially increased since the early 2000s, Whitacre and Rhinesmith note that "un-adopters," or those who choose to discontinue at-home internet service, are likely to cite cost or unwillingness to pay as a reason they disconnect.[17] The high-cost of broadband subscriptions and installation fees, hardware and equipment, and income fluctuations have been noted to impede broadband adoption or continued use. However, cost or affordability is only one characteristic that may influence demand. Although robust infrastructure exists and households may be able to pay for broadband connection, there may still be a lack of demand or reluctance to sign up for broadband connection. In addition, there may be social stigmas or social expectations about certain types of internet access. For example, Dailey et al. note that although some of their low-income participants could afford dial-up connections they refused to sign up for this service because of the reputation of dial-up within their social networks.[18] Clayton and Macdonald have noted how socioeconomic status and occupation shape perceptions of what technologies mean and how they can be utilized to improve quality of life.[19] A 2010 Federal Communications Commission (FCC) study found that along with cost and relevance, digital literacy was also an intervening barrier to broadband adoption and use in the US. As these cases indicate, pre-existing social positions, contexts, and cultural knowledge not only shape decisions around internet adoption, they also shape perceptions of relevance and use.

One factor that has been emphasized in recent literature on digital inclusion is the perceived "relevance" or "usefulness" of internet access. Whitacre and Rhinesmith found that along with cost, "no need" was a major factor in broadband non-adoption and un-adoption. Relatedly, in a study for Pew Research Center, Horrigan found that 22 percent of non-internet users were "not interested in getting online" and categorized 50 percent of dial-up and non-internet users as questioning the "relevance" of at-home broadband internet connection.[20] A Google conducted survey with 3219 Kansas City residents found "lack of relevance" to be a key factor in whether households had internet access at home.[21] In 2012 when low-income neighborhoods didn't sign up for gigabit connection, a Google spokesperson stated that relevance was a major issue: "They don't think they need it. They don't see why."[22]

While "relevance" might be interpreted as not understanding the value in adopting internet and broadband services or a lack of information about how the internet is important in daily life, studies have shown the opposite. Dailey et al. found that low-income populations understand the potential value of adopting broadband services and see these services as required for socioeconomic inclusion.[23] Clearly stated in the report, "No one needed to be convinced of the importance of Internet use or the value of broadband adoption in the home."[24] As access to employment opportunities, government services, education, and communication exchanges move online, the "relevance" of the internet becomes increasingly obvious within social, economic, and political contexts. More recent studies of broadband non-adoption also imply that there may be other social or cultural factors that intervene in rationales and decision-making processes around broadband adoption, non-adoption, and discontinued use that are in need of further research and analysis.

In addition, the category of "non-use" or "non-adoption" is somewhat problematic when applied to lower-income populations and other socioeconomic groups. These categories often specify non-use of fixed, at-home broadband connection. Several participants in the aforementioned studies noted that they routinely used the internet and had access to broadband speeds through mobile devices (such as smartphones) or in places other than their homes (friend's house, community center, school or work, libraries, etc.). The category of "relevance" is also ambiguous. While Pew Research studies have defined relevance as being "too busy," "uninterested in getting online," and "nothing could get me to switch" to broadband, they also note "other unspecified reasons." When mapped onto Rogers' five stages of technology adoption these findings imply that while people are aware of the benefits of internet and broadband access, non-adopters are stalled at versions of the "interest" and "evaluation" phases.[25]

Class in Google Fiber

Google Fiber for Communities used a participatory model in order to identify neighborhoods and households that qualified for Google Fiber. During an early phase of the Google Fiber initiative in Kansas City, neighborhoods were asked to pre-register for services by paying a $10 sign-up fee. Neighborhoods that met prescribed thresholds for household registrations would qualify for Google Fiber installation and services. Areas with the most registrations would receive service first. Class divisions became apparent in the maps and patterns of Google Fiber pre-registered neighborhoods. The neighborhoods that qualified for Google Fiber service were composed of middle to upper middle class, majority white residents who already had an internet service provider and/or broadband internet access. The neighborhoods that didn't qualify for service through the pre-registration process were low-income with majority minority populations.[26]

After the initial round of installation and sign-ups, Google made concerted efforts to remove barriers for low-income communities and encourage more diverse populations to sign up. In addition to canvassing low-income neighborhoods and working with community organizers to spread information about low-cost pricing plans, alternatives to credit card payments, and services available, Google also subsidized connection for schools, community centers, and housing projects. As a result, researchers have found that the geographic availability of Google Fiber has since reached spatial equity.[27] Google Fiber infrastructure now permeates many of the neighborhoods that did not previously qualify for installation during the initial registration phase. In fact, Alizadeh et al. found that although there were no major statistical differences between infrastructure availability in renter versus owner-occupied residences they did find discrepancies in terms of demographics such as race, age, and income. In contrast to the initial pre-registration period, neighborhoods with Google Fiber currently available for purchase are younger, have larger minority populations and lower median incomes.[28]

It is important to note that these statistics refer to availability of infrastructure and *potential* service, not actual subscriptions or demographics of people who signed up for Google Fiber services. A 2014 survey found that while Google Fiber became widely available in previously excluded neighborhoods, only 10 percent of residents in the six low-income, majority African-American neighborhoods surveyed actually subscribed to one of the tiered options for Google Fiber services. An additional 5 percent signed up for a 5 mbps download/1 mbps upload option. This slower speed option was free for seven years after paying a $300 installation fee (an option that was discontinued in May 2016). This 15 percent of residents who subscribed to Google Fiber in low-income neighborhoods pales in comparison with the 53 percent subscription rate of the majority Caucasian, middle and higher income neighborhoods surveyed.[29]

While some Kansas City residents cited the high cost of connection as reasons that they didn't sign up for Google Fiber service, other people I spoke with recognized a range of other social and symbolic factors that signaled that the services weren't targeted at them. Starting in 2012, I began attending Google Fiber promotional events as well as digital inclusion events, meeting with digital inclusion activists, and observing computer training sessions in low-income neighborhoods. I collected video and print marketing and promotional materials and visited demo spaces, such as the Google Fiber Space in the Westport neighborhood of Kansas City, MO. I also attended sign-up and promotional events in Kansas City, KS and Kansas City, MO where representatives demonstrated Google Fiber products and encouraged residents to sign up for gigabit services. Through these materials and events, I observed repeated instances of class-based constructions of the type of internet connection that Google Fiber offered and heard residents speak about the ways in which these discursive constructions affected their interpretation of what services Google was offering and for whom. In particular, discussions and presentations of connectivity, mobility, and home signaled class hierarchies and marked Google services and imagined audiences as fitting within hierarchical strata.

Connectivity

A 2012 introductory spot for Google Fiber showed a series of toy cars, a metaphor for data packets, moving slowly through miniature city streets in the towns of "Dial-Up" and "Broadband." The flow of traffic was restricted by speed limit signs (56K, 10 mbps), halted by railroad crossing barriers that read "Song Downloading," stopped at traffic lights and blockades that resembled buffering or modem connection icons. An instrumental version of The Cars song "Just What I Needed" played in the background. Finally, the toy cars approach a sign that reads "Welcome to Google Fiber" where the speed limit is 1000 mbps and cars speed through gravity-defying highway loops as the song crescendos and the tempo picks up. The ad ends with the promise of a new chapter of internet connection, 100 times faster than current speeds, and with "100 times the possibilities."

Google Fiber advertisements, promotional materials, and pitches to potential customers emphasized gigabit connection speeds as the selling point of the network. The logo for Google Fiber, a primary colored rabbit, implied velocity. In print materials comparing Google Fiber to cable, "Speed" was the heading listed before "Pricing" or "Availability." Speed tests and demonstrations were common practices at Google Fiber sign-up events and when I asked representatives why I should sign up for Google Fiber, they presented a rehearsed pitch about how the speed of the connection would improve the way I worked and accessed entertainment services. They sometimes asked me what I did online and then emphasized download and upload speeds, how frustrating it is to wait for access to content, and how buffering while streaming was simply an unnecessary waste of my time. Promotional materials and representatives at sign-up events explained how email attachments could be uploaded and downloaded in a fraction of a second, large files accessed and exchanged in a blink, video and audio content and gaming experiences streamed without interruption, and feature length films downloaded to devices in seconds.

This carefully constructed message focused on speed and making what someone already does online more efficient and less frustrating, which implies that Google Fiber was geared toward long-time internet users—those who moved from dial-up to broadband and were now ready for the "next chapter." Or, in particular, users who already enjoyed some level of at-home broadband internet connection. In addition to high-speed connection, Google representatives also pointed out that my subscription would come with one terabyte of cloud storage and HDTV service. Representatives at sign-up events told me that their pitches changed when they entered lower-income communities. They de-emphasized speed and focused more on the value of having a stable internet connection at home. While having a consistent, affordable internet connection at home echoed at least one of the pricing plans offered by Google Fiber, this tactic was a deviation from the central promotional message of faster speeds improving quality of entertainment and work life.

One striking feature of Google Fiber's service was that it was a fixed gigabit service to the home. This feature was commonly mentioned in discussions with low-income residents who did not sign-up for service as well as Kansas-based digital inclusion activists. The fixity of the service was seen as a limitation and something that signaled to lower-income populations that Google Fiber was not targeted toward them and their communities. Mainly due to the fact that a fixed, high-speed service exclusively connected to the home was read as "irrelevant" to particular classes and communities of internet users.

Mobility

Many people who have been categorized as "non-users" or "non-adopters" in studies of internet adoption tend to access the internet from a mobile device or from a location other than their place of residence. Google Fiber services offered customers fixed gigabit services to their homes. In advertisements and demonstrations, Google Fiber services were used to power home theaters or stationary entertainment systems at the center of a suburban or spacious living room. The gigabit connection was restricted to the space of the domicile (and as many posts to online forums indicate, the service doesn't always work well within the home). Any tablet or laptops on display might be used in other parts of the house or individual apartment where Google Fiber was installed. This implied that Google Fiber users lived in multi-bedroom residences, had more than one device that needed to be connected to the internet, or more than one internet user within the household.

These images work against the needs and experiences of many low-income internet users and contradict some of their pre-existing relationships to urban place. Google Fiber focused their implementation model on a high-speed connection anchored to a physical space called home. However, for many urban residents it is not uncommon for their residence to change yearly or several times throughout the year. I spoke with several renters who said that it would be a foolish investment to pay for a service that could not move with them when their lease expired. Other potential customers noted that the $300 installation fee and extremely delayed installation appointments signaled that this service was for someone who was making a long-term investment in a particular location and was prepared to stay in their home for years after registration. In addition, images or mention of apartment buildings in Google's promotional materials and implementation plans were initially absent. This absence indicated that Google did not consider diverse experiences and connections to "home" within urban spaces.

Some of the lower income parents I spoke with mentioned that they relocated their families more than once throughout a given school year. These parents confidently stated that their children would benefit from having access to a stable internet connection for schoolwork and educational purposes. However, their children did not always complete their homework at home. Participants that maintained a mobile sense of home noted that they relied on smartphones, Wi-Fi hotspots outside of the home, and institutionalized broadband connections in order to use the internet. Parents' work schedules often meant that students would stay with a variety of friends or family members after school, or attend after-school programs at community centers, libraries, churches, or meet up with other students at the neighborhood McDonald's. A stationary, high-speed internet connection became irrelevant for parents who cared for children who completed their homework at several different venues during the week. The parents and teachers I spoke with readily recognized that a more mobile and affordable internet connection overlapped with the daily travel patterns of many public school students and the adults who cared for them. In Google's broadband plans and service options, high-speed networks were linked to private domestic space rather than public spaces or circulating bodies.

Home

People of color and low-income Americans have historically had a difficult, costly, and precarious relationship with homeownership due to social and economic discrimination. There has been a housing wealth gap in the United States for decades, with African-Americans and Hispanics having lower homeownership rates than Whites, partially due to a series of discriminatory lending policies and housing markets.[30] As a result, members of the American working class and underclass and people of color are far more likely to rent than to own a home.

These demographics apply to the Kansas City region as well. As reported by the Mid-America Regional Council (MARC) in 2016, people of color and single parent households are more likely to rent housing units rather than own a home.[31] In addition, MARC found that high housing cost burden—paying more than 30 percent of income on housing—was nearly twice as frequent among renters than homeowners, indicating that people of color are also more likely to face high housing cost burdens. The percentages of people of color and single parent households that rent an apartment or home in Kansas City, MO are significantly higher than in the region as a whole. In addition, residential loan denial rates were significantly higher (approximately double) for African-Americans, Hispanics, and Native Americans in Kansas City in 2010 as compared with Whites.[32]

Aside from a primary-colored rabbit, a series of houses that were linked via brightly colored underground cables was often used to advertise Google's gigabit network. These houses were nearly identical in size and shape and resembled the single-family homes and landscaping found in the middle class or affluent areas of Kansas City, KS and Kansas City, MO. This iconography presented particular ideologies of home and household. The images evoked private, single-family homes that were presumably owned not rented, in a moderately dense neighborhood surrounded by picket fences and individual internet connections. These simple signs conjured an image of the types of users who were signing up for the service and characteristics and style of the places where they reside. While household and home were equated in Google's campaign, Kansas City residents who resided in the inner city, particularly residents who had never been connected to the internet, understood that an investment in your household did not necessarily mean an investment in the physical space called home.

Images of home and household as self-contained and self-sufficient units evoked a sense of individualism that was evident in Google's implementation and service plan as well. According to Google Fiber policies, registrants were allowed only one connection per household. Communal or shared living conditions such as apartment buildings, the landlords who owned them, and the management companies became cumbersome within Google's implementation model and excluded residents who might have wanted to sign up. According to Google's original implementation plan, the landlord of an apartment building would have to take the initiative to pre-register for Google Fiber service and would be required to pay the registration and flat rate service fee ($300) for each apartment unit. Michael Liimatta the co-founder of the Kansas City nonprofit Connecting for Good from 2011–2016, emphasized that the dependence of a large portion of poor and working class households on landlord-owned housing meant that "literally tens of thousands of families who may have wanted to subscribe were never given the chance."[33]

Creating Class Distinctions in Urban Broadband Projects

Napoli and Obar note that the differences and inadequacies between mobile-only internet use and fixed broadband create a "mobile Internet underclass."[34] By categorizing mobile-only internet users as an "underclass," Napoli and Obar recognize disparities in access to web content, cultural and economic resources based on the device and platforms used to access the internet. The reality that certain populations are systematically excluded from or unable to utilize the institutional and cultural resources provided by at-home broadband services, and where "constraints and opportunities" are shaped by this unequal access applies beyond the use of particular platforms or devices.

Scholars have expanded Bourdieu's notion of distinction to extend to knowledge, access, and use of technology including distinctions based on "technological capital" and digital literacy, the types of technologies or speed of internet connections utilized, and the ways in which digital technologies are incorporated into everyday social relations.[35] More recent studies of non-use and discontinued use have recognized that personal and cultural attitudes and perceptions of technologies influence technology adoption. Biases within social networks, past experiences, or norms about appropriate technology use might influence what types of internet access or internet service provision are adopted within social classes. In Clayton and Macdonald's (2013) study of internet adoption patterns among marginalized social groups, they find that populations struggle to integrate what is understood to be "appropriate use" of technology into their everyday lives, especially when these populations don't dictate what counts as appropriate or "useful."[36] The authors conclude that the boundaries between higher and lower classes and perceptions of technologies reiterated within these classes, impact lower class ability to use digital technologies as a means of social mobility. In some cases, use of digital technologies by members of the urban underclass has been shown to reinforce previous social positions and social networks.

The visual, aesthetic, and rhetorical signs described in previous sections of this chapter, inscribe the idea that certain populations are underprivileged or part of a broadband underclass by linking high-speed, new, and improved internet connection with upper class objects, activities, and lifestyles, while excluding other relationships and experiences of internet access. Google's outreach campaigns and pitches to low-income neighborhoods highlighted the fact that the urban underclass did not sign up for service and suggested that it was because they were information poor in terms of importance or relevance of Google Fiber connection. As Hersberger observed in regard to homeless populations, it is not having access to information about services and resources that is the issue but acting on the information obtained because it does not coincide with one's social context.[37] An analysis of Google Fiber is one example where the inability to act on the services being offered not only because of cost, but because of a disjuncture between pre-existing relationships to home, connection, and mobility, contributed to the making of a broadband underclass.

Differential access to resources, authority to express alternative desires and appropriate forms of broadband use, and pre-existing social inequities codified boundaries of taste and distinction and marginalized populations that didn't fit the at-home gigabit service mold. Internet service provision pricing plans tend to map class structures onto internet access and Google Fiber was no different, offering Gigabit Internet + TV ($130/month), Gigabit Internet ($70/month), and Basic Internet ($0/month + $300 construction fee for less than gigabit service). Within this hierarchy, users who relied on mobile-only, public computing centers, school or work, commercial spaces or other workarounds for internet access or broadband speeds occupied the lowest status of internet user. So much so, that alternate or emerging understanding of home, connectivity, and mobility that overlap with experiences of the urban underclasses were not designed or imagined within the Google Fiber universe. As the pricing plans indicate, cost and not differential experiences of mobility or homeownership were considered as barriers that could be overcome through Google's adjustments.

Kansas City residents were being class-ified based on the places and types of access to broadband they utilized, and these classifications were encoded and reiterated in campaigns to "reach" universal audiences and bridge digital divides. Through the services offered, pricing plans, rhetorical and discursive constructions of lifestyle and fixed gigabit connection, Google Fiber's campaign made class divisions more apparent by hailing populations based on the relevance of certain types of internet connection and relationships to home. The ability to acquire and to use fixed broadband service at home became a signal of class status and was supported by the images of home and community in the Google campaigns, demo spaces, sign-up events and sign-up pitches.

There is a contradiction between the idea that Google Fiber is for "everyone" or for all of Kansas City and the representations of home, connectivity, and mobility being used to sell the gigabit network. Google's urban broadband initiatives coincide with the perspective promoted in broadband adoption reports and measurements that privilege at home access to high-speed internet as a form of social and economic mobility. While at home broadband access is one way to address digital divides and may lead to social mobility and increased digital literacy, fixed broadband initiatives may simultaneously classify groups of people as fixed within class-based structures. Through efforts to make at-home high-speed connection more accessible, these initiatives exposed the ways in which social and economic contexts of the broadband underclass may make technological capital and access to gigabit service at home difficult or untenable.

Conclusion

Cultural processes are central to classification and the creation of class-based distinctions. Through the aesthetics and promotional materials utilized in Google Fiber campaigns, Google created and reinforced a class-based system for broadband use. The social contexts and practices around internet use among marginalized socioeconomic populations contrasted with the images and assumptions about internet use in Google Fiber campaigns. Google Fiber entered a marketplace and environment where low-income populations had limited choices for stable and affordable broadband connections. Through the company's sales pitches, advertising materials, and discursive construction of gigabit networks they erased the experiences of a broadband underclass by constructing high-speed broadband access as simultaneously accessible, but also as a mark of privilege.

The way that Google Fiber conceptualized gigabit connection in its initial service offerings and advertising campaigns represented ideologies and aesthetics that distinguished different classes of internet users and constructed some users and uses as "appropriate" over others. Google Fiber for Communities reduced appropriate internet connection to a particular type of connection (high-speed, at-home broadband) and initially essentialized some of the reasons for lack of internet connection at home (cost and information poverty). Google Fiber promotional campaigns and services privileged at-home internet access as the *only* type of meaningful internet access for urban populations. And if populations can't acquire or act on this type of connection, then they are truly disadvantaged or increasingly disengaged from technological progress and upward mobility.

The type and speed of internet access enjoyed by a particular socioeconomic group does not just indicate distinction or social position but is linked to other social contexts experienced by that group. Although urban broadband initiatives often work toward digital inclusion by offering low-cost pricing options, there needs to be an enriched understanding of cultures of poverty and how experiences of the urban underclasses intersect with digital media access, experience, and use. Experiences of mobility, home, and connectivity are not only connected to cultures and poverty but to digital media as well. In order to construct more equitable methods for designing and advertising urban broadband networks, companies need to recognize intersectional experiences of place, poverty, and digital media. This case study highlights some of the ways that social and material experiences of class (beyond cost) intersect with broadband adoption or the adoption of certain types of broadband services over others.

From the perspective of place and space, digital inclusion is not just about being and feeling included in the segment of the population that is connected to the internet but being and feeling included in the places and spaces where digital technologies and internet connection are being used, taught, and talked about. Where conversations and decisions about digital infrastructure and what they mean for communities are being discussed. As this chapter has demonstrated, urban broadband network campaigns and services construct and reify distinctions between urban broadband underclasses and more privileged classes of internet users. Further research into urban broadband networks could continue to investigate how other intersectional distinctions and differential mobilities are assumed and designed into advertising campaigns, service plans, and policies of network implementation. Researchers should continue to look at the ways that emerging, high-speed services are contextualized and how they differ from urban underclass experiences of place and technology in significant ways that might create obstacles to adopting broadband access at home or at all.

Notes

1 Jane M. Jacobs and Susan J. Smith, "Living Room: Rematerialising Home," *Environment and Planning A* 40, no. 3 (March 2008): 515–519.
2 Enrica Amaturo, Simonetta Costagliola, and Gerardo Ragone, "Furnishing and Status Attributes: A Sociological Study of the Living Room," *Environment and Behavior* 19, no. 2 (March 1987): 228–249.

3. Jon Cook, "Culture, Class and Taste," in *Cultural Studies and the Working Class*, ed. Sally R. Munt (London: Cassell, 2000), 97–112.
4. Annemarie Money, "Material Culture and the Living Room: The Appropriation and Use of Goods in Everyday Life," *Journal of Consumer Culture* 7, no. 3 (2007): 355–377.
5. For further analysis of experiences of speed, mobility, and home in Kansas City's Google Fiber initiatives see Germaine R. Halegoua, *The Digital City: Media and the Social Production of Place* (New York: NYU Press, 2019).
6. Raymond Williams, *Keywords: A Vocabulary of Culture and Society* (Oxford, UK: Oxford University Press, 1976).
7. Mike Savage, "Culture, Class and Classification," in *The SAGE Handbook of Cultural Analysis* (London: SAGE Publications Ltd, 2008), 481.
8. Martin Bulmer, ed., *Working-Class Images of Society* (Routledge, 2016).
9. Pierre Bourdieu, *Distinction: A Social Critique of the Judgement of Taste* (Cambridge, MA: Harvard University Press, 1987), 6.
10. E.P. Thompson, *The Making of the English Working Class* (New York: Vintage Books, 1966).
11. Elliot B. Weininger, "Foundations of Pierre Bourdieu's Class Analysis," in *Approaches to Class Analysis*, ed. Erik Olin Wright (Cambridge, UK: Cambridge University Press, 2005), 82–118.
12. William Julius Wilson, *The Truly Disadvantaged: The Inner City, the Underclass, and Public Policy* (Chicago: University of Chicago Press, 1987).
13. Wilson.
14. John Clayton and Stephen J. Macdonald, "The Limits of Technology," *Information, Communication & Society* 16, no. 6 (2013).
15. A. Smith, "Record Shares of Americans Now Own Smartphones, Have Home Broadband," Pew Research, 2017, www.pewresearch.org/fact-tank/2017/01/12/evolution-of-technology/.
16. Eric Tsetsi and Stephen A. Rains, "Smartphone Internet Access and Use: Extending the Digital Divide and Usage Gap," *Mobile Media & Communication* 5, no. 3 (September 1, 2017): 239–255.
17. Brian Whitacre and Colin Rhinesmith, "Broadband Un-Adopters," *Telecommunications Policy* 40, no. 1 (February 2016): 1–13.
18. Dharma Dailey et al., "Broadband Adoption in Low-Income Communities" (Social Science Research Council, 2010), www.ssrc.org/publications/view/1EB76F62-C720-DF11-9D32-001CC477EC70/.
19. Clayton and Macdonald, "The Limits of Technology."
20. John B. Horrigan, "Home Broadband Adoption 2009," *Pew Research Center: Internet, Science & Tech* (blog), June 17, 2009. www.pewinternet.org/2009/06/17/home-broadband-adoption-2009/.
21. Google and Mayor's Bi-State Innovation Team. "The State of Internet Connectivity in KC: Neighborhood-Based Research Findings," 2012. www.growyourgiving.org/sites/default/files/State%20of%20Internet%20Connectivity%20in%20KC%20Preso%20PDF.pdf
22. Marcus Wohlsen, "Google Fiber Splits Along Kansas City's Digital Divide," WIRED, September 7, 2012. www.wired.com/2012/09/google-fiber-digital-divide/.
23. Dailey et al., "Broadband Adoption in Low-Income Communities."
24. Dailey et al., "Broadband Adoption," 15.
25. E.M. Rogers, *Diffusion of Innovations*, 5th edn (New York: Free Press, 2003).
26. Germaine Halegoua, "Calling All 'Fiberhoods': Google Fiber and the Politics of Visibility," *International Journal of Cultural Studies* 18, no. 3 (2014): 311–316.
27. Tooran Alizadeh, Tony H. Grubesic, and Edward Helderop, "Urban Governance and Big Corporations in the Digital Economy: An Investigation of Socio-Spatial Implications of Google Fiber in Kansas City," *Telematics and Informatics* 34, no. 7 (November 2017): 973–986.
28. Alizadeh, Grubesic, and Helderop.
29. Alistair Barr, "Google Fiber Leaves a Digital Divide; Survey Finds Few Low-Income Residents in Kansas City Subscribe to Superfast Service," *Wall Street Journal* (Online); New York, October 2, 2014, sec. Tech.
30. Mechele Dickerson, *Homeownership and America's Financial Underclass: Flawed Premises, Broken Promises, New Prescriptions* (Cambridge, UK: Cambridge University Press, 2014), 14.
31. Mid-America Regional Council, "Plan for Affirmatively Furthering Fair Housing" (Kansas City, MO: Mid-America Regional Council, October 2016). www.marc.org/Regional-Planning/Housing/Related-Projects/Affirmatively-Furthering-Fair-Housing-Assessment.
32. Mid-America Regional Council.
33. Nancy Scola, "In Kansas City, Few Poor People, Renters Sign up for Google Fiber," *Washington Post*, October 6, 2014. www.washingtonpost.com/news/the-switch/wp/2014/10/06/in-kansas-city-few-poor-people-renters-sign-up-for-google-fiber/.
34. Philip M. Napoli and Jonathan A. Obar, "The Emerging Mobile Internet Underclass: A Critique of Mobile Internet Access," *The Information Society* 30, no. 5 (October 20, 2014): 323–334.

35 Amy Gonzales, "The Contemporary US Digital Divide: From Initial Access to Technology Maintenance," *Information, Communication & Society* 19, no. 2 (2016): 234–248.
36 Clayton and Macdonald, "The Limits of Technology," 949.
37 J. Hersberger, "Are the Economically Poor Information Poor? Does the Digital Divide Affect the Homeless and Access to Information?" *Canadian Journal of Information & Library Sciences* 27, no. 3 (September 2002): 45–63.

21
"SECOND-CLASS" ACCESS
Homelessness and the Digital Materialization of Class

Justine Humphry

Mobile communication has been described as "second-class" access, a term penned by Susan Crawford in a 2011 *New York Times* editorial[1] to designate new patterns of digital exclusion resulting from low or no internet connectivity in poor US neighborhoods. The concept was taken up and developed by Mossberger, Tolbert, and Franko who argued that quality of digital access matters and that having to rely solely on a mobile phone to carry out all online activities is not sufficient to enable full citizenship.[2] Mounting evidence suggests that, for many, the mobile phone is the only form of access. Based on its 2018 survey, the Pew Internet Research Center found that one in five Americans accessed the internet only through their smartphones, predominantly young people, people racialized as non-white and lower-income groups.[3] In Australia, around four million people, or 16 percent of the population, rely exclusively on mobile access to the internet, and these map onto the most disadvantaged groups.[4]

The concept of "second class" access therefore designates ongoing disparities in digital access, countering claims of the disappearance of the "digital divide" as a result of more affordable mobile internet. A key idea here is not only do interrelated inequalities of class, race and geography constrain the nature and extent of people's digital access and engagement, but the mobile phone itself is a poorer quality and lower standard of access. It is this dual-meaning of mobile communication as classed that I address in this chapter. Building on research on digital inequalities and taking cues from a digital materialist approach, I argue for an understanding of class as digitally materialized in mobile handsets, plans and services. Class, as a system of social stratification, is embedded in these media assemblages, resulting in the delivery of more expensive, precarious and substandard digital access to low and no income media consumers, whose communication experiences and prospects are shaped by existing social inequalities. This analysis, which pays close attention to the materialities of people's digital lives, draws on research carried out on the access and use of mobile media by Australian families, adults and young people experiencing homelessness from 2014 to 2016. For those in my study, "second class" access meant having access to cheaper, older and under-powered mobile handsets, more expensive mobile voice and data plans, and confusing and exploitative retail practices; all of which were compounded by insecure and unsafe conditions of use.

The "Digital Material" Turn

We have moved from an era marked by the immateriality of the internet as "cyberspace" to one in which the materiality of digital media is a growing focus of scholarly research. When William

Gibson's sci-fi novel *Neuromancer* was published in 1984, his vision of a global networked dataspace, described in terms of "bright lattices of logic" and a "consensual hallucination," set the stage for imagining the internet as immaterial and placeless, a non-space for the disembodied mind. Progressively, there has been a full about-turn on the internet's immateriality. Feminist and critical race scholars were among the first to recognize the material basis of our online interactions and identities, pointing to their situated and embodied nature grounded in everyday lives and cultures.[5] Various research strands have consolidated this reorientation around the materiality of digital media, including Kittler's "media materialism," Manovich's "new media language," Fuller's "media ecologies," Kirschenbaum's "forensic traces," and Parikka's "media archaeology."[6]

The Marxist Critical Media School has made a major contribution to this digital material turn, exposing the hidden forms of digital labor in the use of social media and in the production of digital devices that reproduce exploitative capitalist structures and ideologies.[7] In this literature, class surfaces as a key concept to show how ordinary media users are part of a worldwide internet proletariat. As argued by Fuchs and Dyer-Witherford, corporate platform owners who dominate the Web 2.0 landscape exploit the activities and content that users generate; these are sold as commodities to advertisers, thereby creating the surplus value upon which the capital of social media firms and internet giants such as Google and Amazon is based.[8]

This Marxist class-analysis has been helpful for identifying and articulating many of the new forms and dilemmas of digital labor; from the extraction of rare minerals by exploited workers in the global south to the manufacturing of smartphones in Chinese factories, from the contradictions of programmers' giving their "free labor"[9] to ordinary users staging their identities and daily communication rituals online. In these accounts, class is recognized as central to this new system of capital with its environmentally degrading and exploitative ideologies, while simultaneously key to its challenge through internet-supported class struggles and collective platform ownership in the form of digital commons.

Nevertheless, for this welcome focus on class, little of this literature addresses the way that class differentially structures digital media access, ownership and use—and how this has very material impacts that reinforce class structures and positioning. While a Marxian class-based analysis provides the basis for a material account of a society transitioning to a new capitalist form, and the digital make up of this form, it says very little about the implications of an already classed society on the communication experiences and inequalities of digital media users with the least capital at hand. To understand this, we must initially, at any rate, turn to the well-established and fast-evolving literature on media, class and the "digital divide."

Media, Class, and the "Digital Divide"

One of the tenets of research on class in media, including that of the "digital divide," is that class is a system of social stratification[10] that is, to varying extents, an external force acting on, in and through media use. Class has been a concern of media scholars for many decades. Audience reception studies applies and extends many of the concepts and insights of media researchers at the famous "Birmingham School" in the 1970s who studied the relationship between the production of media texts and meanings with social categories of class, gender, and race.[11] In this tradition, class is a structural constraint that cannot be "magically resolved," nevertheless individuals and groups produce their own meanings and styles with the media they consume—classically illustrated in the "spectacular" working-class British youth subcultures of the mods and punks in the 1970s and 1980s.[12]

After three decades of research on the "digital divide", there is plentiful evidence that class continues to structure people's digital media access and use, and conversely that digital inequality exacerbates pre-existing social disadvantage.[13] Reviewing the state of the "digital divide" in the United States in 2015, the Pew Research Center found that nearly half of Americans who earn less than $30,000 have neither high-speed internet access nor a desktop computer at home and are much less likely to have multiple devices to go online.[14] Furthermore, digital disparities can be read as contiguous with historically hegemonic forms of geo-spatial social stratification along lines of gender and race. Hong has documented how places in which poor and working-class Chinese Americans have traditionally lived—such as San Francisco's Chinatown—which have historically been used to racially segregate populations, suffer from poor quality and slow internet connectivity. She builds a convincing case that unequal digital access is a product of "enduring legacies of place-based racial formation" and one of the key ways that social inequalities based on race are perpetuated.[15]

What we can learn from these distinct and empirically rich traditions of studying media and digital technology is that people's digital media experiences are highly differentiated by the impact of social inequalities associated with formations of class, gender and race. A broader research program on digital inequalities that has grown out of research on the "digital divide" recognizes the need to tackle these social inequalities to achieve digital inclusion across the multiple dimensions of access, usage and skill.[16] Nevertheless, without close attention to the materiality of digital media, we lose sight of how these social inequalities are materially inscribed into the mediums and services themselves. A digital material perspective foregrounds the agency and effects of media and their constituent elements.[17] In order to show how class is a system that is both internal to media and an external structuring force, I now turn to exploring the way that class is materialized in mobile phone handsets, plans and services, and the implications for those who have little choice but to use this "second-class" form of access. While the mobile phone may be broadly conceptualized as a media assemblage encompassing "objects, practices, symbolic representations, experiences and affects,"[18] I maintain a narrower focus to highlight specific examples and concerns with regards to one subset of disadvantaged media users. In my research on people who are homeless, class and digital media play out in a number of distinctive ways: homelessness itself is a product of class constructs; the media used by people who are homeless embed and reflect these class constructs, and their prospects and opportunities for moving on from homelessness are structured by how and if, media are used.

Homelessness and the Digital Materialization of Class

Homelessness is a growing front of digital inequality that, up until recently, has largely been subsumed within research on other minority groups such as young people, migrants and refugees, indigenous communities, people living with disabilities, seniors and people on low incomes.[19] Definitions of homelessness vary, in part because it is a global phenomenon with divergent national characteristics, and in part because it covers much more than a lack of physical housing. Homelessness is also a lack of a sense of security, stability, privacy, safety, and the ability to control living space—what most people would think of as the core aspects of "home."[20] Importantly, a lack of income is not always the cause of homelessness but there are strong correlations with poverty and other class-related factors, such as poor health and fewer opportunities for education and employment.[21]

As argued by Somerville, homelessness is shaped by class relations because it is itself a condition produced by a social and political system that privileges home ownership, supports evictions and makes housing unaffordable.[22] Class can also determine the opportunities for getting help and finding a pathway out of homelessness. As Hodgetts and his colleagues found in their class analysis of homelessness in New Zealand, people from middle class backgrounds who become homeless after an adverse event or set of experiences are better catered for by homelessness and welfare services than people who drift into homelessness after a lifetime of poverty and disadvantage.[23]

In 2014, I carried out a survey with 95 adults and young people recruited from specialist homelessness services and charities in Sydney and Melbourne. All were homeless or at imminent risk of homelessness, either sleeping rough on the streets or living in temporary, transitional, emergency or supported accommodation. A small number were renting privately. Twenty of these participants took part in a follow up interview carried out in person.[24] Over 2015 and 2016, I carried out another related project, working with eight young people who had recently been homeless and about two dozen representatives from local councils, libraries, charities, telecommunication firms and youth services, to develop digital access solutions using participatory design methods. The design workshops involved story sessions to build understanding of each other's homeless experiences; these formed the basis of problem scenarios for innovating technologies and other access solutions.[25] In both these studies, the vast majority of participants were on government income benefits, in part-time, low-paid employment or without employment. Of those surveyed, 41 percent were from culturally and linguistically diverse backgrounds. More than half (60 percent) were under 25, reflecting the higher proportion of young people in the overall homeless population, although trends indicate this is changing as more people are experiencing difficulties maintaining housing as they age.[26]

One of the most striking features of those homeless participants surveyed in the study was the high level of mobile phone ownership: 95 percent reported that they owned a mobile phone and 77 percent of these were smartphones. Similar statistics in the United States and other countries have been used as support for the delivery of technology-based health and support interventions to the homeless.[27] Nevertheless, it would be a misapprehension to conclude that mobiles are meeting the digital access needs of this population. My account of the lived materialities of those who are homeless highlights ongoing digital barriers, not easily captured in statistics. When it is the only means of phone and internet connection, the mobile phone represents a severely limited form of communication, as well as being a more costly and contingent option.

Cheaper, Older, Under-powered

Despite the high rate of mobile ownership, mobile handsets in the possession of people who are homeless are on the whole cheaper, older (second or third generation handsets), with fewer features, and in poorer condition. Of the almost 100 participants who were surveyed about their mobile phones, 23 percent had basic or feature phones with very limited or no internet access even though a large proportion had smartphones. I also found a large variation in the age and functionality of mobile phones, spanning a number of generations of handset models. The majority of handsets (57 percent) were acquired second-hand from mobile dealers or online ecommerce platforms such as eBay and Gumtree, or were given as gifts by family, friends, a support service or other source.

A lack of internet functionality on mobile handsets corresponded to lower rates of internet use and digital engagement. Those with smartphones used the internet to stay in touch with friends and family, to seek employment, access health services, find accommodation, access social media, create content, and gain new skills.[28] In contrast, basic and featured phones were used for texting and calling, and of the five participants who reported that they did not use the internet, three had basic phones and two were without mobiles altogether. To access the internet, non-smartphone users relied on other internet sources at public libraries, government foyers and community centers or by using a personal computer belonging to a friend or family member.[29]

The reliance on cheaper, older, and under-powered mobiles for accessing the internet meant that digital engagement was restricted to sites and services that supported older features and/or operating systems and slower access speeds. Many of the study participants spoke of their frustrations with their handsets, not being able to see or read material online or snap and upload photos to social media sites. Some of the limitations had been self-imposed by turning off apps and high data use services that operated in the background to strategically manage data use and keep the cost of their mobile service down.

These limitations are not trivial, especially for homeless young people. Studies have repeatedly shown that the preferred social platforms of Facebook, Snapchat and Instagram are much the same for socially marginalized young people as for their non-disadvantaged peers.[30] Far from a case of "selfie" narcissism, these visually oriented apps involve young users in different ways to other more text-based platforms, forming the literal grounds of social membership and a sense of belonging. One young woman spoke of the strengthened self-confidence she had gained from posting photographs of meals she had prepared to her growing Facebook audience, illustrative of the global movement of self-styled young female bloggers and microcelebrities:[31]

> I take photos depending on what I make in the restaurant and here when I get creative. I make butter chicken and I design it, like fancy and plate it up and then I might post it on Facebook or show me friends or send it to them. It makes me feel proud.

Moreover, the free messaging built into these platforms is an important substitute for more expensive communication options such as voice calls on mobile plans. Many of the participants reported that they kept in touch with their family via Facebook Instant Messenger. Yet, full access and engagement to these social media platforms also requires higher quality and consistent internet connectivity—and fully featured phones with cameras—neither of which are readily available to homeless young people as a result of the high cost of data, interrupted connectivity and broken, faulty and cheaper handsets with less functionality and smaller screens.

Another implication of only having access to small screens, more likely to be a limitation of older mobile handsets, is the difficulty accessing, viewing and reading information designed for media devices with larger format screens. For the participants in my research, this created new barriers for participating in education and employment activities. Several of these participants were in the process of studying at the time of the research and explained how they used their phones for enrolling in courses, accessing course content, communicating with tutors and completing assessments and other study tasks. One young man with a mild intellectual disability accessed how-to videos on YouTube while on the job for his apprenticeship as a mechanic: "I look up stuff on YouTube about how to fix things and so it will show me the video, I'll do it. I'll pause it, I'll do it and then wait for the next step and then do that." In this instance, the video sharing platform performed an important supplement to his formal training.

So, on the one hand, mobile phones have proved to be essential for enabling access to education opportunities. On the other hand, the small screen, non-mobile friendly sites, higher cost of mobile data and slow internet speeds set strict limits and disadvantage students with no other regular form of access, who must make do with a platform that is insufficient for the full range of tasks that study involves. This is compounded by the lack of access to safe and comfortable learning spaces and explains why public libraries are so important to people without secure housing. Not unlike the "homework gap" found between children of families who have high-speed internet at home and those who don't,[32] people experiencing homelessness have an "education gap" produced by the limits of mobile only learning.

While it is accurate to say that many of the limitations that people faced in my studies were an outcome of their homeless circumstances, which produces conditions of heightened mobility, insecurity and poverty, this does not provide a full account of these barriers of digital access and engagement. Options for access are also structured by the segmentation of the mobile phone market, differentiated according to a wide range of psychographic and demographic variables, including income, age, gender, education, and ability.[33] One negative outcome of strategies of market segmentation is that consumers with less purchasing power are precluded from features and services that might otherwise be available to them. To illustrate this gap: at the time of writing this chapter, a new Apple iPhone X with a 5.8 inch screen, a 12 megapixel wide-angle and telephoto camera, face ID, Bionic chip and wireless charging, was costed at AUD1579.[34] For a young person on a government youth allowance this represents almost two months of their maximum monthly income, a vastly out-of-reach sum for those for whom a AUD15 spend on data and voice services is a burden.

The structuring of the mobile market around the production of newer more expensive models, and the ensuing "upgrade culture" creates a pool of cheaper handsets available for consumers with less to spend. However, reliance on cheaper, older, and under-powered mobile handsets has a number of negative consequences for people experiencing homelessness. It reduces the range and quality of engagement and potential to leverage digital activities and social networks to connect with peers, expand opportunities, access education, and build capital. It restricts access to only those sites and services that support older features and/or operating systems and slower access speeds. It makes more work and effort to use faulty and under-powered models, peering through broken screens and obtaining replacement models on the hop when older models are lost, stolen or beyond repair. It locks users into a process of having to maintain, repair and replace their handsets more often and at more cost, creating what Gonzalez has described as a culture of "technology maintenance" and resulting in "dependable instability."[35]

Prepaid and Lock In Contracts, Exit Fees, and Bill Shock

"Poverty premiums", or the additional expense charged to people on low incomes for mobile services, is another negative effect of a market structured by segmentation and other kinds of pricing strategies that disadvantage the poor and those in precarious circumstances. A 2016 study carried out on connectivity costs for low-income consumers by the South Australian Council of Social Services (SACOSS), found that poverty premiums in the telecommunications industry were rife across a number of fronts. The study found that one of the key ways that poor telecommunications consumers pay more is through the limited allocation of mobile data in pre-paid plans.[36]

Pre-paid plans are mobile phone plans that allow consumers to pre-purchase selected amounts of data and voice minutes on a needs basis. Because of this capacity to flexibly adjust spending, it's a popular choice among low-income consumers. It is also the preferred option for homeless mobile media users. Out of the participants in my first study, only 18 percent were signed up to mobile contracts, with many having converted to pre-paid after exiting a post-paid contract. However, even with a pre-paid service, a large proportion of users—57 percent—reported having difficulty with their mobile phone payments.

The key problem with pre-paid plans is that the allocation of data and call minutes is not enough for the digital needs of those who rely on mobiles as their main or exclusive form of access. People experiencing homelessness use their mobiles for keeping in contact with friends and family and for interacting with support and government services. Yet, mobile calls to timed numbers and wait times on hold are very costly[37] and a regular feature of contact with these agencies. Some participants reported that they attended centers in person just to avoid the cost of the call and wait time. Others spoke of running out of credit on their pre-paid mobile service and having to sign up to a post-paid plan just to be able to meet the contact and reporting requirements of *Centrelink*, the social security service run by the Australian Government's Department of Human Services. Some had creative ways to save costs and stay connected, such as using public Wi-Fi in shopping centers, cafes and at McDonald's. Others simply ran out of credit, left without the ability to make calls, send texts and access the internet.

The implications of not having a working phone was so adverse when homeless, including immediate risks to physical safety, that people who are homeless are forced into making purchase decisions that ultimately cost more, sometimes resulting in "catastrophic spending." Catastrophic spending, described by Mendoza, is when a purchase of a good or service is made even though it may result in a more extreme outcome, such as missing out on other essential items, like food and housing, or going into further debt.[38] The purchase of a post-paid mobile plan in order to gain immediate access if a handset is stolen or lost, is an example of catastrophic spending, leading to further debt and harm. This happened to a young woman I spoke to:

> When I was young I lived on the street. So I'd lose a lot of phones or they'd get stolen from me. Then when I was old enough to get a phone plan I got them and then I had a lot of trouble with that, so they blocked the phone. I'd get rid of the phone and get another one and then they kept letting me sign up for plans that I couldn't pay. Now they've given me a bad credit rating so a friend had to put a phone in their name for me.

Having the time and wherewithal to seek out longer term affordable options is hardly possible when facing multiple threats and complex life challenges. As a result of mobile contracts with high exit fees, and not being able to meet monthly payments, people who are homeless and already in a situation of extreme hardship, face mounting bills and spiraling debt. Of the 28 percent of participants who reported having a mobile phone debt, I found the most vulnerable and with complex needs—participants with a mental illness or a disability, and single parents—were more likely to have reported difficulties paying bills and had experiences of debt with their mobile phone.

It's important to understand that the heavy dependence on smartphones, while in large part a product of homeless circumstances, is also a result of needing to access services by digital means and to fulfil reporting and compliance obligations that others are not required to satisfy. This pushes up the demand for digital access and data usage. Moreover, as Ogle and Musolino found in their analysis of monthly spend to value of service, many pre-paid plans do not represent the same value per dollar spent than post-paid plans, so that, even when mobile users prudently opt to using pre-paid plans to avoid getting into debt, they end up paying more for their data and voice calls by virtue of needing to purchase top-ups and accruing excess fees over and above their pre-paid mobile allocation.[39] This poverty premium built into the pricing strategies of mobile products and services, working alongside neoliberal regimes that penalize recipients of welfare and other social benefits, reinforces and compounds social and digital exclusion.

The concept and phenomenon of the "poverty premium," also known as the "poverty penalty," while recognized by poor mobile phone users who feel its impacts, is under-theorized and researched. We know from the work of Prahalad and Hammond that this is a feature of emerging economies. Their research found slum dwellers in Dharevi, a slum area in Mumbai in India, paid more for rice, medication, water, credit and telecommunications.[40] Increasingly, the same phenomenon of paying more per unit is the subject of study by economists and social scientists in developed countries.[41] This extra cost paid by lower income consumers goes beyond financial expenditure. A report on *The Price of Poverty* by Anglicare Tasmania, found that, in addition to paying more for telecommunications, poor Tasmanians pay more for food, housing and electricity.[42]

The poverty premium is not isolated to the telecommunications industry, and as Mendoza has argued, is a more generalized function of inequality in participation the market.[43] However, we know that access to an internet-enabled mobile phone has become increasingly essential to social participation, without which it is more difficult to access government services and satisfy service demands and obligations that are disproportionately imposed on some sections of the populations. Poverty premiums built into mobile products and services become an additional burden for people on low incomes and others experiencing various forms of extreme hardship, resulting not only in extra financial expense but additional costs on their time and health.

Consumer Confusion and Exploitative Retail Practices

The number and variation in mobile plans and services has created an environment for consumer confusion and retail practices that target and exploit vulnerable and disadvantaged customers. In interviews carried out with people experiencing homelessness, encounters with retailers and customer service officers produced the biggest cost on their mental health and wellbeing. One young man with a mild intellectual disability explained to me that he owed over AUD10,000 to three different telecommunication companies after being signed up to three contracts in succession shortly after his eighteenth birthday. As a result of not being able to pay for these services, his accumulating debt and difficult customer service interactions, his mental health declined: "Yeah it was a lot of stress. A lot of stress and sleepless nights and stuff like that and them saying, 'I'm sending debt collectors round to your mum's house'."

The ability to navigate this treacherous landscape is highly dependent on cultural and social capital: confidence in making decisions based on consumer expertise of available products and services, and access to a network of friends and family members who can share their tips and know how. Leek and Chansawatkit, in their study of the Thai mobile phone industry, found that handsets, carriers and phone services were a source of considerable confusion to consumers, with older consumers much more likely to experience confusion than those in younger age brackets. Reliance on friends and family as a source of information was the foremost strategy employed to reduce consumer confusion with regards to the mobile phone market.[44] Similarly, in my study, young people in particular relied on peers as well as stories shared on social media to give them information about the most affordable product or tips on how to save on costs.

The problem of unscrupulous mobile resellers signing up vulnerable people without any affordability checks has been widely reported on and interpreted as a failure in the market.[45]

In Australia and elsewhere, various consumer protections have been put in place to try to reduce these practices, including financial hardship policies, the appointment of a telecommunications ombudsman and consumer protection codes. However, I would argue that consumer confusion and exploitative retail practices are more than market failures and are an intrinsic way that access is controlled and commodified within an unequal market system that exposes more cost and harm to those people who need access the most. The greater need for a working mobile, in combination with being in a position of diminished power to access information, negotiate or obtain advice from others, creates what might be described as a "risk premium" that is built into the mobile telecommunications marketplace, which disproportionately disadvantages vulnerable and low-income mobile-only consumers.

Mobile Only Means Second-class Access

People who are homeless are highly dependent on a smartphone, for whom these are the primary, if not the exclusive, form of internet and telephone access. On the surface, smartphones fulfil an access need by making digital connectivity possible for a group who are highly mobile and who lack the resources necessary to have regular access to the internet and telephone. However, mobile only access results in a range of deprivations relating to poorer quality, lower standard, more expensive and contingent access, as well as exploitative retail practices that structure the experience of digital access not only on the cost and quality of the service but also in terms of users' time and health.

Far from mobile technologies providing a bridge for those without home broadband (let alone without homes), mobile phones are an extremely limited form of access compared with the multi-platform access enjoyed by the majority. Pointing out the rise of an "emerging under-class" of smartphone dependent users in the UK, Napoli and Obar argued: "mobile Internet access represents an inferior form of Internet access on a number of fronts—content availability, platform and network openness, speed, memory, and interface functionality among other things."[46] Home broadband is considered the gold standard of access, providing a central hub for a wide range of digital devices and experiences.[47] This multi-platform environment is also increasingly required for full participation and citizenship in a digital society.

We know from the extensive research carried out on digital disparities around the world that being on the digital margins results in being locked out of, or having curtailed access to, a wide range of economic and political activities and ways to enhance their prospects through new skills and opportunities.[48] While the route out of homelessness is not a straightforward matter of securing and capitalizing on digital access, there is little doubt that social members with higher levels of digital access and engagement are likely to be more advantaged social members.[49] People experiencing homelessness, and homeless young people, in particular, have their social worlds and opportunities curtailed as a consequence of having limited, poor-quality second-class access.

The phenomenon of second-class access via mobile internet is starting to gain traction among policy makers and researchers. Donner in his study of mobile internet access in Africa addresses the overlapping set of affordances and experiences he sees contributing to the different internets encountered by Africans. In their comparative analysis of mobile versus PC-based forms of internet access, the aforementioned Napoli and Obar refer to an emerging "mobile internet underclass" to highlight the growing disparities within developed nations. Tsetsi and Rains build on existing research on usage gaps to examine the different uses and outcomes that result from smartphone dependence versus multimodal internet access, finding smartphones to be masking a widening usage gap between low and upper income earners.[50]

My study contributes to this emerging literature by confirming the existence of mobiles as second-class access among Australians experiencing homelessness and by showing how poverty of access is bound up in existing social disadvantage and class positioning as well as its materialization in mobile media products and services. Second-class is a product of homelessness, which makes mobile only access a normal and inexorable feature of everyday digital media use. Second-class access is also an outcome of classification and ordering of media products and services within a system that distributes resources unequally, privileging those who have more of these resources and thus more purchasing power and penalizing those with less. The mobile communication market is very much part of this system of segmentation and punishment, in the way that handsets and plans are designed and costed, and the market organized and controlled. In so doing, a new set of barriers and burdens for people experiencing extreme financial and other forms of hardship is produced.

Conclusion

The rise of second-class access presents a new set of challenges for developing digital inclusion policies and approaches. First and foremost, mobile-only access needs to be recognized for what it is not: it is not a substitute for all other forms of digital access, nor is it a magical salve that will overcome existing inequalities by enabling people to escape extreme hardship and deprivation. Following on from this, we cannot address second-class access without addressing interrelated social inequalities that give rise to it: the need for secure and affordable housing, for an adequate basic income, for affordable and equitably distributed goods and services, and for social support that enables people to belong in a wider sense and build on their social and cultural capital. Without addressing these, there is a risk of perpetuating unstable and inequitable conditions of access, and indeed homelessness, rather than mitigating against these. Finally, in addition to continuing to invest in public connectivity infrastructures, public libraries, subsidy schemes and other access measures, we need to shift our attention towards the market and its construction, to expose the ways that media assemblages embed inequalities in the design and delivery of more expensive, precarious and substandard digital options to low- and no-income media consumers.

Notes

1 Susan P. Crawford, "The New Digital Divide," *New York Times*, (December 3, 2011).
2 Karen Mossberger, Caroline J. Tolbert, and William W. Franko. *Digital Cities: The Internet and the Geography of Opportunity* (Oxford: Oxford University Press, 2012).
3 Mobile Fact Sheet, Pew Research Center, Internet and Technology, accessed 26 July. www.pewinternet.org/fact-sheet/mobile/.

4 Julian Thomas, J. Barraket, Scott Ewing, Trent MacDonald, Meg Mundell, and Julie Tucker, "Measuring Australia's Digital Divide: The Australian Digital Inclusion Index 2016" (Melbourne: Swinburne University of Technology, for Telstra, 2016).
5 For a review of works see: Donna Haraway, "A Cyborg Manifesto. Science, Technology, and Socialist-feminism in the Late Twentieth Century," *The Cybercultures Reader* 291 (2000); Lucy A. Suchman, *Plans and Situated Actions: The Problem of Human-Machine Communication* (Cambridge: Cambridge University Press, 1987); Lisa Nakamura, "Race In/For Cyberspace: Identity Tourism and Racial Passing on the Internet," *Works and Days* 25, no. 26 (1995):13; and Jodi O'Brien, "Writing in the Body," *Communities in Cyberspace* (1999): 76–105.
6 For good overviews see: Nathalie Casemajor, "Digital Materialisms: Frameworks for Digital Media Studies," *Westminster Papers in Communication and Culture* 10, no. 1 (2015); Ramón Reichert and Annika Richterich, "Introduction" in *Digital Culture & Society (DCS): Vol. 1, Issue 1-Digital Material/ism* Vol. 1, eds. Ramón Reichert, Annika Richterich, Pablo Abend, Mathias Fuchs, and Karin Wenz (Bielefeld, Germany: Transcript, 2015).
7 Christian Fuchs and N. Dyer-Witheford, "Karl Marx@ Internet Studies," *New Media & Society*, 15, no. 5 (2013): 782–796; Christian Fuchs, *Digital Labour and Karl Marx* (London: Routledge, 2014).
8 Fuchs and Dyer-Witheford, "Karl Marx@"; Fuchs, *Digital Labour*.
9 Tiziana Terranova, "Free Labor: Producing Culture for the Digital Economy," *Social Text* 18, no. 2 (2000): 33–58.
10 David B. Grusky and Manwai C. Ku, "Gloom, Doom, and Inequality," in *Social Stratification: Class, Race, and Gender in Sociological Perspective* 3rd edition, ed. David B. Grusky (Boulder, CO: Westview Press, 2008), 2–28.
11 Gail Dines and Jean M. Humez. *Gender, Race, and Class in Media: A Text-Reader* (Thousand Oaks, CA: Sage, 2003), 6.
12 Dick Hebdige, "Subculture: The Meaning of Style," *Critical Quarterly* 37, no. 2 (1995), 120–124.
13 Laura Robinson, Shelia R. Cotten, Hiroshi Ono, Anabel Quan-Haase, Gustavo Mesch, Wenhong Chen, Jeremy Schulz, Timothy M. Hale, and Michael J. Stern, "Digital Inequalities and Why They Matter," *Information, Communication & Society* 18, no. 5 (2015): 570.
14 Monica Anderson, "Digital Divide Persists even as Lower Income Americans Make Gains in Tech Adoption," accessed 3 March, 2018. www.pewresearch.org/fact-tank/2017/03/22/digital-divide-persists-even-as-lower-income-Americans-make-gains-in-tech-adoption/.
15 Emily Hong, "Digital Inequality and Racialized Place in the 21st Century: A Case Study of San Francisco's Chinatown," *First Monday* 21, no. 1 (2016).
16 See for example Susan Halford and Mike Savage, "Reconceptualizing Digital Social Inequality," *Information, Communication & Society* 13, no. 7 (2010): 937–955; Paul DiMaggio, and Eszter Hargittai, "From the 'Digital Divide' to 'Digital Inequality': Studying Internet Use as Penetration Increases," *Princeton: Center for Arts and Cultural Policy Studies, Woodrow Wilson School, Princeton University* 4, no. 1 (2001): 4–2; Neil Selwyn, "Reconsidering Political and Popular Understandings of the Digital Divide," *New Media & Society* 6, no. 3 (2004): 341–362; Massimo Ragnedda, *The Third Digital Divide: A Weberian Approach to Digital Inequalities* (Abingdon, UK: Routledge, 2017); Robinson et al. "Digital Inequalities".
17 Reichert and Richterich, "Introduction," 6.
18 Andrew Herman, Jan Hadlaw, and Thom Swiss, eds., *Theories of the Mobile Internet: Materialities and Imaginaries* Vol. 24 (New York: Routledge, 2014).
19 For a selection of works see: L. Leung, "Availability, Access and Affordability Across 'Digital Divides': Common Experiences amongst Minority Groups [Online]," *Australian Journal of Telecommunications and the Digital Economy* 2, no. 2, (2014), 38.1–38.13; K. Ellis and M. Kent, "Disability and New Media," in *Routledge Studies in New Media and Cyberculture* (New York: Routledge, 2011); Katie Ellis and Gerard Goggin, *Disability and the Media* (London. UK: Palgrave Macmillan, 2015); P. Migliorino, "Digital Technologies Can Unite But Can Also Divide: CALD Communities in the Digital Age," *Australian Public Libraries Information Service* 24, no. 3 (2011), 107–110; S. Wise, "Trying to Connect: Telecommunications Access and Affordability among People Experiencing Financial Hardship," *Anglicare Victoria and ACCAN*, September, 2013.
20 Australian Bureau of Statistics 2012 Information Paper—A Statistical Definition of Homelessness, cat no. 4922, ABS, Canberra.
21 Justine Humphry, *Homeless and Connected: Mobile Phones and the Internet in the Lives of Homeless Australians* (Sydney: Australian Communications Action Network, 2014).
22 Peter Somerville, "Homelessness and the Meaning of Home: Rooflessness or Rootlessness?" *International Journal of Urban and Regional Research* 16, no. 4 (1992): 529–539.
23 Darrin Hodgetts, Otillie Stolte, Linda Waimarie Nikora, and Shilah Groot, "Drifting Along or Dropping into Homelessness: A Class Analysis of Responses to homelessness," *Antipode* 44, no. 4 (2012), 1209–1226.

24 Humphry, *Homeless and Connected*.
25 Justine Humphry and Kari Pihl, *Making Connections: Young People, Homelessness and Digital Access in the City* (Melbourne, Australia: Young and Well Cooperative Research Centre, 2016), 6–58.
26 See Specialist Homelessness Services Annual Report 2016–17. Australian Bureau of Statistics, AIHW, last updated February 12, 2018.
27 Harmony Rhoades, Suzanne L. Wenzel, Eric Rice, Hailey Winetrobe, and Benjamin Henwood. "No Digital Divide? Technology Use among Homeless Adults," *Journal of Social Distress and the Homeless* 26, no. 1 (2017): 73–77.
28 Humphry, *Homeless and Connected*, 31–32.
29 Humphry, *Homeless and Connected*, 33.
30 See Amanda Lenhart, "Teens, Social Media & Technology Overview 2015: Smartphones Facilitate Shifts in Communication Landscape for Teens" (Washington, DC: Pew Research Center, 2015); Kira A. Regan, "Socially Marginalized Youths' Experiences with Social Media and its Impact on their Relationships," Electronic Thesis and Dissertation Repository, 2017. 4476.https://ir.lib.uwo.ca/etd/4476.
31 See Teresa Senft, *Camgirls: Celebrity and Community in the Age of Social Networks* (New York: Peter Lang, 2008) for an examination of the phenomenon of young women using social media to do identity work and branding online, and danah boyd for research on teenagers' use of social media in "Why Youth (Heart) Social Network Sites: the Role of Networked Publics in Teenage Social Life," in *Youth, Identity, and Digital Media*, ed. David Buckingham, The John D. and Catherine T. MacArthur Foundation Series on Digital Media and Learning (Cambridge, MA: The MIT Press, 2008).
32 John B. Horrigan, "The Numbers Behind the Broadband Homework Gap", accessed on February 20, 2017, www.pewresearch.org/fact-tank/2015/04/20/the-numbers-behind-the-broadband-homework-gap/.
33 Goggin and Newell have documented the way that early cell phone devices were designed with 'other sorts of imagined users and markets [in mind]' than people with disabilities' in "Disabling Cell Phones," *The Cell Phone Reader: Essays in Social Transformation* 34 (2006): 158.
34 Australian online Applestore, accessed on March 7, 2018. www.apple.com/au//?afid=p238%7CsWvpb2gYZ-dc_mtid_18707vxu38484_pcrid_235072526822_&cid=aos-au-kwgo-brand-slid-.
35 Amy Gonzales, "The Contemporary US Digital Divide: From Initial Access to Technology Maintenance," *Information, Communication & Society* 19, no. 2 (2016): 234–248.
36 Greg Ogle and Vanessa Musolino, *Connectivity Costs: Telecommunications Affordability for Low Income Australians* (Sydney: Australian Communications Consumer Action Network, 2016).
37 The Australian Commonwealth Ombudsmen carried out an investigation into complaints made by customers of Centrelink and found the cost of calling was a heavy financial burden on mobile calling customers. Colin Neave, Department of Human Services: Investigation into Service Delivery Complaints about Centrelink (Commonwealth Ombudsmen, Australia, April 2014).
38 See RU Mendoza, "Why do the Poor Pay More? Exploring the Poverty Penalty Concept," *Journal of International Development* 23 (2008): 1–28.
39 Ogle and Musolino, *Connectivity Costs*.
40 Among other price disparities, Prahalad and Hammond found the price paid for water by slum dwellers was between 4 and 100 times higher than middle and upper class Indians. See Coimbatore K. Prahalad and Allen Hammond. "Serving the World's Poor, Profitably," *Harvard Business Review* 80, no. 9 (2002): 48–59.
41 Frédéric Dalsace, Charles-Edouard Vincent, Jacques Berger, and François Dalens, "The Poverty Penalty in France: How the Market Makes Low-income Populations Poorer," *Field Actions Science Reports. The Journal of Field Actions* Special Issue 4 (2012).
42 Jo Flanagan and Kathleen Flanagan, *The Price of Poverty: The Cost of Living for Low Income Earners* (Tasmania: Anglicare, 2011).
43 Mendoza, "Why do the poor pay more?".
44 Sheena Leek and Suchart Chansawatkit, "Consumer Confusion in the Thai Mobile Phone Market," *Journal of Consumer Behaviour* 5, no. 6 (2006): 518–532.
45 For example, see Flanagan and Flanagan, *The Price*.
46 Philip M. Napoli and Jonathan A. Obar, "The Emerging Mobile Internet Underclass: A Critique of Mobile Internet Access," *The Information Society* 30, no. 5 (2014): 330.
47 Mossberger, Tolbert and Franko, *Digital Cities*.
48 Robinson et al., "Digital Inequalities".
49 Robinson et al., "Digital Inequalities".
50 Eric Tsetsi and Stephen A. Rains. "Smartphone Internet Access and Use: Extending the Digital Divide and Usage Gap," *Mobile Media & Communication* 5, no. 3 (2017): 239–255.

22
MARGINALITY AND SOCIAL CLASS IN MOROCCAN YOUTH MEDIA

Mohamed El Marzouki

In 2017, a homeless, mentally disabled man rose to popularity on social media networks in Algeria. Short videos circulating on Facebook and WhatsApp groups featured the bearded, barefooted man walking up to strangers in the streets of Algiers and asking: "Young man, are you angry?" Or "Why are you angry?" Pedestrian responses often led to glib and amusing exchanges with the unkempt middle-aged man who eventually mutters a prayer for his interlocutors before he asks them for food or change. "May Allah clear away all your anger," or "May Allah gift you with thirty billion dollars," the homeless man asks in some of the viral videos. In the lead-up to the Algerian 2017 local elections, 28-year-old Algerian YouTuber, Anes Tina, shared a six-minute video in which he performs a scripted monologue in response to the homeless man's question: "Young man, why are you angry?" In the video monologue, Anes plays the character of a homeless man in Algiers detailing, in a series of scathing critiques, the social, economic and political roots of his anger.

The monologue is recited in poetry style with somber tunes from the *Titanic* soundtrack playing in the background. The sad melody and Anes' sullen gaze into the camera, his despondent facial expressions and body gestures set an oppressively solemn mood. "I am angry," declares the homeless character before he begins listing the myriad social problems, injustices and sufferings of popular classes and youth in Algeria. From dysfunctional social and political institutions such as schools, hospitals and the parliament to "the Boats of Death," capsizing in the Mediterranean with hundreds of youth migrants from North Africa, the homeless character laments the conditions and manifestations of social injustice. The six-minute video ends with a panning drone shot of the character standing atop a mountain overlooking the city of Algiers. With his back turned to the camera and his arms spread wide open, as if to embrace the city under his feet, the figure turns around to reveal his identity to the camera: Anes Tina. No longer playing the homeless character, Anes speaks mockingly with reference to the then ongoing 2017 elections campaign:

> Theirs are campaigns of the state, and this is a campaign of the people. I love my country; no one shall teach me patriotism. I am no foreign intervention conspiracy. My words are spoken straight from the heart; spoken on behalf of the wretched people living in misery … I declare that I love you my homeland and that I shall love you to the death. But witness, witness oh homeland that *I am angry!*

Building on the popularity and visceral realism of the earlier videos of the homeless man, Anes' video went viral on social media networks across the region, accumulating more than 13 million views (as of this writing) and triggering a hashtag campaign #راني_زعفان (#I_am_angry) across North Africa. The video was featured in social media segments of regional and transnational satellite news media and instigated denouncement from the Algerian regime in the person of a government minister who dismissed the video as pessimistic.

The viral video monologue is part of a growing repertoire of youth media activism that has emerged in North Africa and the Middle East in the wake of what has come to pass as Arab Spring protests. Such youth media documents and critiques manifestations of marginality, exclusion, destitution and political corruption as endured by Arab youth and popular social classes across the region. A case in point, Anes Tina, the creator of the *I am angry* video, started making satirical mash-up videos in 2011 and today he runs a YouTube channel with more than 2.2 million subscribers and over 200 million views as of this writing. His channel features more than 170 short five- to 10-minute videos critiquing and satirizing cultural (marriage, traditions, hair fashion, national TV, etc.), social (racism, domestic violence, aids stigma, illegal migration, petty crime, etc.), and political phenomena (protest, freedom of expression, political corruption, government conduct and policy). While Anes Tina's channel is most followed in Algeria, with occasional videos and hashtags reaching trans-regional popularity, his work is an example of an emerging digital creator culture straddling the line between social media entertainment[1] and a mode of political criticism that is steeped in questions of class, marginality, and citizenship.

With a focus on youth digital media practices in North Africa, this chapter examines how marginalized social groups mediatize the signs, styles and conditions of social inequality and exclusion to contest the discourses and institutions that sustain and reproduce inequality and social class. Drawing on interviews and ethnographic research with young media creators and social influencers in Morocco, the chapter explores how emerging youth media practices harness the symbolic resources of marginality and social exclusion to make demands on the state for social equality and justice. I approach social class as the product of an economic system that manifests as a differential regime of citizenship to reproduce relations of marginality and social inequality. The differential regime of citizenship rights, as I describe below, is produced and sustained in relation to the economic system of capitalism. I argue that the mediatization of marginality and social exclusion plays an important role in building relations of counter-power and online communities of trust that are key to the rise of a networked culture of contentious politics among youth in North Africa and the Middle East.

In what follows, this chapter will first situate the question of marginality and social class in the contemporary debate on citizenship. In the first two sections, I trace the economic roots of marginality and social class in relation to citizenship in liberal democracy. I start with a definition of citizenship as a constellation of civil, social and political rights applied to smooth over the friction between capitalism as a system of inequality and democracy as a project of liberty and equality.[2] In the second section, I go beyond citizenship as a state apparatus concerned with juridical status and formal participation in institutional politics, to examine the rise of new social movements with new sites, scales, rights and acts of citizenship.[3] Here I emphasize the role of digital media technologies as a space for enacting various forms of identity and class struggles and rehearsing new modes of citizenship. In the third and fourth sections, I draw on my fieldwork research with young digital media creators in Morocco to examine how the media are increasingly becoming a space for contesting marginality and social exclusion and demanding rights to liberty, dignity and social justice.

Social Class and Citizenship

Social class as a system of inequality and a by-product of capitalism stands in contrast to democracy, a system of equality and liberty. In order to alleviate the abject realities of destitution and social inequality, liberal democratic theory introduces the concept of citizenship. In liberal theory, citizenship is conceptualized as a set of rights that constitute their bearer as a political subject. In his seminal essay, *Citizenship and Social Class*, British sociologist T.H. Marshall theorizes the citizen as bearer of civil, social and political rights. Informed by the liberal tradition of James Mill, Marshall sees civil rights as concerned with such basic individual freedoms as "freedom of speech, thought, faith; the right to own property and to conclude valid contract; and the right to justice."[4] Since civil rights and especially the right to justice assume equality among citizens before the law, civil citizenship is closely related to legal institutions. In addition to civil rights, the subject-citizen in Marshall's theory of citizenship is also the bearer of political rights, which guarantee *his* right to self-rule. Political rights endow the subject-citizen with the right to exercise political power through representative institutions and local government institutions. The right to vote and to run for office are perhaps the utmost manifestations of political citizenship. The third dimension of citizenship is the right to social security and economic welfare, coupled with the right to live with dignity as a member of a civilized society and partake in the "social heritage" of one's community. The state institutions immediately associated with this element of citizenship are public education and social services (healthcare, retirement benefits, etc.).

Citizenship in this formulation is a form of political subjectivity inasmuch as it endows the individual with a political status. The political subject that is the citizen stands in opposition to an apolitical 'bare life' of non-citizens.[5] As a political subject the citizen, at least in liberal citizenship theory (with a twist of socialism from T.H. Marshall), is guaranteed liberty and equality. Yet, Marshall is aware that citizenship as an ideal of liberty and equality will always be at war with capitalism, an economic system that produces social class and inequality. The apparatus of citizenship (a collection of civil, social, and political rights) is, in turn, deployed to redress the social and political inequalities of a capitalist marketplace and reaffirm equality as a cornerstone of democracy. However, as the offshoots of capitalism, marginality and social class often persist and are sustained by a hollowed regime of citizenship.

Citizenship as a function of state power and a mechanism of social ordering, therefore, sits at the intersection of a liberal democratic polity, a capitalist economic system, and a particular articulation of the individual and society. Liberal normative theories understand citizenship as a set of civil, political and social rights that developed respectively during the eighteenth, nineteenth and twentieth centuries.[6] These rights are developed in tandem with liberal capitalist democracies that perceive the individual as a rational, self-interested actor guaranteed entry to a free-market economy and participation in a democratic process of self-governance in a sovereign state. In capitalist democracies, marginality and social class arise from the uneven interplay between these three components; Marshall, for instance, explains that capitalism is the producer of social class and inequality because a degree of poverty is necessary for capitalism to function.[7] From the labor of the poor working class, wealth is created and with it a capitalist social class. Social rights, in this respect, exist only to moderate the extreme conditions of destitution; their role is not to end social inequality, but to palliate the extreme conditions of poverty and marginality and render inequality less antithetical to democracy.

The over-emphasis on the liberal dimensions of citizenship in the form of civil rights, therefore, results in the gradual erosion of social rights and hence the internal and systematic production of marginality and inequality. The over-obsession with personal civil liberty as the right to own property and to conclude valid contracts justifies a laissez-faire economic system, which in turn undermines the social right of the individual to social dignity and liberty in its positive sense (freedom from hunger, from poverty, from pain, etc.). Fraser and Gordon[8] describe the primacy of civil rights over social rights in the USA as a cultural myth. They argue that "the cultural mythology of civil citizenship stands in a tense, often obstructing relationship to social citizenship," creating a contract-versus-charity dichotomy. Such a dichotomy articulates civil rights as purely contractual property rights, while relegating social rights to the sphere of private charity and community/family bonds. Defining civil citizenship in terms of individual rights to property, therefore, undercuts "ideas of solidarity, non-contractual reciprocity, and interdependence that are central to any humane social citizenship"[9] and sustains marginality and inequality as byproducts of citizenship in liberal, capitalist democracies.

Marxist critiques reject the liberal definition of citizenship as a juridical status that endows the individual with a collection of rights and obligations and, instead, propose a definition of citizenship as a set of *practices*—juridical, political, social, economic, cultural, and symbolic. Turner[10] argues that such practices "define a person as a competent member of society" and "shape the flow of resources to persons and social groups." Emphasizing the historical importance of violent struggles in the construction of citizenship, such a view emphasizes the duality of citizenship as a mechanism of civic association *and* conflict. Because it is situated between capitalism and democracy, citizenship works to foster social bonds within and belonging to a polity and to provide a process through which struggles for redistribution and recognition are enacted. The emphasis on social practices as a mechanism of equal distribution renders citizenship as essentially about the nature of social membership in differentiated polities. The next section traces how these struggles against exclusive notions of social membership continue to challenge normative definitions of citizenship on a much more expansive, digitally networked global scale.

Identity, Media, Citizenship

More recently, the social processes associated with globalization have prompted scholars to rethink the concept of citizenship in light of evolving social and political struggles. The rise of an increasingly interdependent, interconnected global economy and the surge in international flows of capital, people, media and information technologies[11] have arguably led to the expansion and intensification of social relations.[12] Such processes have, in turn, brought into focus new struggles and actors. Citizens of twenty-first century polities are more likely to be affected by an array of shared global issues that exceed the borders of their nation-states (e.g., the environment, security, health). Isin[13] argues these developments have rendered old conception of citizenship that emphasize status and practice "enervated" and have expanded "the rights (civil, political, social, sexual, ecological, cultural), sites (bodies, courts, streets, media, networks, borders), scales (urban, regional, national, transnational, international) and acts (voting, volunteering, blogging, protesting, resisting and organizing)" of citizenship. Such approach to citizenship emphasizes the importance of analyzing the political subjectivities and modes of citizenship that are produced and enacted within and through an emerging gamut of rights, sites, scales and acts of new struggles and social movements.

Such revisionist interventions in the concept of citizenship reflect the ubiquity of identity politics and struggles that have come to characterize social movements in the early twenty-first century. While the politics of class, economic redistribution, welfare and social justice are central to the development of democratic citizenship, current debates tend to emphasize the importance of addressing modes of oppression that proliferate around identity markers of race, gender, ethnicity, nationality, sexuality, age and religion. This trend manifests in the emergence of a list of qualified variants to the concept of citizenship, including activist citizenship,[14] silly citizenship,[15] DIY citizenship,[16] self-actualizing citizenship,[17] alternative citizenship,[18] creative citizenship,[19] and cultural citizenship.[20]

These variations of the concept of citizenship have two elements in common. First, they use the political struggles of contemporary social movements as a starting point for rethinking what citizenship means in multicultural societies. Their investment in the struggles of identity politics, however, does not mean an abandonment of class politics or evacuation of social citizenship. In fact, social rights, combined with legal and political rights, remain the basic tenets of democratic citizenship. But social inequality and oppression are not exclusively tied to social class and its gruesome manifestations of poverty and homelessness. Marginality and social exclusion operate through identity markers of difference just as they are a function of social class—with the increasing commonality of experiencing the two intersectionally of course. In focusing on identity struggles, appraisal accounts such as activist and cultural citizenship articulate the practices, claims, and struggles of a politics of recognition to theorize a more inclusive and substantive definition of citizenship. Second, recent interventions in the concept of citizenship emphasize the centrality of digital media technologies as spaces for making claims, on the one hand, and for enacting new modes of citizenship on the other. Re-formulations such as activist and cultural citizenship retain an interest in the conditions of marginality and social exclusion but with a focus on media culture as a tool for carnivalesque creative expression and a site for enacting counter-hegemonic resistance.

The rise of digital media in the global south is facilitating the emergence of "activist" identities and opening up new spaces for creative cultural expression and production. As digital and social media facilitate the flow of various discourses and counter-discourses online, practices of producing and consuming the discursive symbols, stories, and meanings of counter-hegemonic discourse come to have profound implications on the ways online actors experience citizenship. Anthropological explorations of the connection between cultural practice and citizenship use the concept of *cultural citizenship* to describe sites of social re-production, contestation, and potential transformation; a discursive space where marginalized and minority groups (marked by gender, race, class, religion, or ethnicity) use mundane everyday cultural practices to make claims against the nation-state and thwart dominant discourses of inclusion and exclusion.[21] Because cultural citizenship is a hegemonic site of producing identity and subjectivity, access to the production, distribution and consumption of culture becomes a field of struggle and conflict in late capitalism.[22] The concept of cultural citizenship brings into focus the cultural politics of having access to the means of producing meaning and representations as the basis of claiming equal membership in a polity.

Exploring in further detail the ways in which cultural practices are harnessed to challenge normative and dominant notions of citizenship and belonging, Isin[23] introduces the concept of activist citizenship to describe a mode of citizenship in which actors produce themselves as subjects of rights through the enactment of their citizenship. *Acts* of citizenship are ruptures in a given social and symbolic order that

> disrupt habitus, create new possibilities, claim rights and impose obligations in emotionally charged tones; [acts of citizenship] pose their claims in enduring and creative expressions; and, most of all, are the actual moments that shift established practices, status and order.[24]

Creativity, defined here as a genuine aspiration to openness and a leap of faith into uncertainty, is an important aspect of the subversive nature of activist citizenship. Yet, although *Acts* of citizenship in this formulation may assume a cultural, social or carnivalesque character, they are primarily political because their enactment produces a political subject of rights; a citizen-subject committed to social change. The creative, expressive, and carnivalesque character of activist citizenship, therefore, emphasizes the potential of digital media technologies to evolve into spaces for enacting citizenship.

If social media are increasingly the loci of a new sociality, then that is where evidence of the subversive enactment of citizenship should be excavated. Indeed, there is an expanding compendium of research arguing that the rise of digital media as spaces for the production and consumption of personalized and self-styled media content is shaping new modes of citizenship.[25] Lance Bennett[26] differentiates between dutiful citizenship and actualizing citizenship. In the era of mass communication, traditional media defined the issues of the day for a mass audience whose means of participating in national politics was limited to formal and institutionalized practices such as voting. Participation in national politics through formal channels was considered a duty or obligation that befalls all citizens, and thus produced a dutiful citizenship model.

The actualizing citizenship model of digital media, as opposed to the dutiful top-down model of mass media, places more emphasis on active and substantive forms of citizenship; in doing so, experiences of actualizing citizenship prioritize participation through informal means of political and cultural expression over formal channels and institutionalized practices such as voting or serving on a jury. Instead of leaving it to elite-driven and commercial mass media to set the national agenda and determine the parameters of public discourse and deliberation, collective forms of participation through digital media offer an alternative to elite-driven media. In providing a space for marginalized groups to express common grievances and mobilize support for collective action, social media platforms offer a critique of media power and foster an alternative model of citizenship. But while collective action on the social web may not yield immediate political gains, it nevertheless contributes to the emergence of a more substantive and activist figure of citizenship that is committed to political struggle for group rights.

While this chapter builds on a larger research project that interviewed 23 prominent YouTube creators across nine urban locations in Morocco in 2016 and 2018, the following section will focus on the cases of two creators (Marwan Chakir and Momo Bekri) whose work is driven by the marginality and everyday struggles of the popular social class in Morocco. The *popular* (*shaabi*) social class in local dialect stands in contrast to an urban, educated middle class and the ruling political elites. While populism and populist movements in Western politics champion the interests of the 'ordinary' citizen to circumvent political elites, the *popular* class in Moroccan political discourse lumps together the working class, the poor, the unemployed, and earners in the informal economy of street venders, parking watchmen, and ragpickers, among others. The *shaabi* quality of popular social classes evokes meanings of belonging, humility, and modesty[27] as important aspects of a downtrodden people with little access to cultural and economic capital.

As self-described members of the popular social class, creators Marwan Chakir and Momo Bekri share much in common. At the age of 23, Marwan arrived on YouTube accidentally when his friends uploaded a video of him responding to a then viral rant video about college girls' clothing. Uploaded in 2012, Marwan's video monologue featured a brash (*aroubi*) accent typical of the popular class and quickly became a viral sensation. Like Marwan, Momo was born in the mid-1980s and began creating video content in the wake of the Arab Spring protests at the age of 25, a time when user-generated culture was on the rise in the region. Both creators graduated from high school and started making videos during and after completing post-secondary vocational degrees in technical fields. The next section draws on ethnographic fieldwork I have conducted with Marwan and Momo (among other young digital media creators in Morocco) to examine North African youth's use of digital media technologies as spaces for enacting activist citizenship.

Mediatizing Marginality

Marwan Chakir, a young creator with a focus on critiquing political corruption and social injustice for example, describes his YouTube channel as a site for expressing and amplifying the voices of marginalized groups against the injustice of state institutions and authorities:

> Every day, people contact me with their problems, they call me on the phone and send me documents—dossiers. Some of them have a problem with the hospital, some of them have a problem with inheritance, another one might have problems with injustice in the justice system, some people have a problem with the security service and with the police—you might have been a victim of police abuse; some people have problems with local authorities. Most of the cases and complaints that I received come from people who have issues like these with the state and with the services that the state provides either in healthcare, the justice system, or the police and security services and the Ministry of Interior.
>
> *(Marwan Chakir[28])*

Marwan tells me that in many instances the networked counter-publicity campaigns he participates in pressure the state to address cases of gross injustice, especially when a case or incident becomes the focus of public opinion, press coverage, and offline civil society campaigns. Such immediate, episodic and palliative state response notwithstanding, the true significance of practices of cultural citizenship for social change is not to be understood in linear terms; that is, the articulation and performance of marginality and the making of demands do not automatically translate into permanent social and political changes. Rather, such discursive practices offer an intervention for those often marginalized from formalized processes of citizen action. The practice of producing and circulating youth-produced, politically-inflected new media forms is an intervention in the discursive power dynamics that shape the subjectivities of marginalized groups. Ong[29] argues that strategies of resistance allow poor and cosmopolitan migrants alike a measure of intervention in defining their own subjectivities along the continuum of a racialized regime of citizenship. For the youth of *popular* social classes in Morocco, the practice of cultural/creative citizenship, understood here as the production and circulation of user-generated video as articulations and critiques of the structural conditions of marginality, allow *creators* a space for intervening in the power dynamics that inscribe them in relations of marginality and exclusion by speaking directly to those in power. As Marwan explains:

> The way I see it is that when I publish a video or make a statement, I am not ridiculing the public official as much as I am critiquing, and hopefully, raising the awareness of the official himself. It is like drawing his attention to something that he fails to notice irrespective of his rank. This is democracy for me.
>
> *(Marwan Chakir)*

Rosaldo's[30] work is critical to conceiving of the production of alternative cultural forms as practices of citizenship aimed at challenging structures of exclusion. But the demands articulated in the forms and practices of cultural citizenship are not necessarily achieved through direct confrontation with or contestation against a center of all power and domination. Foucault reminds us that because social power is everywhere and relations of resistance are inscribed in the power network, there is no "single locus of great Refusal, no soul of revolt, source of all rebellion, or pure law of the revolutionary."[31] Another blogger, Momo Bekri, illustrates this point when he distances himself from a more overt form of activist militancy:

> There are activists who have dedicated their lives to political struggle and militancy. They are even ready to die for their big ideas, but for me I prefer to give you one small idea in each video and in the process gradually increase my influence than to give you one grand [radical] idea. Boom! And stop afterwards. I prefer to give more and more. If I share an idea that puts an end to my practice, I will let down my followers. I have to be smart about the way I work if I am to continue in this field.
>
> *(Momo Bekri)*

Momo understands that resistance can only be exercised strategically and incrementally from within the social edifice. He distances himself from the struggles of those "who are ready to die," those locked in relations of force, violence and death with the armies of a phantom social power. In adopting the strategy of micro-struggles, YouTubers such as Momo find in the practices of creative cultural citizenship their ultimate "weapons of the weak."[32] Through such weapons and micro-struggles, resistance is exercised strategically and social change is sought incrementally in the microphysical processes of laughing, articulating, critiquing, and demanding rights:

> As for the question of whether there are direct calls for and a commitment to social change, of course there is. But the change that I imagine cannot happen all at once. That

is not possible for me to effect, but I try little by little and with the limited means that I have available to me.

(Momo Bekri)

The implication of this incremental process is the co-construction of citizenship as a political subject position that values dissent, activism and strategies of resistance as means of improving life-chances and contesting power relations that re-produce marginality and social exclusion. The counter-discursive work of cultural citizenship may not produce results as swiftly as popular uprisings or genuine democratic processes would. But in light of the violent outcomes of most Arab Spring uprisings (and in the absence of genuine democracies), media practices of cultural citizenship remain an important way for marginalized youth to contest regime power and demand meaningful social and political reforms. I turn now to the connection between the creative mediatization of the conditions and signs of marginality and the slow, incremental process of change.

Youth Marginality and Social Change

In addition to their counter-discursive role, the cultural citizenship practices of producing digital media content are intertwined with offline modes of participation in society. This section therefore elaborates on the story of Marwan Chakir, reviewing the negative attention he incurred from the government as a result of his movement between online and offline modes of enacting cultural and activist citizenship.

As a YouTube creator, Marwan combines humor and critique to satirize social, political and cultural policies and figures in Morocco. His crude and populist style of humor notwithstanding, Marwan's offline and online practices often overlap and converge in his unfaltering commitment to social change:

> I have participated in many campaigns and organized many on the Internet including the campaign to kiss the holy book and the campaign for the poor where we distribute food baskets. People respond to these campaigns. There are people who call. People like to do 'good' in this country; they only need someone to trust.
>
> *(Marwan Chakir)*

The two campaigns Marwan references are key to excavating the continuities between online practices of cultural citizenship and offline modes of participation in public life. The two campaigns share a peculiar backstory. In 2013, two high school teenagers aged 15 and 14 from Nador, a small conservative city in northern Morocco, shared a picture on social networking sites. The photograph, which showed an adolescent boy and girl lip-locked in a passionate kiss, circulated widely on social media and led to the immediate arrest of the couple and a third teenager who took the photograph. For local authorities, the kiss was a flagrant public display of affection and indecency and warranted arrest; for the liberal elites in more cosmopolitan centers where the public display of affection is more common, the arrest of adolescent children for a kiss was outrageous. The absurdity and arbitrariness of the arrest provoked liberal activists to stage a protest in front of the parliament building in the capital city, Rabat, where young adult men and women embraced and kissed in support for the teenager's cause and in utter defiance of state authorities. The "kissing protest," which was covered by local and regional media, was, however, interrupted by a conservative young activist, who attacked kissing couples shouting, "This is the land of Islam, you sons of bitches!" While the arrest of the two teenagers prompted bipartisan condemnation of state double standards in enforcing laws of public indecency, the ensuing "kissing" protest drew much criticism and backlash. And it was in this succession of events that YouTube satirist and vlogger, Marwan Chakir, launched his social media campaign to kiss the Qur'an and a subsequent food basket campaign for the homeless and the poor.

While the two campaigns foreground the conflicting ideologies of liberal cosmopolitanism and populist conservatism that structure practices of cultural citizenship, they also reveal a second power dynamic that goes beyond the articulation of counter-hegemonic discourse (discussed above) to contest state legitimacy by competing for social power and influence. In the first social media campaign, Marwan urged his followers to kiss the Qur'an and share a photo of the act on social media as a form of counter-protest to the "kissing" demonstration in the capital. The video call that launched the campaign received almost half a million views and was widely circulated on popular Facebook pages and hyper-local news websites, generating tens of photos of book-kissing supporters. The video that launched the second campaign, which also started in response to the "kissing" protest, featured short interviews with homeless men. The video depicts, in gruesome detail, the abject poverty, grime and hunger that middle-aged homeless men endure in their lives on the streets. In documenting the dire conditions of poverty around his city, the mocking tone of the video ridiculed the futile and perverse motives of liberal, "kissing" activism. Building on these attacks, Marwan preaches a more substantive and worthwhile cause for political activism: he exhorts liberal protesters to organize and protest in support of housing the homeless and feeding the hungry.

Although his call on cosmopolitan liberal elites to organize in support of improving the conditions of the homelessness was rhetorical, Marwan later starts a food drive for the homeless and the poor that will grow popular on social media. The program collected donations and supplied food baskets to needy families and homeless people during the holy month of Ramadan. The food basket program capitalized on Marwan's popularity as a social media personality but was carried out offline under the name of a civic association that Marwan formed. As the program became popular and started to receive generous national and international donations, local authorities launched an investigation into the campaign and ordered Marwan to discontinue all social and charitable activities until the case was closed. Marwan described this chain of events in his interview:

INTERVIEWER: What happened to the food basket program?
MARWAN: You have seen what happened. When I started to grow the program and to reach and give to more and more families, they decided to shut me down.
INTERVIEWER: Why do you think you were being investigated?
MARWAN: Perhaps they thought that this could be the start of a new movement or party of the poor against corruption. You know how the Ministry of Interior follows everything that goes on and what influential actors say, so maybe they think that I'm using the food basket campaign to earn favors with the people so that one day when I asked them to join me in something they will do so happily."

What is striking, however, and perhaps concerning to the state authorities about the food basket campaign, was its close affinity to the national food support programs that the King oversees through his royal charity, Mohammed V Foundation for Solidarity. The royal charity administers food donations to hundreds of thousands, if not millions, of widowed mothers, disabled adults, and poor families. Its special Ramadan food basket program always features the King passing over baskets of food and receiving kisses on his right hand. The event is always covered on state television and national newspapers, with an emphasis on the frame of royal benevolence in the blessed month.

The act of mediatized royal charity is key to the operation of social power in Morocco and to the transmutation of aristocratic wealth into the symbolic capital of reputation and social prestige. "The chief," Bourdieu reminds us, "is a 'tribal banker' who accumulates food only to lavish it on others" and in so doing he builds a symbolic capital of "obligations and debts that will be repaid in the form of homage, respect and loyalty."[33] Indeed, the kiss on the hand or shoulder in Moroccan tradition is a sign of expressing a relationship of gratitude, homage, respect, obligation and moral debt (typically owed to a father figure). Bourdieu explains that while such emotional attachments mask relationships of domination that are based in material and economic inequality, the act of charitable giving disguises relations of material inequality "under the veil of moral relations."[34] In a moment of symbolic violence, the charitable act of giving contains the potential for class antagonism by euphemizing material inequality as moral relations and emotional attachments. In the mediatized act of charitable giving, Moroccan aristocracy cultivates social relations of loyalty, gratitude and moral debt that are, in turn, legitimized and institutionalized in statecraft—and become the basis for social power and political rule.

By this logic, Marwan's mediatized petty charity campaign for the homeless may offer a critique of aristocratic displays of charity, but it may also be viewed as a scramble for social power and influence for himself; it is an attempt to cultivate symbolic capital and gain social prestige and reputation based on online and offline exchanges. Either, or both, may have informed the state's displeasure with Marwan's food basket program. Online, YouTube creators like Marwan are engaged in an online information economy that supplies free, public-spirited and entertaining media content to their followers. The free labor that goes into the expression and articulation of the grievances of marginalized groups in user-generated videos is in many ways a charitable act of giving. What it gives is voice. In a statist media system that is preoccupied with legitimizing its own "chiefs" and institutions, political satire shows and user-generated video are the lifelines of an alternative political voice. To the marginalized, rural and popular voices, the crass expressions of political satire are what the royal baskets of sugar and flour are to the livelihoods of the destitute—they sustain them. In this information exchange of user-generated video, viewers are given voice in the form of humorous articulations of social inequality, oppression, and state double-speak, and creators receive a measure of symbolic, moral authority for their perceived sincerity and courage in speaking truth to power—for being the practitioners of political parrhesia and freedom.[35] By offering both voice and food, Marwan laid claim to the symbolism of authority and largesse that the state might prefer to preserve for itself.

Unlike bread givers who supply sustenance to the bodies of their charity recipients, suppliers of counter-discursive information may not command the same degree of loyalty from their followers. Yet, the relationship of trust that bonds creators of online political satire and their followers is, nevertheless, a moral relationship that bestows a measure of symbolic capital on social media influencers. In light of the global crisis of trust in traditional political institutions, the social relations of trust that digital practices of cultural citizenship are spawning online are the building blocks of what Castells[36] calls counter-power. As Marwan said of the relationship between himself and this counter-power:

INTERVIEWER: So, the volume of people who follow you, your audience … [Interviewee interrupts the researcher]
INTERVIEWEE: they are a form of protection. A shield that protects you. We are like our representatives in the parliaments or our ministers who speak under the protection of community. We have a popular base of audiences and followers that protects us and allows us to speak freely.

In fact, Marwan did enjoy a wide margin of freedom of expression, but his move to organize charitable programs offline clearly did not sit well with state authorities. His counter-discursive practices and scramble for symbolic capital on the nonmaterial, discursive sphere of online content creation was largely tolerated. Yet, the move of contestation from the discursive terrain of information exchange to the materiality of supplying bread to the poor and homeless was alarming to the state. Eventually, when the state launched an investigation into and discontinued his charitable activities, Marwan's base did not come to his support. For at that point the state-subject interaction had moved from a negotiable field of power relations to a far thicker and less negotiable swamp of relations of force, violence and repression.

Conclusion

The practice of producing and circulating youth-produced, politically-inflected new media forms is an intervention in the discursive power dynamics that shape the subjectivities of marginalized groups. Despite state vigilance vis-à-vis (and monopoly on) social processes and practices of building power relations of inequality and social hierarchies, online spaces of cultural citizenship are important sites for rehearsing counter-hegemonic modes of relating to ruling elites and state institutions. As I have outlined above, political satire as a practice of cultural citizenship plays a counter-hegemonic role and contests the legitimacy of institutional channels of official discourse by competing for social power and influence. From the marginal spaces and practices of cultural citizenship, YouTube creators aspire to forge alternative spaces and relations of trust, loyalty and moral association and identification with their base of subscribers and followers. The networked relations and communities of trust spawned through the production and circulation of political satire—among other forms of politically-inflected user-generated culture—challenge legitimized and institutionalized relations of power at the center of society and, often, find themselves in direct confrontation with the state.

This chapter has reviewed the experiences of two North African YouTubers who have been intentional in their desire to enact cultural citizenship through the use of humor and contestation. The networked publics constructed around the media platforms of creators such as Marwan and Momo involve a rapidly growing North African youth population that faces serious challenges and frustrations with regards to access to social and political rights: from quality education to healthcare, employment, and political participation. Combined with feelings of resentment at dysfunctional social services and institutions, the lack of influence on the political decision-making process and frustration with political corruption and authoritarianism fuel expressions of what Zayani[37] in the context of Tunisia calls "networked publics of contention." In line with what has recently been termed an affective turn in the study of politics and emotions, youth contentious politics in North Africa are rooted in feelings of resentment, grievance, and outrage which, in turn, drive forms of citizen contestation and popular protest.[38] While these emotions were central to the Arab Spring uprisings a few years ago, today youth digital spaces of cultural citizenship channel these generative emotions of resentment and outrage into satirical and carnivalesque forms of expression that mediatize marginality and make demands for social and political change.

In Algeria, Anes Tina's I am Angry video has accumulated more than 14 million views in a country whose population is just over 40 million. His initial call of anger (#راني_زعفان) was succeeded by three similarly powerful videos that have become part of the visual repertoire of an ongoing peaceful uprising that ended the 20-year rule of Abdelaziz Bouteflika in early spring 2019. The protests started as an outcry against the wheelchair-confined, octogenarian president's decision to seek re-election for a fifth term and quickly developed into a broader call for le pouvoir (a cabal of military generals and businessmen) to distance themselves from the political process. In his most recent videos (No You Can't and the People Demand), Anes Tina's tone is ever indignant; his words ever honest, visceral and bold; and his monologues ever scathing and cloaked in images of the popular, marginalized and the patriotic. For Algeria and countries across the MENA region, the ebb and flow of citizen-state contestation as epitomized in youth digital media practices and offline forms of collective action will continue to have important consequences for social and political change.

Notes

1 Stuart Cunningham and David Craig, *Social Media Entertainment: The New Intersection of Hollywood and Silicon Valley* (New York: NYU Press, 2019).

2 T.H. Marshall, *Citizenship and Social Class: And Other Essays* (Cambridge: Cambridge University Press, 1950).

3. Engin F. Isin, "Citizenship in Flux: The Figure of the Activist Citizen," *Subjectivity* 29, no. 1 (2009): 367–388.
4. Marshall, *Citizenship*, 94.
5. Giorgio Agamben, *Homo Sacer: Sovereign Power and Bare Life* (Stanford, CA: Stanford University Press, 1998).
6. Marshall, *Citizenship*.
7. Ibid.
8. Nancy Fraser and Linda Gordon, "Contract Versus Charity: Why is There no Social Citizenship in the United States," in *The Citizenship Debates: A Reader*, ed. Gershon Shafir (Minneapolis: University of Minnesota Press, 1992), 113–129.
9. Ibid., 152–56.
10. Bryan S. Turner, "Contemporary Problems in the Theory of Citizenship," in *Citizenship and Social Theory*, ed. Bryan S. Turner (London: Sage Publications, 1993), 2.
11. Arjun Appadurai, *Modernity at Large: Cultural Dimensions of Globalization* (Minneapolis: University of Minnesota Press, 1996).
12. Anthony Giddens, *The Consequences of Modernity* (Stanford, CA: Stanford University Press, 1990).
13. Isin, "Citizenship in Flux," 368–369.
14. Isin, "Citizenship in Flux"; Engin F. Isin and Evelyn Ruppert, *Being Digital Citizens* (Lanham, MD: Roman & Littlefield, 2015).
15. John Hartley, "Silly citizenship," *Critical Discourse Studies* 7, no. 4 (2010): 233–248.
16. Matt Ratto and Megan Boler, *DIY Citizenship: Critical Making and Social Media* (Cambridge, MA: The MIT Press, 2014).
17. Lance W. Bennett, *Civic Life Online: Learning How Digital Media Can Engage Youth* (Cambridge, MA: MIT Press, 2008); Russell J. Dalton, "Citizenship Norms and the Expansion of Political Participation," *Political Studies* 56 (2008): 76–98.
18. Neta Kligler-Vilenchik, "Alternative Citizenship Models: Contextualizing New Media and the New 'Good Citizen'," *New Media & Society* 19, no. 11 (2017): 1887–1903.
19. Ian Hargreaves and John Hartley, *The Creative Citizen Unbound: How Social Media and DIY Culture Contribute to Democracy, Communities and the Creative Economy* (Bristol: Policy Press, 2016).
20. Lori Kido Lopez, *Asian American Media Activism: Fighting for Cultural Citizenship* (New York: New York University Press, 2016); Elke Zobl and Ricardo Drüeke, *Feminist Media: Participatory Spaces, Networks and Cultural Citizenship* (Bielefeld: Transcript, 2012).
21. Vincent W. Flores and Rina Benmayor, *Latino Cultural Citizenship: Claiming Identity, Space, and Rights* (Boston: Beacon Press, 1997); Aihwa Ong, "Cultural Citizenship as Subject-Making," *Current Anthropology*, 37, no. 5 (1996): 737–762; Renato Rosaldo, "Cultural Citizenship, Inequality and Multiculturalism," in *Latino Cultural Citizenship: Claiming Identity, Space, and Rights*, eds. Vincent W. Flores and Rina Benmayor (Boston: Beacon Press, 1997), 27–38.
22. Engin F. Isin and Patricia K. Wood, *Citizenship and Identity* (London: Sage, 1999).
23. Isin, "Citizenship in Flux".
24. Ibid., p. 10.
25. See: Bennet, *Civic Life*; Manuel Castells, "Communication, Power and Counterpower in the Network Society." *International Journal of Communication* 1 (2007): 238–266; Elisabeth Klaus and Margareth Lünenborg, "Cultural Citizenship: Participation by and through Media," in *Feminist Media: Participatory Spaces, Networks and Cultural Citizenship*, eds. Elke Zobl and Ricardo Drüeke (Bielefeld, Germany: Transcript Verlag, 2012), 197–212; Peter Dahlgren, *Media and Political Engagement: Citizens, Communication, and Democracy* (Cambridge: Cambridge University Press, 2009); Peter Dahlgren, *Young Citizens and New Media: Learning for Democratic Participation* (New York: Routledge, 2010); Andy Furlong, "Citizenship and Political Engagement," in *Youth Studies: An Introduction* (New York: Routledge, 2012); Linda Herrera, "Youth and Citizenship in the Digital Age: A View from Egypt," *Harvard Educational Review* 82, no. 3 (2012), 333–352; Linda Herrera and Rehab Sakr, *Wired Citizenship: Youth Learning and Activism in the Middle East* (New York: Routledge, 2014); Bettina Von Lieres and Lawrence Piper, *Mediated Citizenship: The Informal Politics of Speaking for Citizens in the Global South* (New York: Palgrave Macmillan, 2014).
26. Bennett, *Civic Life*.
27. Tarik Sabry, "Emigration as Popular Culture: The Case of Morocco." *European Journal of Cultural Studies* 8, no. 1 (2005): 5–22.
28. All interviewee names have been changed to pseudonyms to protect the anonymity of my research participants.
29. Ong, "Cultural Citizenship".
30. Rosaldo, "Cultural Citizenship".

31 Michel Foucault, *History of Sexuality, vol. 1: An Introduction*, trans. Robert Hurley (New York: Pantheon Books, 1990), 96.
32 James C. Scott, *Weapons of the Weak: Everyday Forms of Resistance* (New Haven and London, Yale University Press, 1985).
33 Pierre Bourdieu, *The Logic of Practice* (Cambridge: Polity, 1990), 125.
34 Ibid., 123.
35 Michel Foucault, *The Courage of Truth: Lectures at the Collège de France 1983–1984*, trans. Graham Burchell (New York: Palgrave Macmillan, 2011); Michel Foucault, *Fearless Speech*, ed. Joseph Pearson (Los Angeles: Semiotext(e), 2001).
36 Castells, "Communication, Power".
37 Mohamed Zayani, *Networked Publics and Digital Contention: The Politics of Everyday Life in Tunisia* (New York: Oxford University Press, 2015).
38 Paul Hoggett and Simon Thompson, *Politics and the Emotions: The Affective Turn in Contemporary Political Studies* (New York: Continuum, 2012).

23

RECONSIDERING MOBILITY

The Competing Logics of Information and Communication Technologies Across Class Differences in the Context of Denver's Gentrification

Lynn Schofield Clark

The city of Denver is becoming gentrified, as anyone who lives there knows very well. An average of 276 people moved into the Denver area every day between 2010 and 2019.[1] Between 1990 and 2010, the city experienced a gentrification rate of 42 percent, placing the city in the top eight urban areas in the world undergoing rapid change.[2] According to several official sources, Denver's growth is attributable to successful collaborations between government, urban planners, and community organizations, each of whom has played a role in bringing increased economic opportunity and stability to the region.[3]

As is true for many cities in the world, the lived experiences of gentrification have been uneven, particularly in relation to mobility and class. By class, I mean to refer to both the shared socioeconomic status and cultural tastes among people, and the practices, societal structures, and embodiment in social dynamics that hold those class distinctions in place.[4] Mobility is one of the dynamics related to class distinctions, as this chapter will discuss. Mobility is "a geographical fact that lies at the centre of constellations of power, the creation of identities, and the microgeographies of everyday life," as Cresswell[5] has pointed out. Mobility refers to our ability to move through space. And those in information and communication studies have long been interested in the ways that communication systems traverse both time and space. The contemporary internet of fiber-optic cables that connects continents around the world, for instance, is based on a system of undersea cables first developed for the telegraph to transport messages, a fact that has long invited analyses both of how the world's systems of transportation and communication are related in our mental maps and how those material relationships meant to traverse both space and time continue to undergird our digital infrastructure regimes.[6] Studies of transportation and geography should be in dialogue with communication studies, as David Morley[7] has pointed out. We in information and communication studies need to pay attention to the distinctions between modes of mobility available to different people in different spheres, not only because communication technologies cross time and space, but because for many people, locality is destiny.

This chapter focuses on the relationship between class and mobility, understood not only in terms of the potential for socioeconomic change in an individual or group's status, but also in terms of one's ability to move across time and space, and the role of communication and data in relation to that movement. This chapter is therefore situated in relation to what Maren Hartmann and her colleagues[8] have referred to as *mobile socialities*, a bridging concept that emphasizes the social and cultural within the overlapping spheres of mobilities and mobile communications. Hartmann and others working in this area are interested in making space for critical thinking and contextualized research on mobile technologies, institutions, and underlying processes and practices of people and media on the move (also see Polson's chapter in this volume). This work follows Morley's[9] admonition to decenter "the media" in media studies and to bring together reflections on communication technologies and transportation infrastructures to questions of how each enable, or constrain, human abilities to bridge between time and space. The concept of sociality, as Magnus Andersson[10] develops it, brings with it the human desire for relationship and connectivity that, as Jose Van Dijck[11] has pointed out, is increasingly mediated by platforms.

I am especially interested in how differing social groups negotiate varied understandings of mobility, class, information and communication technologies, and the relationship between these in the context of gentrification. I adopt Page and Ross's[12] definition of gentrification as "the class-based transformation of urban space involving (a) reinvestment of capital, (b) social upgrade of locale by incoming high-income groups, (c) urban landscape change, and (d) direct or indirect displacement of low-income groups," following the work of Lees, Slater and Wyly.[13] Processes of gentrification are therefore intimately connected to changing relations of time, space, and movement, as those with the greatest access to resources choose to move to the city center, and those with the least access are displaced to areas that are further from places of employment and schooling and may be further from friends, colleagues, and other family members. Denver's gentrification has removed many populations struggling with financial precarity from the urban core, thus securing a perception of city safety among employers, upper middle-class residents, and tourists while also contributing to an intensification of other problems. Among other things, the dearth of affordable housing near employment and education opportunities in the city core has led to the rapid displacement of less financially secure populations from historic neighborhoods and the growth of suburban poverty where infrastructures of transportation and communication are less robust.

Scholars seeking to consider the value of the framework of "mobile socialities" pose it as an alternative to the media-centric and individualistic assumptions embedded in the concept of "networked individualism." Following in that line of thought, in this chapter I look at what I will call *anti*-mobile socialities, exploring the social structures and practices that hold some people in immobility via ideologies, bureaucracies, and other ways power is exercised via transportation and communication technologies.

After an introduction to the historical context of Denver, I focus on two groups of people with differential access to resources of mobility and mobilization who relate to one another in direct and indirect ways. The first group comprises teenaged young people from financially insecure migrant and asylum-seeking families from varying racial/ethnic backgrounds who engaged in collective action to address the daily challenges of mobility that have real consequences in their lives. The second group includes adults from financially secure backgrounds, most of whom are white, and who are involved in progressive urban and transportation planning efforts through their professional or voluntary positions in a major metropolitan city. Ethnographic data exploring the work of these two groups reveals competing logics related to the role of information and communication technologies that play out in relation to class and mobility, a finding that will be presented and then considered to offer a preliminary discussion of what I will refer to as *anti-mobile* socialities at this chapter's conclusion. Underlying this application of theoretical concepts to ethnographic data is a desire to explore the ways that anti-mobile socialities inadvertently work to enable certain kinds of mobilization while simultaneously limiting others. We begin with a discussion of the Denver context.

Denver and Gentrification

Denver's contemporary dense and affluent downtown core of attractive pedestrian malls, tourist-friendly restaurant rows, and active business and entertainment districts dates to changes first brought about with the Urban Skyline Renewal Project of 1967. Using funds made available through the US Housing Acts of 1949 and 1954 to revitalize the downtown area and boost city tax revenues, in the 1960s and 1970s many historic homes and buildings, including the largely Mexican American neighborhood of Auraria, were condemned as "blighted" and replaced with skyscrapers, retail businesses, parking lots, and the joint downtown Auraria campuses of the University of Colorado, Metropolitan State, and the Community College of Denver. Local media were aggressively supportive of the city's revitalization efforts at the time.[14] The revitalization led to the displacement of poor and lower middle-class people to locations outside of the city center and also precipitated a shutting down of what had been a central area of Chicano activism in the 1960s.[15]

While that is the story of the central downtown core, the roots of Denver's current gentrification issues can be traced back even further and are even more directly related to issues of information communication technologies and transportation infrastructure. Denver's oldest city neighborhoods dated to the 1860s and 1870s, which at that time were economically mixed. But with the late nineteenth century introduction of electric streetcars and the influx of automobiles, wealthier residents left those neighborhoods and moved out of the inner city to other city and outer city neighborhoods. By the 1920s, the inner city and some other city neighborhoods were an affordable place for resettlement for Hispanics who were moving from rural Colorado, New Mexico, and Texas in great numbers.[16] The National Housing Act of 1934 made mortgages more readily available, but the Federal Housing Authority only insured those mortgages that were not "redlined." The 1930s-era practice of redlining was a means of organizing and communicating information about homes and homeowners, as the agency drew red lines on the city's map to mark non-white neighborhoods as areas containing housing that was uninsured and uninsurable.[17] Redlining was rooted in the false belief that property values would plummet and crime would rise if African American families moved into the same neighborhoods as white families. Thus, while some wealthier families of color endured discrimination and premium pricing to live in suburban neighborhoods, redlining had the real effect of pushing the majority of Denver's nonwhite and lower income residents into certain less desirable neighborhoods away from the suburbs yet still close to the city center. As Denver became a tech hub for innovation in recent decades[18] and as increased traffic and prices for gas have made public transit and shorter commutes more attractive, it is these older once-redlined city neighborhoods, with charming small homes built from the 1890s to the 1940s, that have come to be desirable in the first decades of the second millennium for their affordability and proximity to the city center. They are the areas seeing the greatest extent of displacement in the contemporary era.

Post-World War Two investment in energy, government, and technology centers south and west of downtown Denver, areas that are known today as the Federal Center to the west and the Denver Tech Center to the south, further fueled suburban expansion in the 1950s–1990s.[19] Then, in 1954, when the Supreme Court decision of *Brown* v. *Board of Education* desegregated US schools, a re-segregation quickly occurred in Denver as remaining white residents moved to further outlying suburban areas and opted into those schools, leaving inner city urban and older city neighborhood schools with a depleted tax base. Wealthier residents and their taxes funded newer schools in suburban and exurban areas and made much greater investments in information and communication technologies than the schools serving the city neighborhoods.[20]

National and state policies favoring highway construction over public transit further calcified the racial, economic, and transportation divides of the city after the city's streetcar system fell into disuse in the 1950s. Recognizing the growing transit issues across Denver's expanding suburban and exurban areas, Denver and several of its neighboring counties initiated a transportation plan and formed what, in 1968, came to be named the Denver Regional Council of Governments (DRCOG). This association then created the Regional Transportation District (RTD) "to develop, maintain, and operate a mass transportation system" in Denver and five of its surrounding counties.[21] Between 1997 and 2004, Denver's RTD worked on implementing rail transit incrementally until, after several proven successes, voters approved what is now one of the largest urban rail transit programs in the USA. This public support was generated in part as a result of massive advertising spending on the part of RTD.[22]

In their analysis of RTD's successful development, Jones, Goetz, and Bhattacharjee[23] have suggested that while the nation state is instrumental in orchestrating city–regional collaborations in more centralized political and economic systems, such as those of the UK or Finland, such efforts occur in the USA 'from below.' This is the case because shortfalls in federal funding for transportation infrastructure mean that state and local taxes and bond issues are the primary source of revenue for major public undertakings such as highways and mass transit projects. Local members of the Board of Directors of the RTD are elected and are directly accountable to their constituents. They therefore hold open meetings and seek input on plans from those who live in their areas.

Smart Young People in the Not-So-Smart City

In Denver, some areas of the city are better served than others by RTD's light rail and bus services. In the book *Young People and the Future of News*, Regina Marchi and I[24] presented the story of a group of young people aged 15–18 in an after-school club who wanted to address the RTD with their concerns about inconvenient and overcrowded bus services. Consistent with worldwide research on digital and mobile media use among young people who live in economically distressed neighborhoods, the students who attended this particular high school and participated in this program were reliant on their mobile phones but lacked access to opportunities linking digital media use to the fostering of political voice, and had encountered little encouragement to use these tools for civic or political engagement.[25] But the students were participants in an after-school program that had experimented with youth-led participatory action research (YPAR) in the past, roughly following a curriculum developed by community engagement expert Cara DiEnno[26] that invited students to (1) identify a problem; (2) conduct research on the problem as well as on the governmental, school, or civic offices and policies that inadvertently exacerbated the problem; and then (3) devise a plan of action for addressing the problem in a manner that could be presented to those who had the authority to change those policies deemed problematic. To this design, the after-school Digital Media Club of Denver's South High School added a media-rich dimension that included utilizing the latest information and communication technologies in both the conducting of research and in the production of a series of messages that comprised a fourth step: (4) designing a communication plan that would present evidence in support of the proposed plan of action developed by the youth in step three. This communication plan would include differing messages, formats, and distribution outlets specifically designed to motivate and persuade a series of differing audiences that might include policymakers, fellow students, members of the public, or all of these.[27] Each of these messages took the form of what Dahlgren[28] had described as *community or grassroots journalism*, as young citizens took the initiative in identifying common problems, communicating about those problems among themselves, and proposing solutions to those problems. But as the projects developed, several of them also evolved into what Dahlgren described as *advocacy citizen journalism*, in that students were introduced to adult members of interest groups, civic and political organizations, and social movements who had been working on addressing the issues that the students had identified and had, therefore, already played a role in both articulating the controversial issues that impacted the community and mobilizing people toward specific political solutions.

Student participants in this effort had come to the Denver area from Somalia, Ghana, Ethiopia, Eritrea, Kenya, Thailand, Bangladesh, Vietnam, China, Mexico, Iraq, and the United Arab

Emirates. Other student participants were members of domestic minority groups, including several who identified themselves as Latinx, Asian American, African American, Native American, and multiracial. Most of the students lived in neighborhoods far from their high school, but were attending there because it was a designated school for English language learners and for neighborhoods where closer schools had been closed.[29]

Angelica, a ninth-grade biracial teen who was new to the club but had been involved in youth media production efforts in the past, mentioned transportation as a possible issue to explore.[30] She had discussed the problems of overcrowded buses and slow transportation routes to city schools with other peers who attended a different high school, and the students in the club enthusiastically agreed that this would be something worth looking into. As she noted:

> I brought up the idea of transportation. It was a bigger issue for us because all of us take the bus. And so we decided that we would investigate it a little bit more. We went to check out the bus stops, and interviewed people off-camera, and we watched the buses pass people, and thought, wow, there are issues!

The students then decided on a general plan of action. First, they decided that they would conduct a survey of their fellow students to determine exactly how well-served students were (or were not) by the current offerings made available through Denver's Regional Transportation District (RTD). Based on their own experiences of an admittedly small and unrepresentative sample, they knew that they and their peers often spent a great deal of time waiting for buses to arrive and were sometimes refused service if a bus was already filled. They therefore began with the idea that they would simply present RTD officials with information on which routes were most overcrowded. They were also interested in learning about whether or not a large number of their fellow students were inconvenienced by existing bus routes that required them to take two or more buses to attend school.

The project quickly took on an investigative thrust with its emphasis on data collection among students and on the processes through which transportation issues were decided within the region. A galvanizing moment occurred when students were discussing the fact that RTD offered all students a discount for monthly bus fares. Rather than paying the $40 monthly fee expected of adult riders, students only paid $20 each month, or a total of $180 each year. The students thought this was a "good deal"—until they started to do research into the amounts that students in other school districts paid to get to school. A sister urban school, they learned, had negotiated an even lower monthly rate for its students. But what really surprised them was when they learned that the school district that served many of the wealthiest neighborhoods in the area offered bus service to students completely subsidized by local taxpayers. It was at this point that their project took on the tenor of a social justice issue. "Why is it that they get bus service for free when we have to ask our parents to help us pay for each sibling's ride to school?," they asked.

Because the school did not want to take up class time for the distribution of the survey, the students themselves arranged to invite students to take the survey using mobile phones in times before and after school and during the lunch hour over the course of several weeks. As the students introduced their fellow peers to the survey, they took the opportunity to inform their peers of what they had discovered about discrepancies between the bus service they received and the services that were available in other areas of the city.

With the assistance of their teachers, area university educators, and graduate student mentors in the project, the students invited several not-for-profit organizations to come and talk with them about citywide initiatives to improve transportation, particularly for underserved populations, including Denver's not-for-profits Mile High Connects and Transportation Solutions (broad-based groups of people and organizations committed to fostering transportation equity in the region). They learned that Denver Public Schools had drastically cut most of its subsidized bus services some

20 years earlier as a cost-cutting measure. This move had indirectly placed the responsibility for transporting students with RTD.

Several students continued to do research on how students across the city got to school, while others focused on analyzing the data from the nearly 400 surveys they collected from their high school peers. Many of the students attended a monthly board meeting of the RTD. Several adult attendees at that meeting offered to introduce students to those who worked in scheduling for RTD, and students learned more about how and to whom to make an effective presentation. The students decided that they wanted to make a presentation to decision makers who could be influenced by the information they desired to share, as they wanted to offer alternative proposals to current arrangements. This presentation, they decided, would be most effective if it included both data from their survey and a short video that conveyed the problem of bus overcrowding so that decision makers would have a better feel for the student experience with public transportation. Their adult mentors made the introduction and arranged the meeting.

In recent years, RTD had been investing heavily in improving the infrastructure that would provide transportation for Denver's burgeoning suburban and gentrifying urban population to get to the airport, located some 20 miles from the downtown area. In fact, in 2016, much fanfare accompanied the announcement of a new rail line that would link the southern suburbs, which contained many of the city's wealthiest neighborhoods, to the airport far to the northeast of the city. Another new line would link the downtown area directly to the airport, travelling through an area to the north of the city. But unfortunately for those living in the east neighborhoods, which is where many of the area's most impoverished citizens and new immigrant communities lived, neither rail line improved their transportation to the city center, which is where most of the city's employment and educational opportunities existed. For the time being, those in the east neighborhoods were going to remain reliant on overcrowded and unreliable bus services. To make matters worse, even some of those bus lines had to be cut for "cost-saving measures," according to RTD, as the city had to locate funds for the larger rail projects. No one would be without service, RTD promised, as they focused on redundancies and cutting poorly utilized lines.

The student survey affirmed that many of the students from the high school, like those students overseeing the transportation project, lived in these east neighborhoods. The survey of transportation needs found that a majority of students travelled 30 minutes or more by bus to get to and from school each day, and many took two buses to get there. Moreover, the survey also found that the bus line most frequently used by English language learning students was among those whose service was scheduled to be drastically reduced. According to an estimate based on the survey, some 100 or more students would now need to take three buses to get to school. Julio, a junior who had moved with his family from Mexico to Denver, noted that he took a first bus shortly after 5 am because he wanted to ensure that he arrived at school on time and knew that if that bus line or either of the other two buses he needed to take were overcrowded, he would risk being late to school.

As it happened, thanks to arrangements made by Transportation Solutions, the RTD scheduler and RTD commissioner had agreed to meet with the club students on an arbitrary day in April—and that date turned out to be four days after the proposed bus service changes went into effect. While a great deal of mainstream media attention had focused on the opening of the rail lines to the airport, very few reporters had looked into the effects of curtailed bus lines (but see Warner[31]). This made the student meeting with RTD officials of particular interest to local journalists, and the largest community-based newspaper in the area covered the meeting, giving extensive coverage to students' concerns and placing the story on its front page a few days later under the headline, "South Students now Commuting Longer."[32] The club's Facebook page linked to this article as well as to the humorous yet poignant video the students had put together illustrating bus overcrowding and frustration over curtailed bus lines. Although nervous, the students had prepared their presentation for the RTD officials by putting together and rehearsing a PowerPoint presentation that included the three-minute video on bus overcrowding.

The RTD scheduler who watched the video and listened to the students' presentation immediately agreed to reinstate the line that affected the large number of students, as documented in the student survey, and the students were very pleased with their success. But we also learned in that meeting that RTD did not receive any data from the schools about the homes and neighborhoods where the students reliant on transit lived. Such information would of course be useful to RTD for planning routes. As the students looked into this further, they learned from Transportations Solutions officials that the data would need to be anonymized before it could be given to RTD, and this was part of the problem: no one at the school district had the time to anonymize the names and addresses of the 40,000 students who were a part of the Denver school district.

The commissioner adamantly noted that they needed such data in order to make good decisions:

> Some of the complaints I get sometimes are, "your buses are running around empty." There's a good reason for that. In the middle of the day, people are not going to and from work. So, we have to figure out how to balance the resources we have as best we can, to serve everyone.… So again, if we have more data, then [the scheduler's] office can crunch the numbers and figure out what we have to spend. And the money we get, by the way, is mostly from tax money. And we have to allocate fairly according to where is the greatest demand. So, organizing yourselves, if you can provide more data for them to do that, then you're likely to get the best result.

This prompted one adult participant to ask: "So, what was the data that made it seem possible or important to cancel the line (that negatively impacted many students)? It seems like 100 or so bus-takers would be a significant amount," to which the scheduler replied, "It's all driven by trying to maintain the budget on the one hand, limited resources, where do people have alternative services." He went on to explain that those students had the option of taking a different bus. But Julio, the student who was affected by this service change, noted that without the reinstatement of the bus service that had been cut, his alternative route would add not only a third bus but also another 15 minutes to his walk to and from the bus. At this point, the scheduler reiterated that he would "check" to ensure that the bus service he had earlier promised to reinstate would, in fact, be reinstated. He also promised to look at adding more buses during the times when the bus service is most in demand in order to alleviate overcrowding. He added, "I can't promise, but it's something else we can look at."

Kwasi, a student who had moved with his family to the United States from Ghana several years earlier, then asked, "Didn't one of you say that you live in [the wealthy school district where the students had earlier learned that bus service was fully subsidized]? I'm just curious. How do your kids get to school?" To which the scheduler noted that in the school district where his children attended, "they provide school buses." "Oh. Okay …" Kwasi replied, allowing the exchange to hang in the air.

As the meeting time was drawing to a close, the RTD commissioner praised the students for their efforts, noting:

> This is a beginning. This is a great idea to have a group like this that represents the school, and it might be good for other schools to have something like this. Because RTD can do its job better if it has more information. So, finding facilities for information to be gathered and organized well, so that they can use it to make good decisions that will serve, and don't have to wait a half an hour, or so that the bus will go to the places at the right times. So, learning from this, doing more of it, maybe talking to other schools. It's a good idea.

The RTD officials expressed gratitude for the opportunity to hear from the students directly. In fact, in the year following, a consultant group hired to work with RTD on a region-wide 10-year transportation plan contacted the group of students again to see if they would be interested in extending their work to other schools. But several of the students who had provided leadership in the bus route project had graduated, and those remaining were not interested in being involved. As there was no remuneration on offer for their time, they thought that other schools could follow their lead, but they could not see the logic in volunteering their own time to these activities. They chose instead to move on to another effort that they felt would provide more direct benefit to the primary communities of their school and their own neighborhoods. They developed a plan to engage more students of color in the Honors and Advanced Placement programs at their school, another project that was ultimately quite successful.

Well-meaning Middle-class Adults and the "Green Field for Experimentation"

Some of the adults who had served as consultants for the students had been working on a regional effort designed to mitigate the effects of Denver's gentrification, and continued their work over the course of the following year. These adults, some of whom were professionals in urban planning and transit design and others who were volunteers and community organizers who lived outside Denver, were focused on the proposed mixed income revitalization of Sun Valley, a Denver city neighborhood with a large immigrant, refugee, and asylum-seeking population. This neighborhood was directly west of the downtown campus and south of The Highlands, one of Denver's gentrifying neighborhoods most recognized for its rapid increase in housing values and displacement. South High school, the school hosting the youth program that successfully changed the bus routes, also served several young people in this neighborhood. The adults involved in this initiative sincerely wanted to involve community members in the processes of revitalizing the neighborhood in a manner that would support and not displace those currently residing there while managing the neighborhood's anticipated influx of attractive retail and business ventures and higher income residents.

It was in the context of ethnographic participant observation in meetings with this group that an alternative logic of information communication and technology revealed itself, along with a contrasting understanding of the role of data in relation to issues of mobility and class. For the young people and their allies, information and communication technologies were understood as tools to use in order to gather data and develop the language appropriate for participation in decision-making; their goal was to be heard and seen. For those engaging in processes of urban planning, information and communication technologies were similarly understood as tools through which they could gather input from historically marginalized groups. However, while they did aim to incorporate insights from community members into revitalization planning, their conversations about information and communication tools and the data collected often focused on their frustrations related to data collection and analysis, as they discussed the problem of people who resisted providing feedback, or provided the wrong kind of feedback at the wrong time, or did not provide enough feedback.

The information and communication goals of the adults involved in planning the neighborhood's revitalization were twofold: first, they wanted to eliminate resistance and to create what they referred to as "smooth" experiences through which they could gather data and convey their plans to the neighbors, and second, they wanted to communicate the city's plans to residents so that those residents would be informed and could therefore participate in decision-making processes. While they held regular community meetings that were poorly attended and invested time in getting to know key community leaders in order to better understand community concerns, they also discussed among themselves the promise of passive data collection that could be developed as part of the neighborhood's revitalization. Fiber-optic cables would be laid under the street grid to provide high-speed internet access while also allowing planners to gather information about transportation flows in order to better anticipate needs, they said. Such information could then inform future plans for the redesign of streets and housing. The need for cumbersome community meetings and survey administration might be lessened in the future, it was implied.

The second goal of those in the urban planning initiative involved developing an information and communication technology infrastructure that would not only gather data, but would also keep members of the community informed of the progress of urban revitalization efforts. Community newspapers, text alert systems, and curated online information about the revitalization project were discussed. Several of the adults became quite excited about the prospects of being able to evaluate the introduction of this communication system into the revitalizing neighborhood. As one middle-class white woman who lived in a different neighborhood declared with enthusiasm, working with this particular revitalizing neighborhood would provide a "green field for experimentation." Several other well-meaning adults similarly embraced this terminology, discussing the introduction of a journalism-like initiative that could demonstrate the value of journalism, understood as a means of keeping neighbors informed so that neighbors could participate in discussions as their community underwent change. Rather than community meetings, what would hold this idea together was the prospect of involving young people from the community as reporters on their own neighborhood, several enthused.

The term "green field" was meant to imply an openness and a lack of existing infrastructure. The term underscored the idea that those who held historical knowledge of information and communication systems, such as professional journalists, could "experiment" in this area. Such language is consistent with the idea of the "city as lab," first embraced by sociologist Robert E. Park in his early twentieth century studies of Chicago that sought to place at the center of inquiry the residents' own perspectives and experiences of life in the vibrant ecosystem of the city. There are several ironies in the use of this particular term of the "green field," however. First, it negated the fact that informal systems of communication already existed in the neighborhood in relation to differing language, culture, and familial groups. These systems had little to do with formal institutions of journalism or of data collection. Flyers pinned to community center bulletin boards, conversations at the elementary school entrance, and weekly gatherings for neighborhood dinners at the community center provided some means for neighbors to learn about and discuss revitalization plans, although in reality those plans mainly came into discussion in relation to current or anticipated inconveniences, skepticism about projected timelines, and fears regarding possible displacement in relation to proposed construction projects.

The use of the term "green field" was also ironic in relation to the lived reality of the neighborhood, where there were few open green spaces save for the fenced school athletic fields, the treacherous banks on the side of the polluted city river, and the weeds and overgrown grass surrounding an abandoned power plant. This second irony pointed to the power of imagining the physical space in the neighborhood itself as a "green field," untrammeled by the eyesores of urban decay and urban mismanagement. The terminology itself suggested the imagined value of an area that could be razed and rebuilt, much like the contested gentrification efforts of the 1960s and 1970s that had led the nearby Auraria neighborhood to experience forced displacement as the areas deemed "blighted" were rebuilt for the steel and concrete campus of the central city.

Both of these ironies point to the ways that those living in the so-called revitalizing neighborhood, some of whom had memories of the razing and rebuilding of the nearby Auraria neighborhood, were not likely to relate the terminology of the "green field of experimentation" to positive developments. Nor were the neighbors likely to share in the enthusiasm for the idea that "youth could be a real communication help for getting the word out," as one well-meaning middle-class adult from a different neighborhood enthused about fleshing out the role of information and communication technologies in the revitalization effort. Those young people living in the neighborhood, as well as their parents, were much more interested in mitigating against the effects of economic insecurity and instability. When they were not in school, the vast majority of the young people between the ages of 16–21 were working or seeking work as a means to bolster their family's and their own income, or were providing child care for family members who were working.

Youth involvement in the proposed communication and information technology plan would, most likely, hinge on the promise of remuneration. Yet among the well-meaning adults who lived in other neighborhoods, the lived realities of economic scarcity and poverty were more difficult to reconcile with plans for the neighborhood's revitalization, and thus were not readily discussed beyond the limits of seeking funding for such a venture. Some young people had volunteered their time to address the bus route problem; this served as evidence that perhaps other young people might similarly volunteer their time. But those volunteers had selected the bus route project. When given the opportunity to work according to someone else's agenda, even on an issue about which they had expertise, they were not as interested. And money for the development of an informed community did not seem forthcoming. After all, the time period of this revitalization discussion was coinciding with the closure of Denver's daily newspaper and the laying off of numerous local journalists. Most discussions about funding for local journalism were centered on how to build a sustainable business model. And those discussions centered on developing strong relationships, or "engagement," between news providers and those news consumers who were willing to, and could, pay for news. A community such as Sun Valley would need a different business model to fund the experimentation involved in designing and implementing a new, or even enhancing an existing, information and communication technology infrastructure. And foundations would not be interested unless such a model were deemed sustainable, which is a challenging prospect for a neighborhood struggling with poverty and the possibility of displacement. In the aftermath of the Trump election and subsequent cuts to not-for-profit and progressive city initiatives, many of these efforts were indefinitely placed on hold.

Discussion

In the previous section, I use the term infrastructure in a manner that follows Lisa Parks'[33] critical methodology for analyzing infrastructural sites and objects in relation to environmental, socio-economic, and geopolitical conditions. I have aimed to make infrastructures "intelligible," to use her term, by breaking infrastructures down into discrete parts, considering the interrelationships between transportation systems, communication and information technologies, urban planners, and those young people and their families and neighbors who live in neighborhoods most directly impacted by gentrification and "revitalization." Parks suggests, following Larkin[34] and Beller,[35] that we explore infrastructure in relation to the technologies that mediate social and political life. The transportation and communication and information infrastructures at the heart of the stories told here therefore involve not only the physical aspects of roads and highways and cables and media channels; they also refer to the bus and rail routes and the daily schedules these follow, and the processes through which decisions are made that put these pathways in place and allow those living in the areas most affected to anticipate and have input into changes that might transpire. Infrastructures also involve the places of focused attention and exchange, such as the points at which drivers and riders or construction workers and neighbors interact, and where urban planners, community leaders, government officials and neighbors meet—or fail to meet—one another in places of employment, schools, community centers, and homes.

It is in these focused points of attention and exchange where feelings of frustration about the limits of the physical structures often emerge. Infrastructures often remain invisible and seamless until people experience disruptions to access, as noted in the case of the bus lines. What is of particular concern in the second case is that the future disruptions that may be experienced by some may be rendered invisible through what Parks has termed the "infrastructural imaginaries" of others. This seemed particularly problematic when the urban planners complained about the ways that community members did not fit their feedback into the channels that had been organized for them, and when some imagined a "green field" devoid of historical relations that offered vibrant possibilities for a yet-to-be-designed information and communication infrastructure.

This chapter has followed Fortunati and Taipale's[36] proposal that research is needed that focuses on the relationships between daily spatial mobility and social mobility and the role of communication and transportation in relation to these. They have pointed out that people must move to where work or school are located, and thus upward mobility is linked to wider and more intensive spatial mobility. This is the "darker side of hypermobility,"[37] in that as humans are required to move in time and space to acquire capital, we incur differential physiological, psychological, emotional and social costs, as is illustrated in the instances of skepticism and fears expressed as well as the complicated workarounds required in order to manage the demands of everyday life in the city. This chapter thus also reinforces the insights in Halegoua's earlier chapter in this section of the book, as she explored the ways that developers struggle with mapping ubiquitous computing onto actual lived experiences.

Both of the cases explored here relate to infrastructures and the ways that data are imagined flowing in and through them. The adults in the urban and transportation planning work for the most part shared my own white cisgender middle-class "do-gooder" and social justice-oriented background. We all tended to emphasize the ways that information and communication technologies could be harnessed for better and more equitable outcomes in the future. In contrast, residents of Denver's city neighborhoods, both those who participated in the student bus project and those opting not to participate in the community meetings of the revitalizing neighborhood, generally shared backgrounds that differed from the first group. Their lived experiences were similar to those community members who had been resistant to the Urban Skyline Renewal Project of 1967 and its use of the eminent domain designation for declaring neighborhoods "blighted," which, in the past, had rendered the displacement of residents as "necessary." The young people in the bus study were only interested in information and communication technologies to the extent that they could be harnessed for concerns they were facing in the present. And those in the revitalizing neighborhoods, while invited to reflect on their present concerns, were largely given opportunities to reflect on what their neighborhoods might face in the future.

Whereas much of this chapter has focused on the movement of data and people across spaces, issues of time are also implicated in each case, as suggested in the observations regarding the past, present, and future, as noted above. It might be useful, therefore, to consider Craig Jeffreys'[38] analysis of what he termed the "politics of waiting" here. Jeffreys chronicles the story of "chronic waiting" as a key experience of life among those in lower income locales in India. He has observed that economic and social changes have rendered some into a state of perpetual waiting: waiting on promised access to political freedoms, or on economic opportunity, that is delayed, sometimes indefinitely. In his argument that pervasive unemployment and chronic waiting has led some young people to engage in political mobilization, Jeffreys ends his own analysis on a hopeful note that echoes the story of the young people told here. And yet, the story of the adults involved in the second case suggests a darker take on the politics of waiting. In that story, too, those most directly affected in the processes of gentrification are similarly asked to wait: for the newer and better neighborhood, with its newer and better transportation, information and communication systems. In this way, it might be argued that the experience of chronic waiting can lead to and reinforce *immobility*.

The imagined possible futures that those with more resources embrace, and that young people, too, are encouraged to embrace, are perhaps best explained as a form of what Lauren Berlant[39] has termed "cruel optimism." Berlant argues that we all remain attached to fantasies of the good life, with promises of upward mobility, job security, political and social equality, and durable intimacy. But through her review of expressions in avant-garde art and film, she argues that we are increasingly recognizing that liberal-capitalist societies can no longer be counted on to provide opportunities for individuals to make their lives add up to something This is cruel optimism's "double bind," she notes; "even with an image of a better good life available to sustain your optimism, it is awkward and it is threatening to detach from what is already not working."[40] Thus, as we wait for these never-to-materialize visions, or even as we experience small victories that make lives somewhat easier in the moment, we are rendered immobile in the face of larger infrastructures, those of the past, present, and future, that limit us in both space and time.

Conclusion

This project seeking to compare the differing logics of information and communication technologies as they relate to class and gentrification came about after publishing a hope-filled and somewhat prescriptive book about what I believed it would take to build the kind of media, education, and digital media literacy environment that would support the inclusion of diverse young people into a working and functional civil society.[41] The second case study took place in the year following my work with young people from lower income and economically distressed neighborhoods who had successfully addressed the transportation infrastructures that were limiting to them and their peers. It was then that I interacted with well-meaning middle-class adults who sought to embrace social justice-informed approaches to urban planning and development.

Both the adults and the young people with whom I had worked shared a deep concern about the negative effects of gentrification on the people who lived in changing neighborhoods. The first story of youth successfully engaging on transportation issues was, importantly, grounded in relation to the adult assistance of mostly middle-class educators, graduate students, and community leaders who were oriented toward supporting the young people in addressing a problem that they themselves had defined. In that case, the youth were able to translate their findings into a logic that made sense to decision-makers. Once the young people had leveraged introductions that their adult assistants were able to facilitate for them with RTD officials, the young people presented those officials with survey data and video evidence in a context that called the officials to account, and provided a space in which to discuss possible solutions. The young people felt ownership in the success of the changed bus routes, and then felt empowered to pursue other activities that they defined and designed in order to address the needs of their community as they understood them.

Yet while the young people sought to utilize ICTs as a means of gathering data and creating stories that would help transportation decision-makers to better understand their challenges, the adults in the urban planning revitalization project had experienced frustration in their own attempts with data gathering, and they envisioned a differing role for ICTs partly as a result. These adults wanted to partner with community members and leaders, but encountered resistance, as community members did not attend community meetings or participate in processes designed to solicit their input. I have therefore noted that both cases produced a "politics of waiting." Those with fewer resources were either placed into a position of waiting due to failing transportation infrastructures, or were asked to wait while also being asked to participate in communication processes that might or might not render positive outcomes for their neighborhoods. Even as hopeful stories of youth mobilization can provide some much-needed encouragement, therefore, this chapter suggests an overarching pessimism with regard to the prospects for social mobility. Even those most attached to visions that might limit the negative outcomes of gentrification might be forgiven for skepticism. For the question of mobility, as David Morley[42] has noted, may be less a question of who is or is not mobile, but rather: who has power over their own mobility?

Notes

1 Denver Colorado Demographics and Population Statistics, "Denver," accessed March 27, 2019. www.hometodenver.com/stats_denver.htm.

2 Jennifer Oldham, "Denver Looks to Curb the Rapid Spread of Gentrification," *Pacific Standard* (January 14, 2019), accessed March 27, 2019. https://psmag.com/economics/denver-takes-on-spread-of-gentrification.
3 Ben Markus, "Hickenlooper's Economy Roars, But How Much of That is Thanks to Him?", *CPR News* (2019, January 2), accessed March 27, 2019. www.cpr.org/2019/01/02/hickenloopers-economy-roars-but-how-much-of-that-is-thanks-to-him/.
4 See Pierre Bourdieu, *Distinction: A Social Critique of the Judgment of Taste* (London: Routledge, 1984), and this volume's introduction.
5 Tim Cresswell, Mobilities I: Catching Up. *Progress in Human Geography* 34(4): 550–558, p. 551. doi: 10.1177/1206331205280144. See also Tim Cresswell, "Towards a Politics of Mobility," *Environment and Planning D: Society and Space* 28, no. 1 (2010): 17–31.
6 James W. Carey, *Communication as Culture: Essays on Media and Society* (New York: Routledge, 1988); John Durham Peters, *Speaking into the Air: A History of the Idea of Communication* (Chicago: University of Chicago Press, 1999).
7 David Morley, *Home Territories: Media, Mobility and Identity* (London: Routledge, 2000); David Morley, "Technologies of Communication: Communities, Mobilities, and Boundaries," Keynote at Mobile Socialities Symposium, Lund, Sweden, April 2018.
8 Maren Hartmann, Annette Hill, and Magnus Andersson, *Mobile Socialities as a Bridging Concept* (Mobile Socialities Symposium Proceedings, Lund, Sweden, April 2018).
9 Morley, *Home Territories*.
10 Magnus Andersson, "Mobile Socialities—A Bridging Concept," Presentation at Mobile Socialities: An International Workshop (Lund, Sweden, April 12, 2018).
11 Jose Van Dijck, *The Culture of Connectivity: A Critical History of Social Media* (Oxford/New York: Oxford University Press, 2013).
12 Brian Page and Eric Ross, "Legacies of a Contested Campus: Urban Renewal, Community Resistance, and the Origins of Gentrification in Denver," *Urban Geography* 38, no. 9 (2017): 1315. https://doi.org/10.1080/02723638.2016.1228420.
13 L. Lees, T. Slater, and E. Wyly, *Gentrification* (New York: Routledge, 2008); L. Lees, T. Slater, and E. Wyly, eds. *The Gentrification Reader* (New York: Routledge, 2010).
14 See: F.C. Abbott, *The Auraria Higher Education Center: How it Came to Be* (Denver, CO: Auraria Higher Education Center, 1999); R.E. Bowen, *The Vision and the Struggle: How Metropolitan State University of Denver Began* (Centennial, CO: REBALS Press, 2015); "Relocation Assistance in Plans, Mayor Says," *Denver Post* (October 30, 1969), 3; and "McNichols Answers Questions on Auraria," *Rocky Mountain News* (November 2, 1969): 5, 10 [as discussed in Page and Ross, "Legacies"].
15 Marianne Goodland, "The Parable of Gentrification," *Colorado Independent* (2015, November 4). www.coloradoindependent.com/2015/11/04/denver-victims-of-gentrification-fret-for-elyria-swansea-and-globeville-residents/.
16 Magdalena Gallegos, *History of the Hispanic Settlers in Auraria: The Forgotten Community* (Denver, CO: Auraria Library Special Collections, 1985), as cited in Page and Ross, "Legacies".
17 Doreen Massey, "Racial Discrimination in Housing: A Moving Target, *Social Problems* 52(2): 148–151.
18 Sasha Galbraith, "Watch Out Silicon Valley! Colorado Primed to Emerge as the Next Hub of Innovation and Entrepreneurship," *Forbes* (December 17, 2012). www.forbes.com/sites/sashagalbraith/2012/12/17/watch-out-silicon-valley-colorado-primed-to-emerge-as-the-next-hub-of-innovation-and-entrepreneurship/.
19 Page and Ross, "Legacies."
20 See *Standing in the Gap*, Four-part documentary, Rocky Mountain PBS (2015). Available: http://race.rmpbs.org/education/watch/.
21 Denver Metropolitan Study Panel, "Metropolitan Change in Denver: Past Approaches," Denver Metropolitan Study and National Academy of Public Administration (1976).
22 Andrew E.G. Jonas, Andrew R. Goetz, and Sutapa Bhattacharjee, "City-regionalism as a Politics of Collective Provision: Regional Transport Infrastructure in Denver, USA," *Urban Studies* 51, no. 11 (2014): 2444–2465.
23 Ibid.
24 Lynn Schofield Clark and Regina Marchi, *Young People and the Future of News* (Cambridge, UK: Cambridge University Press, 2017).
25 L. Gray, N. Thomas, and L. Lewis, *Teachers' Use of Educational Technology in US Public Schools: 2009* (NCES No. 2010040) (Washington, DC: National Center for Education Statistics, 2009); L. Robinson, "A Taste for the Necessary," *Information, Communication & Society* 12, no. 4 (2009): 488–507; Jen Schradie, "The Digital Production Gap: The Digital Divide and Web 2.0 Collide," *Poetics* 39, no. 2 (2011); Jen Schradie, "The Trend of Class, Race, and Ethnicity in Social Media Inequality," *Information, Communication & Society* 15, no. 4 (2012): 555–571; P.G. Tatian, T. Kingsley, J. Parilla, and R. Pendall, "Building Successful

Neighborhoods," *What Works Collaborative* (2012), accessed March 16, 2016. www.urban.org/sites/default/files/alfresco/publication-pdfs/412557-Building-Successful-Neighborhoods.PDF.

26 Cara DiEnno, Personal conversation at the University of Denver's Center for Community Engagement and Service Learning (2015).
27 Lynn Schofield Clark and Margaret Thompson, "Employing Media-rich Youth Participatory Action Research to Foster Youth Voice," *The Handbook of Media and Communication Research*, ed. Klaus Bruhn Jensen (forthcoming).
28 Peter Dahlgren, "Professional and Citizen Journalism: Tensions and Complements," *The Crisis of Journalism Reconsidered: Democratic Culture, Professional Codes, Digital Futures*, eds. Jeffrey C. Alexander, Elizabeth Butler Breese, and Maria Loengo (New York: Cambridge University Press, 2015).
29 Joe Vacarelli, "Denver's Montbello School Ready To Graduate," *Denver Post*, May 20 2014, accessed June 28, 2016. www.denverpost.com/2014/05/20/denvers-montbello-high-school-ready-to-graduate-last-class/.
30 All names of youth and adult research participants have been changed to protect their anonymity in compliance with the guidelines of the University of Denver Institutional Review Board, which reviewed and approved the research project.
31 Ryan Warner, "Politico: Metro Denver Transit 'Miracle' and Missed Opportunity: Is Passenger Rail Across Colorado a Pie in the Sky Vision?" Colorado Public Radio, May 19, 2016. www.cpr.org/news/story/politico-metro-denver-transit-miracle-and-missed-opportunity-passenger-rail-acros
32 Lucy Graca, "South Students Now Commuting Longer," *The Washington Park Profile*, May 5, 2016, accessed June 28 2016. https://issuu.com/washparkprofile/docs/profile_may_2016-fb.
33 Lisa Parks, "Stuff You Can Kick: Toward a Theory of Media Infrastructures," in *Humanities and the Digital*, eds. P. Svensson and D.T. Goldberg (Cambridge, MA: MIT Press, 2015), 355–373.
34 Brian Larkin, *Signal and Noise: Media, Infrastructure, and Urban Culture in Nigeria* (Durham: Duke University Press, 2013).
35 Jonathan Beller, *The Cinematic Mode of Production: Attention Economy and the Society of the Spectacle* (Lebanon, NH: Dartmouth College Press, 2006).
36 Leopoldina Fortunati and Sakari Taipale, "A Different Glimpse into Mobilities: On the Interrelations Between Daily Spatial Mobility and Social Mobility," *The Information Society* 33, no. 5 (2017), 261–270. https://doi.org/10.1080/01972243.2017.1354110.
37 Scott A. Cohen and Stefan Gössling, "A Darker Side of Hypermobility," *Environment and Planning A: Economy and Space* 47, no. 8 (2015), 166–1679.
38 Craig Jeffrey, *Timepass: Youth, Class, and the Politics of Waiting in India* (Stanford, CA: Stanford University Press, 2010).
39 Lauren Berlant, *Cruel Optimism* (Durham, NC: Duke University Press, 2011).
40 Ibid., 262.
41 Clark and Marchi, *Young People*.
42 Morley, "Technologies".

24
CLASS INTERPLAY IN SOCIAL ACTIVISM IN KENYA

Job Mwaura

Participation in social activism is characterized by various socio-political and cultural factors, as discussed in the introduction to this volume. In Kenya, these intersecting social-political factors of social activism include religion, political party affiliations, ethnic affiliation, and class. This chapter will discuss how class issues emerged in two social-political movements in Kenya. I will begin by introducing the context under which these social-political movements occurred, offer some discussion of the framework of class and media in the Kenyan context, and then introduce the two movements (#OccupyPlayground, and #OccupyParliament). I then highlight how class as a socio-political and cultural issue shaped these protests. This chapter interrogates how content produced on social media during activism contributes to constructing these social, economic, political and geographical constructs, which in turn shapes participation in social activism.

Kenya as a Silicon Valley in Africa

Kenya is considered a leader in mobile technologies and technological innovation in the region. Several innovations such as the popular mobile money transfer *M-Pesa* and the crisis mapping application *Ushahidi* originated in Kenya and are now used in several nations worldwide. Indeed, Kenya is considered the "Silicon Savannah."[1] This technocultural transformation began in February 2005 when, under President Kibaki's[2] reign, the Kenyan government adopted the ICT policy,[3] which spelt out priorities to harness the potential for ICTs to achieve Millennium Development Goals (MDGs). The policy accelerated ICT infrastructure projects in Kenya and spurred growth in mobile telephony; because of this, Kenya has one of the highest numbers of mobile users and internet subscribers in Africa.[4]

With the rapid spread of mobile phone and internet in Kenya, social media use has risen exponentially.[5] The use of social media platforms in agitating for socio-political change (activism) is an example of how essential internet technologies have become in Kenya (particularly concerning the social movements arising out of middle-class economic frustrations, as this chapter will discuss). I begin with a review of activism in Kenyan contexts.

Political Activism in Kenya

Activism in Kenya dates back at least to 1921, when what had been known as the East Africa Protectorate (first under German and then British control in the late nineteenth century) became a colony and was renamed Kenya, after the area's highest mountain. Under colonial rule, the Kikuyu had their farmlands taxed and then stolen by British European settlers, leaving them with decreasing lands to farm and prompting an exodus to urban areas. Young Kikuyu men formed the Young Kikuyu Association (YKA) and Kikuyu Central Association (KCA) as they protested against colonial rule and their exclusion from political representation. More rebellions followed from 1952 to 1956, as young Kikuyu peasant farmers mobilized as the Mau Mau movement, to reclaim land and independence from the colonial masters. Colonial leaders mobilized British and African troops, and nearly half of all Mau Mau leaders and supporters were killed or expelled to detention camps.

Native Kenyans participated in Legislative Council elections for the first time in 1957, which brought to power the Kenya African National Union (KANU) and its leader Mzee Jomo Kenyatta, who formed a government and led the movement toward independence in 1963. However, even with the defeat of colonialism, the Republic of Kenya's government has been marked by corruption in public offices, suppression of political movements, ethnic violence, and execution of those who were critical of the government. From the mid-1980s to early 1990s, politicians, students, and religious leaders called for changes to the constitution and a multiparty system. The success of this 'push' was realized in 1992 when President Moi asked Parliament to repeal section 2 (a) of the constitution, which led to the reintroduction of the multiparty system in Kenya.

In 2010, Kenya promulgated a new constitution, which gave new life to civil society organizations, and established institutions such as The Kenya Human Rights Commission (KNHRC), The National Gender and Equity Commission (NGEC), The Independent Policing Oversight Authority (IPOA) as well as The Office of the Ombudsman, each of which was tasked with fighting for the rights of ordinary people. Boaz Waruku, an activist at the time who was interviewed for this study, explained the significance of these elements of the new constitution:

BOAZ: The new constitution then protected activists in a manner that … gives the activists the right to … organize demonstrations, to picket and to also participate in political issues. Human rights works have now been constitutionally appreciated as something you can even develop a career on…. So, a number of those bodies are emerging to offer space for accountability.

(January 5, 2018)

Since 2010, activists have worked with policymakers and government officials to foster policies to end corruption. However, Kenya continues to witness the repression of some individuals and civil society organizations that continue to criticize the current government, and some organizations have been forced into insolvency for suspicion of operating illegally or sponsoring programs not in line with the government's 'agenda.' In 2011, Kenya experienced the worst drought East Africa had seen in 60 years, deepening internal displacements and leading to grave economic impacts that further undermined support both for government and for civil society organizations. During this period, a wave of protests led by civil societies, political parties, and working-class individuals demanded political, social, and economic change. However, global debates about protests have largely ignored African activism, save for the focus on Northern Africa uprisings.[6] The lack of focus on Africa could stem from colonialist western attitudes dismissing Africa as war-ridden, poor, and too rural for any significant protest to take place. Yet, Cohen[7] noted that 50 Africa cities already have more than one million people each; even with these attitudes and alienations, political protests in Africa seem to have diverse issues and angles, echoing the continent's vast diversity.

Brunch and Mampilly[8] argued that, in Nairobi, middle-class activists are leading essential efforts to merge organizational savvy and technical expertise with broader popular movements. However, they point out that unlike the first and second waves of protest mentioned earlier, which culminated in independence and the multi-party political system across Africa, respectively, the third wave of protest lacks viable and new popular agendas. Brunch and Mampilly further posit that the protests might be understood as instigated by people's urge to challenge capitalism and to put an end to liberal democracy—that they are the outbursts of a frustrated middle class whose indignations are fueled by social media-savvy youth. These protests hold some similarities with those that have taken place in Turkey, Brazil, Tunisia, Egypt and, lately, in Sudan, as they have been led by young people who are techno-savvy and use social media to organize. Activists consider themselves globally empowered, oriented, and connected. Further, these young individuals earn an average income have high education levels, and are believed to belong to the middle class.[9] However, it is important to understand the ways that economic differences are perceived in the Kenyan context and how these differences relate to the country's colonial history.

A Conceptualization of Class in Kenya

Scholars on class in Africa view class constructs as a post-colonial phenomenon.[10] The coming of the colonialists established social stratifications with colonial administrators and white settlers owning the means of production and the Africans falling in the working class. Although most of the African countries attribute these social stratifications to colonialism, others have specific and unique ways through which the class system was established. In a country such as South Africa, Cobley[11] argued that the rise of class as a system of social stratification began with the displacement of Africans from the mining fields of Witwatersrand in Johannesburg from 1886, who then converged to form urban centers. He added that this process of urbanization led to the formation of a racially divided industrial working class and an exclusively white capitalist class. Education background also became a new cause of social stratification where Africans who were privileged to receive education during the colonial period were eligible for new social status and positions, which provided more access to power and wealth. These individuals mostly established the nationalist movement in various African nations who helped to push for independence.

In Kenya, individuals such as the first Kenyan President Jomo Kenyatta, and Harry Thuku and Mbiyu Koinange, among others, became members of the nationalist movement after they were educated in missionary schools and some received education in Europe. However, as Iqani[12] has noted, "… one of the socioeconomic legacies of colonialism was the exporting of the class striations to settings previously characterised by other forms of social hierarchy." Thus, it is likely that the ancestors of these individuals, who received education under colonial rule, had ties to community rulers such as chiefs who were culturally endowed and had been differentiated earlier from the rest who were under their jurisdiction before the colonial era. In pre-independence Kenya, Bienen[13] noted that the nationalists who took over power acquired land from white settlers and gave back very little or no land at all to the locals who had been displaced by colonialists and white settlers. This further enhanced class stratifications, which have continued to be seen to date.

Melber,[14] quoting Marx and Engels, argues that social positions are defined by the control of the means of production or via expropriation. He adds that in the case of Kenya, the means of production are capital, labor or land. These three aspects have played out variously since independence in different spaces. For instance, the government and media owners have used media space to appropriate further social stratifications such as class, ethnicity, and religion. How the media successfully appropriates social stratifications has elicited various debates across the globe. In the next section, I discuss the current debates on media and class.

Current Debates on Media and Class

While the study of media and class has for some time focused on media consumption habits, the internet has provided an avenue through which we can study class depictions in the social production of content during certain events—in this case, activism. Such empirical studies have the potential to elicit debates on media and class transnationally to find common ground or differences that help us to appreciate and celebrate global diversity.

The media in Kenya have played a key role in pushing for social-political change. During President Moi's reign (1978–2002), media content was highly censored, and only the state media (Kenya Broadcasting Corporation) had the license to operate countrywide. Those who owned private media such as publications and radio were seen as a threat to government operations. For instance, Gitobu Imanyara, a civil rights lawyer and activist who owned *The Nairobi Law Monthly*, which was shut down several times for criticizing the government; and *Kameme FM*, a radio station broadcasting in the Kikuyu language, faced threats of closure from President Moi's government. Academics such as Ngugi wa Thiongo, Reverend Timothy Njoya, and Dr. Willy Mutunga also faced repression from the government and were either arrested, detained without trial, tortured or exiled. However, during this time, the internet had not taken root.

Towards the end of President Moi's era, the government issued broadcasting licenses to private media owners, who began radio and TV stations countrywide. Radio, particularly vernacular stations, became important in the social transformation of the masses. These vernacular stations provided a space where listeners discussed pressing issues within their communities in languages they were familiar with. For instance, a popular radio talk show named *Crossfire* discussed current political issues in the late 1990s and early 2000s. Radio continues to be the most widely used media in Kenya, followed closely by television.[15] After disputed presidential elections in 2007, the radio played a crucial role in perpetuating ethnic hate and violence in some regions in Kenya that resulted in the deaths and destruction of property of hundreds of people.[16]

Unfortunately, there is little literature on the contribution of social media in interrogating class constructs in activism, especially in Kenya. Previous debates about media and class have looked at patterns of media consumption among the middle class in places such as India and China, which has revealed a tendency to consume sex-related media such as *Playboy*, bridal magazines, media that shows how to be modern and global, and generally media that celebrates urban life and its lifestyle.[17] In South Africa, debates on class depictions have primarily focused on the rise of the black middle class, as scholars consider the representation of black persons amid white capitalism and in the post-apartheid era as well as descriptions that reinforce or challenge stereotypes of class, race, and inequality.[18] In her book on media consumption in the global south, for example, Iqani[19] makes a comparative analysis of documentary film representations of young, upwardly mobile professionals in China and South Africa, noting that, in each case, the emphasis is made on their consumption habits (including the media) and other narratives about success. She further discusses the labelling of the black middle class as 'new' in the English language media, particularly in the first decade after apartheid. She concludes that media narratives about the newness of the black middle class constitute a site of symbolic representation and discursive construction of the consuming class in South Africa. Spronk[20] conducted a study on sexuality and middle-class self-perceptions in Nairobi, observing that the media representation of romantic love reinforced ideals of being urban and modern among young professionals. Whereas each of these studies provides some insights into the relationships between media representation and lived experiences of economic class position (particularly among those of middle-class Kenyans), more research is needed to understand the nexus of class and participation in social activism.

Using social media for activism involves cultural production of various forms of media (textual, video, images) content in discussions and arguments. A critical look at this content reveals different class constructs, with appeals across different layers of social stratifications and concerning differing intersecting identities. This chapter interrogates how content produced on social media during activism contributes to constructing these social, economic, political, and geographical constructs, which in turn shapes participation in social activism.

Methods

This paper adopted qualitative research methods to generate and analyze data from interviews and social media content analysis from two socio-political movements (#OccupyPlayground, and

#OccupyParliament) in Kenya. Individuals closely linked with the cases were interviewed. The key informants included individuals from civil society organizations, journalists, religious leaders, and politicians. Secondary sources of data included analysis of newspaper articles that reported on the movements as well as the social media posts that were generated during the movements. The data were coded according to what was depicted as an aspect or characteristic of class (different social, economic status).

#OccupyPlayground and #OccupyParliament were initiatives of a grassroots organization PAWA254 (PAWA is a corrupted word for 'power' while the '254' digits are the dialing code of Kenya) which brings together young socially conscious artists and activists whose aim is to see a better Kenya by fighting social and political vices. The founder of this organization, Boniface Mwangi, is a photojournalist who has received international acclaims for his photography and mobilization skills. In 2007, while Boniface was working as a photojournalist at the Standard Newspaper, he was tasked with taking photos of the post-election violence that erupted at that time. The distress caused by taking these photos made him quit, and he founded PAWA254. In the last few years, Boniface has become synonymous with Kenyan activism. He has a massive following on Facebook and Twitter and uses the platforms to influence change among young people. PAWA 254 has been involved in various initiatives meant to push for social change as well as protests.

Occupy Playground

#OccupyPlayground protests began in February 2015 when the playground of Langata Primary School was grabbed by the owner of the adjacent Weston Hotel, which belongs to a powerful politician. Earlier media reports[21] had indicated that a shopping mall was to be erected on the playground, but it later emerged that the playground was to be used as a parking lot for hotel visitors. Boniface Mwangi and other activists led the protest. The movement generated a huge debate both online and offline, particularly on the day of the protest. From this moment, #OccupyPlayground became a movement.

Several class issues emerged from the onset of this event. First, elites had the privilege not only to own property but also the power to acquire property legally or through dubious means. It was later reported that the NCC (Nairobi City County) officials had held consultations at the top level with corrupt companies who could afford to pay bribes. The hotel owner, a politician, used his influence to grab the school land and influenced the Nairobi City County officials to approve the construction of a shopping mall, as reported in the *Daily Nation*: "Nairobi County officials played a key role in rushing the approval of a multi-storey shopping mall adjacent to Lang'ata Primary School...."[22]

Second, because of the power held by this politician and his financial capability, he was able to hire youths to build the wall around the school playground and provide "illegal" security for the construction workers, and who were later paid to violently confront the school community, including teachers and parents who had gathered to complain about the encroachment on the school playground.[23] It was later discovered that city officials had illegally given the go-ahead to a company to set up a perimeter wall around the playground in the night with no regard for the children whose playground they were grabbing. The area turned into a battleground between the hired youth and the school community as reported in the *Daily Nation*. The hired youth were poor and lived in the Kibera Slums, informal settlements bordering the Langata residential estate.

A call for action online came in early January 2015: an event created by Boniface Mwangi on Facebook, which read in part:

> Langata Road Primary School playground has been grabbed by a group of known professional land grabbers acting on behalf of a very senior politician in the Jubilee government [the ruling party]. The grabbing took place over the Christmas holiday....

A school playground is a necessity, not a privilege. This is a blatant infringement upon the rights of the pupils, and the community … the future of the pupils is at risk, and their innocence has been violated by the insatiable greed of the owners of Weston Hotel which itself is built on grabbed land. We call on Kenyans to boycott Weston Hotel and all those who are linked to the land grab…. On Monday 19th January we shall go to Langata Primary School to donate sports equipment at Langata Primary School and play on the grabbed playground. The playthings we will carry with us shall be donated to the school….

In this event description, several class issues emerged. Boniface Mwangi mentioned that professional land grabbers had been grabbed the school playground by on behalf of a powerful politician. He also said that the grabbing had taken place over the 2014 December holidays and that a group of about 50 youths had been hired from Kibera to guard construction workers who were fencing off the playground. This confirms that the elite, who are influential individuals in government, employed the middle and the lower-class individuals, who do not have financial means, to commit atrocities. The description of the event also indicated the school board, made up of civil servants (possibly middle-class individuals), had been threatened by senior people in government and their members warned that they would lose their jobs if they kept insisting that the land had been grabbed. Middle-class Kenyans, the majority of whom are civil servants, tend to fear slipping back into poverty and work hard to maintain their status or rise to the elite class. Two of the participants in this study describes this class as follows:

RESPONDENT 2: The middle class in Kenya is always the most contented lot. They are contented because they know they have already climbed above that poverty level. It is very unlikely that they will fall back to poverty. Some of them aspire to be at the top (very rich). As we are talking here, [the] majority of the middle class are now chasing government tenders and county governments since elections are over and there is new leadership. If they are not chasing tenders, they are dealing with buying large parcels of land, sub-dividing and getting rich very fast. They aspire to get richer and richer as quickly as possible. (January 5, 2018.)

RESPONDENT 3: The Kenyan middle-class likes to enjoy the benefits which they have not fought for. The people who fight for change are the most affected by the need for change. The victims of economic injustices. The victims of land grabbing. You find some slums next to palatial homes in some parts of Kiambu county for instance. These are the people the political class exploit during elections. The most vulnerable people you find in informal settlements are the people who bring change in this country. (January 9, 2019.)

Before the day of the protest, #OccupyPlayground had been highly publicized on social media. The Facebook event invitation had attracted over 900 confirmations of attendance. On the day of the event, the mobilization had not worked well, and Boaz Waruku lamented:

RESPONDENT 4: … when I got back from dropping my kids to another school, I came back, and I was hoping to get a lot of people given that there was a massive online campaign saying we must take action, we must do this and that. The teachers themselves had been told that [the] security situation is not good because a big person had been involved in the land case. Even the principal was being threatened. So, I arrived there, and I found few people—Irungu, Boniface—a countable number and I was wondering what went wrong? Thus, the issue [agenda] was there, the media picked it up coz of the big man involved, but [those] who were supposed to be there were not there. Maybe they were cheering and checking online when the teargas and the rest would be thrown.

The low turnout of the event could have been the result of several factors, but class issues emerge in relation to participation in activism. While many expressed interest in attending, most preferred to join the conversation online instead of participating in the street protest. The few activists who turned up mobilized the pupils, whose playground had been grabbed. As the events unfolded, the pupils brought down the wall that had fenced off the playground in full presence of the police. A scuffle ensued, and the children were teargassed by the police who were attempting to disperse them. A policeman was injured, and two of the activists were arrested.

As this was going on, images of the protesting kids started circulating online, and reports indicated that five pupils had been hospitalized.[24] The debate online quickly shifted from land grabbing to blaming the activists, led by Boniface Mwangi, for involving children in the protest and putting them at risk. Facebook commenters also accused the police for the use of excessive force on children.[25] Below are some of the comments from Facebook:

FACEBOOK USER 1: Boniface this is the worst I have seen of you. Fight everyone but please spare the kids for they don't deserve the kind of brutality you exposed them to today. You were prepared to do this ... and watching you on NTV this evening I didn't see any expression of sorry for the ailing children. You have put our country in shame!!!

FACEBOOK USER 2: The children's lives are more important than land & it's our duty as adults to protect them and not to put them in situations that would harm them!

FACEBOOK USER 3: I am a parent and what you did today was wrong. Was any of your kids in the protest? You used other people's kids to get fame! Shame on you!

FACEBOOK USER 4: Land grabbers should be condemned equally as much as people who use kids to push agendas. Boniface, you could have called grown folks to protest. You have done it before. I don't know why this time you endangered the lives of children. Thank God there was no serious accident. This was a bad move bro. Bad move.

This narrative was meant to shame Boniface for his methods, although the backlash also contributed to derailing the campaign by undermining support for the activities. The involvement of the children in the protest was meant to spark interest and scandalize the police forces to hasten the repossession of the land. The playground belonged to the children, and they needed it back. Thus, Boniface and other organizers felt that using the children was well justified.

However, other social media (Facebook) users expressed support for Boniface Mwangi and his colleagues for using children in the protest. Some of the comments read as follows:

FACEBOOK USER 5: ... Kenyans you are full of hypocrisy. Half of us are middle-class people who can afford some expensive play toys to offer our children. They are comfortable playing their PS [Play Station games] as they rest from the comforts of their beds and living rooms. I personally went to a school like Langata Primary School to be precise—Kayole Primary School. It hurts me. One thing that keeps these kids from not thinking of their daily troubles is the games they play on those playgrounds. That is their comfort zone ... some idiotic minds are blaming it on Boniface Mwangi. Common sense ni bure [is free] and clearly not everybody has it....

FACEBOOK USER 6: At least the children made an impact. How many middle class educated people would volunteer to demonstrate on their behalf. In Kenya, we believe that the end justifies the means....

FACEBOOK USER 7: Let's be practical, how do you expect a busy parent to ask for leave from work to go bring down a wall. I support Boniface Mwangi for that.

The above and many other social media comments also revealed several class issues. The school is in a lower-middle-class area in Nairobi and the community around the school, where the stature of the houses indicates a decent income. Given that the government is the biggest employer in

Kenya, we could assume that most of the school community members are government workers or businessmen who earn a decent living. Therefore, the parents who got distraught that their children were involved in protest saw it as an activity that is distant from them or not meant for them and their children (see the Facebook comments above).

Further, the comments describe the carefree attitude of the middle-class who are comfortable even when issues that affect them are happening. In one of the in-depth interviews for this study, a respondent described the middle-class individuals as people who do not participate in agitating for change and only those from informal settlements, who are often poor, oppressed, and unrepresented, attend demonstrations and street protests:

> Kenyans have always been divided along class issues on social media. Those who live in leafy suburbs do not always agitate for change with much vigour like those who live in slum areas such as Korogocho areas and from upcountry and those who are poor. Most of the time, middle-class individuals are not concerned about social change because, for them, they probably get a pay cheque at the end of the month and are comfortable.... When demonstrations are called, middle-class people do not go for protests in the streets. They stay indoors and lock themselves up.... If you look at political rallies at Uhuru Park, people usually walk from Korogocho, Kibera, Mathare but you will not see people walking or being ferried from Runda or Karen.
>
> (April 3, 2018)

These views could offer more insights as to why individuals on social media were agitated by the involvement of pupils in the #OccupyPlayground protests.

The day after the protests, various government representatives responded to the use of excessive force on pupils and blamed the officer who lobbed teargas canisters at the pupils. The then Interior Cabinet Secretary visited the school and personally apologized; elites in government and non-governmental institutions gave statements and press conferences expressing concern. These individuals were only aware of the land grabbing once it happened. They followed events in the media like others. The National Land Commission (NLC), Commission for Administrative Justice (CAJ), and Independent Police Oversight Commission (IPOA) also spoke out.

In the past few years, Kenyan activists have faced intense crackdowns from the government. In 2016, about 900 civil societies were deregistered by the Kenyan government[26] and this has affected how they operate. During #OccupyPlayground, only a handful of civil societies were involved—notably PAWA254, and Society for International Development (SID). From an observation made on the main listserv of the civil societies in Kenya (kptj[27]-communications), the Civil Societies came to life when Irungu Houghton and Boaz Waruku were arrested after the protests. One grassroots activist explained:

> Civil societies have changed and become commercialised. They are full of middle-class individuals whose only interest is to earn a living. Their work is to sit in the office, chase big money and do nothing on agitating for social change. Smaller grassroots organisations such as Mathare Social Justice are the ones doing the actual work of pushing for social change. You will not see some of these individuals in the streets for demonstration but only hear of them in boardroom meetings in expensive hotels.

The respondent suggests that, whereas middle-class individuals were glad to support the movement from a distance and in online ventures, they were not the ones who would have been participating in the first place on the ground. In contrast, it could be that those who were the parents of the school children were either occupied with work or not on social media sites, or both.

As the case evolved, Kenyans online demanded that the Cabinet Secretary of Lands put a face on the professional land grabbers. Days later, The Cabinet Secretary released some of the names, but this was widely considered false. The Vice President was widely linked to the owner of the hotel but denied any involvement, even as an earlier feature on national TV had indicated that he was the owner of the hotel.[28]

Social media users compared and found a sharp similarity between #OccupyPlayground and the #FeesMustFall student movement in South Africa two years earlier.[29] Others used images to point to parallels between the #OccupyPlayground movement and the 1976 student uprising in Soweto,[30] where students took the frontline in agitating for their rights.

Occupy Parliament

The Occupy Parliament protest took place on May 14, and June 11, 2013, after learning that the newly elected Members of Parliament had proposed increasing their salaries, against the constitution and the wishes of many Kenyans. The independent Salaries and Remuneration Commission (SRC) streamlines the salaries of all government officials and civil servants, but members of parliament strived to dictate their salary packages.

The civil society organizations led again by Boniface Mwangi, called for protests. On May 14, 2013, protesters gathered at Freedom Corner at Uhuru Park wearing black T-shirts with different messages and armed with placards and whistles; they marched through the Central Business District to the Parliament building. At parliament, they found the gates heavily guarded by police in riot gear. Outside the gate, protestors released pigs from a truck, which began to eat a red substance that resembled blood to show that members of parliament are as greedy as pigs. Although this tactic was applauded by many, those against it stated the use of pigs showed animal cruelty. On June 11, the activists used the same tactic but only used a huge sculpture of a pig. Although this movement ensured the members of parliament did not increase their basic salaries, they did increase their allowances in a deal that was closed between them and the Salaries and Remuneration Commission. This movement attracted huge media coverage and discussion on social media.

As the movement unfolded, class issues emerged in online media and through offline activities. Civil society organizations first made the call to action through an article on May 3, 2013, which urged citizens to fight the parliamentary salary raises. Planning for the protest was spearheaded by civil society organizations. One of the resolutions was to mobilize people via social media and at a breakfast meeting in a city hotel. The email circulated in a civil society KPTJ communications list serve read in part:

> Dear All,
> I met up with Boniface Mwangi who is organising the "Occupy Parliament" event next week Tuesday, May 14th, 2013 (a protest against the demands by MP's for a salary increase) to see if KPTJ could join in the campaign alongside the other activities we had planned on the same issue—see below
>
> a. A breakfast and briefing meeting with the media to be held this Friday (May 3, 2013, at 7:30 am) at a venue to be confirmed by Transparency International. All EDs and leaders of the above organizations to attend.[31]

While planning and coordination are essential for any movement, this email reveals the plans for the protest had emanated from middle-class civil servants who sought to mobilize those from less advantaged backgrounds. As noted by one of the grassroots activists cited earlier, in Kenya there is a perception, with at least some basis in reality, that civil societies hold planning meetings in exclusive hotels, i.e., breakfast and media meetings, which are inaccessible to ordinary individuals, especially the oppressed working classes. The inaccessibility of such meeting points could be in terms of distance as well as security in those facilities, where ordinary individuals may not be able to afford to pay for hotel services. Since the organizers of such meetings are middle class, they strive or aspire to be in places the upper class frequents. Their use of such spaces could be viewed as a leveraging of cultural capital, as argued by Bourdieu, who posits that cultural capital is accessible to those who have resources for and alliances with culturally dominant individuals and institutions such as education with its access to generating knowledge or ideas.[32] As mentioned earlier, those who attend street protests are primarily working class. Therefore, holding meetings in locations that are inaccessible to those most likely to attend is problematic, and reveals the biases of the organizers who assume their right to organize others. A grassroots civil society member from Mathare said:

> Class issues also play out within the civil societies themselves. There are categories of civil societies—those who are well funded and have offices in palatial parts of Nairobi and those who work at the grassroots levels who are underfunded and often comprise ordinary individuals in informal settlements. The well-funded organisations often incorporate grassroots organisations as their foot soldiers during protests. They work on the background, and their voices are rarely heard. Some individuals in these well-off organisations even pay the media so that their stories can be covered.
>
> *(January 8, 2018)*

The campaign posters for the scheduled street protest were also circulated on email. While strategizing might be done through all means necessary, this approach may have also revealed the limitations and middle-class biases of the organizers. The accessibility of email was, and still is, limited to only those who can afford it. The message in the poster further indicated the dress code for the protest (see Figure 24.1), which was also a likely limitation for working-class participation. In a protest I attended during this research, participants had to purchase T-shirts for the protest at Kenya Shillings 300, equivalent to about US$3.5. With 400 million people living on less than US$1.90 a day in Sub-Saharan Africa according to the World Bank,[33] the ability to buy the T-shirts is beyond the reach of such populations. While it is important to recognize the desire on the part of civil societies to be inclusive of all persons, the limitations revealed in their organizational practices advance the "othering" of those outside the middle classes and thereby exclude many people from such movements who may have otherwise wanted to participate.

On the day of the #OccupyParliament demonstrations, several protesters clashed with the police, and 17 individuals were arrested and charged with an unlawful assembly outside the parliament building. This activity was then condemned by international and local civil society organizations, such as

Figure 24.1 A poster circulated on social media used for the #OccupyParliament protest.

Freedom House and Kenyans for Peace Truth and Justice (KPTJ). This condemnation served to curtail and intimidate the civil society organizations from making further demands to the members of parliament.

The day after the protest, a huge debate in the media ensued about the use of the pigs during the protest. There were arguments that the idea was tantamount to animal cruelty, and social media users argued animal protection should have taken action against the protesters for cruel treatment. Others shifted the dialogue to a religious angle and argued that using pigs as tools of protest was offensive to the Muslim community who consider anything associated with pigs as *Haram*. Like the blaming of Boniface during the #OccupyPlayground movement, these negative reactions discredited the protesters and diverted the conversation away from challenging Members of Parliament's efforts to increase their salary. This backlash may have been orchestrated by the Members of Parliament themselves through social media, as well as the mainstream media, who wanted to discredit the protest.

A month after the #OccupyParliament protests, a call for a fresh protest was made—on June 10, 2013. In this protest, the protesters used an effigy of a pig instead of actual pigs as a protest symbol or tool. While the symbolism of the protest agenda was maintained, one thing that emerged was that the protesters were influenced by those in power to change their protest tactics. This is an example of how movements can outlive orchestrated or incidental instances of shaming that divert attention from protest intentions to protest tactics.

Conclusion

This study began by highlighting the contextual issues that make Kenya a unique space of activism. Experience with digital media is different from any other part of the continent and the world due to unique socio-political and cultural factors. In Kenya, participation in social activism is shaped by issues such as ethnicity, political affiliation, religion, and class. In this chapter, I discussed class as a social construct shaping discussion in digital spaces. Kenyan elites are in constant conflict with the middle class and the lower class. Using their political power, they commit social and political injustices with impunity. Their high economic status means they can afford resources to acquire not only property but also hire laborers. Since the middle-class work for the elite class or for the government, and strive to be like these elites, they often take a back seat when a call to challenge injustices committed by the elite are made, although sometimes they support such calls through social media platforms.

As Bourdieu[34] suggests, injustices occur as people enact assumptions of how life might be outside their field of knowledge and experience. In the case of #OccupyPlayground, perhaps elites do not realize how life would be for children without a playground. In the #OccupyParliament case, perhaps Members of Parliament do not realize how the working and middle-class individuals would be affected by them awarding themselves hefty salaries.

It's possible to conclude that well-meaning middle-class individuals who seek to work with civil societies and the working class to push for socio-political change are unaware of how their own biases undermine their ability to plan protest tactics effectively. In two of these events, protesters used tactics that were considered bad, i.e., using children and using pigs. This enabled those in power to align the dominant narrative with their own position, thereby discrediting activism in ways that would make sense and find sympathy among the very people who might have benefited the most from that activism. While such factors can emerge unconsciously, they may shape the outcome of a protest; civil society organizations need to be aware of this to build sustainable movements.

Notes

1. Jake Bright and Aubrey Hruby, *The Next Africa: An Emerging Continent Becomes a Global Powerhouse* (New York: Macmillan, 2015).
2. Kibaki was the third President of the Republic of Kenya and served from December 2002 to April 2012.
3. Timothy Mwololo Waema, "A Brief History of The Development of an ICT Policy in Kenya," in *At the Crossroads: ICT Policy Making in East Africa*, eds. Florence Ebam Etta and Laurent Elder (Nairobi; Ottawa, Canada: East African Educational Publishers; International Development Research Centre, 2005).
4. Communication Authority of Kenya (CAK) Q3 July–September 2018 report indicates that there are 46.6 million mobile phone subscribers and 42.2 million internet subscribers.
5. Jean-Pierre Afadhali, "Social Networks Reaping from Mobile Internet," *The East African* (April 21, 2017). www.theeastafrican.co.ke/rwanda/Business/Social-networks-reaping-from-mobile-Internet-/1433224-3898780-qjknbjz/index.html.
6. See: Mark R. Beissinger, Jamal Amaney, and Kevin Mazur, "Who Participated in the Arab Spring? A Comparison of Egyptian and Tunisian Revolutions," *Department of Politics, Princeton University* (2012). www.Princeton. Edu/Mbeissin/Beissinger; Nahed Eltantawy and Julie B. Wiest, "The Arab Spring| Social Media in the Egyptian Revolution: Reconsidering Resource Mobilization Theory," *International Journal of Communication* 5 (2011); Philip N. Howard, Aiden Duffy, Deen Freelon, Muzammil M. Hussain, Will Mari, and Marwa Maziad, "Opening Closed Regimes: What Was the Role of Social Media during the Arab Spring?," (2011). https://papers.ssrn.com/sol3/papers.cfm?abstract_id=2595096; Sarah A. Tobin, "Jordan's Arab Spring: The Middle Class and Anti-Revolution," *Middle East Policy* 19, no. 1 (2012): 96–109; Zeynep Tufekci, *Twitter and Tear Gas: The Power and Fragility of Networked Protest* (New Haven; London: Yale University Press, 2017).
7. Barney Cohen, "Urbanization in Developing Countries: Current Trends, Future Projections, and Key Challenges for Sustainability," *Technology in Society* 28, no. 1–2 (2006): 63–80.
8. Adam Branch and Zachariah Mampilly. *Africa Uprising: Popular Protest and Political Change* (London: Zed Books, 2015).
9. A realistically defined middle class would comprise only a narrow slice of Africa's population, set against a backdrop in which nearly half of all Africans live in extreme poverty with their numbers growing. See Divyanshi Wadhwa, "The Number of Extremely Poor People Continues to Rise in Sub-Saharan Africa," *World Bank Blogs* [Data Blog], September 19, 2018. https://blogs.worldbank.org/opendata/number-extremely-poor-people-continues-rise-sub-saharan-africa
10. See Richard W. Franke, "Power, Class and Traditional Knowledge in Sahel, Food Production," in *Studies in Power and Class in Africa*, ed. Irving Leonard Markovitz (New York: Oxford University Press, 1987); Nelson Kasfir, ed. *State and Class in Africa* (London; Totowa, NJ: Cass and Co, 1984).
11. Alan Gregor Cobley, *Class and Consciousness: The Black Petty Bourgeoisie in South Africa, 1924 to 1950* (Santa Barbara, CA: Praeger, 1990), 127.
12. Mehita Iqani, *Consumption, Media and the Global South* (London: Palgrave Macmillan UK, 2016), 27.
13. Henry Bienen, *KENYA: The Politics of Participation and Control* (Princeton, NJ: Princeton University Press, 1974).
14. Henning Melber, *The Rise of Africa's Middle Class: Myths, Realities and Critical Engagements* (London: Zed Books, 2016), quoting: Karl Marx and Frederich Engels, "Das Manifest der Kommunistischen Partei," in: Soziale Ungleichheit: Klassische Texte zur Sozialstrukturanalyse, eds. H. Solga, P.A. Berger and J. Powell (Frankfurt/Main: Campus, 2009).
15. Ipsos Synovate Kenya, "State of the Media Report, 2018," Nairobi (May 2018).
16. Ndirangu D. Wachanga, "Kenya's Indigenous Radio Stations and their Use of Metaphors in the 2007 Election Violence," *Journal of African Media Studies* 3, no. 1 (March 1, 2011): 109–125.
17. See: Beng Huat Chua, "Transnational and Transcultural Circulation and Consumption of East Asian Television Drama," in *Patterns of Middle-Class Consumption in India and China* (Los Angeles: SAGE Publications, 2008), 186; Jacqueline Elfick, "Sex, Television and the Middle Class on China," in *Patterns of Middle-Class Consumption in India and China*, eds. Christophe Jaffrelot and Peter van der Veer (Los Angeles: SAGE Publications, 2008), 207–229; Puay-peng Ho, "Consuming Art in Middle Class China," in *Patterns of Middle Class Consumption in India and China*, by Christophe Jaffrelot and Peter van der Veer (Panchsheel Enclave, New Delhi: SAGE Publications, 2008), 277–291, B-42; Shoma Munshi, "Yeh Dil Maange More. Television and Consumer Choices in a Global City," in *Patterns of Middle Class Consumption in India and China*, eds. Christophe Jaffrelot and Peter van der Veer (Panchsheel Enclave, New Delhi: SAGE Publications India, 2008), 263–276.
18. See: E. Dimitris Kitis, Tommaso M. Milani, and Erez Levon, "'Black Diamonds', 'Clever Blacks' and Other Metaphors: Constructing the Black Middle Class in Contemporary South African Print Media," *Discourse & Communication*, 2018; Jeremy Seekings and Nicoli Nattrass, *Class Race and Inequality in SA*

(New Haven and London: Yale University Press, 2005); Roger Southall, "The ANC & Black Capitalism in South Africa." *Review of African Political Economy* 31, no. 100 (2004): 313–328; Roger Southall, "Political Change and the Black Middle Class in Democratic South Africa," *Canadian Journal of African Studies/Revue Canadienne Des Études Africaines* 38, no. 3 (2004): 521.

19 Iqani, *Consumption, Media*.
20 Rachel Spronk, *Ambiguous Pleasures: Sexuality and Middle Class Self-Perceptions in Nairobi* (New York: Berghahn Books, 2012).
21 See Robert Alai, "Evidence That Links Ruto to Weston Hotel Langata Land Saga," *Kahawa Tungu; Kenya Today* (blog) (January 20, 2015). www.kenya-today.com/opinion/kahawa-tungu-alleged-evidence-links-ruto-weston-hotel-langata-land-saga.
22 Otiota Guguyu, "Police under Fire for Tear-Gassing Children," *Daily Nation* (January 19, 2015). www.nation.co.ke/news/Police-under-fire-for-teargassing-children/1056-2595026-14eoo1nz/index.html.
23 Ibid.
24 Nolan Feeney, "Witness Kenyan Police Use Tear Gas on Protesting Schoolchildren," *Time* (January 19, 2015), accessed June 27, 2019. https://time.com/3673741/kenya-schoolchildren-land-grab-protest-photos/.
25 Guguyu, "Police under Fire".
26 AFP, "Kenya Shuts down US Election Assistance NGO," *Daily Monitor* (December 2016). www.monitor.co.ug/News/World/Kenya-shuts-down-US-election-assistance-NGO/688340-3492302-9nhks6z/index.html.
27 Kenyans for Peace Truth and Justice (KPTJ) is an active civil society in Kenya and owns the KPTJ list serve where members of the civil society organizations exchange ideas.
28 Citizen TV (2015).
29 Christine Hauser, "'Fees Must Fall': Anatomy of the Student Protests in South Africa," *New York Times* 22 (2016); I. Konik and A. Konik, "The# RhodesMustFall and #FeesMustFall Student Protests through the Kübler-Ross Grief Model," *Discourse: Studies in the Cultural Politics of Education* 39, no. 4 (2018): 575–589; Thierry Luescher, Lacea Loader, and Taabo Mugume. "#FeesMustFall: An Internet-Age Student Movement in South Africa and the Case of the University of the Free State," *Politikon* 44, no. 2 (2017): 231–245.
30 Baruch Hirson, *Year of Fire, Year of Ash: The Soweto Revolt, Roots of a Revolution?* Vol. 3 (London: Zed Press, 1979).
31 KP KPTJ, Communications. "Occupy Parliament" (May 6, 2013). https://mail.google.com.
32 Pierre Bourdieu, "The Forms of Capital (1986)," in *Cultural Theory: An Anthology 1*, eds. Imre Szeman and Timothy Kaposy (West Sussex, UK: Wiley Blackwell, 2011), 81–93.
33 The World Bank. *Understanding Poverty* (The World Bank, 2016). Accessed from www.worldbank.org/en/topic/poverty/overview
34 Ibid.

Postscript

Postscript

Postscript
THE VIVID PARTICULARITIES OF CLASS AND MEDIA

David Morley

Grounded Theory, Empirical Research and Contextualized Data

This collection offers a cornucopia of valuable resources to assist in our understanding of the articulation of media technologies and class structures across a range of social and geographical settings. It has a great many virtues—not least, the fact that its authors eschew the kind of generalizing, one-size-fits-all, over-simplistic, media-centric and technologically determinist accounts of these issues which, sadly, have come to dominate our field in the last decade or so.

Thus, in the volume's introduction, the editors offer us an approach which, rather than dealing in ungrounded generalizations, is founded on the analysis of specific examples and of the particularities of the various milieux in which the media and cultural processes to be researched have their setting. This, of course, is the best way to meet the requirements of producing conjunctural analyses of how things work in specific contexts. This kind of carefully grounded analysis, while necessarily arduous and time-consuming offers so much more to any adequate understanding of developments in contemporary media and cultural processes that can be achieved through any kind of abstracted speculation. Of course, there is then the further question of how very carefully one must 'disinter' a set of insights produced in any one situation, so as to be able to deploy them (subject to the relevant re-contextualization) somewhere else, at another time. Thus, to take an example, while it certainly is possible to benefit a great deal, in analyzing regional media cultures today, from considering Gramsci's[1] insights into the problems of Italian regional cultures in the 1930s, that transposition has to be conducted with exemplary care. To that extent, comparative transnational or transcultural work—the material for which is generously provided in many of these essays—evidently involves rather more than a simple cut-and-paste job.

The interdisciplinary spread of the work also helps to guard against the regrettable tendencies towards media-centrism in our field.[2] To argue thus is not at all to downplay the significance of the media, but rather to insist that it is only by setting them in the widest possible contextual frame that one can properly understand their significance. This collection is a fine testament to what good things can be done, if one pays proper attention to the framing of technological development and media use in a variety of different institutional, geographical and cultural settings.

Wisely, it spreads its analytical net wide—covering a good range of what were once called conventional (and which are now sometimes known as 'legacy') media, alongside the latest technological developments. In doing so, this work happily avoids making the naïve assumption that we must "begin again" by reinventing a form of what has been called "Media Studies 2.0." The authors here recognize full well that studies of contemporary technology have plenty to learn from older traditions of media studies. To that extent, this book largely avoids the kind of 'present-ism' which, despite the insights offered by media scholars such as Carolyn Marvin[3] and Lynn Spigel,[4] fails to see the present itself in historical perspective. Such work often then falls prey to the overestimation of the degree of 'special' (or perhaps even magical) power pertaining to today's version of technological newness. Of course, in so doing, that approach also fails to recognize that this newness itself is, in fact, a historical constant which changes only in its surface forms.

From my own point of view, one of the disappointing aspects of much recent work on the new/digital media has been the way in which, despite the deployment of extremely complex theoretical terminology, it mainly depends on an astonishingly simplistic (and long discredited) theory of "hypodermic effects" in relation to media technologies. Thus, much of it is premised on the assumption that the methodological procedure of media studies should be to identify, through a process of philosophical speculation, the supposed 'essence' of any given technology (usually on a McLuhanite model) and then deduce its inevitable effects. Evidently, anyone who proceeded in that way in relation to the study of conventional media would be regarded as hopelessly naïve. Given all that we know from the last 50 years of audience research and technology use, such models of hypodermic effects were abandoned in media studies a very long time ago. In that field, it is abundantly clear, to anyone familiar with the relevant literatures, that media and communications technologies do not, in fact, have necessary, direct or predictable effects. Unfortunately, the study of new media/digital technologies has largely been conducted without the benefit of those involved seeming to have any understanding of audience studies as historically established. Indeed, it is not simply a question of ignorance (however reprehensible that alone might be) but rather, a more thoroughgoing rejection of the need to conduct empirical work on these matters, so as to investigate how, in fact, particular technologies are used. However, as we know, the findings of empirical audience studies have often made a mockery of the presumptions of those who conceptualized and designed the technologies initially.

To offer but one example, very few of those involved in the inception of television had any idea that, in the broadcast form in which it came to dominate the cultural life of many countries throughout the late twentieth century, it was going to become a predominantly acoustic medium, as TV's adaptation to its domestic context of consumption required its re-design as a form of "radio with pictures" in which the soundtrack was in dominance over the visual image. It is to the great credit of the authors involved in this collection that, rather than repeat these elementary errors, their work is based on detailed empirical investigations of how media technologies are themselves deployed in practice, rather than how they might be imagined in theory (with or without the capital 'T' so often deployed to demonstrate its venerable status). As so often, it is only in the study of the ethnographic detail of daily practices that the key issues are revealed.

The Death of Class Analysis?

Over the last decade or so, it has sometimes seemed that the terminology of class had gradually been deleted from media and cultural studies in response to poststructuralist critiques of 'reductionism' and 'essentialism' in the use of social categories as explanatory devices in cultural analysis. However, in the UK, where I live, there has nonetheless been a sustained engagement with the question of class on the part of a small minority of scholars.[5] I have also contributed to this debate[6] and this collection will do much to further the endeavor to return the concept of class to a central place in our analyses.

The question of 'class-ification' points in two directions. In the first place, it is concerned with what happens when a particular set of individuals is classified, by others, as 'belonging together' in some way. Second, it is concerned with the consequences of individuals categorizing themselves—or indeed, failing to do so—as members of a particular class. One unavoidable difficulty here concerns the fact that if we substitute the word 'classes' for 'masses' in Raymond Williams' famous contention that "there are no masses, only ways of talking about other people as masses,"[7] we readily see that there are sometimes very good reasons for speaking of people as members of classes. This is especially so because, contrary to the claims of Ulrich Beck's theories of 'individualization,' classes are still very powerful social institutions.[8] Certainly, in the UK, all the evidence points to the fact that rates of inter-generational mobility are decreasing—thus class position at birth is still a very powerful predictor of a person's likely social status in adult life, and indeed of their life-expectancy.

In the context of debates about the problem of class in media studies, and in the wake of post-structuralist critiques of essentialist models of class, it has often been assumed that the very attempt to make connections between social position and modalities of media practices was *ipso facto* a 'reductionist' waste of time. However, class analysis need not be premised on any such simple 'arithmetic' of *direct* determination, in which people's actions are seen as automatically determined by their class position. Rather, what needs to be explored is how structural position, across a range of dimensions (including, but not restricted to class) might set parameters to the acquisition of different cultural codes, the possession of which may then inflect people's media activities in systematically different ways.[9]

In a period in which some have claimed that class itself is now no more than a 'zombie' category, these issues obviously acquire a heightened pertinence. The question here is less the ontological issue of whether classes still *exist*, but rather the question of *how* a category such as class might be deployed in our analyses—at what level of abstraction, for what purposes and in relation to which theories of causation. Clearly, *any* sociological category—be it class, or gender, or 'race,' or ethnicity—can be deployed in a zombie-like manner. That would be so in any attempt to explain a phenomenon such as differential responses to media material or variations in technology use as if they were a direct result of people being 'prisoners' of class, racial, ethnic or gendered categories.

However, if these analytical categories must be used judiciously, we also need to pay attention to the very high price of not using them at all, for fear of the charge of essentialism or reductionism—that way lie the dangers and limitations of what critical sociologists used to be called "methodological individualism." Thus, to take a different issue, in relation to the status of gender as an explanatory factor in media research, critics of 'essentialism' are quite right that we cannot presume a priori that in any particular instance of media consumption, gender will necessarily be the determining factor. However, to refuse to hypothesize as to *which* factors are most likely to have which sorts of consequences, in which situations, would be to abandon any form of social analysis, which ultimately depends on the use of categorizations, in order to abstract from the details, and thus reveal supra-individual patterns. While categorizations are reductive by their very nature, the point lies in deciding *which* type of categorization devices to use, however provisionally, in analyzing which types of material. Otherwise, we are left floating in an endless play of contextual specificity and infinite difference, in which, by refusing to make any generalizations at all, we disempower our own analyses.

In the context of debates about self-reflexivity in anthropology, Clifford Geertz[10] has written of the disabling effects of the dangers of what he called the "hermeneutics of suspicion." It would seem that in media studies in recent years, we have witnessed a comparable phenomenon, in relation to the "pervasive nervousness" about the use of categories such as class in social analysis. It is for that very reason that I for one find it extremely heartening to see the concept of class redeployed at the center of the analysis in the way that it is in the essays collected in this volume.

Excursions in the Field

In the space available to me here, I can do no more than gesture, encouragingly, towards some of the rich particularities revealed in some of the different essays included in this volume. What I do want to say, in general terms, is what a high standard of work the volume includes—far beyond the specific examples which I go on to mention here.

That selection is no doubt inflected by the nature of my personal research interests—into matters such as the household uses of information and communication technology. In that regard, let me begin by commenting on how very rich I found the material on the implications of class position and residential status in determining differential access to particular levels of technology. The explorations here of the social determinants of urban broadband provision, and of the degree of differentiation between the types of digital access and thus the forms of (increasingly mediated) citizenship available to different categories of people, is particularly valuable in what remains an underdeveloped field of research. In the same way, the analyses here of the interrelations of class, household, generation and forms of techno-literacy provide a valuable set of multi-sited updates to the earlier work in this field.[11] Likewise, the investigations here into the role of class, financial status and age in determining how people navigate mobile technologies is a further valuable contribution to these debates, as are the analyses of the significance of middle-class assumptions in determining the very design of the systems of accessing technology which, because of these limiting, built-in assumptions (for instance, concerning the nature of property ownership), function to effectively exclude many of those who need this access but fail to fit the middle-class stereotype of the potential users created by the manufacturers (on all this see, in particular, the chapters here by Will Balmford and Larissa Hjorth, Germaine Halegoua, and Justine Humphry).

There is also excellent work represented here which articulates questions of transport, communication and mobility in a manner that allows us to grasp the connections between different forms of connectivity or exclusion across both virtual and material geographies. To that extent, the volume makes a valuable contribution to the analysis of the 'politics of waiting'—whether that is a question of waiting in the cold for a bus on a marginalized part of the transport system, or waiting for a governmental agency to answer your call when you are ringing on a high-cost phone line, attempting to comply with that institution's own supervisory requirements. In this spirit, Lynn Schofield Clark investigates a telling example of the ways in which existing institutions work to enable certain kinds of mobilization for privileged categories of persons while denying it for others. Here, we engage with the question of the class-based distribution of (chronic) waiting, especially among marginalized groups living in under-privileged areas. It was in this spirit that the British geographer Doreen Massey[12] critiqued abstracted theories of postmodernity by asking what evidence there was of the supposed conveniences of "time-space compression" in the lives of the poor? In opening up these questions, we thus begin to problematize the interdependent relations between spatial mobility and social mobility. As the book's editors note in their Introduction, we need to examine not only how these technologies reproduce systems of privilege and oppression, but also how they are inserted into pre-existing social hierarchies. Because of this complex set of intermediations, technological 'connectivity' can be seen as both a symptom and cause of inequality. In examining these issues, we move beyond any simple notions of a binary 'digital divide' and begin to address the local works question of variegated modes of access to different levels of material and technological resources. It is, as the editors say, by addressing these issues that we can then better see how a range of identities, religions, lifestyles and geographies intersect all areas of media and class.

This question of the complex modes of the mediation of class differences is also addressed by Holly Kruse in her examination of how practices and places are 'classed' and how class divisions are maintained in and through interactive media practices and in Rohit K. Dasgupta's analysis of the role of a variety of 'media filters' in keeping undesirable 'riff-raff' at bay. From a correspondingly sensitive perspective, Renée A. Botta explores the issue of class differences in the experience of medical problems and in their representation.[13]

The Importance of Differences

The research presented here is particularly valuable when it offers us what are sometimes counterintuitive results. Thus, it is salutary to learn that, just as in the case of refugees whose safety depends on up-to-date information on the situation in the territories through which they are passing, others living in precarious situations—such as the urban homeless—are also compelled to give an extraordinarily high priority in their very limited budgets to maintaining their communications capacities (sometimes in the form of what is called here "catastrophe spending," which they can neither afford nor survive without).

Thus, Justine Humphry explores how class is embedded in media assemblages that provide only expensive—though nonetheless substandard—digital access to low-income consumers. This means that young, poor and/or nonwhite populations studies, living in impoverished neighborhoods are only able to access the internet through a mobile phone as they are excluded from the more sophisticated modes of internet access which are effectively required for full citizenship. Here, we encounter the invidious phenomenon of the "poverty premium" by means of which the disadvantaged are further penalized by having to pay more than others for access to variety of services, and tend, as a result, to get mainly negative (and dispiriting) experiences at a high cost. This is all part of the overall picture of the ways in which class structures people's media access and, conversely, that lack of access itself exacerbates existing inequalities, thus creating barriers to participation in education and employment opportunities.

Similarly, Germaine Halegoua offers a fascinating analysis of the making of broadband classes and, in particular, the creation of a broadband underclass whose experience of the internet is "subpar, circumscribed." This represents a very productive development of the "digital divide" debate to investigate the social stigma attached to—and expectations about—particular types of broadband access. Halegoua successfully articulates the technical questions of internet functionality with material issues concerning the presumptions built into these initiatives. It transpires that built into these initiatives about extending the social reach of broadband technologies, are a set of disabling assumptions about their 'normal' setting for installation: in effect, the forms of housing associated with certain types of privileged populations constitute the necessary ground-base of the market for whom the product is designed. Thus, it seems that for their successful implementation, home *ownership* is required as the assumed conditions for broadband provision. The financial and legal difficulties for anyone living in temporary rented accommodation create a situation where certain populations are systematically excluded from—and are thus unable to utilize—the more reliable forms of broadband.

The collection contains valuable materials on the issue of why members of particular social categories are under- or over-represented in different media spaces, corresponding to Alec Hargreaves' work on how race and ethnicity determine access to desirable "territories"—whether up-market residential areas or the televisual "genres of conviviality" such as comedy and light entertainment. Of course, as Hargreaves[14] argues, persons with the "wrong" skin tones tend to be hypervisible not only in poor areas, but also in the "problem-oriented" genres of documentary and news. This is exactly the point which Hun-Yul Lee makes in their account of how TV shows featuring low-status migrants are usually relegated to the fringes of late-night educational programming in Korea.

All this work offers valuable contributions to debates about the potential for the 'democratization' of media via the widening of participation. Classically, in the recent period it has been argued that the genre of Reality TV has come to play a significant progressive role as a genre that allows more working class people to appear on television. Thus, Annette Hill and Koko Kondo observe, in their essay, that TV talent shows have come to function as a resource to increase "social motility capital," allowing the disadvantaged to achieve greater success in the precarious labor markets of late capitalism. However, as Graeme Turner[15] has observed in this connection the 'demotic turn' represented by the increasing visibility of working class people in certain areas of low-grade television is a different matter from the democratization of the medium, which requires rather more than an extension in the range of its participants, welcome as that might be, in itself. As Hall argued many years ago, in his analysis of the "structure of access" in British television, it may well be that the question of improving access for those who are currently marginalized is, in the end, of less importance than that of curtailing the systematic over-accessing of the currently privileged groups.[16]

The essay by Erika Polson on "privileged mobilities"—in this case, addressing the specific situation of aspirational "digital nomads" who can essentially work anywhere in the world "as long as they have a laptop and a good internet connection"—reminds us that the mobility that is sometimes taken to be an intrinsic characteristic of the contemporary world is, in fact, very unequally distributed as between different categories of persons.[17] In this respect, the key question is that of who has power and control over their own mobility—as opposed to those whose mobility is forcibly thrust upon them by economic or political circumstances which 'displace' them from the locations where they would have preferred to continue to live. Clearly, in the case that Polson addresses, these are people for whom a lifestyle of permanent travel, in which they achieve "location independence" is a highly desirable state of existence. However, as I have argued elsewhere, this is a very particular experience and certainly provides no model of a generalizable kind that would lead us to assume that the world will be increasingly populated by nomads of this kind. Indeed, there is plenty of evidence that most of the world's less privileged citizens—such as, for instance, the denizens of the slums of the megacities of the Global South, will in the future, lead increasingly localized lives, with very little access to mobility in either its virtual or material dimensions.[18]

Looking towards that future, it is clearly important to take account of the increasing centrality of virtual geographies as the infrastructure of forms of citizenship, which are now more dependent on various forms of technological mediation.[19] Evidently, this is no simple matter of the untrammeled roll-out of technology via forms of state or economic power; as Sarah J. Jackson and Brooke Foucault Welles[20] call "hashtag activism" or "truth telling from the margins," citizen activists are creating digital counter publics as networks of resistance to established institutions. As Mohammed El Marzouki observes, in a similar spirit, we must take account of the creation of networked "publics of contention" especially among youth using digital spaces to produce "alternative" cultural practices aimed at challenging structures of exclusion using the "weapons of the weak."[21] These are important points to consider but at the same time we must be careful not to overestimate potentially liberatory capacities of "unfiltered"/social media. Thus, we must also be alert to their ambivalent capacities—which, in the recent period have allowed governmental authorities to more easily enforce systematic modes of surveillance across these forms of oppositional politics (e.g., in the face of electronically networked protest movements in both Cairo and Istanbul, in recent years).

Conclusion

Let me end by returning, in conclusion, to the fundamental issues concerning the relation of class and media which I began by addressing. It is very good to see the concept of class deployed here in sophisticated ways, which recognize that class structures themselves are always articulated with other forms of social organization, whether of race, ethnicity and gender or religion. It is, of course, only within these (as we say today) "intersectional" complexities that we can understand the differential forms and functioning of class structures and produce context-relevant definitions of class (cf. the materials in this collection on the intersection of the class and caste systems in India). Here, of course, we enter the complex (if often badly under-theorized) realm of our own everyday lives, in which we all juggle different identities and deploy the cultural resources at our disposal, within— and at times against—the limits set by the material, political and legal infrastructures that work to constrain us (as many of these authors show). It is within those complex dynamics—where matters of race and ethnicity, class and gender and religion all intersect (and at times 'displace') each other—that our relations to media technologies of our own age (both the familiar and the newly emerging ones) have to be lived out, and only within that context that these matters can properly be understood.

Notes

1. Antonio Gramsci, *The Prison Notebooks* (London: Lawrence and Wishart, 1974).
2. Cf. David Morley "For a Materialist, Non Media-Centric Media Studies," *Television and New Media* 10, no. 1 (2009).
3. Carolyn Marvin, *When Old Technologies Were New* (New York: Oxford University Press, 1990).
4. Lynn Spigel, "Introduction," in *Television After TV*, eds. Lynn Spigel and Jan Olsson (Durham, NC: Duke University Press, 2004).
5. For example, Sally Munt, *Cultural Studies and the Working Class* (London: Cassell, 2000); Andy Medhurst, "Class Identification," in *Cultural Studies and the Working Class*, ed. Sally Munt (London: Cassell, 2000); Beverly Skeggs, *Class, Self and Culture* (London: Routledge, 2004).
6. David Morley, "Mediated Class-ifications: Representations of Class and Culture in Contemporary British Television," *European Journal of Cultural Studies* 12, no. 4 (2009).
7. Raymond Williams, *Culture and Society: 1780–1950* (New York: Columbia University Press, 1958), 298.
8. Ulrich Beck and Elisabeth Beck-Gernsheim, *Individualisation* (London: Sage, 2002).
9. Cf. for a critical review of debates on class and decoding in audience studies: Sujeong Kim, "Re-Reading David Morley's *The Nationwide Audience*," *Cultural Studies* 8, no. 1 (2004).
10. Clifford Geertz, *Works and Lives; the Anthropologist as Author* (Cambridge: Polity, 1988).
11. Roger Silverstone, Eric Hirsch and D. Morley, "Listening to a Long Conversation: An Ethnographic Approach to ICTs in the Home," *Cultural Studies* 5, no. 2 (1991); Shaun Moores, *Media and Everyday Life in Modern Society* (London: Sage, 2000); Elaine Lally, *At Home with Computers* (London: Berg, 2002).
12. Doreen Massey, *Space, Place and Gender* (Cambridge: Polity Press, 1994).
13. Cf. on the complexities and limitations of technologized forms of health education: Thomas Tufte, *Communication and Social Change: A Citizen Perspective* (Cambridge: Polity Press, 2017).
14. Alec G. Hargreaves, "A Deviant Construction: The French Media and the 'Banlieues'," *New Community* 22, no. 4 (1996).
15. Graeme Turner, *Ordinary People and the Media* (London: Sage, 2010).
16. Ibid.; Stuart Hall, *The Structure of Access in British Broadcasting* (University of Birmingham: CCCS Stencilled Paper Series, 1974).
17. Cf. Massey, *Space, Place*; Zigmunt Bauman, *Wasted Lives: Modernity and its Outcasts* (Cambridge: Polity Press, 2003).
18. Cf. David Morley, *Communications and Transport* (Oxford: Wiley-Blackwell, 2017).
19. Cf. Peter Dahlgren, *Media and Political Engagement: Citizens, Communication and Democracy* (New York: Cambridge University Press, 2009).
20. Sarah J. Jackson and Brooke Foucault Welles, "Hijacking #myNYPD: Social Media Dissent and Networked Counterpublics," *Journal of Communication* 65, no. 6 (2015): 932–952.
21. Cf. Michel de Certeau, *The Practice of Everyday Life* (University of California Press, 1996).

INDEX

Page numbers in *italics* denote figures.

Abidin, C. 9
Absolute Poker 82
active audiences 4
Adivasis 143–144, 145
advertising 17–24, 60, 148; AT&T 21; Aunt Jemima 20; Axe Anarchy for Him and Her 22; Brawny paper towels 22; class preferences 18; classified ads for slaves in newspapers 19; Depression-era 19; DirecTV 24; Dollar Shave Club 17, 19, 23; Duluth Trading Company 23; Gorton's of Gloucester frozen seafood 22; intersectionality of class with race and gender 19–21; Luftal anti-gas tablets 23; Marlboro cigarettes 22; post-bellum depiction of African Americans in the US 20; social class in 18–19; State Farm 23; symbolic functions of white working-class males in 21–24; Toyota 21; in Trump era America 24; working-class bodies in 17–24
advocacy citizen journalism 269
African Americans: depiction in post-bellum US advertising 20; in reality TV shows 30; skin tone and status 6
African National Congress (ANC) 161
Agdal, Nina 24
Ahmed, A. 63
Ahmedis 144
AirBnB 6, 171, 173, 197
Albury, K. 112
Algeria 253–254, 263
algorithms 193, 198, 200
Alizadeh, T. 234
All in the Family 18
Altman, M. 204
Amazon 198, 243
Andersson, M. 267
Anheuser-Busch, Super Bowl ad 19

Arab Spring 7, 254, 258, 260, 263
Arroyo, Gloria 218
Asante, G. 70
Ask.fm 136–137
Askanius, T. 53
AT&T 21
Atugala, A. 149
Aunt Jemima 20
Australia 10, 21, 110, 112, 116, 119, 173, 242, 249; mobile technology and class in 110–119; social media and sexual health education in 112
Avatar 21
Axe Anarchy for Him and Her 22

Balmford, W. 9, 298
Banaji, S. 9
Bangladesh 142–145, 148, 150, 213
Banjo, Ashley 54, 58
Bannon, Steve 33
Barthes, R. 4, 56
Basecamp 188
Bayou Billionaires 32
Beck, U. 40, 112
Bekri, Momo 258–260
Beller, J. 275
Bennett, L. 257
Bennett, T. 111–112, 117
Berlant, L. 276
betting *see* horse race wagering
Beverley Hillbillies 32
Beyoncé 6
Bhattacharjee, S. 269
Big Brother 43, 45
Birmingham School 4, 243
Black Lives Matter 7
Black Panthers 6

Index

blackface 21
blue-collar workers 19
Bober, M. 111, 114, 117, 134
Boddy, W. 83
Bollywood 92
Bonaparte, Louis 194
Boston News-Letter 19
Botta, R. 8, 298
Bourdieu, P. 4, 33–34, 39–40, 91, 100–101, 111–112, 134, 139, 157–161, 166, 169, 180, 182, 231–232, 237, 261–262, 289–290
Bourdieusian approach to journalism: the argument 157–158; basic principles 158–159; detailed knowledge of stories 162–163; distinction from other approaches 159–160; journalists' perceptions, social roots 160–166; long-form reporting on social issues 161–162; sensationalism, avoidance of 165–166; telling a story well 164
Boyce, P. 92
Boyle, Susan 54
Brainard, L. 206
Branch, A. 281
Bravo 28, 34
Brawny paper towels 22
A Brief History of Neoliberalism (Harvey) 198
Bring Your Own Device (BYOD) 112, 115, 119
Britain's Got Talent 54
broadband access: class distinctions 229–239; class and urban broadband networks 232–234; and the classification of class 231–232; Google Fiber for Communities initiative 234–237; Google Fiber promotion 229–231; *see also* Google Fiber initiative
Brown v. Board of Education 268
Buddhists 144
bullying 2
Bunker, Archie 18
Burgess, J. 100
Burke, Tarana 2
business process outsourcing (BPO) 213, 216–217
Butsch, R. 18
Byron, P. 112

Cabañes, J.V. 10
call centres 213, 216–217
Canada 149, 174
Cant, C. 193
capital, circles of 100
Cardoso, G. 115
Case, C. 79
caste 1–2, 5–6, 9, 79, 90, 92–95, 97, 143–144, 150–152
catastrophe spending 247–248, 299
celebrity, YouTube and the creation of 102–103
celebrity culture, pervasiveness 99
Centre for Cultural Policy Research (CCPR) 99
Chakir, Marwan 258–260
Chakravartty, P. 3
ChannelNewsAsia 138
Chansawatkit, S. 249

Charm School 32
Chatterjee, S. 91
Chaudron, S. 117
Chayko, M. 90
Chen, G. 204–205
Chennai Pride Walk 92
children, exploration of the risks and benefits of online interaction for 115
Children and Media in India (Banaji) 145
China 2, 41, 128, 283
Christians 144–145
Chugthai, Ali 201
circuits of labour model 7
cis gender normativity 2
citizenship: and identity 256–258; and social class 254–256
Citizenship and Social Class (Marshall) 255
civil rights 166, 255
Clark, L.S. 10, 117, 298
class: American opinions 27; characteristics of construction 101; classification of 231–232; the concept of 1; definitions of 40; discussion of in media and cultural studies 296–297; intersectional approach to media and 5–6; Marxist approach 39; new formations 1–2; origins of contemporary notions 77; as post-colonial phenomenon 282; post-industrial validity of 40; racial perspective of 30–31; shaping factors 5; ways to think about 77; *see also* social class
class formations 1, 7, 101, 180–181, 189, 194, 198
class hybridity, on reality TV 32–33
class mobility 18, 23, 33, 35, 68, 119, 144, 175–176; code switching and 34–35
Class with the Countess (de Lesseps) 32
The Class: Living and learning in the digital age (Livingstone & Sefton-Green) 117
Clayton, J. 233, 237
clickbait 158
Cobb, J. 33
Cohen, S. 84
Cohen, S.A. 170–171
CoinTelegraph 2
colonial infrastructures, inherited inequalities 3
colourism, class-based 6
communication 242–250; apps 132, 136–138; for children 143; role of in political organization 194–195; role of in workplace organization 192, 201; role of the internet and digital devices 133; social media and 188; *see also* broadband access; mobile phone ownership amongst the homeless; mobile technology and class; second-class access
computer literacy, requirements 132
condom use, Kenyan ad controversy 68
Connell, R. 123
Consuming Technologies: Media and information in domestic spaces (Hirsch & Silverstone) 114
Corner, J. 45, 55
cosmopolitan capital 184, 189
Coursera 133
Crawford, K. 7, 112

Index

Crawford, S. 242
Cresswell, T. 266
critical race theory (CRT) 5
Cross, G. 18
crowdsourcing platforms 137
cryptocurrency 2–3
cultural appropriation 21
cultural capital 6, 9, 29, 34, 39, 100, 110–112, 114, 116, 134, 144, 169–170, 172, 175–176, 184, 231–232, 250, 289
Culture, Class, Distinction (Bennett et al) 111
Cyber Proletariat (Dyer-Witheford) 199

Dahlgren, P. 269
Dailey, D. 233
Dalits 6, 92, 143–144, 151
dance talent shows, entertainment mobilization in 51–61 (*see also Got to Dance*; reality talent shows)
Dances with Wolves 21
Daniel, R. 70
Daoudi, O. 9
Darlington, K.-A. 69
Dasgupta, R. 9
Deery, J. 59
Deliveroo 192–193, 200–201; remuneration system 192
demotic turn, Turner's concept 101, 300
Depression-era advertising, class in 19
device literacy, impact of intergenerational differences 114
Diary of a Digital Nomad: How to Run Away with Your Responsibilities (Molloy) 173
DiEnno, C. 269
digital commons 243
digital divide 112, 114, 115–116, 118, 133, 139, 232, 242–244, 298–299
digital domesticity 203–205, 207, 209
digital exclusion 242, 248
digital housewife 203–207
The Digital Housewife (Jarrett) 205
digital inclusion events 234
digital labour 213–223; class and coloniality in the Philippines 215–217; classed and colonial imaginaries 217–222 (*see also under* online freelancers); criticisms 213–214; in the Global South and North 214–215; new forms and dilemmas 243; precariousness 214–215
digital literacy 132–135, 138, 217, 233, 237; the changing face of 132–133; and class 133–134
digital media, materiality of 242–243
digital natives 134, 143, 151
digital nomadism: aspirational class mobility of 168–177; class mobility of the mobile class 175–176; the concept 168–169; digital media and global mobility 171–172; global lifestyle of expatriates 170–171; problems with 172; professional challenges 171; as 'pyramid scheme' 173; resources for 174; role of social media 171–172; selling the nomadic life 172–174; training programme 174

digital queer spaces 90–97; mediation through technological and social differences 90–92; and the role of caste 92–95; and the use of English 95–97; ways forward 97
digital subalternity 203–204, 206–208, 211
DirecTV 24
discrimination 11, 19, 45–47, 79, 90, 93, 95–97, 143–144, 150, 182, 230, 232, 236, 268
disgust, social class and expressions of 23
displacement 144, 268, 273–276, 282
Disposed to Learn: Schooling, Ethnicity and the Scholarly Habitus (Watkins & Noble) 112
disruptive technologies, impact on social class 6–7
Distinction (Bourdieu) 158, 231
Diversity 54
Dollar Shave Club 17, 19, 23
domestic care work 181, 188
domestication theory 114
"Don't Call Me That: A Techno-Feminist Critique of the Term *Mommy Blogger*" (Chen) 204
Doraemon 148
Dreier, M. 117
Dropbox 133
Dubsmash 132, 136, 138
Duck Dynasty 32–33
Duluth Trading Company 23
Duncan, T. 170
Duplic8, 58–59
Durham, A. 6
Dwyer, R. 92
Dyer-Witheford, N. 199, 243

East Asia, YouTube home tour vlogs 122–128
economic capital 6, 68, 100, 106, 169, 176, 258
economic crises 2, 41, 197
economic inequality, in *Shuga* 67–68
education 34, 64–65, 68, 70, 72, 132–135, 143–146, 160–161, 166, 182, 184, 204, 232–233, 244, 246, 268, 277, 282, 289, 299
educational capital 112
edutainment programmes: function 63; necessary considerations 71–72; *see also* HIV edutainment; *Shuga*
Edwards, H. 158
Eighteenth Brumaire of Louis Bonaparte (Marx) 194
84 Lumber, Super Bowl ad 19
El-Marzouki, M. 10, 300
emotional labour 52, 57–58, 61, 205, 207
Endemol Shine 52
Engels, F. 282
English working class, critical reflections 4
"Epistemologies of Doing: E-merging Selves Online" (Gajjala, Rybas & Altman) 204
Espanha, R. 115
Evers, C. 112
!Exclamation Mark 43

Facebook 6, 55, 57, 84, 90, 95–97, 133, 136–138, 147, 174, 180, 184, 186–188, 192, 207, 246, 284, 286

Index

false consciousness 4
family reunion, reality TV format 43–44
Fanning, Shawn 84
Fechter, A.-M. 170
#FeesMustFall student movement 288
female empowerment 70
FIFA Ultimate Team 110
Flamm, M. 58
Flannery, Matt and Jessica 203
Flay, Bobby 80
Florida, R. 214
Fortunati, L. 276
Foxconn 7
Frankfurt School 4
Franko, W.W. 242
Fraser, N. 255
Freelancer.com 213
Fuchs, C. 100, 243
Full Tilt Poker 82
Fuller, M. 243

Gajjala, R. 204, 206
Galarza, L. 8
gambling: problematic 85–86; *see also* horse race wagering
Games of Being Mobile (GoBM) study, methodology 110
Gaul, G. 82
Geertz, C. 297
gentrification 266–277; definition of 267; Denver's experience 266, 268–269; and facilities/services for young people 269–273; mitigating the effects of 273–275; role of transportation and communication in mobility 275–277
geo-tagging 172
Germany 40
Gibbs, A. 69
Gibson, W. 242–243
gig economy: and class (de)composition 192–201; comparative historical context 194–195; and the cycle of struggle 198–200; defining/understanding 197–198; drivers of 195–197; isolation of the work 192, 195; major sources of labour supply 213; organizing in the 192–193, 200–201; *see also* Deliveroo; digital labour; online freelancers
Global Talk Show: The Beauties' Chatterbox 44–45
globalization 2–3, 5, 38–41, 46–47, 196, 213–214, 256
Goetz, A.R. 269
Goffman, E. 55
Golden Bride 43
Goldthorpe, J.H. 28
Google 103, 137–138, 229, 233–234, 236–239, 243
Google Fiber initiative: connectivity messaging 235; creating class distinctions in urban broadband projects 237–238; home messaging 236–237; mobility messaging 236; participatory model of identification 234–235
Goonasekara, A. 142

Gordon, L. 255
Gorton's of Gloucester 22
Got to Dance: audience dissatisfaction 59; audience research 53; auditions 53; backstage *51*; casting objectives 54; ethos and establishment of trust 54–55; invisible labour 56–57; participant observations 53; performance of selfhood 54, 58–59; a performer's experience 58; production company 52; as spectacle of labour 61; viewer disengagement 59; working class audience 54
Gramsci, A. 4, 160
Great Britain 54, 78–79, 83, 192, 200; *see also* United Kingdom
Green, J. 100
Green, L. 113, 115
Gregg, M. 7
Grindr 9, 90–91, 93, 95, 97
Grossetête, M. 159

habitus 33, 125, 166, 182, 184
Hackers 84
Haddon, L. 114
Halegoua, G. 10, 298–299
Hall, S. 4–5
Hammond, A. 248
Hardt, M. 194–195
Hargreaves, A. 299
Hartley, J. 77
Hartman, M. 56, 266–267
Harvey, D. 198
hashtag activism 2
health, impact of socio-economic position on 64
Heffernan, Doug 18
Helsper, E.J. 134
Henderson, L. 90, 92, 95
hijras 92
Hill, A. 8, 42, 52–53, 299
Hill, D.D. 21
Hillrichs, R. 122
Hindus 144
hip-hop 21
historical perspective of media and class 4
HIV, the causes of 69
HIV edutainment 63–72; *see also Shuga*
Hjarvard, S. 67
Hjorth, L. 9, 298
Hodgetts, D. 244
Hogan, Greg, Jr 85
Hoggart, R. 4, 160
Hollingworth, S. 139
Holloway, D. 113
the home: as locale and topic of content production 122; and online gambling 84–86; *see also* YouTube home tour vlogs
homelessness 56, 157, 162, 238, 242, 244–250, 253, 256, 260–262, 299; *see also* second-class access
The Honeymooners 18
Hong Kong 193
Honneth, A. 182
hooks, bell 21

horse race wagering: "classing" of practices and places 77–87; comparison with online poker betting 82; and discrimination against minorities 79; gambling in the home 81–83; Kentucky Derby 80; media and the lives of ordinary people 86–87; racetracks and off-track betting facilities 77; reliance of the horse racing industry on gambling for revenue 80; role of social class in the origins of horse racing 78–81; and segregation of the Victorian home by sex 83; technology and the home 84–86
hot-desking 173
Huggins, M. 78–79
Humphry, J. 10, 298–299
Huws, U. 197, 199
hypodermic effects, of media technologies 296

identity 27, 32, 34–35, 38, 42, 44, 56, 65, 67, 71, 77, 93, 95, 97, 101, 112, 114, 122–123, 128, 145, 150, 157, 169–171, 182, 194–195, 204, 230, 253–254, 256–257
Imanyara, Gitobu 283
immigration/immigrants 19, 38, 40–43, 45, 79, 271, 273
Independent Workers Union of Great Britain (IWGB) 192, 200–201
India: and business process outsourcing 213; discriminated groups 144; enclaves of queer privilege in 90–97; Hindu nationalist discourse 145; movements against sexual harassment 2; poverty in 142; social class and children's media experiences 143; television in 148
Indonesia, hashtag activism 2
Industrial Revolution 77, 231
inequality 24, 40, 63–64, 67–68, 70–71, 111, 119, 133, 143, 149, 211, 232, 243–244, 248, 254–256, 262–263, 283, 298
influencers 122, 128, 173, 217, 220, 223
infrastructure 3, 60, 104, 106, 168–169, 176, 193–195, 197, 203–204, 206, 211, 220, 223, 233–234, 239, 266, 268–269, 271, 274–277, 280, 300
Instagram 132–133, 136–138, 147, 168, 174, 186–187, 246
internet 2, 9, 78, 81–86, 112, 114, 132–135, 138–140, 142–144, 148, 150–152, 195, 231–234, 236–237, 239, 242–243, 245, 247, 249–250, 260, 280, 282–283, 299
Internet Corporation for Assigned Names and Numbers (ICANN) 3
intersectionality 1, 5, 10, 68
Interstate Wire Act 81
intimate citizenship 112, 114
inverse care law 64
invisible labour 56–57, 61, 211
iPhones 7, 90, 113
Iqani, M. 282–283
Irani, L. 218

Jackson, S.J. 300

jananas 92
Jansson, A. 10
Japan 128, 149
Jarrahi, M.H. 171
Jarrett, K. 205, 207
Jaworski, A. 67
Jeffreys, C. 276
Jhally, S. 4
Jonas, A.E.G. 30, 269
journalism *see* Bourdieusian approach to journalism
Jurassic Park 84

Kashmir 145
Kaufman, V. 52, 58
Kendall, D. 18
Kentucky Derby 80
Kenya: HIV edutainment 63–72; social activism in 280–290; *see also Shuga*; social activism
Kenyatta, Jomo 281–282
Keywords: A Vocabulary of Culture and Society (Williams) 5
Khalid, M.Z. 63
Khan, S. 72
Kim, J. 100
The King of Queens 18
Kirschenbaum, M.G. 243
Kittler, F. 243
Kiva 203–204, 206–211
Koinange, Mbiyu 282
Kondo, K. 8, 53, 299
Korea: class and migration in 40–42; class theory in the context of 39–40; history of migration to 38–39; Olympic Games 41, 43; reality TV shows in 42–43; representation of non-Koreans in reality TV 38–48; undocumented workers 41; visitor numbers 42; *see also* non-Koreans on Korean television
Korean War 38–39
kothis 92
Kramden, Ralph 18
Kruse, H. 9, 298
Kuntsman, A. 90

labour exploitation 41, 213
Ladette to Lady 32
Ladies of London 30–31
Lafarge, G. 159
LaFleur, V. 206
Lagae, K. 117
Lahire, B. 33
laissez-faire economic system 255
Lally, E. 113
Lange, P. 100
Lapa, T. 115
Larkin, B. 275
Le Monde 158
Lee, H.-Y. 8, 299
Leek, S. 249
Lees, L. 267
Lerner, D. 4

"Let's Express Our Friendship by Sending Each Other Funny Links instead of Actually Talking: Gifts, Commodities, and Social Reproduction in Facebook" (Jarrett) 207
Levels, Pieter 172
Lewis, B. & J. 70–71
Lewis, T. 112
LGBT perspectives, social media enclaves 90–97
Liechty, M. 175
Ligaga, D. 68
Liimatta, Michael 237
Lim, S.S. 9, 134
LinkedIn 133
Livingstone, S. 7, 111, 114, 117, 134
Loh, R.S.M. 9
Lone Star Park racetrack 81
#LoSHA (list of sexual harassers in the Indian Academy) 2
Love, C. 113
Love in Asia 43
Lowe, Rob 24
Luftal anti-gas tablets 23

Macdonald, S. J 233, 237
Maduro, Nicolas 2
Malay Berita 138
Mampilly, Z. 281
The Man From U.N.C.L.E. 43
Mandela, Nelson 161
Mankekar, P. 151
Manovich, L. 243
Manson, Mark 172
Marchand, R. 18
Marchetti, D. 159
Marchi, R. 269
marginality: mediatizing 258–260; youth marginality and social change 260–262
Marlboro cigarettes 22
Married to Medicine 30–31
Marshall, T.H. 255
Marvin, C. 296
Marwick, A. 84
Marx, K. 39, 159, 194, 197–198
Mascheroni, G. 117
Massey, D. 298
Matthan, T. 144
Mau Mau 281
Maytag Repairman 18
McAllister, M. 8
McGrath, J. 55
Media Studies 2.0, 295
media technology, affordability and reach of 99
Meikle, G. 100
Melber, H. 282
memes 1, 3, 123, 147, 223
Mendoza, R.U. 247–248
Menon, K. 67
#MeToo 2
#metooindia movement 2
microfinance 203, 208–209

Middle East and North Africa (MENA), youth media activism 253–263
middlebrow culture 4
middle-class 18–19, 24, 83, 85, 142–152, 169, 173, 280, 287–288
Mignolo, W. 6
Mills, C. 5
Minecraft 110, 116
mobile phone ownership amongst the homeless: exploitative retail practices 248–249; handset quality issues 245–247; pricing strategies and their impact 247–248; *see also* second-class access
mobile socialities 267
mobile technology and class 110–119; BYOD programmes and the potential for a digital divide 112, 114, 115–116; examples of data management and usage 116–118; framing class 111–113; household management of device use 113–115
mobility: the concept of 266; digital media and global mobility 171–172; mobile career management and family life 184–186; relationship between class and 266, 277; *see also* digital nomadism
Moi, Daniel arap 281, 283
Mojola, S.A. 70
mommy blogging 204–205
monetization, of YouTube content 104–107, 126
Moneymaker, Chris 82
Monopoly (YouTube film) 99
Moodie, M. 208
moral panics, online gambling and 78, 84–85
Morley, D. 4, 10, 160, 266–267
Morocco 254, 258–261
Mossberger, K. 242
mothering, illustration of class through 204
motility 52, 58
MTV Staying Alive Foundation 63
Müller, A. 168
Multicultural Mother- and Daughter-in-Law Stories 43, 44
Murray, S. 42
Musical.ly 132, 136–138
Muslims 144
Mutunga, Willy 283
Mwangi, Boniface 284–286, 288
Mwaura, J. 10

Nagar, I. 92
Nakamura, L. 208
Napoli, P.M. 237, 249–250
Nationwide (BBC) 4
Native Americans, casino businesses 81
Negri, A. 194–195
neoliberal globalization 3
neoliberalism 4, 97, 198
Nepal 142–143, 145, 147–148
Netflix 113, 117–118
Neuromancer (Gibson) 243
newspapers: relationship with class 158; slave advertising in 19

Ngugi wa Thiongo 283
Nintendo Switch 110
Njoya, Timothy 283
Noble, G. 112
non-Koreans on Korean television 43–47; class implications 47–48; migrants 43–44; misrepresentation 45; professionals 44–46; travellers 46–47
Nonsummit 45
"Notes Toward a Politics of Location" (Rich) 176
nouveau riche, reality TV and 28–31, 33
novels, role in class formation 4
Nyong'o, Lupita 63, 71

Obar, J.A. 237, 249–250
O'Barr, W.M. 19
#OccupyParliament movement 288–290
#OccupyPlayground movement 284–288
O'Guinn, T.C. 18–20
Ong, A. 259
online activities, moral panics 84
online freelancers: distinction imaginary 217–218; flexibility imaginary 220–222; transcendence imaginary 219–220
online gambling 78, 81–82, 84–86, 134
online philanthropy 203–211; class and labour in 204–206; Kiva case study 208–209; reproductive labour on digital platforms 207–208; Workaway case study 209–211
online poker industry: indictments 82; revenue 84
Onlinejobs.ph 213
Ortner, S. 92
Ouellette, L. 42
outsourcing 7, 125, 200
Overbergh, A. 65

Page, B. 267
Pakistan 142–146, 148–149, 213
"The Parable of the Democracy of Goods" 18
The Parent App: Understanding Families in the Digital Age (Clark) 117
Parikka, J. 243
Park, Robert E. 274
Park Jeong-Hee 38
Parks, L. 275
Partnership for an HIV-Free Generation 63
Patil, S. 92
patriarchy 70
Paulson, E.L. 18–20
PAWA254, 284
'Performing the Real' (Corner) 55
Peterson, J. 102
philanthropy, online performance of *see* online philanthropy
Philippines 41, 213–216, 218, 220–221, 223
Phiri, Cathy 67
piece-work 197–198, 200
PlanetRomeo 91, 96–97
platform capitalism 193, 195, 197; *see also* digital labour; gig economy ; online freelancers

poker 81–82, 84
PokerStars 82
Polson, E. 9, 267, 300
popular culture 4
poverty premiums 247–248, 299
Poverty Reduction Strategy papers (PRSPs) 3
power relations, Marxist critiques 4
Powers, M. 9
Prahalad, C.K. 248
precarity/precariousness 7, 9, 41, 52, 59, 160–161, 181, 188, 193, 195, 197, 199–200, 214, 216, 218, 222, 236, 242, 247, 250, 267, 299; flexible exploitation and 214; and vulnerability to gentrification-based displacement 267
President's Plan for AIDS Relief 63
The Price of Poverty (Anglicare Tasmania) 248
Privileged Mobilities (Polson) 170
professionally generated content (PGC) 100, 103, 105
proletariat 18, 24, 39, 194–195
prosumerism 7, 137
public visibility, of ordinary citizens 99

Qiu, J. 7
Quijano, A. 5

Racecourse Architecture (Roberts & Taylor) 79
racialized Othered body, white consumption 21
Rajagopal, A. 151
Ralph Kramden 18
reader-response theory 4
Real Housewives 28–29, 31
reality talent shows 51–61; branding opportunities 57; entertainment mobilization 56–59; impression management 54; participation in reality television 59–60; performance in 53–56; performance of selfhood 54–55, 57, 61; researching 52, 52–53; and social mobility 52, 58; Susan Boyle effect 54; *see also Got to Dance*)
reality TV: associated styles and techniques 42; class and labour in 59–60; class hybridity 32–33; class migration and 27–30; class representation of non-Koreans in Korea 38–48; code switching and class mobility 34–35; consumption in the UK 111; contrast of British upper class with American nouveau riche 30; defining 42; Donald Trump's stint on 35; and the effects of alcohol 34; family reunion format 43–44; framing of class 30–32; global surge in popularity 42; habitus clivé and the feminine docusoap 33–34; and the nouveau riche 28–31, 33; origins of 27; preference for vulgarity 33–34; racial perspective of class 30–31; *see also* non-Koreans on Korean television
Reay, D. 204
Rebane, G. 122–123
recognition, technologies of 180–189
redlining 268
reflexive modernization 112
refugees 244, 273, 299
religion 5, 93, 102, 143, 150–152, 256–257, 280, 282, 290, 298, 300–301

Repole, Mike 80
reproductive labour 203, 205–211
Rhinesmith, C. 233
Rice, R. 113
Rich, A. 176
"The Rise of the Precarious Worker" 200
risk society, Beck's theory 112
Roam 174
Roberts, P. 79–80
Rogers, E.M. 4, 234
Rosaldo, R. 259
Ross, E. 85, 267
Ruesch, J. 158
Rybas, N. 204

Sama-Source 213
Sandoval, M. 100
Saudi Arabia, cultural context of YouTube-based programming 99–107
Saudi Vision 2030 101
Saussure, F. 4
#SayaJuga movement 2
SceenTV 99
Schramm, W. 4
Schwartz, D. 79
search engines 137
second-class access 242–250; the concept 242; dependence on smartphones 249–250; the digital divide 243–244; digital materialization of class 244–249; and the materiality of digital media 242–243; *see also* mobile phone ownership amongst the homeless
Secrets of the Southern Belle (Parks) 30
Sefton-Green, J. 115, 117
segregation: by differential pricing 79; in horse racing 78–79; of the sexes 79
Sennett, R. 33
sexual harassment 2
Shark Tank 32
Shuga: case study 65–70; class and economic inequality in 67–68; film location 65; intersectionality of socio-economic position with gender and HIV/AIDS 68–70; men's attitudes to sex in 69; modelling of good and bad behaviour 65–66; portrayal of being tested for HIV 66; social construction and representation of HIV/AIDS 65, 65–67; socioeconomic demographic reflected in 68; spinoffs 63; target audience 63
Simpson, Homer 3, 18
The Simpsons 18
Singapore, smartphones and digital literacy 132–140
Six Million Dollar Man 43
Skeggs, B. 111, 116, 160, 182–183
Skype 147, 173, 186, 188
Slater, T. 267
slavery 6, 19–20, 79
smartphones 9, 90–91, 110, 113, 115, 132–140, 233, 236, 242–243, 245, 248–249; digital literacy, the changing face of 132–133; digital literacy, and class 133–134; homelessness and dependence on 249–250; study findings and discussion 136–139; study methodology 135; and technology adoption 134–135
Smith, Kate 173–174
Smith, N.H. 182
Snapchat 132, 136–138, 246
social activism 280–291; drivers of participation 290; historical perspective 280–282; #Occupy Parliament movement 288–290; #OccupyPlayground movement 284–288; post-colonial perspective of class 282; role of the media 282–283; study methodology 283–284; technological innovation and 280
social capital 68, 91, 94, 99–101, 127, 176, 249
social class: and adoption of new technologies 77; circles of capital 100; citizenship and 254–256; and everyday media use 145–148; lack of scholarly attention 18; role of migration in the de-structuring of 40; *see also* class
social control, mass entertainment culture as 4
social media: and the ambiguities of recognition work 186–189; and career making in the UN system 184–186; classificatory function in mobile careers 180–189; classificatory value of 181; and the commodification of data and culture 100; and ease of publication of diverse content 133; and mass communication 7; organizations' use of 180–181; and political mobilization 56; reality talent shows and 54; recognition theory and 181, 182–184; role in digital nomadism 171–172; role of in social activism 280, 283; and sexual health education 112; and the subversive enactment of citizenship 257
social mobility, talent as resource for 54–55
social movements 1, 4, 56, 256, 269, 280
social status, media/techno-literacy and 114
social stratification 1, 242–244, 282–283
socioeconomic position, meaning of 64
Somerville, P. 244
Soriano, C.R.R. 10
South Africa 63, 161, 166, 282–283, 288
South Asia: children's television programming and viewing habits 148–151; class and caste in 143–144; discriminated groups 144–145; education and schooling 144–145; social class and everyday media use 145–148; technology ownership and media use among the middle-classes 142–152
South Korea 7, 124, 127–128; *see also* Korea
Southern Charm 31
Spigel, L. 296
Spivak, G. 194
Spronk, R. 283
Spyer, J. 122–123
Sri Lanka 144–145, 148
Stanbury, Caroline 30
State Farm 23
Steele, C.K. 6
Strangelove, M. 100
#StrengthHasNoGender 22

sugar daddies 63, 67–68, 70
Super Bowl commercials 19
Survivor 43
Sutherland, W. 171

Taipale, S. 276
Taiwan 128
TakkieSeries 99
Tamils 144
TaskRabbit 192
Taylor, I. 79–80
techno-literacy: impact of generational differences 114–115, 115–116; role of in everyday life 110
technological advances, and the rise of the gig economy 195
technological capital 237–238
technological change, and questions of media and class 2–3
technopanic 84
television: concern about the impact on children 115; domination of cultural life 296
Television and New Media (Jarrett) 205
television commercials, representation of the working-class 18
Thomas, Michael 172
3000 Leagues in Search of Father 44
Thuku, Harry 282
Thulemark, M. 170
Thurlow, C. 67
time-space compression 298
Tina, Anes 253–254, 263
Tolbert, C.J. 242
Toyota 21
transactional sex 69–70
Transnational Courier Federation (TCF) 200–201
Tronti, Mario 199
Trump, Donald 24, 33, 35
Tsai, A. 64
Tudor-Hart, J. 64
Tumblr 137
Turner: B.S. 256; G. 99, 101, 299
Twitter 6, 57, 59, 133, 187–188, 284
Tyler, I. 23

Uber 6, 183, 192, 197–198, 200–201
the underclass 35, 232, 236–237
Undercover Boss 32
United Kingdom 8, 46, 90; *see also* Great Britain
United Nations, social media and career making in 184–186
United States: second-class access to communication 242–250; working-class bodies in advertising 17–24
Unity Academy 55, 57
upper-class 18, 22, 30–32, 34, 67–69, 77–80, 83, 93, 149–150, 158, 231–232
upward mobility, potential problems 33
Upwork 213
user generated content (UGC) 100, 205, 243
Uturn Entertainment 99

Vamplew, W. 78–79
Van Dijck, J. 100, 267
Veblen, T. 4
Venezuela 2–3
Vera-Zambrano, S. 9
Vietnam 41, 173
visibility, of ordinary people through digital platforms 99
vulgarity, reality TV's preference for 33–34

waiting, politics of 276–277, 298
Wallenberg Foundation 52
Wallman, James 171
Wargames 84
Warne, Dan 193
Waruku, Boaz 281
Watkins, M. 112
Wauthier, K. 10
wealth discrepancy, in Trump era America 24
Web 2.0, 243
Weber, H. 39–40
Welcome, First Time in Korea? 46
WeLive 174
Welles, B.F. 300
WeWork 174
What is Your Moonshot? (Sanei) 173
WhatsApp 110, 118, 132, 136–138, 147, 151, 186, 192
Whitacre, B. 233
white supremacy 5
white working-class male, media portrayals 18–19
WiFi 133, 136–137, 171, 174, 233, 236, 247
WiFly Nomads 174
Wikipedia 137
Wilensky, H. 158
Williams, R. 4–5, 77, 231, 297
Wilson, W.J. 232
Wolfson, T. 10
women, depiction in advertising 20
Wood, Douglas 54
Wordpress 133
Words with Friends 110
Workaway 203–204, 206–211
working-class 4, 9, 17–19, 21, 21–22, 23–24, 40–41, 77–79, 144–145, 148–149, 159–160, 193, 195, 197–201, 204, 231–232, 258, 282, 289–290; ideal-types 199; stereotypes 18; in US advertising 17–24
working-class women, portrayal in TV advertising 20–21
World Bank 3, 142
World Series of Poker 82
World Trade Organization 3
World Wars 19
Wright, E. 101
Wyly, E. 267

X-Files 43

yellow journalism 84

York Racecourse, England 79
Young Kikuyu Association (YKA) 281
Young People and the Future of News (Marchi) 269
Yousafzai, Malala 144
youth media activism 253–263; identity and citizenship 256–258; mediatizing marginality 258–260; social class and citizenship 254–256; youth marginality and social change 260–262
YouTube 84, 132, 136–138, 173, 246, 254, 258; positive perceptions 100; professionally generated content 100, 103, 105; user generated content 100, 205, 243
YouTube celebrity, as new online class 101
YouTube home tour vlogs 122–128; everyday routines, narrativizing 124–125; home cafés 126–128; housekeeping principles 125; lifestyle 128; monetization 126; recuperation 125–126; slow living at home 124–126; study context and methodology 123–124
YouTube-based programming 99–107; class perspective 100–101; correlation between socio-economic background and online visibility 100–101; and the creation of a new online class 101; creation of YouTube celebrity 102–103; definition 100; monetization process 104–107, 126; motivations and incentives 103; political context 102; programmes and channels studied 99; research context 101; and the restrictive environment 103; socio-economic context 101–102